INFORMATION SYSTEMS FOR MANAGERS

TEXTS & CASES

GABRIELE PICCOLI

Cornell University

John Wiley & Sons, Inc.

To Margaret: The finest teammate I could have asked for.

To Laura Jean and Erik who always help put it all in perspective.

EXECUTIVE PUBLISHER   *Don Fowley*
EXECUTIVE EDITOR   *Beth Lang Golub*
SENIOR MARKETING MANAGER   *Amy Scholz*
ASSOCIATE EDITOR   *Jennifer Devine*
SENIOR MEDIA EDITOR   *Lauren Sapira*
DESIGNER   *Hope Miller*
EDITORIAL ASSISTANT   *Maria Guarascio*
PRODUCTION MANAGER   *Dorothy Sinclair*
SENIOR PRODUCTION EDITOR   *Trish McFadden*
PRODUCTION MANAGEMENT SERVICES   *Pine Tree Composition, Inc.*
WILEY BICENTENNIAL LOGO DESIGN   *Richard J. Pacifico*

This book was set in Times by Laserwords Private Limited, Chennai, India and printed and bound by R.R. Donnelley/Crawfordsville. The cover was printed by R.R. Donnelley/Crawfordsville.

The book is printed on acid-free paper. ∞

ISBN 978-0470-08703-9

Printed in the United States of America

10 9 8 7 6 5 4 3 2 1

PREFACE

THE PHILOSOPHY OF THIS BOOK

This book is inspired by the notion that, thirty years into the "information age," general and functional managers must be able to *actively* and *knowledgeably* participate in discussions and decisions about information systems and information technology. I have designed this book from the ground up, based on what has worked and proven useful to advanced undergraduate, master of management and executive management students that I have taught over the past nine years. Thus, the topics this book covers, its writing style, the examples, minicases, and full-length cases I use, are all carefully chosen to be both *relevant* and *engaging* to an audience of students who may not plan to become information systems specialists.

I have found in my interactions with executives of large and small firms alike that general and functional managers in modern businesses need to be able to do two things when it comes to information systems decisions:

1. Evaluate the plethora of modern information technology and trends—from a strategic, not a technical standpoint—in order to be able to identify and use the technology that will generate value for the organization.

2. Become effective partners of the information systems function. To this end they need to be familiar with those areas where they will have to come in contact with information systems professionals.

The main focus of this book is therefore on the strategic role of information systems in the modern firm and the design and implementation of IT-dependent strategic initiatives. Over the years I have come to believe that Masters and Executive MBA students need less of a "breadth book" that offers an overview knowledge of technology and technology issues and much more of a "tools focused" book that offers students frameworks and tangible guidance on how to ensure that their firm benefits from information systems and technology efforts. I designed and wrote this book to provide such a toolkit for them.

Thus, this is not a text *about IT* and *how IT works*. This is a book about the information system and information technology resource and how it should be optimally deployed to achieve the objectives of the organization. In other words, this book treats IT like any other organizational resource—an asset that general and functional managers need to understand enough to be able to plan for, select, deploy, and effectively manage so as to be able to create and appropriate value for their organization.

HOW THIS BOOK IS ORGANIZED

The book follows a progression designed to engage students while creating a sound long-term basis for decision making. I have been particularly sensitive to the audience with both the expository approach and content selection. The book uses a more colloquial and engaging writing style than traditional textbooks, with many examples and quotes centering on decision making by general and functional managers. The opening mini-cases, written from the perspective of functional or general managers, reinforce this approach by clearly showing the relevance of the chapter's content while helping to foster discussion at the start of class.

The content of the book is organized in four sections, four stepping stones, that build upon one another in a sequential manner. Part I covers essential definitions and provides the conceptual foundation for the following chapters. Part II describes how new technologies have changed, and continue to change, the competitive landscape and social environment thus creating both opportunities and new threats for established firms and start-ups. Part III represents the defining content of this book. It offers actionable frameworks to help managers envision how to develop value adding IT-dependent strategic initiatives and to gauge whether such initiatives can be protected so as to reap benefits in the long term. Part IV concludes the text by focusing on how to create and implement the information systems at the core of any initiative. It also discusses common systems and major trends as well as security, privacy, and ethical considerations.

Finally, the book provides a number of full-length end-of-chapter cases, written by myself and colleagues, that were expressly designed to use the frameworks and debate the issues covered in the chapter. This tight parallel between content and cases has worked very well in my classes because students see the immediate applicability of the theories and concepts covered.

ACKNOWLEDGEMENTS

While there is only my name on the cover of this book, and I take responsibility for any errors or inaccuracies, a book like this one is a really a joint effort. The ideas and concepts the teaching philosophy, pedagogical approaches, tools and techniques covered came about through observation of, and discussion with, the many colleagues I have had the good fortune of interacting with over the years. Amongst the most influential I want to acknowledge Blake Ives, Roy Alvarez, Erica Wagner, Dick Moore, and Rick Watson. Each of them has helped me shape the courses I have taught and ultimately the content of this book.

I would also like to acknowledge the contribution of the many students who have brought a positive attitude and an open mind to the Information Systems Management course, those who have challenged my own understanding of the concepts in this book, as well those who pushed me to find better way to introduce and discuss them. I would also like to acknowledge the many companies, their management and employees, who recognize that we can't have relevant education without their full engagement and support. These people have kindly volunteered their time to engage with me in discussion of the ideas explored in this book.

Many of them have agreed to let their company serve as case study sites and welcomed my colleagues and I to share their knowledge.

My administrative assistant, Dawn Gonzales, was an invaluable asset in the completion of this project. Dawn sheltered me from many of the time consuming and tedious elements of this endeavor with professionalism and energy. I would like to thank the colleagues who took time from their busy schedules to review earlier versions of the manuscript and to offer valuable and constructive feedback:

Louis Beaubien, Providence College

Ed Christensen, Monmouth University

John Kohlmeier, DePaul University

Blake Ives, University of Houston

Roberto Mejias, Indiana University

Graham Peace, West Virginia University

Cynthia Ruppel, University of Alabama, Huntsville

Paul Licker, Oakland University

Richard McCarthy, Quinnipiac University

Paul Pavlou, University of California, Riverside

John Scigliano, Nova Southeastern University

Michael Wade, York University

Erica Wagner, Cornell University

Ted Williams, University of Michigan, Flint

Last, but certainly not least, I would like to acknowledge the staff at John Wiley & Sons. Without them this book would have never become a reality. Beth Lang Golub, who originally saw the opportunity for this book to be written and was instrumental in its development. Jennifer Devine, who saw the lengthy writing process through and was an indispensable source of suggestions and guidance. Thank you also to Patty Donovan for composing the book layout, to Amy Scholz for her marketing guidance and to all others involved in the production and marketing of the book at Wiley.

FOREWORD

As we all know, the required master level Information Systems course is a very difficult one to teach. I always admire the few faculty teaching this course who can transcend the reluctance, prejudice, and general disinterest too many of us confront from our students. Gabe is one of the talented few. He has enjoyed significant success teaching the required Information Systems course over the years, received teaching awards for his work with both Masters and Executive MBA students. Hopefully, this book will arm the rest of us with some of Gabe's teaching magic.

This book will be a great addition to your arsenal, allowing you to leverage the enthusiasm of students already interested in the material, while energizing those who come in the door with a negative bias toward the "IT course." This book can make your course more compelling to your students thanks to Gabe's very approachable writing style, the wealth of examples he uses, the opening mini-cases that quickly create excitement and buzz, and the many unique full-length cases (several of which we wrote together). Most helpfully, Gabe has identified both the foundation and leading edge content that is most relevant to Management students. With this book you will find it much easier to demonstrate the relevance of Information Systems to your students and to create a positive learning environment in your classes.

Blake Ives, Ph.D.
C.T. Bauer Chair in Business Leadership
Director, IS Research Center
C. T. Bauer College of Business
University of Houston

CONTENTS

CHAPTER 8

CHAPTER 9

P A R T

I

Foundations

In Part I we lay the foundations for the study of information systems. Although the press and commentators devote much attention to information technology (IT) and the (often substantial) IT investments that organizations make, modern general and functional managers don't have the time, and often the inclination, to become IT experts. After all, that's why organizations hire and pay information systems and information technology professionals.

Yet with information technologies becoming increasingly present in both business and society at large, modern general and functional managers can no longer abdicate their obligation to make decisions about this crucial organizational resource. The good news is that you can be an effective manager without knowing a huge amount about IT, without knowing how the technology works, and without having to keep up with the barrage of new technologies that are constantly being commercialized. To be an effective general or functional manager, a user of the IT resource, and a productive partner of the firm's information systems and technology professionals, you need a strong grounding in the fundamentals of information systems (IS) management and decision making.

As we describe in Chapter 2, information systems are sociotechnical organizational systems that encompass technology, the people who will be using such technology, and the business processes they execute to accomplish their daily tasks and carry out business activities. User managers can rely on IT professionals when it comes to choosing among programming languages or the appropriate structure of a new database being implemented, but general and function managers must be able to design the appropriate information systems for their organization, plan and budget for the use of IT resources, and analyze whether a given information system creates a competitive advantage and whether such an advantage is sustainable over time.

This is not a book about IT and how it works. This is a book about information systems and the IS decisions that general and functional managers are routinely called on to make.

In Part I we lay the foundations upon which you will build your information systems knowledge. Specifically,

- *Chapter 1: Introduction.* The first chapter defines some basic terms and makes the case for why general and functional managers must be intimately involved in information systems decision making.
- *Chapter 2: Information Systems Defined.* The second chapter defines what an information system is (the central concept in this book), places this definition in the organizational context, and draws a crucial distinction between IT and IS.
- *Chapter 3: Organizational Information Systems and Their Impact.* The third chapter categorizes the different information systems found in modern organizations and provides the vocabulary you need in order to communicate with other managers and the information systems professionals in your firm. This chapter also provides you with a foundation to consider the impact of various information technologies on the organization.

Information Systems and the Role of General and Functional Managers

What You Will Learn in This Chapter

This chapter focuses on the role that general and functional managers play in the organizational use and management of information systems. The chapter also describes the meteoric rise to prominence of information technologies and the role advanced IT plays today in the modern organization.

In this chapter you will learn

1. To define the terms *general manager, functional manager* and *end user.* You will also learn to to articulate the difference between these two concepts.

2. To define the role of modern chief information officers (CIOs).

3. To identify organizational and information technology trends that have led to the current popularity of IT-based information systems.

4. To identify why it is important for general and functional managers to be involved in decision making pertaining to information systems.

5. To identify, and avoid, the risks engendered when general and functional managers decide to abdicate their right (and duty) to make important information systems decisions.

MINI-CASE: FACING TERMINATION?

The silence was beginning to become uncomfortable as you searched for words to answer the question from your chief executive officer (CEO). This boardroom had never looked so big, and it seemed her words were still echoing: "How could it get to this? You sat here telling us how this new software program would dramatically improve our marketing efficiencies and customers' repurchase frequency. It has been over two months, and the bloody thing is not even working!"

As you searched for the right way to respond, the whole incident flashed through your mind. It was over two months ago when you sold the board on the benefits of a new salesforce automation tool. You had just been promoted to vice president of marketing, taking over for Tom Vecchio. Tom was an old-fashioned salesperson, with a huge personality and an incredible memory. He was employee number 4 when the company launched, back in 1982, and had been instrumental in its early growth via personal networking—phone calls, rounds of golf, and birthday calls. He had surrounded himself with very similar people. You understood that culture, you had been one of the young guns a few years ago, and now you had replaced the master.

But things had changed in your industry, competition was much tougher, and markets were now global. "How could a firm the size of this firm run sales and marketing without any IT support?" you wondered once promoted. How ironic that you'd be the one to usher in the "new IT-enabled world." You had managed never to concern yourself with all that techie computer stuff. You were a pretty good user: e-mail, Web, some Excel . . . the usual. But now your bonus depended on the performance of the whole function, not just the number of contracts you closed, and it seemed you had been getting all the heat about efficiencies that they could not put on Tom . . . they could scream all they wanted, he was untouchable. But you weren't!

It all seemed to have fallen into place when you went to the National Convention of the Sales Executives Association. At one of the booths you had seen VelcroSoft and the salesforce automation product VelcroSFA. There was a lot of buzz around their product both at the conference and in the press. The attendant at the booth told you about all of the great features of VelcroSFA: automated recording of information at each stage in the sales process, automated escalation and approval, contact management, lead sharing for team selling, in-depth reporting. It could even integrate with human resource systems for immediate computation of commissions, reduced data entry, and increased speed.

After you returned to the office, you read some more material about VelcroSFA and called a couple of friends who had installed it in their organizations. It seemed to be the right application. You showed the brochure to some of the best-performing salespeople. They did not seem impressed, and they raised a bunch of issues. Joe, one of the old-timers, said, "The Rolodex did wonders for me throughout my career; what do I need a computer for?" Joe never liked you anyway since you had taken Tom's spot, you thought. Amanda, a younger associate, seemed more positive: "I am willing to give it a shot, but it seems quite convoluted. I am not sure I need all those functionalities." You recall thinking that they would change their mind once they saw their commissions go up because the software would allow them to spend more time with customers. You did not like computers after all, but you liked the software more as you found out more about it. They would, too.

Jenny Cantera, the IT director, had pledged her help with the installation and, after looking at the brochure, had said, "Should take a weekend to install this application and write the interface to the HR system. I am busy with the implementation of the new accounting system for the next three or four weeks, but I should be able to do this afterward." You had some doubts about Jenny. She was very smart and technically gifted, but she was the very first IT director in your firm and she had little experience in the position.

The board had been sold pretty easily on the purchase, even though at $55,000 it was a sizable investment for your firm. You had used the return on investment (ROI) calculations provided by VelcroSoft. Granted, VelcroSoft personnel were very aggressive with assumptions underlying their calculations, but with a bit of effort on everyone's part you truly believed you could achieve strong results. As soon as you got the go-ahead, you contacted the vendor and obtained the installation package. Everything had gone perfectly up to that point, but your fortune seemed to turn right after.

First, you had the software installation disks sitting on your desk for over a month. Jenny was running into unexpected trouble with the accounting software. Once she finally got around to implementing your product, she took one weekend to complete the installation and created the user accounts. The interface to the HR application was not operational yet—something about a "software conflict," you did not quite understand. However, you pressed on. Over the following week, you had encouraged your sales rep to "play around with the applications." You had even sent an e-mail with the subject line "Up and running in the brave new world of Sales Force Automation!" But response had been cool at best. Only a few accounts had been accessed, and overall people you spoke to said they were too busy and would look at the software once the quarter closed.

Last weekend, when Jenny wrote the interface to the HR systems, all hell broke lose. On Monday (yesterday) the HR database was locked and the HR system was down. Jenny was scrambling to bring it back up, and she was now saying she may have to reinstall the program. She

had already uninstalled VelcroSFA, and at this point it looked like the application would not be a priority for a while. You did not really mind; you had bigger fish to fry . . . you were concerned about getting fired.

DISCUSSION QUESTIONS

1. Who do you think is to blame for the current state of affairs?
2. What do you think is the most critical mistake you made over the last two months? What were the principal mistakes made by others involved?
3. How could these mistakes have been avoided, if at all?
4. Should you take this opportunity to say goodbye to everyone and resign now? If not, what should you say in response to the CEO question?

INTRODUCTION

It is hard these days to escape the hype and publicity surrounding information technology (IT) and its business applications. IT has become more affordable and pervasive then ever before; just think about the wide array of technologies that you use for work and pleasure on any given day.

For businesses, IT has become a critical resource, and for many organizations it represents over 50 percent of capital spending. As important as technology is to today's general and functional managers, don't be misled, this is not a book about IT and how it works. This is not a book written exclusively for IT professionals. This book is written from the standpoint of, and to serve the needs of, the modern manager.

GENERAL AND FUNCTIONAL MANAGERS

A manager is a knowledge worker of modern business and not-for-profit organizations who is in charge of a team, a functional area (i.e., functional managers), or the entire organization or a business unit (i.e., a general manager). These individuals are typically trained in management schools, and particularly in larger organization and entrepreneurial ventures they often hold a master's degree in management or business administration.

General and functional managers have, through schooling and on-the-job experience, developed strengths in a business area such as operations, marketing, finance, human resources, accounting, and the like. Those of you who plan for a career in business consulting will develop a similar set of expertise. However, with the unrelenting pace of IT innovation and its widespread adoption in organizations, the personal success of general and functional managers and of their area of responsibilities increasingly depend on making optimal decisions about the use and management of information. Information is a critical organizational resource. As Thomas Watson, Jr., the legendary chairman of IBM, recognized over thirty years ago, "All the value of this company is in its people. If you burned down all our plants, and we just kept our people and our information files, we should soon be as strong as ever."[1]

To manage information effectively, the modern firm must adopt and use information systems and information technology resources. Selecting, designing, and managing these resources is no longer exclusively the job of the technology professional, but it is the shared responsibility of all modern and functional managers. General and functional managers must work in partnership with information systems and technology professionals—those individuals with substantial technical training and majors in management information systems, computer science, and engineering—when it comes to carrying out these decisions. Partnership is the key word here; it is no longer acceptable for general and functional managers to claim ignorance of IT and delegate all IT decisions to technologists. This course of action is not acceptable, as we will see, because the firm's success in today's environment depends on the interplay of the information systems and information technology with the other organizational resources (e.g., labor, brand, capital).

Let's look at examples of what happens when this partnership works well:

■ Consider Harrah's Entertainment, now the largest casino resort operator in the world. In the mid-1990s, Harrah's found itself unable to compete with new resorts that were wowing gamblers with elaborate buildings and attractions (e.g., the Mirage, Treasure Island, the Bellagio). At that time Harrah's chairman and CEO, Philip Sartre, sensed that customer knowledge and customer loyalty could become the firm's core competency and differentiation driver. Working with its IT department, an external consultant, and a newly founded group of decision scientists, Harrah's spent over $100 million to build and use a business intelligence infrastructure that enabled its new positioning and financial success.

■ As it became clear that the Internet would be a viable channel for economic transactions, Michael Dell, founder and CEO of Dell Computers, Inc., challenged his team to take advantage of the opportunity. The Internet offered Dell the chance to sell directly to the consumer (not just to business accounts), without having to compromise its direct model. In charge of the efforts was thirty-year-old Scott Eckert, a recent MBA graduate. Working closely with the information systems and technology group, Eckert developed Dell Online, the online store, and an application that allowed customers to configure their machine. As they say, the rest is history. Dell Computers is now the largest computer maker in the world, helped in part by the success of the Dell Online initiative. Fueled by the staggering growth rates of the Internet itself, the online store generated $1 million in revenue per day in six months, $2 million/day in nine months, and $3 million/day in a little over a year since opening for business.

The preceding examples highlight a few critical lessons for prospective general and functional managers:

■ The general and functional managers in the examples were making educated decisions about the deployment of IT in their organizations.

---

[1] Quinn, S. B. (1992). *Intelligence Enterprise: A Knowledge and Service Based Paradigm for Industry.* New York, NY: Free Press, p. 244.

■ The objective of IT deployment was business driven. In other words, the new technology was brought in to serve the growing or changing needs of the business. The people who perceived and understood the need for this new way of doing things were the general and functional managers.

■ These general and functional managers were not IT professionals and had no specific training in technology, but they worked in partnership with the IT professionals in their organization to ensure the successful deployment of the needed information systems and technology functionalities.

■ The general and functional managers did not use the new technologies firsthand once introduced. Rather, other employees, the end users, had direct contact with the hardware and software programs that had been introduced.

The last of the preceding points is important as there is a clear difference between general and functional managers and the role of end users.

General and Functional Managers versus End Users

End users are those individuals who have direct contact with software applications as they use them to carry out specific tasks. For example, I am an end user as I use word processing software (i.e., Microsoft Word™) to write this book. You, as a student, are an end user as you engage in spreadsheet analyses using Microsoft Excel™ in your statistics, operations, or finance courses.

Clearly, most general and functional managers in modern organizations are also end users. Most managers today use software programs to improve their own personal productivity—from the very basic such as e-mail and calendars, to the most advanced, such as using a Blackberry to keep in touch on the road, using reporting applications, and using management dashboards to keep a real-time pulse of the business' performance. Although being a sophisticated end user is an important asset for the modern manager because effective use of software programs can lead to increased productivity, it is far more important for you to have the skills and knowledge to make appropriate information systems decisions at the organizational level.

It should now be clear why this book is not an IT training book and its focus is not on end-user skills. This book is expressly designed for current and future managers, for those individuals who have general management and/or functional management responsibility, for those who serve, or will one day serve, on the board of directors of an organization. The promise of this book is that to be an effective manager you need not know an inordinate amount of information about IT, or how technology works, even though some of this IT-specific knowledge undoubtedly helps.

Rather, what you really need to know and feel confident with is knowledge of information systems and the role that IT plays in them (see Chapter 2 for definitions). You need to know how to identify opportunities to use information technologies to your firm's advantage; how to plan for the use of information systems resources; and how to manage the design, development, selection, and implementation of information systems. These are the skills that separate the effective modern managers—those who can be productive partners of the IT function—from ineffective ones—those who delegate critical IT decision making and, more often than not, live to suffer the negative consequences of this decision. In the words of Rob Solomon, Senior Vice

President of Sales and Marketing of Outrigger Hotels and Resorts, "Every manager must have an IT strategy. You can't delegate to technologists and only worry about your allocated cost or what training your employees need. You must understand how to be master of your own destiny and make IT work best for you. Too many managers still don't get that."

THE NEXT WAVE OF CIOs

Another interesting trend that makes this book relevant to management school students is the increasing permeability of the boundaries of the IT function. That is, the chief information officer (CIO) position is increasingly seen not as the endpoint of a career but as a stepping stone to the chief executive officer (CEO) or president posts. The old joke "CIO stands for Career Is Over" no longer rings true. Examples of CIOs being promoted to the role of CEO or to other executive level positions now abound—and there is even a Web site to keep track of these upward-moving CIOs.[2] For example, David Bernauer, former CIO at the pharmacy chain Walgreens, was promoted to chief operating officer (COO) after four years in the top IT post. He then became CEO and is currently the chairman of the board at Walgreens. Maynard Webb, CIO at Gateway Computers, was hired as COO by online auction giant eBay. Kevin Turner, former CIO of Wal-Mart, became CEO at Sam's Club and is now COO at Microsoft Corporation. Two primary reasons are fueling this trend:

- The increasing prevalence of IT and the consequent need for those who serve on the executive teams and the board of directors to have some understanding of how to use this crucial resource. In the words of a British headhunter, "CIOs are the only ones with a helicopter view of the business and they have a great deal of operational experience of the business."[3]

- The fact that the prevalence of IT and information systems throughout the organization gives CIOs a broad view of operations, business processes, interorganizational coordination challenges and opportunities, and a broad understanding of how the firm is positioned to execute its strategy. As Tom Murphy, former CIO of Royal Caribbean Cruise Lines and current CIO of pharmaceutical supply chain services provider AmerisourceBergen, put it, "Information technology is everywhere; we touch almost every process in the firm. We must intimately understand operations to enable them; I have a complete view of the organization and its operations."

On the flip side, forward-looking firms no longer view the IT function as the province of technologists who speak a foreign language that nobody else understands. Individuals with strong technical skills represent irreplaceable assets, of course, but the information systems function is increasingly staffed with businesspeople, individuals who were trained in management schools, who share an excitement for the potential of technology to solve business problems, and who are relatively well versed in information systems issues and vocabulary. These are individuals who are increasingly joining the IT function as business analysts, system analysts, and project management specialists to complement software designers and developers, IT architects, and other professionals with more technical profiles.

---

[2] http://www.baselinemag.com/article2/0,1540,2095044,00.asp
[3] http://www.silicon.com/cxoextra/0,3800005416,39155417,00.htm

Modern CIOs are required to exhibit many of the skills of their chief executive counterparts while maintaining priorities that are focused on keeping the lights on and IT operations running. This convergence of skills is perhaps best captured by Scott Heintzeman, CIO of Carlson Marketing, the marketing services arm of the Carlson Companies conglomerate. He identifies the following skills as the trademark of successful modern CIOs:

- Perpetually develop the team/organization
- Effectively manage change while in pursuit of
  - Marketplace innovation
  - Process improvement
  - Maximum agility
  - Leverage of legacy systems
- 100 percent customer satisfaction
- Consistently improve business performance

At the same time, CIOs are focused on delivering information services and enabling the business, as shown by the Gartner Group's 2005 survey of the top 10 business and technology priorities for CIOs (see Table 1.1).

Table 1.1   Top 10 Business and Technology Priorities for CIOs

Top 10 Business Priorities
1. Business process improvement
2. Security breaches and disruptions
3. Enterprise-wide operating costs
4. Supporting competitive advantage
5. Data protection and privacy
6. The need for revenue growth
7. Using intelligence in products and services
8. Focus on internal controls
9. Shortage of business skills
10. Faster innovation and cycle times
Top 10 Technology Priorities
1. Security enhancement tools
2. Business intelligence applications
3. Mobile workforce enablement
4. Workflow management deployment and integration
5. Enterprise resource planning (ERP) upgrades
6. Storage management
7. Voice and data integration over IP
8. Customer relationship management (CRM)
9. Business process integration tools
10. Server virtualization

Source: Gartner EXP (January 2005)

Consider this as you begin this course: As much as you don't think you will ever be an integral part of the IT group, you may find yourself becoming a CIO one day on your way to the CEO position. Whether you are trying to position yourself for this career path or just looking to be a successful general or functional manager, this book is for you.

FUNDAMENTAL IT TRENDS: THE STAYING POWER OF MOORE'S LAW

Information systems (ISs)—those organizational systems that enable the processing and management of an organization's information—have now become the backbone of operations. These information systems are increasingly powered by more or less advanced information technologies (IT) at their core. This evolution of IT is important for you as a general and functional manager because new technologies constantly enable new strategies, new initiatives, and the effective management and use of greater and greater amounts of information.

The popularity and growing importance of IT-based information system is self-evident twenty years into the "information revolution." For those in need of further convincing, we need only show statistics that capture the breathtaking rates at which IT has become, and continues to grow into, a critical tool for modern organizations and for consumers and individuals alike. For example, in 2005 there were an estimated 1.08 billion people with access to the Internet.

Q4   Another source of evidence is the precision that has characterized Moore's law over the forty years since its enouncement by Gordon Moore. In 1965 Dr. Moore, who three years later cofounded Intel Corp., commented at a conference that if the current rate of improvement in the production process of transistor-based microprocessor continued, the number of transistors that could be etched on an integrated circuit (i.e., a microchip) would double every one to two years. What is remarkable about Moore's law is not so much how Dr. Moore arrived at it, but rather how precisely it has held over the last forty years (see Figure 1.1) and the fact that it is expected to hold true for a decade or two more.

The unrelenting pace of performance improvement in the process of microchip design and production has a number of important managerial implications, discussed below. Paraphrasing Professor Warren McFarlan of the Harvard Business School, IT will continue to enable organizational and strategic innovation. Taking advantage of this continuous technological progress is the responsibility of general and functional managers.

Processing Power and Storage Capacity Have Increased

The processing power of microprocessors has increased exponentially. Because a transistor is the basic unit of computational ability of a microprocessor, more transistors equates to more computational power in any device that use a microchip—your personal computer, of course, but also your music player, your cellular phone, your digital camera, your car, even your microwave, and increasingly your fridge.

Storage capacity of memory chips has also increased exponentially. With transistors serving as the basic component of memory chips as well, higher density of transistors makes for increased memory capacity and performance.

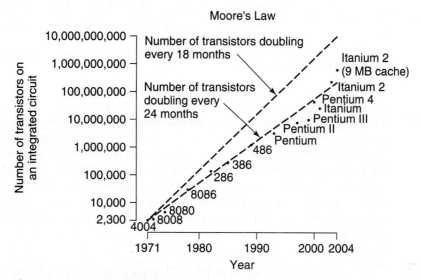

Figure 1.1   Moore's Law

Costs Have Steadily Declined and Battery Life Increased

The cost of computing power and storage has declined at breathtaking rates (see Figure 1.2). As Moore's law has taken effect, the cost of computing performance has declined dramatically. By some estimates, all the power of a mainframe that cost over $10 million in 1965 had been incorporated in a $7 chip by 2002. The cost of that same chip is projected to drop to about 1¢ in 2017. It is this amazing combination of power and affordability that has led to the spreading of "intelligence"—here defined as computational ability—in products ranging from the more advanced to the more mundane.

   As the dimension of transistors decreases, and more of them are printed on a chip, the battery life of increasingly powerful devices has continued to grow. This trend has enabled the development of countless new devices—most notably portable devices such as iPods,

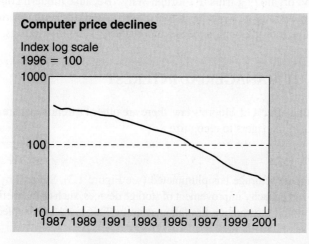

Figure 1.2   Declining Cost of Computing Power.
(*Source*: National Science Board. 2006. *Science and Engineering Indicators 2006*. Arlington, VA: National Science Foundation (Volume 1, MSB 06-01).)

palm-top computers, and the like—and the computerization of products that had no intelligence before, such as smart cards, radio frequency ID (RFID) tags, and so on.

Computers Have Become Easier to Use

As computers become more powerful, they become easier to use. This is an interesting side effect of Moore's law and one of the most intriguing characteristics of information technology. Because software is an extremely malleable tool, as computers become more powerful and are able to process more and more operations in a unit of time, they can be asked to do more work, freeing users from this burden. If you had the (sometimes painful) experience of using computers before the arrival of graphical user interfaces (i.e., the Apple Macintosh, Microsoft Windows) you know how difficult it can be to have to memorize a command—with perfectly correct syntax!—in order to have the computer perform a task. For example, in MS-DOS, in order to copy a file from the CD-ROM to the hard disk, you would have to issue a command with the following structure:

COPY [/Y|-Y] [/A][/B] [d:][path]filename [/A][/B] [c:][path][filename] [/V]

Failing to remember the preceding syntax would yield a cryptic error message and, typically, little hint as to how to go about fixing the error. Conversely, when using modern graphical user interfaces, copying a file from one location to another is as simple as identifying the right icon and dragging it to the target location. Voice recognition interfaces are becoming more common, and we can increasingly issue commands to a computer by simply telling it what to do.

The simplicity of user interfaces is just an example of how IT, as it becomes more sophisticated and complex, becomes easier to use. This is because as more powerful computers can process more and more sophisticated software code, they are able to interact with humans in ways that are closer and closer to our natural behavior—such as the interpretation of visual cues and the use of vocal commands. It is not a coincidence that seniors represent a sizable portion of the online population. Note that these are individuals age 65 and older who are often considered to be too old to learn to program a VCR. Yet they are connected to the Internet, e-mailing and chatting with their grandkids, sharing pictures, and organizing trips to Florida. Why? Because modern computing devices offer things they want (e.g., keeping in touch with grandkids), are affordable, and shelter them from much of the complexity of the machine's inner workings.

OTHER IT TRENDS OF MANAGERIAL INTEREST

Beyond the lasting effects of Moore's law, there are other IT trends that are critical for general and functional managers to recognize.

Storage Costs Are Declining

The cost of computer storage has plummeted (see Figure 1.3). Spurred by the continuous miniaturization and capacity improvement of storage devices, such as magnetic hard disks, the cost per unit of stored information has fallen steadily. This trend has enabled the emergence

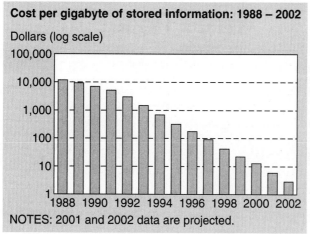

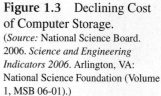

Figure 1.3   Declining Cost of Computer Storage. (*Source:* National Science Board. 2006. *Science and Engineering Indicators 2006.* Arlington, VA: National Science Foundation (Volume 1, MSB 06-01).)

of a whole host of strategic initiatives predicated on the collection and analysis of significant amounts of data. Consider, for example, one of the major cruise lines in the world. On each voyage each ship in the line's fleet collects a significant amount of data about its customers (e.g., spa services they take, drinks they have, excursions they book). In the past, once the ship docked, the data were downloaded to shore-side systems, consolidated, and rolled up. Most of the details were lost in the process. While the firm always recognized that the individual-level data may be valuable, it was not economically feasible to save such data. Since 2002, with the declining cost of storage, the firm has been able to cost justify keeping the detailed voyage data. The firm has yet to devise an analytical strategy to use the data, but it knows that saving data from past voyages will be invaluable when the firm finally decides how to use this wealth of historical data.

Network Access Is Becoming Ubiquitous

Ubiquitous networks are now a reality. In the early 1990s the Internet, and its most visible services such as the World Wide Web and electronic mail, took the world by storm. "The Internet changes everything" was the rally cry that spurred the emergence of a thousand new business models and sent billions of dollars through the hands of venture capitalists and into those of high-tech entrepreneurs all over the world.

The dot-com era, as it is sometimes called, has now come and gone. What remains is the Internet: a global network of networks relying on distributed ownership and openly available standards and communication protocols. Access to the Internet is increasingly pervasive. We can already imagine a world in which we will not wonder whether we will have access to a high-speed Internet connection when we travel, we will assume so—just like we do today with access to electricity.

Network access is not only becoming ubiquitous, but the costs of data transmission are becoming negligible. The convergence of these trends is spurring an amazing array of initiatives. Consider the recent trend to enable cell phones to receive a text message when your bus is approaching your stop (no more waiting in the cold!) or to enable payments for small purchases at vending machines via cell phones (no more being thirsty due to lack of correct

Wi-Fi® Phone
for Skype™
FREE unlimited phone calls
over Wi-Fi networks

Figure 1.4   The Belkin Wi-Fi[4]
Phone for Skype

change!). Some startups are anticipating this brave new world (see Figures 1.4 and Figure 1.5).

These are simple examples, but they highlight how dramatically these trends can change the competitive and social landscapes in which your firm will compete and your career will take place.

Intelligent Devices Are Becoming the Norm

As IT costs and storage costs have plummeted, and as global data networks have become widely available, more and more devices are now intelligent (i.e., able to store and process data) and connected (i.e., able to communicate with other devices). The smart home is now a reality, with smart refrigerators that can tell you what they have in store, alert you when food is going bad, suggest recipes that use ingredients you have on hand, and even order food (Figure 1.6); smart heating systems that you can control over the Internet from your office; and bathtubs that will allow you to start running a bath before you get home.

Modern automobiles often pack as much computing power as your personal computer; and, through satellite networks and telemetry technology, some can self-diagnose and e-mail

Figure 1.5   Wi-Fi
Phones use the Internet
to Place Free Calls

[4] Wi-Fi is a set of technologies that enables wireless networking of computing services.

Figure 1.6   The Lexicle Smart Fridge

you alerts about preventive maintenance and potential trouble you may experience down the road (see Figure 1.7).

This proliferation of smaller, more powerful, interconnected devices, summarized in Figure 1.8, has had a few direct and indirect effects. First, computing devices are smaller and increasingly embedded in everyday products. As a consequence, digital content and services have increased dramatically and will continue to increase over time. Moreover, we increasingly see the convergence of multiple devices into one. Chances are you carry a cell phone that doubles up as a planner, a digital still camera, a digital video camera, an e-mail client, a music player, and who knows what else.

Second, the rapid proliferation of easy-to-use computing equipment has spurred more and more digitization—the process by which content and processes become expressed and performed in digital form. Finally, as computing devices become increasingly easy to use and interconnected, they become pervasive. These trends have important implications for the manager of the future.

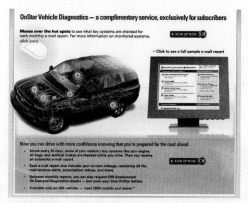

Figure 1.7   OnStar Vehicle Diagnostic

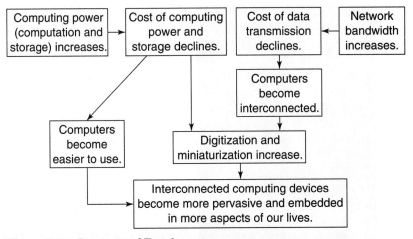

Figure 1.8   Summary of Trends

HOW DO THESE TRENDS AFFECT TODAY'S MANAGERS?

The discussion in the previous section depicted the world in which you, as a modern general and functional manager, will operate. You will increasingly be challenged to devise strategies and implement processes that enable your organization to take advantage of these trends and better serve your increasingly IT-savvy customers.

Perhaps, though, the most important implication of the pervasiveness of computing for today's management is to be found in the amount of money that is spent on IT equipment, software, and services. This amount makes other capital expenditures pale in comparison (see Figure 1.9).

The ever-increasing amount of money being spent on IT is largely due to one of the most interesting characteristics of software. Software is an extremely malleable tool that can be

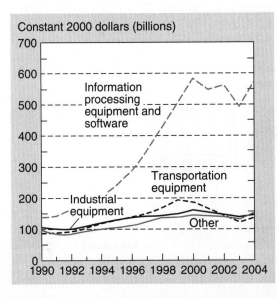

Figure 1.9   Industry Spending on Capital Equipment.
(*Source:* U.S. Bureau of Economic Analysis (http://www.bea.doc.gov/ bea/dn/nipaweb/). Science and Engineering Indicators 2006.)

molded into almost anything. Through the infinite combinations in which software code can be written by talented software designers and programmers, digital devices can be molded into an infinite number of applications, many still left to invent! As a consequence, the number of opportunities for innovation and business success that depend on the appropriate use of IT is literally skyrocketing. If you think for a moment about the different types of software you come in contact with on a daily basis, you'll see that they support a huge variety of tasks.

For example, we use e-mail, Instant Messenger, and Voice over IP (VOIP) applications such as Skype to communicate with our friends, family, and colleagues. With these applications, IT acts as a communication device, replacing our traditional telephone or penned letters.

Many of us listen to streaming radio and watch videos on our personal computers; we play video games and organize our pictures using Web sites such as Flickr.com. With these applications, our IT behaves like an entertainment device, replacing our radio, stereo, television, and scrapbooks.

We use word processing, spreadsheets, and presentation software to carry out our work. With these applications, our IT takes on the role of a productivity tool for the office, replacing typewriters, calculators, and flipcharts.

Finally, and most important for you as a manager, IT can embed intelligence and decision-making capabilities previously required of employees or organizational functions. For example, modern check-in kiosks used by airlines and hotels replace the work of front-line employees; forecasting software and automatic inventory reorder software used in retail embed some of the intelligence and the decision-making ability of skilled inventory managers.

Beyond replacing earlier ways of doing business, new technology creates a constant stream of new possibilities. For example, it is now possible for us to get custom-made apparel by simply typing in some measurements and a few style preferences at the Lands' End Web site. Behind the scenes, far from view, software from Archetype Solutions, Inc. goes to work to create unique patterns that will be automatically fed to cutting machines that will generate your custom-made, perfect-fitting jeans.

WHY CAN'T WE JUST HIRE GOOD IT PEOPLE?

One of the most enduring results of research in information systems has been the degree of discomfort that executives claim when it comes to making decisions about information systems and information technology. The great number of acronyms—increasing daily, it seems—the pervasiveness of technical language, and the unique blend of skills that are required to understand computing can be very intimidating. As a consequence, we often hear executives wonder why it isn't enough to hire "good" IT professionals and let them worry about all the IT stuff.

This stance immediately raises the question, How do you know if an IT professional is indeed good without knowing a minimum amount about what IT professionals do? More important, how can you establish a good partnership with your firm's IT group if you are not equipped to prove useful in the relationship? Just as most general and functional managers are not trained in the design and implementation of IT the way computer scientists and engineers are, most computer scientists and engineers are not trained in marketing, management, finance, or accounting.

This diverse training leads to much communication difficulty. Because the skills and knowledge of general and functional managers are complementary to those of the information systems professionals in the organization, communication and a good relationship is a critical to the firm's success.

As a simple example, imagine being the vice president of marketing for a retail chain (e.g., Best Buy, Inc.) that wants to be able to measure customer spending patterns precisely and rank shoppers based on the customer life-time value[5] they contribute to the firm. Business intelligence technology and techniques (discussed in Chapter 12) will enable this strategy. However, how can your IT group build the appropriate infrastructure, track all the relevant data, perform accurate analyses, and best segment the customer base unless you and your team are intimately involved in the design and development of this technology and analytical infrastructure? The IT professionals in your organizations are not as familiar as you are with the retail operations, and they are certainly not well versed in marketing segmentation and customer valuation techniques.

The only recipe for success in this case is to have a productive partnership. You contribute the marketing specific knowledge and make decisions about the critical requirements and capabilities of the initiative and the information systems. The information systems and technology professionals make decisions about platforms, interfaces, programming languages, and hardware performance.

While you clearly should not delegate information systems decisions to technologists, there is good news. You need not know an inordinate amount of IT-specific information to be a good user of the information systems and technology resource or a good partner of the IT function. The sheer size of the information technology expenditure, however, commands the attention of today's managers. This ever-increasing budget means that as you hit the workforce you will find yourself making decisions that have an increasingly large IT component. Moreover, as IT becomes an increasingly important business tool, you will find that a larger and larger stake of your function's (and your personal) success rides on making good decisions when it comes to investing in and using, or not investing in and not using, information systems and IT. Exploiting business opportunities and managing threats increasingly require accurate information systems decisions.

■ SUMMARY

This chapter laid the groundwork for this book by identifying the managerial and technology trends that make it imperative for the modern general and functional manager to get involved in decision making pertaining to information systems and information technology. In this chapter we learned that

■ General and functional managers, those individuals in organizations who have responsibility to lead a

---

[5] Customer Life-time value is a metric used to estimate the value of a customer over the complete history of his or her interaction with the firm.

functional area or a business, can no longer abdicate their right, and duty, to be involved in information systems and IT decisions. They should act in partnership with the firm's information systems and technology professionals.

■ The information systems skill set required of the modern general and functional manager pertains to decisions about identifying opportunities to use information technologies to the firm's advantage; planning for the use of information systems resources; and managing the design, development, selection, and implementation of information systems. While end-user skills (i.e., the ability to use computers proficiently) are an important asset for any knowledge worker, the critical skills for modern

managers relate to the organizational, not personal, uses of information technology.

■ Chief information officers (CIOs), the leading figure in the information systems and technology function, are increasingly being selected from the functional and managerial ranks rather than from the technology ranks.

■ The enduring effects of Moore's law have led to increasingly powerful yet cheaper computing power, declining costs of computer memory, and a dramatic improvement in the ease and breadth of use of digital devices. Moreover, increasingly available network connectivity and storage capacity, improved battery life for portable devices, and the proliferation of intelligent devices have contributed to dramatically change the business and social landscape.

STUDY QUESTIONS

1. Define the following terms: *general manager, functional manager, CIO, end user.* Explain how these roles differ and the skill set each role requires.
2. Explain why it is critical to the success of modern firms that general and functional managers be directly involved in information systems and technology decision making.
3. Explain why modern firms are increasingly selecting CIOs from the managerial ranks rather than from the technology ranks.
4. Describe Moore's law and its direct and indirect effects on organizations.

FURTHER READINGS

1. Huff, S. L., Maher, P. M., and Munro, M. C. (2006). "Information Technology and the Board of Directors: Is There an IT Attention Deficit?" *MIS Quarterly Executive* (5:2) pp. 1–14.
2. Leavitt, H. J., Whisler, T. L. (1958). "Management in the 1980s." *Harvard Business Review* (November–December), pp. 41–48.
3. Nolan, Richard, and McFarlan, F. Warren. (2005). "Information Technology and the Board of Directors." *Harvard Business Review* 83, no. 10 (October) pp. 96–106.
4. Ross, J. W., and Weill, P. (2002). "Six IT Decisions Your IT People Shouldn't Make." *Harvard Business Review,* November pp. 84–92.

GLOSSARY

■ **Chief information officer:** The individual in charge of the information systems function.

■ **Digitization:** The process by which content and processes become expressed and performed in digital form.

■ **End user:** Those individuals who have direct contact with software applications as they use them to carry out specific tasks.

■ **Information system:** Formal, sociotechnical, organizational system designed to collect, process, store, and distribute information.

■ **Information technology:** Hardware, software, and telecommunication equipment.

- **IT professionals:** Those employees of the firm who have significant technical training and are primarily responsible for managing the firm's technology assets.
- **Manager:** A knowledge worker of modern business and not-for-profit organizations who is in charge of a team, a functional area (i.e., a functional manager), or the entire organization or a business unit (i.e., a general manager).
- **Polymediation:** The process of convergence of multiple digital devices into one.

2

Information Systems Defined

What You Will Learn in This Chapter

This is one of the most important chapters of this book because it defines the key concepts. Specifically, in this chapter you will learn

1. The definition of *information system* (*IS*) and *information technology* (*IT*) and the difference between the two.

2. The definition of *information system success* and *information system failure*.

3. The principal reasons why modern firms create and deploy information systems.

4. The influence of the firm's context and the external environment in which it is embedded on organizational information systems.

5. The four components that make up an information system and the manner in which they interact.

6. How to design successful information systems and how to troubleshoot problematic information systems implementations.

MINI-CASE: WIRELESS CONNECTIVITY AT McDONALD'S

One morning, as you take another sip of the bitter brewed coffee they make at WizConsult, the consulting firm you have recently joined, you stare out the window and begin daydreaming. As a connoisseur of gourmet coffee, you remember your days as a student, when given your flexible schedule you could walk to that independent specialty coffee shop near campus and work while sipping your favorite cup of double-latte vanilla-cinnamon-spice-mochaccino-delight. You loved everything about the experience—the comfortable couches, the music, the hip atmosphere, the ambiance, and the other people reading a book, doing some work, or discussing life. Then, when Wi-Fi wireless laptop connectivity was introduced, you didn't have any reason to leave—you could do all of your work there!

You are rudely awakened from your daydreaming when your boss walks in and asks you to follow him immediately. You take one last sip of your pretty bad and almost cold office coffee and go. Your boss is on the phone with a large McDonald's franchisee who operates 42 McDonald's restaurants in the upstate New York area. They quickly bring you up to speed: McDonald's has been quietly joining the Wi-Fi hotspot bandwagon. After testing the concept, it began rolling out the technology to stores in 2004. McDonald's even built a dedicated section on its Web site explaining the concept, a pay-per-use approach currently starting at $2.95 for two hours of connectivity.

Your client explains that McDonald's doesn't expect to earn money initially from its Wi-Fi service. He quotes the words of Don Thompson, president of McDonald's West Division: "What we're banking on is that more customers will visit McDonald's."[1] Also, taking a page out of Starbucks own playbook, McDonald's Corp. thinks that Wi-Fi hotspots will encourage customers to stay longer and increase consumption.[2] The program seems to be strongly supported by corporate; corporate has even added information about wireless to the online restaurant locator.

The franchisee has heard mixed reviews from his fellow franchisees at a recent conference. He does not want to miss out making extra revenue, as every bit helps. However, he does not want to waste money on the latest high-tech gizmo just for the sake of staying on trend.

As an early adopter of hotspots, you are now on the hot seat as your boss and the franchisee turn to you for a recommendation.

DISCUSSION QUESTIONS

1. Drawing on your own Wi-Fi experience in coffee shops, do you think that Wi-Fi connectivity will work at McDonald's restaurants? Justify your answer.
2. Given your answers to Question 1, can you see exceptions or do you believe your answer applies to all restaurants? What about McDonald's restaurants in other countries?
3. What do you suggest WizConsult's client do tomorrow?

INTRODUCTION

Despite the well-documented challenges associated with achieving satisfactory return on information technology (IT) investment, modern organizations around the world continue to spend significant amounts of money on IT, lured by its promise to yield efficiencies and improved competitive positioning. With IT spending on the rise, there is little doubt that

---

[1] Fried, I. (2003) "McDonald's serves up wireless web access," C|Net News.com. Available 6/29/2006
http://news.com.com/McDonalds+serves+up+wireless+Web+access/2100-1039_3-1023844.html?tag=nl

[2] Shim, R. (2004) "McDonald's Wi-Fi recipe could define industry," C|Net News.com. Available 6/29/2006
http://news.com.com/2100-7351_3-5172630.html?tag=nefd_pop

being able to wring value from these investments is critical for the modern organization. However, a narrow focus on IT investments is problematic. Instead you should focus on information systems (ISs) and their design. To do so we must first cover some important background information and introduce some key definitions.

INFORMATION SYSTEMS: DEFINITION

In order to refocus our attention from the IT investment perspective to a more comprehensive IS design perspective, we must first define an information system and how it differs from IT.

IS Not the Same As IT

Without doubt, information technology engenders a plentitude of confusing lingo, technical terms, and acronyms—a problem compounded by the many half-prepared, fast-talking individuals using terminology incorrectly. Of all the potentially confusing terms, none is more insidious than the term *information system*, usually abbreviated IS. In this context, information system is often used as a rough synonym for information technology. But there is a critical difference between IT and IS!

Consider a simple example. The famous Plaza Hotel in New York City opened its doors on October 1, 1907 (Figure 2.1). Did the Plaza have an information system when it was inaugurated as hotel?

The answer is yes, of course. The Plaza's information system allowed it to take reservations, check guests in and out, keep track of room status, and manage its inventory of amenities and equipment. Using books and ledgers (Figure 2.2), The Plaza was able to keep track of employee schedules and pay them appropriately while also maintaining financial records for legal and tax purposes.

Yet the first known implementation of computerized technology in a hotel did not occur until June 27, 1963, when the New York Hilton introduced its card-reader-based,

Figure 2.1   The Plaza Hotel

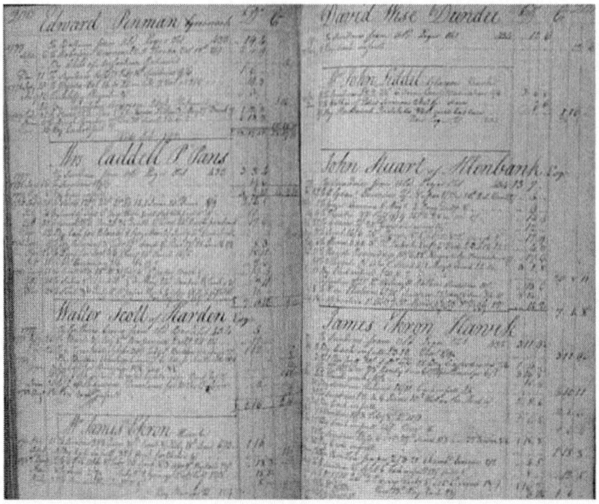

Figure 2.2   An Eighteenth-Century Ledger. (*Source*: Trustees of the National Library of Scotland.)

batch-processed front-desk system.[3] Overall computer systems began to appear in business organizations after World War II, but all kinds of business—from car manufacturers to laundry services, from banks to soft drinks makers—had been conducting businesses for decades (in some cases, centuries!). Clearly, while IT is a fundamental component of any *modern* information system, IT and IS are not synonyms.

Information Systems as Sociotechnical Systems

Information systems are formal, sociotechnical, organizational systems designed to collect, process, store, and distribute information. Within this book we primarily concern ourselves with formal organizational information systems, those that are formally sanctioned by a company or not-for-profit endeavor. For example, while as students you are very familiar with the valuable informal information system at your school (i.e., the "grapevine" that you tap into for networking contacts and to find out the scoop about a professor or a class), such a system is beyond the scope of this book. Facebook.com, the social networking site born on the Harvard campus as a tool for students to establish connections and exchange information, is another example of an informal information system (Figure 2.3).

The key aspect of our definition is the notion of sociotechnical system. Sociotechnical theory has a long tradition of research dating back to work done at the Tavistock Institute in London, England. Sociotechnical theory questioned the overly optimistic predictions about the potential benefits of new technology and suggested that the impact of new technologies on work systems was not a direct one but depended on the interplay of technology with other aspects, or components, of the work system.

---

[3] See Charles I. Sayles, "New York Hilton's Data-Processing System," *Cornell Hotel and Restaurant Administration Quarterly*, Vol. 4, No. 2 (August 1963), p. 41; and Roy Alvarez, Dennis H. Ferguson, and Jerry Dunn, "How Not to Automate Your Front Office," *Cornell Hotel and Restaurant Administration Quarterly*, Vol. 24, No. 3 (November 1983), pp. 56–62. Interestingly, the system was not speedy enough for the New York Hilton's needs, and within a year the hotel had to remove the front-desk computers—until technology processing power and speed caught up with the hotel's information processing needs.

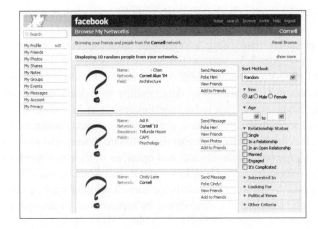

Figure 2.3   Facebook.com Web Page

The Four Components of an Information System

While sociotechnical theory is general in nature and applicable to any work system, it has been applied to IT-based information systems. Specifically, we can represent any formal organizational IS as having four fundamental components that must work together to deliver the information processing functionalities that the firm requires to fulfill its information needs.

The four components of an IT-based information system are IT, people, process, and structure (see Figure 2.4). They can be grouped into two subsystems: the technical subsystem and social subsystem. The technical subsystem, comprised of technology and processes, is that portion of the information system that does not include human elements. The social subsystem, comprised of people and people in relation to one another (i.e., structure), represents the human element of the IS.

As a general and functional manager, you will be called on to make information systems decisions as they impact your sphere of influence (e.g., your department or functional area). In order to make appropriate decisions in this realm, you need to have a solid understanding of each of the four components and how they relate to and interact with one another.

Information Technology   Information technology (IT) is defined here as hardware, software, and telecommunication equipment. The IT component is a cornerstone of any modern

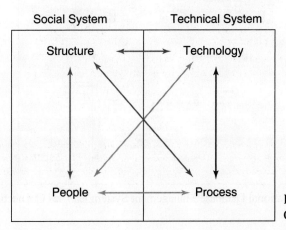

Figure 2.4   Information System Components

IS, enabling and constraining action through rules of operation that stem from its design. For example, if you choose to collect and analyze data using spreadsheet software such as Microsoft Excel rather than using a relational database management system such as Microsoft Access (Figure 2.5), you are limited by the design of the spreadsheet software. Microsoft Excel cannot create meaningful associations between separate pieces of data. The result is substantial duplication of data, leading to redundancy, inconsistencies, and inefficient data management. This is because the design of Microsoft Excel is focused on computations and formulaic calculations, not on efficient data management.

In addition, it is important to remember that software design, still as much an art as a science, is driven in large part by the choices and opinions of the developers and programmers who create it. InfoWorld columnist Bob Lewis put it well when he said, "Every piece of software is an opinion." Software, particularly custom developed applications, represents the developers' viewpoint on how the data should be represented, organized, and manipulated.

To relate to Lewis's quote, you need to only think about the last time, on the phone with a customer representative, you heard the phrase, "The system won't allow that." In such a circumstance the software design team did, knowingly or unknowingly, restrict the functionality of the software to enforce a given behavior. Note, however, that this ability to enforce rules through software is a double-edged sword. For example, some car rental companies do not allow a rental contract to print unless the customer provides two distinct phone numbers. The design of the software seeks to ensure that the customer can be easily contacted if needed and that valuable customer contact data can be tracked. However, those customers who do not have (or do not want to provide) more than one number, and rushed employees trying to move quickly through the cue of customers waiting, find it easy to produce "phantom" phone numbers—thus defeating the very purpose for creating the restriction in the software.

Process   The process component of an information system is defined here as the series of steps necessary to complete a business activity. Consider the job of a small, family-owned grocery store manager and the process he engages in when restocking inventory. The store manager must (1) check the inventory and identify the needed items; (2) call individual suppliers for quotations and delivery dates; (3) compare the various quotes; (4) select one or more suppliers for each of the needed items based on the terms of the agreement (e.g., availability,

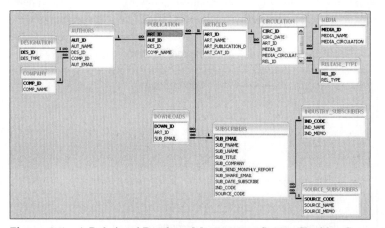

Figure 2.5   A Relational Database Management System Enables Connections Among Data

quality, delivery); (5) call these suppliers and place the orders; (6) receive the goods upon delivery, checking the accuracy and quality of the shipped items; and (7) pay the suppliers.

Note that the same activity may be performed using a variety of different business processes. Note as well that gaps can exist between the official business process that forms the basis of training programs and customer service protocols, and the informal ways in which these processes are actually performed. This discrepancy is due to the fact that, while many business processes are codified in procedure manuals and training materials, they are enacted by people. Consider again the case of the rental car company mentioned previously. While the stated business process calls for the collection of two separate customer phone numbers, you can imagine an employee who sees a long line and is attending to a customer who is not willing to provide two numbers; rather than waste time arguing, the employee types in a fictitious number to speed things along.

This potential discrepancy between the business processes as designed by the organization and the manner in which they are actually enacted is often the root cause of IS failure. When confronted with IS failure, it often helps to think about what possible obstacles exist that may make it difficult for employees to accurately follow the business process.

People   The people component refers to those individuals or groups directly involved in the information system. These individuals—whether they are end users, managers, or IT professionals—have their own set of skills, attitudes, preconceptions, and personal agendas that determine what they are able to do and what they will elect to do as part of the IS. A genuine understanding of the people involved, their skills, interests, and motivations is necessary when designing and implementing a new IS or when troubleshooting an existing IS that is not performing as expected.

Consider the example of a national government intent on rationalizing and improving communication between the local administrations (e.g., school districts) and the central institutions (e.g., ministry of education). As part of this initiative, e-mail addresses are produced for the school district superintendents and each school's principal and assistant principal. You quickly realize that this simple initiative is more likely to be successful today than it was ten or fifteen years ago when computer skills were scarce and computer anxiety was high even among highly educated individuals.

Structure   The organizational structure component (structure for short) refers to the organizational design (hierarchy, decentralized, loose coupling), reporting (functional, divisional, matrix), and relationships (communication and reward mechanisms) within the information system. Understanding the structure component is crucial because user resistance, incentive systems, and relationships are often silent enemies of IS success that go undetected before and even after IS failure becomes apparent.

Consider the famous case of a large IT consulting firm. The firm, with global operations, recognized the potential for knowledge sharing among its stable of consultants. If we introduce a knowledge management system, the thinking went, we can create repositories of knowledge to which our consultants will contribute upon completing a project. This will enable us to surface and share best practices, rather than having to reinvent the wheel with similar projects just because they are in different regions and involve a different team of consultants. Moreover, we will be able to identify subject matter experts to whom we will direct questions on specific topics. The outcome of this IS implementation will be increased turnaround time on projects, better quality results, and more satisfied clients.

A few months after the rollout of the system, it became clear that usage was spotty at best. Upon careful analysis the firm realized that there was little incentive for consultants to contribute to the knowledge base. In the fast-paced world of IT consulting, the road to success was the "billable hour," which was gained by spending productive time working on client projects. Moreover, the organizational culture was such that individual behavior and superior skills were valued over teamwork and knowledge sharing. The inevitable conclusion was that, in order for the knowledge management systems to reap the expected benefits, the tangible reward structure and the traditional mentality of the organization would need to change.

Systemic Effects

It should be clear from the preceding discussion that all four components are necessary to ensure that the information system is successful and delivers the functionality it was intended to provide. Imagine dropping any one of the four components in any of the preceding examples—the system would not work. More subtly, the four components of an information system don't work in isolation, but instead interact with one another—as noted by the arrows in Figure 2.4. This notion of interdependence of the components goes by the name *systemic effects*, indicating that changes in one component (e.g., the introduction of a new software application, a process redesign, a new organization chart, turnover among employees) affect all other components of the system and, if not properly managed, its outputs. Tim Harvey, CIO of Hilton Hotels, when speaking about the key challenges in information systems management, captured this idea: "First, by far, I think, it's the people adapting technology . . . technology is not very good unless it's used and embraced and the information it provides really infiltrates the business processes."[4]

Because of systemic effects, when called on to design a new IS or modify an existing one, you should focus not on optimizing the technology (i.e., adopting the most innovative and cutting edge technology) or any other component individually. Rather you should optimize the IS as a whole (i.e., selecting components that create the best chance to deliver the needed information processing functionality). This focus on information systems design, rather than IT investment decisions, also suggests that there are multiple ways to achieve the same information systems goal—as demonstrated by the many different ways in which similar organizations meet their information processing needs.

Understanding the importance of systemic effects is critical not only when designing a new system, but also when troubleshooting an existing one that is underperforming, in order to diagnose the root causes of the failure and to devise the appropriate intervention. Consider a restaurant that introduced hand-held ordering devices only to face discontent and rejection by the waitstaff, who complain about the fact that the system is not intuitive, is difficult to use, and gets in the way of their interactions with the guest—the source of their tips! How would you solve this problem if you were the restaurant manager? There may be a number of options here:

- You could deem the new system a failure and cut your losses by dropping the use of hand-held technology.
- You could ascribe the failure to the quality of the user interface of the hand-held ordering devices. You could then negotiate with the provider to improve the interface. This solution focuses on the IT component.

---

[4] Shein, E. (2003) "Hilton Hotels CIO Talks 'OnQ'," *CIO Magazine*, July 15, http://www.cioupdate.com/insight/article.pup/

■ You could ascribe the failure to the quality of the user interface of the hand-held ordering devices, but choose a different solution. You could work with your staff and convince them that the system is not as awkward as it seems and a bit of training will solve all their issues. This solution focuses on the people component.

■ You could ascribe the failure to the fact that your staff, comprised mostly of old-fashioned gum-chewing waiters and waitresses, just does not have the knowledge and skills to adopt computerized devices. You would then turn over your staff, replacing them with iPod-carrying cell-phone-toting college students. This solution focuses on the people component.

■ You could ascribe the failure to human inertia and your staff's resistance to change. You could then call a meeting and inform staff that the hand-held devices are going to stay and the next person who complains is going to go (you may offer incentives if you are more of the positive-reinforcement management type). This solution focuses on the structure component.

WHY DO ORGANIZATIONS BUILD INFORMATION SYSTEMS?

Now that we know what an information system actually is, we should step back and question why organizations build ISs in the first place. Simply put, a firm's objective when introducing IT-enabled information systems is to fulfill its information processing needs. Sometimes external requirements, such as financial reporting, maintenance logs, or tax documents, mandate the introduction of a new IS. More typically an organization introduces information systems in an effort to improved efficiency[5] and effectiveness.[6]

In order to fulfill its information processing needs, the organization must capture relevant data that are then manipulated, or processed, to produce an output that will be useful to the appropriate users, internal or external to the firm (e.g., customers). These data and information are typically accumulated, or stored, for future retrieval and use (see Figure 2.6). Thus, while not a component of the information system per se, information plays a critical role in modern organizations.

Note that, while the focus of this book is on IT-enabled information systems, processing of information does not necessarily require IT support to happen. Consider the last time you contributed to the in-class discussion of a case study. In order to produce valuable comments for the class, you gathered substantial information (i.e., you read the case, you read assigned articles and other class materials, you actively listened to the professor setting the context for the discussion, and you listened attentively to your classmates' comments). You then processed the information (i.e., during preparation you thought about the case issues in the context of the information presented in the readings, during class discussion you thought about how your classmates' comments supported or questioned your point of view). Finally, you produced some output—your insightful analysis for the whole class to hear. In other words, you engaged in significant information processing without ever using a computer.

---

[5] *Efficiency* is defined as the ability to limit waste and maximize the ratio of the output produced to the inputs consumed. In other words, a firm is more efficient when it produces more with the same amount of resources, produces the same with less resources, or produces more with less resources.

[6] *Effectiveness* is defined as the ability to achieve stated goals or objectives. Typically, a more effective firm is one that makes better decisions and is able to carry them out successfully.

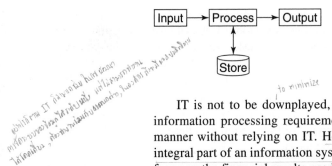

Figure 2.6 Information Processing

IT is not to be downplayed, as all but the most trivial of today's organizational information processing requirements can be fulfilled in a reliable and cost-effective manner without relying on IT. However, IT can only be successfully leveraged as an integral part of an information system, not in isolation. Moreover, while managers often focus on the financial results produced by the design and introduction of a new IS, you need to be aware of nonfinancial outcomes as well, both planned and unexpected.

Successful Information Systems

Any information system should be built according to an explicit goal (or a set of goals) designed to fulfill specific information processing needs of the implementing organization.[7] Examples of typical IS goals include

■ *For a large retail store (e.g., Wal-Mart)*: To increase the efficiency and speed of customer check-out by using self-check-out stations.

■ *For a high-end car manufacturer (e.g., BMW)*: To improve customer service by allowing individual customers to select finishing and accessories on their car, and quote in real time price changes and delivery date changes.

Consider the opening mini-case. The wireless connectivity project is being promoted by McDonald's corporation based on the expectation that it will help increase the number of customers visiting locations with Wi-Fi, it will help increase consumption by customers who have an incentive to stay longer, and it will generate new revenue from purchased wireless time.

The McDonald's franchisee seeking your input was attempting to understand whether introducing wireless connectivity would make his operations more efficient and/or effective. Even with the minimal information provided in the case, it should be clear that just purchasing the equipment (i.e., the IT) would not be enough to reap the benefits. At the very least, if customers felt that McDonald's plastic seats were too uncomfortable to sit on for more than fifteen minutes and that the food was too messy to fumble with their laptops during or after the meal, the systems would be largely unused, hence delivering little benefit to the franchisee that paid for it.

Information Systems Success: Definition   The case provides insight as to what should be considered information systems success and failure. We can unequivocally deem an information system a failure if it is abandoned (i.e., the information system is never completed) or not used (i.e., the information system is completed only to be rejected by its intended users). In either case, the system is a failure because, due to nonuse, it will yield none of the promised benefits (e.g., efficiency improvements). Figure 2.7 highlights some high-profile failures.

Beyond nonuse, discriminating successful information systems from failed ones requires an evaluation of whether, and to what extent, the system has delivered the

---

[7] Note that, while the IS goals should fit with the firm's strategic goals, the IS cannot ensure that the correct business objectives have been chosen. In other words, an IS is deemed successful when its information processing goals are achieved—even in the face of business failure due to the pursuit of a flawed strategy.

YEAR	COMPANY	OUTCOME (COSTS IN US $)
2005	Hudson Bay Co. [Canada]	Problems with inventory system contribute to $33.3 million* loss.
2004-05	UK Inland Revenue	Software errors contribute to $3.45 billion* tax-credit overpayment.
2004	Avis Europe PLC [UK]	Enterprise resource planning (ERP) system canceled after $54.5 million[†] is spent.
2004	Ford Motor Co.	Purchasing system abandoned after deployment costing approximately $400 million.
2004	J Sainsbury PLC]UK]	Supply-chain management system abandoned after deployment costing $527 million.[†]
2004	Hewlett-Packard Co.	Problems with ERP system contribute to $160 million loss.
2003-04	AT&T Wireless	Customer relations management (CRM) upgrade problems lead to revenue loss of $100 million.
2002	McDonald's Corp.	The Innovate information-purchasing system canceled after $170 million is spent.
2002	Sydney Water Corp. [Australia]	Billing system canceled after $33.2 million[†] is spent.
2002	CIGNA Corp.	Problems with CRM system contribute to $445 million loss.
2001	Nike Inc.	Problems with supply-chain management system contribute to $100 million loss.
2001	Kmart Corp.	Supply-chain management system canceled after $130 million is spent.
2000	Washington, D.C.	City payroll system abandoned after deployment costing $25 million.
1999	United Way	Administrative processing system canceled after $12 million is spent.
1999	State of Mississippi	Tax system canceled after $11.2 million is spent; state receives $185 million damages.
1999	Hershey Foods Corp.	Problem with ERP system contribute to $151 million loss.
1998	Snap-on Inc.	Problems with order-entry system contribute to revenue loss of $50 million.
1997	U.S. Internal Revenue Service	Tax modernization effort canceled after $4 billion is spent.
1997	State of Washington	Department of Motor Vehicle (DMV) system canceled after $40 million is spent.
1997	Oxford Health Plans Inc.	Billing and claims system problems contribute to quarterly loss; stock plummets, leading to $3.4 billion loss in corporate value.
1996	Arianespace [France]	Software specification and design errors cause $350 million Ariane 5 rocket to explode.

Figure 2.7   Some of the Worst Systems Failures in the Recent History of Business Computing.

(*Source*: Adapted from *Business Week, CEO Magazine, Computer World, Info Week, Fortune, The New York Times*, and *The Wall Street Journal*.)

continued

1996	FoxMeyer Drug Co.	$40 million ERP system abandoned after deployment, forcing company into bankruptcy.
1995	Toronto Stock Exchange [Canada]	Electronic trading system canceled after $25.5 million** is spent.
1994	U.S. Federal Aviation Administration	Advanced Automation System canceled after $2.6 billion is spent.
1994	State of California	DMV system canceled after $44 million is spent.
1994	Chemical Bank	Software error causes a total of $15 million to be deduced from 100,000 customer accounts.
1993	London Stock Exchange [UK]	Taurus stock settlement system canceled after $600 million** is spent.
1993	Allstate Insurance Co.	Office automation system abandoned after deployment, costing $130 million.
1993	London Ambulance Service [UK]	Dispatch system canceled in 1990 at $11.25 million**; second attempt abandoned after deployment, costing $15 million.**
1993	Greyhound Lines Inc.	Bus reservation system crashes repeatedly upon introduction, contributing to revenue loss $61 million.
1992	Budget Rent-A-Car, Hilton Hotels, Marriott International, and AMR [American Airlines]	Travel reservation system canceled after $165 million is spent.
		Adapted from © 2006 IEEE

Figure 2.7   *continued*

expected results. This is why it is so important to articulate information system goals during the design and justification phase. Yet as thorough a job you do in defining the intended IS goals, there are many situations when unintended results, positive and negative, will emerge. The best-known case of a strategic information system, the celebrated SABRE reservation systems pioneered by American Airlines, was originally introduced simply to enable inventory control in response to a very tangible operational problem: American Airlines found itself unable to manage and sell the increasing number of seats it supplied in response to mounting consumer demand for commercial air flights.

Information Systems Outcomes

Beyond efficiency and effectiveness improvements and the associated financial considerations, information systems have other direct and indirect effects on people within and outside the firm (e.g., employees, customers, suppliers). These effects can be positive, including employees' empowerment and the widening scope of their responsibility; or negative, including deskilling (i.e., the reduction of the scope of an individual's work to one, or a few, specialized tasks), loss of responsibility, and the creation of a monotonous working environment.

Another important outcome of information systems use pertains to their effect on future opportunities available to the firm. The introduction of a new information system may enable or constrain future information systems and strategic initiatives available to the firm. This is due to the fact that future systems typically rely on, or connect with, preexisting ones. Consider a grocery store that has introduced check-out scanners. This information system often becomes the basis for automatic reorder initiatives when the firm has achieved a satisfactory level of reliability and precision of scanner data.

Beyond an appreciation of their goals and outcomes, successfully designing and implementing information systems requires recognition that any information system that you envision or propose exists in a unique and very specific organizational context.

INFORMATION SYSTEMS IN THE ORGANIZATIONAL CONTEXT[8]

Consider a five-star hotel chain with sixty-two properties within the United States, and a small Silicon Valley start-up outsourcing part of its software development to high-tech firms in Ireland and India. Imagine that management in each organization heard about the potential for virtual teaming and collaboration at a distance. At the hotel company, executives pushed to have general managers from each of the locations work together as a team to share best practices and help one another respond to emergencies, such as the recent widespread blackouts in New York City or an approaching hurricane. At the start-up, the objective is to enable programmers in the three locations to share their knowledge and help each other with coding questions. Both firms introduce a groupware solution supporting the following functionalities: shared calendar, contact manager, personal e-mail, discussion forum and chat functions, resources and content management system, file manager, knowledge-base engine, and a shared whiteboard. Will the same system yield comparable results in each of these firms? Where is the "virtual teaming" vision most likely to come to bear?

Every Organization Is Unique

The simple example just described should clarify that organizations are unique in many respects. This is not only true for companies in different industries but also of otherwise similar firms that compete head to head. Microsoft and Apple Computers were the two most recognizable names in the software industry throughout the 1990s, vying to establish their operating system as the dominant platform. Yet the two firms had dramatically different images and cultures. Even starker is the difference between two of today's Dallas, Texas–based airlines—Southwest and American Airlines.

At the highest level of abstraction, a firm is characterized by its strategy, its culture, and its current infrastructure, stemming from the organization's history, size, product line, location, values, and so on.

---

[8] The following discussion is largely influenced by the following article: Silver, Mark S., M. Lynne Markus, and Cynthia M. Beath, "The Information Technology Interaction Model: A Foundation for the MBA Core Course," *MIS Quarterly*, vol. 19, no. 3 (September 1995), pp. 361–390.

Firm Strategy   A firm's strategy represents the manner in which the organization intends to achieve its objectives. In other words, understanding a firm's strategy tells us what the firm is trying to do and what course of action it has chartered to get there.

Consider two other head-to-head competitors: Dell Computers and Hewlett-Packard (HP). Dell and HP are the number 1 and number 2 makers of personal computers, respectively. Yet they have two drastically different strategies. On the one hand, Dell focuses on highly customizable made-to-order devices that are assembled upon receipt of orders directly from consumers and business clients. Conversely, HP and its recently acquired Compaq subsidiary have historically focused on producing standardized devices to be sold through a channel of distribution (e.g., Circuit City). Dell and HP are two direct competitors in the same industry, with very different strategies.

Firm Culture   A firm's culture is defined as the collection of beliefs, expectations, and values shared by the members of an organization. The firm's culture, a broad representation of how the firm does business, is an important characteristic of the organization because it captures the way, often unspoken and informal, in which the organization operates. Practices that are deemed appropriate in one organization may not be in another one.

Consider the recent merger between software titans Oracle, Corp. and PeopleSoft, Inc. Announcing the merger, the *San Francisco Chronicle* posed the question, "What do you get when you combine a company run by an Armani-clad executive known for take-no-prisoners tactics with a firm led by a fatherly founder who hands out bagels and lets his workers wear flannel to work? . . . For the merger to succeed, Oracle faces the tough task of creating a cohesive company out of two firms with distinct, even contradictory, cultures." Quoting a Forrester Research analyst, the article concluded, "Pretty quickly, the PeopleSoft employees are going to divide themselves into those who say 'I think I can work for Oracle' and 'I don't ever want to work at Oracle.'"[9]

Infrastructure   When it comes to making information systems decisions, it is also important to consider the current IT infrastructure of the firm. The existing IT infrastructure, defined as the technological backbone of the firm, constrains and enables opportunities for future information systems implementations.

The preceding example of check-out scanners at grocery stores highlights this point. Once the infrastructure is in place, the grocery store can consider future initiatives that rely on it, such as automatic inventory reorder, but also check-out coupons (i.e., the ability to print coupons at check-out based on the items the customer bought), frequency shopper cards, and basket analysis (i.e., the ability to identify correlations among items purchased by the same customer).

The External Environment   Organizations themselves don't exist in a vacuum, but instead are embedded in the external environment that encompasses regulation, the competitive landscape, and general business and social trends (e.g., outsourcing, customer self-service).

Consider three competitors, such as the Sony Corporation, Philips Electronics, and Samsung Group headquartered in Tokyo, Japan, Amsterdam, Holland and Seoul, South Korea, respectively. While these three firms compete, at least in part, in the world market for consumer electronics, they have to contend with widely different local labor and taxation laws, governmental incentive, and so on. The external environment is fairly removed

---

[9] Pimentel, B. (2004) "When firms merge, a clash of cultures Oracle, PeopleSoft managing styles couldn't be more different," *San Francisco Chronicle*, 12/15/2004.

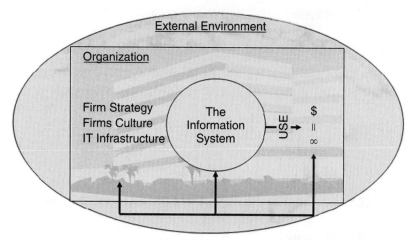

Figure 2.8 Information Systems Exist in an Organizational Context

from day-to-day operations, yet these factors have an influence on the firm and, as a consequence, on the type of information systems the firm will need to introduce.

Bringing It All Together

The previous discussion of the outcomes associated with information systems use and the information systems in context is summarized in Figure 2.8.

The model in Figure 2.8 indicates that the first-order effect of information systems is whether they are used or not. If they are used, then intended and unintended outcomes ensue, including financial results, effects on people, and effects on the future opportunities and constraints available to the firm. The model also shows that information systems do not exist in a vacuum, but they are embedded in a specific organizational context, defined by the firm strategy, culture, and IT infrastructure. Moreover, the organization itself does not exist in isolation, but it is embedded in the external environment, including social and competitive forces. The feedback loops represented by the solid line reminds us that whatever outcomes produced by the information system, positive or negative, will affect organizational characteristics and future information systems decision making.

This model is important for you as a general or functional manager because it draws to your attention all of the external influence that will aid or undermine information system success.

INFORMATION SYSTEMS AND ORGANIZATIONAL CHANGE

As a general or functional manager, you must pay close attention to organizational change. With the widespread adoption of IT by modern organizations, increasingly this organizational change is brought on by the introduction of new IT. The definition of information systems as sociotechnical systems is instrumental in helping you better manage organizational change. Specifically, we can identify three levels of organizational change brought about by the introduction of a new IT.

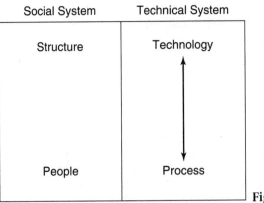

Figure 2.9   First-Order Change

First-Order Change: Automate

The simplest order of change ensuing from the deployment of technology is automation. This level of change involves technology and processes but does not affect the sphere of the social subsystem (Figure 2.9). First-order change occurs when an IT innovation is introduced that changes how an existing process is performed.

Consider those online banking tasks previously executed through a touch-tone phone interface—such as checking balances or transferring money between accounts. Many of us now perform those same tasks through a Web interface. What has changed with the move to the Web is the manner in which these processes are performed, not the tasks themselves or the individuals involved (e.g., customers). With the introduction of the Web as a customer interface, the process has become simpler and more intuitive.

Managing-first order change   The limited scope of first-order change makes it relatively easy to envision, justify, and manage. General and functional managers understand how the new technology impacts the firm's operations, and the project is straightforward to justify since the financial benefits of the change, in terms of the return on investment, can be estimated with some precision. Thus, first-order change requires little executive sponsorship and involvement.

Second-Order Change: Informate

Second-order change has major implications for the people component of the information systems as well as IT and processes (Figure 2.10). With second-order change, not only the manner in which the process is performed changes, but also those individuals who performed the process are affected by the change—either their role is modified or a different set of people is involved. Moreover, the manner in which people interact with the technology also undergoes modification. This level of change typically occurs when the information intensity of the process being performed changes substantially due to the introduction of new IT. For this reason, this level of change is called *informate*.

A good example of second-order change is IT-enabled customer self-service. Consider airline check-in kiosks. Traditionally as an airline traveler you'd have to go to the airport, cue up, and interact with an agent, who would authenticate you by checking your ID card and then would provide you with a seat and boarding passes. The advent of check-in kiosks, and now online check-in, has dramatically changed this process. First, it is now the

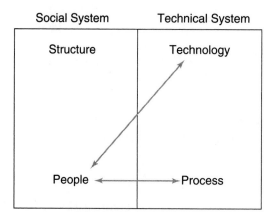

Figure 2.10   Second-Order Change

machine that authenticates you—using a credit card or frequent flier card. Then you can proceed to select a seat and print the boarding passes (see Figure 2.11).

For anyone who is very tall and used to implore the agent for an exit row seat, the kiosk has opened a wealth of new possibilities. More important, the kiosks have had a dramatic impact for the agents themselves, who now serve more of a training and troubleshooting role, helping travelers solve any problems they encounter with the system, rather than completing the check-in process on behalf of the travelers.

Managing Second-Order Change   The primary impact of second-order change is on the people dimension of the sociotechnical system. As such, second-order change provides much more of a challenge to managers who seek to implement it than does first-order change. Those affected may include employees as well as customers. Thus, appropriate training and overcoming the human tendency to resist change are key challenges.

The objectives of second-order change are typically far reaching as well. While first-order change is focused on automating existing tasks, informate level change is often seeking to take advantage of available market opportunities. Thus, justifying this level of change is more difficult and requires a more speculative analysis.

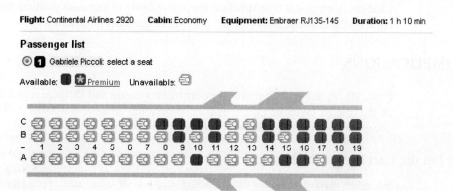

Figure 2.11   Web Check-in Allows You to Choose Seats From the Comfort of Your Home

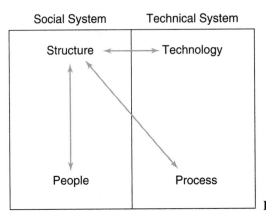

Social System   Technical System

Structure ←——→ Technology

People   Process

Figure 2.12   Third-Order Change

Third-Order Change: Transform

Third-order change represents the most pervasive and radical level of change—as such it is often referred to as *transform*. Third-order change subsumes first- and second-order change while also causing organizational structures disruptions (Figure 2.12). The interaction between structure and technology is substantiated by a change in the way the organization selects, uses, and manages technology. The interaction between the organizational structure and the people generally results in a change in the reporting and authority structure of the organization. A flatter or more permeable organizational structure usually emerges after the technology implementation. The interaction between the organizational structure and tasks manifests itself in a novel way of task accomplishment or a new set of tasks.

Consider the example of OLAP tools (see Chapter 12 for a more in-depth discussion). The commercialization of OLAP tools and powerful workstations enabled analysts and end users to have easier access to organizational data for analytical purposes. The introduction of this new technology created dramatic changes in some organizations, where the information systems function used to be the gatekeeper of data access.

Managing Third-Order Change   Third-order change requires significant managerial and executive involvement. Championship by the top management team is necessary both for signaling purposes and to provide the necessary political impetus to complete the transition. Changes in organizational structure are in fact likely to engender political battles and resistance by those whose authority and political influence is diminished.

IMPLICATIONS

From the preceding definitions of information systems and IS success and the discussions of the role of systemic effects and organizational context, a number of implications of interest to general and functional managers follow:

Don't Put the Cart before the Horse

We often receive inquiries from former students or other managers asking our opinion about one or the other IT solution (e.g., what is the best CRM software). However, you

การ คิด ก่อนว่าอยากทำอะไร แล้ว ค่อยหาวิธีทาง (IT , software) ที่จะนำมาใช้ให้ไปสู่จุดหมาย (จุดหมาย) ไม่ใช่นา software ที่ต้นแบบ แต่ตัวไม่รู้ว่าจะทำอะไร ต้องการผล

now recognize that asking such questions is equivalent to putting the proverbial cart before the horse by letting technology drive decision making.

While it is common for strategy to be inspired by the functionalities of a powerful software product, the selection of a specific IT product should not be the point of departure, but the point of arrival of your information system design effort. When asked to express an opinion about a software program or other technology, you should always start by asking, Why are you investigating this software program (i.e., what is the firm strategy?)? What are you attempting to do with the software (i.e., what is the IS goal?)?

In our opening mini-case, the firm's intention was to be able to improve its volumes (i.e., increase the number of customers and their level of consumption). This can be classified as the strategic goal. From this goal the firm should derive a precise set of IS goals that specify what information processing functionalities are needed to achieve the strategic objective (e.g., to create a comfortable working space for restaurant patrons by deploying the infrastructure to enable them to connect to the Internet using their personal computing devices, such as laptops and hand-held devices). Once the goals are set, the IS design team can identify, shape, and deploy the appropriate components of the system, of which IT is one.

The Rock in the Pond

คือถ้ามีการเปลี่ยนระบบการจัดการข้อมูล (IS) มันก็เหมือนการโยนหินลงน้ำ เพราะจะต้องมีการเปลี่ยนแปลง ไปยัง หน่วยงานอื่น, ในองค์กรด้วย

As in any other system, the components of an IS mutually influence one another (systemic effects). Similar to the ripples resulting from the act of throwing a rock into a pond, changes to one or more IS components impact, sooner or later, all other components.

Let's return to the example of airline check-in kiosks. When kiosks are installed, the business process of identifying travelers and assigning them seats must change for those customers who prefer this method. The role, and the skills required, of check-in agents is modified as a result of the change in the business process—at a minimum they must be able to explain the kiosk operations and provide helpful support as customers learn to use them.

Information Systems Are in Flux

flow , continuous movement

IS มีการเปลี่ยนแปลงตลอดเวลาเนื่องจาก กลยุทธ์ทางธุรกิจ & ปัจจัยสิ่งแวดล้อมภายนอก

fixed เครื่องมือที่เป็นเทคโนโลยีคงที่

ถ้าขั้นแรกจะมีการ update & เปลี่ยน แปลงข้อมูลอยู่ตลอดเวลา และปรับระบบ IS ให้เข้ากัน กับระบบ เพื่อให้ทำงานได้ เกิด efficiency มากสุด ไม่จำเป็นต้องปรับทุกแบบให้ดีเลิศ ที่สุด แต่ต้องปรับ ให้ในมวลรวมมาก ที่สุดกับองค์กร

An information system is not designed "once and for all" as if it were a static artifact. Business strategy and the external environment evolve continuously. This evolution calls for a constant reevaluation of IS goals and needed information processing functionalities. In turn, this reevaluation will at times engender the need for changes to the design of an existing information system.

The design and use of an IS should be seen as an iterative process involving the cyclical evaluation of individual IS components and the assessment of how different organizational systems work together to support the business. The synergy among IS components, as well as among discrete organizational ISs, can be maintained over time only if there is a willingness to modify aspects of this IS configuration as needed. Anytime a change occurs, the current IS design must be reevaluated and the system must be optimized once again.

Optimize the Whole   As mentioned earlier, you should never lose focus of your objective: to optimize the information system rather than any of its constituent parts. Optimizing the system as a whole often requires that one or more components be deoptimized (i.e., they are not as powerful or cutting edge as they could be). This fundamental insight is one that is often forgotten when managers get caught up in the IT investment mentality—the most effective information system need not be comprised of all the best parts.

To the contrary, examples abound of firms that deployed cutting-edge technology where there was no need for it to deliver the desired information processing functionalities. In some cases, the adoption of cutting-edge technology in fact reduces the effectiveness of the IS as a whole, making the achievement of the needed information processing function-alities more difficult.

CONCLUSION

Like all frameworks, those presented in this chapter are valuable because of their ability to support systematic and disciplined analysis of specific issues (e.g., software selection, IS design, system failure diagnosis). They don't offer cookie cutter answers, but they provide the support necessary for a disciplined and thorough analysis. By using them to guide your thinking, you can be sure to complete a comprehensive analysis rather than being tempted to stop upon identifying the first or second most obvious explanations, perhaps those com-municated by the most vocal members of your organization.

Furthermore, working with the models challenges conventional wisdom and man-agement fads and fashions that may lead you to reach simplistic conclusions that, while true, often only reveal part of the story (e.g., "You must train your employees when new software is introduced"). The alternative—being driven by a best practice mentality, benchmarking your organization against the performance of competitors—is a risky strategy, and always beware of so many buzzwords in one sentence! You as a manager must always consider how new IT fits within the context of your own company. Does it suit the unique people, processes, and structures of your firm? If not, is it a wise strat-egy to make changes to these components in order to fit with the IT? Or do you need different IT? All too often when selecting a system, considering change initiatives, or troubleshooting underperforming information systems, the focus is on IT and system functionality. The frameworks presented here challenge you to think in terms of overall IS design instead—perhaps a more difficult task, but certainly a more appropriate and productive one.

SUMMARY

This is a critical chapter in the book because it pro-vides fundamental definitions and sets the stage for the discussion in the next chapters. The chapter defined information systems as sociotechnical sys-tems comprised of four components: IT, people, processes, and structure. This definition and its implications provide the basis for this book.

Specifically, in this chapter we learned that:

■ Information systems are designed and built with the objective of improving the firm's efficiency and effectiveness by fulfilling its information processing needs. Successful information sys-tems are those that are used and achieve their intended goals.

■ Information systems exist in an organizational context, characterized by the firm strategy, cul-ture, and IT infrastructure. The organization itself is subject to influences of its external envi-ronment, including regulatory requirements, social and business trends, and competitive pres-sures.

■ Information systems are subject to systemic effects, defined as the notion that the different components of a system are interdependent and that changes in one component affect all other components of the system. Thus, when designing a new information system, or troubleshooting an underperforming one, you can devise multiple ways to achieve the system's goal.

■ Increasingly in modern firms, organizational change stems from the introduction of new information technologies. Depending on the objectives and reach of the new system, we identify three levels of change—first-, second-, and third-order change—each requiring different levels of commitment and sponsorship to be successfully managed.

STUDY QUESTIONS

1. Describe the difference between information systems and information technology. Provide an example of each.

2. Provide an example of two organizations in which you think a similar information system would engender two very different outcomes. Explain why.

3. Provide two examples, from your personal experience, of information systems that generate positive and negative unintended results.

4. Define the concept of systemic effects. Explain why it is important for you as a general or functional manager to be aware of this concept.

5. Describe first-, second-, and third-order organizational change induced by the adoption of new IT. Provide an example, real or imagined, for each of these three levels of change.

FURTHER READINGS

1. O'Hara, Margaret T., Watson, Richard T., and Kavan, C. Bruce. (1999). "Managing the Three Levels of Change." *Information Systems Management Journal* 16(3):63–70.

2. Zuboff, S. *In the Age of the Smart Machine: The Future of Work and Power*. New York: Basic Books, 1988.

GLOSSARY

- **Efficiency:** *Efficiency* is defined as the ability to limit waste and maximize the ratio of the output produced to the inputs consumed. In other words, a firm is more efficient when it produces more with the same amount of resources, produces the same with less resources, or produces more with less resources.

- **Effectiveness:** The ability to achieve stated goals or objectives. Typically a more effective firm is one that makes better decisions and is able to carry them out successfully.

- **External environment:** The world outside the firm that creates influences such as regulation, the competitive landscape, and general business and social trends (e.g., outsourcing, customer self-service).

- **Firm culture:** The collection of beliefs, expectations, and values shared by the members of an organization.

- **Firm strategy:** The manner in which the organization intends to achieve its objectives.

- **Information system:** Formal, sociotechnical, organizational system designed to collect, process, store, and distribute information.

- **Information technology:** Hardware, software, and telecommunication equipment.

- **IT infrastructure:** A firm's technological backbone that constrains and enables opportunities for future information systems implementations.

- **Organizational structure:** The organizational design, reporting, and relationships within the information system.

- **Process:** The series of steps necessary to complete an organizational activity.

- **Systemic effects:** The notion that the different components of a system are interdependent and that change in one component affects all other components of the system.

INTRODUCTION

In early May 2006, after the first year in the master's program at the Very Famous University (VFU), Blake Cantera landed a summer internship with Fancy Consultants & Company (FC). Upon receiving FC's call, Blake was thrilled. FC was a highly regarded local IT consulting firm serving the needs of clients ranging from independent mid-sized hotels to large multinational grocery chains.

While small and nimble, FC afforded the opportunity to work with large clients on cutting-edge projects. It also offered significant potential for personal growth and, with its flat organizational structure, FC prided itself on picking independent and self-reliant young consultants who'd work immediately on projects rather than toil in the "analysts limbo" for years. This was the most appealing aspect of FC for Blake, who knew that he would be able to do some real work over the summer.

After a brief introduction to FC systems and culture and a two-week orientation discussing the FC approach to consulting, Blake was assigned to his first account. As expected, this was a relatively small account. On the bright side, Blake was sent alone to manage the whole project, from start to finish. He was thrilled; July had not even started and he was already doing some real work!

THE ROYAL HOTEL

The Royal Hotel in New York City was a luxury all-suite hotel primarily serving an executive clientele visiting Manhattan on business. Typically, these business guests stayed for three to six days, during which time they used their suite as a temporary office. Thus, Royal Hotel's management had positioned the property to cater to the many needs of this busy and demanding audience. Amenities included in-suite plain paper fax, printer, and copier; three two-line telephones with voice mail and remote message alert; high speed Internet access; and plasma TVs and entertainment centers in each of the 482 guest suites. The Royal Hotel also provided three restaurants and a coffee shop on the premises, a 24-hour business center, a fitness center, suite dining, laundry service, complimentary shoe shine, and dedicated high-speed elevators.

This made for a fairly complex operation that needed to run smoothly and consistently. Given the high percentage of repeat guests it was important that guest rooms be spotless and consistently in working order.

THE TASK

As he arrived to the property for a one-week assignment, all expenses paid, Blake thought to himself with a smile, "I can get used to this . . ." But, with just the time to take a shower, he had to get ready for a dinner meeting with the general manager (GM).

The Royal Hotel's GM was a no-nonsense old-school hotelier with a distinctive German accent. He quickly zeroed in on the task, in response to Blake's comment about the "very good" quality of service provided by the Royal Hotel:

> Our level of service is unacceptable! We are very good by most hotels' standard, but we are not "most hotels." Our guests are extremely discerning; it is completely unacceptable to have a light bulb out in the bathroom when the guest checks in, particularly if she is a returning guest. And that's not as bad as a stain on the carpet or a clogged toilet. I had one of my best customers call down to report a clogged toilet last week; can you imagine? Unacceptable! I need you to make sure this never happens again.

As he sat listening to the GM, Blake briefly questioned the wisdom of taking on so much responsibility so quickly; he had not even finished his master's! But this was a brief moment of doubt, and he remembered one of his father's famous sayings: "Did you want the bicycle? Now you have to pedal!" Blake silently chuckled to himself and tuned back into the GM's tirades with a confident smile. He already had the answer to the problem.

THE SOLUTION

After examining the property and interviewing a number of people, including the directors of housekeeping, maintenance, and IT, Blake recommended that the Royal Hotel purchase and install M-Tech's Espresso! Rapid Response Solution (see Case Appendix for a description of the product). In his presentation to the executive team, highlighting the main advantages of the proposed information system, he mentioned the following:

- *Rapid response*: The Espresso! application enabled the use of a phone interface, allowing housekeepers to report problems with the room (e.g., light bulb out) as soon as the problem was identified rather than having to wait until the housekeeper ended the shift and verbally communicated the problem to the maintenance department.

- *Quality control*: Since the new information system allowed immediate reporting of problems, it reduced the chance of "slippage through the cracks" occurring when housekeepers at the end of the shift forgot to communicate the problem. It also eliminated the risk that maintenance would forget or claim it did not receive the request.

- *Preventive maintenance*: The maintenance department would be able to identify recurrent problems and stop them before they occurred.

- *Reporting*: Management would be able to extract a number of extremely valuable reports from the system (see Case Appendix for details). This would allow managers to reward best performers and motivate employees.

Upon receiving the go-ahead from the executive team, Blake negotiated with the vendor for the application license, configuration and start-up costs, ongoing maintenance and support, and a week of onsite training. But as he was preparing for the upcoming roll-out and implementation, he was called to a new account. This unexpected call was bittersweet. Yes, he would not be able to see his very first project through, but the partner at FC must have noticed his performance since he was being reassigned to a project with a regional credit union in Cortland, New York. Not quite New York City, but the project was larger and more high-profile. This was a good move for a summer intern!

As Blake handed the Royal Hotel project to his replacement and classmate at VFU, Jack Scarso, he was a bit nervous. Having been on a couple of teams with Jack back at school, Blake did not hold him in the highest esteem. Yet, telling himself that Jack deserved a fair shake, Blake turned over all the paperwork and his draft information system design, adding a word of caution:

> Jack, the GM is very impatient about this project. Make sure you don't let his anxiety for an operational system rush you into a half-baked design. This is a complex operation, there is a heck-of-a-lot going on here.
>
> Good luck, Jack!

SIC TRANSIT GLORIA MUNDI[10]

A month and half had gone by since Blake left the Royal Hotel. While he heard from Jack a couple of times regarding minor questions, he assumed everything had gone well. He felt good about the quality of the material he had left with Jack as well as the quality of the Espresso! application and the contract he had negotiated.

He had missed staying at the Royal Hotel, having traded down to a Ramada Inn across the street from the bank headquarters. But he felt good about the project as he wrapped up the documentation. A full-time offer was a sure bet!

"Here it comes," Blake smiled as he recognized the cell phone ring tone associated with his boss's personal cell phone. As he picked up, Blake quickly realized he was in for a surprise. Blake's boss sounded quite unhappy as he said,

> What happened at the Royal Hotel? I just got a call from the GM over there. He said that they did what you and Jack proposed and they wasted a bunch of money on a system nobody is using! I had my doubts about Jack, but I thought you'd have no problem with this project. You don't start school for another two weeks, right? My assistant just booked you on a flight back to NYC; you should have confirmation in your inbox.

Blake realized that this was not the time to voice his own doubts about Jack. Rather, he simply took ownership of solving the problem and began modifying his plans on the fly. Out were the pre-class barbeques and trading summer internship stories with classmates. Two weeks was probably just enough to attempt to straighten out the mess made by Jack.

Blake's attempts to get in touch with Jack were futile. Jack's internship had ended and he was backpacking through the woods of Utah to, as he put it, relieve stress and recharge his batteries before school started again.

Upon returning to the Royal Hotel, Blake found that the machine running Espresso! was sitting in a corner collecting dust. It looked like it was abandoned soon after roll-out, a suspicion confirmed by the director of IT, who mentioned that the installation and training session had been smooth sailing. Employees had been very eager to learn about the system but seemed to lose that interest rapidly afterward.

The director of housekeeping and the director of maintenance did not have much to add, simply noting that employees found the old manual system to work much better for their needs. The GM, on the other hand, had much to say, his German accent more pronounced than ever. The words were still ringing in Blake's ears as he left the meeting: "I invested a lot of money in this software. You better deliver all the results you promised in your presentation."

---

[10] A phrase meaning "*thus passes away the glory of the world*" used to remind us that nothing is permanent and that we must stay humble. As Blake found out, so fleeting can be the fortunes of a summer internship.

continued

CASE STUDY (*continued*)

As Blake prepared to troubleshoot this failed information system and to devise a solution to make it work, he remembered the words of his information systems professor at VFU: "Focus on the information system design, not the technology investment!" "Therein lay the solution," Blake thought with a tinge of hope.

[handwritten annotations: "term, plan in the mind", "small, slightly", "in that place, in that circumstance"]

APPENDIX: BROCHURE OF M-TECH ESPRESSO!

Solve tomorrow's issues today

⚡ Rapid Response

No matter how comprehensive your preventive maintenance program is, issues like burnt light bulbs, leaks, and guest requests are unavoidable in any hotel. Espresso! Rapid Response helps your staff report, respond to, and resolve issues like these faster than ever before!

Reporting

Housekeepers are in the guest rooms everyday and they must be the hotel's eyes and ears. With Rapid Response, they can report deficiencies directly to the computer. *[handwritten: (inadequacy, incompleteness)]*

- No more hard to decipher work order tickets. *[handwritten: read, interpret (ambiguous)]*
- No more busy signals or holding for a dispatcher. *[handwritten: (someone who administers sth on schedule)]*
- No more language barriers.

An automated attendant walks them through the reporting process step by step in the *language of their choice* - English, Spanish, French, and Chinese, to name a few. In a matter of seconds, Rapid Response automatically generates, prioritizes, and dispatches a work order to a printer, fax, or alphanumeric pager. *[handwritten: lettered numbers]*

Response and Resolution

The resulting work order contains all of the information that response personnel need to complete the call. Whether it's a toilet overflowing, or a guest who needs towels, your staff will be able to respond faster

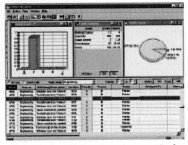

The Espresso! Command Center

than ever before! Response staff can then use the same automated attendant to tell you when they've started and completed the work.

Meanwhile, at the Hotline

Instead of spending their time answering employee calls and entering data into a computer, your hotline operators and guest service agents are now free to focus on guest requests and monitor all pending calls at Espresso!'s visual Command Center (shown above). In the end, the issue is resolved, often *before a guest ever even notices*, and the detailed work order history is being maintained by the computer automatically.

Espresso! Rapid Response, turns your hotel staff into a proactive team working together to maximize guest satisfaction by solving tomorrow's issues today!

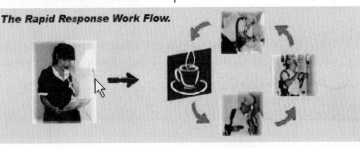

The Rapid Response Work Flow.

Preventive Maintenance

Plan your work. Work your plan.

A well-managed, targeted, preventive maintenance program is the foundation of any quality management system. If your hotel is in great shape, your guests are sure to notice. Espresso! PM Center and Sidekick make managing this traditionally difficult and time-consuming part of hotel operations easier than ever before.

The PM Challenge
No one has ever doubted the importance of a solid preventive maintenance program. On the contrary, hundreds of computerized systems have been designed to help create and manage your preventive maintenance program. Why, then, do most of these systems wind up collecting dust on a shelf? Because the information required to get these computerized systems going is difficult to compile, enter, and maintain.

We've Done The Hard Part For You
Forget about defining and entering detailed PM tasks for every piece of equipment. The PM Center already includes a comprehensive library of PM Tasks predefined for you by equipment type. Each task includes a list of Smart Steps which detail preventive maintenance measures needed for each task. All that you need to worry about is getting your property specific equipment and location information into the system.

The Startup Wizard Gets You Running - FAST!
The unique Startup Wizard guides you through the process of entering your equipment, locations, and employee information and setting up a load-leveled calendar. Following the Wizard's six easy steps you can have a comprehensive, load-leveled PM program ready to go in minutes - not days.

Get to Work With Sidekick
Once your calendar is ready, you can quickly issue PM tasks to your crew on their Sidekick handheld units. Using the Espresso! Sidekick software on the Symbol SPT 1700 Palm Pilot, your engineers take all of their assigned work with them to the field. Sidekick walks them through each PM procedure step by Smart Step. A barcode scan is required at each piece of equipment to start and complete each work order and ensures that the

Symbol SPT 1700

technician actually visited the scheduled location. Data collected with the Smart Steps and labor information is stored on the Symbol SPT 1700 and then uploaded to the PM Center at the end of the day.

More Wizards, More Magic
Sidekick can also be used with the PM Center Survey and Rounds Wizards. These wizards create work orders for taking equipment inventory, collecting plate information, and performing daily rounds. The Sidekick software and Symbol SPT 1700 make it easy to gather data in the field and perform daily rounds. Since each inspection point must be scanned with the barcode reader, you'll know that your technician actually visited each location during his rounds.

Espresso! PM Center and Sidekick guarantees your property a targeted, comprehensive, preventive maintenance program and a solid foundation to the property quality management system. Espresso! - plan your work. Work your plan.

PM Calendar Preview

Features

- Telephone-based data entry
  - *Work Order Request*
  - *Order Assignment*
  - *Start Work*
  - *Complete Work*
  - *Close Order*
- Multilingual voice prompts
- Hotline Command Center
  - *User defined desktop configurations*
  - *Bidirectional sorting and keystroke searching*
  - *Meaningful graphics*
  - *Single screen operation*

- Dispatch Options
  - *Alphanumeric paging*
  - *Network printing*
  - *Fax*
- Automatic escalation dispatch
- Intelligent duplicate work order prevention
- User defined security groups
- Quick page alphanumeric paging
- Automatic system event and action error logs
- Color coded priorities and selectable audible alarms
- Remote system support
- Microsoft SQL version available

BENEFITS

Improve Response Time
Espresso!'s unique telephone interface and alphanumeric pagers can log and dispatch work requests in under a minute and without human intervention.

Eliminate Lost Calls
Whether entered over the telephone or at the terminal, Espresso! tracks and ages work orders until they are completed.

Save Data Entry Time
Dispatchers save data entry time and focus on guest requests by enabling personnel to enter work requests and complete work orders using the telephone interface.

Ensure Proper Follow-up
Real time graphs of work order aging facilitate the follow up process for dispatchers.

Expand Reporting Pool
Multilingual prompts and deficiency cards empower non-English-speaking personnel to report problems in their native language.

Improve Guest Service
Espresso! helps you discover problem areas in service or the property. With this information, your proactive measures can prevent guest dissatisfaction.

REPORTS

With the Espresso! Report Generator you'll easily be able to see:

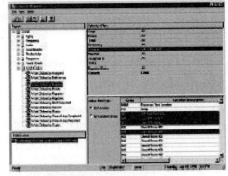

- Most frequently occuring or recurring issues

- Top reporting and/or completing performers

- Guest room histories

- Response time reports

- System utilization graphs

- Productivity reports

- Labor reports

- Aging reports

3

Organizational Information Systems and Their Impact

What You Will Learn in This Chapter

This chapter completes our introductory series on the foundations of information systems. In Chapter 1 we made the case for this book's value to general and functional managers. In Chapter 2 we provided important definitions. In this chapter we discuss the vocabulary and concepts that will enable us to categorize different types of information systems and to communicate with other managers and IS professionals.

Specifically, in this chapter you will learn:

1. How to categorize systems according to the hierarchical, functional, and process perspectives. You will also learn the rationale for each perspective and its limitations.

2. The definition, underlying principles, and applications of business process reengineering (BPR), as well as the advantages and disadvantages of BPR.

3. The definition of *integration* and its role in the modern firm. We will explore the pressures toward integration and the challenges integration creates. We will also discuss business and systems integration trends and the relationship between the two.

4. The information systems cycle and the progression of business data, from its inception in transaction processing systems, to its storage in data repositories, and finally to its use in analytical tools.

MINI-CASE: ONLINE DISTRIBUTION AT THE INDEPENDENT

Another morning, another bad cup of coffee at the office . . . you are seriously considering buying an espresso machine for your floor; you may even turn a profit after you convert all your bad-coffee-drinking colleagues. Before you can even begin to long for the old college days of decent morning coffee (see Chapter 2 mini-case), your boss calls you in. He is sitting with an old friend, the general manager (GM) of The Independent, a renowned upscale property in New York City without any chain affiliation but with a strong brand and good name recognition.

As they fill you in on the discussion and reminisce for over twenty minutes about all the pranks they pulled in college, you discover that management at The Independent was very forward looking and had attempted to cash in on the potential offered by online distribution early on. It created its first Web site in the mid-1990s, when only the large chains were doing it, and developed a channel strategy to improve its online exposure. In addition to its own Web site, The Independent purchased placement and banner ads on large search engines (e.g., Google) and developed relationships with online distributors such as Travelocity and Expedia. As the GM put it, "If you want to drive traffic, you no longer open your doors and wait for people to show up. These days you must be an online player or travelers won't even know

you exist. Online distribution is the wild, wild, west; every other day there is a new intermediary on the Internet with different revenue models, contracts, and ideas about how to reach an audience. You must play, or customers won't find you. It's a brave new world for a traditional hotelier like me, I tell you; it is a full-time job just to keep the online channels humming!"

With such attention devoted to online distribution, management at The Independent was unsure about the implications of recent developments. "I am not sure what's going on here," the GM said. "We were getting a nice steady flow of bookings from our Web site, and now we don't. We have done customer surveys, and I regularly walk the lobby to talk to my guests. They are very satisfied with our product and how informative and fast our Web site is. With the cost of third-party online distribution, we must regain a steady flow of Web site bookings!"

Your boss suggests that you are the right person for this job, with your knowledge of service industries and information systems . . . and you don't mind going since you heard the café at The Independent makes great cappuccino!

Upon your arrival, life is good, the cappuccino is all it was cracked up to be, and your brain is firing on all cylinders. As you perform some simple analyses on historical traffic by channel (Figure 3.1)[1] and booking flows

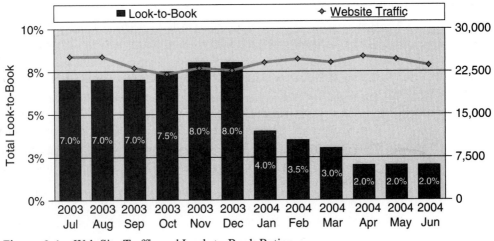

Figure 3.1   Web Site Traffic and Look-to-Book Ratios

---

[1]Web site traffic represents the number of unique visitors to the site. The look-to-book ratio measures the hotel's ability to convert these visitors (lookers) into paying customers who book reservations.

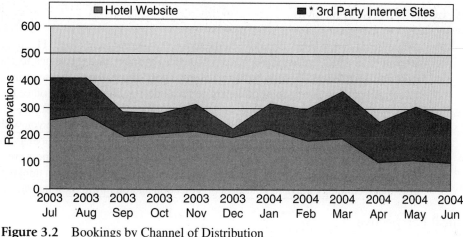

Figure 3.2   Bookings by Channel of Distribution

by channel (Figure 3.2), you realize that the answer was there all along in the data.

For all the attention that The Independent paid to the online channels of distribution, hotel management seemingly failed to realize the value of the footprints left by its online travelers as they shopped the Web.

DISCUSSION QUESTIONS

1. What do you think was the root cause of shifting market share of reservations (i.e., bookings) made directly on the proprietary Web site to reservations made on the third-party channel of distribution (e.g., Travelocity, Expedia)?

2. What recommendation will you make to the GM of The Independent once you finish sipping your cappuccino? What should the Independent do tomorrow? What should it change about its operations, if anything?

3. What do you think is the key lesson learned by The Independent? What general guidelines would you have for your many other clients in and outside the lodging industry?

INTRODUCTION

In Chapter 2 we formally defined information systems (IS) as those sociotechnical organizational systems designed to collect, process, store, and distribute information. We identified the four components of an IS and introduced the notion of systemic effects to represent the mutually interdependent relationships among the four components. We also discussed how information systems fit within the organization in which they are embedded and within the larger external environment.

In this chapter we rely on those definitions to explore the organizational impacts of information systems. This chapter is important for two main reasons. First, information systems pervade the modern organization, so understanding how they are classified and organized is a prerequisite to becoming a successful manager and being able to navigate the infrastructure of the modern firm. Second, because you are ultimately responsible for the success of your company or the organizational function that you are heading (e.g., finance, marketing), it is critical that you optimally manage organizational change when it occurs. Increasingly today, the impetus behind organizational change comes from the introduction of new IT and the implementation of information systems. Moreover, even when IT is not providing the impulse for change, organizational change calls for information systems adaptation. It is therefore paramount that you understand the impact of information systems and the firm on each other.

CATEGORIZING SYSTEMS

Since Levitt and Whisler popularized the term *information technology* (IT) in the business literature in 1958,[2] researchers have advanced a number of approaches to classify and describe the role that IT plays in organizations. These efforts focus on categorizing the software applications as the point of departure for understanding the function of the information systems built around the applications in the organizations of interest.

Classification models are useful for two reasons. First, they provide you with a vocabulary to interact with your colleagues and with IS professionals—a vocabulary that is used extensively and taken for granted in modern organizations and in the business press. Second, the models described below provide the basis for you to develop your own thinking about the role that technology plays in your own organization and on how to best manage its impacts.

Hierarchical Perspective

ตามลำดับชั้น,ขั้น

The hierarchical perspective recognizes that decision making and activities in organizations occur at different levels. At each level the individuals involved have different responsibilities, make different types of decisions, and carry out different types of activities (see Table 3.1). As a consequence, the type of information systems introduced to support each level must take these differences in account.

Operational Level   The operational level of the organization is mostly concerned with short-term activities, typically those that occur in the immediate term. Operational personnel are focused on performing the day-to-day activities that deliver the firm's value proposition. For example, in a grocery store, operational personnel concentrate on keeping the shelves stocked, keeping the store clean, addressing customer questions and requests in a timely fashion, and ensuring speedy transaction processing at checkout.

Decision making at the operational level is typically highly structured by means of detailed procedures, and, traditionally, front-line employees enjoy little discretion. The objective here is efficient transactions processing under a limited degree of uncertainty.

Table 3.1   Activities by Hierarchical Level

Activity	*Time Horizon*	*Hierarchical Level*	*Characteristics*
Strategic	Long term	General management	Externally focused
		Functional management	Ad hoc
			Highly unstructured
Tactical	Mid term	Middle management	Repeatable
			Semistructured
			Recurrent
Operational	Short term	Front line employees	Low discretion
			Highly structured
			Transaction focused

---

[2]Leavitt, H. J., and T. L. Whisler (1958), "Management in the 1980s," *Harvard Business Rev.*, Nov.–Dec., 41–48.

We refer to the information systems that support this organizational level as transaction processing systems (TPSs). The information technologies underpinning a TPS are typically used to automate recurring activities and to structure day-to-day operations, ensuring that they are performed with speed, accuracy, and as prescribed by the procedures. The scanner checkout system in the aforementioned grocery store represents a classic example of a TPS. Another example, in any retail store, is represented by the inventory management system.

Transaction processing can occur in batch, when transactions are acquired, and stored before being computed all at once (e.g., payroll processing), or online, when transactions are processed as they occur, in real time (e.g., credit card authentication).

Managerial Level   The managerial level of the organization is mostly concerned with mid-term decision making and a functional focus. The activities performed tend to be semi-structured, having both well-known components and some degree of uncertainty. Returning to our grocery store example, consider the job of the store manager. Store managers in large chains are typically responsible for selecting that portion of the inventory that experiences regional and local demand. The store manager therefore must be able to monitor demand for these products, forecast future demand, and make inventory management decisions. In manufacturing contexts, such as a chemical plant or a factory, middle management is charged with decision making that pertains to optimizing plant operations (e.g., inventory management, production schedules, labor utilization) given the overall production goals.

Decision making at this level is typically semistructured but characterized by repeatable patterns and established methods. The focus is on tactical decision making characterized by some discretion. The objective is to improve the effectiveness of the organization, or one of its functions, within the broad strategic guidelines set by the executive team.

The information systems that support this organizational level are typically called decision support systems (DSSs).[3] DSSs provide the information needed by functional managers to engage in tactical decision making. The objective is to produce recurring reports (e.g., daily sales reports, monthly customer service reports) and exception reports (e.g., items that are running low and may cause a stockout). DSSs typically focus on internal operations, and the data they use for analysis stems from the firm's TPS (see Figure 3.3).

Executive Level   The executive level of the organization is concerned with high-level, long-range decisions. Executives are focused on strategic decision making and on interpreting how the firm should react to trends in the marketplace and the competitive environment. Continuing the example of the grocery store chain, the executive team is focused on judgments such as where to locate new stores, what to do with underperforming stores, what long-term contracts to sign with suppliers, and at what price.

Decision making at this level is highly unstructured, often ad hoc, and reliant on internal as well as external data sources. The objective is, as much as possible, to predict future developments by evaluating trends, using highly aggregated data and scenario analyses. Little structure and formal methodologies exist for activities at this level.

We refer to the information systems that support this organizational level as executive information systems (EISs). A recent development in EIS is offered by the use of software applications known as executive dashboards. These tools enabled rapid evaluation of highly

---

[3] There is some confusion about terminology at this level, with some sources referring to information systems in support of middle management as management information systems (MISs). The term *MIS* can be confusing as it is often used to refer to the collection of all the information systems used by the firm. We therefore use the term *DSS*.

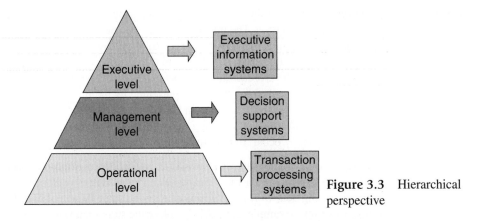

Figure 3.3 Hierarchical perspective

aggregated organizational and trend data while still providing drill-down features that enable executives to view detailed information (see Figure 3.4 for an example).

Evolution of the Hierarchical Perspective The hierarchical perspective has proven very useful over the years in enabling managers and IS professionals to easily identify the main characteristics and purpose of information systems and the information technology products designed to support them. However, this perspective is becoming increasingly less representative due to the recent organizational trend toward the adoption of flatter hierarchies with fewer layers between front-line operations and strategic decision making. Moreover, we have recently witnessed a trend toward the empowerment of operational personnel who increasingly enjoy decision-making discretion. (prudence)

Another limitation of the hierarchical model stems from the fact that it is difficult to separate information systems in clear-cut categories. For example, while the defining characteristic of TPSs is their operational focus on day-to-day transaction processing. The software applications that support many modern TPSs provide extensive reporting functionality, increasingly giving these systems the traits and functionality that characterize DSSs.

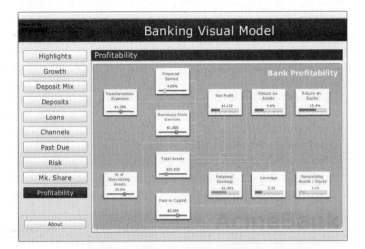

Figure 3.4 Executive Dashboard for the Banking Industry

Functional Perspective

As the post–World War II years created significant impetus for the growth of American businesses, the centralized organizational forms could no longer cope with the increasing managerial complexity brought on by size and diversification. As a consequence, there was a trend toward decentralization, with organizations creating business units and distinct functional areas within them (e.g., accounting, finance, human resources).

This decentralized management structure was very successful because it solved the coordination problems brought on by increasing size. Each unit was able to maintain its operations to a manageable degree of complexity while the corporation grew larger. The functional organization within business units is typically represented in the form of the organizational chart (see Figure 3.5 for an example).

With every function managing its own budget independently and having its unique information processing needs, functional information systems emerged.

Functional Systems   Functional systems are expressly designed to support the specific needs of individuals in the same functional area (see Figure 3.6). Functional systems are based on the principle of local optimization, which suggests that information processing needs are unique and homogeneous within a functional area. Thus, the optimal systems are tailored to those highly specific needs and use a language that is familiar to the professionals in that area. As a result, today there is a vast software industry catering to the information processing needs of every functional area in almost any industry sector.

The functional perspective, in conjunction with the hierarchical approach (see Figure 3.7), worked reasonably well for a number of years, until the recession of the late 1980s put pressure on U.S. firms to both increase efficiency and offer superior customer service.

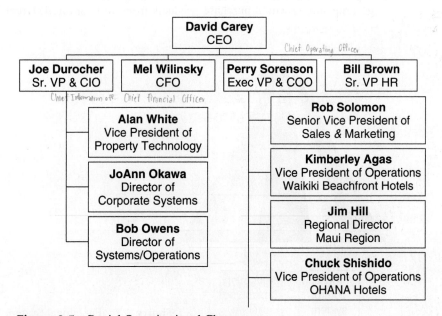

Figure 3.5   Partial Organizational Chart

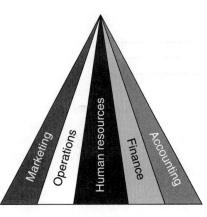

Figure 3.6 Functional Perspective

Process Perspective

The primary limitation of the functional and hierarchical perspectives is their lack of integration among separate systems and the introduction of considerable redundancy. This redundancy often created inefficiency, with duplication of similar efforts in separate business units, and substandard service, with customers often being referred to different representatives of the same organization for service. From a technology perspective, the functional approach led to the development of silo applications. Like silos used in farms to store and keep different grains separate (Figure 3.8), these applications would serve a vertical (i.e., functional) need very well but made it difficult to enable communication across functional areas.

Consider the case of Johnson and Johnson (J&J), the highly diversified health care products maker, with product lines ranging from beauty-care goods to medical and diagnostic devices. After engaging in some internal research, J&J found that a number of its customers (e.g., drug stores) would purchase products from up to seven different business units.

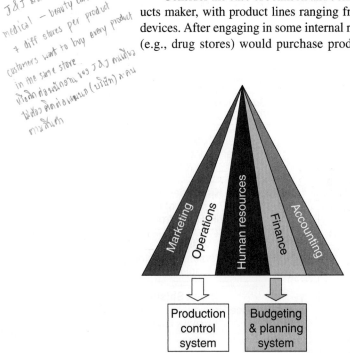

Figure 3.7 Functional Systems

Figure 3.8   Silos on a Farm

Customers began to ask why they could not interact once with a J&J representative for all their needs. This change would make it easier for the customer to do business with J&J, and it would also enable customers to negotiate volume discounts, coordinate shipments, and experience superior customer service.

Business Process Reengineering   Business process reengineering (BPR) emerged in the early 1990s as a way to break down the organizational silos in recognition of the fact that business processes are inherently cross functional. A business process is defined here as the series of steps that a firm performs in order to complete an economic activity (see Figure 3.9).

BPR is a managerial approach that employs a process view of organizational activities. BPR was codified in a methodology for achieving internal business integration using a top-down approach to business process redesign and seeking dramatic performance improvements through rationalization of activities and elimination of duplication of efforts across separate functions and units. As Michael Hammer put it in the article that first popularized the term *BPR,* "We should 'reengineer' our business: use the power of modern information technology to radically redesign our business processes in order to achieve dramatic improvements in their performance."[4]

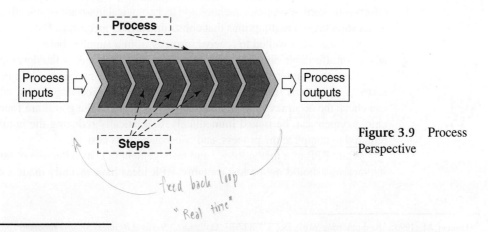

Figure 3.9   Process Perspective

---

[4] Hammer, M. (1990), "Reengineering Work: Don't Automate, Obliterate," *Harvard Business Review,* July/Aug., pp. 104–112.

The BPR methodology focuses on activities internal to the firm and requires that managers in charge of the redesign effort question old assumptions regarding how the business should operate. Such redesign should be driven by a process focus—defined as a way of organizing work that centers on the steps necessary to create value for customers, without regard for what functional areas would traditionally be responsible for the process steps.

The proponents of BPR suggest that it is this process focus that enables the firm to eliminate redundancy and inefficiency associated with the multiple handoffs of tasks from one area to another. The firm should therefore reorganize its work in a series of processes designed around the intended outcomes. In charge of each process is a processes champion, who oversees the process from start to finish.

Finally, the BPR methodology is radical in nature, requiring total disregard for existing processes to make room for the redesigned ones. Only with this approach could the firm "stop paving the cow paths"[5] and achieve drastic performance improvements.

The Dark Side of Reengineering   As with any far-reaching transformation process, there were significant risks associated with BPR efforts. First, radical third-order change (see Chapter 2), as required by BPR efforts, engenders significant resistance by those involved. Changes in the individuals' scope of work, responsibility, and position within the organizational structure require abundant retraining and careful planning. People tend to be very comfortable with the way they operate, and changes in their job role, scope, or responsibility require the development of new sets of skills and training. This often engenders confusion.

Second, the BPR methodology developed a bad reputation over the years due the significant amounts of downsizing and layoffs that followed BPR efforts.

Finally, BPR initiatives are very expensive because they often require the firm to retire its legacy systems and develop a costly integrated technology infrastructure. Applications that had been developed to enable a functional perspective rarely can be adapted to support a process perspective. The rise to prominence of BPR was seized by the software industry and spurred the development of a number of integrated applications. New classes of software programs, such as enterprise systems and supply chain management systems (see Chapter 12), built to support a process focus emerged at this time.

The Role of IT in Business Process Reengineering Efforts   The main catalyst for BPR efforts is modern information technology; technological innovation typically enables the firm to question the old assumptions that constrain current operations. For example, while traditionally firms have waited to receive invoices from a supplier before issuing payment, the advent of affordable and comprehensive networks has enabled the development of secure extranets (see Chapter 5). Such extranets have allowed the redesign of billing processes, with many organizations installing networked computers at receiving docks, where employees can check the accuracy of a shipment as it is received. If the goods are found to be acceptable, payment can be issued immediately, dramatically reducing the number of handoffs required to complete the process, and consequently its cost.

While BPR as a methodology and management fad has fallen out of favor, its underlying message should not be lost (notably, BPR ideas have recently made a comeback).[6] As

---

[5] Hammer, M. (1990), "Reengineering Work: Don't Automate, Obliterate," *Harvard Business Review,* July/Aug., pp. 104–112.

[6] Hammer, M. (2004), "Deep Change: How Operational Innovation Can Transform Your Company," Harvard Business Review, *April.*

organizations and technology evolve over time, traditional business processes may become obsolete and need to be reevaluated. The interplay of new technologies, and the opportunity they afford, with the redesign of business processes to take advantage of these technologies has the potential to yield substantial performance improvements. Note that while BPR was developed as an internal methodology to the organization, the same idea has been extended to interorganizational relationships.[7]

THE INTEGRATION IMPERATIVE

The emergence of the process perspective, and the promise it held for streamlining business operations and thereby creating substantial efficiencies and effectiveness improvements, is at the heart of the current impetus behind integration efforts. Integration efforts have held center stage for the last decade and continue to rank among the top issues of interest to business and information systems executives.

The Reasons behind Nonintegrated Operations

As we discussed above, lack of integration finds its roots in the historical evolution of organizational structures and the increasing coordination costs associated with managing larger and larger companies. As new, increasingly powerful technology became available, with its ability to reduce coordination cost by handling large amounts of information at a negligible marginal cost, it became increasingly feasible to reunite previously separate units.

Another source of lack of integration is mergers and acquisitions. Many of the promised synergies that justify mergers and acquisitions are predicated on the ability to meld together information systems that had been developed independently by previously separate organizations. While the costs associated with such endeavors have often been underestimated, the importance of systems integration following mergers and acquisitions is now widely acknowledged.

A testament to the continued importance of integration to the modern business is the fact that many of the trends discussed in Chapter 12 are based on the integration imperative. In this section we provide a definition and an overview of integration.

Defining Integration

The Merriam-Webster online dictionary defines the act of integrating as "form, coordinate, or blend into a functioning or unified whole" or "unite." Thus, integration is the process that an organization, or a number of related organizations, uses to unify, or join together, some tangible or intangible assets. Assets here represent physical possessions, like computer networks and applications, or intangible assets, like data, knowledge, or business processes.

The overarching goal of integration, in any of its forms, is to organize, streamline, and simplify a process or an application. Alternatively, the firm's integration effort seeks to modify processes, applications, or assets so that they better represent the realities of the

---

[7] Hammer, M. (2001), "The Superefficient Company," *Harvard Business Review,* September, 82–91.

organization and are more closely aligned with the current business objectives and strategic orientation of the firm.

The Dimensions of Integration

We can categorize integration efforts on two dimensions: their locus and object (see Figure 3.10). The locus of integration can be internal or external. In the first case the firm is seeking to unify and coordinate owned assets that reside within the boundaries of the firm. For example, a bank may take loan applications at a branch, by phone or by asking customers to fill out paper-based applications and mail them to the bank. Once an application has been collected, it is checked for accuracy and sent to the bank's administrative office for processing. There, a clerk collects any documentation still needed, such as the applicant's credit score, and passes the application on to a loan officer, who makes a decision.

Using an expert system and networked computers, such a process can be redesigned to achieve dramatic improvements in speed. The application can be completed online or input directly into a computer application by an agent if the applicant prefers to call or visit a branch. Its accuracy can be immediately enforced by rules in the software application that do not allow the process to continue without the needed data. The system, connected to the credit rating agency, can immediately obtain credit scores and any other relevant information. For the majority of loan applications, where decisions are fairly straightforward, this is typically all that is needed to issue a recommendation, and the expert system can do so in real time. More complex applications can be escalated to an experienced loan officer, who, accessing the information through a networked computer, makes a decision.

In the second case, the assets being integrated are not all owned by the firm, and interorganizational integration efforts are involved. Consider the example of General Mills and Land O'Lakes, two companies with different product lines but a similar customer base of grocery stores and similar needs for refrigerated warehousing and transportation. Realizing the potential for synergies and efficiencies, the two firms now coordinate their logistics efforts. As a consequence, General Mills warehouses Land O'Lakes products and delivers

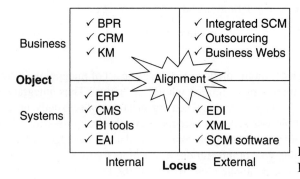

Figure 3.10   Object and Locus of Integration Efforts[8]

---

[8] Adapted from Markus, M. L. (2000) Paradigm Shift: eBusiness and Business/Systems Integration, *Communications of AIS,* 4, 10 (November)

them with fuller trucks that make fewer stops. Integrating their distribution and logistics has proven beneficial to both firms.

The second dimension of interest is the object of integration (i.e., what assets the firm is looking to unify or combine). With respect to the object of integration, we distinguish between business integration and systems integration.

Business Integration   Business integration refers to unification or the creation of tight linkages among the diverse, but connected, business activities carried out by individuals, groups, and departments within an organization. The outcome of business integration is the introduction of cohesive, streamlined business processes that encompass previously separate activities.

Consider the experience of a large computer manufacturer describing how its financing processes have recently changed: "The last thing we want to do is make customers fill out paperwork and [then] call them at a later date to say, 'you are not qualified' [. . .] This is no longer a satisfactory way to deal with the customer—we need to qualify the customer on the spot."[9] This degree of responsiveness can only be achieved thorough an integration of the sales and financing processes.

Business integration is considered critical to the survival of the modern firm. Many observers have suggested that in order to stay competitive today's business ventures must be able to present one face to the customer, provide solutions, and achieve global inventory visibility.

Presenting One Face to the Customer   Increasingly we hear that organizations must organize around their customers' needs, rather than in functional areas or around product lines. With the continuous speeding up of competition, they must be able to react and respond quickly and effectively to customer requests and make it as easy as possible for customers to work with the firm. A request by the firm to call a different department or a different location to have questions addressed is increasingly met with discontent by customers.

Barnes & Noble and other retailers with both online and offline channels are attempting to better integrate their diverse channels of distribution (Figure 3.11). As customers we have come to expect the ability to shop online, but still check to see if an item of interest is available at the local store. When we have an item to return, we don't understand why we can't simply drop it off at the local store rather than having to fumble with packaging and the postal service. If these are different channels of distribution of the same company, we argue, why can't we work seamlessly with the one that makes it easiest for us at the time?

Providing Solutions   Companies are now expected to provide solutions, not an array of products or services. Hotels, for example, are increasingly defining their business as "travel support" rather than lodging. This redefinition of the firm's value proposition from a product to a solution creates a wealth of opportunity for creating new services, like airline check-in and baggage pickup at the hotel.

The sporting goods store Finish Line provides another example for solving a nagging problem: Shoes on sale often are missing some of the sizes. At Finish Line, customers who are eyeing a nice pair of sneakers at the right price but find out that their size is missing are

---

[9] Brohman, M. K., Piccoli, G., Watson, R., and Parasuraman, A. (2005), "NCSS Process Completeness: Construct Development and Preliminary Validation," *Proceedings of the Thirty-Eighth Hawaii International Conference on System Sciences,* Hawaii:HI.

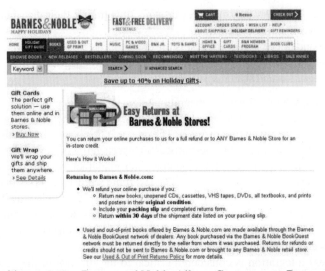

Figure 3.11 Barnes and Noble Allows Customers to Return to Local Stores Books Purchased Online

not at a loss. The Finish Line associates can look up the availability of the same item at other stores affiliated with the chain. If they do find it, they charge the customer and issue a request for direct shipment of the item to the customer's address. This initiative recasts the inventory clearance process from a local store affair to a coordinated chainwide integrated process. Incidentally, the initiative not only leaves customers more satisfied, but also moves old inventory more quickly by increasing the reach of the sale—a happy note for the company itself.

Global Inventory Visibility With the increasing rate of speed at which business moves, customers are also progressively coming to expect fast and precise response from the firm to questions about customization and modification of the firm's products. This trend, perhaps more typical of manufacturing industries and business-to-business relationships, rewards firms that have achieved global inventory visibility. Global inventory visibility represents the knowledge of current inventories and the ability to rapidly estimate price and delivery schedule changes in response to requests for customization. At the now famous Dell Online store, you can customize your new computer system and receive a precise estimate of the date you will receive it—such a delivery date will change based on the actual components you request in your machine.

Business Integration Trends In reaction to the pressures described above, a number of business integration trends have emerged (see Figure 3.10). These trends are discussed in depth in Chapter 12.

Systems integration With the business integration imperative taking center stage, information systems professionals and the software industry have sought ways to enable integration. It is evident that without information systems and technology infrastructure to support them, business integration strategies cannot be feasibly implemented.

The term *system integration* refers to the unification or tight linkage of IT-enabled information systems and databases. The primary focus of systems integration is the technological component of the information systems underpinning business integration strategies. The outcome of system integration is a collection of compatible systems that regularly exchange information, or the development of integrated applications that replace the former discrete ones. More precisely, when the systems integration effort seeks to enable communication between separate software programs, we speak of *application integration.* When the systems integration effort seeks to enable the merging of data repositories and databases, we speak of data integration.

Internal integration pertains to the unification or linkage of interorganizational systems, while external integration pertains to interorganizational ones. Internal and external systems integration substantiates itself in custom-developed applications or off-the-shelf commercial products and tools with names that you probably heard before: enterprise resource planning (ERP), enterprise systems, business intelligence tools, supply chain management software, service-oriented architecture (SOA), eXtensible Mark-up Language (XML), and so on. These trends will be discussed in depth in Chapter 12.

Integration Trade-Offs

Like many business and organizational trends that you will find yourself assessing in your position as a general or functional manager, the integration imperative has created its share of hype and buzz. Integration is, of course, no panacea; more integration is not necessarily better or advisable. Rather the integration trend engenders trade-offs that need to be evaluated.

Benefits of Integration   An organization undertakes integration efforts because they offer a number of benefits. First and foremost, integration promises a drastic reduction of duplication of efforts and redundancy of operations. For example, once a firm integrates its receiving and inventory applications, it no longer needs data to be keyed into separate databases multiple times. This reduces not only direct costs, but also the potential for errors and inconsistencies leading to further expenditures of time and money.

Second, integration offers advantages in terms of access to information, speed, and response time. It also serves to increase coordination across organizational units and to enforce standardization.

Drawbacks of Integration   The advantages mentioned above come at a cost. Aside from the costs of achieving integration itself—expenses that can be substantial both for business and systems integration efforts—successful integration requires that organizations bear a number of coordination costs that the decentralization movement was designed to eliminate in the first place. While modern information technologies have helped reduce such costs, many of them are still significant. Let's return to the General Mills and Land O'Lakes example. Both firms clearly benefited from the integration of their logistics and distribution processes. Now, however, each firm has to coordinate with the other to ensure that the right products are warehoused and ready to go according to the agreed upon schedule.

Moreover, the standardization advantages mentioned above also bring about limitations of flexibility that are all the more relevant for larger firms with unique local operations. With highly integrated operations, the needs for change of a business unit or function need to be weighed against the needs of the other units and the costs that they will have to bear to accommodate the change.

Consider the example of Barnes and Noble. Barnes and Noble originally established its online unit as a separate organization. While customers may demand cross-channel integration between the physical stores and the Web, this level of integration requires compromises between the units involved, a level of coordination that is harder to muster the more independently the units are run (e.g., separate profit and loss statements). For example, ensuring that a book purchased online can be returned to a store requires that stores be willing to collect and resell books that they otherwise may not carry due to a lack of sufficient local demand.

THE INFORMATION SYSTEM CYCLE

When describing the various categories of systems found in modern organizations, we described transaction processing systems as those concerned with automating routine day-to-day activities that happen in the present. Attentive managers though have long recognized that, while the implementation of these systems is typically justified with arguments focused on efficiency improvements, the value of the data that they capture should not be underestimated.

The information systems cycle portrays the progression of business data from their inception in transaction processing systems, to their storage in data repositories, and finally to their use in analytical tools (see Figure 3.12). Data are typically produced as a byproduct of daily operations and transactions (e.g., gamblers playing a slot machine at a casino, shoppers purchasing items at a retail shop) the firm completes as it handles the present. Such organizational data, when not disposed of, can be accumulated in data repositories and create a record of past transaction (i.e., the data are used to remember the past). Using analytical tools, the firm can then make sense of the accumulated data to find patterns, test assumptions, and more generally enable decision making in an effort to better prepare for the future.

Often these decisions directly impact the firm's information systems, with the introduction of new systems (i.e., new IT, new people, new processes, new structures) or the modification of existing ones in an effort to position the firm to achieve its future objectives in an ever-changing competitive environment.

Consider again the example of a grocery store introduced earlier. As customers come and go, a wealth of transactional data is generated. This information is necessary for the store to manage its daily operations (i.e., handle the present). Customers need to find shelves stocked

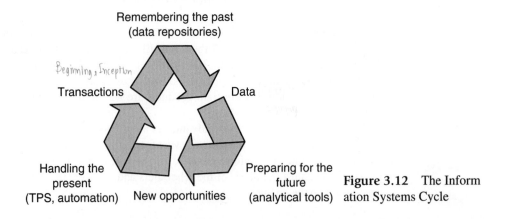

Figure 3.12   The Information Systems Cycle

with popular items. Managers must optimize inventory in order to minimize working capital and spoilage of perishable items. Correct billing, taking into account promotions and discounts, must be generated at checkout. All these instances describe events that happen during the normal course of business in the grocery store. When customers leave, and the present has been handled, all the data generated that are not subject to legal requirements may be thrown away.

Alternatively, the store can create data repositories that catalog and hold this information—now historical in nature. This act of "remembering the past" is of course only meaningful if the data can be used at a later stage to prepare for the future (e.g., gain beneficial intelligence through analysis of the data). For example, management may commission basket analyses seeking to identify items that sell well together, and, based on the results, change the product mix or the location of some items. Management may also use inventory data to optimize reorder schedules and limit chances of stockouts.

SUMMARY

This chapter completed our introductory series on the foundations of information systems, by explaining the vocabulary and concepts you need in order to categorize different types of information systems and to communicate with other managers and IS professionals. Specifically, in this chapter we learned

- That different organizational information systems can be characterized through a hierarchical perspective. This perspective identifies three types of systems: transaction processing systems, decision support systems, and executive information systems. These systems are designed and built to support different activities—operational, tactical, and strategic, respectively.

- That different organizational information systems can be characterized through a functional perspective. This perspective identifies vertical organizational systems focused on the specific needs of each unit (e.g., accounting, marketing, finance, receiving).

- That more recently a process perspective has emerged. According to the process perspective, the firm and its operations are seen as a set of processes, rather than functional areas. The functional

perspective underpins many of the most recent managerial trends, including business process reengineering (BPR) and business systems integration efforts, as well as information systems trends, such as systems integration initiatives.

- BPR, defined as a managerial approach calling for a process view of organizational activities, was one of the principal management trends of the mid-1990s. While its popularity has faded somewhat, you should not forget the key lessons of BPR: Firms evolve over time, as do technologies; old assumptions may no longer be valid today; and you have an opportunity to use IT to dramatically improve the efficiency and effectiveness of the firm's business processes.

- The information system cycle, an analytical model that portrays the progression of business data from their inception in transaction processing systems, to their storage in data repositories, and finally to their use in analytical tools, can help you realize the full potential of your firm's technology investments. The IS cycle reminds you that the data generated by your transaction processing systems in the normal course of business may have value if opportunely stored and analyzed at a later stage.

STUDY QUESTIONS

1. Describe the principal differences among transaction processing systems, management information systems, and executive information systems.

2. Identify the three types of organizational activities. For each one, describe its typical time horizon, hierarchical level, and principal characteristics. Provide an example for each type.

3. Provide an example of functional systems. What is the defining characteristic of these systems?

4. Define the concept of BPR. Can you provide an example, real or imaginary, of a company operating under old assumptions no longer valid? How would you propose to redesign the firm's business processes? What information technology would you expect the firm to adopt to enable the redesigned process?

5. What are the principal limitations and drawbacks of BPR?

6. How have we defined the concepts of business and systems integration? What is the relationship between the two? Can you provide examples of each?

FURTHER READINGS

1. Davenport, T. H. (1992) *Process Innovation: Reengineering Work through Information Technology.* Boston, MA: Harvard Business School Press.

2. Hammer, M. (2004). "Deep Change: How Operational Innovation Can Transform Your Company." *Harvard Business Review,* April, pp. 84–93.

3. Hammer, M. (2001). "The Superefficient Company." *Harvard Business Review,* September, pp. 82–91

4. Hammer, M. (1990). "Reengineering Work: Don't Automate, Obliterate." *Harvard Business Review,* July/Aug., pp. 104–112.

5. Leavitt, H. J., Whisler, T. L. (1958). "Management in the 1980s." *Harvard Business Review* (November–December), pp. 41–48.

6. Markus, M. Lynne (2000). "Paradigm Shifts—E-Business and Business/Systems Integration." *Communications of the AIS,* (4:10).

GLOSSARY

- **Business integration:** Unification or the creation of tight linkages among the diverse, but connected, business activities carried out by individuals, groups, and departments within an organization.

- **Business process:** The series of steps that a firm performs in order to complete an economic activity.

- **Business process reengineering** (BPR): A managerial approach calling for a process view of organizational activities. The BPR methodology calls for internal business integration and seeks dramatic performance improvements through rationalization of activities and the elimination of duplication of efforts across separate functions and units.

- **Executive information systems (EIS):** Systems designed to serve the long-range planning and decision-making needs of senior managers.

- **Functional systems:** Systems expressly designed to support the specific needs of individuals in the same functional area.

- **Information systems cycle:** An analytical model that portrays the progression of business data from their inception in transaction processing systems, to their storage in data repositories, and finally to their use in analytical tools.

- **Integration:** The process that an organization, or a number of related organizations, uses to unify, or join together, some tangible or intangible assets.

- **Decision support systems (DSS):** Systems designed to provide information needed by functional managers engaged in tactical decision making in the form of regular reports and exception reports.

- **System integration:** The unification or tight linkage of IT-enabled information systems and databases.

- **Transaction processing systems:** Systems mainly concerned with automating recurring activities and structuring day-to-day activities to ensure that they are performed with speed and accuracy.

CASE STUDY: DSL PROVISIONING: REDEFINING "CUSTOMER SERVICE"[10]

INTRODUCTION

In July 2001, Brian Cantera and his wife Marie arrived in Center City. There they would take up positions as faculty at a local university. Their teaching responsibilities would include classes in the Executive MBA program. Brian would also serve as the director of a research center whose members included information systems executives from many of the largest firms in Center City.

Brian Cantera held a Ph.D. in management information systems as well as a Master's in computer science. A computer user since 1967, he taught with and about them for over thirty years. Between office and home he had four computers. His wife had two computers. Cantera's Apple Titanium Powerbook and his wife's IBM Thinkpad were both connected to a wireless network in their apartment, the base station for which used Apple's AirPort technology. A router connected the Air Port Base station and his desktop computer to a broadband modem.

The Canteras found that moving grew ever more complex because of the personal information system infrastructure that, like many other Americans, they surrounded themselves with. The old burdens included change of address forms, connecting and disconnecting telephone and power service, updating insurance policies, choosing retirement programs, registering to vote and drive, acquiring parking details and a new driver's license. But now there were also digital cable systems to be uninstalled, returned to the provider, and reordered, web pages stored on the cable system's servers that needed to be transferred elsewhere, cellular phone service to be transferred, e-mail addresses to be updated, and so on. As professors and well-connected professionals, the Canteras encountered these infrastructure issues both at home and the university, though in the latter location, support personnel were available to sort out some of the problems.

CELLULAR PHONE INFRASTRUCTURE

Upon arriving in Center City, the Canteras discovered that their cellular phones provided poor reception in parts of town and no service at all in their 31st-floor apartment. A clerk in a local Sprint retail shop explained that the cell phone numbers would have to be changed and the phones reprogrammed for Center City. While the phones were being reprogrammed, Cantera was directed by the retail representative to a side-room where he was told to pick up a telephone connected to Sprint's central order processing center.

After nearly 30 minutes on the phone, he was provided with Center City's phone numbers and other identifying information, which he then was required to provide the retail clerk after the clerk finished with other customers.

While in-town cellular service appeared to improve marginally, Cantera was still unable to use the service in the apartment building. A neighbor lent Cantera his phone for a day and Cantera found the phone's Verizon service did work from the apartment. The following day he purchased two new phones and signed up for Verizon service at a local Radio Shack.

Several days later Cantera called Sprint to cancel the original service. After entering his phone number into an automated system, he waited on hold for ten minutes. When an operator came online she asked for his phone number and then asked to confirm his address. Cantera read to her the address appearing on his latest phone bill from Sprint—his new Center City address. She questioned the address, telling him a Baton Rouge address was listed in the file. She said she was not authorized to discontinue the service but would forward him to someone who was. But first she asked why he was shutting off the service. He provided the answers, and after another five-minute wait another representative came online. She appeared to know the reasons Cantera gave for discontinuing but tried, nevertheless, to retain his account. She also told him that he was required to pay a $150 termination fee as he apparently, and without being orally informed, signed an agreement to keep the service for one year when he transferred the service from Baton Rouge to Center City. He was also told that the service would stay in operation until the billing period ended. Cantera searched the Sprint web site, in vain, for an email address to submit a complaint to.

COMPUTER INFRASTRUCTURE

Prior to leaving Baton Rouge, Cantera also experienced considerable problems with his Macintosh Titanium computer. An Apple technical support rep requested the machine be sent back to Apple, where it was given a new motherboard as well as a new hard drive. Still problems persisted. Upon arriving in Center City, Cantera spent nearly two days on the phone with various Apple service representatives. On three different occasions and following their instructions, he completely reloaded the computer's operating system. It still was not working properly, but Cantera felt he did not have any more time to spend on the phone with the representatives from Apple—each of whom seemed to treat his call as if it was their first.

[10] This case was originally published as Ives, B., Loiacono, E., and Piccoli, G., "DSL Provisioning: Redefining 'Customer Service,'" *Communications of the AIS* (Vol. 7 Article 21), 2001.

continued

CASE STUDY (*continued***)**

Near the end of September, fully two months after he originally sent the computer to Apple for repair, Cantera received an e-mail from Apple requesting him to complete "a follow-up web survey regarding your recent Mail-In Repair experience." Cantera cut and pasted the survey into an open-ended question on the survey form. Two months later he had received no response.

BANKING INFRASTRUCTURE

In Louisiana, Cantera and his wife both banked with Bank One and, increasingly, were relying on it for more and more automated and online services. Their mortgage payments as well as several other payments were made automatically, their payroll checks were automatically deposited, and Cantera used the system to pay monthly bills. About 25 payees were now listed, and he valued being able to pay a bill in just a few seconds.

Cantera had initially been relieved to find that Bank One operated banks in his new home state. That relief was cut short, however, when told he could not make a deposit into his Louisiana account from a Bank One office in Center City. He would have to either mail the money to Louisiana or open a local account. As he would have to change banks anyway, Cantera went to the Wells Fargo Web site to see what was entailed in registering for their online banking services. Here he found a bewildering array of products, but no easy way to put together the package of accounts and services he already had with Bank One. He called Well Fargo's service number and, after being asked to enter the first three letters of the name of his state, was automatically forwarded to a line that was neither answered nor equipped with a reassuring recording.

Several days later he visited a Wells Fargo retail outlet. Eric, a young banker moonlighting as an undergraduate major in computer science at the University of Center City, quickly and competently set up his account. To assist him in making the sale, Eric produced a brochure promoting packages of services, including one that duplicated Cantera's services with his Bank One account. Cantera suggested that this kind of service packaging was missing from the Web site. Eric smiled and said that the bank encouraged its employees to use and provide feedback on the online use of their own personal accounts. He said he had raised this same issue but, thus far, saw no improvements in the site.

At his previous home Cantera paid for high-bandwidth ISP service through the local cable company. The Canteras waited almost six months longer than they had initially been told before the service became available in their new home. But, once it was installed, they were quite satisfied with it. The

only negatives were occasional downtime, some slowing down in the late afternoon and early evening, and the need to keep a separate ISP provider for times Cantera was on the road. His wife also used the dial-up ISP connection as she found it inconvenient to move to a different part of the house to access the wide-band service. The cable service provided the Canteras with one static IP address and, for an extra five dollars a month, a second one that Brian used with a second computer. The IP addresses meant that Cantera could access his desktop computer from outside the house—for example, he could run programs from his home desktop computer while using his laptop machine in a classroom. However, he chose not to put his Web pages on his desktop machine but instead relied on server space provided by his Internet provider. Access speed from the cable modem exceeded that of Cantera's connection at the university.

Initial investigation of the cable provider in Center City suggested that it would be more expensive to duplicate the arrangement in his previous home. After only a cursory examination, he instead chose to install DSL service as provided by MightyFone, the local phone company. Several levels of service were available. Cantera decided that Extended Service best met his needs. While Basic Service provided only a single dynamic IP address, the extended service included five IP (Internet protocol) addresses. The provider rated the systems speed as varying between 384,000 and 1.5 million bits per second (bps) for download and 128,000 bps for upload. He would thus be able to connect two of his computers and his wife's computer directly to the network. Two other IP addresses were still available. One, for example, might be used for a baby-monitoring camera that Cantera could use to check on the couple's soon-to-be-born baby. Cantera also made a note to buy an extra cellular card so that overnight guests could use the last IP. He also briefly considered "lending" the last IP address to a neighbor who lived one floor below them; he suspected, however, that this act would probably be a violation of the DSL provider's service agreement.

Provisioning

Near the middle of July 2001, Cantera placed an order with MightyFone for Extended DSL service. It would cost him $64.95 per month. He decided he neither needed nor, at $179.95 per month could afford, a higher-speed option, which promised download speeds of 1.5–6 million bits per second and an upload speed of 384 kbps. Several days later the self-installation box arrived. In it were three pamphlets, each describing installation procedures for a different computing environment, a SpeedStream® modem, a CD containing the necessary software, and six filters that had to be used with any other device in the house that was to be connected to phone lines. These would filter out the special codes required to operate DSL. Cantera installed the filters, wired up the modem, loaded the software, and waited. Nothing happened. The four lights on the front of the modem were all on; three were green but the fourth continued to blink red.

According to MightyFone's online documentation, DSL service required the subscriber to be located within 14,000 cable feet of the central office. Even within that range, the Web site warned, only 60 to 65 percent of lines would be of sufficient quality. Cantera initially thought the line distance or quality might be the problem, but, given that there were over one hundred apartments in his building and that many of the tenants were professionals like he and his wife, it seemed likely that MightyFone would have already informed him if there were a known problem with the building's wires. While the technical support representatives appeared to know nothing about the connectivity within the particular building, the problem turned out instead to lie with the need to make some connections in the local switching office. After about two weeks and several phone calls, the service finally came online.

Through this process, Cantera began to realize that at least some aspects of the service were not being provided locally through MightyFone but rather by some of the BigFone (MightyFone's parent company) "brands" or other divisions. Several times he spoke with representatives who were located in California. One of the support phone lines to which he was referred opened with the recorded message, "You have reached the WayOutFone Internet Provisioning Group."

A recorded message at another line welcomed Cantera to BigFone Internet Services, serving DessertFone, WayoutFone, and MightyFone. Still another, of the five support numbers, added a fourth brand, USAFones, to those apparently being supported by BigFone Internet Services. And one of the online screens Cantera had seen (see Figure 17 below), and several calls with technicians suggested that, Proisp, a large national Internet service provider, was also involved. In 2000, BigFone had acquired a 43 percent share of Proisp.

Whichever organization handled the calls, they all required listening to a series of recorded messages and then selecting from various options, which usually led to more recordings and still more options. Cantera learned, and sometimes was prompted by service representatives, to write these options down to speed his way through the maze. He also had begun taking down employee numbers and keeping track of how long he was on hold.

The Call Center

A typical call required anywhere from ten to thirty minutes to get through to a human and, once there, Cantera was again

usually put on hold four or five times. The total time required from the usual call varied from an hour to two, with little more than a few minutes of it actually talking to a service representative. When they did put Cantera on hold, which was much of the time, representatives almost unfailingly came back on the line every three minutes to indicate that they themselves were on hold with a higher-level technical representative and did Cantera mind waiting longer. In several instances there were as many as a dozen of these interactions before the conversation was completed—usually with a request to call back a day or two later.

The representatives were very polite. They first asked for the subscriber's phone number and name followed by the name of the person they were speaking to. They then asked if they could use Cantera's first name in the conversation. They then would ask questions like the make and model number of the digital modem, and the operating system being used. On one occasion Cantera asked them why they always asked for this same information and was told that it might have changed since the previous call.

Technicians sometimes gave Cantera "case numbers," which appeared to be linked to particular calls. Sometimes they would ask for these when he called back. Technicians on two occasions seemed befuddled when Cantera was unable to provide a case number even though the previous representative did not provide one. He began to ask for the case number before he got off the phone.

While the Canteras eventually were able to get the service installed, a number of hiccups occurred along the way. The hiccup with the most far-reaching implications was the failure of the original order taker or an order fulfillment representative to realize this installation was Enhanced DSL rather than Basic DSL service. A technical support representative confided to Cantera that, because his order was mistakenly initially set up as Basic DSL service rather than Enhanced DSL, they now had "to work their way backward to sort out the problem."

In his many conversations with level-one technical representatives, several of whom seemed as frustrated by their organization and systems as Cantera had become, Cantera learned several interesting things. For instance, one representative informed him that, contrary to Cantera's own experience, Enhanced service was always installed by an on-site technician. Still the representative comforted him by telling him that he was better off with self-installation as the home installers often didn't know what they were doing. Scheduling also seemed to be a problem. The representative mentioned a customer who he claimed he had talked with earlier that day who, apparently due to a scheduling snafu, was besieged by eight different installers in a single day. It also seemed clear to Cantera that the level-one technicians

continued

CASE STUDY (*continued*)

were poorly trained and often appeared unable to do anything other than basic triage. They could usually figure out whom to call or escalate the problem to, but they seemed either unable or unauthorized to solve his problems.

When asked, one representative described the organization structure as consisting of three levels of technical support—level one, level two, and operations. Unfortunately, it proved to be almost impossible to directly speak to a level-two representative. Instead, the level-one support personnel relayed information from the customer to level-two or proposed actions from the level-two representative back to the customer. Each time Cantera called it was like calling for the first time.

Accessing the Account Management Tool

Cantera experienced problems in almost every step of the original provisioning, including learning on one occasion that the previous representative had mistakenly closed out his record and, in doing so, apparently deleted the entire past record of his calls. Nevertheless, by the second week in August Cantera was connected to the Internet. And each of his allocated five IP addresses was activated. He could now surf the Internet and, using e-mail forwarding services provided for free by Apple, send e-mail. He also set up his Web home page on his desktop computer.

He could not, however, reach the login screen for the DSL Account Management Tool. As a result, he was unable to ascertain what his login ID and password were and,

without them, was unable to set up his MightyFone e-mail account or access other online resources, such as instructions for accessing the service from other dial-up lines or setting up Web pages on the provider's central server.

Cantera once again called up the BigFone DSL service line and began a long and tortuous process of trying to gain access to the Account Management Tool. Various technical support representatives provided him with several different Web addresses for registering for the Account Management site. Two of these were incorrect.

When he finally connected to the appropriate site, he saw the screens shown in Figures 3.13 through 3.15. As noted in Figure 3.14, the user is required to enter both the subscriber phone number and a customer number. The directions called for the subscriber phone number to be entered in a precise format, with a space after the area code and a hyphen separating the next three digits from the last four. Cantera had learned that entering the number any other way resulted in an error. Cantera had been directed to retrieve the customer number from his phone bill. Unfortunately, as a new subscriber, Cantera had no bill to refer to and would not for another week. After several phone calls, however, he was able to reach a service representative to provide this number over the phone. After several more failures and subsequent phone calls, he was told that, while that was indeed his customer number, it had not been properly entered in the system when the order had initially been set up. He was assured that this problem had been escalated and would be resolved within twenty-four hours.

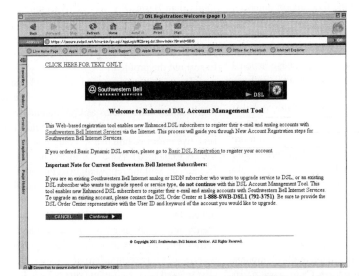

Figure 3.13 DSL Account Management Tool Welcome Screen

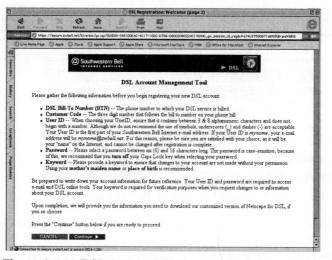

Figure 3.14   DSL Account Management Tool Instruction Page

It wasn't. Several days later, however, Cantera found that he could now see a new screen (Figure 3.16) rather than the screen that he had terminated on previously (Figure 3.15). A follow-on screen (Figure 3.17) indicated a new error condition. A call to the service representative led to promises that the problem would be escalated and would be fixed in twenty-four hours. Two days later the problem persisted. Cantera called again. This time he was able to get through, for the first time, to a level-two technical support person. The representative assured him that the problem had been re-escalated. This time the anticipated delay was reported as forty-eight hours. Another call, three days later, indicated that the anticipated delay was seventy-two hours and, as this was Labor Day weekend, the delay would naturally be longer. This time the representative noted that the case was already "on the spreadsheet" and that further escalation might only confuse things. The representative also said he has seen similar problems in recent days and felt certain that Operations would quickly sort the problems out.

Four days later the service was still not working and no one had called from BigFone Internet Services. Cantera called again and managed to get the call elevated up to Operations, apparently the highest level in the technical scheme. He was told that the problem was "a registration problem" and that the registration people, located in another office, only worked from 8 A.M. to 5 P.M. The representative suggested calling back during business hours so this problem could be followed up on immediately. Again "the spreadsheet" was mentioned, and Cantera asked the representative if there were dozens, hundreds, or thousands of entries on it. He was assured that it was a small number and certainly not in the thousands.

Hearing Cantera's frustration with both the lack of service and the need to work his way each time through the cumbersome service hierarchy, the representative provided a direct dial-in number to operations. At 9 A.M. the next day, Cantera called that number. A recording indicated that this number was

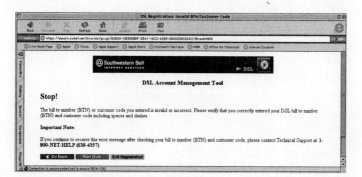

Figure 3.15   Account Management Tool Login Error Screen One

continued

CASE STUDY (*continued*)

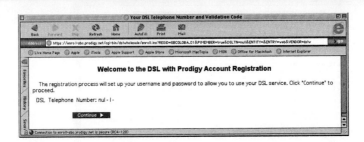

Figure 3.16 DSL Account Management Tool Login Welcome Screen

for internal use only and that customers should dial another number. Cantera stayed on the line and started working through this new hierarchy of recorded messages. The representative he finally reached said that the registration office was in California and was not yet open. He said that he would call once the office was open and then call Cantera back. Cantera asked, "Are you *really* going to call back?" The representative said he would. Cantera added his employee number to those of the two level-two support personnel he was able to get through to.

CIRCUMVENTING THE HIERARCHY

Forty-eight hours later, Cantera's frustration was running high. Two days passed and the Account Management Tool was still not accessible and the promised callback once again did not materialize. Cantera, recalling seeing a follow-up e-mail (Sidebar 1) from a marketing arm of the DSL provider, decided to take action.

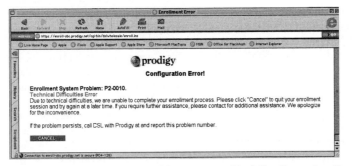

Figure 3.17 DSL Account Management Tool Configuration Error

SIDEBAR 1. REQUEST FOR CUSTOMER FEEDBACK

From: survey.research@acme.com

Date: Mon, 13 Aug 2001 12:40:52-0400 (EDT)

To: BCantera

Subject: Your MightyFone DSL Self-Installation Experience

Dear Brian Cantera:

On behalf of the BigFone DSL technical help desk, Acme Marketing Research would like to thank you for your recent telephone inquiry on 8/10/2001. The voice of the customer is very important to BigFone Advanced Solutions Inc. as it continually monitors and improves its customer service. Your feedback is key to evaluating the BigFone DSL technical help desk team's performance. We invite you to provide feedback about your recent telephone interaction with the BigFone technical help desk on 8/10/2001. You can provide your opinions by completing a brief 5 minute survey. Please click on the URL hyperlink.

http://www.sendyourfeedback.com/bigfoneemail

or cut and paste the address into your Internet browser. When you reach the login screen, enter the following login ID and password.

Your login ID is: xxxxxx

Your password is: xxxxxx

For your convenience, the survey is available 24 hours a day, seven days a week through 08/27/2001, and can be accessed from any computer with Internet access. Please contact Acme Marketing Research with any survey questions at survey.research@acme.com

Sincerely,

The Acme Marketing Research Team

Cantera composed a short e-mail message to the state's Public Services Commission (PSC) requesting information on how to report the inferior service from the DSL provider. He included his phone number in the note and also noted that if the PSC was unable to assist, he would take the matter up with the Better Business Bureau.

In addition to the PSC, he sent a copy of the note to the e-mail address attached to the service follow-up note he previously received from the marketing staff. The previous evening Cantera sent an e-mail message similar to an e-mail address he found on the MightyFone site (see Sidebar 2 for the note and response).

continued

SIDEBAR 2. NOTES TO AND FROM MIGHTYFONE SUPPORT DESK

From: support
Date: Fri, 7 Sep 2001 12:53:33 -0700 (PDT)
To: BCantera
Subject: Re : Internet Services: Internet Service

Hello User BCantera

I have received your email regarding your mail problem.

Unfortunately, you have reached the wrong department to have these issues resolved.

Please contact the Self Install Department at 1-999-999-9999.

Thank you for choosing MightyFone Internet Services.

Regards,

Shawn

Technical Analyst

BigFone Internet Services

Try our online help at <http://.bigfone.proisp.net>.

Remember, it's quick, hassle free, and is always available!

~*~

You Wrote:

To: support @bigfonel.net
Customer Name: Brian Cantera
Email Address: BCantera
City: Center City
State: QQ
Phone: 000-999-9999
Zip: 99999

Email Tracking Number: 82450
Message:

I have been trying to get my DSL account registered for over one month. I have probably called over 20 times and each time I am told the problem is being "escalated." This morning employee VA2187 told me he would call me back later in the day. He did not.

If someone does not call me with a guaranteed solution in 24 hours and if that solution is not in place in 72 hours I will write a complaint to the state public service commission, the Better Business Bureau and the CEO of MightyFone.

Twenty-four hours after he sent the second message, at 9 A.M. on a Saturday, the phone rang. It was Aaron calling from MightyFone Internet Services. He said that he was following upon the previous day's e-mail and that things would now be brought under control. He tried to reassure Cantera, saying that this was now a "one-stop shopping" situation and that he would personally ensure that the service was established. He then, apparently reading from the computer record, noted that the system was installed successfully on August 6. Cantera pointed out to him that there had been many subsequent calls and that, while the system was installed, he was still unable to register with the Account Management Tool. Aaron mentioned a more recent date when a representative called and, encountering an answering machine, left a message saying that he had called.

After politely listening to Cantera fume for several minutes about the poor service and his impression about the inadequacy of BigFone's systems, Aaron reaffirmed his intention to get to the bottom of the matter. Within an hour Aaron called back. He noted that the problem appeared to be solved and that he was just going to go through the final registration process with Cantera to ensure there were no problems. He asked Cantera to go to the site to register while they stayed on the phone together. The Account Management Tool remained inaccessible. Aaron said he would need additional time and would call back.

When he called back, later that afternoon, he reported that the problem was with the customer number. Previous representatives apparently did not enter the correct customer number in the system. Cantera informed him that this particular problem was discovered several weeks before and was supposedly fixed. Aaron replied that the fix apparently did not go through and that the request was now being escalated to the proper office, where it would be fixed within twenty-four hours. Aaron assured him that that he would personally track this over the next twenty-four hours. Cantera asked Aaron if he would share the complete record of Cantera's previous calls to the provider. This request would be difficult to meet, he was told, as the messages were not in a form that could easily be e-mailed. He did, however, agree to provide his direct phone number.

Cantera then asked him for the dates of his own previous calls to the service center. He was told there were six case records in the record. These occurred on July 31 and August 1, 6, 10, 28, and 29. Incredulous, Cantera asked about the call only three days before in which he had obtained the employee number for the second-tier tech support representative, the representative who had not returned his call. No, Aaron admitted, there was no record of that call. Cantera reminded him that he had made at least a dozen other calls that were not included in the record. Yes, said Aaron, who said that he had been suspicious of that when he had found no record of the call Cantera had mentioned. He then suggested that technical representatives who were unable to fix a customer's problem might sometimes not enter them into the system.

Cantera then complained about the computer systems, noting that MightyFone personnel should, by just entering his phone number, automatically be able to pull up every single contact he ever had with a support representative. Aaron replied that this was impossible as there was not one software tool that was being used, but rather many different ones. The recent merger and the need to integrate the systems from each of the partners to the merger, he said, really caused much of the problem.

By Monday morning at 9:45 A.M., forty-eight hours after Aaron's first call, there were no further callbacks and Cantera was still unable to log in. Unable to stay home to wait any longer for the call, Cantera decided to call Aaron. The number he had written down appeared to be a wrong number—it was neither Aaron's name nor voice on the recorded message, nor was there a company affiliation. Cantera did not leave a message. By 6:30 P.M. on Monday, there was still no contact.

The following afternoon, Aaron left a message with Cantera's wife. "Everything," he said, "was now ready to go." Cantera tried to register—once again without success. At 9 the next morning, Wednesday, Aaron called. Cantera asked Aaron to confirm his phone number, which proved different than the number he previously provided. Aaron explained that the first number was that of another representative. Cantera then asked why Aaron did not return his call within twenty-four hours as he promised. Aaron explained that he was pulled off the case on Sunday and only was reassigned to it on the previous day. Together Cantera and Aaron then went through the registration process, and again Cantera was unable to logon. Aaron said that, even though he had been off the case, he had checked on the registration process and been told that it was complete. He promised to check again and then call back. At 11 A.M., feeling he could wait no longer for that call, Cantera called the second number Aaron gave him. He reached the voicemail for yet another support person, though this message did properly identify the firm.

Cantera mused to an observer about his quandary:

This has been very frustrating. I have spent a minimum of thirty-six hours trying to get this sorted out. I have stayed home, waiting for calls that often never came. With the exception of Aaron, I have not dealt with

continued

anyone at BigFone or MightyFone who seems either willing to take or capable of taking responsibility for getting something fixed. And now he has let me down. BigFone's systems seem to preclude anyone taking responsibility. Every call is a transaction, with the service representative seemingly far more attentive to how the call will influence her or BigFone's productivity statistics than on actually solving the problem. First-level technicians appear unable to actually fix problems, while second-level representatives seem to have a strong aversion to even talking to customers.

I'm a newcomer in Center City, but neighbors, students, and colleagues have not been particularly generous in their assessment of MightyFone's service record. My dean told me he waited weeks to get his DSL account activated after the system itself had been installed. At least three students in my Executive MBA class have had similar experiences. Others have raved about their positive experience with RoadRunner, the local cable alternative to DSL.

Unfortunately, my attempts to get problems fixed in my cable TV programming suggest that their provisioning service may be even worse than I have experienced with DSL. With the local cable company, I have a hard time just getting past the busy signal.

Cantera pondered what to do. He felt he had given the firm every chance, but BigFone's DSL organization seemed incapable of self-regulating, self-monitoring, or conducting internally driven process improvement. He felt his options included actually filing a report with the state Public Service Commission or contacting the Better Business Bureau. But first he felt he had one last responsibility—to give the senior management of BigFone and MightyFone an opportunity to fix his immediate problem and, far more importantly, address the broader systemic problem. He decided to write the BigFone Chairman and CEO, Whitney Edwards, and send a copy of the correspondence to Alexander Wainwright, the CEO of MightyFone, the local phone company. On Wednesday afternoon the two letters went in the mail (Sidebar 3).

SIDEBAR 3: LETTER TO BIGFONE CHAIRMAN AND CEO

September 9, 2001

Whitney Edwards.

Chairman and CEO

BigFone

175 E. Center City Street

Bowie, QQ 99999-2233

Dear Mr. Edwards:

I read in an article published on you in Business Week that you had landed your first job at MightyFone through determined tenacity. I have followed your lead during a six-week marathon attempt to get my DSL service established through MightyFone in Center City. As a professor of Business I have written many case studies, indeed having learned to do so while a fellow at the Great Eastern School of Business several years ago. Such cases can be instructive for our students but also for the organizations that are featured in the cases. Attached is such a case, this time providing "a customer view" of the DSL provisioning process at BigFone. I intend to use it in several of our MBA and Executive MBA classes this fall and, assuming it is well received, shall draw the case web site to the attention of colleagues at other B-Schools.

I suspect there are several people on your management team who might value reading the case, which highlights potential problems in organization design, employee assessment, systems design, and, most of all, customer service. Many of these difficulties, of course, appear related to the challenges that must be faced in merging computing and operations systems from the several firms that make up BigFone. Others, however, appear to have emerged from the faithful execution of a rather narrow view of customer service. Still, I am sure there are also explanations that might make the story appear less one-sided. I would be pleased to publish with the case such responses as BigFone personnel might care to prepare describing some of the root causes and systemic improvements planned. I would also be most pleased to have a member of your team attend one or more of our discussions of the case later this fall.

I hope you will pardon my taking a small amount of your attention with this matter. My actions were inspired by the creative whirl that emerged from the sensory depravation accompanying the long hours I spent on the phone waiting for BigFone representatives. Lemons to lemonade!

I do look forward to hearing from you or a member of your staff.

Cordially,

Brian Cantera

Professor of Business Leadership

Director, Information Systems Research Center

CC:

Alexander Wainright

President, MightyFone

continued

The following day, Cantera received a bill for services from MightyFone. The bill included August 3 charges for a Basic DSL Internet Package ($49.95) and a DSL Modem ($99), and September 3 charges for Enhanced DSL Internet Service ($113.01), a DSL Modem ($99), and $200.00 for technician installation.

On Friday, September 7, Cantera left a message for Aaron describing the billing problems. Aaron's return message assured Cantera the billing problem would be fixed and that he was still working on the registration problem. He also said that another employee who specialized in registration problems had joined the hunt.

On Monday morning, September 10, Aaron called again. He said that he had sorted out the billing problem and was continuing to work on the registration issue.

Three days later Cantera received a call from BigFone Internet Services. The caller, Martin Bell, identified himself as an operations manager. He assured Cantera that, while he was a novice on the help line, he had a technical support person sitting with him. He told Cantera that they had not yet been able to resolve the registration problem but, in the meanwhile, would set him up with a MightyFone Dial-Up Internet account. This would be accessible over DSL and permit him to see password-protected Web pages and send e-mail through a MightyFone net account. He assured Cantera that the following day, the dial-up and e-mail accounts would be merged, for billing purposes, into a single account. Bell provided him with the server addresses for incoming and outgoing e-mail as well as the local Center City dial-up number. He told Cantera that dial-up numbers for other cities were available on the MightyFone Web site, though calls from outside the area would cost 4¢ per minute.

Bell said that he did not anticipate problems, but there was a slim chance that there might be a duplicate billing for the dial-up service and the DSL service. If so, he instructed Cantera to call him.

The next morning Cantera received a call from Terrell Bunker from Advanced Solutions, a subsidiary of MightyFone. Bunker identified himself as a network center technician within the executive complaints department of customer service. He said he had received the letter but without the subscriber number had been unable to actually find anything out about the problem. After Cantera gave him the number, Bunker promised to follow up on those problems which were within his area of responsibility.

He explained that his organization provided the DSL service but that the various brands (e.g., MightyBell) provided the ISP service. The registration problem, Bunker explained, was probably outside of his area of responsibility, but he was nevertheless going to track down any issues that might relate to his business and send a memo "to the Presidents." Cantera noted that while he experienced considerable difficulties even getting the DSL service installed, those early problems were less well documented in the case.

Bunker mentioned that there had been problems due to the recent alliance between BigFone and Proisp, including some problems with file integration. It was therefore not possible to tell how many times a customer had actually called. He also acknowledged that terminology used with customers across the several organizations was not consistent—one unit, for instance, referred to "trouble ticket numbers" while another called them "case numbers." Bunker also reiterated an issue previously raised by Bell, that FCC regulations further compounded integration problems among MightyFone, BigFone, Proisp, and the other BigFone brands. Bunker asked Cantera to call him if there were any further problems, including problems getting reimbursement for the services inadequately provided over the previous two months.

A few minutes later Cantera's phone rang again. The caller was Hamilton Diaz, President of BigFone Internet Services. Diaz apologized for the service failings and asked about the current status of the service. He also offered to come to Cantera's Executive MBA class to shed some further light on the case. He also mentioned regulatory issues as a barrier to full coordination among the various businesses.

That evening, Cantera received a voicemail from Martin Bell. Bell was calling to verify that the e-mail was working. He said that the service was now "completely set up on our site," and that there was "absolutely nothing that could cause us any additional issues." He left his number in case anything did come up.

The following Friday, four days since his last call, Aaron called and left two messages. He indicated he knew that the e-mail had been set up and confirmed the e-mail address.

A week, later a MightyFone marketing representative called Cantera to see if he might be interested in subscribing to MightyFone's DSL or long-distance service. A few days later, in early October, Cantera received a letter from

MightyFone's collection's department. If the "undisputed portion of his" unpaid bill was not paid by October 15, his service would be cancelled. The letter did not indicate what the amount due was.

As the October bill was due to arrive, prior to the October 15, Cantera decided to hold off paying the bill until the new one arrived. Several days later, on October 10, Martin Bell called and mentioned the letter. He said that the only portion of the unpaid bill that Cantera would be required to pay was the phone charges and the cost of a router. Cantera said he had received a modem but no router. Indeed, he had his own router. Bell apologized and said that the only charge would be $99 for the modem plus the regular telephone charges.

That afternoon the October bill from MightyFone arrived. The two modem charges had disappeared but there were now, listed for September, two charges of $378 each for CPE Premises Charges, two more for $64.95 each for DSL Internet Package–Enhanced1, two of $200 each for Technician Installation Charge, two fees of $50 for Service Order Processing, and two $100 fees for DSL Installation and Set-Up. A separate section of the bill showing charges for October included a third charge, this time for $83.79 for DSL Internet Package–Enhanced. Cantera's, total current charges, due by October 26, were for $1938.81.

Elsewhere in the bill Cantera noted that his previous month's bill for $758.99 had been adjusted by a credit to MightyFone Internet Services of $1515.62, leaving him with a credit of $756.63. This credit had been applied to the more recent charges, leaving him with a bill of $1182.18. Based on his conversation with Martin Bell earlier in the day, Cantera estimated that the real amount he owed was probably somewhere between $190 and $330.

On October 26, four people (Hamilton Diaz, Martin Bell, a customer services manager, and an external public relations consultant) entered Cantera's Executive MBA classroom. Per their request, Cantera agreed that there would be no audio- or videotaping and no visitors in the classroom.

P A R T

II

Competing in the Internet Age

The rallying cry of enthusiastic engineers, entrepreneurs, venture capitalists, investors, and just about everyone else during the late 1990s, or, as it became known, the dot-com era, was, "The Internet changes everything."

In such a statement there was certainly quite a bit of "the emperor has no clothes" syndrome, as Netscape Corp. cofounder Marc Andressen described it. In other words, while most people were unsure as to how the Internet was going to change everything, they did not want to miss out on it . . . if it did. The frenzy took the NASDAQ—the tech-focused electronic equity security market—past 5000 points in March 2000, before seeing it tumble down to 2000 points in about a year. The market crash notwithstanding, the dot-com era ushered in what some have named the "network economy." The Internet, and the many related information technologies and innovations that are built on the Internet infrastructure, dramatically changed the competitive landscape for almost every company. Today we see a resurgence of the positive mentality that drove the growth of the Internet. The driving force today is a set of technologies that go under the label of Web 2.0 (see Chapter 5).

What is the network economy? Simply put, a network economy is one where ubiquitous global networks drastically reduce geographic and time constraints, enabling organizations to truly compete on a global basis. This notion is at the center of a recent book by *New York Times* columnist Thomas Friedman. The main thesis of the book, titled *The World Is Flat*, is that the technology revolution that took place during the dot-com era has changed modern business and has enabled work to move seamlessly around the globe. The consequence is that the global competitive playing field has been leveled, leading to an unprecedented degree of globalization.

The most apparent changes brought about by the network economy took place at the front end of company interaction with their clients, in what is called the business-to-consumer space. You could not imagine running an airline or a hotel today without a professional and functional Web site that your customers can use to learn about your offer, book reservations, and even check in. The same goes for banks, retailers in the widest variety of sectors, publishers, newly released movies, and even for celebrities a Web site seems to be a must! However, while the front end grabbed all the headlines, the bulk of the "Internet revolution" took place behind the scenes, within company walls, and in what is termed the "business-to-business" space. This trend is captured by a quote attributed to Jack Welch, the iconic former CEO of General Electrics. Welch, referring to the potential for efficiencies ushered in by the Internet is rumored to have said, "Where does the Internet rank on my priority list? It is number one, two, three, and four. I don't think there's been anything as important or more widespread in all my years at GE."[1]

Whether the Internet does indeed "change everything" or not is really not the issue. There is no doubt that the Internet, and the many technologies that leverage it, is today a critical business enabler. Thus, you as a modern general and functional managers must be able to appropriately use it to benefit your firm. In order to do so, you must be able to answer two broad questions:

1. What impacts do Internet technologies have on the competitive landscape? How do they change the environment your firm is, and will be, competing in?

2. How have the Internet and related technologies been used by organizations before? How can they be used by your firm to improve the business efficiency and effectiveness?

Part II of this book is devoted to answering these two questions. Specifically,

- *Chapter 4: The Changing Competitive Environment.* This chapter focuses on the first question and provides you with a background on the Internet and related technologies. It then discusses how networks and information differ, as economic entities, from traditional and physical goods. With this backdrop, the chapter discusses how Internet technologies have changed the modern competitive landscape and the implications for strategy in the modern firm.

- *Chapter 5: Electronic Commerce: New Ways of Doing Business.* This chapter tackles the second question and provides you with a vocabulary with which to understand electronic commerce trends, past, present, and future. The chapter also discusses the role of the Internet, and related technologies, both within and outside the modern firm.

---

[1] Fingar, P., and Aronica, R.C. (2001), *The Death of "e" and the Birth of the Real New Economy: Business Models, Technologies and Strategies for the 21st Century*, Tampa, FL: Meghan-Kiffer Press.

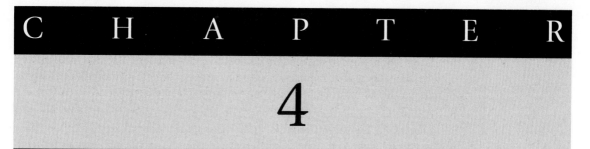

CHAPTER

4

การเปลี่ยนแปลง สภาพแวดล้อม ที่แข่งขัน

The Changing Competitive Environment

What You Will Learn in This Chapter

This chapter focuses on the revolutionary changes that have occurred in the global economy since the advent of the commercial Internet in the mid-1990s. A networked world is widely different from a pre-networked one because networks have peculiar economic characteristics. Moreover, in the presence of pervasive networks, the amount of data and information that can be generated and transferred in real time is literally exploding. The successful firm, and the successful manager, must be able to design and implement strategies to take advantage of, rather than suffer from, these changes. The concepts and examples discussed in this chapter will help you do so.

Specifically, in this chapter you will become well versed in the language of network economics, information economics, and disruptive technologies. You will

1. Be able to define what the Internet is, its defining characteristics, and the principal services it makes available to users.

2. Broaden your definition of the Internet from a network of computer networks to an information grid connecting a staggering range of intelligent devices, both wired and wireless.

3. Understand the basic principles of network economics, including the sources of value in networks and the definitions of physical and virtual networks. You will also learn how to apply these concepts to strategy and managerial decision making.

4. Become familiar with the concepts and vocabulary of network economics, including positive feedback, network externalities, and tippy markets. Be able to recognize when network effects occur and what makes a market tip, as well as what market will not tip toward a dominant player.

81

5. Be able to identify the basic principles of information economics and the role that information plays in the modern competitive environment. Become familiar with the concepts and vocabulary of information economics, including the ability to define classic information goods and information-intensive goods.

6. Be able to explain how the advent of pervasive networks has enabled information to break the constraints imposed by traditional information carriers. You will also be able to explain what the richness/reach trade-off is and its implications for modern organizations.

7. Be able to draw the difference between disruptive and sustaining technologies. Be able to identify each kind and draw implications for decision making in organizations faced with the emergence of disruptive technologies.

MINI-CASE: AMAZON.COM VERSUS EBAY, INC.

"You always had an entrepreneurial streak" you told yourself with a chuckle as you reflected in front of a hot cappuccino at your favorite coffee shop. With an undergraduate degree in computer engineering and a soon-to-be-granted Master's of Management degree, an Internet company sounds like a perfect way to jump back into the real world . . . "too bad you are a few too many years late on the venture capital funding," you tell yourself! However, good ideas still get funded, and the payoff can be handsome—just a few weeks back the YouTube deal became public. YouTube was picked up by Google for $1.65 billion after a little more than two years in operation and little to show in the form of revenues. And what about Skype, sold to eBay, Inc. for $2.6 billion before it reached its third year of existence!

Speaking of eBay, you had just read an interesting article about it. It drew a parallel between eBay, Inc. and Amazon.com. "EBay and Amazon.com, the Internet's top two e-commerce sites, are taking opposite approaches to growth. EBay raised its prices this month for the fourth year in a row, while Amazon renewed its pledge to keep cutting prices even if it means lower profits."[2]

Meg Whitman, eBay chief executive officer, was quoted in the article as saying, "The eBay marketplace is a powerhouse [. . .] We continue to enjoy ever-bigger, ever-faster cycles of success, fueled by the unlimited opportunity of our huge addressable market." Conversely, Amazon's founder and CEO Jeff Bezos was quoted in the same article as saying that his firm would continue to stay close to its customer needs: "The things that matter to them are convenience, selection and lower prices," he mentioned. "We will, for years and years and years, consistently give back the gains we get in lower operating costs to our customers in the form of lower prices" he promised.

As you pondered these statements, you couldn't help but think that Ms. Whitman came across in the article as quite the shrewd character, while Bezos sounded like a really nice guy. Of course, you know better than to think that this was the reason for the difference in the firm's pricing behavior and overall strategies (Figure 4.1). There had to be something else, but what?

On the one hand, eBay spent lots of money on advertisement to drive traffic to its marketplace, but Amazon had a strongly recognized brand as well. In fact, they were 60th and 66th, respectively, on the 2004 *Business Week* Top 100 Brands list.[3] Both companies, as the article mentioned, were electronic commerce powerhouses with significant information systems and IT competencies. Yet they differed dramatically in their approach and financial performance.

The article painted a stark picture of their differences: "But any way you look at it, eBay is the giant. Its sellers moved $7 billion worth of merchandise in the fourth quarter last year, while Amazon's gross sales totaled $1.94 billion. EBay's gross profit margin—its revenue minus the cost of sales—was 82 percent. That's after subtracting the cost of running its Web site, customer support and payment processing operations. And eBay's bottom-line profit stood at

---

[2] Walker, L. (2004), "A Study In E-Commerce Opposites," *The Washington Post Company*, January 29.

[3] *Business Week* (2004), "The Global Brand Scorecard," *Business Week* (vol. 72) August, 2.

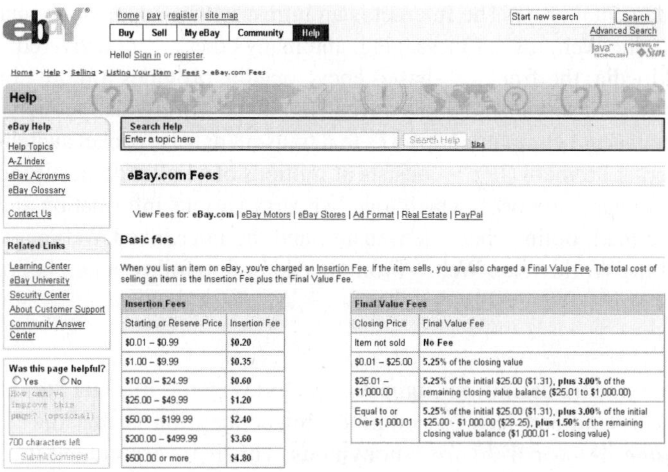

auction   amazon ⇒ retailer.

Figure 4.1 eBay's Fee Structure

they have
1.) different on business model

22 percent of its revenue after subtracting all other expenses, including the hefty $172 million that eBay forked over for marketing and sales expenses. Amazon's gross profit for the same quarter, by contrast, was 22 percent, and its bottom-line profit was under 4 percent."

"Wow," you exclaim out loud, drawing looks from the other coffee shop guests. "I sure should go find me an eBay deal!!!" you say—lowering your voice. "But how do you recognize one when you see it?"

DISCUSSION QUESTIONS

1. As you reflect on what you have read and your knowledge of the impact of new technology on the competitive landscape, you ask yourself why these two companies have taken such diametrically opposite approaches. Cause ebaY → auction while amazon is retailer. so amazon has to keep their price competitive

2. Would you behave any different if you were Meg Whitman? What if you were Jeff Bezos? while ebay can keep rise the price for auction.

- Trust worthy is not a pb for both, amazon & ebay, 2 of them are trust worthy.

INTRODUCTION

Whether you believe that "the Internet changes everything," as dot-com enthusiasts vigorously maintained during the late 1990s rally of the NASDAQ, or you take a much more conservative stance, it is undeniable that the Internet and the many information technologies that the global network has spawned are important tools in the strategic arsenal of the modern firm.

Understanding how to appropriately deploy these technologies requires a basic appreciation of what the Internet is and how it works. More importantly for general and functional managers, being able to use the Internet and related technology requires an understanding of the economic characteristics of networks and of information, as well as their impact on the competitive landscape and strategy of the firm. In the remainder of this chapter we discuss each of these issues in turn.

THE INTERNET

A brief look at any information systems textbook quickly reveals that the Internet is, simply put, "a network of networks." In other words, the Internet is broadly defined as a collection of networked computers that can "talk to one another." This simple definition points to a fundamental issue: The Internet is an infrastructure upon which many services—such as e-mail, the Web, instant messaging, and many others—are delivered.

Wikipedia, the free Web-based encyclopedia, provides a more complete definition: "The Internet (also known simply as the Net) is the worldwide, publicly accessible system of interconnected computer networks that transmit data by packet switching using the standard Internet Protocol (IP). It consists of millions of smaller domestic, academic, business, and government networks, which together carry various information and services, such as electronic mail, online chat, file transfer, and the interlinked Web pages and other documents of the World Wide Web."[4] From this definition follow a number of observations.

Internet Services

As the Wikipedia definition suggests, the nodes of the Internet "together carry various information and services." A common misconception is that the terms *Internet* and *World Wide Web* (or *Web*) are synonymous. This is incorrect, and it is important to differentiate the two. The Internet is the infrastructure on which many services are made available. Typically, you will connect to the Internet, the infrastructure, to access and use the services you want to use.

The Web is a service available on the Internet and, alongside electronic mail, the most popular. However, there are many other services that many of us use on a daily basis—for example Instant Messaging (IM), Voice over IP (VoIP), Blogs, Real Simple Syndication feeds (RSS), (Figure 4.3) discussion groups (asynchronous electronic discussion), chat rooms (synchronous electronic discussion), and File Transfer Protocol (FTP) (Figure 4.2). As technology innovation continues at a relentless pace, new services become available.

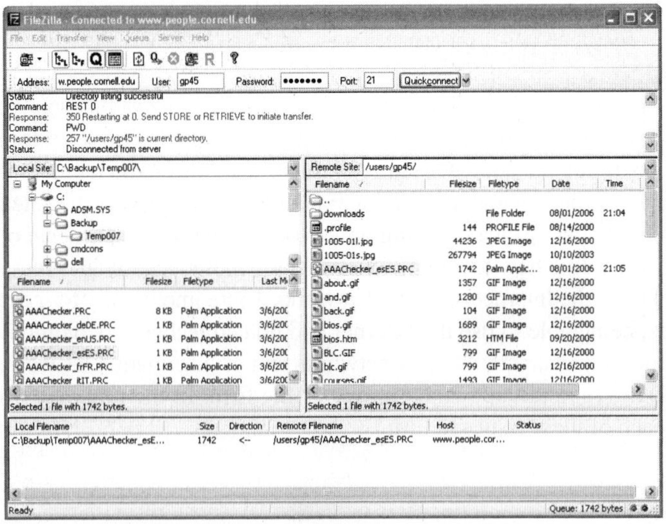

Figure 4.2 FTP Client

---

[4] http://en.wikipedia.org/wiki/Internet (Accessed 1/12/2007).

TechCrunch

[>] Zune as Part of Microsoft's "Broader Picture"

Lots of new details are emerging about Zune, Microsoft's new music/video device and related service.

The news about Zune broke last week in a Billboard article where Chris Stephenson, Microsoft's new GM of marketing for MSN Entertainment Business, said Zune will be an umbrella brand for what he says is "a family of hardware and software products" targeting various digital entertainment services. The somewhat creepy-yet-strangely-soothing "comingzune" site launched as well, with no real information whatsoever.

On July 25 Microsft CEO Steve Ballmer spoke about Zune at a Retail Vision Summit in Seattle:

it's all about how do multiple groups of people, friends, interact together in various entertainment experiences, whether it's watching the British Open, whether it's enjoying movies, and music, and other video entertainment, whether it is involved in an interactive gaming session, a lot of the IQ we're putting into is how you view community and entertainment together.

log in   register

username
password
remember me?

log in

options
show oldest first
group by item

Figure 4.3   Feeds.Reddit, an RSS Reader

Distributed Ownership

The Internet is "publicly accessible," meaning that no single entity owns it, regulates access to it, or otherwise controls it. In fact, the Internet has many owners but no one who centrally controls it. In other words, different portions of the Internet (i.e., different networks connected to the other networks) are owned by different entities—literally millions of them.

For example, your university network, while connected to the public Internet, is privately owned by your university. Your university manages and pays for it. Similarly, if you decide to launch your start-up upon graduation and need it to have a Web presence, you may decide to run your own infrastructure rather than purchase it as a service. In this case, you would maintain your own Web server and your own dedicated connection to the Internet, thus becoming one of the many entities owning a small piece of the global network.

Distributed ownership has been perhaps the main strength of the Internet, limiting regulation, fostering experimentation, and ensuring widespread access leading to significant growth. The Internet was the fastest-growing technology ever, reaching the 50 million adopters milestone (Figure 4.4). It did so in about five years since the advent of the commercial Web. By some estimates it took television thirteen years to achieve the same milestone, while radio took thirty-eight.

Multiplicity of Devices

The Internet is a digital network consisting of millions of smaller digital networks. Each of these smaller digital networks encompasses a collection of digital devices, called nodes. The simplest digital network to visualize is perhaps a home network (Figure 4.5). Your home network may be comprised of a couple of personal computers and a printer to which both computers can send documents. Using a home router, wired or wireless, and a broadband modem (e.g., cable or DSL), you connect to the Internet. Each of these

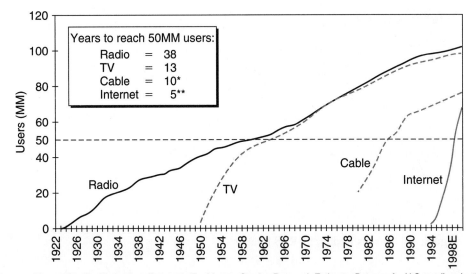

Source: *Morgan Stanley Technology Research. E – Morgan Stanley Research Estimate. Data are for U.S. media adoption.*
* We use the launch of HBO in 1976 as our estimate for the beginning of cable as an entertainment/advertising medium. Though cable technology was developed in the late 1940's, its initial use was primarily for the improvement of reception in remote areas. It was not until HBO began to distribute its pay-TV movie service via satellite in 1976 that the medium became a distinct content and advertising alternative to broadcast television. ** Morgan Stanley Technology Research Estimate.

Figure 4.4 Adoption of Technology Over Time

digital devices—the two computers, the printer, the router—are nodes on your home network.

Your home network is a tiny contributor to the larger Internet. The fancier ones among us may have more cutting-edge devices, such as wireless VoIP phones to make free Skype-powered phone calls all over the world, a wireless media center to stream MP3 music from a computer through the living room stereo or to listen to Internet radio stations, a wireless Web cam to monitor the front door, and even cooler stuff!

A car equipped with a GPS device or the OnStar system is another example of a networked node, as is a modern cell phone (Figure 4.6). As the price of microchips and bandwidth keeps dropping (see Chapter 1), the number and type of devices that become nodes of a network will continue to increase. In other words, the Internet is in continuous expansion.

Open Standards

The Internet relies on open technology standard and protocols. A protocol is an agreed-on set of rules or conventions governing communication among the elements of a network (i.e., network nodes). For example, case study discussion in your class follows a (stated or implicit) protocol. Typically the professor sets the stage for the case discussion. You listen and, when the floor is open for discussion, you might raise your hand. When you are called, you contribute your perspective. You may disagree with the professor or classmates, but you do so in a polite manner, addressing ideas rather than individuals. Respect of the protocol by all is necessary to enable constructive communication rather than unproductive classroom chaos.

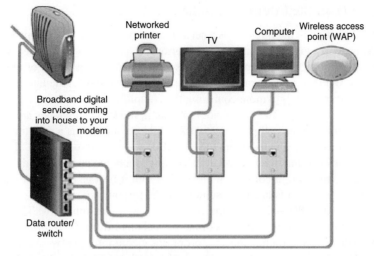

Figure 4.5   A Simple Home Network

Similarly, in order to communicate, network nodes need to follow an agreed-on set of rules. On the Internet such a set of rules is the TCP/IP protocol mentioned in the Wikipedia definition. Nobody owns the TCP/IP protocol; as such, it is an open (i.e., freely available) standard as opposed to a proprietary one.

The same holds true for the other technologies that enable the Internet and its services, such as HTML (the language used to write Web pages). While there are standard-setting bodies that decide how each of these technologies should evolve (in the case of HTML it is the World Wide Web Consortium, W3C), no entity can charge for their use. Thus, anyone who wants to embed support for these standards in their applications can do so . . . and innovation continues to thrive on the Internet!

Figure 4.6   Modern Cell Phones Connect to the Internet and Access Its Services

The Network, More Than the Internet of Today

The definition of the Internet, as a network of networks, can be very misleading. It typically conjures up a vision of computers, of various shapes and sizes, hooked together by a maze of cables of different shapes and colors—the Internet as a bunch of interconnected computers. While this image more or less correctly captured what the Internet looked like in the past, it is increasingly more confusing than helpful.

For example, while it may not look like it, modern cell phones are full-fledged digital computers, and the cell phone network, while not a cable, is a data transmission channel. Similar examples abound, from the BlackBerry you may soon be (or already are) carrying (Figure 4.7), to intelligent appliances coming to a home near you in the immediate future.

Don Tapscott, a consultant and author, put it best as he wrote in 2001 that it is "an all-too-common mistake [to assume] that the Internet we see today—a network that connects desktop PCs—is the same Internet we will see tomorrow. This is nonsense. The Internet of tomorrow will be as dramatic a change from the Internet of today as today's Internet is from the unconnected, proprietary computing networks of yesterday."[5]

He went on to describe a vision that has, in large part, already become reality: "Mobile computing devices, broadband access, wireless networks, and computing power embedded in everything from refrigerators to automobiles are converging into a global network that will enable people to use the Net just about anywhere and anytime. No facet of human activity is untouched. The Net is a force of social change penetrating homes, schools, offices, factories, hospitals, and governments."

Others have discussed a similar vision using the term "grid."[6] The idea is that distributed intelligent devices and high-volume network connections will soon make it possible to turn computing into a utility, much like water or electricity. In the near future, the proponents of grid computing claim, we will not have to wonder whether we will have access to the Internet and all its services when we travel, just like we don't worry about whether we will have access to electricity or a phone.

Figure 4.7 The BlackBerry 7730

---

[5] Tapscott, D. (2001), "Rethinking Strategy in a Networked World," *Strategy and Competition*, Third Quarter.

[6] Heingartner, D. (2001), "The Grid: The Next-Gen Internet?" *Wired News* (Accessed 7/12/2006 http://www.wired.com/news/technology/ 0,1282,42230,00.html).

With such a pace and magnitude of evolution awaiting you as you hit the workforce and get ready to make decisions as a general and functional manager, you must be equipped with some fundamental concepts to navigate the new environment.

NETWORK ECONOMICS

With a clear grasp of what the Internet is and how it works, we now turn to discuss how its advent has impacted the competitive landscape and business strategy. In order to do so, we first introduce the topic of network economics, focusing on the question, How is value created in networks? As we will see, networks have some unique characteristics. We also introduce the vocabulary needed to discuss these concepts.

We then expand once again our definition of *network* beyond the notion of interconnected devices, but also to include people that are mutually dependent in some way. Finally, in this section we draw some implications of interest to you as general and functional managers. Specifically, we discuss the organizational impact of these network dynamics for basic strategic choices and value creation.

Value in Scarcity

The opening minicase was very telling. How can a firm like eBay, created in 1995, go on to dominate its industry in only a few years? How can a little piece of software like Skype, for as useful or brilliantly coded as it may be, enable the firm that owns it to fetch billions of dollars in only three years?! How have these firms created so much value so quickly? Much of the answer is to be found in the economics of networks.

Anyone who has recently gotten engaged can easily rattle off key statistics about diamonds. The value of a diamond depends on its physical attributes: Color, clarity, cut, shape, and, of course, size (measured by its weight in carats). Interestingly, while jewelers may try to convince you that a diamond has a soul, spirit, and personality (!?!), diamonds are cataloged and measured quite precisely in the United States by the Gemological Institute of America (GIA). The price of a diamond is a fairly precise function of its physical characteristics. A quick online search reveals that as diamonds become harder to find, their value increases. For example, a superior round diamond, of ideal cut, D color, and IF clarity, will run you about $3800 for half a carat, $16,000 for one carat, $56,000 for two carats, and cool $150,000 for three carats.

The lesson is clear: The value of a diamonds is proportional to their rarity. In fact, diamonds are a great example because they have little use outside the jewelry domain. What you are paying for is indeed scarcity, which is a function of the physical characteristics that determine its beauty, brilliance, and fire. Ironically, oxygen and water are much more valuable than diamonds. After all, if you couldn't breathe or were dehydrating, you would hardly notice the beauty of that diamond you bought! However, water is cheap and oxygen is free because they are plentiful.

To be sure, the relationship between scarcity and value of a resource is the rule, not the exception. Skilled labor and managerial talent, the resource you sell to your employer, is no different. While we can debate the morality of sky-high executive compensations, it is clear that they are justified with the argument that few people in the world have the talent and experience to run large, complex business operations. The same argument is used for professional athletes in popular sports—there was only one Michael Jordan, who could fill seats in an arena, make people tune into the games he played, and have kids clamoring for his shoes and jerseys. Like scarce diamonds, these people command a premium price for their services. As the scarcest attraction in basketball, Jordan fetched the highest one-year contract in the sport during his last year with the Chicago Bulls—$34 million for the single 1997–1998 season.

The above examples represent the norm rather than the exception. Value is typically found in scarcity, and the heart of strategy is about being unique in a positive way (see Chapter 7).

Networks Are Different: Value in Plentitude

While fax technology has been around in one form or another since the early 1900s, fax machines did not become a common sight in organizations until the 1970s. How much would you have been willing to pay for the very first fax machine rolling off the assembly line then? If value is found in scarcity . . . would you have paid hundreds of thousand of dollars? Probably not!

In fact, you probably would take a pass and pay nothing for it. The very first fax machine is valueless. On the other hand, if a business associate of yours had a fax machine, you may consider purchasing one if the price were low enough given the amount of real-time document exchange you had to engage in with this associate. If many of your business associates had fax machines and were already communicating back and forth, you would see significant value in it and you would consider paying a considerable amount for it.

Where does the fax machine draw its value from? Not scarcity, rather plentitude (Figure 4.8). In fact, the value of a network is proportional to the number of connected nodes. Similar arguments can be made for network technologies, like the telephone, instant messengers, railroads, and the telegraph. The insight underlying these examples is that networks differ dramatically from most other goods, as their value is tied to how many other nodes are in the network (plentitude) rather than how few (scarcity).

Physical and Virtual Networks

In the previous section we talked about computer networks and the Internet. There are, of course, other types of networks, like the telephone network or the railroad network. We call these physical networks, where the nodes of the network are connected by physical links (i.e., railroad tracks, telephone wires). However, network economics apply also to "virtual" networks.[7] The defining characteristic of a virtual network is that connections between network nodes are not physical, but intangible and invisible. The nodes of a virtual network are typically people rather than devices.

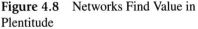

Figure 4.8   Networks Find Value in Plentitude

---

[7] We adopt the term *virtual networks* following the definition used in Shapiro, C., and Varian, H. R. (1999), *Information Rules*, Boston MA: Harvard Business School Press.

Whether tangible or intangible, network connections enable network nodes to share and communicate. In a virtual network the people in the network can share information (i.e., share files of the same format) with other members of the same user network (e.g., eDonkey file-sharing users), or they can share expertise (e.g., information on how to use a given software program is the reason why you would join a certain community of practice). Note that a virtual network is generally sponsored by an organization or technology that enables it, controls access to it, and manages its evolution. Apple Computer, Inc., for instance, sponsors the iTunes network, while Skype controls the Skype network of VoIP users. Maintaining control of the network puts the sponsor in a position of advantage.

Consider the writing of this book as an example. We are writing this book using Microsoft Word on a Wintel platform.[8] If you were also a Microsoft Word user, it would be easy for you to become a coauthor on our next edition. This is because we could easily exchange versions of the chapters for comments and editing. Conversely, if you used the Linux operating system and the StarOffice 8 Writer text editor (Figure 4.9) it would be much harder to work together. Documents may not convert correctly, images may be rendered differently, we may lose special formatting in the exchange, we would not be able to easily track, approve or reject each other's changes, and so on.

Another example of a virtual network is provided in the opening mini-case: the eBay network of users—buyers and sellers. If you buy or sell on the eBay marketplace, you are a member of the eBay network because you can share information and transact with other eBay users. The eBay network is sponsored (i.e., created and controlled) by eBay, Inc.

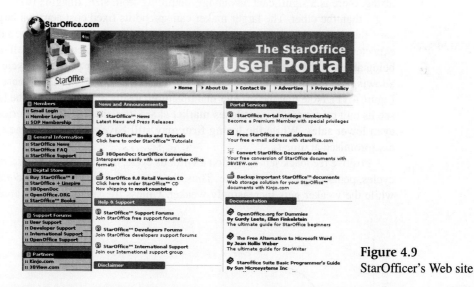

Figure 4.9
StarOfficer's Web site

<hr>

[8] A platform is a combination of a hardware architecture and operating system. The Wintel platform refers to the dominant personal computer platform using Microsoft Windows running on machines using the Intel microprocessor.

Size Still Matters   Whether physical or virtual, the value of the network for its members is a function of its size. That is, the more nodes the network has, the more valuable it is to its members. Consider the Wintel platform example again. If you are getting ready to buy a new computer, you will likely not make the decision in isolation. Rather, you will look at your immediate circle of friend and coworkers and make sure that you purchase a computer that allows you to interact with them.

For example, as a student you write papers with your team members, you exchange spreadsheet models, you swap notes, and so on. As a consequence, if most other people at your school are using a Wintel platform or a compatible one (e.g., Apple Macintosh), then you would most likely choose the same so as not to be left out of the network.

Key Concepts and Vocabulary

To move beyond an intuitive level, in order to understand how networks operate and to explore their implications for firm strategy, we need to introduce some vocabulary and key concepts.

Positive Feedback   Adoption of a new technology product or service typically follows the pattern represented by the S-curve (see Figure 4.10). Positive feedback is simply defined as that self-reinforcing mechanism by which the strong gets stronger and the weak gets weaker. It is very similar to the process by which return in a microphone quickly becomes louder and louder until it is deafening (i.e., a high-pitched sound due to interference is picked up by a microphone and amplified, the now louder sound is picked up again by the microphone and amplified some more, etc.).

Positive feedback is a well-known economic phenomenon at the heart, for example, of economies of scale. In industries with strong economies of scale, say automobile manufacturing, there is a significant advantage stemming from size. Imagine two car makers, one larger than the other. The larger maker can spread its fixed cost across a larger volume of cars, thus being able to reduce its prices—assuming everything else is the same, including expected profit margins. With lower prices, the larger manufacturer will sell more cars, thus being able to further spread its fixed costs. With even lower prices the cycle begins again, allowing the dominant manufacturer to further reduce unit cost and increase volumes (see Figure 4.11). Note that the smaller manufacturer, losing market share to the larger one, will see its unit cost increase as it loses market share, thus having to raise prices and seeing even lower sales. While the losing firm may still have a chance at time t_1, things look compromised at time t_2.

Positive feedback sets in motion a virtuous cycle, benefiting the larger firm, and vicious cycles, penalizing the smaller one. Thus, the stronger gets stronger and continues to grow while the weaker gets increasingly weaker. Unless the smaller firm is able to identify a

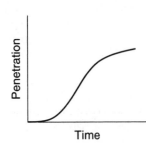

Figure 4.10   Classic Technology Adoption Curve

งูด tipping point เกิดใน ช่วงแคบๆ และยังในตัวนี้ (p.95)

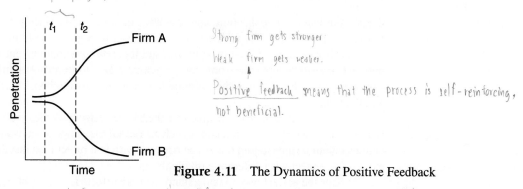

Strong firm gets stronger

Weak firm gets weaker.

Positive feedback means that the process is self-reinforcing, not beneficial.

Figure 4.11   The Dynamics of Positive Feedback

ข้อง,ไม่มา,ออก   เปลี่ยนแปลง/ทำให้แตกต่าง   mignาน, extinction, eclipse
(ถอ-ลิ-เวิน)

profitable niche or somehow differentiate its product, it will likely fade into oblivion, unable to sustain itself as a viable business.

Negative Feedback   The above discussion should clarify that there is nothing inherently positive (i.e., good) about positive feedback—particularly for the firms on the losing side of it! In other words, positive feedback simply means that the process is self-reinforcing, not beneficial.

Negative feedback is the term used to refer to the opposite dynamic. If negative feedback is at play, the stronger gets weaker and the weaker gets stronger. Negative feedback typically characterizes economies of scale and takes effect when the dominant firm has reached a significant size. After a certain size, economies of scale no longer reduce unit cost and, due to coordination costs and increasing overhead, further growth is hampered. In other words, past a certain size, the dominant firm encounters difficulties that limit further growth.

Network Effects   Positive and negative feedback play a crucial role in physical and virtual networks because the value of a network to its members is a function of the number of nodes in the same network. Positive feedback dynamics that occur in networks go under the name of network effects, network externalities, or demand-side economies of scale.

Network effects occur when a new node (e.g., a new Skype user), while pursuing his or her own economic motives, creates value for all the other members of the network by making the network larger, and thus more valuable. Network effects have the characteristic of economic externalities[9]—hence the name *network externalities*. That is, they create spill-over effects that have an impact on other individuals, positive for those members of the growing network and negative for the members of the other ones.

Consider once again the example of Skype. Skype software enables those who download it to call, chat, and exchange files with other Skype users. If you are a Skype user, you were probably alerted to its existence by a friend or colleague who had already downloaded it. Once you downloaded the application and started using it, you probably began to recruit your own friends and colleagues. The reason is that any one of them who downloads Skype

---

[9] As you may recall from your introductory economics courses, an externality occurs when an economic actor, pursuing his or her own economic motives, affects other actors' economic position. Consider the example of a large resort able to charge $500 a night. If a pig farm is opened upwind of the resort, with no intention to hurt the resort simply to pursue a business opportunity, the resort will no longer be able to charge premium prices . . . or any price at all! This spill-over effect is called an externality—a negative externality in this case.

Ex of spill-over effect could be both +/-.

makes your using the application more valuable. In other words, since you can now interact with more people, the Skype software is more useful to you. The term *evangelist effect* has been coined to describe this dynamic and the incentive that current members of the network have to "spread the word" and convince others to join it. A similar dynamic has fueled the growth of many other applications you may use today: MySpace, Facebook, and the like.

Note as well that the more people join the Skype network, the less valuable become, in relative terms, competing applications such as Yahoo! messenger. You would rather try and convince your friends to join the Skype network with you rather than install multiple applications to connect with different individuals.

Perhaps the easiest way to understand network effects is to look at the service offered by those organizations that sought to build an explicit business model around it. Mercata (Figure 4.12), a firm backed by Microsoft cofounder Paul Allen, pioneered the "group-shopping" business model along with MobShop. In this model groups of strangers seeking to purchase the same product (e.g., Palm Treo 750) would come together via the Internet to form a Mercata-enabled buying group. As the number of new customers joined the buying group, the price for the item would drop for each member of the group.

The Mercata Web site showed the current price and future prices available to all once targets in the number of customers were hit (e.g., $550 per item once the size of the group reaches 10, $540 at 15, etc.). The network effect at play here is clear. Every new customer who joins the buying group, while seeking his or her own economic benefit, lowers the price for all. While both Mercata and MobShop were casualties of the dot-com bust, their business model offers a great example of network effects at play.

Positive feedback associated with traditional economies of scale typically exhausts itself well before one firm can achieve market dominance, but this is not the case for network effects. Positive feedback associated with network effects can play out, without limit, until one firm dominates the network and all others disappear, a situation typically referred to as a "winner-take-all" dynamic (see Figure 4.11).

A firm that finds itself on the losing side of network effects can survive under two conditions:

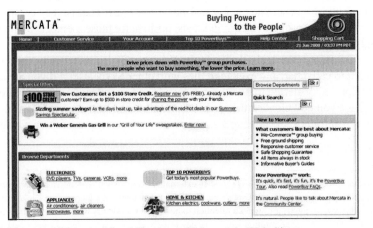

Figure 4.12   Archived Version of Mercata's Web Site

Losing side of network effects can survive under 2 conditions

1) ■ Become compatible with the dominant player, thus being able to connect to the dominant network and tap into its value. When Apple Computers found itself on the losing side of the battle for dominance of the personal computer platform, it was forced to seek compatibility with Wintel products—sponsor of the dominant network.

2) ■ Find a niche that is different enough from the broader market and big enough to sustain the firm. Before Apple became compatible with the dominant Wintel platform, it was able to survive by offering a far superior product for designers and publishers, who found the Macintosh computer and software far superior to Windows machines for their needs (Figure 4.13).

The dominant network sponsor may react by trying to either block or limit compatibility. It may also try to take over the available market niches. Being able to do so will depend on the characteristics of the market it competes in and the demand for product variety that characterizes it.

Tipping Point and Tippy Markets   A tippy market is defined as one that is subject to strong positive feedback, such that the market will "tip" in favor of the firm that is able to reach critical mass and dominate it. A tippy market is therefore a market with "winner-take-all" tendencies.

We define a tipping point as as the watershed of dominance. In other words, the tipping point is that moment in the evolution of a market where one organization or technology reaches critical mass and goes on to dominate it—the point of no return where winners and losers are defined. In Figure 4.11 the tipping point occurred some time between times t_1 and t_2.

The lower the cost of production and distribution of a product, the quicker the onset of the tipping point (Figure 4.14). Software programs such as Skype represent a good example. A random check of your Skype application may reveal that there are seven or eight million users currently connected—not bad for a company with only a three-year-old product.

Not All Markets Tip   During the dot-com days, there was a prevalent misguided perception that any business that used the Internet would be able to harness strong network effects. As a consequence, many firms focused on ramping up their user base at any cost, trusting that, once they reached critical mass, they would be able to dominate the market and figure out how to turn a profit.

Figure 4.13   The Original Machintosh Released in 1984

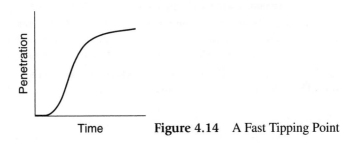

Figure 4.14   A Fast Tipping Point

Unfortunately, not all markets tip, and winner-take-all dynamics are more the exception than the rule—even on the Internet. Consider, for example, Buy.com (Figure 4.15), the online retailer vying for market share against Amazon.com. Buy.com, made famous by a Superbowl in 1999, employed the retailing tactic of drawing customers with heavily discounted popular items in the hope that they would then make multiple purchases. This tactic was also thought to increase the size of the buy.com network, by increasing the numbers of its customers. But is the online retail an industry characterized by strong network effects? This is a crucial question because the strategy would otherwise backfire.

Applying the definition of network effects, it becomes clear that the online retailing market is not a tippy market. If you purchase a computer monitor from buy.com (i.e., you join the buy.com network), your doing so does not make buy.com more valuable to me—another buy.com customer. While it is true that as the customer base grows Buy.com may be able to negotiate lower prices with its distributors and pass on some of the savings to its customers, this is by no means an immediate or significant effect.

Contrast the above example with that of Resort Condominiums International, LLC (RCI). RCI is a well-established timeshare company founded in 1974 to enable "exchange vacations." In the timeshare model, customers buy a right to one or more vacation weeks to a condominium unit in a specific property and a specific location (e.g., Unit 235 at The Outrigger Palms at

Figure 4.15   Buy.com Store

Wailea, on the isle of Maui, Hawaii). Those who own a timeshare can enjoy it during their allotted time. Alternatively, when seeking variation in their vacation, timeshare owners can exchange the right to use their unit with others. RCI, and other companies that support exchange vacations, create the market and facilitate the process of finding suitable trading partners, managing credits (e.g., a week in high-end Maui resort may be worth two weeks in a midscale Florida property), and providing the many other services to enable the exchange.

RCI has a membership base of over three million timeshare owners with more than 3700 affiliated resorts in over one hundred countries. RCI now has a Web site that supports many of its interactions with its members and prospective timeshare owners (Figure 4.16), but it is certainly not a "network business." Is RCI's industry characterized by strong network effects?

The answer here is yes. Every new member that joins the RCI network increases the network's value for the entire current (and prospective) membership because the new member's unit increases the pool of available options. Moreover, it increases the potential pool of people interested in current members' own units—thus making current RCI member's units more likely to be requested for exchange. It follows that for prospective timeshare buyers, joining the largest timeshare exchange network offers the highest value.

How to Recognize a Tippy Market   The two examples above show that "being on the Internet" is no guarantee of being able to harness network effects and that even non-networked businesses can benefit from network effects. How can we recognize a tippy market a priori? How can you tell if your firm has the potential to harness positive feedback?

Whether a market will tip toward a dominant technology or a dominant player depends on two factors:

- *The presence and strength of economies of scale.* Strong economies of scale, whether traditional economies of scale or network effects, provide an advantage to larger firms.

- *The variety of the customer needs.* Customer demand for variety creates the potential for the development of distinct market niches that the dominant player may be unable to fulfill.

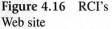
Figure 4.16   RCI's Web site

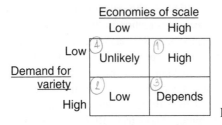

Figure 4.17   Likelihood of Market Tippyness

When economies of scale are significant and customer needs are fairly standard, then the conditions for market tippiness are strongest. Consider our first example, the fax machine. As we discussed, there are strong network effects in the faxing industry. Moreover, the need for fax machines is a very standardized one—customers don't need much variety in the service. It follows, then, that one dominant fax network will emerge. While more than one fax standard may be vying for dominance in the early days, the market will tip toward one. The others will disappear. A similar dynamic has played out for modems and videocassettes recorders in the past and is currently playing out in the high-definition DVD market.

When economies of scale are limited and the market has a wide range of different needs, the potential for market tippyness is the weakest. This is because not only is there a small advantage associated with increasing size, but there are also a number of smaller niches that can support multiple smaller focused players. Consider sports cars, for instance. Typically the top manufacturers, such as Ferrari, Lamborghini (Figure 4.18) Lotus, and the like, make a limited number of cars. Thus, economies of scale are small. Moreover, those who seek to purchase high-end sports cars do so partly to differentiate themselves from the crowd. Those who purchase exclusive goods seek variety—at times even uniqueness. This is therefore a market that is likely to sustain a number of relatively small players.

When economies of scale are significant and demand for variety is high, the potential for market tippiness depends on the number and size of the available market niches. The ability to tap into a sizeable market niche seeking a product with unique specifications

Figure 4.18   The Lamborghini Murcielago

(e.g., graphic designers) is what allowed Apple Computers to survive prior to ensuring compatibility with Microsoft-dominant products.

Ⓐ When economies of scale are limited, even if the demand for variety is low, the potential to create positive feedback is small and the market is unlikely to tip.

Two-Sided Networks

Now that we have discussed the dynamics of networks in their purest sense, we can complicate the picture a bit. When network effects are present, the addition of one node to the network directly creates value for all the existing members. However, positive feedback can occur also in what we term two-sided networks, networks that have two types of members, each creating value for the other.

Consider, for example, Adobe, the firm that in 1990 invented the now ubiquitous Portable Document Format (PDF) standard. Documents that are converted to PDF are guaranteed to look exactly the same on any platform. Chances are that you are a heavy user of PDF documents, reading them with Adobe's Acrobat Reader, for which you paid exactly nothing—not because you are a user of pirated software but because Adobe gives the software away for free. In similar fashion, Microsoft gives away its Windows Media Player, as do all other streaming audio/video makers. Why is it so? Does it make sense for a company to give away its product?

The strategy described above is sensible, particularly as the firm tries to establish its product as the standard. As you realize when you move from wanting to read PDF files to wanting to create them, Adobe Acrobat is not free. In other words, Adobe created a market for software programs that would ensure documents' cross-platform accuracy of display. Then it proceeded to establish its technology as the standard by creating a market of users, all those who downloaded and used the free reader. As the number of users grew, fueled by some early adopters of the authoring software (i.e., PDF documents makers), organizations that produce and publish documents (e.g., the Internal Revenue Service) decided to adopt Adobe Acrobat. In turn, the increasing number of PDF documents available for download created even more demand for the reader software, aided by the "Free: Download Acrobat Reader" link that would be placed next to it.

You immediately recognize this process as an example of positive feedback. If you tried to break into the cross-platform document maker market as of today, you would be taking on a next-to-impossible feat. On the other hand, Adobe today provides a whole family of "ePaper solutions," including, of course, the ubiquitous (and free) Acrobat Reader. Adobe also offers various versions of the PDF maker, such as Acrobat Elements, Acrobat Standard, Acrobat Professional, and Acrobat 3D, each with different functionalities and price points.

More generally, in a two-sided network, the value of the network to one type of member depends on the number of members from the other side that take part in the network (Figure 4.19). An example is offered by electronic procurement exchanges (see Chapter 5). In these marketplaces, whether catering to consumers or businesses, buyers are interested in the number of suppliers they will be able to reach (i.e., selection) while sellers are interested in the number of buyers they will be able to reach (i.e., potential sales volume). In this case as well, the firm that enables the marketplace (i.e., the sponsor of the network) and is first to reach critical mass (i.e., passes the tipping point) will dominate the industry, leaving little room for any competitor (i.e., any competing marketplace).

Figure 4.19   The Hotel Booking Solutions Network Brings Together Supply and Demand for Hotel Rooms

Implications for General and Functional Managers

Network economics have substantial implications of managerial interest. As networks become more ubiquitous, you must take these implications into account.

Network Effects, Not Just Networks   As we have seen in the many examples provided above, network effects, and, more generally, positive feedback, create the precondition for winner-takes-all dynamics. Network effects occur in the presence of technology standards, like the fax machine or a computer platform, but are not restricted to the technology arena. They also occur in the presence of virtual networks and communities of interest.

Consider, for example, the great success enjoyed by dating communities, such as Match.com, or employment search sites, such as Monster.com (Figure 4.20). While these

Figure 4.20   Monster.com Matches Job Seeker with Organizations Looking for Talent

[handwritten margin notes at top:] How do these (match.com or Job search sites) companies make money from ? — ทุกคนเข้าไปใช้ website ได้ฟรี ไม่ต้องเสียเงินทำให้มี ยอดใช้, เอากำไร/รายได้จากทางไหน ??—

communities do not use or require their members to purchase any specific technology or buy into any technical standard, their value is directly proportional to the number of users they can attract and, as a consequence, enjoy strong network effects.

[handwritten margin note:] Tipping point meaning / ก. ลำกัญใน การเริ่มต้น หรือ เปิดตัว สินค้า

The Threshold of Significance   We defined the tipping point as the watershed of dominance, that moment in the evolution of a market where one organization or technology reaches critical mass and goes on to dominate it. Traditionally, the onset of the tipping point would take some time, as the dominant technology slowly gained acceptance and became adopted by more and more users. For example, in the now famous battle for dominance of the videocassette recorder (VCR) market, Sony and JVC struggled to establish their standard, Betamax and VHS, respectively (Figure 4.21). The battle between these competing standards lasted over a decade and, as we know today, was won by Sony's VHS technology. Today a similar battle is replaying in the DVD market between two technologies vying for dominance: Sony's Blue-Ray and NEC's High Definition DVD (HD-DVD).

The new generation of general and functional managers will not have a decade to monitor competitors before the onset of the tipping point. Particularly for digital products delivered over the Internet, the market can tip very rapidly. In some cases, by the time a competitor realizes that a technology is emerging (i.e., the new technology reaches the threshold of significance), it is too late to react. In these markets, being the innovator and the first mover may be critical. ICQ, the firm that popularized Instant Messaging and went on to dominate that industry, reached critical mass before there was even one competitor. While formidable competitors have since emerged, such as Yahoo! and Microsoft, ICQ remains the dominant platform.

Users Select a Network   One of the most important implications of the above discussion is that customers will pick a network, not a product or a service provider. Let's return to your decision to buy a personal computer. If all your friends are in the Microsoft Windows network, you are most likely to join them in that network. Yet, while many of your friends may be using Dell laptops, you could chose a Compaq machine or even a Mac—which now enables you to be a member of the dominant network. In other words, you will not care about what hardware or software you use, as long as it enables you to tap into the resources of your network of interest.

Figure 4.21   A Betamax Tape and a VHS Cassette

Controlling the Network Provides Competitive Advantage   Firms are willing to engage in standards battles and invest significant resources to achieve critical mass because sponsoring a dominant network provides the firm with a position of competitive advantage.

Consider the recent court battle involving America Online (AOL), sponsor of the dominant Instant Messenger (IM) network after having bought ICQ, and rival IM software providers. AOL found itself having to defend why it resisted making its IM network compatible with Yahoo! Messenger and Microsoft MSN. While the firm claimed that it wanted to be able to control its network to offer the best possible experience to its users and to limit security and privacy concerns, it was clear that AOL's decision was a business decision designed to maintain and strengthen its advantage as the sponsor of the largest network.

The Importance of Mutual Exclusivity   Up to this point, we have treated competing networks as mutually exclusive. This is true for many of them. Consider the VCR standards battle once again. Very few individuals would be willing to purchase two VCRs, one using the Betamax standard and the other one using the VHS standard. This is because not only would they need to purchase two devices that cost money and take up space, but they would also have to maintain separate movie collections with some titles in one format and some in the other.

Simply put, there are costs associated with being a member of both networks. The steeper these costs, the more valuable it is to be able to control and retain ownership of the network. Consider Skype and the Voice over IP (VoIP) market. Skype is a small piece of software that can be installed quickly and requires little configuration. Once installed, Skype runs as a service in the background until the user decides to make a call. If a competitor with very similar characteristics were to emerge, it would not cost users much to run both applications simultaneously. It is a bit of a nuisance to have to install and run two VoIP applications, but the two networks would not be mutually exclusive and the power associated with controlling the dominant network (i.e., Skype) would be largely diminished.

THE ECONOMICS OF INFORMATION

As networks of interoperable digital devices have continued to grow, one of the most important results of managerial interest has been the unprecedented amounts of data and information that are being captured, stored, processed, and distributed by modern organizations. Andy Cohen, former senior vice president of sales and marketing at Instill, said it best: "The information you can derive from e-commerce is as interesting as the commerce itself."

However, in order to be able to wring value from data and information, you must understand its economic characteristics. Information, like networks, has some interesting idiosyncrasies that differentiate it from the physical goods that we are commonly used to. These unique characteristics of data and information have significant implications for firm strategy and competition.

Data and Information

Information systems researchers typically draw a distinction between the terms *data* and *information*. *Data* is defined as codified raw facts—things that have happened (e.g., a customer has made a reservation in a hotel) coded as letters of the alphabet and numbers and stored, increasingly, by way of a computer (see Figure 4.22).

85903380 1 Aug 29 2004 Aug 30 2004 99.00 DR GABRIELE PICCOLI

Figure 4.22   A String of Data

Information is defined as data in context (see Figure 4.23). In other words, data becomes information when they have been given meaning and can therefore be interpreted by individuals or other technology (i.e., be employed by a software program). It follows, then, that information is audience dependent; one person's data is another person's information.

Classic Information Goods

The unique characteristics of information are best understood by first looking at products where information is the heart of the value proposition. We define classic information goods as those products that a customer purchases for the only purpose of gaining access to the information they contain.

For example, this book (and any other book) is a classic information good. The only reason you purchased it was to be able to gain access to its content. The same goes for movies. The only reason you go to the theater or rent a movie is to gain access to the experience that a film provides. The news represents yet another example. Whether you read the newspaper, watch the television, or visit a news agency Web site, the only reason to do so is to acquire the information provided. Other classic information goods are music, stock quotes, class lectures, software programs, and the like (Figure 4.24).

A simple test for recognizing information goods is to verify whether the product can be digitized (i.e., can be encoded into bits and stored in digital format). If so, the product is an information good. You are probably holding a paper copy of this book, but the same content could be delivered online, as an eBook, or as sound if we decided to publish an audio book version. I have a version of this same book in my computer in Microsoft Word format, while the publisher has a version on its computers in Adobe FrameMaker.

Now consider the chair on which you are sitting as you read the book. Could that be digitized? The answer is no, of course. The plans and drawings for making the chair could be digitized (another example of information good), but the chair itself is a physical product that you purchased not for its information content, but for its ability to support you in a comfortable sitting position.

The Economic Characteristics of Information

The fairly specific definition of classic information goods provided above is important because information has some unique and interesting characteristics.

Information Has High Production Costs   The first copy of an information good is very expensive to create in terms of time and money. Consider this book once again. Writing this text required a substantial amount of time in front of a computer typing a first draft, editing

Conf.# Type	Arrival	Departure	Rate	Guest name
85903380 1	Aug 29 2004	Aug 30 2004	99.00	DR GABRIELE PICCOLI

Figure 4.23   Data that have been Contextualized Become Information

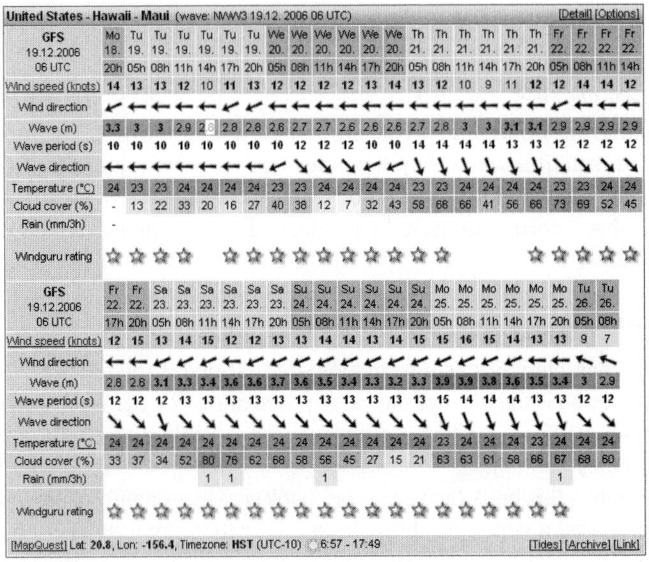

United States - Hawaii - Maui (wave: NWW3 19.12. 2006 06 UTC)																						[Detail] [Options]
GFS 19.12.2006 06 UTC	Mo 18.	Tu 19.	Tu 19.	Tu 19.	Tu 19.	Tu 19.	We 20.	We 20.	We 20.	We 20.	We 20.	We 20.	Th 21.	Th 21.	Th 21.	Th 21.	Th 21.	Th 21.	Fr 22.	Fr 22.	Fr 22.	Fr 22.
	20h	05h	08h	11h	14h	17h	20h	05h	08h	11h	14h	17h	20h	05h	08h	11h	14h	17h	20h	05h	08h	11h
Wind speed (knots)	14	13	13	12	10	11	13	12	12	12	12	13	14	13	12	10	9	11	12	12	14	14 12
Wind direction																						
Wave (m)	3.3	3	3	2.9	2.8	2.8	2.8	2.6	2.7	2.7	2.6	2.6	2.7	2.8	3	3	3.1	3.1	2.9	2.9	2.9	
Wave period (s)	10	10	10	10	10	10	10	10	12	12	12	10	10	14	14	14	14	13	13	12	12	12 12
Wave direction																						
Temperature (°C)	24	23	23	24	24	24	24	23	24	24	24	24	23	23	24	24	24	23	23	24	24	
Cloud cover (%)	-	13	22	33	20	16	27	40	38	12	7	32	43	58	66	66	41	56	66	73	69	52 45
Rain (mm/3h)	-																					
Windguru rating	☆	☆	☆	☆		☆	☆	☆	☆	☆	☆	☆	☆	☆			☆	☆	☆	☆	☆	

GFS 19.12.2006 06 UTC	Fr 22.	Fr 22.	Sa 23.	Sa 23.	Sa 23.	Sa 23.	Sa 23.	Sa 23.	Su 24.	Su 24.	Su 24.	Su 24.	Su 24.	Su 24.	Mo 25.	Mo 25.	Mo 25.	Mo 25.	Mo 25.	Mo 25.	Tu 26.	Tu 26.
	17h	20h	05h	08h	11h	14h	17h	20h	05h	08h	11h	14h	17h	20h	05h	08h	11h	14h	17h	20h	05h	08h
Wind speed (knots)	12	15	13	14	15	12	12	13	13	14	14	13	14	15	15	16	15	14	13	13	9	7
Wind direction																						
Wave (m)	2.8	2.8	3.1	3.3	3.4	3.6	3.6	3.7	3.6	3.5	3.4	3.3	3.2	3.3	3.9	3.9	3.8	3.6	3.5	3.4	3	2.9
Wave period (s)	12	12	12	13	13	13	13	13	13	13	13	13	13	15	14	14	14	13	13	13	12	12
Wave direction																						
Temperature (°C)	24	24	24	24	24	24	24	24	24	24	24	24	24	23	24	24	24	23	24	24	24	
Cloud cover (%)	33	37	34	52	80	76	62	68	58	56	45	27	15	21	63	63	61	58	66	67	68	60
Rain (mm/3h)					1	1				1										1		
Windguru rating	☆	☆	☆	☆	☆	☆	☆	☆	☆	☆	☆	☆	☆	☆	☆	☆	☆	☆	☆	☆	☆	☆

[MapQuest] Lat: **20.8**, Lon: **-156.4**, Timezone: **HST** (UTC-10) 6:57 - 17:49   [Tides] [Archive] [Link]

Figure 4.24 Wind and Wave Forecast—an Example of a Classic Information Good.
(*Source:* http://www.winguru.cz)

it multiple times, selecting appropriate examples, responding to reviewers' comments, and performing further editing as necessary. More subtly, before the writing process even began, substantial time was invested in studying these ideas, learning frameworks proposed by other authors, developing the unique frameworks and analytical models that are original to this text, doing the interviews and writing up the case studies, teaching the material, and taking notes about what seemed to work well in the classroom and what did not. After the draft of the book was completed, editors from the publishing house edited it, paginated it, and so on.

While this book was a big undertaking, you can envision projects that are even more costly and time consuming. Think about the latest big-budget film you have seen, a project that easily cost hundreds of millions of dollars and involved a large number of people who spent years developing their craft. All that work went into creating a less than two-hour-long experience.

In summary, information goods are very costly to produce. This is particularly true in relative terms, when the cost of producing the first copy is compared to the cost of producing the second one.

Negligible Replication Costs   This is where information goods begin to differ drastically from physical goods. For as long as it took to create the first copy of this book or the blockbuster movie you last saw, the second copy could be produced at a fraction of the cost.

Consider software, say the copy of Microsoft Word we are using to write this book. By some accounts Word is made up of millions of lines of code, written by hundreds of Microsoft programmers over the years. The first copy of such a complex software program takes a significant amount of time and money to produce, but what about the second copy? Producing the second copy of Microsoft Word was essentially free. It simply took up a few megabytes of storage space on a hard disk somewhere at Microsoft Corp. or on a compact disk (CD) (Figure 4.25).

Figure 4.25   A CD-ROM is the Carrier of Information Goods such as a Software Program

For many information goods the second copy, and all subsequent ones, has such a low cost of production that it is essentially free. This is not true of physical goods, such as the chair discussed above, or a car, or a meal. In a restaurant, for example, food cost is the second largest component of variable cost, second only to labor. Thus, no matter how many steaks the restaurant cooks that evening, each one will consume roughly the same amount of ingredients. The second copy of a physical good is not free.

The Information Is Not the Carrier   Note that the cost of the CD that is used to hold the second (or third or hundredth) copy of a software program is not, strictly speaking, to be considered a cost of the copy. The CD is simply the "carrier" of the information, not the information. In other words, when you purchase a new software program, you purchased the CD because it allows you to get to what you are buying, the information. When the Internet became a viable channel of distribution for digital goods, shrink-wrapped software programs on CD became less and less popular.

The same holds true for all classic information goods, such as the DVDs you rent at the store so that you can access the movie experience, and paper books that you carry so that you can access the content of the book. This is an important point because sometimes the economics of the carrier constrain the economics of the information.

Consider, for example, the recently announced service of CinemaNow, Inc., which allows movie buffs to download a copy of their favorite movie to be burned on a blank DVD and be added to their library. While the DVD has not been eliminated in the process, as in the case of movies on demand offered by cable companies, this service separates the movie being bought and paid for and the carrier of the information. Aside from speed and convenience, the cost structure for CinemaNow more accurately reflects that of distributing an information good and is reflected in its proposed pricing scheme (from \$8.99 to \$14.99 depending on how new the title is).

Negligible Distribution Cost   As with replication costs, the distribution costs associated with information goods are very low. Distribution costs are defined here as the costs associated with delivering the information good to the customers so that they can use it, not as marketing costs (which can be significant for information goods).

Consider once again the example of a big-budget movie. How does the movie get to the theater for your enjoyment? Traditionally the studios copied films onto reels (Figure 4.26) —a movie fits on five or six reels—and shipped them in film cans to the theaters. However, strictly speaking, the cost of distributing the cans is the cost of distributing the carrier of the information, not the information itself. In fact, modern delivery systems for in-room entertainment in hotels, for example, rely on digitized movies that are downloaded onto servers

Figure 4.26 Movie Reels Carry the Movie to a Theater Near You

that in turn stream them to the TV sets in the rooms. High-definition movie theaters also have done away with the reels.

Where the infrastructure for digital distribution has been created (for example, for digital music sales through the iTunes store), the distribution cost of the information goods is indeed negligible—free in practice. The same happens for software programs and audio books you can play on your iPod (e.g., audible.com).

Information goods are therefore characterized by high fixed costs and very low marginal costs. The cost of producing the first copy is steep while making and delivering incremental copies is almost free.

Costs Are Sunk Unrecoverable costs, those expenses that the firm has incurred to create its product or service but cannot be recuperated, are termed sunk costs. For example, if you are remodeling your kitchen and purchase some new flooring, only to find out that your significant other hates it and vetoes your installing it, you can return the material and recover the expense, but you can't recuperate the costs (in terms of time, effort, and gasoline in this case) you spent in selecting and transporting the flooring. Your time and the gas you wasted are sunk costs.

Information goods are unforgiving. If nobody is interested in reading our book, we will be unable to recover all the costs associated with writing it and publishing it. If you have dreams of making it big in the music industry, all the time and money you sunk into making your first CD is lost if nobody cares for your form of artistic expression.

The costs of information goods are mostly sunk costs. It follows that there is significant risk involved in producing information goods, and therefore a good deal of attention and research needs to be devoted to gauging and creating demand for them. The reason why movie studios spend so much money on marketing is to create demand for a product; the cost of which is mostly unrecoverable (i.e., sunk cost) once the movie hits theaters.

No Natural Capacity Limits While the creation of new information goods entails the significant risk that the investment will not be recovered, the upside is also significant. Information goods face almost no constraints to reproduction.

Let's return to the example above and imagine that your songs struck a nerve with the executives at Shady Records, who see in you the next hip-hop star. When your songs make it into the iTunes music store, there is no limit to how many times they can be downloaded (i.e., how many digital copies can be generated for next to zero cost).

Not Consumed by Use   Perhaps the most intriguing characteristic of information is that it can be reused multiple times. Physical goods, like an apple or one night in a hotel room, are destroyed through their use. That is, if you eat the last apple in the room, there is nothing left for any of us. If you occupy room 235 at the Four Seasons New York on March 19, 2009, that room, that night, will not be available for anyone else to enjoy.

Conversely, information goods are not consumed by use. All the people in the theater with you can enjoy the movie alongside you. The fact that you read the news this morning does not preclude me from learning the same facts from the nightly news . . . or even from the very same newspaper you left on the subway on your way to work. This characteristic of information is at the heart of the widespread music pirating phenomenon—or sharing, as those who engage in it call it. While two thirsty people will think twice before sharing their water, music lovers don't think twice about sharing their music. That's because after you upload your MP3 collection to a peer-to-peer file-sharing network and others start downloading your tunes, the songs are not consumed, instead they multiply!

Experience Goods   Information goods are experience goods, defined as those products or services that need to be tried (i.e., experienced) before their quality can be assessed. All new products and services are experience goods; in fact, perfumes trials and samples of shampoo have been used for decades to entice people to buy. However, information goods are experience goods every time. If you are happy with the scent of the Acqua di Gió by Giorgio Armani (Figure 4.27) perfume you sampled, you can confidently make it your perfume of choice and purchase it forever (or at least until the manufacturer changes the formula).

But how do you know if tomorrow's copy of the *Wall Street Journal* is as good as today's? Can you be sure that the next book by Dan Brown is worth reading, or that the BBC international newscast is worth watching tonight?

Implications

The unique economic characteristics of information and classic information goods described above have some important implications for you as a general or functional manager:

- *Information is customizable.* Information goods can often be modified with relative ease. For example, movies are typically edited for different showings or different audiences. Bonus cuts and extra material are often included in DVD releases. This

Figure 4.27   Physical Goods Need to be Evaluated Only Once

book partly draws from original material that has been published before in different venues in the form of reports, case studies, or lecture slides. Physical goods are typically much more difficult to customize before or after they are produced (e.g., a car, a house).

- *Information is reusable.* Because information is not consumed by use, it is reusable multiple times and, because it is customizable, in multiple forms.

- *Information is often time valued.* The value of information is tied to the user's ability to employ it. Often timely use of the information is necessary to reap the potential value. Stock quotes represent a perfect example. Stock quotes on a fifteen-minute delay are useless information to a stock trader.

    Another example is represented by book publishers, who often release hard-cover versions of popular novels and business books before releasing paperbacks that sell for much less. The cost of production of hard covers is not the reason for the price difference. Publishers are simply "versioning" their product to capitalize on the fact that some customers are willing to pay a premium to read the book as soon as it is released.

- Information goods can achieve significant gross profit margins: Because of their economic characteristics—high production costs and low replication and distribution—firms that produce successful information goods can enjoy vast profit margins. Microsoft Corporation has enjoyed legendary profits over the years thanks in large part to its two cash cows: Microsoft Windows, the dominant operating system software for personal computers, and Microsoft Office, the dominant suite of productivity tools.

Information-Intensive Goods

As you followed the above discussion about classic information goods, you may have wondered what applicability it has to industries that don't deal directly with classic information goods. That is, how useful is the above discussion to executives in industries such as restaurant franchising, car manufacturing, cruise ship operations, or health care? In each of these industries, you may reason, the value proposition customers seek is a tangible product or service, not information. While this is true, a quick look "under the hood" will reveal that information plays a critical role in these businesses as well.

Authors Evans and Wurster, from their vantage point at the Media and Convergence practice of the Boston Consulting Group, claim that "every business is an information business."[10] As an example they cite health care, an industry that offers a very "physical" service but where one-third of its cost is "the cost of capturing, storing and processing such information as patient's records, physicians' notes, test results, and insurance claims."

Most industries, while not dealing directly with information goods, rely on information to create and bring to market their product or service; from research and development, to logistics, to distribution, to sales and marketing, information is the glue that holds together business operations. That is, most products and services are information-intensive goods. For information-intensive goods, while information is not exclusively what the customer seeks

---

[10] Evans, P. B., and Wurster, T. S. (1997), "Strategy and the New Economics of Information," *Harvard Business Review*, Sept./Oct., 70–82.

Figure 4.28   Computer Embedded in a Car's Dashboard. (*Source:* www.fuel cellmarkets.com)

when purchasing the goods, information is either one of their critical components or a necessary resource during their production process.

The role that information plays could be at the periphery of the product or service (e.g., informational material about the features of a product, marketing messages, a brand) or could be embedded in the product itself as knowledge (e.g., modern cars). Consider, for instance, McDonald's Corporation, the franchiser of the popular fast-food restaurants. Is McDonald's in the "restaurant business" or is it in the "information business"? While you may opt for the first answer, a careful analysis reveals that the second is a more accurate label. What McDonald's Corp. sells to its franchisees around the world is sales volume through customer traffic due to its strong brand (i.e., information in the consumer mind), management know-how (i.e., information about optimal practices ranging from pricing, to purchasing, to human resource management), and various other support services (e.g., training, bulk purchasing contracts). Thus, much of what the franchisor offers is in the form of information and knowledge.

Information is also embedded in the production and organizational processes that enable the transformation of inputs into products and services to be sold. Moreover, products and services in today's economy are increasingly "augmented" by information services. Recall the example discussed in Chapter 1 of car manufacturers embedding self-monitoring and self-diagnosing components on automobiles that can then proactively communicate with their owners via e-mail (Figure 4.28).

Because of its pervasiveness, information has become a clear source of competitive advantage. Many of the most admired modern organizations draw their advantage from a superior ability to capture, manage, and distribute (or use) information. We will discuss ways to think about how to create value using organizational data and information in Chapter 8.

INFORMATION IN NETWORKS

As we have seen, information has unique economic characteristics. However, it has traditionally had to rely on physical carriers in order to be delivered. Film reels carry movies to the theater, books carry text and images to readers, professors carry lecture content to a class of students. The fact that information has had to rely on a physical carrier has acted as a constraint, limiting its ability to behave accordingly to its inherent characteristics.

Consider the process of organizing your honeymoon prior to 1993, date of the commercialization of the Internet. Back then you would likely visit a travel agency with your spouse and, after waiting in line for your turn to speak with an agent (the carrier of the information you were seeking), you would tell the agent your likes and dislikes and receive some suggestions. Based on these suggestions and your reaction to them, a skilled travel planner would narrow his or her suggestions, asking increasingly specific questions and offering advice based on his or her superior knowledge of destinations and even individual resorts.

This example suggests that, when information is constrained by a carrier, such as the travel agent, it is not allowed to behave like information. That is, while information is not consumed by use and is cheap to reproduce and distribute, since it has to be delivered by a person, it has to follow the economics of the carrier—only one person can speak with the agent at one time. The travel agency could hire and train new agents to reduce the lines, but this would be a costly proposition.

Even in 1993, you could have organized your honeymoon independently. You could have collected brochures and publications (Figure 4.29), telephoned individual resorts for pricing and suggestions, called multiple airlines, and put all the information together—quite a risk for a newlywed since independent planning would leave you unable to blame the travel agent if your spouse were to have a bad experience! More importantly, this would have been a time-consuming (i.e., costly) proposition on your part.

The travel agency could also reach a larger audience—for example, by creating brochures with suggestions and sample packages and distributing them by mail (Figure 4.29). Or it could purchase TV time and run some infomercials. However, such brochures and infomercials provide only limited content when compared with the personalized, interactive exchange that an experienced travel planner could offer.

The Richness and Reach Trade-Off

The travel agency example above is representative of a phenomenon known as the trade-off between richness and reach. Richness represents the amount of information that can be transmitted, the degree to which the information can be tailored to individual needs, and the

NEWLYWEDS SAVOR THE UNTOUCHED ISLANDS OF FRENCH POLYNESIA

By Sherri G. Hoke

Figure 4.29   Magazines and Brochures Often Describe Fantastic Honeymoon Packages

Richness : the amount of information that can be transmitted (depth of message)
Reach: number of recipients of the message

level of interactivity of the message. Reach represents the number of possible recipients of the message. Traditionally, as information has been constrained by its physical carrier, a firm would have to make a trade-off decision between the number of people it wanted to communicate a message to (i.e., reach) and the depth of the message (i.e., richness).

pervasive = widespread.
Ubiquitous

Before the advent of widespread information networks, a firm with a fixed budget would have to decide whether it was willing to reach a smaller audience with a richer message (e.g., individual consultations with a travel agent) or use a leaner message to reach a larger audience (e.g., create a brochure to be mailed to perspective travelers). This trade-off, a "compromise" that constrains information to behave like its physical carrier, is represented by the line in Figure 4.30. The line on the graph represents the frontier of optimal decisions. That is, the firm will be able to choose any point below the frontier, but the optimal decisions, those that offer the highest return in terms of reach and richness, are those on the frontier. Because of the constraints identified above, the firm cannot go beyond this frontier.

With the advent and widespread adoption of a cheaply and easily accessible information infrastructure, such as the Internet and the services it makes available, these constraints are increasingly being lifted. Ubiquitous communication networks and powerful computers are quickly enabling firms to decouple information from the physical objects that traditionally carried it.

For example, digital music no longer needs a CD, novels and stories no longer need books, lectures and meetings carried out on a platform like WebEx no longer need the physical co-presence of participants. The Internet and the technologies that leverage it have mitigated the trade-off between rich information and reach of the message.

Note that the trade-off between reach and richness has not been eliminated. There are still compromises to be made between reaching a large audience and offering a very rich exchange. However, new technology is making it increasingly possible to reach many people with more information-intensive, interactive, and personalized messages (see Figure 4.31).

Consider the travel agency example once more. As travel products have moved aggressively to the Internet platform, now you have increasing access to 360-degree views of resorts (see Figure 4.32), live chats with agents (see Figure 4.33), travel blogs, communities of interest where people share their experiences, and travel products packaged by an online agency (see Figure 4.34).

Yet while these technologies are increasingly pushing the reach/richness frontier and encroaching on travel agents' territory, they have yet to be able to fully replicate the face-to-face interaction and high degree of personalization that a knowledgeable, skilled travel agent can offer.

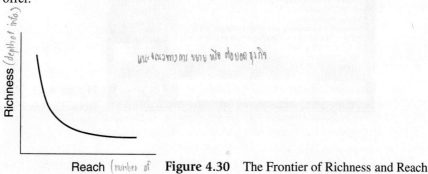

Figure 4.30   The Frontier of Richness and Reach

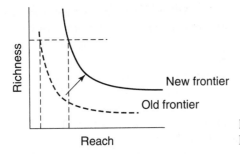

Figure 4.31   Technology Pushes the Richness/Reach Frontier

Figure 4.32   360-Degree Views of a Resort Lobby

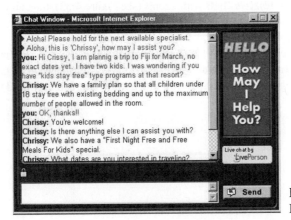

Figure 4.33   Live Chat with Booking Agent

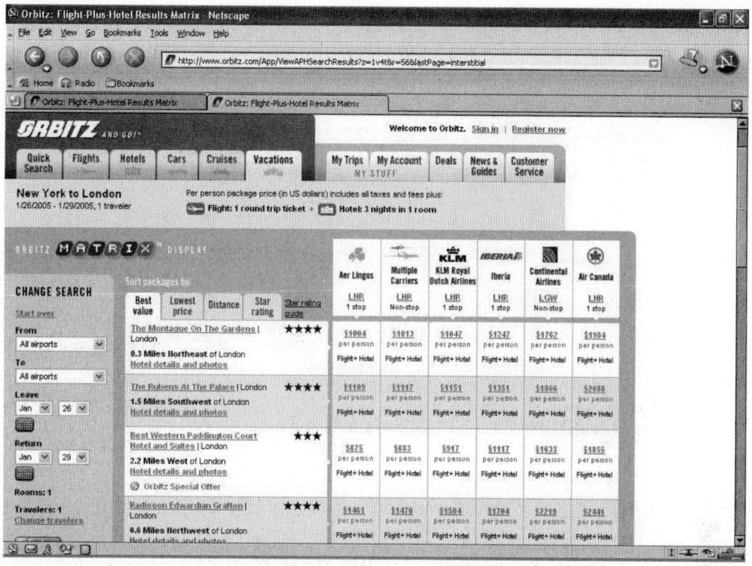

Figure 4.34 Dynamic Packages

Implications

As the emergence of new technology eases the trade-off between richness and reach a number of implications for you as a general or functional manager emerge.

Traditional Business Models Continue to Be Questioned   A number of "traditional" business models were predicated on the fact that information was constrained by its carrier. Such business models have been facing and will continue to face challenges from focused organizations that exploit emerging information technologies.

Consider the traditional travel agent business model once more. Many travel agents do an outstanding job of providing valuable consultation and advice to prospective travelers. Others base their value proposition on the fact that most travelers don't have the ability to book their own travel. As airlines, hotels, and car rentals created their own bookable Web sites and travel intermediaries such as Kayak.com (Figure 4.35) made it easy to quickly query multiple providers, the latter kind of travel agents faced significant pressure. With technology advancing relentlessly, even those travel agents who offer valuable information and expertise will come under increasing pressure.

The effect of widespread adoption of computer networks is particularly threatening to organizations that historically bundled services, using one to subsidize the other. Consider the daily newspaper industry. By some accounts, a typical newspaper collects 20 to 25 percent of its revenue from the classifieds section. Yet the classifieds account for only 5 percent of the cost of operating a newspaper. As a consequence, the classifieds are subsidizing many other aspects of the newspaper business, such as reporting and editing.

With the advent of the Internet and Web sites such as eBay, newspapers have seen and continue to see a loss of revenue from the classifieds—after all, what is eBay if not a global classified ads section with an auction twist? While newspapers are unlikely to become

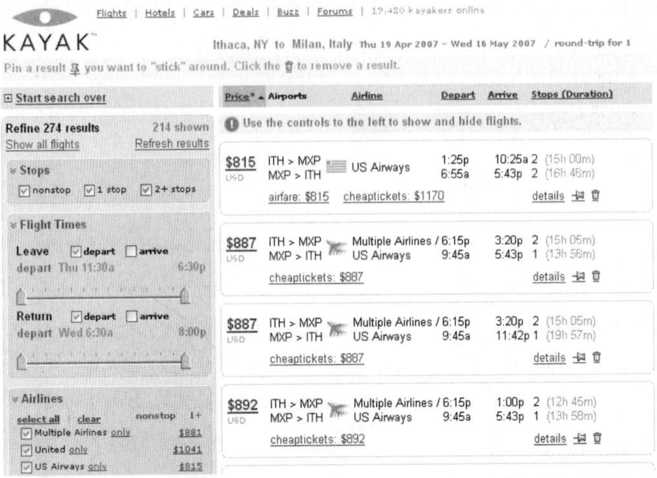

Figure 4.35 Kayak.com is a Metasearch Engine for Travel Products

extinct anytime soon, this example shows that the unbundling of information from the physical carrier can have far-reaching consequences—particularly for those firms where the current business model is predicated on the need to bundle information with a physical carrier.

Consider another example, the movie rental business. With high-capacity broadband networks coming to the home in the form of digital cable, we are now able to order movies on demand and start, pause, and restart them at will—just like rentals but without the late fees. Unbundling the information customers want (the movie) from the carrier (the tape cassettes or DVD) has enabled superior convenience, in the form of easy billing in the monthly statement, no late fees, and no need to leave the home, stand in line, or find that the movie we want is sold out.

The Importance of the Customer Interface   If information is increasingly allowed to travel independently of its carriers, it becomes feasible to unbundled traditional products and services (as described above) and bundle products that could never be brought together before. Consider the retail banking industry. Traditionally a customer would purchase a bundle of services from her retail bank, say a checking account, saving account, certificates of deposit, mutual funds, car loan, and a mortgage. An important value driver of this bundle would be the convenience of one-stop shopping (i.e., being able to visit one branch to address a number of financial needs).

Today that same customer may use Quicken to manage her finances, thus being able to interact directly with individual providers of each of the services she needs (Figure 4.36). She may have checking and saving accounts with the local bank, a car loan with another local provider, a mortgage through LendingTree.com, mutual funds and retirement planning with Schwab.com, and some stocks with Ameritrade. Being able to easily download monthly statements to Quicken, she can easily keep the pulse of her financial standings and easily switch providers, as long as the new one also enables downloads to Quicken. The old adage, location, location, location, is in many industries based on information friction and is being challenged by technologies that mitigate the trade-off between reach and richness.

Figure 4.36   Quicken is Now Available for Portable Computers. (*Source:* With Permission from Pocket Quicken.)

In the environment described by the above example, having a direct relationship with the customer, or owning the customer interface, may become critical. In the banking case it is Quicken, a software company, that is in the strongest position. Customers may become more loyal to Quicken than to any of the providers of financial services in the background.

The example seems a bit futuristic still, and significant obstacles remain to the widespread adoption of these arrangements (see below), but we are beginning to see a number of organizations vying to control the customer interface. Consider Progressive insurance, for instance. In its advertisement the firm promises that its agents will seek to find you the best insurance plan, even shopping and suggesting competitors for you. The objective of this approach is to ensure that you think about them when seeking to purchase insurance, thus allowing them to preserve the control of the customer interface.

The Decreasing Value of Asymmetric Information   Perhaps the most evident implication of the emergence of technologies that ease the trade-off between reach and richness is the amount of information modern customers have available to them. This has put significant pressure on organizations that benefit from asymmetry of information.[11] If an organization bases its value proposition on the inability of individuals to obtain and use information at low costs, the position is increasingly untenable as the richness/reach frontier is increasingly pushed outward. Today, for example, within a few minutes, you can shop for a car online, find out the factory price from Edmunds.com, research various dealer packages, find out the value of your trade-in used car, and walk into a dealership ready to negotiate.

Obstacles

While there are many examples of industries where the effects of the easing trade-off between reach and richness are being felt, there are a number of obstacles that have been slowing and will continue to slow this process.

---

[11] Asymmetry of information is the condition where one party to a transaction has more information than the other party. Purchasing a used car is a classic example, where the seller knows the history of the car while the buyer has to rely on the seller or use other imprecise means to gauge the quality of the car (e.g., take it to a mechanic).

New Technology Must Replace All Characteristics of the Old One   Consider again the example of newspapers. Newspapers do not offer the best platform for consuming the news; they are not as timely as the television news or the Internet, they support neither video nor high-quality images, they offer limited space, and they have many other drawbacks. Why do we still buy them and read them? Why don't we all read the news online? Most newspapers have Web sites anyway.

The answer is simple: With all the drawbacks newspapers have due to the constraint of printed paper, the broadsheet is still the most portable, most convenient, and easiest to read device for accessing the news. It will not be until new technology is able to supplant these advantages that the newspaper will disappear, its limitations notwithstanding. The lesson is clear: Old technology goes away only when the new one has replaced all of its relevant characteristics. Until then the new and old technology tend to coexist—as do newspapers and online news today.

Retaliation from Incumbents   As we attempt to envision how new technology changes society and the competitive environment, seeking ways to create value in the new environment, it is easy to commit a critical fallacy: ignore incumbent's retaliation. This was one of the main mistakes many observers made during the dot-com days. Retaliation can come in a number of forms:

- Legal means, such as those used by the music industry in reaction to the advent of digital music and the mp3 compression standard.
- Legislative means, such as the lobbying efforts of car dealership networks to stave off direct sales by car manufacturers.
- Hybrid offers, such as those provided by retailers with physical stores and online operations so as to leverage their existing infrastructure.
- Heightened competition, such as that started by telecommunications companies in reaction to the offering of Voice over IP solutions.

While it is enticing to think about the promise of the new technology and the opportunities it offers, you need to always remember that the road from today's landscape to the future reality is paved with competitive battles.

Human Resistance to Change   Perhaps the most powerful bottleneck to some of the changes discussed above is human inertia. New technologies and new ways of doing business, while offering advantages, entail costs in the form of learning to use the new technology or simply stopping the old routine. While easily dismissed, these considerations can spell the difference between success and failure of a fledgling business. The history of IT is full of great ideas that fell pray to the "if we build it they will come" mentality and failed to address and manage human resistance to change.

Attention Challenges   A byproduct of the unprecedented availability of information is the increasing difficulty people encounter in keeping up with it. Customers' attention is not only required for your product or service to be considered, but it is also required to educate customers about its advantages and how they can best use it. People's time and attention is perhaps the scarcest resource an organization has to deal with. The scarcity of attention leads to slow adoption rates for all but the most revolutionary innovations.

Consider, for instance, online grocery shopping, an industry mostly remembered for having produced the largest failure of the dot-com era. Webvan, the poster child for online grocery shopping, burned through $1.2 billion in funding before it closed up shop to the dismay of its few but enthusiastic customers. Yet online grocery shopping is alive and well in many locales, the torch being carried by traditional brick and mortar grocery chains.[12] The lesson of the Webvan story is not so much that online grocery shopping was an ill-conceived idea, rather that the consumer adoption rate of this radically new way of performing a task that is thousands of years old is much slower than the adoption rates Webvan needed to survive as an online-only grocery operation.

THE INTERNET CHANGES EVERYTHING?

Considerable debate still remains with respect to what the impact of the Internet and the technology that are built on it has been and will continue to be on organizations and the competitive environment. On the one hand are those who claim that "for all its power, the Internet does not represent a break from the past; rather it is the last stage in the ongoing evolution of information technology."[13] On the other hand are those that consider the Internet a force that goes far beyond technology, such that "no facet of human activity is untouched. The Net is a force of social change penetrating homes, schools, offices, factories, hospitals, and governments."[14]

Where you choose to fall on this debate is largely up to you. It is clear, however, that the network economy has ushered in a new wave of opportunity for firms that are able to take advantage of, rather than resist, the changes. While the boundaries of a firm have historically been fairly fixed, the adoption of global networks has enabled these boundaries to become increasingly permeable under the guise of outsourcing arrangements and partnerships.

Consider, for instance, the relationship between HEB, the tenth largest grocery chain in the United States, and Procter & Gamble (P & G). While traditionally P & G sold its goods to HEB, who then would resell them to consumers, the two firms have now moved to a consignment model whereby P & G places its goods on HEB's shelves and, once they are sold, receives payment from HEB. HEB benefits from reduced working capital requirements and risk, while P & G benefits by having real-time consumption data that allows it to streamline both production and logistic processes.

A NOTE ABOUT DISRUPTIVE TECHNOLOGY

Beyond the role of the Internet in changing the competitive landscape and the role of information and network economics, it is important that, as a general or functional manager, you are aware of the potential disruptive impact of new technologies. Specifically, you should be able to identify and, to the extent possible, manage the impact of emerging disruptive technologies.

---

[12] http://www.internetretailer.com/internet/marketing-conference/27475-online-grocery-showing-fortified-strength-study-says.html (Accessed August, 10th 2006)

[13] Porter, M. (2001) "Strategy and the Internet," *Harvard Business Review*, March, 62–78.

[14] Tapscott, D. (2001), "Rethinking Strategy in a Networked World," *Strategy and Competition*, Third Quarter, pp. 1–8.

Sustaining Technology

The innovation literature has investigated for decades the characteristics of new technology. Recently, though, Clayton Christiansen's[15] work has identified a classification that has important implications for strategy: the differentiation between sustaining and disruptive technologies.

The defining characteristic of sustaining technologies is that they maintain or rejuvenate the current rate of performance improvement of the products and services that use them. The performance trajectory of a new product (e.g., electric cars) is typically captured visually by the use of the S-curve (see Figure 4.37). The S-curve suggests that, as the product is first introduced its performance is limited. With design refinements comes a growth period where substantial improvements in performance are achieved, until the technology underpinning product performance plateaus and further performance improvements become marginal.

Sustaining technologies are those new technologies that enable a product's performance to continue to grow—in other words, sustaining technologies extend the useful life of the product as the market demands further and further improvements (see Figure 4.38). A sustaining technology will therefore be a good candidate to replace a previous generation because it offers the same set of attributes, but it yields superior performance. Thus, firms that are using the existing technology in their product will find it appealing to switch to the sustaining technology as they seek to improve their products along the established performance trajectory.

Consider, for instance, the mechanical excavation industry. The tool of choice in this industry at the turn of the century was the steam shovel. Steam shovels used a steam engine to generate the required power to pull the cables that would lift buckets full of dirt to be moved.

In the early 1920s, the steam shovel began to be replaced by gasoline-powered shovels that offered superior performance on the critical performance dimension: the ability to move dirt in a fast, reliable, and cost-effective manner. This is an example of sustaining technology since the new technology (i.e., gasoline engines) enabled manufacturers of dirt-moving equipment to improve performance of their product on critical performance dimensions.

Disruptive Technology

Disruptive technologies are defined by the following two characteristics:

- The technology offers a different set of attributes than the technology the firm currently uses in its products.

- The performance improvement rate of the technology is higher than the rate of improvement demanded by the market (see Figure 4.39).

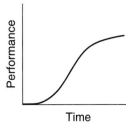

Figure 4.37   Product Performance Improvement Over Time

---

[15] Christiansen, C. (1997) *The Innovator's Dilemma: When New Technologies Cause Great Firms To Fail*, Botton, MA: Hbs Press .

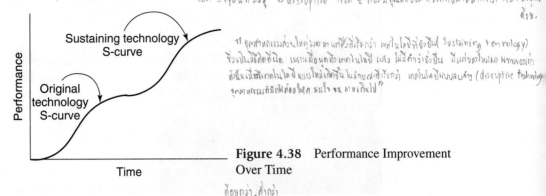

Figure 4.38 Performance Improvement Over Time

While a disruptive technology has an inferior performance with respect to current market demands and what is delivered by existing technology, it offers two advantages: a different set of performance characteristics, and a high rate of performance improvement on the critical performance dimensions.

Consider the example of the hard disk industry. The critical performance dimension for customers of hard disk drives (i.e., computer manufacturers) is the storage capacity of the disk (Figure 4.40). With remarkable precision, hard disk drive manufacturer have been blindsided by the emergence of architecture design that enabled smaller and smaller drives to be produced—from the original 14-inch drives, to the 8-, 5.25-, 3.5-, 2.5-, and 1.8-inch architectures. This is because these changes were disruptive in nature.

Each generation of smaller disk drives did not at first offer the same storage capacity of the established one. Yet each generation offered a performance rate of improvement on this dimension (the critical performance dimension) far superior to the speed with which computer manufacturers required greater storage capacity. As a consequence, when the storage capacity of the smaller drives reached market needs, the incumbent's mainstream customers switched to the new entrants. No longer having storage capacity concerns, they now valued the other characteristics offered by the new technology (i.e., smaller size, reduced power consumption, etc.).

Implications for Managers

Familiarity with the dynamics of disruptive technologies is important for modern general and functional managers because disruptive technologies typically blindside leading firms, who see their position of dominance lost to those upstarts that were able to ride the disruptive technology wave.

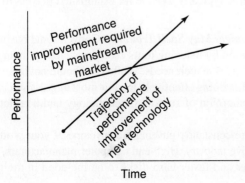

Figure 4.39 Differential Rate Associated with Disruptive Technologies

Figure 4.40   An 8" Hard Disk Drive by IBM

Differential Rates of Improvements   The deadliest characteristic of disruptive technology is their rate of evolution on the currently established performance metrics. As shown in Figure 4.39, a disruptive technology begins with performance that is well below the needs of the firm's mainstream customers. Moreover, the disruptive technology will likely not improve at a rate sufficient to overcome the existing or sustaining technologies available. However, this is misleading information for a manager!

It is irrelevant whether the disruptive technology will ever outstrip the current one on key performance metrics. Rather, you should estimate whether, in the foreseeable future, the disruptive technology will catch up to market needs on the critical performance dimensions (i.e., become good enough for mainstream customers).

It is often the case that, focused on its most demanding and most advanced customers, a firm will push the performance of its products using new generations of sustaining technologies. However, such relentless focus on the most demanding customers may end up pushing the firm to increasingly overshoot the needs of its mainstream customers. When this is the case, the incumbent firm becomes particularly vulnerable to disruptive technologies.

Different Sets of Attributes Become Relevant   As disruptive technologies close the gap between the performance level they offer and mainstream customer needs, the novel set of attributes they offer may become increasingly attractive to potential customers. In other words, as the disruptive technology closes the gap on the primary performance metrics, their other characteristics may become a source of positive differentiation. At this point customers defect from established suppliers offering the standard products and begin to adopt the new technology—but it is typically too late for established players to make the switch to the new technology.

Listening Closely to Customers May Spell Trouble   Conventional business wisdom suggests that a firm is well served by listening to its customers closely in an effort to develop the products and services that serve their needs. While you should not ignore this suggestion, we add a word of caution: Listening attentively to your most aggressive customers will create a bias toward prompt adoption of sustaining technology and a reluctance to buy into disruptive technology.

Your best customers are constantly pushing the envelope of your product performance. Consider again the hard drive industry. High-end computer manufacturers, seeking to outdo each other, will seek larger and faster hard disks to be included in their machines. As a consequence they will create an incentive for you to adopt those technologies that offer improved performance on the accepted set of performance metrics. A technology that enables the development of smaller hard disks is not valued, even though these smaller devices have other interesting characteristics, such as compact size, lower energy consumption, and less need for heat dispersion. They simply are not good enough on the "important" dimensions that your best customers are clamoring for. However, if the new, smaller hard disks are a disruptive technology, their performance will soon meet the needs of your mainstream customers. When this happens, all those other characteristics may become valuable and you'd be left with a rapidly shrinking market.

What to Do?

Those studying disruptive technology change suggest the following approach to managing organizations that face the emergence and development of disruptive technologies:

- Monitor market developments for the emergence of new technologies and determine whether they are of the sustaining or disruptive kind.

- When disruptive technologies emerge, envision the new market they would likely be best suited for. One of the greatest challenges faced by the incumbent firm is to identify what customers will likely appreciate the new blend of features and functionalities that the disruptive technology supports. While a producer of large mainframes does not care much about the power requirements and the physical size of hard disks, these are critical characteristics for laptop manufacturers.

- Spin off a new division that focuses exclusively on the commercialization of products based on the disruptive technology. Separating the group that is blazing the trail for the new technology may be necessary to create the appropriate financial incentives. Disruptive technologies start off serving the needs of a small niche market. As such, it is difficult for large companies to get excited about, and more importantly divert resources to, such small markets. A separate entity, focusing on that business and competing with the other small firms in the new market, would have no difficulty creating the appropriate incentives.

SUMMARY

This chapter provides you with a framework to understand how new technologies are shaping the competitive landscape you will encounter as you enter the job market. Specifically, in this chapter we discussed three broad topics: network economics, information economics, and disruptive technologies.

- The Internet, traditionally thought of as a network of computer networks, is evolving into a global information grid enabling ever-changing devices, and those who use them, to easily connect and disconnect from it. The rapid pace of evolution and innovation on the Internet is enabled by its characteristics: distributed

governance and the reliance on publicly available open standard supporting a multiplicity of compatible devices and offering a number of services.

- Value creation in networks, physical ones such as the telephone network and virtual ones such as eBay's online community of buyers and sellers, is created by plentitude. This value driver is the opposite of the principal value driver of most other goods and services: scarcity.

- Because the most valuable networks are the largest ones, the act of joining a network by an individual creates value for the other members of the network—a phenomenon termed network effects. In industries subject to strong network effects, particularly when demand for variety is low and networks are mutually exclusive, winner-take-all dynamics ensue and the market is dominated by one organization.

■ Information, a prevalent resource in the modern competitive landscape, has unique economic characteristics. In its pure form, information has high production costs, which are sunk, and negligible replication and distribution costs. The production of information faces no natural capacity limits, and information is not consumed by use. As a consequence, information is infinitely reusable, highly customizable, and often time valued.

■ When discussing information as an organizational resource, it is important to distinguish the information from the carrier of the information. Historically, information as a resource or product has been constrained by the economics of the carrier. The advent of the Internet, a global infrastructure for information exchange, has in many cases separated the two. New technology continues to push the frontier of the richness/reach trade-off

and in the process threatens established business models in information industries and beyond.

■ New technologies can be characterized as sustaining or disruptive. Sustaining technologies are those that maintain or rejuvenate the current rate of performance improvement of the products and services that use them. Conversely, disruptive technologies are those that offer a different set of attributes than the technology the firm currently uses in its products, and their performance improvement rate is higher than the rate of improvement of market needs. Disruptive technologies are particularly dangerous for established firms, which typically tend to underestimate their potential impact on their current business. Proper monitoring and management of disruptive technologies by the incumbent is necessary because, due to the rate of performance improvement and the different set of features they offer, once a disruptive technology has achieved acceptable performance improvements on the traditional dimensions of performance, customers quickly defect to products that use it.

STUDY QUESTIONS

1. Define the term *Internet* and offer examples of its principal services. What is the difference between the Internet and the World Wide Web?

2. What do you see as the likely evolution of the Internet in the near future?

3. Explain each of the following concepts: positive feedback, network effects, and tippy market. Explain how the three concepts relate to one another.

4. Offer an example of a tippy market and an example of a market that does not tip.

5. Can you differentiate physical and virtual networks? Can you provide examples of each?

6. Explain the defining characteristics of a two-sided network and provide an example.

7. What is the defining characteristic of classic information goods? How do they differ from information-intensive goods? Provide examples of each.

8. Information, as an economic entity, behaves quite differently than traditional goods. Identify the principal economic characteristics of information and draw the principal implications for strategy.

9. Explain what we mean by the richness/reach trade-off. Why is this concept important today for general and functional managers? Provide examples of recent technologies that have pushed the richness/reach trade-off frontier further out. What industries or organizations are under pressure as a consequence of this development?

10. Do you believe that "the Internet changes everything" or is it "just another technology"? Be sure to defend your position.

11. What is the difference between sustaining and disruptive technologies? Can you offer one example of each?

12. What would you advise an incumbent firm to do in the face of the emergence of new technology? For example, if you were an executive for American Airlines, what would you do about the recent introduction of Very Light Jets (VLJ)— such as the 2000 preordered Eclipse 500 from Eclipse Aviation able to reach 300 mph and a range of 1125 nautical miles?[16] Is "air taxi" a disruptive technology? What should major airlines do about it, if anything?

---

[16] http://edition.cnn.com/2006/TRAVEL/03/31/private.jet/ (Accessed 20/8/2006).

FURTHER READINGS

1. Bower, J. L., and Christensen, C. M. (1995). "Disruptive Technologies: Catching the Wave," *Harvard Business Review*, January–February, 43–53.
2. Christensen, C. M. (1997). *The Innovator's Dilemma: When New Technologies Cause Great Firms to Fail.* Boston, MA: Harvard Business School Press.
3. Evans, P. B., and Wurster, T. S. (1999). *Blown to Bits: How the New Economics of Information Transforms Strategy.* Boston, MA: Harvard Business School Press.
4. Evans, P. B., and Wurster, T. S. (1997). "Strategy and the New Economics of Information." *Harvard Business Review*, Sept./Oct., 70–82.
5. Porter, M. (2001). "Strategy and the Internet." *Harvard Business Review*, March, 62–78.
6. Rayport, J., and Sviokla, J. (1994). "Managing in the Marketspace." *Harvard Business Review*, Nov./Dec., 141–150.
7. Shapiro, C., and Varian, H. R. (1999). *Information Rules.* Boston, MA: Harvard Business School Press.
8. Tapscott, D. (2001). "Rethinking Strategy in a Networked World." *Strategy and Competition*, Third Quarter, pp. 1–8.
9. Shirky, C. (2001). "The Internet Revolution Rages On," *Business 2.0*, March.

GLOSSARY

- **Classic information goods:** Those purchased for the only purpose of gaining access to the information they contain.
- **Data:** Codified raw facts—things that have happened—coded as letters of the alphabet and numbers and stored, increasingly, by way of a computer.
- **Disruptive technologies:** Technologies that offer a different set of attributes than the technology the firm currently uses in its products, and whose performance improvement rate is higher than the rate of improvement of market needs.
- **Information:** Data in context.
- **Information-intensive goods:** Those tangible products and services (i.e., not classic information goods) for which information is either one of the critical components or a necessary resource during the production process.
- **Internet:** A global, publicly accessible network of digital networks relying on distributed ownership and open standards.
- **Message reach:** The number of possible recipients of the message.
- **Message richness:** The amount of information that can be transmitted, the degree to which the information can be tailored to individual needs, and the level of interactivity of the message.
- **Negative feedback:** The self-reinforcing process by which the strong get weaker and the weak get stronger.
- **Network effects:** The process by which a network becomes more valuable as its size increases. That is, when a new node, while pursuing his or her own economic motives, joins the network, the network is more valuable for all the other members.
- **Network node:** Any device connected to a network.
- **Physical networks:** Networks where the nodes are connected by physical links (e.g., railroad tracks, telephone wires).
- **Positive feedback:** The self-reinforcing process by which the strong get stronger and the weak get weaker.
- **Protocol:** An agreed-on set of rules or conventions governing communication among the elements of a network (i.e., network nodes).
- **Sustaining technology:** Technologies that maintain or rejuvenate the current rate of performance improvement of the products and services that use them.
- **Tipping point:** That moment in the evolution of a market where one organization or technology reaches critical mass and goes on to dominate it—the point of nonreturn where winners and losers are defined.
- **Tippy market:** A market that is subject to strong positive feedback, such that the market will "tip" in favor of the firm that is able to reach critical mass and dominate it. A tippy market is therefore a market with "winner-take-all" tendencies.
- **Virtual networks:** Networks where the connections between nodes are not physical, but intangible and invisible. The nodes of a virtual network are typically people rather than devices.
- **World Wide Web:** One of the most popular services available on the Internet. It consists of "pages" and other resources that can be easily created and published as well as accessed by way of uniform resource locator (URL) addresses.

CASE STUDY: ONLINE EDUCATION[17]

Thirty years from now the big University campuses will be relics. Universities won't survive. It is as large a change as when we first got the printed book.

— Peter Drucker[18]

INTRODUCTION

As the Internet revolution raged on and the effects of the network economy manifested themselves in industries as diverse as elevator manufacturing and financial services, the above quote by Peter Drucker sounded, in January 2007 on the snowy campus of Ivey University, like a relic of the dot-com days. Erica Wagner, dean of the School of Information Management, saw the quote while scanning a recent article in *The Economist.*

The Internet, the new technology that only ten years before had administrators like Dr. Wagner worrying about the future of the institution they had been entrusted to lead, now seemed to have had minimal effect on prestigious research universities such as Ivey. Enrollment in undergraduate programs was more selective than ever, due to rising demand. Campuses were teeming with construction workers developing new buildings, adding to existing ones, remodeling teaching and office space, equipping ever more sophisticated labs, and, most importantly it seemed, developing more parking space!

While the number of students in executive education programs had been declining steadily over the last decade, forcing the School to shorten some of its programs from five to three-days, many blamed the recent recession for these results. However, one of the passages in the article brought back some of Dr. Wagner's own uneasiness:

The innate conservatism of the academic profession does not help. The modern university was born in a very different world from the current one, a world where only a tiny minority of the population went into higher education, yet many academics have been reluctant to make any allowances for massification.[19]

Was everyone missing the forest for the trees? Was the Internet a disruptive technology in the education industry, simply brewing under the surface to soon blindside slow-to-react incumbents?

EDUCATION AND RESEARCH AT IVEY

Like its peers, Ivey University had a complex mission and a large community of stakeholders, ranging from students and faculty to alumni and the local and global community. At the highest level of analysis, Ivey performed two main activities: the creation of new knowledge (i.e., research) and the dissemination of knowledge (i.e., education).

As a prestigious Research I institution, Ivey spent a considerable amount of resources supporting the development of new knowledge by hiring some of the brightest young faculty members and accomplished researchers. Among its faculty it counted 12 Nobel Prize winners, and boasted many world-class research centers.

While the research mission was pursued in basement labs and offices throughout campus, the most evident manifestation of Ivey's contribution to society was its teaching mission. A large school like the School of Information Management at Ivey University had truly global reach.

Its largest population was about 2200 undergraduate students. The School also trained Master's students, leaving the workforce for one or two years (a substantial opportunity cost on top of the direct costs of going back to school) to gain an advanced degree and the skills to accelerate their career. Ivey had a medium size, but very selective, Master's program with about 300 students enrolled. Finally, the School educated the next generation of faculty and researchers by way of its Ph.D. program.

A very recognized brand in the business world, Ivey also offered a number of executive education and professional education programs. These were typically highly condensed courses, held on Ivey's own campus or satellite locations, designed to serve the needs of corporations seeking to update the skills of their workforce or to offer working students a chance to access the wealth of knowledge that the School's faculty had to offer without having to resign their job.

GLOBAL EXPANSIONS

Because of its brand recognition around the world, the School of Information Management and a number of other schools at Ivey had been focused on global expansion

---

[17] This is a fictitious case developed with the exclusive intent of supporting class discussion.

[18] For PJS.com (1997). Seeing Things as they Really Are (Accessed 6/2/07) http://members.ForPjs.com/forPjs/1997/0310./5905122p.Print.html

[19] "The Brain Business," *The "Economist* (Sept. 8, 2005).

through partnerships and the opening of satellite campuses. The School had partners in Asia and Europe and was currently evaluating whether to enter the South American market.

The reason for global expansion was simple: With the skyrocketing demand for high-quality education in emerging markets around the globe, there was great opportunity to extend the Ivey brand. Expansion was not without challenges, with revenue models being at times challenged and a myriad of logistics and quality assurance hurdles to be overcome. However, with almost every other recognized education brand entering the new markets, a wait-and-see attitude could be extremely risky.

ONLINE PLAYERS: A REAL THREAT OR A NUISANCE?

Since Peter Drucker's prediction, there had been a significant amount of development in online educational offerings. University of Phoenix, the largest for-profit institution, had about 300,000 students. While quality concerns lingered, not just on prestigious university campuses, online universities seemed to be gaining power, at least in the legislative arena. The *New York Times* reported,

> It took just a few paragraphs in a budget bill for Congress to open a new frontier in education: Colleges will no longer be required to deliver at least half their courses on a campus instead of online to qualify for federal student aid. That change is expected to be of enormous value to the commercial education industry.[20]

A whole industry developed around online educational opportunities, much like the well-established one surrounding traditional university education.

Not all online educational offerings were by upstarts. Indeed, traditional universities had their own offerings, and Ivey itself had launched its own online education effort

during the late 1990s: iIvey. While the number of courses offered at iIvey had slowly but steadily increased, and some of the School's programs required them as prerequisites, the iIvey effort seemed to have lost steam after the bursting of the dot-com bubble. Yet with about forty courses available, a price tag between $1000 and $1500 per course, and a global reach, iIvey still offered quite a bit of potential, if nothing else, for revenue.

THE FUTURE

As Dr. Wagner watched the snow drop a fresh dusting of white powder on the roof of the gothic buildings across the quad, she pondered some of the words of the article:

> A few years ago a report by Coopers & Lybrand crowed that online education could eliminate the two biggest costs from higher education: "The first is the need for bricks and mortar; traditional campuses are not necessary. The second is full-time faculty. [Online] learning involves only a small number of professors, but has the potential to reach a huge market of students." That is nonsense. The human touch is much more vital to higher education than is high technology. Education is not just about transmitting a body of facts, which the Internet does pretty well. It is about learning to argue and reason, which is best done in a community of scholars.[21]

That was promising news for a top-ranked university like Ivey, but what if the author were wrong? As the dean of the School of Information Management, Dr. Wagner was not only entrusted with the future of the School she led, but she also felt a responsibility to help the university community at large thrive in the network economy. Could Ivey miss the wave of the future? "Not on my watch!" Dr. Wagner told herself while getting ready for the first of many of the day's meetings.

---

[20] Dillon, S., "Online Colleges Receive a Boost From Congress," *The New York Times*, March 1, 2006.

[21] "The Brain Business," *The Economist* (Sept. 8, 2005).

5

Electronic Commerce: New Ways of Doing Business

What You Will Learn in This Chapter

This chapter covers over a decade of electronic commerce history and trends. The objective is to help you develop a sound grounding in electronic commerce concepts and vocabulary—a vocabulary that is no longer the exclusive province of Silicon Valley insiders, but an integral part of the language of modern business. After laying the foundations, we look ahead to coming electronic commerce trends. Specifically, in this chapter you will

1. Be able to define and differentiate the terms *electronic commerce* and *electronic business* and provide examples of each. Identify the enablers of electronic commerce trends.

2. Categorize electronic commerce phenomena on a number of dimensions, including the type of transactions taking place and the structure of the organizations involved.

3. Define the term *business model,* and explain why the Internet has led to so much business model experimentation. Identify the principal revenue models employed in electronic commerce and explain the dominant business model in use today.

4. Describe the principal implications of electronic commerce for both established firms and new entrants.

5. Discuss some of the more relevant future electronic commerce and electronic business trends.

MINI-CASE: THE QUEST FOR DIFFERENTIATION AND PROFITS AT EPICTRIP.COM

The phone started ringing as you arrived in the office. You picked up the receiver and immediately recognized the familiar soft voice: "Hey there, it's Steve-O!" You had not heard from him in a few months, but in a split second the whole history flashed in your brain. Steve Yu, Steve-O as his closest friends called him, went to work for a large corporation right after college. As the executive assistant to the president of one of the largest hotel chains in the United States, he had the luxury to be involved in high-stakes strategic decisions, without much of the responsibility. But an entrepreneur and a dreamer at heart, Steve quickly became disenchanted with the corporate lifestyle. As a former Marine, he was fond of saying, "Life's too short not to chase your dream."

The genesis of Epic Trip started from Steve's interest of collecting television commercials while attending college. He believed commercials told compelling stories when emotionally connecting with consumers about the possibilities of what the product could help the customer realize or achieve. About a year and half ago, Steve resigned and founded his own firm. With one childhood friend and a lot of ramen noodles, they began developing what would soon become EpicTrip.com (see Figure 5.1). An arts enthusiast, Steve brought significant design sensitivity to the team while his partner brought

the technical skills. The vision behind EpicTrip.com was to revolutionize how people purchase travel.

The Epic Trip Web site read, "Epic Trip is a new and unique way for travelers to know what their destinations and their hotels are all about, even before setting off. By connecting our travelers with videos, virtual tours, reviews, and the wealth of experience brought to bear by the very users of Epic Trip, it is our mission to spark people's desire to discover their own epic trip."

As the Internet travel market was crowded with sites that focused on listing as many options and finding customers the "best deals," Steve believed there would be value in focusing on the experience of travel, even before the trip started. Through the use of rich media (videos, virtual tours, photos, and audio), Epic Trip was designed to help travelers get a feel for the unique offerings of their destination before arriving—and to dream about new ones. With the number of broadband Internet connections rapidly growing (and surpassing dial-up connections in 2006), Steve believed that the timing was now. Epic Trip also focused on community, with tools for members to share their experiences and photos and to connect with other like-minded travelers.

Still in beta version, without having begun any formal marketing campaign, EpicTrip.com was attracting some

Figure 5.1 EpicTrip.com Home Page

continued

attention from bloggers, travel industry insiders, and travel enthusiasts. The consensus was that the Epic Trip site was visually appealing and extremely easy to navigate.

"What's up, Steve-O!" you screamed in the receiver, a bit too loud for the early hour. "I know that you have been doing some eCommerce consulting for the travel industry as of late," said Steve, adding with a chuckle, "I keep up with you, my friend." You fire back: "I have been monitoring your progress. I see you have launched in beta already."

"We are at a cross road," Steve said, his voice becoming serious. "We have the site up and running, we have the partnerships in place with the major travel distributors. The site is fast and we have rolled out the members' area and the platform for featured destinations" (Figure 5.2).

"Nice going Steve-O!" you exclaim, excited about the progress. "Time to make some dough, buddy," Steve replies. "As you know, we originally thought about a referral model, making a cut when people follow a link from our site and purchase some travel product."

"That's a tough business," you interject. "Exactly," Steve replies. "It appears we have people doing research on the site, but they don't go straight through. They may come back over and over and later book or even call an agency or a hotel. We don't get paid that way. In addition, we just learned that Expedia is now offering hotels free production of virtual tours to be featured on their site."

With very limited resources, Steve knew he had to quickly come up with a solid value proposition that differentiated Epic Trip and a revenue model to approach potential investors. "You are my eCommerce guru; I need some guidance. I have some ideas, but I would love your take. I need to start monetizing this platform we have built."

"Absolutely!" you reply without hesitation. "Give me until the end of the week to study this and I will call you with some ideas." Steve answers, "Thanks bud, I knew I could count on you. Talk to you at the end of the week."

DISCUSSION QUESTIONS

1. What kind of information do you think you need to seek out as you formulate your recommendations to Steve?
2. How do you suggest that Epic Trip think about driving revenue? What are some of the options? How would you rank them relative to each other?
3. What would you suggest Epic Trip do to differentiate? How can Steve ensure the long-term viability of Epic Trip?

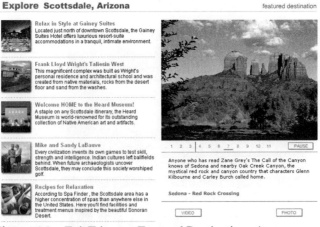

Figure 5.2   EpicTrip.com Featured Destinations Area

INTRODUCTION

In the previous chapter, we introduced concepts and techniques to understand the implications of recent technological advancements for the modern firm. We introduced the notions of network economics and information economics and the role of disruptive technologies in shaping the competitive landscape. These concepts are critical for general and functional managers, who increasingly find themselves managing in the network economy.

We now focus more specifically on the business innovations that have been spurred by the widespread adoption of the Internet and the technologies that leverage it. Our objective here is to help you become familiar with the language, history, and manifestations of the electronic commerce phenomenon by providing useful categorizations and examples.

THE ECOMMERCE VOCABULARY

The concept of electronic commerce (or eCommerce for short) has been widely investigated since its advent in the early 1990s. We recall a quote we read in the late 1990s that suggested "in five years there will be no eCommerce, just commerce." This statement is perhaps a bit bold and certainly designed to be attention grabbing. However, history has proven it largely true. It is hard to imagine organizations today, beyond those of very small size, that would be well served by ignoring the Internet as a vehicle for commerce, be it as a tool for back-office operations (e.g., purchasing and logistics), a channel of distribution (e.g., online sales), or a complement to the customer service experience.

eCommerce and eBusiness

A number of definitions of the terms *electronic commerce* (eCommerce) and *electronic business* (eBusiness) have been proposed over the years. Perhaps the simplest definition of the term *electronic commerce* is the broadest one: an online exchange of value. A more comprehensive one, adopted in this book, is the following: Electronic commerce is the process of distributing, buying, selling, marketing, and servicing products and services over computer networks such as the Internet.

This definition succinctly captures the essence of the electronic commerce phenomenon as the coming together of parties in an exchange that is mediated by networked information technologies.

The term *electronic business* originally referred to the digital enablement of internal organizational business processes, such as logistics and the use of Intranets. However, recognizing the increasingly interconnected nature of business operations upstream and downstream in the value chain, the term rapidly evolved to encompass interorganizational processes spanning such as electronic purchasing and supply chain management. Thus we broadly define the term *electronic business* as the use of Internet technologies and other advanced IT to enable business processes and operations.

Today the definitional boundary between the two terms, *electronic commerce* and *electronic business,* has largely blurred, and regardless of definitional differences both phenomena rely on the same set of enablers.

The Enablers

While much of the attention-grabbing electronic commerce headlines date to the dot-com era (1993–2000),[1] electronic commerce and electronic business concepts, as defined above, are not a new phenomenon. Electronic transactions have been completed over computer networks since their early development in the 1970 and 1980s.

Consider, for example, the Minitel in France, launched in the early 1980s by France Telecom (see Figure 5.3). The Minitel, launched as a way to check telephone directories, quickly evolved into a platform for accessing a wide range of services, from ordering flowers to purchasing train and airline tickets—even chat rooms to socialize with other Minitel users.

Another early example is offered by Electronic Data Interchange (EDI) technologies, pioneered conceptually in the late 1960s. EDI enabled the computer-to-computer exchange of structured data by two or more organizations that agreed on message standards to be used by their respective applications. In fact, in a business-to-business setting, electronic business has been around since the introduction of telecommunication and networking technology. The hospitality industry, often regarded as a technology laggard, was engaging in electronic business as early as the 1970s using proprietary networks to sell reservations.

Yet if electronic commerce and electronic business transactions have been around for so long, why have the last fifteen years been so ripe with innovation and opportunities? A number of enablers, discussed in previous chapters, are at the heart of the meteoric rise to prominence of eCommerce and eBusiness. We briefly summarize them here:

■ *Affordable computing equipment.* The most recent Census Bureau data indicate that in 2003 more than 61 percent of U.S. households had a computer. The number increases when access at work or in public venues (e.g., schools, libraries, Internet cafés) is considered.

■ *Access to the Internet.* The same report shows that over 54 percent of U.S. households have access to the Internet.

Figure 5.3   The Original Minitel Terminal (1982)

---

[1] While there is no agreed-on timeline of the dot-com era, we can think of it as beginning with the commercialization of the Web in 1993 and ending with the crash of the NASDAQ security market in March of 2000.

- *Ease of use.* Technology adoption is strongly influenced by its perceived usefulness and ease of use. The emergence of the World Wide Web created an easy-to-use, graphical method of navigation of the Internet. This tool broadened dramatically the potential audience for the Internet and its services.

- *Open standards.* Open standards—technology standards that are freely available and can be used for free—created the bedrock for the expansion of the Internet.

Categorizing Electronic Commerce Initiatives

The electronic commerce and electronic business landscape literally exploded during the dot-com era. It was a unique period of time when venture capital was plentiful and a sense of possibility pervaded Silicon Valley and other hotbeds of eCommerce innovation. To make sense of the seemingly endless number and types of innovations, a specific vocabulary was introduced. This vocabulary has now become part of the language of business circles, and you should therefore master it.

Note that the process of creating categories is useful in that it enables us to identify and quickly refer to different entities. However, categorizations are a simplification of reality and, as a consequence, you may find that the different categories introduced below overlap somewhat.

Categorizing Ventures by Transaction Type   The most immediate way to classify different types of electronic commerce ventures and innovations is to identify the parties involved in the transaction.

Business-to-Consumer (B2C)   Business-to-consumer transactions are those that involve a for-profit organization on one side and the end consumer on the other. This category includes online retailers, such as Amazon.com or Target.com, as well as business models where a firm offers value to a consumer without selling any physical goods. Take, for instance, Edmunds.com. Edmunds.com provides information and referrals to consumers seeking to purchase automobiles. Edmund's revenue model is based on referrals and advertisement revenue (see Figure 5.4).

We recall a conversation with an executive at uBid.com, the online auction pioneer, who told us that the biggest question in 1995 for electronic commerce trail blazers was "whether consumers would feel comfortable providing their credit card information to a web site." That question, with many similar others, has long been answered, and the B2C electronic commerce model is now a mature one as well as the most visible kind of eCommerce.

Business-to-Business (B2B)   Businesses-to-business transactions are those is which two or more business entities take part. The transactions can range from one-time interactions, very similar to the ones described above (e.g., your company purchases printer toner through Staples.com), or they can be highly unique and tailored to the relationship between two firms.

For instance, Dell.com offers a B2C site, where all consumers can purchase computing equipment. Dell also offers an extensive B2B site, called Premier Pages, which offers services tailored to the individual needs of its larger business customers (see Figure 5.5). On Premier Pages authorized employees can access tailored services, such as maintenance history and a knowledge base of identified issues, and purchase items with agreed-on contract terms (e.g., warranty, returns) and preferred prices due to volume discounts.

Figure 5.4 Edmunds.com Web Site. (*Source:* Copyright Edmunds Inc. All rights reserved. Used with permission.)

Consumer-to-Consumer (C2C) Consumer-to-consumer transactions are those that enable individual consumers to interact and transact directly. The classic example of a firm that enables C2C transactions is eBay, Inc., the marketplace that lets any one of us trade goods with other consumers. Business models built around community and social networks, such as YouTube or mySpace (Figure 5.6), fall into this category as well.

For example, Yahoo! recently launched Yahoo! Answers, a Web site where individuals can post questions that other people respond to. Interactions occur between members of the Yahoo! community, while the firm benefits from the traffic they generate.

Consumer-to-Business (C2B) Consumer-to-business transactions occur when individuals transact with business organizations not as buyers of goods and services, but as

Figure 5.5 Dell Premier Pages

Figure 5.6   MySpace.com's Web Site

suppliers. eLance.com represents an example (see Figure 5.7). The company enables firms to upload the specifics of a project or job needed and allows individuals (or other firms) to offer their services to complete the project or job. Typical projects are those amenable to simple outsourcing and delivery, like graphic design, research, or programming, but any type of project can be posted.

eGovernment   Electronic government, or eGovernment, refers to all transactions involving legislative and administrative institutions. eGovernment transaction can occur with individual citizens, businesses, or other governments. An example of an eGovernment

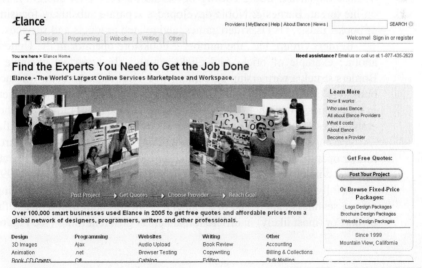

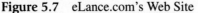

Figure 5.7   eLance.com's Web Site

transaction may be electronic filing of income tax. Another example is offered by electronic voting or the use of Web portals to solicit public input on upcoming regulation and legislation.

Categorizing Ventures by Company Structure Beyond the type of transaction being investigated, another way in which observers have been trying to make sense of the electronic commerce landscape is by categorizing the companies involved in it on the basis of their structure.

Brick and Mortar Brick and mortar is a term used to refer to "traditional" organizations—in other words, those firms that have physical operations and locations (i.e., stores) and don't provide their services exclusively through the Internet. In the early days of the dot-com era, brick and mortar firms were regarded by many observers and commentators as dinosaurs soon to be swept away by nimble online firms. This prediction proved incorrect, and today most brick and mortar organizations have substantial eBusiness and eCommerce operations.

Consider, for example, General Electric (GE), the largest company in the United States. GE is certainly a business with substantial brick and mortar operations. Yet, under the leadership of Jack Welch, GE moved very aggressively to incorporate the Internet in the very fabric of its operations.

Bricks and Clicks Bricks and clicks, or click and mortar, is a label used to refer to organizations that have hybrid operations. These are typically brick and mortar operations that saw the potential offered by the Internet and aggressively used the new channel. Bricks and clicks operations evolved in one of two ways.

Some developed independent ventures to take advantage of the opportunities, and capital, available to online ventures. A classic example of this model is offered by Barnes & Noble, the largest bookseller in the United States. Barnes & Noble was thrust, much to its dismay, into the eCommerce limelight once Amazon.com opened its virtual doors selling books as its very first category. In response to the online threat, Barnes & Noble developed a separate subsidiary focusing on online sales of books, music, DVDs, video games, and related products and services.

Borders Group, Inc., the number 2 bookstore operator in the United States, provides another example of bricks and clicks strategy. In a perfect example of co-opetition,[2] Borders struck a partnership agreement with rival Amazon.com, who now runs its online bookstore (see Figure 5.8). The firm preferred to outsource its online operations to the best in the business—which also happened to be a competitor—rather than shoulder the considerable investment necessary in creating its own online selling and fulfillment capabilities.

A competing approach consists in running the online channel as part of the bricks and mortar operations in a highly integrated fashion. An example of this strategy is offered by the drugstore chain CVS/pharmacy. The firm launched CVS.com in 1999 with the objective of fully integrating the online pharmacy with store operations. Doing so enabled it to offer a seamless experience to shoppers, allowing them to interact with the firm online, offline, or (most likely) in different manners at different times (see Figure 5.9).

---

[2] The term *co-opetition* is a combination of the terms *cooperation* and *competition*. It represents situations where competitors strike mutually beneficial partnerships agreements.

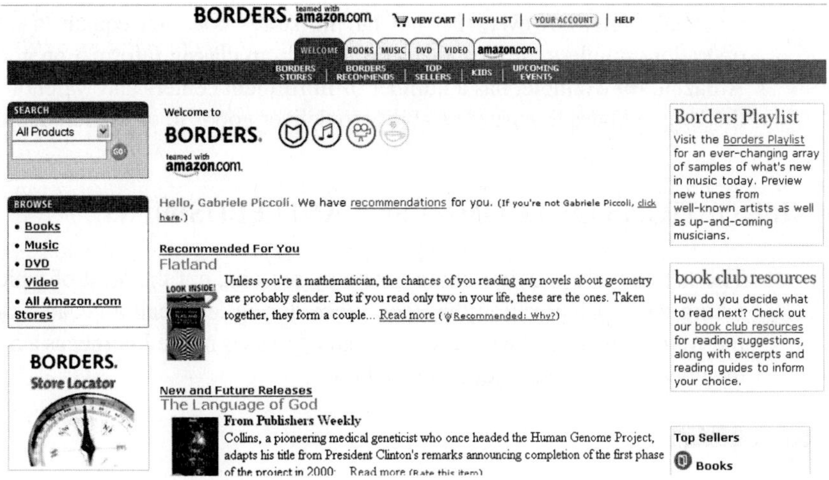

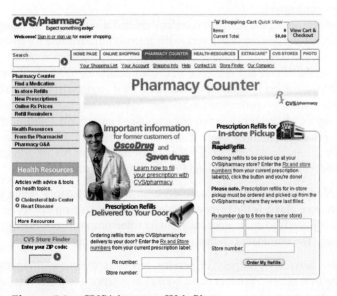

Figure 5.8   Borders' Online Store

Whichever approach is better for bricks and clicks firms is a matter of debate. On the one hand, the independent operation allows the online channel to make decisions with only limited concern for the impacts on the store operations. On the other hand, proponents of the integrated model point out that combining online and offline operations yields potential synergies.

Pure Play   Pure play is a term used to identify those organizations "born online"— that is, firms that have no stores and provide their services through the Internet. Google, Amazon.com, Yahoo!, Monster.com, Match.com, and eBay are some of the traditional pure play brands. Skype, YouTube, Facebook, and many others have more recently

Figure 5.9   CVS/pharmacy Web Site

emerged. Note, however, that not having stores does not equate to not having physical operations—unless the firm deals exclusively in classic information goods (e.g., Google). Amazon, for example, has a number of fulfillment centers and warehouses located around the United States to ensure its ability to deliver goods to customers rapidly.

MANIFESTATIONS OF ECOMMERCE AND EBUSINESS

The dot-com era was intriguing for many reasons, not the least of which was the breathtaking pace of innovation that took place during less than a decade. Beyond technology innovation, much of the creativity pertained to uses of the Internet as a business platform—the notion of business model innovation.

Business Models: Definition

A business model captures the firm's concept and value proposition while also conveying what market opportunity the company is pursuing, what product or service it offers, and what strategy the firm will follow to seek a dominant position. The business model may also identify what organizational capabilities the firm plans to leverage to turn the concept into reality. In short, the business model tells us what the firm does for its customers, how it does it, and how it is going to be compensated for what it does.

The term *business model* acquired prominence with the emergence of electronic commerce because up to the emergence of the Internet, with few exceptions, it was clear what a firm did and what its value proposition was (i.e., its business model) once we knew its industry. The statement "I produce beer," or "I sell groceries," or "I am a real estate agent," clearly conveyed what the firm did, what its cost structure was likely to be, and, most importantly, how the firm would create and sustain a revenue stream. The underlying business model was implicit.

The emergence of the network economy created a seemingly unending stream of new business models and new ways to leverage the Internet infrastructure for business opportunity. Consider Priceline.com, for example. The Priceline name-your-own price business model is predicated on the notion that real-time B2C communication made available by the Internet would enable customers to trade-off convenience for discounts. In other words, travelers with more time than money—perhaps students—can communicate to Priceline how much they are willing to pay for a ticket between two city pairs (see Figure 5.10). Priceline then shops for the customer's price at top airlines to see if anyone is interested in selling a ticket with such characteristics (e.g., city pairs, dates, price). If any provider accepts the price, the customer's credit card is billed, the flight is ticketed, and Priceline collects a commission.

Revenue Models   An important consideration for organizations doing business online, particularly pure plays, is the revenue model they adopt. A firm's revenue model specifies how the firm intends to draw proceeds from its value proposition—in short, how it plans to make money. The dominant revenue models include the following.

Pay for Service   The pay for service model is the most straightforward revenue model. The firm offers a product (e.g., books) or a service (e.g., insurance) for sale and it is compensated much like a traditional store or service provider.

Your Trip: Depart: Return:
Ithaca, NY to Milan, Italy change cities   Fri, August 25   Sat, December 23

Name Your Own Price® and Save on Flights
THE BEST PRICE AND QUALITY GUARANTEED!   *details ›*

You can save up to 40% over leading online sites when you Name Your Own Price® for your flight.[1] We guarantee you a quality travel experience at the best price possible.

Select Departure and Arrival Airports

Departure Airports	Arrival Airports
⑤ ☑ Ithaca - Tompkins County, NY (ITH)	⑤ ☑ Milan - Malpensa, Italy (MXP)
☐ Syracuse - Hancock Intl, NY (SYR)	☐ Milan - Linate, Italy (LIN)
☐ Greater Buffalo Intl, NY (BUF)	☐ Milan - Orio Al Serio, Italy (BGY)
☐ Newburgh - Stewart Intl, NY (SWF)	
☐ Allentown - Lehigh Valley Intl, PA (ABE)	
☐ Albany - County, NY (ALB)	

⑤ Best deal airport option   Ⓝ Not available for this trip

Name Your Own Price® and Save Up to 40% on Your Trip[1]   ⒭ THE BEST PRICE AND QUALITY GUARANTEED!

Name Your Own Price℠ Per Round-trip Ticket $ 780 .00	Not Flexible? Choose exact flight times and prices
Total charges, including taxes and fees, are displayed on the following page.	

Figure 5.10   Priceline's Name-Your-Own Price Model

Subscription   The subscription revenue model is similar in nature to the pay for service model, in that customers pay for the service they receive, which in this case is content (e.g., news, sport highlights). Unlike pay for service, though, subscription models are typically based on access rather than usage. In other words, customers pay for the right to access the content and then are able to use as much of the service (i.e., content) as they need.

Advertisement Support   Perhaps the most used (and abused) revenue model of the network economy is the advertisement-supported model. The firm's content or services are made available for free in an effort to attract a large audience. The firm then "sells access to its audience" to interested advertisers, much like radio stations do (Figure 5.11). A critical difference between the traditional and online ad-supported models is that traffic to, and behavior on, a Web site can be tracked very precisely at the individual level—something that print media, television, and radio advertisement could never offer.

The unprecedented level of accountability offered by online advertisement, however, proved to be a mixed blessing. On the one hand, advertisers value the ability to monitor

Google™
AdSense   Change Language:

Discover your site's full revenue potential.

Google AdSense is a fast and easy way for website publishers of all sizes to display relevant Google ads on their website's content pages and earn money. Because the ads are related to what your visitors are looking for on your site — or matched to the characteristics and interests of the visitors your content attracts — you'll finally have a way to both monetize and enhance your content pages.

It's also a way for website publishers to provide Google web and site search to their visitors, and to earn money by displaying Google ads on the search results pages.

Figure 5.11   Google AdSense

who is consuming their message, when, how, and what they are doing afterward. Specifically, sites that require logon id (e.g., *New York Times*) can collect precise demographics and serve up targeted ads. On the other hand, precise data quickly demonstrated that most sites did not get the significant traffic (i.e., hits) they expected. More importantly, precise click-through data (the percentage of people who take action spurred by Web-based advertisement) shows that very few of the people visiting a Web site respond to the ads online by clicking through.

Affiliate   In similar fashion to the advertising model, the affiliate model, pioneered by Amazon.com, seeks to generate revenue from a third-party based on customer traffic to the firm's Web site. In this case the referring site receives a commission once a customer who originated from the site makes a purchase on another site. This model is enabled by the ability to link pages directly to products (Figure 5.12).

Dominant Business Models

As the Internet and the Web emerged as a stable platform for commerce, a number of business models were proposed by entrepreneurs and organizations seeking to profit in the "network economy." The sense of possibility offered by the new technology (and plentiful cash from venture capitalists!) and the limited knowledge of the new landscape created the precondition for significant business model experimentation. Some of these business models spawned successful and profitable companies, while others proved flawed. We address the most relevant below. Note, however that, just like industrial age conglomerates, modern firms may have a portfolio of business models and you may not be able to categorize them neatly in one or the other.

Online Retailing   The poster child of eCommerce business models, due in large part to the attention garnered by Amazon.com, is online retailing. Examples abound with both pure play, such as Buy.com, and bricks and clicks organization, like Staples.com or BestBuy.com. The defining characteristic of online retailers is the fact that they take control of inventory they then resell at a profit. Fulfillment is a critical capability for these organizations. The revenue model is pay for service.

Figure 5.12   Amazon's Affiliate Program

Infomediaries   Information intermediaries, or infomediaries, are organizations that use the Internet to provide specialized information on behalf of product or service providers. The value proposition of the infomediary consists in the gathering of product and service specifications and reviews and creating a system to quickly search and organize the data. Unlike online retailers, though, infomediaries do not sell the goods and services they review or take ownership of inventory. Rather, they link to online retailers and receive compensation for referrals as well as advertisement. Infomediaries are typically segment or product focused, so as to offer domain-specific expertise.

Examples of infomediaries abound, from consumer electronics (e.g., MySimon.com) to travel (Kyak.com) to autos (e.g., Edmunds.com).

Content providers   Content providers are organizations that develop and publish content. The content offered ranges from news (e.g., Reuters.com), to current information (e.g., Eonline.com), historical and reference information (e.g., Britannica.com), and travel information and tips (e.g., EpicTrip.com). Traditionally content providers relied on largely owned content generated by the organization's staff, but there is an emerging trend toward user-generated content (Figure 5.13). User-generated content offers two advantages. First, it is considered more honest and less prone to marketing influence or manipulation. Second, it has a limited cost of production, since the community typically volunteers its input.

The technologies used by content providers are increasingly converging, with most providers employing a mix of text, images, animations, streaming audio, and video. Because the product being offered by these organizations is information based (i.e., classic information goods), fulfillment is not a major concern. The revenue model for content providers can be advertisement supported, subscription, or pay per download.

Online Communities   An online community is a group of people brought together by a common interest (e.g., windsurfing) or goal (e.g., initiate a class action lawsuit). The community is virtual in that its members primarily interact using information technologies and are brought together through a network.

Figure 5.13   EpicTrip.com Offers Travel-Related Content

Virtual communities work because they alleviate one of the constraints of the physical world: physical distance. Imagine three cities—say, Ithaca, New York, Durham, North Carolina, and Phoenix, Arizona—and three individuals who share a passion for windsurfing (e.g., Gabe, Fernando, and Anthony). Before the advent of the Internet, these three individuals would have likely never met each other. However, by virtue of being members of the same online community, they can trade tips, pick each others' brain about equipment and repairs, and even coordinate trips together to meet (physically) in world-class windsurfing destinations.

Before the advent of the Internet, these individuals may have been isolated in their city, unable to find a critical mass of like-minded persons who share the same interest (see Figure 5.14). Today you can find thriving online communities devoted to almost any interest.

Virtual communities are particularly valuable for niche interests, where critical mass of community members can only be found in large cities. In many cases they offer business opportunities, but, perhaps more importantly, they have created unprecedented opportunity for non-mainstream interests to thrive because those who share them can now easily find each other.

Business models crafted around online communities became extremely popular once the business community realized their potential to harness network effects (see Chapter 4). One of the most interesting recent examples of online community is offered by Yahoo! Answers (Figure 5.15). The site allows anyone with a Yahoo! account to post questions that are immediately read by other members of the community. The wealth of content on Yahoo! Answers, ranging from where to find historical weather data to how to best exact revenge, is generated by the community at no cost to Yahoo!, the sponsor of the network.

Exchanges Exchanges are organizations that create a marketplace for buyers and sellers to come together and transact. Thus, an exchange does not take control of inventory or worries about fulfillment. Yet the exchange provides a "market making" service and is compensated with fees, commission on sales, or consulting fees on more complex business-to-business transactions.

The prototypical example of an exchange is eBay. Others include uBid.com (Figure 5.16), an online auction house mainly focused on business-to-consumer transactions, and FreeMarket (now owned by Ariba), also targeting the business-to-business domain.

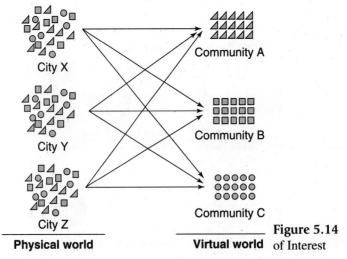

Figure 5.14 Virtual Communities of Interest

Figure 5.15   The Home of the Yahoo! Answers Community

Infrastructure Providers   Under the label of infrastructure providers fall a number of diverse companies that have been able to create value by developing and managing the infrastructure of electronic commerce. This infrastructure includes both technological and financial assets and services providing the preconditions to commerce.

Examples in this category include hardware companies that manage the Internet backbone (e.g., MCI WorldCom, now owned by Verizon) and produce specialized networking equipment (e.g., Cisco Systems), and Internet service providers (ISPs), which enable access to the Internet and its services (e.g., AOL). Organizations that enable secure transactions on the Internet also belong in this category—for instance, payment service companies (e.g., PayPal), organizations that offer privacy or security certification (e.g., TRUSTe), and the many other business and nonprofit concerns that provide the lubricant that makes

Figure 5.16   The uBid.com Exchange

the electronic commerce machine work smoothly. A traditional pay for service revenue model is typically what for profit infrastructure providers use, even though some ISPs like NetZero attempted to generate revenue through advertisement.

ECOMMERCE IMPLICATIONS

As we discussed in the introductory chapters, the emergence of new technologies often has dramatic impacts on organizations. The rapid adoption of the Internet and the emergence of the network economy proved to be no exceptions. General and functional managers must proactively manage these effects.

Disintermediation

The hallmark of the Internet is connectivity. As such, its emergence and widespread adoption by consumers enabled any organization that so chose to establish (at least technically) a direct relationship with its customers. All of a sudden it was practical for companies as diverse as hotels and computer manufactures, automakers, and insurance companies to reach customers directly rather than through one or more middlemen.

The term *disintermediation* refers to the process by which a firm's distribution chain is shortened through the elimination of one or more intermediaries. Disintermediation has a direct impact on those organizations that find themselves threatened by it, such as travel agents and car dealers. If you find yourself managing one of these organizations, you will need to recast its value proposition.

For example, many travel agents have found it difficult to stay in business after airlines, and increasingly hotels, have eliminated commissions. Many others, though, have been able to leverage superior knowledge about the travel product and rules and are now prospering using a consulting, rather than commission, model (i.e., they receive fees from travelers who value their service and knowledge). In the worst-case scenario, a firm facing disintermediation may be forced to harvest and close the business.

Disintermediation has less direct impacts on organizations that, while unable to dismantle their distribution chain, can circumvent some parts of it (for example, by improving after-the-sale service).

Reintermediation

As managers and observers tried to make sense of the Internet as a business tool, many thought that disintermediation would lead to the demise of distribution channels in most industries. While disintermediation failed to eliminate traditional intermediaries in most industries, the Internet created opportunities for new intermediaries to exist alongside their brick and mortar counterparts—a process known as reintermediation.

Consider the insurance industry, for instance. Today, insurance companies reach consumers directly (e.g., Progressive.com), through traditional insurance brokers, and through independent online insurance brokers (e.g., insure.com).

Another example is offered by many of the infomediaries discussed above. While it is true that traditional travel agents have been forced to reinvent their value proposition, a number of Internet travel agents (e.g., Orbitz, Travelocity) have emerged and are thriving due to their ability to help travelers gather information and uncover low prices. Similar dynamics have occurred in traditional retail and many other industries.

Market Efficiency

Since their advent, information technologies have contributed to reduce search costs and improve the efficiency of markets. The Internet and its related technologies continued and perhaps accelerated this process, empowering customers with the tools to sift through large amounts of product and service data.

Prior to the arrival of the Internet, customers faced significant costs when searching for products and services. They would have to either visit physical stores or call multiple outlets to describe what they were looking for and inquire about availability and price. In either case the process would be fairly time consuming and, therefore, costly. The outcome of this process has been heightened competition and an increasing difficulty to profit from strategies rooted in asymmetry of information or high search costs.

Channel Conflict

The emergence of the online channel created a conundrum for many organizations that had an established distribution chain. Should they disintermediate, following the promise of reduced distribution costs and a direct relationship with customers, or should they work with the channel in an effort to identify mutually beneficial Internet-enabled initiatives? At the heart of this dilemma is the inherent difficulty of moving distribution from the traditional channel, the one currently producing the revenue stream the organization needs to survive, to the online direct channel, the one that promises the highest profitability in the long run. The term *channel conflict* captures the dilemma.

Two examples highlight the difficulty faced by organizations confronting channel conflict. When Dell began selling computers through its Web site, it faced no objections from distributors because it had none. When Compaq, Dell's principal competitor, sought to respond by creating its own direct-sale Web site, it faced significant resistance from electronics store chains carrying its devices (e.g., Circuit City).

Renaissance Cruises had an even more traumatic encounter with the channel conflict dilemma. Taking a page out of the airline and lodging industries, the company decided to embrace the Internet channel in the late 1990s and drastically reduce travel agent commissions. In retaliation, the travel agent community boycotted the Renaissance product and the firm quickly encountered financial difficulties. A public apology in the pages of the *Wall Street Journal* notwithstanding, these difficulties culminated in bankruptcy once the events of September 11, 2001 severely hampered the travel industry.

Customer and Employee Self-Service

Another important implication of the widespread adoption of electronic commerce and electronic business has been the emergence of customer and employee self-service. Aided by easy-to-use Web sites and the increasing degree of comfort that the general

Figure 5.17   Self-Service Kiosks

public has developed with information technologies of all kinds, IT-enabled self-service is a growing trend requiring managerial attention.(Figure 5.17)

Examples of this trend abound, from kiosks at airline counters, in hotel lobbies, and in fast food restaurants, to self-checkout counters at grocery stores and Web-based software that allows you to compute fairly complex tax returns without ever speaking to a professional.

ECOMMERCE AND EBUSINESS TRENDS

In a little over ten years since the Internet opened for business, electronic commerce and electronic business have become mainstream. No modern organization would ignore the impact of the Internet and the technologies that leverage it. However, innovation has not stopped; both technology advances and business innovations continue to emerge at a rapid pace. Below we discuss some of the most recent trends.

Technological Innovation

A number of technologies supporting novel Internet services have recently emerged under the umbrella term of *Web 2.0*. While some see the term *Web 2.0* as a vaguely defined catch-all buzzword, it has the value of grouping the new wave of technologies that are helping to move the Web from a static platform made of flat (i.e., not interactive) pages, to one that is more functional and more akin to the desktop of personal computers and media experiences offered by television.

Perhaps the defining characteristic of Web 2.0 technologies is their ability to enable services that are free and easy to use, less structured, and more interactive than traditional Internet services. Interestingly, these services do not lack structure but they instead allow for structure to emerge, based on the interest and objectives of the community that uses the services. The following are some examples of these services:

Wiki   Wiki is a technology, introduced by Ward Cunningham in 1994, that enables simple coauthoring and editing of Web content. Wikies are extremely conducive to online collaboration, they can be set up as private or public, and they can require authentication or enable anyone to write and make changes to the Wiki.

The primary example of a Wiki is Wikipedia (Figure 5.18), a global, free community-written encyclopedia. Wikipedia is literally a phenomenon, having started with little funding in 2001. Wikipedia does not commission any articles; the writing, editing, and quality assurance is all done by the global virtual community of Wikipedia contributors.

In early 2007 Wikipedia counted over 150,000 encyclopedia entries in each of ten languages and over 1.5 million entries in English alone. As a community-supported encyclopedia, with a staff of less than ten people and no professional or editorial staff, it is legitimate to wonder about the quality of the entries in Wikipedia. A recent article in the journal *Nature* asked the question and concluded, based on a peer-review test, that Wikipedia is of equivalent quality to the Encyclopedia Britannica Online, a repository of knowledge with a decidedly more august pedigree.[3] The test by *Nature*, while certainly not definitive, suggests that harnessing the knowledge and efforts of a huge community may lead not to anarchy, but instead to robust content of quality comparable to that produced by experts—an argument used by the proponents of Open Source software as well (see Chapter 12).

Blogs   Blogs, a shorthand for Weblogs, emerged along with the public Internet. Despite the techie-sounding term, a blog is nothing but an online journal that an individual keeps and publishes on the World Wide Web for the whole world to enjoy. While the early blogs were just static Web pages laboriously updated by their authors, today setting up a blog is matter of minutes using tools such as those provided by Blogger—a company now owned by Google (see Figure 5.19).

As a Web 2.0 technology, blogs enable their authors to modify their structure by including other media types beyond text—such as video and images. More importantly, blogs enable hyprlinking and discussion, thus making them not just a one-way communication medium but one able to support interactive "conversations."

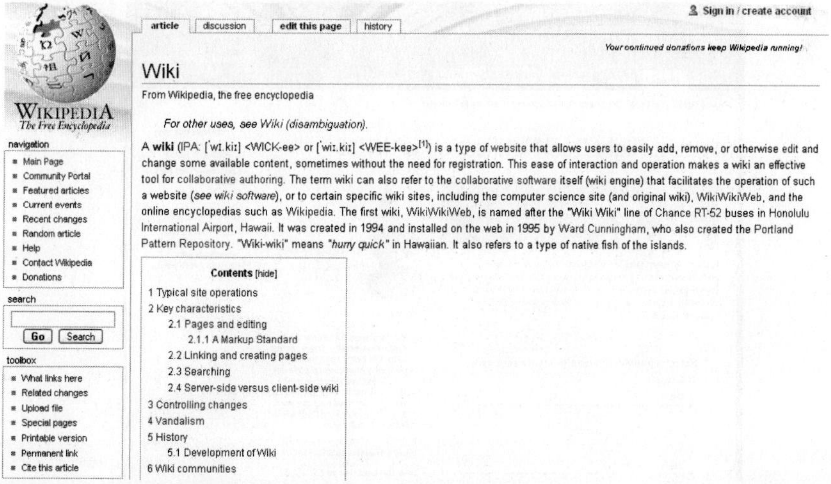

Figure 5.18   Wikipedia on Wiki

[3] Giles, J. (2005), "Internet Encyclopedias Go Head to Head," *Nature,* 439, pp. 900–901.

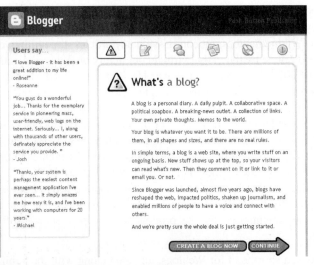

Figure 5.19   Blogger.com on Blogs

RSS   RSS stands for Real Simple Syndication (RSS). RSS technology enables an organization to create Web feeds, short summaries of content with a link to the full-fledged version that are broadcast to all those who subscribe to the feed once a trigger event occurs. For example, as a blogger you may want to use RSS to inform your faithful readers every time the blog is updated. Travelocity uses RSS to alert customers who signed up and provided information about their preferred city pairs and destinations about changes in fares of interest to them (Figure 5.20).

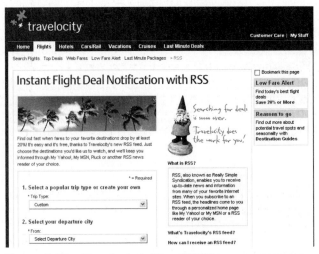

Figure 5.20   Travelocity's Use of RSS. (*Source:* 1996–2006 Travelocity.com LP. All rights reserved. TRAVELOCITY, TRAVELOCITY.com, The Roaming Gnome and Stars Design are trademarks of TRAVELOCITY.com LP.)

In many ways RSS is a new twist of an early Internet idea: push technology. Push technology emerged in reaction to the explosion of Web content and the increasing difficulty of searching for relevant content. Instead, push technology enabled users to specify what content they were interested in, and such content would be delivered to them.

Tags   Tags, short descriptors associated with an object, are not a new technology by any means. However, tags are beginning to be widely used on the Internet to give structure to and to categorize the increasing amount of available content. A particularly novel use of tags is demonstrated by sites such as Flickr, the online photo management and sharing application (Figure 5.21). Instead of providing users with a fixed set of predefined tags to use, Flickr allows individual users to create their own tags to categorize the pictures they upload as they please. Subsequently, Flicker uses software to identify the emergent structure of the aggregate image database by identifying sets of tags that correlate highly. This approach creates an intriguing emergent structure.

For example, the tag Ithaca, NY is associated with Cornell (the university located in Ithaca), lake (Ithaca is in the beautiful Finger Lakes region), and . . . snowy winter weather!

Business Innovation

Web 2.0 technologies, as well as continuing the trend in the evolution of traditional Internet technologies (e.g., wireless networking), continue to spur business innovation driven by firms seeking to create value in the evolving environment.

M-commerce   With the increasing miniaturization of devices, digitization of content, and emergence of wide area wireless and cellular networks, organizations are seeking to extend their reach and use mobile devices for enabling transactions with customers. The term *mobile commerce* (or M-Commerce, mCommerce) refers to the ability to complete commercial transactions using mobile devices, such as cellular phones or personal digital assistants (PDAs).

Consider the following example. You booked your flight with Orbitz, the online travel agency. As you are driving to the airport, you receive a text message informing you that the

Figure 5.21   Flickr on Ithaca, NY

Figure 5.22   The Evolution of Commerce

aircraft due to come into your airport had a mechanical problem. As a consequence, your own flight is delayed. The message also carries a link to a page where you can see what other flights are scheduled to your destination. You tap on the link, choose the first available flight out, and you have a new confirmed reservation before you even arrive at the airport. This scenario may seem a bit futuristic, but it highlights the promise of M-Commerce initiatives.

M-Commerce has existed conceptually since the advent of electronic commerce, but it has recently received significant impetus as consumers have shown its viability by adopting electronic commerce and self-service through digital devices. The main advantage offered by M-Commerce is the ability to reach consumers in real time, at the point of service, based on their current location. Imagine walking down the street in a new town; it is 9 A.M. and you could really use a coffee. Your cell phone beeps, you check the message, and you see an electronic coupon for the local coffee shop, just one block off your current path. You would have missed it, and the shop would have missed the revenue, if not for the alert being sent to you based on your location.

The advantages of M-Commerce are appealing, but a number of obstacles to its widespread adoption persist. First, mobile devices offer very limited screen real estate and small keyboards for data input. Second, there are at the moment a number of technologies vying to become the standard for online connectivity. Third, access speeds (i.e., bandwidth) for mobile devices are still slow. Moreover, beyond the technical limitations, significant security and privacy concerns remain.

U-Commerce

U-commerce, a term coined by Professor Rick Watson, refers to the latest evolution of commerce (see Figure 5.22). U-commerce refers to the use of ubiquitous networks (i.e., the information grid described in Chapter 4) to support personalized and uninterrupted communications and transactions.

U-commerce is predicated on four requirements: ubiquity, uniqueness, universality, and unison. Ubiquity enables users to access resources anywhere at any time. Uniqueness enables users to be univocally identified by the requested resources both with respect to who they are as well as where they are. Universality enables users to use their devices anywhere using commonly accepted standards. Unison enables a consistent, cross-platform, and device-independent view of the available resources.

█ SUMMARY

The years between 1993 and 2000 saw the dawn of the network economy, a landscape of economic activity characterized by pervasive information networks. While the frenzied pace of experimentation has slowed since 2000, electronic commerce and electronic business trends and innovations spurred by the widespread adoption of the Internet have become mainstream.

In this chapter we sought to provide you with the tools to make sense of past developments and to understand future trends.

■ While today the two terms are used largely as synonyms, we defined *electronic commerce* as an online exchange of value and *electronic business* as the digital enablement of internal organizational business processes. Electronic commerce and electronic business find their roots in the development of information technology and networking over the last forty years. But the recent acceleration of innovation in this area has been enabled by affordable computing equipment, widespread access to the Internet, the increasing ease of use of information technologies, and the availability of open standards.

■ We have categorized electronic commerce phenomena on two dimensions. By looking at the type of transaction taking place, we classified electronic commerce as business-to-consumer (B2C), business-to-business (B2B), consumer-to-consumer (C2C), consumer-to-business (C2B), and eGovernment. Focusing on the company structure of the organizations involved, we classified concerns involved in electronic commerce such as brick and mortar, bricks and clicks, and pure play.

■ We defined a business model as the document that captures the firm's concept and value proposition while also conveying what market opportunity the company is pursuing, what product or service it offers, and what strategy the firm will follow to capture a dominant position. The dominant business models that have emerged in the network economy are online retailing. Infomediaries, content providers, online communities, exchanges, and infrastructure providers.

■ A key feature of a business model is the revenue model—the firm's plan for building a revenue stream. The dominant revenue models that have emerged are pay for service, subscription, advertisement support, and affiliate.

■ The rapid adoption of the Internet and the emergence of the network economy have had some significant implications for both established organizations and upstarts. Disintermediation (the process by which a firm's distribution chain is shortened through the elimination of one or more intermediaries), reintermediation (the process by which new online intermediaries carve a niche for themselves alongside their brick and mortar counterparts), channel conflict (the dilemma faced by organizations deciding whether to disintermediate their legacy distribution channels), and the emergence of widespread IT-enabled self-service are the most relevant.

■ While the dot-com boom may have slowed down, technology and business innovation is alive and well in the network economy. New technologies such as Wiki and RSS continue to redefine business models and how organizations can create value in the network economy.

STUDY QUESTIONS

1. What is the difference between the terms *electronic commerce* and *electronic business?* Why has the distinction largely faded recently?

2. What are the principal enablers of the continued importance of electronic commerce trends?

3. Define each of the following terms and provide examples: *business-to-consumer (B2C)*, *business-to-business (B2B)*, *consumer-to-consumer (C2C)*, *consumer-to-business (C2B)*, and *eGovernment.*

4. Define each of the following terms and provide examples: *brick and mortar, bricks and clicks,* and *pure play.*

5. Explain what we mean by the terms *business model* and *revenue model.* How do the two differ? What are the principal business models and revenue models adopted by modern organizations?

6. What are the principal impacts of the network economy for both established organizations and upstarts? Define each and provide examples.

7. Identify and provide examples of the most important recent technology and business innovations in the network economy.

FURTHER READINGS

1. Anderson, C. (2006). *The Long Tail: Why the Future of Business Is Selling Less of More,* Hyperion, New York, NY.

2. McAfee, A. (2006). "Enterprise 2.0: The Dawn of Emergent Collaboration." *Sloan Management Review,* Spring, 20–28.

3. Rayport, J. F., and Jaworski, B. J. (2004). "Best Face Forward." *Harvard Business Review,* December, 47–58.

GLOSSARY

- **Brick and mortar:** A term used to refer to "traditional" organizations, those firms that have physical operations and don't provide their services exclusively through the Internet.

- **Bricks and clicks:** Organizations that have hybrid operations involving both physical and online operations.

- **Business model:** A business model captures the firm's concept and value proposition while also conveying what market opportunity the company is pursuing, what product or service it offers, and what strategy the firm will follow to capture a dominant position.

- **Business-to-business (B2B):** A form of electronic commerce involving two for-profit organizations in the transaction.

- **Business-to-consumer (B2C):** A form of electronic commerce involving a for-profit organization on one side and the end consumer on the other side of the transaction.

- **Channel conflict:** A term that captures the dilemma faced by organizations deciding whether to disintermediate their legacy distribution channels.

- **Consumer-to-business (C2B):** A form of electronic commerce enabling individuals to transact with business organizations not as buyers of goods and services, but as suppliers.

- **Consumer-to-consumer (C2C):** A form of electronic commerce enabling individual consumers to interact and transact directly.

- **Disintermediation:** The process by which a firm's distribution chain is shortened through the elimination of one or more intermediaries.

- **eGovernment:** A form of electronic commerce involving legislative and administrative institutions in the transaction.

- **Electronic business:** The digital enablement of internal organizational business processes.

- **Electronic commerce:** An online exchange of value.

- **Pure play:** Organizations that have no physical stores and provide their services exclusively through the Internet.

- **Reintermediation:** The process by which new online intermediaries carve a niche for themselves alongside their brick and mortar counterparts.

- **Revenue model:** Specifies how the firm intends to draw proceeds from its value proposition—in short, how it plans to make money.

PART

III

The Strategic use of Information Systems

The potential for the strategic use of IT-enabled information systems has been the source of debate since it became clear that information technologies had important business applications. The love-hate relationship between business and information systems continues to this day, with stark examples of companies that have successfully harnessed the potential of ever-more-powerful information technologies grabbing headlines, market share, and profits, and others who have famously squandered large sums of money with little visible benefit.

For example, eBay Inc., the multinational company managing online marketplaces in twenty-seven countries around the globe, has built an empire around the novel and clever use of information systems to enable the connection of far-flung buyers and sellers.

The ability of mega-store operator Wal-Mart, Inc. to manage information for competitive advantage is the stuff of legends. The firm built its own satellite-based telecommunication network to support real-time communication with its stores located in rural areas of the United States in the 1970s. As a testament to the faith in the potential of information systems pervading the company, founder Sam Walton declared in 1992, "We've spent almost $700 million building up the current computer and satellite systems we have. . . . What I like about it is the kind of information you can pull out of it on moment's notice—all those numbers."[1] Wal-Mart's traditional competitor, K-Mart, never reached the same level of proficiency with information systems and IT use. Its inability to compete in the battle for low prices took it perilously close to bankruptcy more than once.

So why are some firms able to exploit information systems for sustained competitive advantage while others cannot? Perhaps the most enduring research result that can help in answering this question is offered by executives' surveys, which show remarkable consistency with the finding that the average non-IT senior manager feels that technology and

---

[1] *Sam Walton: Made in America*, Sam Walton with John Huey, New York: Bantam, p. 271.

information systems decisions are well outside his or her comfort zone. To this day, many general and functional managers are uncomfortable with planning for the use and management of information systems. This state of affairs is best captured by the following quote: "What can I do? I don't understand IT well enough to manage it in detail. And my IT people—although they work very hard—don't seem to understand the very real business problems I face."[2]

Compounding the above problem is the fact that the information systems function has traditionally been led by technologists. Because of the vastly different background and knowledge base of the business executives and the technology executives, the result has often been failed communication and a delegation of "all IT issues" to technologists. More recently, we have witnessed a trend reversal, with the IS function being led by many "new school" CIOs, who are well versed in the inner workings of the business. While this is a step in the right direction, it is hardly enough because, as talented as today's CIOs are, they are not spending their time addressing operations problems the way COOs do, marketing problems the way CMOs do, or financial problems the way CFOs do.

The above call to action is particularly important when it comes to using information and information technology to underpin value-adding strategic initiatives. General and functional managers must feel comfortable with planning and setting direction for the use of information systems resources, with identifying opportunities to use technology to create and appropriate economic value, and with deciding under what circumstances these initiatives can be protected against competitive retaliation.

Part III speaks to general and functional managers and covers the key information systems decisions that all modern managers must be comfortable in making. Specifically,

- *Chapter 6: Strategic Information Systems Planning.* This chapter provides an overview of the strategic information systems planning process, from the definition of an overall information vision to the identification of strategic initiatives.

- *Chapter 7: Value Creation and Strategic Information Systems.* This chapter sets the background for analyzing the use of information systems and technology to create and appropriate value. We define key terms and explain the framework used to analyze value creation and appropriation potential of specific strategic initiatives.

- *Chapter 8: Value Creation with Information Systems.* This chapter discusses a number of frameworks and analytical models that have been advanced over the years to help managers envision how to use information systems and technology to create and appropriate economic value.

- *Chapter 9: Appropriating IT-Enabled Value over Time.* This chapter completes the puzzle by focusing on sustainability. Once a firm has successfully created value with information systems and technology, it must be able to defend its position of advantage and appropriate the value created over time.

---

[2] Nolan, Richard, and McFarlan, F. Warren (2005), "Information Technology and the Board of Directors." *Harvard Business Review,* 83, no. 10 (October), pp. 96–106.

Strategic Information Systems Planning

What You Will Learn in This Chapter

This chapter focuses on the strategic information systems planning process and the role that general and functional managers need to play in it. Strategic information systems planning is a fundamental aspect of information systems management because it ensures that information systems and technology decisions are not made in a haphazard fashion. Rather, decisions are made with a clear understanding of business strategy and an overall sense of direction with respect to what the firm is trying to achieve with its use of information systems resources.

Specifically, in this chapter you will learn

1. Why general and functional managers must be involved in information systems planning decisions despite their lack of technical expertise.

2. The purpose that strategic information systems planning serves in modern organizations.

3. What the key components of the strategic information systems planning process are, including information systems assessment, information systems vision, and information systems guidelines.

4. How to perform an information systems assessment.

5. How to decide what role information systems resources should play in your firm using available analytical tools to develop an information systems vision.

6. What role information systems guidelines play in the planning process, and how to develop them upon having established an information systems vision.

7. To evaluate how well positioned your organization is to achieve its information vision following the guidelines, and to develop consistent strategic initiatives.

MINI-CASE: STRATEGIC INFORMATION SYSTEMS PLANNING AT THE MONEYMAKER

As you return to your hotel room, tired from the first day at the client site, you start thinking about the challenge ahead. Your consulting firm was called in by an upstate New York resort and casino—The MoneyMaker. The property is very nice; in addition to the casino, the resort has a large salon and day spa, seven restaurants, and a theater that books comedy acts and singers, many of them who used to play much larger venues in the 1980s.

The MoneyMaker's operation is centered on the hotel and tower, comprising 453 rooms and suites, with many of the luxuries typically found in the large Vegas resorts. The hotel also offers meeting space for conference and company retreats. But, as you suspected and your meeting today confirmed, the resort's bread-and-butter customers are drive-in local guests.

Your consulting firm has been engaged by the client to "develop a strategic information systems plan." Yet the series of meetings you had today left you with the distinct impression that the client has already formulated some ideas. In a meeting with you, the senior vice president of marketing said, "We are missing the boat. Large chains like Harrah's target our customers with precise marketing offers. We must invest in Business Intelligence and CRM tools or we will not survive." From the director of technology services you heard mostly frustration: "They want me to deliver a world-class infrastructure on a shoestring. The CFO, to whom I report, makes me justify every IT investment. ROI and net present value calculations are all he cares about! Yet two-thirds of my budget goes to keeping the lights on, and the remainder is spent on various pet

projects for one or the other of the executives. How am I going to modernize our archaic infrastructure under these conditions?"

The CEO seemed to recognize some of these issues and thought your help would be instrumental in changing things for the better. In the opening meeting, he said, "Your firm is the best at this and you know our industry well. We need you to assess our current operations and draft a strategic plan; we will follow it at once!" As you organize your notes, a nagging feeling overcomes you— the firm does not seem to have great unity of purpose at the moment, so how does it expect you to be able get all members of the firm on the same page? Plans are vacuous without the commitment of those who have to follow them.

"Well," you tell yourself, "one step at a time." You have certainly been in more difficult situations.

CRM : CUSTOMER RELATIONSHIP MANAGEMENT,

DISCUSSION QUESTIONS

1. What do you see as the major pitfalls of the current manner in which the information systems budgeting and prioritization process is run?
2. What do you believe are going to be the major challenges you will encounter on this assignment?
3. Do you agree with the CEO's seeming belief that the strategic information system planning process can be outsourced to a consulting firm?
4. What should be your next step as you get to work tomorrow morning?

INTRODUCTION

With information technologies increasingly embedded in all aspects of business operations, the most successful organizations are the ones that are able to establish a productive partnership between IT executives and their functional counterparts. Results of a recent ComputerWorld survey indicate that in all of the firms classified as "world-class businesses" in the study, the CIO had a seat on the primary management committee (e.g., executive committee), compared to only 56 percent of typical companies.[4]

Being able to establish such partnerships is predicated on recruiting the right people and devoting significant attention to the development of the relationship. However, whether you will be able (and lucky enough) to establish a productive partnership with the information

---

[4] Eckie J. (2006). What it takes to be world class. Computer World (accessed http://www.computerworld.com/careertopics/careers/story/0,108901,108974,00.html

systems professionals in your organization, you must be involved in the strategic planning and management of information systems in your firm. Failing to do so, and leaving all information systems decisions to your IT counterparts, will simply result in your joining the ranks of the unsatisfied and disappointed general and functional managers.

Strategic Alignment

A firm that has been able to achieve a high degree of fit and consonance between the priorities and activities of the IS function and the strategic direction of the firm has achieved strategic alignment. Research in this area has consistently shown that alignment has a direct impact on firm performance, and alignment is perennially on the top-ten list of CIO priorities. Yet strategic alignment is very difficult to achieve and maintain, particularly in those highly competitive environments where opportunities arise and fade quickly and strategic priorities change constantly. Thus, ensuring a high degree of strategic IS alignment requires as much improvisation as careful planning.

SIX DECISIONS REQUIRING MANAGERIAL INVOLVEMENT

Jeanne Ross and Peter Weill, of MIT's Center for Information Systems Research (CISR), suggest that senior management get involved in IS management by taking the leadership role on six key information systems decisions (Table 6.1).[5]

1. *How much should we spend on IT?* This is perhaps the critical question you, as a general manager or as a member of the executive committee, will be called on to ask because the answer informs all subsequent IT-related decision making.

    As we saw in Chapter 2, organizations are widely different with respect to their strategy and objectives, their culture, their history, their current infrastructure, and

Table 6.1   Six Key Information Sytems Decisions Managers Must Be Involved With

How much should we spend on IT?	This question is designed to force senior executives to discuss and decide what the role of information systems and technology should be in the organization.
Which business processes should receive the IT dollars?	This question requires executives to decide what business processes are most important to the firm at a given point.
Which IT capabilities need to be companywide?	This question requires executives to weigh the cost/benefits of standardization and flexibility.
How good do our IT services really need to be?	This question forces executives to make conscious decisions about the degree of service the firm needs and that they are willing to pay for.
What security and privacy risks will we accept?	This question forces executives to make conscious decisions about privacy and security risk management.
Whom do we blame if an IT initiative fails?	This question forces executives to clearly identify and assign responsibility for information systems projects.

[5] Ross, Jeanne W., and Weill, Peter (2002), "Six IT Decisions Your IT People Shouldn't Make," *Harvard. Business Review,* November, pp. 84–92.

so on. It follows that even two head-to-head competitors may need very different investments in IT—different both in terms of quantity (i.e., how much to spend) and quality (i.e., what initiatives should be the recipient of the IT budget).

This question is designed to force senior executives to discuss and decide the role of information systems and technology in the organization—something that most executive committees don't do. Failing to ask and answer this question puts the firm's IT department in a reactive mode, having to decide on individual project with little guidance as to the overall picture.

2. *Which business processes should receive the IT dollars?* This question requires executives to decide what business processes are most important to the firm at a given point—clearly a business decision—and as a consequence should attract IT funding. In other words, it is within the purview of business managers to decide on the allocation of resources among the many possible projects the firm can pursue—information systems and technology projects are no different!

3. *Which IT capabilities need to be companywide?* Large organizations constantly battle the trade-off between standardization and flexibility. Increasing standardization enables the firm to manage operations efficiently, while flexibility enables the firm to react more quickly and more effectively to local needs. Because information systems often enable the standardization or flexibility of operations, IS professionals are often left with the responsibility to make this decision. Yet this is a business decision that general and functional managers should not hand over. After all, the executive committee is in the best position to weight the cost/benefits of standardization and flexibility.

4. *How good do our IT services really need to be?* The quality of service provided by an organization's information systems department is measured by the reliability and uptime of the IT infrastructure, data accessibility and flexibility, responsiveness to user needs, and the like. This question forces executives to make conscious decisions about the degree of service the firm needs and that they are willing to pay for.

5. *What security and privacy risks will we accept?* Remember the old adage, "You get what you pay for"? When it comes to computer security and privacy risks, this proverb is more accurate then ever. Security and privacy decisions are about managing, not eliminating, risk (see Chapter 13). Different organizations face different threats and have different degrees of risk aversion. For example, while a hospital cannot afford to skimp on redundancy and uptime of life support systems, a restaurant may not need to worry about (and pay for) more than basic security and backup procedures. The critical point is that security and risk management decisions are not information systems decisions. Rather, they are business decisions that can have a dramatic impact on the future viability of the business and, as such, need the full attention of the executive team.

6. *Whom do we blame if an IT initiative fails?* This question draws attention to the need to identify business sponsors for most information systems projects. Any project that involves users and organizational departments beyond the information systems group should have a clearly identified business sponsor who is responsible for its successful implementation. It is the job of senior executives to allocate resources (e.g., create time for business managers to be involved with relevant information systems projects) and assign responsibility.

Note that these are wide-ranging business decisions, necessitating senior executives' input, but they require technical understanding of the various alternatives, costs, and implications. Thus they need to be made in partnership with the information systems professionals and the IS function. The planning process helps structure this partnership.

THE PURPOSE OF STRATEGIC INFORMATION SYSTEMS PLANNING

The six decisions mentioned above are based on the premise that general and functional managers need to be involved in the decision making that affects the investment in, and use of, information systems and information technology resources. In order to be an asset on the planning team, you must understand the planning process, its purpose, and the type of decisions to be made as it unfolds.

As we have established in this book, information systems are complex organizational systems that exist at the intersection of business and technology. For this reason, setting direction for their use and management requires a blend of skills, technical and organizational, that are rarely housed in one organizational function or department. The planning process must occur as a partnership among those with technical skills, the information systems group, and general and functional managers.

The planning process has a number of objectives, chief among them that of clarifying how the firm plans to use and manage information systems resources to fulfill its strategic objectives. Note that we used the term *planning process,* not *planning document.* As most executives will attest, the *process of planning* is as important as, if not more important than, the final documents that represent its output. The planning process requires discussion, clarification, negotiation, and the achievement of a mutual understanding. While these documents can serve to bring new hires, consultants, and vendors up to speed on what the company is looking to achieve with its adoption and use of IS resources, the time spent discussing and writing the documents is what cements mutual understanding of the individuals involved. The planning process offers a number of advantages, discussed next.

Plans Enable Communication

Perhaps the most important outcome of the information systems planning process is to enable and support intraorganizational communication. As the planning team members, composed of IS professionals as well as general and functional managers, assess current IS resources and set guidelines for their future use and management, a shared mental image of the role of each member of the team emerges. This communication is critical since individuals typically have different expectations, speak different languages, and often have different objectives and priorities.

Consultants are sometimes brought into the planning team because they bring significant experience and knowledge of the planning process and they can serve as catalysts for discussion and facilitators of the communication process. Yet their firm-specific knowledge is limited, and it will be easy for the organization to dismiss a plan that is formulated by a consulting firm. Thus, it is critical that consultants serve as members of the planning team rather than as delegates of the firm.

Plans Enable Unity of Purpose

Business firms achieve their best results when a clear strategy and clear goals have been identified and lead to concerted efforts from the organizational units and employees. The information systems plan serves as a contract of sort, where the objectives of information systems deployment are specified and clear responsibilities are agreed on. When this happens, coordinating action and achieving unity of purpose become simpler.

Plans Simplify Decision Making over Time

When a firm has not developed an IS plan, it has failed to create a context for decision making. Under these circumstances (all too common, unfortunately), the firm will find itself selecting projects to fund as part of the yearly budgeting process, with little sense of overall direction and purpose. As a consequence, projects will be funded year-to-year in a haphazard fashion, resulting in an uncoordinated infrastructure and redundancy of systems and efforts and thus leading to a heightened risk of missing opportunities and wasting resources.

■ THE STRATEGIC INFORMATION SYSTEMS PLANNING PROCESS

While strategic information systems planning can be a lengthy and complex process, particularly for large organizations, its basic structure is fairly straightforward. It consists of gathering information about the current availability and performance of IS resources. It also involves a series of decisions, increasingly specific, designed to provide a roadmap for decision making about information systems. The strategic IS planning process typically evolves in five phases:

1. *Strategic business planning:* A strategic business plan consists of an organization's mission and future direction, performance targets, and strategy. Strategic plans are a prerequisite to information systems planning. Note, however, that strategic planning is itself informed by available IT and current IS trends. As discussed in Chapter 2, IT is a critical enabler for modern firms, often determining the strategic opportunities available to them.
2. *Information systems assessment:* An information systems assessment consists of the process of taking stock of the firm's current IS resources and evaluating how well they are fulfilling the needs of the organization.
3. *Information systems vision:* An information systems vision consists of a concise statement that captures what the planning team believes should be the role of IS resources in the firm. It provides an articulation of the ideal state the firm should strive for in its use and management of its resources.
4. *Information systems guidelines:* Information systems guidelines represent a set of statements, or maxims, specifying how the firm should use its technical and organizational IS resources.
5. *Strategic initiatives:* Strategic initiatives are long-term (three- to five-year) proposals that identify new systems and new projects or new directions for the IS organization.

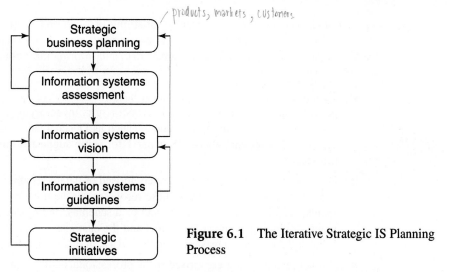

products, markets, customers.

Figure 6.1   The Iterative Strategic IS Planning Process

Note that while we are presenting the strategic planning process in a sequential manner, this is a simplification of reality and the process is really an iterative one (see Figure 6.1). In other words, downstream analyses may lead to a reevaluation and change in decisions made earlier. We now discuss each step in greater depth.

Know Who You Are: Strategic Business Planning

Information systems are enablers of business strategy and operations. They allow a firm to achieve its stated goals while also creating opportunity for new strategic directions and initiatives that new technologies make possible. Thus, effective information systems planning can only occur in concert with business planning. In other words, unless the planning team has developed a clear understanding of the firm and what makes it successful and a deep understanding of the business strategy and its future goals and objectives, planning for the use and management of information systems resources is an exercise in futility.

Imagine trying to decide what car you should rent for your upcoming vacation before you have decided where you will go, with how many friends, and at what time of the year. A sporty two-seater may do wonders for you and your better half on a weekend trip to Miami, but it won't help much if you and your four ice fishing buddies planned a two-week outing roughing it in upstate New York.

Know Where You Start: Information Systems Assessment

Once the planning team has a clear grasp on the strategic direction the firm intends to pursue, more research is needed. The team needs to perform an information systems resource assessment that includes taking an inventory of the IS resources the firm is currently using and critically evaluating them in terms of how well they are meeting the business needs of the organization. The planning team should assess the firm's current use of, and satisfaction with, these resources. The objective is to understand what resources are available and whether they are currently satisfying organizational objectives. Note that we refer here to an information systems assessment, not an information technology assessment, as including technical resources, data and information resources, and human resources.

- Technical resources are comprised of hardware, software, and networking components that make up the firm's IT infrastructure. Inventorying of these resources can be done by examining documents, such as IT schematics and speaking with selected IS professionals (see Sidebar 1 for some suggested questions to ask at this stage).

- Data and information resources are comprised of databases and other information repositories. An assessment of these resources can be done by examining documents, such as database structure and data schemas, and by speaking with informants, including technical personnel and the customers of the data resource (see Sidebar 2 for some suggested questions to ask at this stage).

- Human resources are comprised of IS professionals—those individuals who are responsible for creating and managing the IT resources—and the user community—including general and functional managers as well as end users. An assessment of these resources requires an examination of the individuals and their skills, attitudes, and preconceptions, as well as an examination of reporting structures and incentive systems. This can be done by examining documents, such as the firm's organization chart, and speaking with informants from the various hierarchical level of the IS function and the business (see Sidebar 3 for some suggested questions to ask at this stage).

SIDEBAR 1

Technical Resources

- What hardware comprises the organization's IT infrastructure?
- What platforms are currently in use?
- What is the current application portfolio?
- Are there any redundant systems?
- What networking infrastructure is currently in place?
- Does the IS organization provide any shared services to the business?
- Is the IT infrastructure centralized or decentralized?
- What systems are on site, what systems are off site?

- Are any components of the IT infrastructure outsourced?
- How do the existing applications relate to one another as a system?
- What is the age of the current application portfolio?
- How applications are normally obtained (in-house development, acquisition)?
- Who owns the IT infrastructure?
- What rules are followed to determine ownership and responsibilities?

SIDEBAR 2

Data and Information Resources

- What data are currently collected?
- Where and how are the data collected?
- Where are the data stored? In what format?
- Are data shared across applications? How?
- What applications access the data?
- Who owns the data (e.g., the IS organizations, local departments)?

- Who is in charge of maintaining the accuracy of the data?
- Who is in charge of ensuring the security and backup of the data?
- What rules are followed to determine data ownership and responsibilities?

SIDEBAR 3

Human Resource

- How many full-time IS professionals are currently employed by the organization?
- How is the IS function organized?
- Who does the head of the IS organization report to?
- In what role has the IS organization been explicitly assigned in its mission statement?
- What is the current skill set of the in-house IS professionals?
- What is the IS sophistication of the end users and user-managers?
- What are the industry performance benchmarks?

- How does the organization compare against industry benchmarks?
- Who are the leading competitors?
- What performance levels have leading competitors attained?
- What are the user-managers' opinions of the current IT infrastructure and application portfolio (e.g., alignment with the business objectives, accurate and comprehensive information)?
- What are the users' perceptions of the current IT infrastructure and applications (e.g., usability, reliability, information accuracy)?

During the assessment stage, the planning team reviews company documents and public literature and interviews key informants. The documents reviewed and individuals interviewed depend on the size and structure of the organization. Note that obtaining the needed information requires skilled questioning. Often it is not enough to ask informants a direct question (e.g., how is the IS function performing); they may not be willing to share the information or, more likely, they may be unable to answer. But skilled questioning and probing from a number of angles usually will surface the needed information (e.g., what IS services do you need that are lacking today).

The output of the assessment stage should be a snapshot, using both text and graphics, of the current "state of IS resources" in the organization. A well-developed assessment document should clearly convey to the reader what IS resources are currently available and how well they are serving the needs of the organization. It should also inherently suggest potential areas of concern.

Know Where You Want to Go: Information Systems Vision

With a clear understanding of the organization's business strategy, an inventory of current resources available, and a solid assessment of their current performance, the planning team begins its real work—looking forward.

The first step at this point is to clearly spell out the role that information systems should play in the organization. In some organizations information systems operations and technology resources are critical to the firm's survival, let alone its success. For other firms, information systems operations are not so critical to the survival and continued success of the organization.

Consider the case of eBay, Inc. In June 1999, a 22-hour outage at eBay's popular auction Web site cost the firm between $3 and $5 million in revenue and a 26 percent drop in stock price, resulting in a $4 billion decline in capitalization. Flawless IT operations at eBay are a must, at least according to the stock market!

Contrast the above case with that of Morton's Restaurant Group, Inc., the world's largest owner and operator of company-owned upscale steakhouse restaurants, running seventy-seven upscale steakhouses in the North American, Singapore, and Hong Kong markets. The company has several systems, ranging from unit-level point of sale to corporate procurement and financials systems. Disruptions to the performance of these applications, even if protracted, do not endanger the viability of the organization. Imagine, for example, a 22-hour outage of the network or of the point of sale systems. Morton units can revert to a manual system and continue with operations. While this is certainly not a scenario that Morton's executives would like to experience, the impacts are much less severe than those that eBay experienced.

With more and more organizations relying on computer based information systems, protracted disruptions to the firm's IT infrastructure are going to create problems. However, the impact of these disruptions can vary dramatically from organization to organization.

Aside from the impact on day-to-day operations, information systems play a more strategic role in some firms and a tactical one in others. Some organizations' success in the marketplace depends heavily on their ability to introduce IT innovations and manage information systems strategically. Google and Apple, Inc. come easily to mind, as do United Parcel Service of America (UPS) and Federal Express.

For these firms, information systems must play a strategic role, and the organization must constantly look for IS solutions that enable it to be more competitive. For others, typically those organizations in more mature and less IT-intensive industries, being cutting edge is less important. In fact, in some firms information systems are nothing more than a "necessary evil"—a resource the firm needs to have and use, but not one that will give the firm a leg up on the competition.

Information Systems Vision Whether information systems are crucial to the firm's success, or merely useful, whether they are strategic or a necessary evil, it is important that the planning team is able to clearly articulate what the role of IS *should be* for the firm. We refer to this statement as the information systems vision (see Sidebar 4).

Information Systems Vision of The Large Cruise Line

The IS function will assume more of a leadership role within the corporation. While the IS function will continue to service the organization by providing a solid IT infrastructure, supporting and maintaining existing systems, the IS function will no longer be considered exclusively a support arm to the rest of the organization.

In order to maintain our leadership position, we must use information to

■ Set the customer service standard in the industry for consumers and business partners by using customized

and personalized information, beginning with the first contact and continuing throughout the relationship.

■ Enable the company to be the employer of choice in our industry by empowering a workforce with accurate, timely information and thus to accelerate change and innovative decision making.

■ Assume a leadership role as innovators in the use of the Internet as an enabling technology that drives business growth, internal and external communications, operating efficiencies, and new sources of revenue.

The IS vision is a concise statement that captures what the planning team believes should be the role of information systems resources in the firm. It provides an articulation of the ideal state the firm should strive for in its use and management of IS resources.

The information systems vision must be aligned with and reflect the firm's business strategy and, as a consequence, will be unique and highly specific to your firm. While the industry your company competes in, the product or service you offer, and the competitive environment will have some influence on the role that information systems should play in your organization, the position of the IS function should depend on a conscious decision by senior management and the planning team. Thus, companies that compete in the same industry, even head-to-head competitors, will have different information visions as reflective of their strategic posture.

For example, while the Ritz-Carlton and the W Hotels compete in the luxury segment of the lodging industry, the former positions itself as a firm that offers traditional luxury while the latter has a much more edgy image catering to a younger and more tech-savvy customer base. We can expect the two firms to have developed very different IS visions.

Deciding what the role of information systems in your organization should be and developing a concise IS vision that encapsulates it is a difficult task. Two analytical tools that have been developed to help managers involved in this process are the critical success factors (CSF) methodology[7] and the strategic impact grid.[8]

Critical Success Factors   A technique that has been used over the years to help focus managers' attention to the firm's information needs is the critical success factors (CSF) methodology. Critical success factors are defined as the limited number of areas, typically three to six, that executives must effectively manage to ensure that the firm will survive and thrive. CSFs represent those fundamental things that "must go right" for the business to flourish. At the risk

---

[6] Sidebars 4 to 7 all refer to the same company, a large cruise line operator with multinational operations. The examples are adapted from the actual firm's 2000 information systems planning document. We refer to this company as The Large Cruise Line.

[7] Rockart J., "Chief Executives Define their Own Data Needs," *Harvard Business Review,* 57 (March–April 1979), pp. 81–93.

[8] Nolan, Richard, and McFarlan, F. Warren (2005) "Information Technology and the Board of Directors," *Harvard Business Review,* 83, no. 10 (October), 96–106.

of oversimplify things, the CSF methodology has the merit of focusing attention on fundamental issues and of helping to ensure that the planning team is able to prioritize. Note that the CSF methodology asks that managers focus not on information systems, but on business objectives. That is, the CSF methodology asks that you identify what the firm must do right (not what the IS department must do right) to ensure the ongoing success of the organization. With the CSFs identified it becomes easier to think about the role of IS in achieving them.

Let's return to the eBay example. Given that eBay's revenue stream is highly dependent on its Web site being operational and given the significant disruptions (and stock market reaction) that follows protracted downtime, one of eBay's CSFs will likely be "to ensure the optimal performance (i.e., reliability and speed) of online store operations." Other CSFs we could imagine for eBay are as follows:

- Continue to grow the size of the marketplace in terms of buyers and seller.

- Increase online buyer and seller confidence and trust in the marketplace by ensuring the security of transactions, reliable payments, and high levels of customer service.

The Strategic Impact Grid Another tool that helps in defining the role of information systems in a specific company is the strategic impact grid. The main advantage offered by the strategic impact grid is its ability to enable simultaneous evaluation of the firm's current and future information systems needs. This is achieved by plotting the firm on the following two dimensions: the firm's current need for reliable information systems and the firm's future need for new information system functionalities.

Current Need for Reliable Information Systems This dimension focuses on current day-to-day operations and the functionalities of the existing systems. Not all organizations, even fierce head-to-head competitors, need the same information systems and the same degree of reliability of their technology infrastructure. The planning team should achieve some consensus about where the firm falls on this dimension by determining whether

- There is the risk of a tangible loss of business if one or more systems fail for a minute or more.

- There are serious negative consequences associated with even small degrading response time of one or more systems.

- Most core business activities are online and require real-time or near-real-time information processing.

- Even repeated service interruptions of up to twelve hours, while troublesome, cause no serious consequences for the viability of the business.

- The company can quickly revert to manual operations for the majority of transaction types when systems failure occurs. While unwelcome, such disruptions do not endanger the business as a viable concern.

Future Needs for New Information System Functionalities This dimension is forward looking and is concerned with the strategic role that new IT capabilities play for the organization. While the industry the firm competes in has some bearing on this question, different organizations pursuing different strategies will fall on different locations of the spectrum. The planning team should achieve some consensus about where the firm falls on this dimension by determining whether

■ New systems and new functionalities of existing systems promise major process and service improvements.

■ New systems or new functionalities of existing systems promise major cost reductions and efficiency improvements.

■ New systems or new functionalities of existing systems promise to close major gaps in service, cost, or process performance with competitors.

■ Systems work is mostly maintenance of the current state of the art and functionalities. The firm foresees no major new systems that are crucial to business success within the current planning horizon.

■ New systems promise little strategic differentiation and customers do not expect any major new functionalities or services.

At the intersection of these two dimensions we find four possible roles that information systems can play in the organization (see Figure 6.2). A common misconception is to use the strategic impact grid to map the firm's current and future position (i.e., where the firm is today and where it should be). The strategic impact grid simultaneously captures current operations and future impact. Therefore, if used correctly, it will show where the planning team thinks the firm falls and, as a consequence, what the use of information systems resources should be going forward.

Support Quadrant   The organization falls in the support quadrant when information systems are not mission critical for current operations and this state of affairs is not likely to change in the foreseeable future. A mining company may be an example of a firm that falls in this quadrant, as is the Morton's Restaurant Group, Inc. discussed above.

When a firm finds itself in the support quadrant, it should view information systems as a tool to support and enable operations, but one that offers little potential to significantly harm or benefit the organization. As a consequence, firms in this quadrant are typically cost conscious and conservative in their IS investments decision making, with the head of the IS function typically reporting to the chief financial officer.

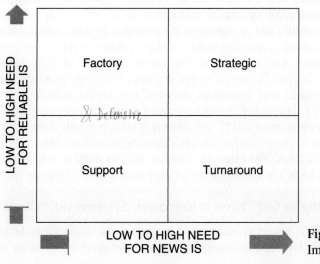

Figure 6.2   The Strategic Impact Grid

Factory Quadrant   The organization falls in the factory quadrant when it currently has a technology infrastructure that enables the business to operate with the needed degree of efficiency and effectiveness. Disruptions to this infrastructure, even small ones, can endanger the firm's well-being and future viability. Yet within the planning horizon under consideration, the firm appears to be in a stable state and the planning team foresees a limited potential for new systems and functionalities to make a substantial contribution. Like a factory working steadily, if the current state of information systems affairs is maintained, the firm will be in good shape. NASDAQ, the company that runs the largest U.S. electronic stock market, is an example of a firm that must ensure flawless operation of its current systems. Airlines and large chemical plant operators represent other examples.

When a firm finds itself in the factory quadrant, it must closely monitor its current systems and must be willing to fund their maintenance and upgrade. Yet because of the minor future potential for impact of new systems, the organization may take a conservative stance toward future investments.

Turnaround Quadrant   The organization falls in the turnaround quadrant when information systems are not considered mission critical for current operations. Yet unlike firms in the support quadrant, the planning team believes that the current state of affairs is due for a change in the near future and new information systems or new functionalities of existing systems will be critical for the business's future viability and continued (or expected) success. As the term *turnaround* suggests, the firm is (or should be) readying to change its information systems posture. Consider, for example, Harrah's Entertainment, the Las Vegas–based casino operator, in the late 1990s. A firm historically in the support quadrant, Harrah's foresaw the opportunities afforded by emerging business intelligence techniques and spent over $100 million to secure a leadership position in guest data analysis.

When a firm finds itself in the turnaround quadrant, it typically needs to engage in some reorganization (for example, by reevaluating its organizational structure and creating a CIO position with a seat on the executive team). The firm will also need to take an aggressive stance with respect to IT investments and the acquisition of the necessary skills.

Strategic Quadrant   The organization falls in the strategic quadrant when information systems are both critical to the firm's current operations and the planning team foresees new information systems or new functionalities of existing systems to be critical for the future viability and prosperity of the business. In other words, outstanding IS operations and a relentless attention to information systems innovation are a must for companies in this quadrant. Amazon.com and eBay are two examples of organizations whose survival depends on flawless IS operations and that must constantly be on the lookout for new systems. Large banks find themselves perennially on this list as well.

When a firm is in the strategic quadrant, it must be extremely proactive with respect to information systems and IT investments. This is typically done by having CIOs with a strong voice on the executive team. For these organizations, information systems are part of the firm's DNA. For example, Amazon defines itself as a technology company that happens to be in the retail business, rather than a retail company that uses technology.

Know How You Are Going to Get There: Information Systems Guidelines

While the information systems vision articulates the destination, the ideal state the firm should strive for when it comes to using and managing information systems resources, it provides little guidance as to how the firm should deploy its resources to achieve this goal. Thus, the next stage in the information systems planning process consists of identifying a parsimonious set of guidelines that, if followed, will enable the firm to achieve its information vision. This set of guidelines, sometimes referred to as the information systems architecture, is prescriptive in nature—identifying the guiding principles that the firm will follow when using and managing information systems resources.

Why Develop Information Systems Guidelines?   The building of a custom home offers a good metaphor for understanding the role of information systems guidelines. While you have a vision for what you'd like your dream home to be like—including location, style, size, number and types of rooms—you probably know very little about construction codes, materials, and the like. Thus, you engage an architect to whom you describe your vision and rely on him or her to formalize it in the form of blueprints and schematics.

When the architect delivers the drawings and the floor plans, you will be able to see if he or she captured your vision and to suggest any changes. A good architect will also make suggestions about what changes will make the house better, reduce cost, speed up construction, and so on. Once you sign off on the blueprints, they become binding—a sort of contract. Armed with them you, or your architect on your behalf, will engage a builder who will actually create the house.

The blueprints enable the contractor to develop the house according to your vision, without having to interact much with you—or even knowing what your overall vision was. Contractors will know where they should locate the rooms, their size, and where to install plumbing, windows, door frames, and electrical outlets. They will also know what materials they should use. If you change your mind during construction and request changes, you will be responsible for their cost. If the builder makes a mistake and forgets to create a window opening in the master bedroom, he or she will be responsible for the cost of the modifications. The blueprint serves as the guideline for what should happen and for dispute resolution.

The process and purpose of creating information systems guidelines are very similar to those described above in the context of custom home building. The firm executives have a vision for what they want the business to achieve and how they want it to operate. Working in partnership with information systems professionals, as part of the planning team, they will refine their vision and establish a blueprint that will enable communication, establish responsibility, and guide future decision making.

Communication   The primary objective of the information systems guidelines is to simplify tactical and operational decision making and to ensure that future decisions are aligned with the information systems vision. By establishing a coherent set of rules stemming from the information systems vision, these guidelines ensure that future information systems and technology decisions are made in accord with the overall objectives of information systems use and management in the firm, rather than haphazardly and in an uncoordinated manner.

Imagine, for example, an organization that opted for a strictly supporting role of information systems. Such company will likely strive to buy low-cost IT products (e.g., buying refurbished or older hardware) and to be conservative when it comes to IT innovation (e.g., waiting to buy applications when they have become a competitive necessity).

Conversely, an organization in the strategic quadrant of the strategic impact grid that has identified flawless personalization of the customer experience as a critical success factor may decide to move to a centralized architecture with centralized servers that gather all customer data in one location for easy retrieval and analysis.

Identify Responsibilities   The information systems guidelines also set expectations for behavior, serving a similar binding purpose as policy rules or the custom home building blueprints and schematics described above. Decisions that are made in accord with the information systems guidelines are in line with expectations and will typically be deemed appropriate. Decisions that are made outside of the guidelines are treated as exceptions and will typically need substantial justification. If the firm finds itself regularly making exceptions, it will need to reevaluate the quality and accuracy of the information systems guidelines.

Long-Range Decision Support   Because the firm will not engage in the IS planning process every year, the information systems guidelines must be general enough to provide direction over a number of years. Yet it is crucial that they be actionable. Thus, they need to be specific enough to clearly spell out what the firm should do, and, as a consequence, what it should not do, when it comes to the deployment of information systems resources.

Imagine that you just got an internship with The Large Cruise Line (discussed previously). You are eager to make a contribution and, after reading the company's information systems vision (see Sidebar 4), you remember your long-lost cousin Vinnie, who just launched a startup. The brochure of his flagship product reads, "Our personalization software solution enables your company to track customer preferences and offer outstanding service." The light bulb goes off, and you run to your CIO and suggest, "We should buy and implement this software; it is perfectly aligned with our vision!" She ponders your suggestions for all of five seconds and then denies your request, adding, "I am glad you read the planning document, but you seem to have stopped reading too early." The second technical guideline (see Sidebar 5) rules out relationships with new and not established vendors for core systems like those housing customer data.

Technical and Organizational Guidelines   Information systems guidelines address every aspect of information systems decision making, both technical and organizational. While the technical guidelines and organizational guidelines are deeply intertwined, it helps to separate them out during the planning process and in the planning documents.

Technical Information Systems Guidelines   The information systems guidelines that focus on the technical components of the firm's information systems must address future decisions pertaining to the hardware and software infrastructure, networking services, and the storage and protection of organizational data and information (see Sidebar 5 for an example).

Technical guidelines will not typically specify vendor to be used or particular platforms or applications. Instead they are broad enunciations of direction for the technical components of the infrastructure. As the example in Sidebar 5 shows, the statements produced by the planning team of the cruise line are aligned with the firm's information systems vision (see Sidebar 4) and are both general, thus making them relevant and useful for years to come, and precise, thus specifying what decisions are legitimate and what decisions should not be made.

SIDEBAR 5

Technical Information Systems Guidelines of The Large Cruise Line

1. The movement toward standardization will evolve over time, and we will remain flexible in our approach. However, our major objective is to achieve centralized and standardized products that are more easily managed and controlled, especially across multiple continents with limited staff to maintain them.

2. We will follow the trends of dominant vendors and be guided by these leaders rather than the niche market players for both hardware and software core systems.

3. We will buy software packages (rather than develop custom code) that provide generic solutions for business functions that are not part of our core competency and not part of what constitutes our competitive advantage.

4. We will not obtain monolithic packages that drive significant duplicate code and data.

5. We will store data centrally for all mission-critical applications.

6. Mission-critical systems will have complete fall-back solutions to redundant systems to minimize the impact of any disaster.

Organizational Information Systems Guidelines   The information systems guidelines that focus on the organizational components of the firm's information systems must address those decisions that pertain to human resources, the organization of the information systems function, reporting and hierarchical structures, and the like (see Sidebar 6 for an example).

These statements focus on IT governance issues (e.g., the relationship between the IS function and the other departments in the organization, who is responsible for proposing and sponsoring application development, how maintenance and new purchases should be

---

SIDEBAR 6

Organizational Information Systems Guidelines of The Large Cruise Line

- We will focus our expenditures on projects of strategic value and importance over short-term fixes that deviate from our overall strategy.

- Outsourcing will be considered for IS operations and legacy applications where possible and feasible.

- Business-supported projects will be governed by the business case and will be evaluated by the full project costs and values in terms of people, process, and technology.

- Business-supported projects will require the participation of the business throughout the engagement.

- While the IS function will be developing systems, at all times our mindset will be that of a business professional first and will always consider the business opportunity and or impact of systems that we develop or purchase.

- The IS function will create a mixed environment of both seasoned professionals and new, eager, recent graduates. The persona of [company name]'s IS function will be that of a levelheaded, technologically excited individual.

- We will strive to avoid silos of data and silos of skill sets within our company and thus enable our staff to grow and to minimize disruption when specialized staff are moved to other assignments and/or leave the company.

evaluated), on outsourcing and vendors relationships, on human resource decisions (e.g., what type of individuals the IS function is looking to hire, the type of IS skills that the firm deems necessary), and the like.

Know How Well Equipped You Are to Get There: Information Systems SWOT

Having defined the information systems vision and the broad maxims to achieve it—the information systems guidelines—the planning team must now review how well equipped the firm is to achieve the vision in accord with the stated guidelines. This step is the last piece of analysis before the team develops an action plan and proposes tangible initiatives. It consists of a Strengths, Weaknesses, Opportunities, and Threats (SWOT) analysis focused on the firm's current information systems resources and capabilities.

The iterative nature of the planning process becomes clear at this stage. As the planning team members evaluate how well positioned the firm is to attain the information systems vision, they may realize that they are attempting to do too much and the vision, as stated, is not achievable given the current set of strengths and weakens and the landscape of opportunities and threats. In this case, the information vision should be revised to be more realistic. Failing to do so will create an unattainable, not actionable, vision that will make people cynical and defeat the purpose of the planning process.

SIDEBAR 7

Information Systems SWOT at The Large Cruise Line
Strengths:

- The IS staff is competent in the implementation and maintenance of new technology.

- User-managers, on average, understand information systems concepts and have a good relationship with the IS function.

Weaknesses:

- There are currently four nonintegrated systems housing customer data.

- The current IT infrastructure supports a silo, function-centric approach and does not support flexible timely response to customer needs.

Opportunities:

- New technology, such as the XML standard and data warehousing applications, is now robust enough to warrant migration to integrated data repositories.

- No competitor is currently offering IS-enabled integrated customer solutions.

Threats:

- [Competitor's name] is moving swiftly to establish itself as the customer service leader in our industry through the deployment of integrated, channel-independent customer service systems.

- Our preferred suppliers have developed the capability for electronic data communication, but we are currently unable to connect to their systems. This inability to communicate hampers our efficiency and may drive suppliers to the competition.

As shown in the example (see Sidebar 7), this stage of the analysis is designed to surface the internal factors that can be exploited to achieve the vision, as well as highlight the internal weaknesses that must be carefully managed. It also enables an externally focused analysis that seeks to uncover new technologies and trends that generate opportunities for the firm, as well as threats that may undermine the ability of the firm to achieve its information systems vision.

In a well-developed plan, this section of the analysis is consistent with the previous ones and forms the basis for the next section. In other words, having read the SWOT analysis, and given the proposed vision and the guidelines, it should become clear what the firm needs to do during the current planning cycle.

From Planning to Action: Proposed Strategic Initiatives

After so much discussion and analysis, it is time to move to action. The last component of the strategic information systems plan is the identification of strategic initiatives. Strategic initiatives are long-term (three- to five-year) proposals that identify new systems and new projects (e.g., supply chain management) or new directions for the IS organization (e.g., create a CIO position reporting directly to the CEO). These initiatives need not be precisely articulated, but they need to identify a set of future avenues for exploitation of the IS resources. They also must be tightly aligned with the information vision and the proposed role of IS in the organization. For example, it would not be appropriate for the planning team to propose a change to the organizational structure, seeking to establish a new CIO position who reports to the CEO, after having decided that information systems play a support role in the organization and having crafted a defensive information system vision.

A number of frameworks and techniques have been developed to support the identification and analysis of strategic initiatives, and they will be discussed in the remaining chapters of Part III.

■ SUMMARY

This chapter provides the basis for the ensuing chapters and describes the strategic information systems planning process. Specifically, in this chapter we discussed the goals of the strategic information system planning process and its component, with a focus on the role played by general and functional managers.

■ Strategic information systems planning is the process by which the firm, by way of the planning team, develops a shared understanding of the role of information systems resources use in the organization.

■ General and functional managers play a crucial role on the planning team, despite the fact that they typically lack technical knowledge. Their role is to help identify the firm's strategy, and, in light of the business strategy, how information systems resources should be used to achieve it.

■ General and functional managers should also take the lead in answering questions such as how much money should be spent on IT, to what business processes these funds should be directed, what IT capabilities should pervade the organization, what levels of IT service should be achieved, what degree of IT risk will the firm accept, and who is responsible for IT initiatives.

■ As critical members of the planning team, general and functional managers will help in crafting the firm's information systems vision and guidelines. The information systems vision provides an articulation of the ideal state of information systems resource use, while the guidelines offer a context for decision making.

■ With the basic planning mechanisms in place, the firm moves to action and identifies strategic initiatives to be implemented to achieve the stated information systems vision. These strategic initiatives often stem from what the organization believes are opportunities available and weaknesses that must be managed.

STUDY QUESTIONS

1. Why should general and functional managers be involved in information systems planning decisions despite their lack of technical expertise?

2. Jeanne Ross and Peter Weill, of MIT's Center for Information Systems Research (CISR), suggest that senior managers be involved in six information systems management decisions. What are these decisions? What is the guiding principle behind this need for senior executives' involvement?

3. What is the purpose of strategic information systems planning? Who needs to be involved in this process? Why?

4. What are the key components of the strategic information systems planning process? Can you define and describe each one?

5. What purpose do the critical success factors methodology and the strategic impact grid play in the planning process? Can you provide examples of firms in each of the four quadrants of the strategic impact grid?

6. What is the purpose of the information systems vision? Can you provide an example?

7. What is the purpose of the information systems guidelines? Given the information systems vision you have proposed in response to Question 6, can you provide an example of guidelines that are aligned with it?

FURTHER READINGS

1. Nolan, Richard, and McFarlan, F. Warren. (2005). "Information Technology and the Board of Directors." *Harvard Business Review*, 83, no. 10 (October), 96–106.
2. Ross, J. W., and Weill, P. (2002). "Six IT Decisions Your IT People Shouldn't Make." *Harvard Business Review*, November, 84–92.
3. Yolande E. Chan. (2002). "Why Haven't We Mastered Alignment? The Importance of the Informal Organization Structure." *MIS Quarterly Executive*, 1(2) pp. 97–113.

GLOSSARY

■ **Information systems assessment:** The process of taking stock of the firm's current information systems resources and evaluating how well they are fulfilling the needs of the organization.

■ **Information systems guidelines:** A set of statements, or maxims, specifying how the firm should use its technical and organizational information systems resources.

■ **Information systems vision:** A concise statement that captures what the planning team believes should be the role of information systems resources in the firm. It provides an articulation of the ideal state the firm should strive for, in its use and management of information systems resources.

■ **Planning team:** The set of individuals, company employees and hired consultants, who work together to develop the firm's strategic information systems plan.

■ **Strategic alignment:** The degree of fit between the priorities and activities of the IS function and those of general and functional managers involved in the day-to-day operations of the business.

■ **Strategic information systems planning process:** The process by which the planning team develops the planning documents.

■ **Strategic initiative:** A long-term (three- to five-year) proposal that identifies new systems and new projects, or new directions for the IS organization.

■ **Strategic plan:** An organization's mission and future direction, performance targets, and strategy. Strategic plans are a prerequisite to information systems planning.

CASE STUDY: OUTRIGGER HOTELS AND RESORTS[9]

I am involved with every decision that senior management takes. They look to me for an IS slant to it—whether an IT solution can capitalize on opportunities or eliminate threats. They also expect my team to independently develop an IS strategy that will further the business.

—Joe Durocher, SVP & CIO

Every manager must have an IT strategy. You can't delegate to technologists and only worry about your allocated cost or what training your employees need. You must understand how to be master of your own destiny and make IT work best for you. Too many managers still don't get that.

—Rob Solomon, SVP Sales & Marketing

OUTRIGGER HISTORY

On Black Friday, September 13, 1929, Roy C. Kelley arrived in Hawaii with his wife Estelle. An architect by training, Mr. Kelley joined the firm of C.W. Dickey and was responsible for designing many of Honolulu's landmark buildings, including the main building of the old Halekulani Hotel and the Waikiki Theater on Kalakaua Avenue.

Nine years later Kelley set out on his own and opened his architecture firm, building numerous homes, apartment buildings, and hotels on the island of Oahu. In 1963, Kelley took over the land occupied by the old Outrigger Canoe Club and Outrigger Hotels became a reality with the mission of bringing the dream of a vacation in Paradise within the reach of the middle-class traveler. Included in the agreement were leases on three Waikiki lots that later became the Outrigger East, Outrigger West, and Coral Reef hotels. The Outrigger Waikiki Hotel was built on the site of the old canoe club, arguably the prime spot on Waikiki beach, in 1967. Throughout the next two decades, Outrigger Hotels Hawaii, as the company was named, continued its expansion in Waikiki. When in the seventies the zoning authority put a cap on new construction in Waikiki, Outrigger began to expand through acquisition rather than construction, ultimately becoming the largest chain in the State of Hawaii with over 7,000 rooms and a total of 15 properties concentrated in Waikiki (see Exhibit 1). Thanks to its clustered configuration, Outrigger Hotels Hawaii was able to maintain a centralized management structure fitting Mr. Kelley's 'management by walking around' style.

Exhibit 1   Properties Managed by Outriggers Hotels and Resorts (Hawaii)

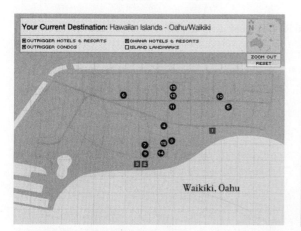

Figure 6.3   Properties Managed by Outriggers Hotels and Resorts (International)

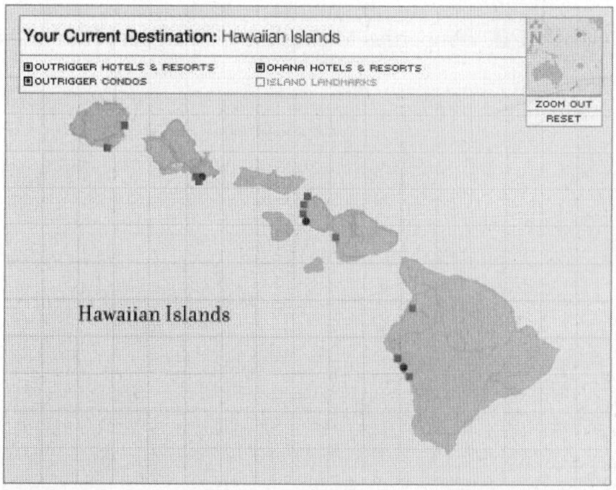

Figure 6.4   Properties Managed by Outriggers Hotels and Resorts (International)

---

[9] This case was originally published as Piccoli, G. (2005), "Outrigger Hotels and Resorts: A Case Study," *Communications of the AIS* (Vol. 15, Article 5), pp. 102–118.

continued

In 1989 Outrigger Hotels Hawaii, now under the leadership of Roy Kelley's son Dr. Richard Kelley, took over management of The Royal Waikoloan Hotel on the Big Island of Hawaii. When hurricane Iniki, heading for Waikiki in 1992, barely missed Honolulu and ravaged the island of Kauai, it provided further impetus for Outrigger's geographical diversification strategy to and beyond neighboring islands. The firm, now expanding into management agreements with third party owners, added properties on Maui and Kauai and ultimately grew to a total of 26 locations in the Hawaiian Islands (see Exhibit 1). In 1996 the firm made its first international foray, opening the Outrigger Marshall Island Resort on Majuro Atoll in the Republic of the Marshall Islands. Through partnerships, joint ventures, acquisitions, and new developments the firm continued to grow internationally, adding properties in Guam, Fiji, Tahiti, Australia, and New Zealand (see Exhibit 2).

While growing geographically, Outrigger Hotels Hawaii also began to diversify its product portfolio with the addition of condominium resorts beginning in 1990. Because of its geographical and product diversification, in 1995 Outrigger Hotels Hawaii changed its name to Outrigger Hotels and Resorts, and in 1999 re-branded fifteen of its hotels in Waikiki to launch a new hotel brand called OHANA Hotels of Hawaii. Reflecting on the decision, President and CEO David Carey commented:

We had an identity crisis because the market moved up, we upgraded the on-beach properties where we had higher demand and bought some nice properties in neighboring islands. But we had huge variation in the portfolio—if you stayed at a budget property vs. a beach front property, you'd be very confused as to what an Outrigger was.

In an effort to bank on the name awareness that the Outrigger brand had developed with consumers, the on-beach properties became upscale full-service hotels under the Outrigger brand. The condos, also typically on-beach upscale locations, maintained the Outrigger brand. Conversely, the OHANA brand was positioned to cater to the budget traveler looking for value on off-beach properties. Perry Sorenson, COO, explained the OHANA value proposition:

OHANA hotels are something between a Holiday Inn and a Hampton Inn. No expectation of restaurants, but expectations that you have a friendly staff, that the room is going to be clean, and you will be taken care of. Not a lot of extras, but good value.

Condominiums represented an increasingly important share of the total portfolio of properties (see Exhibit 3),

Exhibit 2   Properties Managed by Outriggers Hotels and Resorts (Hawaii)

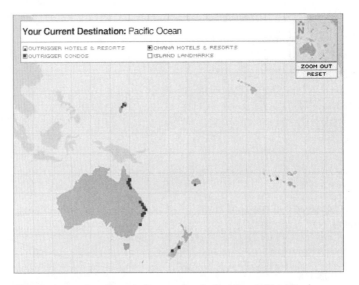

Figure 6.5   Outrigger's Properties in the South Pacific

Exhibit 3 Rooms Breakdown in Each of the Three Products

Outrigger Resorts

Outrigger Waikiki On the Beach	Oahu	525 Rooms
Outrigger Reef On the Beach	Oahu	858 Rooms
Outrigger Guam Resort On Tumon Bay	Guam	600 Rooms
Outrigger Reef Fiji	Fiji	207 Rooms and 47 bures
Te Tiare Beach, An Outrigger Resort	Tahiti	41 Bungalows

OHANA Hotels

OHANA East	Oahu	445 Rooms
OHANA Islander Waikiki	Oahu	283 Rooms
OHANA Reef Lanai	Oahu	110 Rooms
OHANA Waikiki Tower	Oahu	439 Rooms
OHANA Waikiki Village	Oahu	442 Rooms
OHANA Waikiki West	Oahu	663 Rooms
OHANA Reef Towers	Oahu	480 Rooms
OHANA Waikiki Malia	Oahu	327 Rooms
OHANA Waikiki Surf East	Oahu	102 Rooms
OHANA Royal Islander	Oahu	101 Rooms
OHANA Waikiki Surf	Oahu	302 Rooms
OHANA Maile Sky Court	Oahu	596 Rooms
Best Western The Plaza Hotel	Oahu	274 Rooms
Honolulu Airport	Oahu	307 Rooms
OHANA Maui Islander	Maui	360 Rooms
OHANA Keauhou Beach Resort	Hawaii (big Island)	309 Rooms
OHANA Oceanview Guam	Guam	191 Rooms
OHANA Bayview Guam	Guam	148 Rooms

Outrigger Condominiums

Outrigger Waikiki Shore	Oahu	25 Apartments
Outrigger Luana Waikiki	Oahu	N/A
Outrigger Palms at Wailea	Maui	89 Apartments
Outrigger Maui Eldorado	Maui	100 Apartments
Outrigger Royal Kahana	Maui	191 Apartments
Outrigger Napili Shores	Maui	101 Apartments
Outrigger Kiahuna Plantation	Kauai	190 Apartments
Outrigger at Lae nani	Kauai	60 Apartments
Outrigger Kanaloa at Kona	Hawaii (big Island)	83 Apartments
Outrigger Royal Sea Cliff	Hawaii (big Island)	61 Apartments
Outrigger Fairway Villas	Hawaii (big Island)	78 Apartments
Outrigger at the Beacon, Queenstown	New Zealand	14 Rooms, 23 Apartments
Outrigger at Clearwater Resort	New Zealand	N/A
Outrigger on the Beach at Salt Kingscliff	New South Wales	N/A
Outrigger Ettalong Beach Resort	New South Wales	N/A
Outrigger Heritage Port Douglas	Australia	15 Rooms, 42 Apartments
Outrigger in the Village Port Douglas	Australia	8 Rooms, 13 Apartments
Outrigger on the Inlet Port Douglas	Australia	10 Rooms, 21 Apartments
Outrigger Beach Club & Spa Palm Cove	Australia	104 Rooms, 195 Suites

continued

Exhibit 3 *continued*

Cairns Resort by Outrigger	Australia	127 Rooms
Outrigger 1770 at Agnes Water	Australia	N/A
Outrigger Hervey Bay	Australia	27 Rooms, 139 Suites
Outrigger Mooloolaba International Beach Resort	Australia	201 Apartments
Outrigger Sun City Resort	Australia	266 Apartments
Outrigger Coolangatta Beach Resort	Australia	90 Apartments

even though the firm had sort of stumbled upon the opportunity condominiums offered. Condominiums appealed to the independent traveler who would do much research and planning on his own. Condominiums were also very complex, non-standard products that travel agents and wholesalers found hard to sell. As Sorenson explained:

> The addition of condominium properties was a customer driven initiative. We kept receiving inquiries about condominium vacations and had to direct customers to competitors who also ran hotels. That did not make any sense.

As the firm learned over time, condominiums were very different than traditional hotel and resort operations. While management agreements with condominiums varied substantially, unit owners typically had the option to join a pool of units that Outrigger was responsible for marketing and managing. Owners typically received 55% of the gross income the units generated and Outrigger funded its operations with the remainder. Beyond labor costs, the primary expenses included the costs of marketing and selling the properties, front desk and housekeeping operations, and in-unit maintenance. Maintenance of the common areas, defined as anything from the unit's inside wall paint outward, was the responsibility of the AOAO (the owners association) and was funded through annual dues. This state of affairs was simpler in the Australian condominiums—referred to as strata title properties. There, the management company had to buy and control the lobby area, and the contracts were generally 25 years in length and required standardization of revenue splits. This approach created simplicity and clarity that

made it more efficient for the management company to operate.

Because condos were rarely built as business ventures, but rather were designed as primary or vacation homes for the tenants, they offered little office or staging space for management companies to operate in. They also lacked many of the typical hotel services and departments such as food and beverage, room service, laundry, and daily maid service. Working with a relatively unsophisticated and widespread ownership base, with some condominiums having almost one owner (i.e., one contract) per unit, presented significant challenges. Jim Hill, Regional Director–Maui, summarized the challenge:

> The thing that is hardest to do in condos is to change anything. You'll sit in a board meeting with the association and they'll say no, no, no, when the next property over offers a more appealing layout and better amenities. But that same person will ask you in another meeting why isn't the revenue higher?

These difficulties notwithstanding, Outrigger found the condo business appealing when it made its first foray into it in the early 1990s, because it provided a means for expansion through management contracts without the need to acquire expensive properties. Condo products varied widely, ranging from studios to two bedroom apartments, and did not have all the services typically associated with a hotel, like room service, on-property restaurants, and retail shops.

Outrigger had grown to a sizable firm, encompassing about 3,600 employees (of which about 230 were at corporate), a portfolio of properties exceeding US $1.4 billion,[10] and approximate revenues of U.S. $45 million.

---

[10] "Outrigger's President and CEO David Carey Named Hotel Person of the Year by Travel Agent Magazine" (2003, January). Hotel Online Special Report. Retrieved June 1, 2004 from the World Wide Web: http://www.hotel-online.com/News/PR2003_1st/Jan03_DCarey.html.

THE HOTELS AND RESORTS INDUSTRY

As the new millennium dawned, the global lodging industry was estimated to exceed $295 billion in sales, about 11% of the world's economic output, and employed more than 250 million workers (see Table 2 for performance indicators).[11] The leisure travel segment accounted for about 45% of total volume.[12]

With respect to the Hawaiian market, which was Outrigger's traditional stronghold, recent figures showed performance levels above the average of the global industry (see Table 3). Being quite isolated from any large population pool, Hawaii was a classic destination market with an exclusive fly-in customer base. The major feeders were U.S. westbound traffic and Japanese eastbound traffic. These markets were thought to yield very high return rates—estimated by some to be around 50% westbound and over 65% eastbound. This trend made for a very location-savvy customer base. Peculiar to this market was also the trend of multi-island stays, with guests visiting more than one destination during the same trip.

Because the Hawaii and Pacific Rim markets were exclusive destination markets, the use of packages—including air and accommodations—was pervasive. Historically, packages were assembled and sold by wholesalers and tour operators who purchased both air and hotel rooms in bulk and remarketed them to the traveling public. With the widespread adoption of the Internet, a new type of package was emerging under the leadership of large online travel agencies: dynamic packages. A dynamic package was one that enabled the guest to choose air, hotel, car rental, and even activities, ticket them independently, and then price them out as a bundle. Dynamic packages were appealing to suppliers because the price of each item was not disclosed, making price comparison difficult and alleviating commoditization fears. They were appealing to perspective travelers because they increased choice and fostered flexibility. Finally, they appealed to online travel agents because they built upon their value proposition—customer choice—and had the potential to improve their margins.

As a mature destination, Hawaii had been entered by many of the larger branded hospitality and resort companies. The largest hospitality firms, such as Marriott International, Hilton Hotels and Resorts, and Starwood, had a significant presence with eight, five, and eleven properties, respectively. But the largest operators in Hawaii were geographically- and leisure-focused players such as Outrigger, ASTON Hotels & Resorts Hawaii (with twenty-eight properties), and Marc Resorts Hawaii (with eleven properties).

Table 6.2   Performance of Global Hotel Industry

Occupancy	63.5%
Avg. number of rooms	706
ADR	$91.62
RevPAR	$58.18

Table 6.3   Performance of Hawaii Hotel Market

Occupancy	72.1%
Avg. number of rooms	706
ADR	$198.41
Revenue*	$78,488

* Amounts per available room

---

[11] "Hotels and Other Lodging Places." Encyclopedia of Global Industries, 3rd ed., 2003. Business and Company Resource Center. Infotrac. http://infotrac.galegroup.com/itweb/nysl_sc_cornl?db=bcrc

[12] Worldwide Hotel Industry Study, 2002, Horwarth International.

continued

OUTRIGGERS ORGANIZATION

Outrigger Hotels and Resorts was a management company wholly owned by a holding corporation called Outrigger Enterprises. Reflecting its real estate development roots, Outrigger Enterprises also owned a real estate ownership company called Outrigger Properties (Exhibit 4). Outrigger Properties wrote and managed real estate contracts with third party owners and supervised the owned assets (accounting for about a third of all properties in the Outrigger portfolio), as well as the development of new properties. The firm also monitored the real estate market for optimal times to invest in available properties or sell assets in the portfolio and raise needed capital. Outrigger Properties managed leasing contracts with the many independent retailers occupying food and beverage outlets—rarely run internally by Outrigger—and shops within the hotels and resorts in its portfolio. Sorenson explained the tradeoffs associated with this decision:

We are the third largest retail landlord in Hawaii, with about 300,000 square feet of retail space, so we have access to the best restaurant operators. Leasing restaurants allows us to focus our energies on hospitality and [the] profitability of the rest of the hotel, but of course you lose some control when you outsource. It takes a hotel mentality to do room service very well for example.

Outrigger Hotels and Resorts, the operating arm of Outrigger Enterprises, was responsible for the writing of new management contracts, as well as overseeing property renovations, and operations of the managed hotels, resorts, and condos. Outrigger Properties generally negotiated a base and a percentage of revenue with tenants; revenues from leased space were assigned to the hosting property's own Profit & Loss statement. Room revenue made up the bulk of each property's revenue, with rental income as low as 5% in hotels with little retail space and as high as 20%

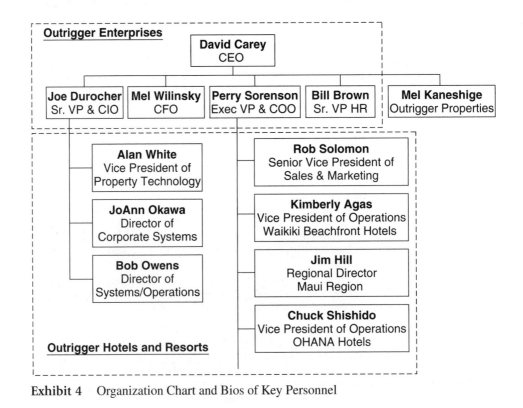

Exhibit 4   Organization Chart and Bios of Key Personnel

Exhibit 4   Organization Chart and Bios of Key Personnel

W. David P. Carey III, President and Chief Executive Officer
David Carey joined Outrigger Enterprises, Inc. as executive vice president and general counsel in 1986, and was named president of the company in 1988 and chief executive officer in 1994. After graduation in 1982, Carey moved to Honolulu and was an attorney specializing in corporate and real estate law at Carlsmith Wichman Case Mukai and Ichiki, where Outrigger Hotels was one of his major clients. Carey is a member of numerous business and community organizations, including the Hawaii Tourism Authority, Hawaii Hotel Association, and others. Carey has a B.S. in electrical engineering from Stanford University, a J.D., cum laude, and an M.B.A., with distinction, from the Santa Clara University. He was a member of the Beta Gamma Sigma Honor Society.

Joe Durocher, Senior Vice President and Chief Information Officer
Joe Durocher first joined Outrigger in 1986 as vice president of information systems. During his tenure, he was instrumental in the installation and maintenance of the company's Stellex reservations and front desk computer system. After 10 years with Outrigger, Durocher left the company to join Hilton Hotels Corporation as SVP and CIO, where he was responsible for data processing and related strategies for all of Hilton's non-gaming hotels, amounting to well over 300 properties with over 110,000 rooms worldwide. While with Hilton, Durocher was instrumental in the replacement of Hilton's Hiltron central reservation system with Hilstar, a new state-of-the-art central reservations system. Durocher rejoined Outrigger Enterprises in 2000. Born and raised in Hawaii, Durocher received his B.S. in Electrical Engineering and M.B.A. from the University of Hawaii. He is a Certified Systems Professional (CSP) and Certified Data Processing Professional (CDP). Durocher is also a member of the Beta Gamma Sigma honor society.

Perry Sorenson, Chief Operating Officer
In his position as a chief operating officer, Perry Sorenson is responsible for all aspects of hotel operations as well as Outrigger's current expansion across the Pacific. He joined Outrigger as executive vice president in 1991. Sorenson's career spans over 20 years in the hospitality industry. He was previously EVP and COO for Embassy Suites, Inc., the world's largest all-suite hotel chain. Sorenson directed the rapid growth of Embassy Suites operations as it expanded from 5 to 105 hotels in five years. Prior to joining Embassy Suites, Sorenson was vice president of operations for Holiday Inns Inc., where he was the recipient of the Holiday Inn Corporation Chairman's Award for Service Excellence. He has also held management positions with Radisson Hotel Corp. and Rockresorts, Inc. He is currently a member of the Native Hawaiian Tourism and Hospitality Association and sits on the board of various other community and industry organizations. Sorenson received his B.A. in psychology and M.B.A. from the University of Utah.

Robert L. Solomon, Senior Vice President, Sales and Marketing
Before joining Outrigger, Solomon spent 15 years with Dollar Rent A Car as senior vice president, with additional responsibilities as vice president, Pacific sales. Solomon's professional career has also included senior management positions in California with various corporations as well as government agencies in California. Solomon is well known within Hawaii's visitor industry, having served on numerous boards and committees, including the research and marketing committees of the Hawaii Visitors and Conventions Bureau and the Oahu Visitors Bureau. He is the immediate past chair of the Marketing Committee for the Oahu Visitors Bureau, and presently chairs the Internet Subcommittee for the Hawaii Visitors and Convention Bureau Advisory Committee. Solomon holds Master's degrees from Princeton and Yale universities in the fields of public and international affairs and Southeast Asia studies.

Alan White, Vice President of Operations–Information Technology
White joined Outrigger Hotels & Resorts in 2001 and is responsible for all data processing for hotel operations. In his time with Outrigger, he has produced numerous new interfaces to the company's proprietary Central Reservations System (CRS) and Property Management System (PMS). White also created electronic interfaces to more than 13 different suppliers, who account for nearly 30% of the

continued

Exhibit 4 *continued*

total reservations for Outrigger and OHANA Hotels. White has extensive operation experience in hotels ranging from the F&B area to the front desk to general management. Prior to joining Outrigger, White worked at Pegasus Solutions, Inc. for over a decade. Born in Paris, France, White was educated at Providence College in Rhode Island, the Universitat Freiburg in Switzerland, and George Washington University in Washington, D.C. He did his advanced graduate studies at the Sino-Soviet Institute and the Osteuropa-Institut.

Kimberly Agas, Vice President of Operations, Waikiki Beachfront Division
Agas joined Outrigger in 1984 while attending college and has worked at eight different properties throughout her years with the company. Prior to her tenure at the Outrigger Waikiki, she was hotel manager for the OHANA Village and OHANA Coral Seas hotels. Recently, she was promoted to the newly created position of Vice President–Operations, Waikiki Beachfront Division, and she will assume the duties of general manager of the Outrigger Reef on the Beach. Agas is a graduate of Liberal Arts program at Leeward Community College and the University of Hawaii at Manoa, where she studied Economics. Since joining the company she has been awarded the company's prestigious President's Award six times.

Chuck Shishido, Vice President of Operations, OHANA Hotels and Resorts
Chuck Shishido, CHA joined the company in 1972 as a part-time worker in the housekeeping department of the then Outrigger Reef Towers while pursuing an accounting degree at the University of Hawaii. In 1975, Shishido was promoted to assistant hotel manager at the Outrigger Reef. A year later, he transferred to the Outrigger Reef Towers as hotel manager. For the next thirteen years, Shishido moved between six different Outrigger properties as hotel manager. He was promoted to Group Manager in 1990 and was responsible for four properties in the Lewers Street area. In 1994, he was appointed general manager of the Outrigger Waikiki on the Beach and remained there until he was called upon to assist in the launch of OHANA Hotels & Resorts. Shishido holds a Bachelor of Arts degree in accounting from the University of Hawaii and is a member of the Hawaii Hotel and Lodging Association.

Jim Hill, Regional Director, Condominium Operations, Maui
Jim Hill is responsible for the daily operation of the Outrigger Royal Kahana, in capacity as General Manager, as well as overseeing operations for Outrigger's three other condominium resorts on Maui—the Outrigger Napili Shores, Outrigger Maui Eldorado and the Outrigger Palms at Wailea. Hill, who has been with Outrigger for over 17 years, previously served as General Manager for the Outrigger Kiahuna Plantation located on the island of Kauai.

in some of the most appealing locations. Other more marginal revenue lines were parking, in-room entertainment, telecommunications, and kids' clubs operations.

Outrigger Hotels and Resorts had historically maintained a highly centralized organizational structure. As the firm grew in size and geographical distribution a more traditional structure emerged, but, reflecting its roots, Outrigger Hotels and Resorts remained consolidated where possible. For example, the two beach-front Outrigger Hotels on Waikiki beach were managed as one.

As Chuck Shishido, OHANA Hotels VP of operations and a 33-year veteran of the company, explained:

We have centralized services—accounting, IT, finance, engineering, purchasing, and special projects—that support all the properties on Oahu, as well as indirectly the neighboring islands. There is also one executive housekeeper in charge of all properties. We run the OHANA Hotels like a 4,200-room distributed hotel. It is very efficient.

Since each property in the Outrigger family had its own P&L, these shared services were charged back to them based on room count, revenue, or usage, depending on the service. As the firm expanded internationally it became more decentralized, with resorts in the Pacific Rim working much more like independent operations and organized like traditional resorts. Recognizing the significant advantages offered by its centralized structure, Outrigger was looking at the possibility of better integrating its international resorts. However, distance presented new challenges—1,800 miles separated its southernmost Australian property from its northernmost property alone. Sorenson explained:

> We need a reservation solution for Australia, a real-time coordination with a central reservation service. They are operated as individual hotels; the central 800 number today is just switched to the correct hotel. A centralized system would offer tremendous value because we get drive-in business and substantial potential cross-property traffic.

THE OUTRIGGER CUSTOMERS AND COMPETITION

Outrigger's original mission was to bring the opportunity for a vacation in paradise within the reach of middle-class families. As the firm began to diversify its portfolio, the profile of its customers and the competition changed as well. The typical Outrigger guest was often a multigenerational customer with a sense of loyalty to the Outrigger family (about 25% of guests were returning to Outrigger) and an annual income exceeding $75k. Outrigger guests were almost exclusively leisure travelers, with some mixing business and travel (e.g., attending a conference and extending the stay for some leisure time with the family afterward). This customer base created seasonality, with winter and summer being the high seasons when properties like the Outrigger Waikiki on the Beach reached an ADR of $260 and an overall occupancy around 90%. Group business was limited, with some overflow from the conference center looking for meeting space for break-out events. Solomon profiled Outrigger's customer base:

> Our customers are independent-minded and look for an experience that is more regional and attuned to the destination, but still within their comfort zone. They may stay with big brands in their road warrior capacity, but that's not what they are looking for in a tropical destination.

Competing for these customers, Outrigger went head-to-head with such major brands as Marriott International, Hilton Hotels and Resorts, and Starwood Hotels and Resorts—the latter having a big Sheraton presence in Waikiki. These brands enjoyed name recognition, significant brand awareness among the traveling public, a flow of customers redeeming points, available capital, and availability of programs for employees such as discounted travel beyond Hawaii and the Pacific region. In response, Outrigger leveraged some of the premier locations in the markets it competed in, like the Outrigger Waikiki on the Beach, strong name recognition and long-term relationships with the travel distribution network, a strategic focus on vacation destinations, a deep local knowledge and community ties, and good employee relations. Kimberly Agas, VP of Operations for Outrigger's Waikiki Beachfront Hotels and a 20-year veteran with the company, explained:

> Our employees are trusted to help the guests have a wonderful stay, and have the flexibility to act on their initiative. The teams of employees include our partners in the retail, restaurants and activities. We are concerned with the holistic experience, an all encompassing experience. In much of our unionized competition everyone has a narrow job [description] and outside of that they will refer you to a colleague, out of respect, because of contract restrictions, or because that's how they look at it: "this is all I have to do."

The typical OHANA guest was a value-minded and Hawaii-savvy leisure traveler with income below $100k a year. Typically, OHANA guests had visited Hawaii multiple times, stayed longer than average, and visited more often. Business travel was mainly comprised of military and corporations with operations on multiple islands. Groups accounted for less that 10% of OHANA's overall traffic. Shishido explained:

> We have about 50% return guests. Your first trip you want a beach front hotel, the atmosphere, the ambiance—you want the full Hawaii experience. When you come more often, you still want the experience, but you look for more value and instead of spending $250–$300 a night for a beachfront you can stay longer off-beach for $70–$80 a night.

With seasonality similar to that of the full service Outrigger Hotels, OHANA Hotels typically achieved an ADR around $66 and approximate occupancy levels of 75% over the year. A number of small regional chains (such as Marc Resorts and Castle Resorts) and many off-beach independent hotels existed in the Waikiki market. But Outrigger's senior management thought that OHANA hotels had no direct competition. Solomon explained:

continued

There is no quality branded competitor for OHANA. Because of the real estate costs and lack of efficiencies, competitors like Holiday Inn, Cendant, and Choice can't build and operate their product at their price point here. There are many independent no-name products.

Pricing for off-beach properties was much harder to manage because of the commodity nature of the hotels not enjoying a premium location, even though wholesalers concerned about their own brand and customer satisfaction were more willing to carry the OHANA brand over independents because Outrigger backed OHANA's quality promise. OHANA was the largest operator in Waikiki and the largest Hawaii-owned operator.

Two types of customers were typically staying at the condominiums. On the lower side of the $90k to $160k income brackets were families visiting during school breaks and looking to control expenses and control their vacation experience. They valued the full kitchen—a standard in every unit—and the two bedrooms and two baths. This was substantiated by the fact that condos had four times as many reservations coming from the Internet directly and tended to recover faster after a soft economy. On the upper side of the spectrum were "newlyweds" and "nearly dead" couples who liked the privacy and space afforded by a condo. As Hill explained:

> On the upper end of the scale people like the convenience to have a full size refrigerator and kitchen amenities but they may never cook. If they want to cook the kitchen is available, but chances are they'll never use it. That's why, against conventional wisdom, the new trend is to put restaurants with more resort services in condominium properties.

While high degrees of variability existed between properties, returning guests to the same property ranged typically between 20% and 40%. With its expanding portfolio, Outrigger believed it enjoyed significant cross-property traffic as well, but it had little hard data on this.

Condominiums enjoyed almost no branded competition. Instead, because of the need to convince individual owners to join the pool of Outrigger-managed units, the firm competed with small local management companies and individual owners' beliefs that they could do a better job alone. This idiosyncrasy of condominium operations amounted to having two customers—the unit owners and the guests—[the latter] who, unaware of the workings of condo operations, were looking for the same level of service they would receive at a resort. On average, a condominium with mostly two bedroom units would achieve ADRs around $175, while properties with mostly studio and one bedroom units would settle around $140.

Outrigger operated a Central Reservation Office (CRO) in Denver, Colorado with anywhere from 40 to 70 reservationists (FTEs [full-time employees]), mainly depending on the volume of business. A corporate marketing staff of 12 people, allocated about 6% of revenue, was responsible for managing the brand and for going to market. An additional 2% of revenue was used to fund reservation and other distribution costs. Reservations were centralized for all properties in Hawaii. Outrigger Hotels had a staff of two or three people at each property to follow through (e.g., to reconcile inconsistencies, create rooming lists, and identify VIPs). For the OHANA hotels this was done as a shared service. Beyond Hawaii reservations were only taken at each property.

Outrigger executives believed that distribution was a cornerstone of its success, with about 50% of the business coming from wholesalers (classified as anything that is on a contract basis) who often sold Outrigger products as part of a package. Consumer direct (via voice or the Web), travel agents, government and military, and corporate clients made up the difference. For international properties the source of business percentage from wholesalers was close to 80% and almost all reservations were faxed to the property. But the lines were blurring with the increasing prominence of online travel agents (e.g., Expedia) and the advent of dynamic packages. Solomon explained:

> We strive to make distribution as broad as possible, and for each pipeline (voice, Web direct, GDS, fax) we want to make it as efficient and user friendly as possible. The customer is in control; more than half of those who transact in the wholesale channel can pick the hotel.

The firm felt that it had been able to capitalize on the use of technology to increase distribution efficiencies in the face of ever rising labor costs. Conversion rates at the CRO had improved from 20% to 45%–50% with widespread consumer adoption of the Internet. The firm estimated that as much as 60% of callers had already researched the Outrigger Web site and had made a purchase decision but, as Solomon put it, "had one more question." In an effort to provide support right on the Web site, the firm introduced live chat functionalities and also offered email confirmation for significant savings in labor and postage costs.

OUTRIGGER STRATEGY

At the heart of Outrigger Hotels and Resorts' strategy was a drive to position its properties in places where people could enjoy a vacation experience leveraging Outriggers' own core competencies. The firm was very careful not to create a cookie cutter approach, but instead to deliver an experience that was respectful of the culture and the special characteristics of the localities in which it operated—a "sense of place" as the firm called it. As Carey put it:

> Our business is really about being a "window" to an experience, not the experience itself. We are the enabler through which people can engage in the leisure experience they desire. We don't try to export Hawaii when we go elsewhere, but we do honor the same values in the places we operate hotels and resorts.

The firm was embarking in a $315M renovation of the heart of Waikiki that required the leveling of five existing OHANA hotels—almost 2,000 rooms—that required significant investment in asset maintenance. In this area the firm planned to create about 500 rooms—a substantial reduction in room count—with a sizeable retail component. The firm's real estate ownership in the area totaled 7.9 contiguous acres and, with its biggest real estate investment being in Waikiki, a renewal of the area had benefits beyond the creation of new hotels and retail space. This bold project limited the firm's ability to expand in the short term, but Outrigger remained committed to growth and expansion once the renovation was completed. Carey explained the rationale for the firm's growth strategy:

> Given our key competencies, expanding to Guam, the Pacific, and Australia was a source-customer or distribution-driven growth strategy. It leveraged both markets where the customers knew us because they had experienced our hotels before and [markets] where we had relationships with global distribution channels.

Outrigger's senior management felt that its key competencies resided in providing hospitality to guests visiting their properties and successfully marketing those properties through leisure distribution channels, which before the widespread adoption of the Internet by consumers had accounted for over 80% of travel to Hawaii and other fly-in leisure destinations. To complement these basic competencies, Outrigger felt it had developed a superior capability to manage in a multicultural environment, including multicultural and multilingual employees and guests.

Outrigger had its roots in the economy segment of the market, but the firm's executives believed that it was not feasible to compete on price alone and had begun to focus on service delivery as well to build customer preference. Aided by a turnover rate in the single digits in the tight Hawaii labor market, and an average of 25 years of employee tenure with the company, it implemented a value-based management system that called for upward evaluation of managers and a focus on helping employees understand the principles behind Outrigger's service delivery strategy. As a testament to the firm's ability to fulfill its employees' needs, Outrigger had managed to be a mostly non-union shop in the heavily unionized Hawaii labor market. Carey summarized the firm's positioning:

> We operate properties that have good locations, we have a strong travel distribution network, and our employees really provide hospitality from the heart. That creates a differentiated product making price less important.

Beyond maintenance of the product under capital constraints, at the operational level three dimensions were deemed fundamental for success: providing guests with a rewarding experience and a sense of place, enabling employees to reach their potential, and being an integral part of the community. These dimensions were reflected in the firm's Management Incentive Plan (MIP), structured along three dimensions: Operating Cash Flow, guest satisfaction surveys (using reports produced by the independent research firm Leisure Trends), and employee satisfaction.

Beyond these critical success factors within the firm's control, Outrigger was wedded to the success of its destination markets given the proliferation of competing choices for consumers' entertainment budgets. Moreover, the firm was dependent on airlines. As leisure decisions became more and more impulse-driven it became more difficult for travelers to find available seats at suitable times and prices. Carey summarized these challenges:

> If Hawaii does well, so do we. I spend a lot of time working with local tourism authorities to improve the appeal of the destinations we operate in. But airlines can be a bottleneck. We may not have available lift at times when we need it. If the airlines are full or they have decided in their yield model that

continued

they are going to only sell their top fares, there is nothing we can do. From purely the hotels' perspective, the best thing for us is an airline price war to Hawaii.

The major carriers, those driving the most traffic into Hawaii and the Pacific region, were under constant financial pressures. The events of September 11, 2001 and the recession that had hit the United States had depressed airline travel and had negatively impacted Outrigger's own financial performance. While the firm had been able to recover from these setbacks and was seeing high occupancies, terrorist threats and alerts remained a significant concern.

OUTRIGGER IT INFRASTRUCTURE

Joe Durocher, the CIO of Outrigger Enterprises, was hired by David Carey in 1986. Durocher recalled his early days with the firm:

Mr. Roy Kelly was a hands-on manager. He once told me he hated two things: computers and vice presidents. As the VP of IT, I had two strikes against me. Yet, in 1986 I was brought in to overhaul Outrigger's IT infrastructure and we built Stellex—our integrated CRS/PMS. At the time all our properties were in Waikiki, within one square mile of each other.

Stellex, introduced in 1987, was a COBOL application running on a Tandem NonStop platform and a proprietary Enscribe database management system that guaranteed complete redundancy and 24 × 365 uptime. In 1992 Outrigger introduced Stellex 2.0, its first major update to Stellex, which ran on a Sun Microsystems UNIX platform and provided revenue management functionality and reservation center support. Because of its unique need for substantial wholesale interaction, Outrigger engaged Opus to build their revenue management module for Stellex 2.0. Outrigger retained control of the source code and over the years made substantial enhancements, mainly to manage wholesale relationships. The firm felt that its centralized IT infrastructure was a source of competitive advantage. Durocher discussed the trade-offs associated with centralized IT:

Decentralizing IT would decrease our capabilities while increasing overall costs. But centralized IT

creates friction at times. When a hotel is sold for example, the IT allocation may increase for other properties.

Stellex provided the anchor to which all other operational systems, including telephone switches, call accounting, and in-room entertainment, connected. All of the properties in the Hawaiian Islands had access to Outrigger's centralized IT systems, served from the Honolulu-based data center, through the firm's proprietary Wide Area Network (Exhibit 5). Stellex, for example, was accessed using an ASP model by all the properties in the Hawaiian Islands, the firm's Denver-based CRO, and the Portland-based Web servers, greatly simplifying the achievement of single image inventory, disaster recovery, and overall IT management. This enabled the properties to operate with PCs (as few as 12 in a typical 500-room property) and networking equipment. The point of sales (POS) systems were not centralized, since Outrigger leased retail and restaurant space. This state of affairs generated some friction at times, as Alan White, VP of Property Technology, explained:

We offer to interface their POS to Stellex and pay for interfaces to automate room charges. But many of those POS are old and can't interface; they must be upgraded first. Restaurants have to write a manual charge voucher and walk it to the front desk for input. It's not a popular or efficient way to do it.

Due to the need for local support, the high telecommunication costs, and the reliability of international networks deemed unacceptable, Outrigger had yet to extend this centralized model to its operations in Australia and the Pacific. The properties in Australia and New Zealand, all condominiums, used a highly specialized PMS particularly well suited for strata title properties and their special tax code requirements. Durocher explained:

None of the properties in Hawaii has a server on property. In the outer regions we have standalone PMS's and on-property reservations. We don't even try to keep Stellex in sync, they just open and close. If a date is getting full, they issue a stop-sell. Reservations that are taken centrally are automatically emailed.

Outrigger's IT function comprised a staff of 26 full-time employees, including 4 data entry operators and 3 developers housed in a separate limited liability company designed to help Outrigger take advantage of tax incentives offered by the state of Hawaii. One corporate IT

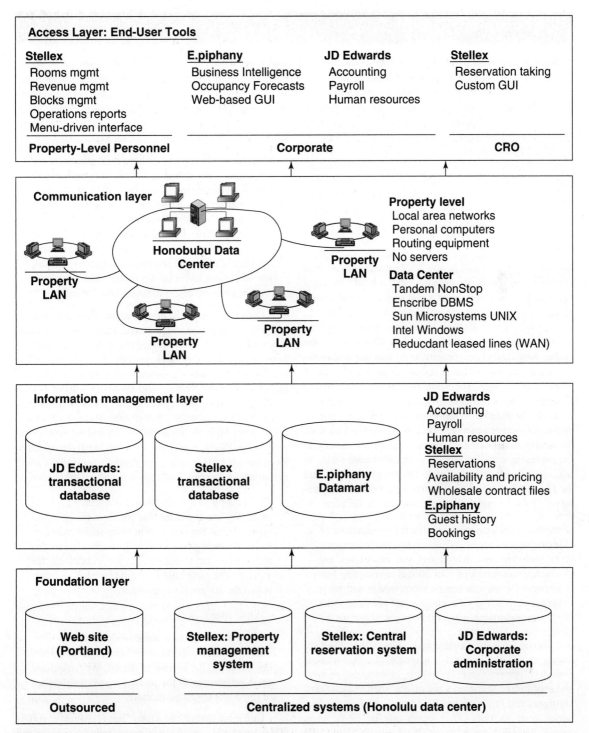

Exhibit 5 Property-Level IT Infrastructure (Hawaii Properties)

continued

professional supported the Australian properties' application needs. Hardware support was contracted out to local vendors. The function was organized along user needs rather than traditional departmental lines (e.g., data entry, application development, support). Alan White, VP of Property Technology, led the group in charge of creating and supporting IT solutions for the hotels. JoAnn Okawa, Director of Corporate Systems, led the group in charge of creating and supporting IT solutions for the firm's back-office needs (e.g., general accounting, HR, payroll, purchasing). Bob Owens, Director of System Operations, and his group managed the data center and supported the other two groups. They also performed advisory work for the international properties that had local MIS managers in charge of procuring and managing technology solutions locally. This organization enabled operations personnel to unequivocally ask the Property Technology group for support, while administrative personnel referred to the Corporate Information Service group.

The IT function at Outrigger was designated a cost center. Its operations were funded through allocations to the business units and to each property using four different methods. A charge, based on room count, was assessed for use of property technology. The same mechanism was used to account for use of administrative systems. Group sales software (i.e., Newmarket's Delphi) was charged based on each property's meeting space. Finally, any ad-hoc solution (e.g., the writing of a specialized report) was charged directly to the requesting unit. Traditional metrics to measure success (e.g., on-time and on-budget project delivery) were used, and the IT function had recently introduced service level agreements. Durocher explained the rationale for the decision:

> Service level agreements enable the management of expectations, increase accountability, and offer choice to user-managers. If you feel you are paying too much, you can reduce your allocation accepting less service. Or you can request more service and we'll adjust your charge. Of course, we still get some of the "I want more service but I don't want to pay for it."

Beyond maintaining and upgrading Stellex, Outrigger's IT professionals engaged in minimal application development—mainly writing customized reports, and configuring and interfacing off-the-shelf applications. Outrigger had implemented JD Edwards ERP as the cornerstone of its back-office operations in 1990, years before the ERP craze swept the business world. JD Edwards ran on an IBM AS 400—a very mature and stable platform. The use of outsourcing was limited to the Web

site, developed and hosted by a third party in Portland, Oregon. Yet, in order to maintain the integration of direct channels, Stellex served as the Web site's booking engine through an XML interface that Outrigger's IT group used as the proof of concept for the interfaces with wholesalers—a key initiative for Outrigger. Durocher explained:

> With many wholesalers we have real-time electronic interfaces—they can check availability and we get their reservations instantaneously. Without the interface, if they create a reservation six or three months out, we don't see it until reporting time, ten days out, when we receive a fax and manually input it. It is virtually impossible to revenue manage like that. Many big brands have great revenue management systems, but don't have real-time wholesaler data. Moreover, we can write wholesale contracts brand-wide.

Outrigger felt that its electronic interfaces afforded it a competitive advantage and preferential treatment from interface-enabled wholesalers, a relationship that proved particularly important during slow periods or a soft economy. Electronic interfaces generated substantial efficiencies, including automatic billing and invoicing without human handling, lowering estimated costs to $0.75 from an estimated $10 for manually handled ones. But not all wholesalers were able or interested in automating reservation processing. This was particularly true for small operations or those for whom Hawaii and the Pacific represented a small percentage of business. Solomon summarized the challenge:

> The industry is a mess from a connectivity standpoint. We are fortunate that we have the in-house expertise and the recognition from senior management of how important this is. Even the big companies often don't understand the conditions for success. The dirty little secret of the travel industry is that the fax machine still rules.

White added:

> I spend 30–40 hours a week working with wholesalers on interfaces. There are many legacy systems out there; the fax is state of the art. We have made great progress with the more advance wholesalers or those that upgraded recently.

Outrigger found the Open Travel Alliance (OTA) XML standards, specifying common message format and common content, of great help. But being able to pick the right partner, and avoid costly failures, remained the major challenge. While Outrigger felt it had been successful to date, with an estimated 33% of total reservations received electronically through the various channels, it still handled more than half a million faxes a year—about eight hundred a day from its largest wholesaler alone before its recent migration to the electronic interface.

The firm had recently acquired business intelligence software, a data mart, and analytical tools from E.piphany running on a Windows 2000 platform. The data mart held detailed data for three years, enabling analysis down to the individual guest folio. Data were consolidated afterward, enabling only aggregate analyses. While E.piphany was a recent purchase, Outrigger had been disciplined in collecting data for some time. White explained:

> We had 10 years of high quality data from Stellex; we are very rigid about data capture standardization like room category, naming conventions, request codes, [and] what goes where. For example, postal and country codes are mandatory fields. Our employees' long tenure helps, and peer pressure is a great asset—nobody wants to be the one that ruins the value of these reports for all.

The data collected by Stellex, including source of business, stay information, and consumption, were extracted every night by load programs that scrubbed (i.e., cleaned) them, and transferred them to JD Edwards for accounting and E.piphany for analysis. Feeding historical data and forward looking availability and reservation activity, Outrigger had learned to harness the analytical power of E.piphany to do forecasts and generate business intelligence both at the source of business and at guest levels. White elaborated:

> We want the marketing data. It is stupid to have a treasure trove like that and not use it. We mine it. We send thank you letters to recurring guests, we can give you history on who visited, how they got here, what in-flight magazine we should hit. We sold a resort once and they figured they would have to hire 3 people to achieve manually what our reports gave them automatically. They even set their rates based on E.piphany forecasts.

The IT group served as custodian of the data, but any user with security clearance had access to E.piphany data though a web interface; the data was used for marketing and operational analysis (e.g., analysis of call patterns to evaluate the appeal of Voice over IP solutions). More challenging was to incorporate the information into daily operations. Outrigger found it hard to justify a frequent guest program—with an average repurchase cycle for returning guests of three years, a once-a-year purchase was considered

very high in resort operations. Speaking about recognition programs, Sorenson explained:

> Individual properties have their own customer database and a strong informal recognition system. We haven't been able to justify the investment technologically to do it brand wide. It would be a natural extension of the recognition we give our return guests, but it must be cost-effective.

Agas added:

> If a guest did not tell us he is returning when making the reservation, our current system does not have a database with guest history. Many times we recognize our frequent return guests at the door, or during check in at the front desk, but without any guest history in on current system a new employee may not acknowledge the return guest or their special occasion. We have special programs (e.g., for honeymooners, wedding anniversaries), but we need to know their history to appropriately acknowledge them.

IS ASSESSMENT

Outrigger's senior executives found technology to be a great asset to enable communication, as Outrigger's operations spanned 11 time zones, and felt confident that the IT function was enabling the firm to compete effectively. Carey indicated:

> We think that our IT capability in the leisure travel space exceeds the major chains and we have an ability to implement things very quickly. [That's] the advantage of being small.

The IT function was thought to be able to operate more efficiently than the competition, often offering the same level of service with one or no property-level IS professionals when the competition needed three to six. Outrigger also felt that its size enabled it to move faster than the competition. Bob Owens, Director of Systems/Operations, explained:

> We don't do anything slow here. Major systems in other firms take a year to plan, a year in committees that assign responsibilities, and two or three years to build. A year is a really a long time here to develop and implement anything. But we are not a huge company, and capital is a constraint, so we are always challenged to get way ahead of the curve, speculate, and build with a forward thinking mentality. You don't get bored here.

As the firm was expanding aggressively, and had yet to find an integrated solution for its international properties, some questioned the viability of reinvesting in Stellex. Its

continued

rapid geographical and product growth notwithstanding, the IS group felt that its legacy technology—specifically its mature ERP, integrated PMS/CRS, and electronic interfaces with distribution partners—was serving the firm well. White explained:

> Stellex is 18 years old. So three years ago we developed the business case for PMS and CRS functionalities. We could not find anything better, with one exception—Stellex is a green screen application that needs a windows GUI.

The firm was prompted to reevaluate the role of Stellex after a failed attempt to migrate to a more modern platform thought to simplify connectivity with the other off-the-shelf computer systems in the portfolio. After testing in two properties over an eight-month period the project was aborted, principally [due to] the difficulty in effectively managing wholesale relationships and billing manually with the new PMS.

Outrigger engaged in limited formal technology training and relied mainly on on-the-job training when it came to software applications. While this created difficulties for people who were hired from outside the firm, Sorenson explained:

> Our people have been working with Stellex so long that they have effective workarounds when necessary, and we have very low employee turnover. If someone new comes in we have many experienced employees to help them; this makes training easier.

As guests became used to ever increasing technology choices and availability both at home and on the road, even resorts focused on the leisure traveler felt the pressure to provide it to guests—whether they used it or not. But for a mid-size company like Outrigger, chasing the technology curve could be dangerous. Agas articulated the challenge:

> Our guests say: "I do wireless at home, why can't I do it here?" As a company we use our buying power to do what's best for the company. But as two beachfront properties with guests paying the highest ADR and expecting more, sometimes we are held back when it gets to technology as we explore what is best for all.

THE FUTURE

Outrigger's senior management felt that the firm could leverage its hospitality and marketing expertise, as well as big brand name recognition, by entering into management

agreements with third party owners and large brands. While it remained committed to growing and strengthening the Outrigger family of brands, it also had plans to engage in this type of partnership.

Another important trend affecting Outrigger's future strategy was the rapidly changing hospitality distribution landscape and the role of the retail travel agent. Travel agents had historically provided significant amounts of information, counseling, and reassurance to leisure travelers, but more and more consumers were now turning to the Internet for this information. This presented Outrigger with the challenge of populating the new electronic world. The emergence of powerful online agencies (e.g., Expedia, Orbitz) was creating significant opportunities and threats. Carey captured them:

> We have grown up with wholesalers; we know how to yield manage the merchant model. The major chains are not yet embracing the capabilities of the internet. They look at Internet bookings through third party providers as a threat. We see it as just another wholesaler; we know how to revenue manage the merchant model. We all must recognize the consumer's desire to shop before they buy. The single web site solution will not work in my opinion.

This was particularly true with wholesalers using electronic interfaces. With these partners, Outrigger was able to open and close rates dynamically. Yet, questions remained as to the long term effects that powerful online intermediaries were having on customer loyalty and brand preference. As some senior managers put it: "Whose customer is it, Expedia's or ours?" For a company with relatively small scale and a niche positioning, the commoditization threat could be quite dangerous. Durocher summarized the challenge:

> In the days of Mr. Kelley and Dr. Kelley, Waikiki was running at 98% occupancy annually. Get the reservations in accurately was the main concern. That world has changed, now we compete in mature destinations.

With the increasing competition in its key markets, Outrigger felt that strengthening electronic relationships with distributors, improving its trademark hospitality and customer service, better managing inventory yield, and better integrating its international properties were crucial stepping-stones to the firm's continued success. The right information systems strategy was crucial to enabling these goals.

CHAPTER

7

Value Creation and Strategic Information Systems

What You Will Learn in This Chapter

This chapter focuses on the strategic role of information systems and the information technologies that enable them. The definitions, analytical frameworks, examples, and exercises in this chapter will help you develop a knowledge base that allows you to confidently identify and evaluate the added value creation potential of IT-dependent strategic initiatives.

Specifically, in this chapter you will become well versed in the language of the added value analysis and strategic information systems. You will learn

1. To define key terminology, including the concepts of total value created, customer willingness to pay, supplier opportunity cost, and added value.

2. To compute total value created and added value.

3. To estimate the portion of the total value created that will be appropriated by each of the entities who contributed to its creation.

4. To differentiate between strategic information systems and tactical information systems.

5. To define and utilize the concept of IT-dependent strategic initiatives.

MINI-CASE: CONSULTING FOR THE ROYAL HOTEL

The Royal Hotel in New York City is a luxury all-suite hotel primarily serving an executive clientele visiting Manhattan on business. Typically, these business guests stay for three to six days, during which they use their suite as a temporary office. Thus, Royal Hotel's management has positioned the property to cater to the many needs of this busy and demanding audience. Amenities include in-suite plain paper fax, printer, and copier, three two-line telephones with voicemail and remote message alert, 24-hour business center, wired and wireless Internet access in rooms and public areas, fitness center, suite dining, laundry service, complimentary shoe shine, complete stereo system with CD and cassette player, dedicated high-speed elevators, and more.

Even though most suites feature an in-room combo device (fax, printer, and copier), and the Royal Hotel has the technical ability to route incoming faxes to the combo devices, most guests prefer to have faxes sent to a central number. In-room combo devices are used mainly for sending outgoing faxes. In order to fulfill the demand for incoming faxes, the IT department at the Royal Hotel runs four "industrial strength" Canon fax machines (twenty pages per minute or ppm), with rollover numbers (i.e., one incoming fax number automatically allocated to the available machine). On a typical day the fax machines run almost nonstop. The fax machines cost the Royal Hotel $1000 each and have operating costs of about $200/year each (e.g., toner, electricity, maintenance). The fax machines have a usable life of five years.

The Royal Hotel has developed over the years a formal process for delivering the faxes and maintains a full-time "fax operator" position. The process has the following steps: (a) retrieve the fax; (b) log the receipt in a dedicated log book recording time of receipt, recipient, recipient's room number, and sending fax number; (c) place the fax in a bright orange envelope; and (d) make it available to the bell staff for immediate delivery to the guest's room.

WizTech, a California-based hi-tech firm specializing in printing solutions, has recently contacted the Royal Hotel. This contact is very timely as the Royal Hotel was about to replace the four Canon fax machines and assume the costs discussed above. WizTech is beginning to commercialize a "driverless printing" solution that enables regular printers to be contacted by fax machines without any need to install drivers (a driver is a software program that manages the interaction between two devices). Thus, the printer equipped with driverless printing software is a *perfect substitute* for the industrial strength fax machines. Moreover, to ensure a degree of redundancy, WizTech offers, free of charge, a backup service that enables temporary rerouting of incoming faxes to any other printer in the hotel if the main printer fails; this service is secure and managed seamlessly by WizTech until the main printer is back in operations. WizTech's high-end solution offers a "driverless printer" performing at eighty ppm with annual operating costs of $500. The printer's useful life is comparable to that of the industrial strength fax machines (five years). Each printer equipped with the software costs WizTech $1500 to produce.

DISCUSSION QUESTIONS

1. What should Royal Hotel's IT department do?
2. Does WizTech enjoy a competitive advantage (or disadvantage) in this market?
3. Can you quantify such advantage (or disadvantage)?

INTRODUCTION

Perhaps the primary role of functional and general managers in business organizations is to contribute to the *creation* and *appropriation* of economic value by their firm. Consider, for example, the following episode as recounted by Jack Shewmaker, former President and COO of Wal-Mart Stores, Inc.:

Figure 7.1   A Satellite Network Operation Center

Glen Habern was our data processing manager, and he and I had this dream of an interactive [satellite-based] communication system on which you could communicate back and forth between all the stores and the distribution centers and the general office. Glenn came up with the idea and I said, "Let's pursue it without asking anybody."[1]

This quote speaks to the importance of a strong partnership among a firm executive, the COO, and an IT professional who together envisioned a better way to manage information and to create economic value in their organization—in the case of Wal-Mart this satellite network (Figure 7.1) became the backbone of many of the firm's future strategic initiatives and competitive advantage.

But what does it mean to create value? Why would an organization want to engage in value creation? And, perhaps most importantly, how can you ensure that your organization benefits from its value creation strategies and initiatives?

THE ANALYSIS OF ADDED VALUE

Added value is one of those terms that we all too often hear being used in presentations and press releases to convey the idea that a firm is doing something worthy of attention. Consider the following:

- From the Web site of a State Information Technology Agency: "We will work hard to make sure that everything we do is "value-add" for our customers and achieves [the agency's] vision."

- From the 2006 list of *Top Ten Industry Trends* of a luxury resort operator: "Luxury is back! Guests are spending more and expecting luxury, first class amenities and added value in return for their money."

- From the title of an article published by *The Washington Times:* "Wi-Fi Going from an Added Value to an Expected Amenity."

- There is even a multinational consulting firm called ADDEDVALUE!

---

[1] *Sam Walton: Made in America,* Sam Walton with John Huey. New York: Bantam, p. 270.

The Benefits of Disciplined Analysis

What does it really mean to create or to have added value? Can you carry out a disciplined analysis or compute a number for the value added by an initiative you have envisioned? What would this number mean? What decisions could you make based on this analysis?

The analysis of added value is a formal mechanism that managers and analysts use to answer these questions and to evaluate how much of the value created the firm can appropriate in the form of profits. While the analysis of added value can be applied to any firm's initiative, we will constrain our focus to those projects that leverage IT at their core. This analysis is an essential step in the decision of whether you should go ahead with the initiative or not. It stands to reason that, if the proposed initiative creates no tangible value, you should shelve it. More insidiously, if the initiative does contribute to the creation of value, but your firm will be unable to appropriate such value created, then you should also not go on with it, in most cases.

This type of analysis is useful not only when you are innovating—in other words, when you are endeavoring to create value in novel ways and offering things that no competitor is currently offering, but also when you are evaluating how to respond to a competitor who took the leadership position. The analysis of added value can help you measure how much benefit your competitor is drawing from the innovation and what benefits are likely to accrue to you if you choose to replicate the initiative.

The Definition of Value

Economic value is generated when *worthwhile things* that did not exist before are created. Thus, value is created not only when something novel is done, but only when this "something novel" is deemed worthwhile by someone else. As entrepreneurship scholars have long recognized, this is the crucial difference between inventors and entrepreneurs. Inventors are those individuals who create new products and new technologies—in short, new things. These new technologies or products can be amazing, technically flawless, and beautifully engineered, but they will not create value until they solve a problem in some market. Entrepreneurs know this full well and focus on *market opportunities* and the development of *solutions* to meet these opportunities—that is, entrepreneurs look for new ways to create value rather than new technologies or new products. Often the novel solution being marketed relies on a new technology, but it is the invention that serves the market opportunity, not the other way around. While the solution offered may not be technically superior or beautifully engineered, it will be commercially appealing precisely because it does create economic value.

The Firm's Transformation Process Economic value is created through a transformation process when some input resources that have a value of $x in their next best utilization are transformed in outputs for which customers are willing to pay $x + $v. When such transformation process takes place, it can be said that value, in the amount of $v, has been created. In other words, this new value was not there before and would not come to be, unless the transformation process did occur since the input resources would remain untransformed and simply maintain their original worth of $x. Enacting the transformation process is typically a firm that engages in it seeking to monetize (at least) some of this value created in the form of profits.

Input resources are represented by any factor of production such as raw materials, labor, equity and debt capital, managerial talent, support services such as transportation or storage, and so on. In other words, anything that is used to generate the product or service, market it, sell it, and support it is to be considered an input resource.

Figure 7.2 Busy Checkout Lanes at Wal-Mart

The output of the transformation process is the product and/or service that the firm engaging in the transformation process is seeking to sell and a customer is interested in acquiring.

Let's return to the Wal-Mart, Inc. example (Figure 7.2). As a retailer Wal-Mart uses input resources such as labor, physical stores, warehousing facilities, trucks and transportation equipment, energy sources (e.g., diesel fuel for the trucks, electricity for the stores), equity and debt capital, and so on. By employing these resources in its transformation process, which consists of acquiring products in bulk, warehousing them, and distributing them to conveniently located stores, the firm is able to offer something that its customers are willing to pay for: convenient access to a large selection of mainstream products, at everyday low prices.

Defining the Components of Value Created

A formal analysis of added value requires some key definitions:

- *Supplier opportunity cost (SOC):* Supplier opportunity cost is the minimum amount of money the suppliers are willing to accept to provide the firm with the needed resources.

- *Firm cost (FC):* Firm cost is the actual amount of money the firm disbursed to acquire the resources needed to create its product or service.

- *Customer willingness to pay (CWP):* Customer willingness to pay is the maximum amount of money the firm's customers are willing to spend in order to obtain the firm's product.

- *Total value created (TVC):* The total value created in the transaction is computed as the difference between customer willingness to pay and supplier opportunity cost. TVC = CWP – SOC.

Supplier Opportunity Cost Supplier opportunity cost, the lower bound of value creation, is an important figure as it represents the value that the needed resources would have in their next best use. For this reason it is defined as an opportunity cost. A rational supplier will only provide the firm with its services (e.g., labor, managerial talent, raw materials) if it receives at least the same sum of money it would have received from any other buyer (i.e., another firm seeking to use the resource the supplier offers).

Note, however, that suppliers will typically not be paid an amount equal to their supplier opportunity cost. This is because the firm acquiring the resources will not be able to precisely estimate supplier opportunity cost—in fact, in most cases the suppliers themselves may not have a precise estimate available—and the suppliers will happily accept any offer exceeding their opportunity cost.

For an example, think back to the latest job offer that you received and accepted. During the interview, you, the supplier of labor to the hiring firm, formulated some idea regarding your willingness to work for the company and how much you'd want to get paid. When the offer came through it most likely exceeded this minimum requirement you had established, and you took the job . . . without returning the "excess salary" you received.

The simple example above addresses a very important issue. Supplier opportunity cost is a theoretical minimum; the actual amount of money the firm will pay to acquire the needed resources (i.e., the firm cost) is the outcome of a negotiation effort in the presence of an asymmetry of information between the negotiating parties. We will see that this important point resurfaces later when we discuss price considerations.

Customer Willingness to Pay The other end on the value continuum is represented by the customer willingness to pay. As we noted above, an inventor is someone who generates a new idea and creates a new product or technology. An entrepreneur is someone who matches a novel product or service to a market opportunity. This difference should be clear now with the terminology of value creation. Unless some customer is willing to part ways with money to acquire whatever the inventor has created, and this amount is larger than the supplier opportunity cost, no value has been generated and no economically viable venture has been created. In other words, value is in the eyes of the customer. The most elegantly engineered and technically beautiful product is valueless unless a customer is willing to pay for it.

The history of information technology products and services is littered with examples of innovations that, while perhaps technically amazing and even breakthrough, met with cool customer response and dwindled into market oblivion as a consequence: Do you remember the picture phone (Figure 7.3), the Apple Newton, Audrey (3Com's Internet appliance) (Figure 7.4), WebTV, and Webvan's online grocery service?

NEW LOOK PICTUREPHONE
Now you can *see* as well as talk
The Picturephone has Touch-Tone controls to make calls
and control the television screen so you can see the person
you're talking to, be seen yourself, or have a darkened
screen. Attended service between New York, Washington
and Chicago began in 1964.

Figure 7.3 The PicturePhone—an Innovation Introduced Thirty-Five Years before Its Time

Figure 7.4   Audrey, the Internet Appliance

Computing the Total Value Created

Simply defined, value is the difference between customer willingness to pay and supplier opportunity cost. That is, value is created when resources that in their next best use would be worth a given amount are transformed into something that a customer is willing to pay more for.

Consider a simple example.[2] Your grandmother was famous for baking a great-tasting cake. In her will, she entrusts the secret recipe to you, so you decide to become an entrepreneur and start baking the specialty cake. You can bake a cake using amounts of eggs, flour, sugar, and the secret grandma ingredients worth about $4.00 total. An hour of your time invested in making the cake is valued at $6.50 under the assumption that you only qualify for minimum-wage jobs (i.e., if you used the same amount of time to work for the best other job you qualify for, you would earn $6.50). Finally, you use electricity to bake the cake and some gas and wear and tear on your car to deliver it, in the amount of 50¢. The local gourmet coffee shop, whose owner knew your grandma personally and who had tasted the cake, is willing to pay you as much as $20.00 for each one of your homemade cakes. This is because she thinks that she can get twelve slices out of every cake and sell each one for $2, thereby making a nice $4.00 profit.

This information allows us to precisely compute the total value created in this *cake making and selling* transaction, computed as TVC = CWP − SOC (see Figure 7.5). That is, TVC = $20.00 − ($4.00 + $6.50 + $0.50) = $9.00. Or, more formally, taking resources valued at $11.00 in their next best use and producing a good valued at $20.00 by a customer, you have contributed to creating value for $9.00 through a "cake-making transformation process."

Appropriating the Value Created

To this point we have discussed the process of value creation—a process in which suppliers, the focal firm (i.e., you), and the customer partake. However, total value creation only tells us if there is *an opportunity* to make a profit. That is, if the total value created is greater than zero, someone will benefit, but we still don't know who.

---

[2] While this example could be considered trivial, we encourage you to pay close attention since it elucidates every aspect of the analysis of added value. The example is clearly fictitious in that it assumes perfect information by all parties involved.

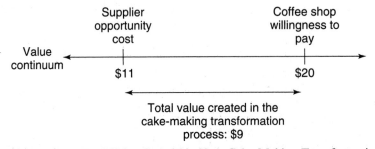

Figure 7.5   Total Value Created in Your Cake-Making Transformation Process

Q4

Value appropriation is the process by which the total value created in the transaction is split among all the entities who contributed to creating it (i.e., suppliers, the firm, and the customer). It is typically the outcome of a negotiation process between the firm and the suppliers, to determine the firm cost, and between the firm and the customer, to establish product prices (see Figure 7.6). When a firm appropriates value, it does so in the form of higher profits. When customers appropriate value, they do so in the form of savings (i.e., paying less than what they would have been willing to pay).[3]

Let's return to the example of your grandma-recipe cake-making venture. Note that at this point we have said nothing about either your actual cost to making the cake (i.e., the firm cost) or the price you and the coffee shop have agreed on for each cake you will deliver. In other words, at this point we know how much total value has been created (a theoretical amount), but we know nothing about how this value is going to be realized and who is going to appropriate it.

Let's assume that, while the store that provides you with the ingredients for your cake may be willing to drop the price to about $4.00 per cake because of your bulk buying, you are unaware of the store's supplier opportunity cost and do not negotiate hard. You simply pay the published price of $5.00 per cake in ingredients. Thus, your firm cost[4] equals ($5.00 + $6.50 + $0.50) = $12.00.

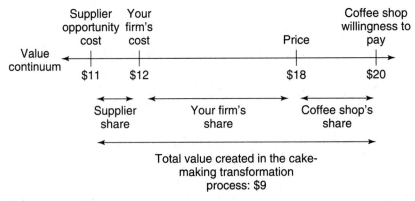

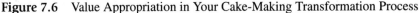

Figure 7.6   Value Appropriation in Your Cake-Making Transformation Process

---

[3] As customers we have all come across a "good deal" a few times in our life. A good deal is nothing but a situation where the price we are asked to pay is lower than our customer willingness to pay.

[4] Note that in this simplistic example you are playing two roles. On the one hand, you are a supplier of the labor resource. At the same time, you are the entrepreneur, the firm, who will retain any profits the business is able to generate.

Now, since you do not know that the coffee house's actual customer willingness to pay is $20.00 (they certainly are not going to tell you!), you accept the coffee house's first offer and do not negotiate hard . . . should you consider a negotiation class at this point?!? The price you agree on is $18.00 (see Figure 7.6).

We now have all the information we need to compute value appropriation and to determine how much of the total value created each of the entities involved will retain. Here is how the total value created, $9.00, would break down in this case:

- The suppliers appropriate $1.00 in excess profits—that is, one dollar more than the minimum amount of money they would have been willing to accept to provide you with the needed resources (i.e., supplier opportunity cost).

- You appropriate $6.00 in excess profits—that is, six dollars more than the minimum amount of money you would have been willing to stay in this venture for (i.e., your firm cost).

- The customer, the gourmet coffee shop, appropriates $2.00 in savings—that is, two dollars less than the maximum amount of money it would have been willing to disburse to acquire your specialty cake (i.e., their customer willingness to pay).

The Definition of Added Value

With the terminology of value creation and value appropriation now in place, we are ready to discuss added value. A firm's added value is defined as *that portion of the total value created that would be lost if the firm did not take part in the exchange.* That is, the firm's added value is measured as that portion of the value created in the transaction involving the firm minus the total value that could be created if the firm did not exist. A firm's added value is therefore the unique portion of the total value created that is contributed by the firm itself. Added value depends on the effects of existing competition.

Recall the example of your cake-making venture. In that example your firm was the only one in the market that could take the ingredients that were valued at $11.00 and, using the secret grandma recipe, transform them into a final product, this one-of-a-kind cake that customers would be willing to pay a maximum of $20.00 for. We established that the total value created in the transaction was $9.00.

What was your firm's added value then? It was the full $9.00. If you decide to not bake the cake, as the only person who has knowledge of the secret recipe (i.e., the unique transformation process), none of the potential value would be realized. That is, all the $9.00 of new value would be lost as we would be left with the raw resources worth the original $11.00.

Added Value in a Competitive Market

Let's now assume that you were not the only one who had been given the secret recipe in your grandma's will. Much to your surprise, your estranged cousin Bettie also received the secret and, you just found out she is entering the cake-baking business in your area! In fact, she just contacted the gourmet coffee shop you have been in talks with and is attempting to undercut you. She has the exact same cost structure as you do and produces a cake that is no different in any respect than yours. In other words, you and Bettie produce two products that are perfect substitutes for one another.

Mapping this scenario to the value creation model demonstrates that the total value created has not changed (see Figure 7.7), since both you and Bettie encounter the same supplier opportunity cost[5] and produce a cake that the coffee shop owner would pay the same for.

What has changed in this scenario is your firm's added value. In the first scenario you were the only one who could create the cake. Now, if your firm were to leave the exchange, Bettie's firm could step right in and, using the exact same resource, could produce the exact same cake. You do *nothing unique* and, as a consequence, your added value is now $0.00.

Pricing Considerations

Again, while we don't need to know price to compute added value (a theoretical value), price becomes important to gauge what portion of the value created each entity partaking to the transaction can appropriate. In our first scenario, when you were the only person who knew the secret recipe for the cake, we assumed you'd agree to the first price the coffee shop owner proposed (see Figure 7.6)— $18.00. It should be clear, though, that you were in a position of bargaining power and could have pushed the envelope. In fact, since we know the coffee shop owner's customer willingness to pay, we can assert that you could have charged as much as $20.00.

Once your cousin Bettie enters the market and begins to offer her cake, a perfect substitute of yours, you are no longer in a position of bargaining power. We can therefore expect a price war to cause prices to drop as low as your firm cost since neither of you offers anything unique (your added value is zero). Under this circumstance any price you quote that exceeds your firm cost would provide an incentive to the coffee shop and cousin Bettie's firm to strike a deal to cut you out. Cousin Bettie would quote a price lower than yours to get the business and a lower price would be a better deal to the coffee shop. This would force you to underbid Bettie, and the process would only end when either one of you is willing to quote a price equal to the firm cost. In this case, neither competitor will make any extra profit, while the customer, the coffee shop, will reap big savings.

The lesson is clear: No matter how much value your firm contributes to creating, unless you can be (at least in part) unique in your value creation, you will quickly compete

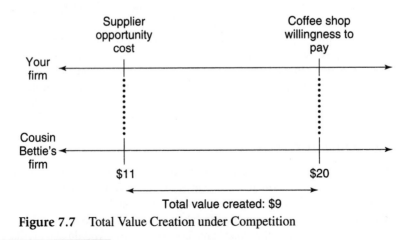

Figure 7.7   Total Value Creation under Competition

---

[5] This assumes that Bettie also has a minimum-wage job as the next best use of her time.

this value away to customers. This is, of course, the essence of competition and a force that in your capacity as a manager you need to learn to manage.

The Relationship between Added Value and Competitive Advantage

The insight about pricing discussed above is critical and it should clarify that a firm should focus on creating value, through innovation and the use of IT, not for the sake of doing so, but in order to be able to appropriate at least a portion of the total value created. In theory, the maximum amount of value that a firm can appropriate equals its added value. Thus, the imperative when engaging in new strategic initiatives is for a firm to create *added value*. The firm's added value is also a measure of its competitive advantage because it measures the extent to which the firm is able to do something unique and valuable.

How Is Added Value Created?

Imagine now one last twist in the story of your cake-making venture. Imagine that, since you have some artistic talents, you are able to garnish the cake with some icing that makes it unique. The coffee shop owner thinks that she can sell each slice of your "personalized" cake at a premium, say $2.25, claiming that the cake is a "coffee shop exclusive."

Personalizing the cake takes you fifteen minutes in extra labor, and the value of the extra ingredients needed is 37.5¢. In this case, your supplier opportunity cost has risen by $2.00. But the extra investment of resources leads to an increase in customer willingness to pay of $3.00. Cousin Bettie has no artistic talents and is unable to personalize her cakes. Your firm's added value is now positive (Figure 7.8).

Perhaps a bit simpler is to focus on the value of the different characteristics of your product. That is, with an incremental investment of $2.00, you create an increment in customer willingness to pay of $3.00, over what the competition can do, thus generating added value in the amount of $1.00. Note that price will be once again determined as a consequence of a negotiation process, but you certainly now have a competitive advantage versus Cousin Bettie's firm and you can expect to appropriate as much as one dollar (e.g., charging the coffee shop no more than $14.00).

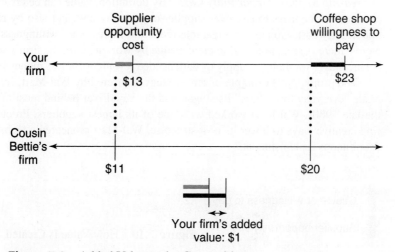

Figure 7.8   Added Value under Competition

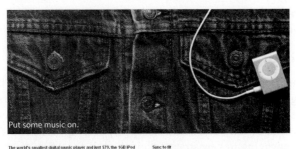

The world's smallest digital music player and just $79, the 1GB iPod shuffle lets you wear up to 240 songs(1) on your sleeve. Or your lapel. Or your belt. Clip on iPod shuffle and wear it as a badge of musical devotion.

One size fits all
You know what they say about good things and small packages. But when something 1.62 inches long and about half an ounce holds up to 240 songs, "good" and "small" don't quite cut it. Especially when you can listen to your music for up to 12 continuous hours.(2) In fact, iPod shuffle just may be the biggest thing in small.

Sync to fit
The first step to wearing 240 songs on your iPod shuffle is downloading iTunes — free. Then you can download 99¢ songs from the iTunes Store or import music from your CDs. When it's time to sync, plug the included dock into your Mac or PC's USB port and transfer your music from iTunes just by docking iPod shuffle.

Remix and match
Got more than 240 songs in your iTunes library? No problem. Let iTunes autofill your iPod shuffle and get a new musical experience every time. Pop follows jazz. Rock follows rap. iPod shuffle loves to improvise. Take the Shuffle switch, for instance. Even if you've synced a particular playlist, you can shuffle songs with a flick.

Figure 7.9 Apple's Explanation of the Key Features of the iPod Shuffle

Two Ways to Create New Value

More important than the calculations produced above is the meaning of this analysis and the considerations that follow from it.

Increasing Customer Willingness to Pay   Added value is created by doing something of value for customers, thereby increasing customer willingness to pay, through an investment of resources that does not exceed customer willingness to pay—otherwise we would be simply destroying value and wasting resources.

The most visible competitive battles take place on this end of the value continuum. The firms that have innovated use marketing to educate customers about their new products and services and drive up customer willingness to pay (Figure 7.9). However, this focus on customer facing initiatives can be misleading.

Decreasing Supplier Opportunity Cost   By definition, value can be created by increasing customer willingness to pay over supplier opportunity cost, but also by reducing supplier opportunity cost without a comparable reduction in customer willingness to pay. In other words, there is great potential to create value by working with the firm's suppliers and create incentives for them to supply us with needed resources for less money (see Figure 7.10).

The prototypical example of this strategy is offered by Wal-Mart, Inc. a firm that has made "everyday low prices" its slogan and the key driver behind most of its decisions. In the late 1980s, Wal-Mart worked with one of its largest suppliers, Procter & Gamble, to find creative ways to lower its cost structure. Wal-Mart pioneered a technique now called "continuous replenishment."

⬆ Customer willingness to pay

⬇ Supplier opportunity cost

Figure 7.10   How Value Is Created

Continuous replenishment is based on the idea of "pulled logistics" whereby a supplier (e.g., P&G), not a customer (e.g., Wal-Mart), is in charge of managing the customer's inventory. In the specific case of the Wal-Mart/P&G partnership, leveraging its data network (remember the opening quote?), Wal-Mart provided P&G with real-time purchase data from each of its stores. That is, anytime a box of Pampers or a carton of Tide detergent were bought at any Wal-Mart store, P&G was notified. This near-real-time knowledge of actual consumer demand enabled P&G to optimize its production schedules and its supply chain operations. As a consequence, P&G's own costs decreased and P&G became willing to supply Wal-Mart for less money than it charged other customers who could not engage in continuous replenishment. In other words, P&G supplier opportunity cost for dealing with Wal-Mart, and only Wal-Mart, decreased thanks to this data-sharing initiative. On the other hand of the value continuum, where Wal-Mart serves us the end consumer, no change occurred as customers didn't need to know about continuous replenishment or see any changes in what Wal-Mart offered, and Wal-Mart still commanded the same customer willingness to pay for its service.

Some Considerations about the Analysis of Added Value

The above discussion of the analysis of added value and the above examples suggest a few important concluding remarks.

Value Is in the Eye of the Customer   We define customer willingness to pay as the maximum amount of money that a *customer* is willing to give the firm to acquire its products or service. Unless there is a market for the innovation, no value has been generated.

Customer Willingness to Pay Is Not the Same as Price   Price is a consequence of a negotiation between the firm and the customer depending on the available information and the degree of competition in the market. Note, however, that a firm that is able to create higher customer willingness to pay does not *need to charge* higher prices to benefit. Imagine two firms vying for customer business and charging the same price. If one is able to command a slightly higher customer willingness to pay, for example by having a stronger brand, it will get the customer's business.[6]

Value Can Be Tangible or Intangible   Our cake-making example suggests that the coffee shop is willing to buy your cake because it can resell it and turn a profit. We buy clothes because of the tangible outcomes they provide (e.g., warmth). However, we also buy them for looks, style, fashion, for the way they make us feel, to fit within a certain group, to support a particular manufacturer, and so on. All these "intangible" drivers of value are as important as the tangible ones. As much as possible, goodwill, brand effects, loyalty, and all other intangible drivers of value should be estimated and measured. Techniques such as focus groups and market research are typically used to do so.

---

[6] Note that in some industries (for example, the lodging or airline industries), where the cost structure involves significant fixed costs and small variable costs, attracting more customers, even if at the same price as the competition, can result in significant profitability gains. This is because any revenue from incremental business will mostly flow through to the bottom line.

Creation of Value Is Not Appropriation   Beyond increasing customer willingness to pay, there is much opportunity to create added value by focusing on suppliers' opportunity cost and by providing advantages to suppliers to work with the firm. Yet, as a firm, it is crucial only to create value that you can appropriate (i.e., added value). Creating value can be done even in circumstances when this value can be appropriated by others (often customers). You must have added value (which is unique to your firm) to be sure to appropriate it.

Competitive Advantage and Added Value Are Closely Related   While the framework for the analysis of added value is a simplification of reality as it assumes perfect information of all entities involved and the absence of switching costs, it highlights what a firm must do to gain a competitive advantage. True competitive advantage is a function of added value. (see SideBar 7-1) Note, however, that the analysis of added value is focused on the short term and tells us nothing about the long-term resilience (e.g., resistance to erosion) of the firm's competitive advantage. An analysis of sustainability, the focus of Chapter 9, is the tool needed to evaluate if any added value we create can be appropriated over time. As we learned in this chapter, it is not enough to be able to create value; we must be able to appropriate it. To do so we must protect any added value we created from erosion by competitors.

SIDEBAR 1: HOW TO PERFORM ADDED VALUE ANALYSIS

Depending on the specific characteristics of the initiative under investigation, the analysis of added value can be more or less straightforward. You should:

Clearly Define the Initiative and Understand What It Entails

The first step in the analysis requires that we are very clear about what the firm will do for customers and what resources are necessary to create the product or perform the service being sold by identifying the intended customers and value proposition.

Identify the Comparison

Because added value is defined in comparative terms, it is critical to identify a baseline comparison. This baseline can be the competitor's initiative or the firm's own offers—when the firm is innovating with products or services that improve on the current state of the art in the industry.

Estimate Customer Willingness to Pay

Estimating customer willingness to pay can be a very complex process requiring substantial approximation and research. In order to simplify and focus this process, it helps to start by listing all the positive customer willingness to pay drivers—defined as those things that the firm does, as part of its offer, to increase customer willingness to pay. Note that any initiative has both positive and negative effects. That is, any initiative entails trade-offs; as the firm does some things of value for its customers, it also forgoes doing other things. It is critical to surface these negative customer willingness to pay drivers and discount their effect.

Estimate Supplier Opportunity Cost

This analysis is similar to the one above and includes both positive and negative change. When the initiative's main contribution to value creation is on the supplier opportunity cost side, supplier opportunity cost must be used. When the main effect of the initiative is on customer willingness to pay, then a simplifying assumption using firm cost as a proxy for supplier opportunity cost is acceptable.

Estimate Added Value

With the above information in hand, you can measure added value and begin to draw value appropriation considerations.

STRATEGIC INFORMATION SYSTEMS

Without doubt, information systems and technology engender a plentitude of confusing lingo, technical terms, and acronyms—a problem compounded by the wealth of half-prepared, fast-talking individuals using terminology incorrectly. In Chapter 2 we were very careful in defining what an information system (IS) is and in differentiating it from information technology (IT). We defined an information system as a sociotechnical system that includes IT, processes, people, and organizational structure.

The distinction between IT and IS is a critical prerequisite to understanding the strategic potential of information systems and the role that information technologies play in the creation and appropriation of added value. This distinction also shows why the firm that focuses solely on IT investments to become competitive (i.e., blindly purchasing computer systems) is wasting its money. IT investments are only appropriate within a larger IS design and only as components of information systems.

Definition: Strategic Information Systems

As you may intuitively expect, not all information systems an organization seeks to design, develop, and use may be strategic. The foremost objective of strategy in for-profit business ventures is to achieve and sustain superior financial performance. To do so the firm uses its resources to create value by either reducing supplier opportunity cost or by increasing the customers' willingness to pay for its product and services, or both. A firm achieves competitive advantage when it is able to generate added value by creating a unique and positive difference between customers' willingness to pay and the supplier opportunity cost. At that point, the firm is in a position to appropriate, in the form of profits, the added value it has created. In short, competitive strategy can be defined as the art and science of *being unique.*

We define *strategic information systems* as those information systems used to support or shape the competitive strategy of an organization. More succinctly, with the terminology discussed in this chapter, we can define *strategic information systems* as those that enable the creation and appropriation of value.

Strategic or Not? Depends on the Purpose   Strategic information systems are not defined by their functionality or the organizational function they support (as categorized in Chapter 3), but instead they are defined in terms of their objectives and the purpose they serve (e.g., improving the firm's competitive standing). Consider two examples from American Airlines:

- The SABRE reservation, typically considered the foremost example of a strategic information system, was originally created as an inventory system (i.e., a transaction processing system).

- The SMARTS system, also considered a tool that enabled American Airlines to gain a competitive advantage, was expressly designed to enable AA regional sales representatives to craft highly tailored incentive schemes for travel agents. SMARTS was an analytical tool (i.e., a decision support system).

No Need for Proprietary IT   Contrary to conventional wisdom, strategic information systems do not have to rely on proprietary technology. eBay, Inc. has provided the starkest example

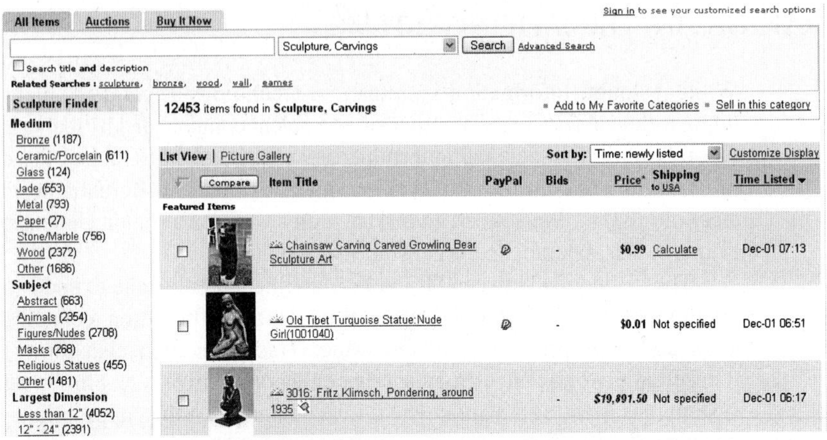

Figure 7.11   eBay's Auction Site

of this rule (Figure 7.11). eBay has dominated the online auction market since its inception using commonly available technology; namely, Internet technologies and the Web.

A simple look at a competitor's auction site (Figure 7.12) shows remarkable similarities and that the competitor offer comparable functionalities. eBay deploys little in the way of proprietary IT, and its technology has been duplicated by competitors. However, such replication of the technology is not enough, as it is the whole of eBay's initiative, and its information system, that underpins the firm's value-creating strategy and determines its added value. As we discuss more fully in Chapter 9, replicating the IT at the core of defendable strategic information systems is often a useless move.

Strategic versus Tactical Information Systems   The definition of strategic information systems we use is helpful in discriminating and identifying the many systems that are not strategic. These are systems that do not position the firm to create added value, even

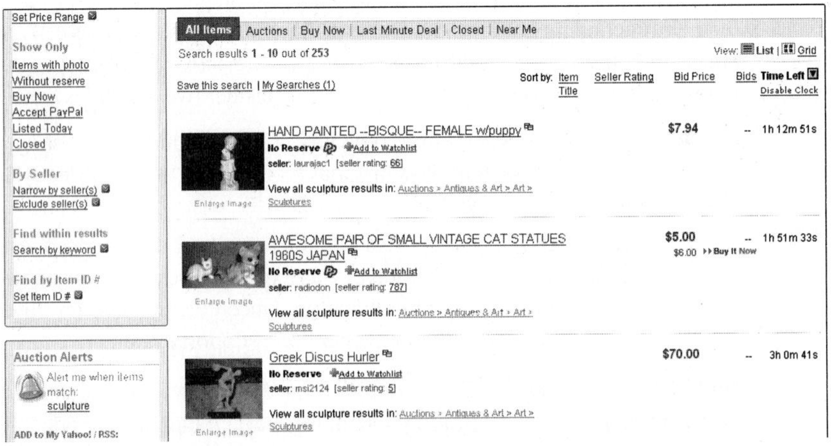

Figure 7.12   Yahoo's Auction Site

though they are important (often crucial) for the business's operations. We refer to these as *tactical* information systems. Consider the following examples:

- All the organizations that have salaried or hourly employees must pay them and maintain a complex set of records to compute tax withdrawals, accrued vacation time, sick leave, and so on. These information systems, typically called human resource systems, are critical for the smooth operations of organizations. Can you imagine working for a company that consistently sends you a paycheck with errors? You'd be looking for another job soon! Human resource systems are critical. Yet they are not strategic. They typically do not enable the creation of added value—rare is the firm that offers a unique value proposition based on its ability to correctly cut paychecks!

- A restaurant's primary information system, anchored by its point of sale (POS), is used to manage reservations, seating, order taking and delivery, and billing. Clearly, most modern restaurants could not operate as effectively without such system. Yet POSs are generally tactical in nature, not strategic, because they rarely allow the restaurant to create unique value.

- Similarly, no matter how well it is run, an e-mail system is unlikely to be the foundation of a strategic information system, and the same argument can be made for productivity software such as Microsoft Word and Excel, no matter how advanced their features may be.

No modern organization could run without e-mail and productivity software such as Microsoft Excel. Yet it is important to recognize that, important as they are, these systems are not strategic, and implementing or upgrading tactical systems will not create competitive advantage.

IT-Dependent Strategic Initiatives

As a general or functional manager, you may often propose new initiatives that need information systems and IT to be enacted. You will also be called on to help in the analysis, design, and development of strategic information systems early in your career. As a graduate of a management school, you will be paid for your analytical and decision-making abilities. This will likely include being involved with strategic information systems decisions.

In this capacity, you will be focusing on specific projects and initiatives. We use the notion of *IT-dependent strategic initiatives* in this book to refer to identifiable competitive moves and projects that enable the creation of added value and that rely heavily on the use of IT to be successfully implemented. IT-dependent strategic initiatives have three defining characteristics:

Initiative   IT-dependent strategic initiatives consist of specific projects, with clear boundaries that define what the initiative is designed to achieve, what it is designed to do and not do. For example, a freight shipper's package tracking initiative has very clear boundaries. It is designed to allow customers to gain visibility with respect to the current location of their parcels by logging onto a Web site (Figure 7.13).

Strategic   The firm introduces IT-dependent strategic initiatives with the definite objective of producing new value that the firm can appropriate. In other words, the firm seeks to create

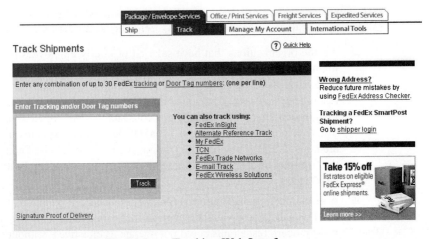

Figure 7.13 FedEx Package Tracking Web Interface

competitive advantage through the initiative. The freight shipper's package-tracking initiative, originally pioneered by Federal Express in the mid-1990s, was primarily designed to improve customer service (and therefore customer willingness to pay). Note, however, that, as it happened, this initiative also had the potential to shift much of the current volume of tracking inquiries away from call-center operators and to the Web, thereby reducing firm cost as well.

IT Dependent IT-dependent strategic initiatives cannot be feasibly created and executed without the use of information technology at their core. Note that this IT core needs not use cutting-edge or new breakthrough technologies, as was the case at FedEx, where the technology core of the initiative was certainly not of the bleeding-edge sort. While the Internet and the Web were relatively new to the shipping public in the mid-1990s, the technology at their core had been around for over twenty years. FedEx's package-tracking initiative is clearly IT dependent, as it would not be feasible for the freight shipper to heavily promote a call-center-based package-tracking system due to the high costs of call-center operations versus online automated tracking systems.

Examples of IT-dependent strategic initiatives abound in modern businesses and include some of the most important and most recent trends: ERP-enabled business integration, supply chain management, customer relationship management, electronic commerce, and electronic business initiatives. However, as we see in the FedEx example above, IT-dependent strategic initiatives can have much more limited scope, including projects such as introducing Internet cafés on cruise ships or online retailers creating recommender systems (e.g., Amazon).

IT-Dependent Strategic Initiatives Not IT Investments The notion of IT-dependent strategic initiative is a critical one to plan for the use and management of strategic information systems. Using this definition forces us to shift attention away from investments in technology and to recognize that IT investments can only pay off if they are part of a larger and cohesive information system design. It is the ability of the IT-dependent strategic initiative to create added value that we must focus on, not the uniqueness or innovativeness of the technology at its core. Thus, IT-dependent strategic initiatives do not simply consist of the building of a computer system or application that, allegedly, generates competitive advantage until it is successfully replicated; rather, they consist of the configuration of an activity system, dependent on IT at its core, that fosters the creation and appropriation of economic value.

SUMMARY

This chapter provides the background for understanding strategic information systems decisions by discussing fundamental concepts and analytical frameworks. Specifically, in this chapter we introduced the notion of value creation and appropriation.

- Economic value is created when some input resources that have a value of $x in their next best utilization are transformed in outputs for which customers are willing to pay $x + $v.

- The value thus created is partitioned amongst those entities involved in its creation: a firm, its suppliers, and its customers—a process known as value appropriation.

- A firm is able to appropriate that portion of the total value created that would be lost if the firm did not partake in the exchange—a figure we termed added value.

- Strategic information systems are those that are designed and developed to create and appropriate value. They differ from tactical information systems, those systems that, while often critical for the

firm's operations, do not enable the creation of distinctive value.

- IT-dependent strategic initiatives consist of identifiable competitive moves and projects that enable the creation of added value and that rely heavily on the use of information technology to be successfully implemented. They should be the focus of the search for new value creation.

- General and functional managers, because of their understanding of the firm's processes and customer needs, take center stage in the identification and analysis of opportunities to create value with information systems. When doing so, they should focus on IT-dependent strategic initiatives rather than taking a narrow focus on IT investments.

This chapter laid the foundation for the analysis of value creation and appropriation of IT-dependent strategic initiatives. In the next chapter we examine frameworks and analytical tools designed to help you envision, and take advantage of, opportunities to deploy IT-dependent strategic initiatives.

STUDY QUESTIONS

1. Explain the value creation process. How does a firm contribute to the creation of economic value?

2. Provide two examples of firms that you think have been able to create value using information systems. The first one should be a firm that has done so mainly by focusing on customer willingness to pay. The second one should be a firm that has done so mainly by focusing on supplier opportunity cost.

3. Think about the last time you bought something that you felt was "a great deal." Why did you think the product or service was such a great deal? Do you believe that the transaction was considered "great" by the firm you acquired the product or service from? Why or why not?

Explain using the framework of value creation and appropriation.

4. What is the difference between value creation and value appropriation? Why is this difference important?

5. Provide an example of a well-known firm that you think currently has added value. Explain your example using added value analysis.

6. Define the concept of strategic information systems and provide an example.

7. Define the concept of tactical information systems and provide an example.

8. Define the concept of IT-dependent strategic initiative and provide an example.

▮ FURTHER READINGS

1. Brandenburger, A. M., and Stuart, H. W. (1996). "Value-Based Business Strategy." *Journal of Economics and Management Strategy* (5:1), pp. 5–24.

2. Porter, M. E. "What Is Strategy?" *Harvard Business Review* (November–December 1996).

▮ GLOSSARY

■ **Added value:** That portion of the total value created that would be lost if the firm did not partake in the exchange.

■ **Competitive advantage:** The condition where a firm engages in a unique transformation process and has been able to distinguish its offerings from those of competitors. When a firm has achieved a position of competitive advantage, it is able to make above average profits.

■ **Customer willingness to pay:** The maximum amount of money the firm's customers are willing to spend in order to obtain the firm's product.

■ **Firm cost:** The actual amount of money the firm disbursed to acquire the resources needed to create its product or service.

■ **IT-dependent strategic initiatives:** Identifiable competitive moves and projects that enable the creation of added value and that rely heavily on the use of information technology to be successfully implemented (i.e., they cannot feasibly be enacted without investments in IT).

■ **Strategic information systems:** Information systems that are designed to support or shape the competitive strategy of an organization. Those information systems that enable the creation and appropriation of value.

■ **Supplier opportunity cost:** The minimum amount of money suppliers are willing to accept to provide the firm with the needed resources.

■ **Tactical information systems:** Systems that do not position the firm to create added value. In other words, they do not enable distinctive initiatives that enable the firm to create unique economic value.

■ **Transformation process:** The set of activities the company engages in to convert inputs, purchased from suppliers, into outputs, to be sold to customers.

■ **Total value created:** The difference between customer willingness to pay and supplier opportunity cost.

■ **Value appropriation:** The process by which the total value created in the transaction is split among all the entities who contributed to creating it (i.e., suppliers, the firm, and the customer).

■ **Value creation:** The process by which new economic value is generated through a transformation process.

CASE STUDY: RICE EPICUREAN ONLINE SHOPPING: DECADENCE OR DESTINY[7]

INTRODUCTION

With his ten-month-old daughter asleep on his shoulder, Larry Cantera[8] hit the return key on his PowerBook computer and quietly closed the cover. Another week's grocery shopping finished! The following afternoon a Rice Epicurean delivery van driver would arrive at the Cantera's apartment door. Their nanny would check the items against a receipt, give the driver any coupons, and put the groceries away.

The previous day, Cantera had told a friend about the scheme.

> Since Julie was born, our lives have become more hectic. With both of us working, grocery shopping

---

[7] This case was written from public sources and, unless otherwise noted, materials were not provided nor approved by Rice Epicurean managers. The case was originally published as Blake Ives and Gabriele Piccoli. (2002) "Rice Epicurean Online Shopping: Decadence or Destiny" Communications of AIS (9:18) pp. 314–329.

[8] A fictional name for a real Rice Epicurean customer.

became even more of a burden. On most weeks my wife or I were going to the grocery store twice a week. I did one big run on Saturday, when everyone else in the world was in the store. From the time I stepped out the door until I had the groceries home and in the fridge took about two hours. Later in the week we'd be shopping for bread, cold cuts, milk, and whatever we had forgotten.

Last week I spent fifteen minutes completing the on-line order. My wife maybe spends another five minutes going over with me anything special she thinks we need. After six weeks I have pretty much everything we ever order on our master list at Rice Epicurean.

Cantera defended paying a $15 delivery charge.

Our first order hit a free delivery promotion scheme. We paid full price for the second delivery but then received three more delivery promotions. So our out-of-pocket costs for grocery delivery for the first month were pretty modest. The grocery store is about 4 miles away, so I could come up with a small savings on gas and wear and tear on the car. And when Julie is a bit older, we won't miss talking her out of candy purchases at checkout. But the real benefit is our time. If we can save three, or even only two hours a week, it's worth the 10% premium—particularly if we end up spending that time with our daughter.

RICE EPICUREAN BACKGROUND

In September of 2002, Rice Epicurean Markets was the self-reported oldest family-owned chain of supermarkets in Houston, Texas. It traced its roots to Rice Boulevard Market, opened in 1937 by William H. Levy, grandfather of the current owners. In 1937 Rice Boulevard was a dirt road in a largely undeveloped future suburb of Houston. Sixty-five years later, that store, considerably increased in size, sat in the middle of one of the most desirable living areas in Houston. In 1957 a second store was opened. Its first customers included rice farmers living west of Houston; by 2002 those rice fields had become Houston's prestigious Galleria area. Rice Epicurean's other four stores were located in similarly well-to-do neighborhoods, including one almost across the street from a recently

opened giant HEB Central Market. The six stores ranged in size from 20,000 to 42,000 square feet.[9]

Founder William Levy sought to provide quality products and personal service to his customers. With its founding in 1988 the Rice Epicurean chain continued that tradition.

For Rice to now compete with the larger chains, we re-created ourselves in a successful effort to be the best grocery store in town . . . each store operated by Rice Epicurean Markets is still merchandised to be in tune with its particular neighborhood. The charge card system with monthly billing, introduced in 1964, remains in effect. Rice Epicurean Markets prides itself on the growing number of employees who have been with the chain for 20 years or more and can tell you by name, the customers and their families who have shopped with them for many, many years.[10]

The stores, while smaller than other Houston chains, sought to maintain a rich inventory of typical grocery store items as well as gourmet products, chef-prepared foods, high-quality bakery products, and, in most stores, full-service meat departments. Home delivery was not new to Rice Epicurean, as Phil Cohen, director of loyalty marketing and customer services, explained.

People don't know this, but we've been delivering groceries for a very long time. . . . We have customers who've been faxing in their orders for years. We have our own delivery vans, and we deliver out of each store. [DeMers, 2002]

Customers could also join the chain's loyalty card program. The "Experience Card" provided lower prices on promotional items, discounts on products and services from Epicurean's Experience partners around Houston, and, in some instances, rebate coupons for a certain level of purchases.

ONLINE SHOPPING

In the summer of 2002, Rice Epicurean announced, primarily through in-store promotions, its new Home Runs online shopping program. It was not the first online grocery in Houston, but, in September of 2002, it was the only one still operating in the city.

---

[9] This section draws on material from the History page [http://www.riceepicurean.com/about_rice/about_home.html] of the Rice Epicurean Web site.

[10] http://www.riceepicurean.com/about_rice/about_home.html

continued

CASE STUDY (*continued*)

Home Runs had two online shopping options. One, priced at $15, was home delivery. This was available from individual stores to customers in designated zip codes. The second option was in-store pick-up. This $7 option was available to any customer who could reach the store. Orders could be placed from Rice Epicurean's Web page seven days a week, twenty-four hours a day. They could be picked up or delivered in one-hour time slots as selected by the customer; pickup was available from 9 A.M. until 7 P.M. seven days a week and home delivery from noon until 6 P.M. Monday through Friday.

Customers wishing to try out online shopping were directed by a brochure to go to the Rice Epicurean home page [Rice Epicurean, 2002] and click on "Shop Online." A Web page identified the four stores that were participating in the program as well as the zip code areas each store provided home delivery to. Once a store was selected, the customer was automatically redirected to the Rice Epicurean virtual store run for them by a third-party application service provider, MyWebGrocer.[11]

Once at the MyWebGrocer (MWG) site (see Exhibit 1), a new customer first set up an account by providing her e-mail address, a password, and, if she were a member, her Experience Card number. After registering, the customer

could begin to shop. Items could be selected from the Groceries, Health & Beauty, and Home Supplies links in an index panel extending down the left quarter of the screen (see Exhibit 2). A customer selecting the Grocery option, for instance, would then be shown a list of twenty-some categories of groceries (e.g., baby store, bakery brands, dairy, deli). Clicking on "Produce" would then reveal subcategories for Fresh Fruit, Fresh Vegetables, Organics, and so on. A subsequent click on "Fresh Fruit" would reveal a list of fruit (apples, bananas, berries . . .).

Clicking on one of these then revealed in the middle half of the page an alphabetized list of the products. Each entry included a picture of the product (if one was available), the vendor and name of the product (e.g., Chiquita® Bananas), some descriptive or instructional information (e.g., "please order the number of individual bananas you want"), the size or weight of a typical purchase (e.g., average 8 ounces each), the price[12] per pound (e.g., $.49,) the average price each (e.g., $.25), the price for non–Experience club members (e.g., $.30 each), and buttons to "buy," to "add to [shopping] list," or for "Details" to get a richer description of the product. In some cases, a pull-down menu was displayed for specifying the weight of the desired order (e.g., for sliced ham from the deli). The "Details" button

Exhibit 1   Rice Epicurean Home Page

Exhibit 2   Aisles in Virtual Store for Rice Epicurean

---

[11] http://www.mywebgrocer.com

[12] Prices were sent via ftp (file transfer protocol) from the store to MyWebGrocer at midnight once a week.

revealed the products UPC code and, where available, bigger pictures and further descriptive information.

Having found the product, either by drilling down as described above or by using a search feature,[13] the customer could either add a product to the shopping basket by clicking on the "buy" flag next to a product or instead add it to a shopping list that was then available in the current or subsequent visits. From the master list the customer could add items to the shopping cart, vary the number of items, or remove the item from the master list (see Exhibit 3). Other lists could also be created—for instance, for Thanksgiving dinner or the items necessary for a favorite recipe.

Once the order was completed, the customer would go to checkout, where, if it were her first visit, she would provide billing and delivery information including name, address, phone number, and credit card information. A secure server at MWG then processed this information.

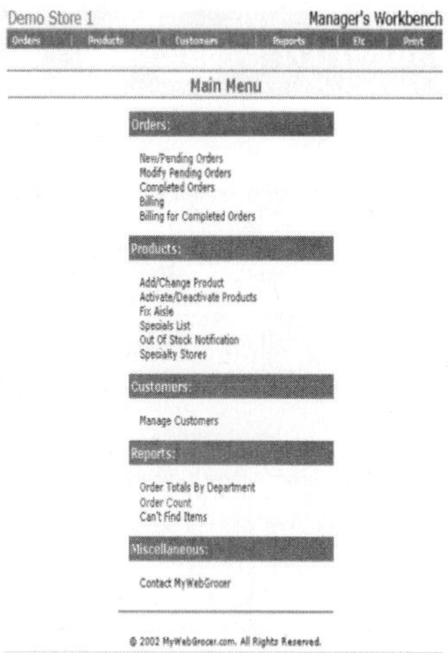

ORDER FULFILLMENT

Customer orders were accessible to the store from a password-protected electronic workbench located on a secure MWG server (see Exhibits 4–6).

Once retrieved from the site, the orders, sorted in shelf-sequence order, could either be printed or loaded onto handheld devices.[14] These then guided the pickers in pulling the items from the store shelves. Once picked, the

Exhibit 4   MWG Manager's Workbench: Main Screen

order items would be scanned and the Experience Card and Credit Card info entered. A printed point of sale receipt was then available to accompany the order, as was an exception report providing in preprinted form a six-digit order number, the scheduled time and date of delivery, and the name, address, and phone number of the recipient. There were also blanks for filling in the local details about the order, including the number of bags and their location

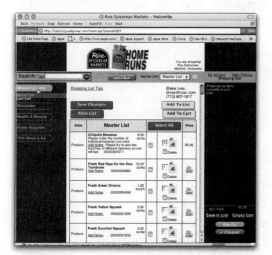

Exhibit 3   Master List for Customer of Rice Epicurean

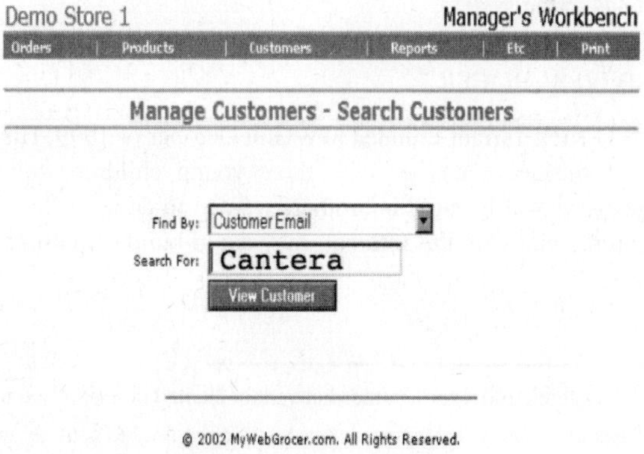

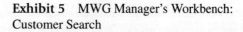

Exhibit 5   MWG Manager's Workbench: Customer Search

---

[13] Searches could be done by brand name (e.g., Cowboy Caviar), product name ("Original Recipe") or UPC code (e.g., 9171700100).

[14] If stores had handheld devices available, these could direct pickers to the appropriate shelf and, by scanning, ensure that the correct product had been picked.

continued

Demo Store 1				Manager's Workbench	
Orders	Products	Customers	Reports	Etc	Print

Manage Customers

Customer:	Actions:
	Edit Customer Account
	Create Customer Discount/Charge
Larry Cantera	View Customer Discounts/Charges
1 Main St	Shop for the Customer (password will be requested)
Houston, TX	Select A Different Customer

© 2002 MyWebGrocer.com. All Rights Reserved.

Exhibit 6   MWG Manager's Workbench: Customer Functions

(e.g., freezer, cooler). Handwritten on this form were any substitutions made by the picker. This latter form was printed from a secure server on the MWG site.[15]

Technology requirements for the store were minimal. In addition to the optional handhelds, stores required an Internet-connected PC for accessing the workbench and for transferring prices, weekly ads, and so on. A small kernel of code was also necessary for interfacing the handhelds to the system.

MYWEBGROCER

CEO Rick Tarrant founded MWG in October of 1999. His sister-in-law, a mother with three young children, suggested that if he and his brothers wanted to do something commercial with the Internet, they could build something

so that she could shop at her local grocery store without ever having to get out of her SUV.

At the core of Tarrant's business was the information processing engine behind the online shopping experience now available at Rice Epicurean and many other stores throughout the United States. Offering a nonexclusive relationship and operating on a fee per transaction basis, MWG played the role of application service provider for chains that could either not afford or did not wish to develop an online shopping application. In October of 2002, MWG's retail partners were all grocery stores or chains, but the firm saw long-term opportunities in other forms of retail [Spindler, 2002b].

A sample store on the MWG site provided prospective retail partners first-hand experience with online shopping. The MWG Web site also explained some of the benefits to prospective shoppers.

> The easy-to-use customer interface will accurately reflect each store's inventory and pricing, including specials and frequent shopper program discounts. The Shopping Solution has been designed to work for multiple stores in different geographic areas, offering different inventory at varying prices. Inventory and price changes are made easier than in traditional brick and mortar stores!

MWG claimed that the time required to set up a virtual store varied from two weeks to forty-five days.[16] MWG personnel, including an account executive, would "install and setup the Internet Shopping Solution and train store personnel, or fulfillment center management, in the most efficient methods for order fulfillment" (see Sidebar 2 for examples of tasks necessary in the implementation). The sheer number of items carried by each store complicated this process.[17]

---

[15] See [Intel, 2002] for a somewhat vendor slanted description on MyWebGrocer's technical architecture.

[16] Retailers, however, reported that the time required to actually get ready for going online could be considerably longer, particularly for multiple-store operations. Among the issues were working with grocery wholesalers to set up the price list to be transferred to MWG. One retailer estimated it had spent between six months and a year getting the system in place.

[17] Typical grocery stores carry anywhere from 35,000 to 50,000 stock keeping units (SKUs), including many such as deli or bakery items or store brands that are store or chain unique. It has been estimated that there may be a total of 700,000 or more unique SKUs across U.S. grocers and that approximately 25 percent are replaced each year. Splinder [2002b] reported that MWG had about 140,000 SKUs in their database thus far.

SIDEBAR 2: PARTIAL LIST OF STEPS IN GETTING A STORE ONLINE [SPINDLER, 2002A]

1. Grocer provides a file of products handled in each store. This includes UPC code, description, size, unit-of-measure, department, and movement over some period of time. MWG matches this against their own library of products, identifies the non-matches or poor descriptions, ranks them by sales volume, sorts by department, and returns to retailer for better descriptions of the most important items.

2. MWG has a discussion with the grocers IT department about how often prices change, including weekly specials, and arranges to get a feed of information matching what the grocer uses to feed his POS in-store. We begin getting these files, either by email or FTP, as soon as possible. Once set up, this process is automated.

3. In cases where the retailer has a planogram of the store, MWG aligns aisles with products. If they do not have accurate data, MWG asks the store manager to fill out an electronic survey. Pickers can update changes from the handheld.

4. Grocers provide MWG with files of new products and of discontinued products. This too is eventually automated.

5. For new products MWG asks retailers to use a scheme called content exchange to ensure new and revised products descriptions, images, ingredients, sizes are correct and current. Using UPC codes, grocers could check to see if the item was in the MWG database. If not, they, or a third party, could provide a graphic, description, and so on.

6. MWG works with store category managers to make sure descriptions of perishables are kept current.

7. MWG works with operations and merchandising managers to set up rules of engagement for such issues as privacy policy, hours of operation, substitution policy.

8. MWG sets up each store using the above factors and tests it with real orders from employees. Here pickers are taught how to pick efficiently and how to handle customer service issues.

9. MWG provides advice on how the store should market the program.

10. Online shopping at the store is launched.

THE ECONOMICS OF ONLINE SHOPPING

MWG felt the economics of the scheme were compelling. Among the new costs were labor for picking and delivery, equipment, storage space, and a transaction fee paid to the service supplier. Mike Spindler, president of MyWebGrocer, explained the breakdown of costs [MyWebGrocer.Com, 2002]

> Generally we have found that a picker can pick two, $100 orders each hour from beginning to putting them into the car, if they are picking single orders. If loaded labor costs are $15.60 that means labor runs about $7.80 per order. If they are picking multiple orders simultaneously, then that cost/order decreases significantly.

Most grocers already have ample computing and communication systems in store. Incremental gear would include a handheld picking device, a drive-up call box and when volume warrants a cooler/freezer combination up by the pickup aisle. If delivery is contemplated, a vehicle is necessary.

In September of 2002, the MWG site described a per transaction fee of $4.00 and a minimum number of transactions per month. The fee was the same for home delivery or in-store pick-up. There is also a small installation fee and whatever money the retailer chose to spend on advertising and promotions.[18] The hand-picking systems, provided by

---

[18] The installation fee for a single store varied in October of 2002 from $2,000 to $2,500 but for chains of forty or more stores the fee could be as little as $250 per store [Spindler, 2002b].

continued

Symbol Technology, cost about $1,250 per machine,[19] and a call box and coolers and freezers at the pickup location could run anywhere from $8,000 to $12,000 per store.

HARVESTING THE BENEFITS

According to Spindler, there were compelling benefits to the retailer.

> The average order is greater than $100 per basket for online shoppers. Even the top 10% of in-store customers average only about $60 per basket. [Spindler, 2002b]

Spindler's supposition about increasing market basket size had been reported [MyWebGrocer, 2001] as having been independently verified:

> A Bain & Company study looked at very loyal Jewel shoppers who had switched to Peapod (offered, at the time, through Jewel). Those shoppers where spending 45% of their overall replenishment requirements budget at Jewel each week when shopping in store. After the switch to the online purchase/delivery combination offered by Peapod, these same shoppers bought 65% of their weekly requirements through that outlet.

While MyWebGrocer explained the increased per basket revenues by increased purchases of products that might previously have been bought elsewhere, Cantera's experience suggested an alternative explanation.

> We are trying to get by on just one delivery each week. I suppose paying with real money rather than with my time may make us keener to reduce the number of weekly transactions with the store. First, because I didn't want to spend $1,500 a year on grocery deliveries and second because I wanted to get the maximum benefit out of the $750 that we were proposing to spend. We are also trying to buy things at the grocery store we might have, in the past, bought from the drug or baby store—particularly heavy things like formula or bulky things like diapers.

That means we are freezing more things, looking at alternative storage schemes—say to keep bananas from ripening too fast—and also asking for help from Rice Epicurean. For instance, each week I order a dozen bananas in two bunches. The system allows me to attach a note to any item ordered. In this case I have a standing request to the picker to look for two bunches that are of varying degrees of ripeness.

In addition to greater revenues per existing customer, Spindler felt that retailers would get even greater benefit from new customers attracted by the online option.

> Most customers are incremental to the store. In most cases we find that the grocer offering online service will receive the inverse of his normal store market share in incremental customers. In other words if a store has 20% market share in its area, 80% of its online customers have been shopping at other stores . . . . The customer base is small, generally around 1% or less of total store business, but is growing rapidly, as much as doubling every 6–8 months.

The MWG team also felt the online format tended to attract shoppers who were "willing to pay a premium for the offered service" and who were "not nearly as likely to switch out items already in their shopping lists for similar items that are 'on deal' " [MyWebGrocer, 2001]. That, as Mike Spindler explained, translated into higher profits.

> Given that 50% of your online customers are new and a labor rate of about $16 per hour (loaded), the average order yields a pre-tax profit of between $8 and $13—better by far than in-store current yield. [Spindler, 2002a]

Providing exceptional customer service was a major objective for Rice Epicurean and, for Cantera at least, the online shopping appeared to provide a convincing way to deliver on that promise.

> One thing that surprised me was the level of personal service—far more than I ever experienced in any store, including Rice Epicurean. They have

---

[19] Handheld-equipped chains, depending on volume, had from one to five handhelds per store, usually with a spare device available at headquarters. The Symbol SPT 1800 was a rugged PDA running the Palm operating system and able to sustain up to a four-foot drop to a concrete floor. The devices included bar code scanners and wireless connections that could be configured for local or wide area use. Further information on the SPT is available at http://www.symbol.com/products/mobile_computers/mobile_palm_spt1800.html.

called to confirm product switches and I have called them to request changes. For instance, we are on the border, but just outside of the store's delivery area, so I called to ask them to make an exception and deliver to us—which they agreed to do. When the groceries are ordered you get both a Web page and e-mail confirmation of the order and, when they are delivered, are asked to check them off against the receipt.

Some retailers, however, had found this richer interface to offer more problems than opportunities, as John A. Catsimatidis, the chief executive of Red Apple Group, described.

It's a pain in the neck. . . . What is particularly tough . . . is trying to guess a customer's tastes. "Is it ripe, is it too ripe? What size tomatoes do they want?" I'm not saying that some day online grocery shopping won't become a reality, but not within the next decade.[20] [Pristin, 2002]

In the middle of August in 2002, Spindler announced numbers that must have been reassuring to investors, retail partners, and hooked customers:

We have three record volume weeks in a row and each of the last four weeks have doubled our year ago comparable store volume. [MyWebGrocer, 2002b]

MWG's Web site listed over thirty chains and markets throughout the United States that had implemented the scheme. Among these were D'Agostino in New York; Langanstine's and Robérts in New Orleans; Potash Brothers in Chicago; a Piggly Wiggly in Rome, Georgia; and Supermarketbutler.com in Sacramento.

MWG also had the opportunity to sell manufacturing programs, including advertising and favored product positioning, on the Web site, but had yet to aggressively promote this with manufacturers. They were running programs, promoting the program for their retail partners, and were doing so for free. Among the promotions were follow-up surveys, instructions for new customers such as drawing the search feature to their attention if they have not used it, weekly reorder e-mails (which now accounted for about 40 percent of weekly online orders), promotions based on behaviors such as promoting infant formula, if diapers were purchased, and mass promotions the grocer chose to participate in. For instance, a customer who might complain about overripe bananas could be informed, via

the system, that he had been given a $2 off coupon on his next banana purchase. Pickers could also be alerted, via the handhelds, to customer concerns.

COMPETITION

Internet Grocery Shopping had been among the biggest casualties of the dot-com meltdown of 2000–2001. Among the dead and wounded had been Webvan, Kozmos, Streamline, and HomeRuns.Com [Intel, 2002]. Hoovers.Com described the demise of Webvan:

In summer 2001 [Webvan] turned off the lights and quit filling orders. It's reported 2000 sales were about $178 million, but it reported a loss of nearly a half-billion dollars . . . stopped filling orders, shuttered its Web site, and fired its workforce. It later filed for Chapter 11 bankruptcy protection, and in October sold its distribution technology and some warehouse assets. [Hoovers.Com, 2002]

Another Internet startup, Peapod, was still competing in Chicago, New York, Connecticut, Massachusetts, and Washington, D.C. Founded in 1989, Peapod had initially pulled items from affiliated supermarkets, but the company had more recently turned to centralized distribution from its own warehouses.

In April of 2000, Royal Ahold International, a Netherlands-based firm with 9000 stores in 25 countries, acquired a controlling interest in Peapod for $73M, the amount of Peapod's previous year's revenues. In July of 2002, Ahold bought out the remaining 52 percent of Peapod for $35M. Peapod became a subsidiary of Ahold USA, with some 1600 stores primarily in the Carolinas and the Northeastern United States, and the online shopping and delivery arm for Ahold USA stores, including Giant Food and Stop & Shop.

Ahold's CFO, Michiel Meurs, defended the decision to acquire the remainder of the Peapod stock at 72 percent above preannouncement market value:

By bringing Peapod fully into the Ahold family, we are best positioned to further grow the company successfully and meet increasing customer requirements. Strategically, we are convinced that the Web-based grocery business combined with our store network under strong local brands will prove to be a powerful concept to attract and retain loyal customers.

---

[20] Red Apple Group is parent to Gristede's, a New York store using the EasyGrocer.com solution for online shopping [Pristin, 2002].

continued

Despite the failures of the dot-coms, several large chains had announced online trading initiatives and some, such as Ahold USA, were built on the bones of dying dot-coms.[21] Safeway, with 2001 sales of $34 billion, was offering, in September of 2002, home delivery for $9.95 in San Francisco; Sacramento; Portland, Oregon; and Vancouver, Washington. It had yet to announce any plans for extending the scheme, including into its Houston stores.

Safeway's online shopping engine was developed by GroceryWorks.Com, a Dallas-based firm that at one time had distribution centers in Dallas, Fort Worth, and Houston. Safeway acquired for $30 million a 50 percent interest in the firm in the spring of 2000, with the UK-based retailer Tesco in June of 2001 acquiring another 32 percent for $20 million. At the time Tesco reported already having almost 1 million registered customers in the U.K. and was processing approximately 70,000 orders per week and operating its online business profitably on sales of about $420 million a year [Macaluso, 2001].

In 2001 Albertsons, with $38 billion in annual revenues, began offering home delivery for $9.95. By September of 2002, the program had been extended to six West Coast markets as well as nationwide delivery of non-perishables through its Savon.com site. However, in March of 2002 Albertsons exited the Houston market. H.E. Butt, with over 250 stores in the Southwestern United States, Mexico, and Houston, had shelved plans for an eight-digit investment in online shopping in December of 2000, just a month before the scheduled rollout of its first pilot store in Austin, Texas [McFarlan and Dailey, 2000].

All three of these chains, Safeway, Albertsons, and HEB, were also members of the World Wide Retail Alliance, a B2B organization whose mission, according to its Web site was

> To enable participating retailers and suppliers to simplify, rationalize, and automate supply chain processes, thereby eliminating inefficiencies in the supply chain. Today, the WWRE is the premier Internet-based business-to-business (B2B) exchange in the retail e-marketplace. Utilizing the most

sophisticated Internet technology available, the WWRE enables retailers and suppliers in the food, general merchandise, textile/home, and drugstore sectors to substantially reduce costs across product development, e-Procurement, and supply chain processes. Current membership consists of 62 retail industry leaders from around the world with combined revenue of over U.S. $845 billion. [Worldwide Retail Exchange, 2002]

MWG itself faced competition, and using MWG or its online competitors, other smaller Houston chains could relatively easily enter the home delivery business. One of the alternative ASPs was EasyGrocer.Com,[22] serving less than 100 stores, primarily in New England. Another, WhyRunOut, served a small market segment in Los Angeles [Viejo, 2001].

While Rice Epicurean currently appeared to face no major local competition in the home delivery grocery business, there were other retailers in Houston that provided home delivery for many of Rice Epicurean's product categories (e.g., flowers, catering). Specs Liquors, a popular wine retailer, for instance, offered online ordering and courier delivery to most of the same areas served by the Rice Epicurean chain.

Within the Houston grocery industry, Rice Epicurean was a relatively small player, failing to make the *Houston Chronicle*'s February 2001 list of the top ten grocers in town. At the top of that list were Kroger ($1.57B in revenues, 81 stores), Randalls ($1B, 42), H.E. Butt ($.7B, 50), Fiesta Mart ($.6Bm 33), and the since departed Albertsons ($.56B 33) [*Houston Chronicle,* 2001]. Rice Epicurean had last appeared on the *Houston Chronicle*'s top ten grocers list for the twelve months prior to February 1999 [*Houston Chronicle,* 1998] at that time its eight stores and 621 employees were reported as having a 1.9 percent market share on sales of $96.8 million.

THE FUTURE OF HOME DELIVERY

A friend asked Cantera if he thought he would still be buying his groceries online in a year or two.

---

[21] Further details on the early online grocery shopping business models are available in [Palmer, 2000].

[22] http://www.easygrocer.com/

We likely will if someone is there to provide the service, though it would be complicated when our nanny is no longer here to receive the delivery. When we buy a house the store pick-up might be attractive if the store is closer or on the way home from work. It's unlikely we will stop because of the expense. Today my wife and I have a fair amount of disposable income, but I wouldn't have been doing this when I was living from paycheck to paycheck.

If someone offered delivery at $9.95, a wider choice of groceries, or some other significant inducement, we might switch. On the other hand, if we find our store carrying products we have a hard time finding,[23] our incentive to stay will increase.

Cantera had already faced one test of his loyalty to Rice Epicurean. He had recently registered as a member of Upromise,[24] a cross-industry loyalty program that rolled up frequent shopper rewards into savings for kids' education. By shopping with particular merchants, banks, realtors, phone companies, and so on, he could increase the size of that contribution. Consumer products manufacturers, including Coca Cola®, were participating, but to earn reward points for purchases of those products, Upromise members also had to be members of participating grocer's loyalty programs. Thus far, Rice Epicurean was not participating in the Upromise program, but Cantera had noticed Upromise logos on the advertisements of several other Houston chains.

Cantera's wife had raised some concerns about the privacy of the family's purchase data. Privacy was obviously a concern at Rice Epicurean, which included several separate privacy notices on its Web site (see Sidebar 3).

Setting his computer aside, and with daughter Julie still dozing on his shoulder, Cantera pondered the future of online shopping. Would it remain a small niche market for the decadent or would in-store grocery shopping go the way of bank clerks, gas jockeys, and pay telephones, largely pushed aside by more customer convenient or cheaper order fulfillment alternatives? And, if it is to attract large numbers of consumers, what would be the impact on the still largely fragmented and regional grocery industry? And what role would intermediaries such as MyWebGrocer play; could they survive and prosper in the face of large chains with their own online shopping systems?

SIDEBAR 3: PRIVACY NOTICES FROM RICE EPICUREAN WEB SITE

Privacy Related Questions and Answers Related to Rice Epicurean Experience Card

"What else are you going to try to find out about me or my family?"
  "Your family's grocery purchases are the only thing we want to track. This will enable us to reward you with additional savings customized especially for you and your family."

"Will you give my name, address, and e-mail address to other people?"
  Absolutely not! Your name, address or e-mail address will NEVER be sold or given to any other marketing agency."

Rice Epicurean Home Run Customer Privacy Policy
  "Our customers' privacy is of utmost importance to Rice Epicurean Markets. We do not sell, trade, or rent personal information about individual members (such as name, address, e-mail address) to third parties. During registration and checkout a user is required to give their contact information (such as name, phone number and e-mail address). This information is used to contact the user about the services on our site for which they have expressed interest and to get in touch with the user if we have trouble processing an order. We value our customers and we take their privacy concerns seriously."

---

[23] A button at the top of the ordering screen (see Fig. 3) encouraged customers to request items they could not find. The store had recently begun to carry one of those Cantera had requested.

[24] http://www.upromise.com

REFERENCES

DeMers, J. (May 20, 2002). "Online Groceries Give It Another Try," *Houston Chronicle,* http://www.mywebgrocer.com/news_05-23-02_HoustonChronicle.htm.

Hoovers.Com (September 5, 2002). "Webvan Inc, History," http://www.hoovers.com/premium/profile/boneyard/3/0,5034,59643,00.html (current October 18, 2001).

Houston Chronicle (February 1998). "The Chronicle 100: Leading Companies in Houston (Largest Grocery Chains)," http://www.chron.com/content/chronicle/business/chron100/99/100grocery.html.

Houston Chronicle (February 2001). "The Houston 100: Largest Grocery Chains (2001)," http://www.chron.com/content/chronicle/special/01/100/charts/grocery.html.

Rice Epicurean (2002). "Rice Epicurean Markets," http://www.riceepicurean.com (current October 18, 2001).

Intel Corporation (2002). "MyWebGrocer.com: Bagging Customers in a Difficult Sector," Intel Business Computing Case Study, http://www.intel.com/eBusiness/pdf/cs/webgrocer0221.pdf, (current October 18, 2001).

Macaluso, N. (June 25, 2001). "Safeway Brings in Tesco as Online Grocery Partner," *E-Commerce Times,* http://www.ecommercetimes.com/perl/story/11499.html (current October. 18, 2001).

McFarlan, W., and M. Dailey, M. (April 14, 2000). "H.E. Butt Grocery Co.: The New Digital Strategy (A)," Harvard Business School Case, Boston, MA: HBS Press. #9-300-106.

MyWebGrocer (February 2001). "Online Grocery Shopping: Learnings from the Practitioners: Executive Summary," http://www.fmi.org/e_business/webgrocer.html (current October. 18, 2001).

MyWebGrocer (June 2002a). "Grocers Find Profitable Growth in the Darndest Places," MyWebGrocer.Com News, http://www.mywebgrocer.com/news_06-14-02_GrocersFindProfitableGrowth.htm (current October 18, 2001).

MyWebGrocer (August 19, 2002b). "Guess What the Fastest Growing Food Channel Is? (Hint: It Isn't Supercenters)," MyWebGrocer News (current October 18, 2001).

Palmer, J. (2000). "Online Grocery Shopping Around the World: Examples of Key Business Models," *Communications of the Association for Information Systems,* (4)3, December.

Pristin, T. (May 3, 2002). "Ordering Groceries in Aisle 'WWW,'" *New York Times.*

Spindler, M. (September 10, 2002a). Personal communication.

Spindler, M. (October 18, 2002b). Personal communication.

Viejo, A. (July 14, 2001). "Why RunOut Outlasts Larger Rivals," *Los Angeles Times,* (Accessed 10/18/2001) http://www.angelstrategies.com/news/whyrun.htm.

Worldwide Retail Exchange (September 4, 2002). "Overview," Worldwide Retail Exchange, http://www.worldwideretailexchange.org/cs/en_US/index.html (current October 18, 2001).

C H A P T E R

8

Value Creation with Information Systems

What You Will Learn in This Chapter

In the previous chapter we laid the foundations for our discussion of strategic information systems and IT-dependent strategic initiatives. In this chapter we continue this discussion by focusing on theoretical and analytical models that have been developed over the years to identify opportunities to create value with IT and to design and develop value adding IT-dependent strategic initiatives.

Specifically, in this chapter you will learn

1. How to use traditional models of value creation with information systems and information technology to identify and craft IT-dependent strategic initiatives, including industry analysis, value chain analysis, and the customer service life cycle framework.

2. How to incorporate data resources in your search for opportunities for value creation using emerging frameworks, including the virtual value chain and the customer data strategies framework.

3. How to devise and select initiatives that create value using business data.

MINI-CASE: RADISSON EXPRESS YOURSELF

On September 17, 2004, Scott Heintzeman, chief information officer of Radisson Hotels and Resorts, announced an industry first: The "Express Yourself" initiative (see Figure 8.1). The cornerstone of this initiative was the ability of reservation-holding Radisson's guests to check into the property as early as a week prior to their stay.

As some competitors were focusing on installing check-in kiosks, marking the third attempt by the industry at making kiosks work after failures in the 1980s and 1990s, Radisson decided to differentiate itself by taking a page out of the airlines playbook—24-hour anywhere Web-based check in.

Describing the rationale for the initiative, Bjorn Gullaksen, Carlson Hotels Worldwide executive vice president and brand leader, explained: "Radisson is taking a bold step to transform what consumer research has consistently shown as the least desirable experience in the hotel stay—standing in line for a slow check-in or slow check-out"[1] (see Figure 8.2 for the online check-in process).

In order to take advantage of the initiative, Radisson guests had to

1. Book a reservation any way they chose (online, toll-free reservation number, travel agent, or with the hotel directly).
2. Check in online on Radisson.com (see Figure 8.2) from seven days to six hours before arrival, choose stay preferences (see Figure 8.3), and print the Check-In Pass (see Figure 8.4).
3. Hand the Check-In Pass and ID to the Express Yourself front desk staff person (using a separate line from regular onsite check-in) when first arriving at the property.
4. Receive an envelope with a welcome packet and the room key.
5. Go on to their room.
6. If guests had signed up to receive an e-mail of the bill following departure, they could avoid check-out at the hotel.

In order for Radisson to deliver on the promise of the initiative, a number of changes were needed. For example, guests who checked in online must be preassigned to rooms, and their key must be made ahead of time and placed in the welcome packet.

DISCUSSION QUESTIONS

1. Do you believe that Radisson Express Yourself is an example of an IT-dependent strategic initiative? Explain.
2. Do you believe that this initiative has the potential to create added value? Substantiate your answer.
3. Do you believe that the Radisson Express Yourself initiative improves customer service? How?
4. What would you do next if you were put in charge of the initiative?

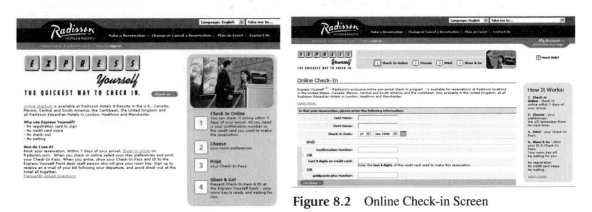

Figure 8.1 Description of the Radisson Express Yourself Initiative

Figure 8.2 Online Check-in Screen

---

[1] Available (2/7/05): http://www.radisson.com/news/category.jsp?category=hotel&releaseid=expresslaunch

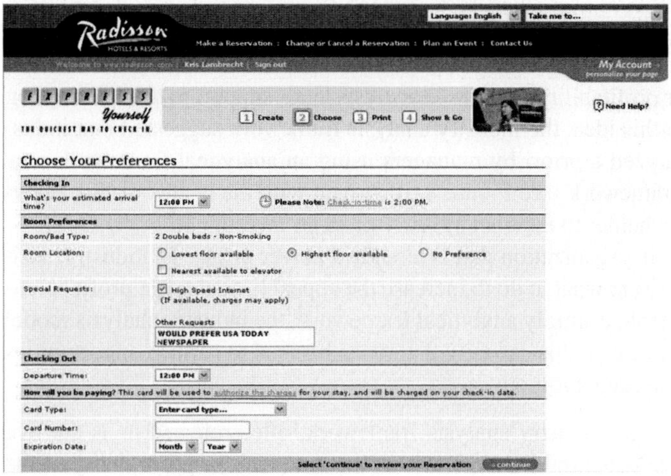

Figure 8.3   Choosing Preferences

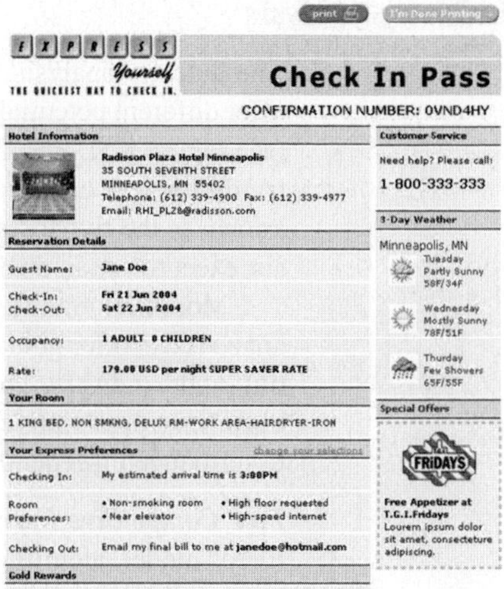

Figure 8.4   Confirmation Screen

INTRODUCTION

We concluded Chapter 6 by showing how the strategic information systems planning process is designed to create an overall context for information systems decision making. The planning documents conclude with the identification of strategic initiatives. In Chapter 7 we laid the foundation for our discussion of strategic information systems and IT-dependent strategic initiatives by explaining how you can analyze the impact of such initiatives. In this chapter we get to the heart of the matter and introduce the frameworks and analytical models that information systems professionals, as well as general and functional managers, use to identify opportunities, to design, and to evaluate IT-dependent strategic initiatives.

TRADITIONAL MODELS OF VALUE CREATION WITH IT

Considerable attention began to be devoted to the strategic potential of information technology in the mid-1980s. It was at this time that, prompted by a critical mass of success stories and case studies, academic researchers and consulting firms began to systematically explore and document the role of information systems and IT beyond automation of work and the creation of efficiencies. The use of IT as a "competitive weapon" became fertile ground for research and practice alike.

Prompting this attention toward the strategic role of information systems was the emergence of influential strategic models focusing on competitive positioning and competitive advantage. Three analytical tools were introduced or adapted to the search for strategic information systems opportunities:

- Industry analysis
- Value chain analysis
- Customer service life cycle analysis

Industry Analysis

The industry analysis framework is grounded in the basic notion that different industries offer different potential for profitability.[2] A simple analysis lends support to this assumption (see Figure 8.5). Based on this idea, the industry analysis framework suggested that industry differences can be analyzed a priori by managers using an analytical framework now known as the five forces framework (see Figure 8.6). Armed with the results of this analysis, executives can decide whether to enter an industry or forgo investment.

More importantly, for an organization that is already a player in a given industry, such analysis can offer guidance as to what to do to increase the appeal (i.e., average profit potential) of the industry. Thus, from a simply analytical framework, the industry analysis model becomes a prescriptive one. It is in this capacity that it can be used to surface opportunities to introduce IT-dependent strategic initiatives.

Five Competitive Forces   The industry analysis framework, often referred to as the five forces model, identifies five structural determinants of the potential for profitability of the average firm in a given industry. Each is discussed next.

The Threat of New Entrants   This force represents the extent to which the industry is open to entry by new competitors or whether significant barriers to entry make it so that the existing firms need not worry about competition from outside.

Consider car manufacturing for an example. Car manufacturing is characterized by a substantial need for capital investments in research and development and a need for significant

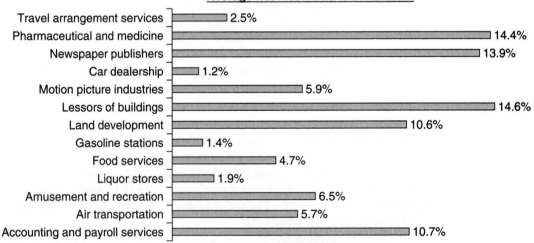

Average Net Income as % of Revenue

Industry	%
Travel arrangement services	2.5%
Pharmaceutical and medicine	14.4%
Newspaper publishers	13.9%
Car dealership	1.2%
Motion picture industries	5.9%
Lessors of buildings	14.6%
Land development	10.6%
Gasoline stations	1.4%
Food services	4.7%
Liquor stores	1.9%
Amusement and recreation	6.5%
Air transportation	5.7%
Accounting and payroll services	10.7%

Figure 8.5   Interindustry Differences in Average Profitability[3]

---

[2] Porter, M. E. (1980) *Competitive Strategy: Techniques for Analyzing Industries and Competitors,* Free Press. New York NY

[3] Author's research (2005).

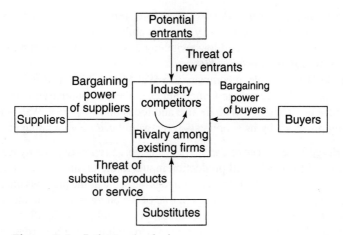

Figure 8.6 Industry Analysis

production capacity. Moreover, the automotive industry is characterized by strong economies of scale, such that it is important to produce a large number of vehicles to stay competitive. For these reasons, the auto industry is characterized by a low threat of new competitors due to strong barriers to entry.

The Threat of Substitute Products or Services This force represents the extent to which the products or services marketed by the firm in the industry of interest are subject to potential substitution by different products or services that fulfill the same customer needs.

For example, new products such as the iPod and digital music files, introduced by firms traditionally in the computer industry, are rapidly substituting CD players (Figure 8.7) and other devices traditionally offered by consumer electronics firms.

Figure 8.7 Will CD Players Go the Way of the Gramophone and the Vinyl Record Player?

The Bargaining Power of Buyers   This force represents the extent to which customers of those organizations in the industry have the ability to put downward pressure on prices. Highly concentrated buyers and low switching costs (see Chapter 9) typically conspire to increase the bargaining power of buyers.

Consider, for example, a company like Wal-Mart, which, because of its huge sales in its more than 3500 stores in the United States alone, can purchase the bulk of a manufacturer's production capacity. With its size and focus on low prices, Wal-Mart is famous for influencing prices set by its suppliers—some would even say dictating prices to them!

The Bargaining Power of Suppliers   This force represents the extent to which those individuals and firms who sell production inputs to the organizations in the industry have the ability to maintain high prices. This force is the same as the previous one, where the firms in the industry of interest have taken the role of the buyer rather than the seller.

As a future supplier of labor resources, you should pay significant attention to this force. If you can put yourself in a position of bargaining power toward the industry of your interest (for example, by choosing to concentrate in a field of study that is highly sought after but in short supply), you stand to reap significant benefits in terms of salary due to your position of strength in bargaining power.

The Rivalry among Existing Competitors   This force represents the extent to which fierce battling for position and aggressive competition occur in the industry. The degree of competition in an industry can vary dramatically. The term *hypercompetition* refers to industries characterized by fierce rivalry among existing firms and a very rapid rate of innovation leading to fast obsolescence of any competitive advantage and a consequent need for a fast cycle of innovation. The search engine industry may be an example of a hypercompetitive one (Figure 8.8).

Industry Analysis and the Role of Information Systems   Researchers and consultants who have adapted industry analysis to the search for opportunities to introduce IT-dependent

Figure 8.8   The Online Search Industry is Widely Considered a Hypercompetitive One

strategic initiatives suggest looking for ways to use information systems to affect one or more of the industry forces, thereby tipping it to the firm's advantage. The following are some of the questions that are typically asked:

Can the Use of IT Raise or Increase Barriers to Entry in the Industry?   Investments in information systems may be such that they reduce the threat of new entrants—consider, for example, the need for an automated teller machine (ATM) network in the banking industry (Figure 8.9). Entry into the banking industry nowadays requires access to a network of ATMs and, increasingly, online banking facilities. Access to the lodging industry requires access to a computerized central reservation system (CRS) and a substantial number of interfaces to the plethora of traditional and emerging distribution channels.

Can the Use of IT Decrease Suppliers' Bargaining Power?   With the emergence of the Internet and its related technologies as viable business tools, examples abound of information systems that have contributed to shift power away from suppliers and toward buyers. Consider, for example, Ariba (Figure 8.10), the sourcing, procurement, and expertise provider that enables companies to analyze, understand, and manage their corporate spending to achieve increased cost savings and business process efficiencies. Among other services, Ariba offers auction facilities that enable buyers in a number of industries to manage the sourcing process and realize significant savings.

Can the Use of IT Decrease Buyers' Bargaining Power?   As much as the Internet has helped firms strengthen their bargaining position toward suppliers, it has also reduced their bargaining power toward customers. Just as companies can rapidly shop for alternatives when looking for production inputs, so can their customers. Yet some opportunities to strengthen relationships with customers, thus reducing their incentive to shop around still exist.

Consider travel intermediaries like Orbitz.com. While competitors are literally one click away, by storing personal preferences (e.g., preferred airlines), personal data (e.g., frequent flier miles) and billing information, travel intermediaries can levy switching costs and reduce their customers' bargaining power.

Figure 8.9   ATMs are a Ticket to Entry in the Modern Banking Industry

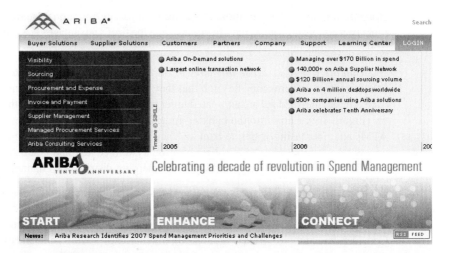

Figure 8.10   Ariba's Web Site

Can the Use of IT Change the Basis of Industry Competition?   The introduction of a new information system by a firm, whether an incumbent or a new entrant, sometimes spurs a revolution that forces competitors to take notice and react. A stark example of this dynamic was presented by the advent of online retailing in the mid-1990s.

When Amazon.com burst onto the scene, with its ability to offer huge selection and high levels of customer service without a single store, shock waves reverberated in the retail sector. Firms such as Amazon that seized the opportunity presented by the Internet to sell direct to consumers trained consumers to self-serve in ways unheard of before and changed forever the notion of what it means to be a retailer. Today, it would be a grave mistake for any large retailer to neglect the online channel of distribution. We can find similar examples in online banking and throughout the travel and tourism sector.

Value Chain

While useful in identifying potential opportunities to improve the profitability of the industry and suggesting ways in which managers can deploy information systems to neutralize or minimize the unattractive features of an industry, much of the potential for the employment of strategic information systems concerns intraindustry competition. In other words, much of the time that you, as general or functional managers, will be spending analyzing opportunities to deploy strategic information systems will be with respect to the ability to create added value. Thus you will not worry so much about average industry performance; rather, given the industry that you are competing in, you will seek to outperform your competitors by using information systems to create added value and competitive advantage.

In Chapter 7 we stated that value is created when a firm employs its transformation process to use resources that have a value of \$*x* in their next best use and to generate a product or service that customers are willing to pay \$*x* + \$*v* for. If what the firm does is unique, such that no competitor is able to offer comparable value, the firm creates added value and has achieved a position of competitive advantage. But what does the firm "transformation process" look like? How do these input resources become the final product or service that customers pay for?

Primary and Support Activities The classic framework that has been used to logically represent a firm's transformation process is the value chain (Figure 8.11).[4] The value chain model maps the set of economic activities that a firm engages in and groups them into two sets: primary activities and support activities.

Primary Activities Primary activities represent the firm's actions that are directly related to value creation. These are the activities that define the firm's unique transformation process, such that they are typically performed by all firms engaged in the same, or similar, transformation processes. The classic value chain identifies five primary activities: inbound logistics, operations, outbound logistics, marketing and sales, and service. It is the sequential execution of these activities that enables the transformation of the input resources in final products or service—and, as a consequence, the creation of value.

Let's return to the automotive industry. We can think of the car manufacturing transformation process in terms of these five primary activities. A car manufacturer needs to procure and receive component parts (i.e., inbound logistics), have assembly lines that take these components and put them together in the various car models (i.e., operations), deliver the vehicles to the distribution channel and its dealership network (i.e., outbound logistics), create a demand for its make and models (i.e., marketing and sales), and ensure that problems with its products can be addressed by a network of repair shops (i.e., service).

Support Activities Support activities represent the firm's actions that, while not directly related to the transformation process, are nevertheless necessary to enable it. These activities do not define the organization's unique transformation process, such that they are typically performed by a wide range of firms offering diverse products and services. The classic value chain identifies four support activities: firm infrastructure, HR management, technology development, and procurement.

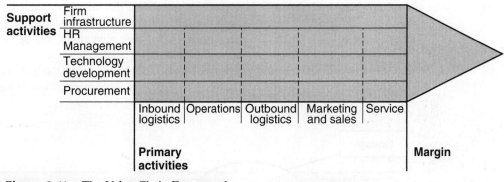

Figure 8.11 The Value Chain Framework

---

[4] Porter, M. E. (1985), *Competitive Advantage: Creating and Sustaining Superior Performance,* New York, NY: Free Press.

Take HR management, for example. Any firm that relies on labor resources, from car manufacturers to hospitals, must be able to recruit, train, evaluate, pay, promote, fire, and generally manage the labor force.

As we discussed in Chapter 7, competitive advantage stems from the ability of the firm to transform input resources into a product or service that is both valuable and unique—thereby having created added value. Thus, in order to have a competitive advantage, the firm must perform a different set of activities than competitors, or it must perform the same set of activities but in a different (and value adding) manner. Information systems and IT have a long tradition of enabling such unique transformation processes.

Value Chain Analysis and the Role of Information Systems   Using the value chain to identify opportunities to deploy IT-dependent strategic initiatives requires managers to identify, understand, and analyze the activities the firm performs so that they can be enhanced or transformed using IS resources. This approach is grounded in the assumption that a firm's value chain has both physical and information processing components and that information is a critical enabler of the firm's activities. Thus, the search for the strategic deployment of IT should focus on the role that information technologies can play in transforming current activities.

An example is offered by an IBM commercial. A malicious-looking character is seen walking the isles of a supermarket stuffing various goods in his trench coat under the suspicious eye of a security guard. As he walks out of the store, apparently without paying, he is called by the guard, who, after some suspense-inducing delay, says, "Sir! You forgot your receipt."

This is an example of how the grocery store checkout process may change in the future using radiofrequency identification (RFID) chips embedded in everyday goods. If this vision comes to bear, grocery stores no longer will have checkout lines, but we will simply walk out the door and our bank account or credit card will be charged with the full amount of our purchases. In this case the checkout process is radically transformed, leading to substantial efficiency improvements and creating the potential for new initiatives (e.g., tracking household purchases over time).

The Value Network   Another insight that emerged from the introduction of value chain analysis is that a firm has relationships both upstream and downstream. In other words, the firm's own value chain exists in a larger value network that comprises the firm's suppliers upstream and the firm's customers downstream (Figure 8.12). The points of contact between these separate value chains are called linkages, and they offer significant opportunities for the deployment of IT-dependent strategic initiatives.

For example, the inbound logistics activities of your firm can be thought of as an extension of the outbound logistics activities of your suppliers. Recognizing these linkages enables

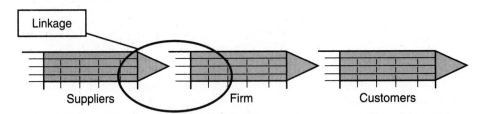

Figure 8.12   Linkages in the Value Network

firms to create partnerships and develop interorganizational systems that may benefit all parties involved. Continuous replenishments, the initiative pioneered by Wal-Mart and Procter & Gamble and described in Chapter 7, is a classic example.

A Word of Caution   Managerial frameworks are designed to map and simplify the complexity of real organizations in order to enable a disciplined analysis of complicated phenomena. In the case of the value chain model, the objective is to help you as a manager to identify opportunities to change the transformation process your organization engages in and thus uncover ways to create new value. It is therefore critical to recognize that a general framework, like the value chain, often needs to be adapted to the specific realities of your organization.

For example, the original model portrayed in Figure 8.11 is clearly best suited to represent the realities of manufacturing companies where raw materials and component parts are transformed into final products that need to be marketed, sold, and later serviced. Service businesses (e.g., consulting and law firms, banks, entertainment venues, laundry services, restaurants) typically work very differently and, while they also have to complete primary and secondary activities, the activities they perform and the sequence of events can be very different. Figure 8.13, for example, portrays the value chain model mapping the sequence of primary activities as they occur in a hotel or resort.

It is imperative that when using the value chain, or any other managerial framework, you do not simply apply it "as is," but, using your in-depth knowledge of the specific firm you are analyzing, you adapt the model to your needs. After all, as supplier of managerial talent, this is what you are paid to do!

Customer Service Life Cycle[5]

The customer service life cycle (CSLC) was originally introduced as a tool to spur managerial thinking about the potential of advanced information technologies under the label of customer resource life cycle.[6] While the CSLC framework has a time-honored tradition, its

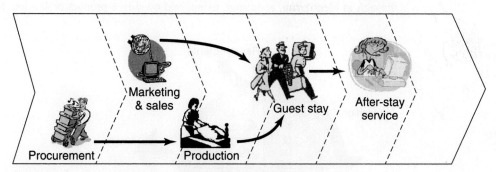

Figure 8.13   Sample Value Chain of a Lodging Outfit

---

[5] Portions of this section are adapted from Piccoli, G., Spalding, B. R., and Ives, B. (2001), "The Customer Service Life Cycle: A Framework for Internet Use in Support of Customer Service," *Cornell Hotel and Restaurant Administration Quarterly* (42:3), pp. 38–45.

[6] The Information System as a Competitive Weapon," with G. P. Learmonth, *Communications of the ACM,* Vol. 27, No. 12 (December 1984), pp. 1193–1201.

fundamental premise that a firm can use information systems to create value by offering superior customer service has received new impetus via the commercialization of the Internet and the introduction of the Web as a viable business tool. As more and more organizations have been able to establish direct relationships with customers (see Chapter 5), the potential for new value creation through superior customer service has increased.

The CSLC breaks down the firm-customer relationship into thirteen stages, grouped into four primary phases; for each one it shows how you can craft IT-dependent strategic initiatives to respond to customers' needs and create economic value.

Four Phases The CSLC framework suggests that managers step into their customers' shoes and think about the needs and problems that customers experience at each of four major phases in their relationship with the firm: requirements, acquisition, ownership, and retirement (Figure 8.14).

During the requirements phase, the customer realizes the need for a specific product or service and begins to focus on its attributes. During the acquisition phase, the customer orders, pays for, and takes possession of the product or service. The next major phase is ownership; here the customer has the product or is receiving the service and must deal with issues regarding its efficient and effective use. The final phase is retirement, in which the customer may begin to think about buying again, trading in, or dismissing old products.

Thirteen Stages Each of the four main phases is then further broken out in subphases, or stages (Table 8.1). These thirteen stages represent typical needs that customers encounter when obtaining, using, and retiring a firm's product or service. The primary objective of the CSLC is to help management identify stages where their organization's customers are frustrated or underserved, and where the interaction can be improved through the use of the Internet or the deployment of IT-dependent strategic initiatives. As a creative planning framework, the CSLC is designed to stretch your thinking and help you view your business with a fresh perspective.

Note that the life cycle model covers the entire range of activities a customer goes through in identifying, acquiring, using, and owning a product or service. However, it is

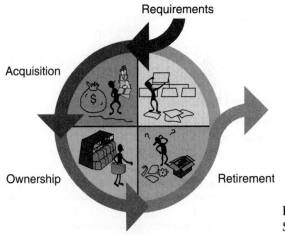

Figure 8.14 The Customer Service Life Cycle (CSLC)

Table 8.1   Customer Service Life Cycle (CSLC) Stages

Requirements

Establish requirements	Establish a need for the product or service
Specify	Determine the product or service attributes

Acquisition

Select Source	Determine where to obtain the product or service
Order	Order the product or service from a supplier
Authorize and pay for	Transfer funds or extend credit
Acquire	Take possession of the product or receive service
Evaluate and accept	Ensure that the product or service meets specifications

Ownership

Integrate	Add to an existing inventory or integrate with existing internal business processes
Monitor	Control access and use of the product or service
Upgrade	Upgrade the product or service if conditions change
Maintain	Repair the product as necessary

Retirement

Transfer or dispose	Move, return, or dispose of product or service
Account for	Monitor expenses related to the product or service

typically a subset of these thirteen stages that present particular challenges for the firm's customers—and therefore particular opportunity. Moreover, the stages that have the potential to yield the highest payoff will vary by customer segment, product, and over time.

Consider a firm that has recently developed an innovative new product. In this case the very first stage, establish requirements, may be ripe for innovation. Priceline.com, with its innovative model for purchasing airline tickets, hotel rooms, and other products, encountered early problems in educating both consumers and operators about its benefits. On the other hand, for a mature product competing in a fiercely competitive industry, the real potential may lie in managers' ability to differentiate their product and services by identifying unresolved customer problems—such as the need to effectively *account for* the total cost of ownership or use of the product or service.

Stage 1: Requirement   In the first stage of the CSLC, the customer identifies a need for the firm's product or service. In many cases, at this point in the life cycle the customer may not even be aware of the emerging desire or may have a limited idea about what possible products or services he or she needs. The ability to reach and communicate with a customer at this stage may enable the firm to gain his patronage.

Site 59, the last minute week-end getaway site now part of Sabre holdings, bills itself as "your source for spontaneous escape and entertainment." It does so by cleverly positioning its offering in the requirement stage. You tell Site 59 what mood you are in and ask, "What should we do this weekend?" Site 59 will respond with offers ranging from half-day suggestions as simple as going to visit your local museum to an elaborate night out, including prepaid dinners and theater tickets. Site 59 recognizes that with more disposable income and less free time, customers appreciate novel suggestions prepackaged and ready to go.

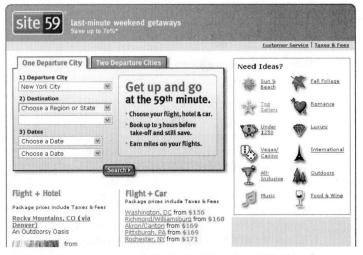

Figure 8.15   Site59.com Offers Travel Solutions Based on Customers' Mood and Interests

Stage 2: Specify   Once customers have established the need for a new product or service, they need to specify the characteristics of that product or service in order to know which particular one to acquire. In the specification stage, customers select the product features that best suit their needs.

A nice example is offered by Nike, the sports apparel manufacturer, which allows prospective customers to customize many of the features of its sneakers (Figure 8.16). Using the Internet to interact with customers in the specification stage is, of course, something

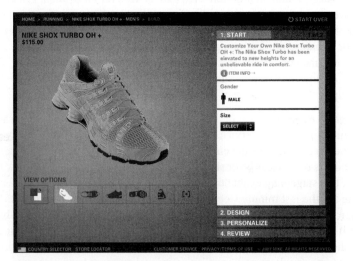

Figure 8.16   The Nike Configuration Enables Buyers to Customize their Shoes

that is now fairly common. Today consumers can purchase made-to-order personal computers, consumer electronics, and even clothes online.

Stage 3: Select a Source   The Internet provides a new source for finding desired products, and one that can significantly reduce the vendor's distribution costs. The emergence of the Internet and the Web has created significant opportunity for new intermediaries in a wide range of industries to create value by focusing on this stage. Consider firms like MySimon.com that provide information and tips about buying popular products to attract traffic and then enable customers to rapidly find and rank purveyors of the chosen product.

Stage 4: Ordering   After selecting a source for their product or service, customers must order it. As with all other stages of the CSLC, the primary objective of the firm is to make it as easy as possible for clients to do business with it. This is often easy to do for returning customers, as certain elements of their second and subsequent orders typically are repeated from the first.

Wyndham Hotels and Resorts uses a dedicated application and the Internet to allow customers enrolled in its frequent guest program, Wyndham ByRequest, to configure rooms to their liking. Guests can select whether they want upper or lower floors, whether they want to be near or far from the elevator, even what kind of pillows they would like and what drinks or snacks they prefer to receive as welcome tokens. This customer service design has a number of potential far-reaching advantages and risks, yet it also helps to ensure that Wyndham differentiates itself at the ordering stage of the CSLC. If Wyndham can deliver the room as configured by customers, they are more likely to be satisfied.

Stage 5: Authorize and Pay For   Once customers have placed an order, they need to authorize and issue payment. Convenience and security are the determinants of customer service and satisfaction at this stage. Most firms that accept online orders enable clients to store payment method, shipping location, and preferences details for quick and easy future reorder. Amazon.com was among the pioneers of this process under the label of 1-Click shopping.

Stage 6: Acquire   At this stage the customer takes possession of the product or begins to use the service. Some perishable or sensitive products may not be able to be shipped, while some information-based products or services may be delivered online directly. Information-based products are far more widespread than most of us realize. They include financial, medical, legal, and accounting services as well as airline tickets, reservations, music, education, books, software, magazines, games, films, and so on—a very sizable, and growing, percentage of the economy.

One of the most familiar products that have dramatically changed the traditional acquisition stage is the digital song. Consider Napster, for example. After its early days as an outlaw, Napster now offers a legal service enabling subscribers to gain access to its database of digital songs. The "song acquisition process," once confined to complete albums on physical CDs available for purchase in stores, is now available for individual tunes on a subscription basis from the comfort of your home.

Figure 8.17 Napster has Changed the Acquisition Stage in the Music Industry

Stage 7: Evaluate and Accept After customers have acquired their new product or service, they may test it out to verify that it works as expected. This is particularly true for businesses purchasing equipment, but it is also the case for consumers purchasing big ticket items, such as cars. When a very innovative product or service is introduced, customers need to be extensively educated about its features and how to maximize the benefits of its use. This is particularly important for products and services that require the customer to undergo a certain degree of process change.

Although the evaluate and accept process historically has taken place after purchase, we increasingly see firms in service- and information-based industries letting customers "try out" products prior to purchase. Examples include virtual tours, sample consulting reports, or demo software.

Stage 8: Integrate Once the product or service is acquired and accepted for use, the customer must add it to his or her existing inventory of resources. Often customers must also adjust their internal business processes to take full advantage of the new product or service.

Fed Ex offers Ship Manager, a Web-based tool for the creation and editing of Fed Ex labels. Using Ship Manager, customers can develop an address book of frequent shipment receivers and seamlessly create package labels, automatically price the shipment, and print package labels. Through Ship Manager, Fed Ex devised an IT-based solution to the challenge that customers face when they integrate the Fed Ex service in their existing operations.

Stage 9: Monitor Use and Behavior Customers must ensure that resources remain in an acceptable state of operation while they are in use or during the time they receive service. Using the Internet, suppliers can provide customers with the facilities to simplify this monitoring stage. By reducing clients' effort in monitoring usage of the product or service, the provider may be able to command a higher price or simply create a tight bond that customers may find difficult or costly to forego.

Otis Elevators mastered this stage long ago. During the 1980s, Otis introduced self-monitoring equipment that reduced unavailability, service calls, and overall maintenance

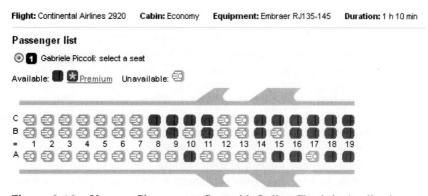

Flight: Continental Airlines 2920   **Cabin:** Economy   **Equipment:** Embraer RJ135-145   **Duration:** 1 h 10 min

Passenger list

Gabriele Piccoli: select a seat

Available: Premium   Unavailable:

Figure 8.18   You can Choose your Seat with Online Check-in Applications

costs. The new version of this service, called e*service, is now Web based and allows customers to monitor their elevator system through a Web browser and place service calls as needed, 24 hours a day.

Stage 10: Upgrade   When customers are using the product or service, it may become necessary to modify or improve it so that it can better fit their unique needs. As competition has heated in the airline industry under continued pressure from low-cost carriers, the legacy airlines have attempted to differentiate service for their best customers. Many of them now offer preferential seating (for example, in exit rows) and automatic upgrades to their best customers, who can request upgrades and receive confirmation online (Figure 8.18).

Stage 11: Maintain   Helping the customer to analyze, diagnose, and repair the product or service, or suggesting solutions to problems as they occur, affords the firm many opportunities to take what would be a source of dissatisfaction and offer outstanding service.

The software industry has led the way in this area. Microsoft Windows, the software program we all love to hate and the favorite target of hackers and virus authors, has a facility that will automatically identify, download, and install security patches and bug fixes.

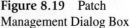

Figure 8.19   Patch Management Dialog Box

Stage 12: Transfer or Dispose   Customers will eventually transfer, resell, return, or dispose of the product or service. As this sometimes happens after a considerable amount of time, the original supplier may not be involved. In some occasions this step may be complicated by regulation and restrictions (for example, with regard to disposal of old computer equipment).

Some organizations have made support of this process a staple of their offering, recognizing that a customer problem, the need to dispose of an item no longer needed, may be the start of another customer service life cycle. Dell is a firm that realized this very early with its business clients. With its Dell asset recovery service, the company will pick up, within two days and at the client's site, any end-of-life machine, format its hard disk to eliminate all of the customer's data, and dispose of it according to current legal requirements. At the end of the process Dell sends a statement to the client detailing what was done and certifying that the equipment was disposed of correctly.

Stage 13: Account For   The final stage of the life cycle focuses on evaluation and accounting of the experience. This stage is particularly important for large corporations that are constantly attempting to better measure, manage, and control their travel and entertainment (T&E) budgets. Given the complexity and magnitude of this process, an organization may willingly limit its portfolio of T&E suppliers in exchange for the ability to precisely monitor and control total spending while enforcing company policies.

Large travel agents, such as American Express, have long recognized this fact and developed Web-based products designed to offer tools for accounting and control of travel expenses to their large customers. Armed with these tools, the organization achieves better control of its travel budget while being able to use a larger pool of providers.

Organizations achieve competitive advantage through their ability to envision and implement value adding strategic initiatives. The most innovative ideas are often not the most costly or resource intensive, but simply those based on the best understanding of how customer needs can effectively be satisfied. The CSLC provides you with a basis for evaluating a firm's relationship with customers, benchmarking against competitors, and uncovering opportunities to use the Internet and advanced IT to improve customer willingness to pay through outstanding customer service.

Traditional Models, Not "Old" Models

The analytical frameworks discussed above have been in use for many years and have helped spawn numerous business innovation and IT-dependent strategic initiatives. They continue to accurately represent the way in which many companies organize their work and therefore offer significant insight to those seeking to apply increasingly powerful and evolving IT in the never-ending quest for competitive advantage. Note that the value chain and CSLC are somewhat complementary. The value chain mostly focuses internally while the CSLC draws attention to the relationship between the firm and its customers.

EMERGING FRAMEWORKS

The strategic role that information systems and IT can play in the modern organization was acknowledged over twenty-five years ago. However, recent trends have provided new impetus for the search for IT-dependent strategic initiatives. Perhaps the most important event was the commercialization of the Internet in 1993, an event that took the global network of computers from an unknown tool used by scientists and the military to business organizations. The Internet took the world by storm, and today many of us, both consumers and businesses, could not imagine working (and living?) without it.

Parallel to this upsurge of global networking was the continuance of trends we discussed in Chapter 1—the declining cost/performance ratio of computing equipment, the declining cost of storage, and the consequent widespread adoption of computing in consumer and business life.

One of the most successful users of IT for strategic advantage is Dell Computers, Inc. Michael Dell, founder and chief executive officer of the firm, in describing how his firm had been able to dominate the computer hardware industry, said, "We substitute information for inventory and ship only when we have demand from real end consumers." This quote captures the power of information to create economic value and competitive advantage.

Inventory of parts in a manufacturing company are typically held to reduce uncertainty of demand and inbound logistics. Clearly this insurance against uncertainty comes at a cost, the cost of capital tied up as well as the cost of write-offs for obsolete inventory. A firm that is able to gather and use superior information, and thereby reduce uncertainty, can limit its inventory stocks and run a leaner operation. This is all the more important in computer manufacturing, where technological innovation is rapid and the value of inventoried parts drops significantly when a new, more powerful component is developed (e.g., new generation microchips). Dell has significantly reduced uncertainty by turning the production process on its head and gathering demand before building, rather than manufacturing computers it then sells through a distribution channel.

Affordable, powerful, interconnected computers and cheap storage have created the backdrop for a number of new ways to create economic value with information systems. Traditional models were characterized by a view of information as a support resource to the production and transformation processes that the firm engages in. Thus, the search for value creation with IT-dependent strategic initiatives focused on using IT to affect physical activities.

Recently developed frameworks recognize that the data that modern organizations generate through their day-to-day operations may have significant value in their own right. These frameworks therefore are designed to help managers identify opportunities to harness information for value creation.

Virtual Value Chain

The virtual value chain (VVC) model[7] is designed to map the set of sequential activities that enable a firm to transform data in input into some output information that, once distributed to the appropriate user, has higher value than the original data (Figure 8.20). The virtual value chain builds on the generally understood value chain model. In a value chain, through a series of logically sequential activities, raw materials are transformed into products

[7] Rayport, J. and J. Sviokla, J. (1995), "Exploiting the Virtual Value Chain," *Harvard Business Review,* 73 (November–December 1995), pp. 75–85.

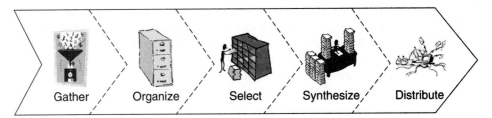

Figure 8.20   Virtual Value Chain Framework

or services that are then distributed to customers. The process is a value adding one such that the products or services being distributed have a higher value (and command higher customer willingness to pay) than the inbound material and services.

The critical insight underpinning the VVC is that information is no longer just a support resource for physical activities, those described by the physical value chain model,[8] but can itself be treated as an input of a productive transformation process. In the physical value chain information is treated as a support element, designed to enable the physical activities of the value chain. The virtual value chain model uses the same logic but recognizes information as the entity being transformed (the value of which is being enhanced) through the chain of activities. When fed through the activities of the virtual value chain, organizational data can be transformed into valuable insights, new processes, or new products or services.

Five Activities   The proponents of the virtual value chain identify five sequential activities that must be complete in order to harness its power:

- *Gather.* The first activity in the value chain deals with the collection of information from transaction processing systems and any other sources—both internal to the organization (e.g., orders received) or external (e.g., census data).

- *Organize.* The organization stores the gathered data in a way that makes later retrieval and analysis simple and effective.

- *Select.* When it comes time to utilizing the stored data, users identify and extract the needed data from the data repository created in the previous step.

- *Synthesize.* The selected information is then packaged so that it can be readily used by the intended consumer for the specific purpose to which it is directed (i.e., decision making, sales, etc.)

- *Distribute.* Finally, the packaged information is transferred or sent to its intended user or customer.

Three Classes of Strategic Initiatives   The proponents of the virtual value chain offer three classes of strategic initiatives that firms typically create once they adopt virtual value chain thinking: visibility, mirroring capabilities, and new customer relationships. These three

---

[8] In this section, to avoid confusion, we use the term *physical* value chain to refer to the traditional value chain model.

classes of activities are in increasing order of complexity and uncertainty of results, with visibility being the most intuitively appealing and easy to justify financially and new customer relationships being the toughest to sell to senior management.

Note that the five value adding activities of the virtual value chain are performed with each one. What changes is the level of complexity and departure from the traditional way of doing business of the organization.

Visibility   The first application of the virtual value chain is termed *visibility*. In this case the firm uses the sequential activities in the virtual value chain to "see through" organizational processes it was previously treating as a black box.

An example of visibility is offered by online retailers such as Amazon.com. Because their customers' behavior is computer mediated as the consumers shop and purchase online, Amazon collects significant amounts of individual and aggregate data. These data include what Web pages a customer views, which Web pages seem to go unused, what path through the site customers are taking as they shop, whether and where they abandon the transaction, how customers react to advertising and banners, and so on. In other words, online retailers have significant visibility in their customers' shopping and purchasing process, a degree of accuracy and detail that was unprecedented in brick and mortar stores.

As more and more devices become "intelligent," by embedding microchips and running software, the firms that use them have more opportunities to harness the power of visibility. Imagine a firm that manages vending machines (Fig. 8.21). What decisions could you make if the vending machines where able to maintain real time communication with a central server about sales and inventory level? How much more efficient could your firm be with this information? What new strategic initiatives would you implement with this infrastructure in place?

Mirroring Capabilities   A further application of the virtual value chain, termed *mirroring capabilities,* consists of shifting some of the economic activities previously completed in the physical value chain to the information-defined world of the virtual value chain. That is, some of the activities that were previously physical in nature (i.e., completed by employees) become completely information based.

Figure 8.21   Vending Machines are Becoming Smarter

Examples of mirroring capability are pervasive in firms that need to perform much testing and simulation. For example, a recent trend among drug manufacturers is to test the effect of new drugs using computer models rather than real patients, thereby drastically speeding up trials and reducing the cost of new drug development.

Another example that may be particularly dear to your heart, as busy students, is offered by electronic library reserves. Typically your instructor will place some materials on reserve in the library so that you can check them out for a short period of time and study them. Due to copyright restrictions, only a few copies of the material can be put on reserve. As you painfully know, the day before the exam, the early bird gets the worm, and if you are late, you will be unable to consult the readings. Electronic reserves solve this problem (Figure 8.22). Because material that is digitally uploaded is not tied up when checked out (information goods are not consumed by use; see Chapter 4), all those who want to consult it can, and can do so at any time they like, day or night, from their own room.

Note that mirroring capabilities are beneficial when transferring the activity to an information-based platform if they enable the firm to perform them more efficiently and effectively. They are also beneficial when the activity can be transformed with significant performance improvements. For this reason a mirroring capability approach is different from a mere automation of the existing activity using computers.

New Digital Value   The above two types of strategies, visibility and mirroring capabilities, are mainly concerned with internal operations and the creation of value within the confines of the organization. The third stage, new digital value, is instead concerned with the organization's relationship with the customer and the firm's ability to increase customers willingness to pay, using the information generated through the virtual value chain to create new value in the form of new information-enabled products or services.

Recent examples of this strategy abound. Consider, for example, the recent impetus behind personalization strategies such as Amazon.com's suggestive selling initiative (Figure 8.23). Using your individual purchase history, as well as a technique known as collaborative

Database Name: Cornell University Library
Search Request: Course Reserve = Course=HADM 772: Information Technology Hosp.
Search Results: Displaying 1 of 2 entries

previous   **next**

(Brief View) (Long View) (MARC View)

Electronic Reserve Readings for HADM 772 Fall 2006 Piccoli

Database: Cornell University Library
Title: *Electronic Reserve Readings for HADM 772 Fall 2006 Piccoli
Electronic Access:
Making It Happen / Gabriele Piccoli / Working Paper Series No. 12-05-02 / The Center for Hospitality Research (PDF-Displays using Adobe Acrobat Reader)
Login Required
No holdings information available. Check with Reference or Circulation.

previous   **next**

Record Options		
Select Download Format	Brief View ▾ Format for Print/Save	Save Search Query
Enter your email address:		Email
Save results for later:	Save To Bookbag	

Figure 8.22   A Library's eReserve Application

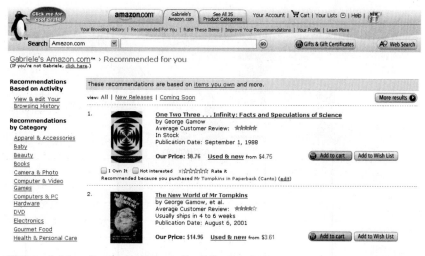

Figure 8.23   Amazon's Personalized Suggestions

filtering that compares your purchases to those of others with similar interests, Amazon is able to suggest items that may be of interest to you.

Value Matrix   When introduced to the virtual value chain and the potential for value creation through the use of organizational data, it is natural to gravitate to this way of thinking. However, it is important to remember that most organizations today need to pay significant attention to the traditional environment and their traditional operations. For as relevant as the potential to create value through information is, much of the opportunity for value creation remains in the firm's physical transformation processes.

Thus, combining the traditional (physical) value chain and the virtual value chain offers a cohesive framework, termed the *value matrix,* that general and functional managers can use to seek and exploit opportunities for the deployment of IT-dependent strategic initiatives in their organizations (see Figure 8.24).

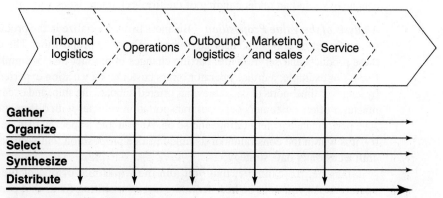

Figure 8.24   The Value Matrix

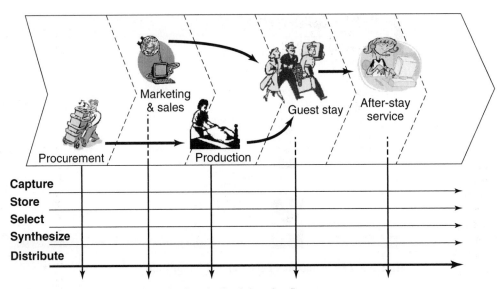

Figure 8.25   Sample Value Matrix of a Lodging Outfit

By being mindful of the five steps of the virtual value chain as they apply to data generated throughout the physical value chain, managers can uncover opportunities for new creation and appropriation of value. The caveat expressed before about analytical frameworks holds here as well, and you need to map the value matrix that more accurately represents your firm's individual context (see, for example, Figure 8.25).

Value Creation with Customer Data

One of the classes of initiatives that the proponents of the virtual value chain model have identified is the creation of new customer relationships and new digital value. The objective of these types of initiatives is to use customer data and information to do something of value for them—thereby increasing their customer willingness to pay. To do so requires significant analysis and an understanding of the firm's characteristics and value proposition.

Analysis of the Value Proposition   Business firms specialize in the production and sale of a specific set of goods and services—the firm's value proposition. The characteristics of these products and services are, barring changes in product mix or significant innovation, fixed. For example, a cruise operator offers customers a vacation experience characterized by length of time, ports of call, amenities offered onboard the ship, and excursions; a car manufacturer offers customers personal transportation vehicles with different characteristics of size, performance, safety rating, and so on. As you join a specific firm, in a specific industry, it is within the constraints of its unique value proposition that you may be called on to craft a customer data strategy.

Imagine, for example, that you join the workforce of one of the large cruiseline operators. As you do, you hear from the large consulting firms that personalization and customization are all the rage and that "customers are demanding it"— you must "go personal!" Their argument is that because you can collect so much data about your customers' habits and preferences, you can create extensive profiles of your returning customers.[9]

Once you know that Joe Cruiser likes Corona beer, you can have a few chilled bottles waiting for him in his cabin. It is hot at the port of Miami, he is tired from the embarkation process, but as soon as he checks in he can unwind with his favorite drink. He'd love you for that and will never want to cruise with another line!" But, how do you know if a personalization strategy is the best way to use customer data?

Repurchase and Customizability: The Dimensions of Decision Making   An analysis of your firm's value proposition and characteristics of customer behavior in your industry helps in identifying initiatives that fit with the context and those that don't. Specifically valuable is information about the theoretical repurchase frequency in the industry and the degree of customizability of the product or service being offered.

Theoretical Repurchase Frequency   The dimension of theoretical repurchase frequency represents the regularity with which the average customer acquires goods and services offered by the firms in the industry or segment of interest (e.g., how often do people repurchase the cruise product). Note that this measure is concerned with the potential for high repurchase frequency, not with the actual repurchase rates any one individual firm is experiencing—hence the use of the term *theoretical repurchase frequency.* A firm that has very few returning customers in an industry characterized by high theoretical repurchase frequency is doing a poor job or missing an opportunity.

Imagine going to a McDonald's in your neighborhood and finding it dirty and painfully slow in service. If this state of affairs is not quickly rectified, you most likely will not return

Figure 8.26   Magnetic Strip Key Cards

---

[9] If you have recently cruised, you know that there is no cash onboard a modern cruise ship. Rather, every cruiser has a card that serves as an identification document when leaving or returning to the ship at various ports of call, as a room key, (Figure 8.26) and, most importantly, as a debit card to pay for any one of the hundreds of on-board services. Since the introduction of these cards, cruise lines have the ability to unobtrusively collect large amounts of individual level behavioral and preference data.

to the same store. However, you will not stop patronizing fast food restaurants—you'll just shift your demand to a store that does an acceptable job. The key point here is that theoretical repurchase frequency is a function of the industry the firm is in and the characteristics of the value proposition it offers. It is not a characteristic of any one individual firm's current performance.

Car manufacturing and real estate are typical examples of industries characterized by relatively low theoretical repurchase frequency. Perhaps the ultimate low repurchase frequency is the "Master of Business Administration (MBA) product"— once you have obtained one MBA, no matter how satisfied you were with the experience, you have no need for another. Coffee shops and grocery stores are at the other side of the spectrum and enjoy high theoretical repurchase frequency.

Degree of Customizability   The degree of customizability represents the extent to which the product or service your firm offers can be tailored to the specific needs and requirements of individual customers or a segment of the customer base. This dimension is a function of the complexity of the product or service itself.

Gasoline, as most commodities, is an example of a product with a very low degree of customizability. Airline service and vending machine operations also belong in this category. At the other end of the degree of customizability spectrum are large resorts and destination spas. The Grand Wailea Resort Hotel and Spa, on the Hawaiian island of Maui, is a perfect example (Figure 8.27): Along with top-notch accommodations in paradise, the Grand Wailea offers high-end shopping at the Grand Wailea Shops, seven dining options, a world-class spa with hundreds of services, a golf course, a tennis club and fitness center, a number of pools, beach services, excursions, and events, all immersed in a setting characterized by beautiful scenery and art pieces.

Cruise lines, meeting and conference planning, and home building represent other example of industries selling products and services characterized by a relatively high degree of customizability.

Figure 8.27   The Grand Wailea's Web Site

General Customer Data Strategies   Based on the specific theoretical repurchase frequency of an organization and the degree of customizability of the product and services it offers, we can identify four general customer data strategies (see Figure 8.28). Note, however, that these strategies are not a prescription or a silver bullet solution. Like any analytical framework, the matrix presented is a thinking tool designed to help you analyze the potential offered by an organization's operations.

The matrix does offer insight as to what strategies are likely to fit best with the characteristics of a given industry and a firm's value proposition. This does not mean that other strategies will not work, but simply that they will encounter obstacles and may be difficult to implement—something that as a general or functional manager responsible for their success you'd rather know up front.

While the firm you are analyzing may or may not fit neatly in one quadrant, the matrix will help you evaluate the advantages and disadvantages of each general strategy and, more importantly, the natural fit of each of the four approaches to your firm's characteristics and value proposition.

Personalization Strategy   A typical service personalization or product customization strategy is most appropriate for firms competing in industries characterized by both a high theoretical repurchase frequency and a high degree of customizability. Under these conditions the potential is there to collect significant individual-level data because of the repeated interactions the firm has with its returning customers. Moreover, the high degree of customization affords management many opportunities to use this information to tailor the product or service to the specific needs—learned or inferred—of the returning customers. Thus the firm can use the information to modify its operations and differentiate its product or services.

Event planning may be a good example of an industry that fits in this quadrant—particularly those firms that work closely with customers who need the organization of many recurrent events (e.g., large investment banks). Another example may be large IT vendors (e.g., Sun Microsystems) catering to business customers with complex business and IT requirements.

Rewards Strategy   A rewards strategy is predicated on the notion that the firm's product and service will be purchased frequently. Yet these same products are fairly standardized, and it is difficult for the organization's managers to tailor them to specific customer requests.

Figure 8.28   Customer Data Strategies

Under these circumstances the firm can use customer data to evaluate the profitability of each customer—actual and potential—and use this information to reward behavior in an effort to increase customer loyalty or boost share of wallet (i.e., make sure that customers consolidate their purchase behavior in the industry by sourcing from the company rather than competitors).

The firm can also use the individual level data collected to generate accurate reports and improve its operations (e.g., grocery stores performing basket analyses). Note that this means understanding customer profitability as well as customers' propensity to repurchase without incentive—a strategy much more complex and sophisticate than the "buy nine coffee cups and receive the tenth one free" that many firms seem to settle for (Figure 8.29). The airline industry represents a classic example for this quadrant.

Acquisition Strategy   Even in the face of low theoretical repurchase frequency, a firm in an industry with a high degree of customization may benefit from an acquisition strategy. Following this approach, the firm collects exhaustive data about its current customers in an effort to profile them and develop predictive models to identify and attract new profitable customers while avoiding nonprofitable or marginal ones.

A good example of an industry that falls in this quadrant is the wedding reception business (Figure 8.30)— an industry offering highly customizable products but typically enjoying low repurchase frequency.

Another example may be the Grand Wailea Resort Hotel and Spa profiled earlier (Figure 8.27). Given the significant cost of a vacation in Hawaii, and even more so in a luxury resort such as the Grand Wailea, theoretical repurchase frequency for such product may be very low. Yet given the complexity of the product and the high degree of customizability it offers to talented managers, an acquisition strategy may work well in this case.

No Potential   When a firm is in an industry characterized by low theoretical repurchase frequency and relatively low degree of customizability, there seems to be little potential for crafting a strategy around customer data. This is because very little data will likely be generated and managers' hands are tied with respect to what they can do with it.

A chain of budget or limited service tourist hotels in an exclusive fly-in destination (e.g., Hawaii, Fiji) offers an apt example. Midscale hotels in these locations are generally a

Figure 8.29   Coffee Punch Card

Figure 8.30   The Uniquely Complex Choreography of a Wedding Reception.
(*Source*: Courtesy of www.flowershopnetwork.com)

"window on an experience" rather than the experience themselves, and their value proposition is to offer guests an affordable opportunity to experience a great location. Because of the time commitment and cost of reaching these destinations, repurchase is relatively infrequent. Thus, there is little opportunity to enact any of the three strategies discussed above. Under these conditions the firm may be better off focusing on efficiency and low prices and avoiding the cost of collection, management, and analysis of customer data.

Applying the Model   Let's return to the scenario we used earlier: your job at the cruise line. When analyzed through the lens of the general customer data strategies matrix, it becomes clear that a personalization strategy, while intuitively appealing, is probably not optimal.

The cruise product is characterized by relatively low repurchase frequency—for as affordable and mainstream as cruises have become, they remain a fairly expensive vacation option, and the cycle of repurchase is relatively long (e.g., honeymoon cruise followed by a five- or ten-year anniversary cruise).

How likely is your company to be able to profit from the (considerable) investment in a personalization strategy? Would it not be better to focus on an acquisition strategy designed to attract profitable first-time cruisers based on what the firm learns analyzing and clustering the profile of its past cruisers?

Acquiring the Needed Data: The Third Dimension   The strategic initiatives described above are predicated on the firm's ability to capture the needed customer data in a format and a manner that make them amenable to the needed analysis. As with theoretical repurchase frequency and degree of customizability, the immediacy with which customer data can be captured and used varies by industry and context.

The expanded model acknowledges that different industries, because of the general norms about how business is conducted within them, offer a different potential for data capture. In other words, the degree to which data collection can be done easily can vary dramatically by industry and is an important early consideration.

Consider a simple example. When purchasing hospital services (something that we typically prefer not to do!) we don't think twice about providing our social security number and intimate details about our personal life. In fact, if the doctor came in, looked at us, and said, "take these pills twice a day, they'll fix you up," we would be outraged. Given the nature of hospital services, it is part of the natural course of good business to be asked many (personal) questions about our medical history, allergies, and symptoms before making a diagnosis.

Compare the hospital experience with the "get paid for your opinions!" e-mail that clog our inboxes, the guest satisfaction surveys we rarely fill out in hotels, or the dreaded twenty-minute dinner-time phone call on behalf of a company we recently transacted with asking us to rate service. We largely consider them all to be a disruption and a waste of our time. Of course, the firm would be quite happy to gather the information in a different manner, but for many of these companies it is just not natural to provide lots of information during the interaction.

Customer expectations as to what the encounter with the firm should be like—the norms within the industry—that determine what options the firm has when collecting data. While it is OK for a hospital to ask us for our social security number, as it is for a bank or an insurance company, we would be startled if the coffee shop, the restaurant, or the grocery store in our neighborhood did so.

These simple examples show that some firms are highly constrained when it comes to gathering customer data, and may have no better way to obtain it than pay a representative sample of customers to take time to respond to survey. Others have more data than they can ever hope to use. We refer to this as the degree of unobtrusive data capture. Despite being a mouthful, this is a largely intuitive concept that indicates the extent to which, in the normal course of business, customer data are collected and stored in a readily usable format (see Figure 8.31).

An early analysis of practices in your industry can be illuminating. Imagine, for example, a fine dining restaurant. Fine dining is an industry with relatively high repurchase

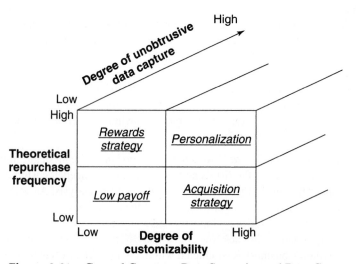

Figure 8.31 General Customer Data Strategies and Data Capture Constraints

frequency and a relatively high degree of customizability of the experience. A personalization strategy is highly suitable for such an establishment, yet much of the data needed to carry it out are generated in fleeting customer-server exchanges that are difficult to capture and codify for easy storage and retrieval. Add to this mix the high turnover typical of the food service industry and it becomes clear why for as much patronage we give to our favorite restaurants, we generally don't receive a commensurate degree of personal service.

Compare the difficulty a restaurant has with collecting and storing its customer data in a readily usable format to the relative simplicity of the same task at an online retailer—such as Amazon.com. Granted, the potential depth of the relationship is lower, but the ease with which Amazon can collect, store, and process the data you provide is much greater—enabling them to provide a more personalized experience than your favorite restaurant.

The degree of unobtrusive data capture for a firm is largely given at any point in time. However, technology improvements and innovation may pay off here if you are willing to shoulder the cost of changing people's habits. For example, while much of the information about customers' gambling behavior in casinos was traditionally left to busy and fallible casino hosts and pit bosses, the advent of electronic slot machines ushered in a new era. Casino executives realized that a modern slot machine is in essence a digital computer and that a computer records all the transactions it performs with great speed and accuracy.

Tying these transactions to individual customers once they were convinced to use magnetic strip cards was a relatively small step. Today the natural course of business in the casino industry is such that a company can have an accurate, real-time picture of each of its customers' slot-playing behavior. With the declining price point of RFID tags (Figure 8.32), this same level of precision will soon be extended to table playing as well, not just slots.

Crafting Data-Driven Strategic Initiatives

Given the wealth of information available to the modern business, it can be extremely confusing to decide where to start looking for opportunities. The amount of data and information generated by the IT infrastructure of modern organizations often overwhelms those who look for opportunities. As a result, general and functional managers often face frustration when they attempt to extract value out of the business data locked into their computer systems. "All this software comes with great reporting capabilities, but who has time to look at them" they often lament.

Figure 8.32 RFID-Enabled Chips may be the Future in the Casino Industry. (*Source*: Courtesy of Texas Instruments.)

In this section we present a methodology that can be used to identify opportunities to create value with organizational data and then select the ones that hold the greatest potential for value creation and appropriation.

1. Identify relevant transaction processing systems.
2. Inventory data currently available in these systems.
3. Conceptualize initiatives that use the available data.
4. Prioritize among the selected initiatives.

Identify Relevant TPS   This first step is designed to allow you to narrow the scope of the analysis and focus on the systems that are most likely to hold relevant data—given your functional area and scope of responsibility. For example, a hotel revenue manager is mainly focused on decisions pertaining to room pricing and stay restrictions. While this narrowing of the scope may not be necessary in smaller operations, like a small independent retail store, it is crucial in larger outfits where functional areas must be clearly defined. At this stage the primary objective is to focus attention on the computer systems that hold data relevant to the area you are focusing on—typically a relatively small set of software programs.

Inventory the Data Currently Available   Once the relevant TPS have been identified and listed, you can inventory the data that are currently readily available in them. A first step in this phase may be to gain access to the system and explore its reporting functionalities. The key here is to focus not so much on the analyses that the reports yield, but instead to identify the underlying data that are tracked by the application in the natural course of business.

When you are not very familiar with the application, this step may be best accomplished by meeting with power users, those individuals who have intimate familiarity with the software, its capabilities, and the data it stores. This is often the best alternative because power users in your area will speak the same language and will be intimately familiar with the opportunities and challenges that you are likely to focus on. Alternatively, particularly in larger organizations, a meeting with the IT professionals who support the software may be necessary. The outcome of this phase should be a comprehensive list of data items that are reliably tracked within each TPS.

Conceptualize Initiatives   Having laid out all the available data currently being tracked by your TPS, you can simply ask yourself, "Given what I have, what would I like to know?" For this phase very little formal guidance can be offered; there is no substitute here for creativity and insight.

Figure 8.33   In the Retail Industry the Point of Sale (POS) is a Major Source of Valuable Data

As you examine the data you have inventoried, some ideas and potentially beneficial analyses will emerge. This is a crucial part of the brainstorming stage, and you should focus at this point on generating ideas without worrying much about their feasibility or financial viability.

Prioritize Initiatives   Once you have articulated a number of potential initiatives, it is time to evaluate their actual feasibility. At this stage you should make a series of pragmatic decisions regarding the order in which the suggested initiatives should be implemented. This is because justifying data-driven initiatives to acquire the necessary funding is a very difficult task. Financial justification measures, typically requested by executives, are illsuited to the task. Initiatives that are based on data analysis are qualitatively different from automation initiatives, where ROI is much easier to compute. As a consequence, the reputation of the initiative champion and the trust executives put in his or her judgment is of paramount importance. How do you establish such a reputation in the domain of business data initiatives?

The prioritization matrix described in Figure 8.34 may help. It is based on the evaluation of two dimensions: upside potential and data availability.

Upside Potential   The first dimension provides an assessment of the financial benefits associated with the initiative in terms of revenue lift or cost reduction. The extent to which data analysis initiatives have upside potential typically depends on their

- *Time sensitivity:* The degree to which the impact of the decisions that analysis of the data allows depends on how closely to the time of data collection it is made.

- *Impact immediacy:* The degree to which the information is directly usable after it is generated as opposed to needing aggregation or manipulation.

- *Aggregation requirements:* The extent to which the benefits of the analysis are dependent on substantial aggregation of multiple data sources.

- *Trending requirements:* The extent to which the benefits of the analysis are dependent on substantial trending of data over time.

Data Availability   The second dimension provides an assessment of the immediacy with which the initiative can be implemented and a measure of the costs associated with it—the higher the availability of the needed data, the cheaper and more immediate the initiative's successful implementation. The following are critical dimensions of data availability:

- *Accuracy:* The extent to which the available information is reliable without duplication, inaccuracies, or outdated elements.

- *Comprehensiveness:* The extent to which the data needed to carry out the initiative are complete and free of missing elements and/or values.

Note that this dimension becomes crucial when resources are limited and/or executives are not easily sold on the potential of data as a strategic resource. Developing initiatives around high-availability data enables the firm to establish a track record of project success.

When the initiatives identified earlier are mapped to each of the four quadrants, it becomes apparent which ones can be quickly implemented, maybe as proof of concept or to gain support from other executives. It will also become clear what initiatives are resource intensive and require a much higher level of organizational commitment.

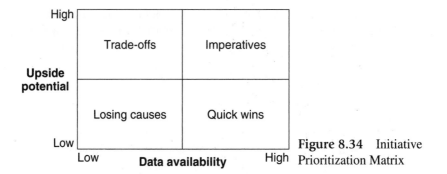

Figure 8.34 Initiative Prioritization Matrix

Imperatives In this quadrant, classified as imperatives, fall projects that have significant upside potential and rely on readily available information. These initiatives can be implemented quickly and with limited investment of resources beyond sunk costs.

Consider, for example, a grocery store that has been using checkout scanners for quite some time. With a relatively small investment, the store could compile checkout data and, after comparing it to current inventory levels, provide the store manager with an exception report flagging items that are running dangerously low. While the incremental investment is minimal, the potential upside of this initiative, reducing costly stockouts, can be significant.

Quick Wins In this quadrant fall projects that, while not having much upside potential, can be readily implemented based on immediately available information. These initiatives are labeled quick wins because they do not require significant resources and a demanding approval cycle. In the absence of clear imperatives, these initiatives can often be used as proof of concept to gain momentum and to establish a track record of successful implementation designed to build credibility with other executives. The credit so built can then be put to use when making the case for harder-to-sell trade-off initiatives.

Consider a firm running an online store that uses banner ads on referring sites. Further, imagine that your firm receives a limited amount of traffic and business from these referrals. Using currently available data and log analyzer software, the various referral sites can be evaluated, enabling a ranking with respect to the volume of traffic and business each one provides. If customers referred by one Web site consistently leave the online store after a few seconds, there is a mismatch between your offer and the referring Web site's audience. This type of analysis can be very valuable in contract negotiations, even though given the limited amount of traffic coming from referrals in this example, upside potential is limited.

Trade-Offs In this quadrant fall projects that have significant upside potential but rely on information that is not readily available and consequently tend to be quite costly. This may be because the information is not easy to capture, it is not in a readily usable format, or the initiative requires the pooling of substantial information from multiple sources and substantial data integration. These initiatives are called trade-offs as they require substantial cost benefit analysis and a rigorous approval cycle before the allocation of the needed resources can be justified.

Consider, for example, customer preferences elicited through the waiter-guest interaction at a restaurant. While such data can be very valuable to improve customer service and elicit loyalty, the data are hard to capture and store in a manner that makes them easily usable for analysis.

Losing Causes In this quadrant fall projects that are deemed to have little upside potential and rely on information that is not readily available. Initiatives that fall in this category should not be implemented unless the cost associated with making the needed data available can be justified and assigned to other projects with positive ROI. In other words, these initiatives should be shelved until a change in circumstances moves them to another, more attractive quadrant.

CONCLUSIONS

In this chapter we continued our discussion of strategic information systems, initiated in Chapter 7 with foundation concepts. Crafting successful IT-dependent strategic initiatives is part art, requiring creativity and insight, and part science, requiring disciplined analysis and attention to detail. The primary goal of this chapter was to support both the creative and analytical aspect of this process by introducing you to traditional and recent frameworks for value creation with information systems and IT. Each of them offers a different focus and a different perspective which, collectively, should provide you with a comprehensive toolset.

SUMMARY

In this chapter we focused on IT-dependent strategic initiatives, discussing the frameworks and analytical models that have been proposed over the years to help you identify opportunities to create value with IT and to design and develop value adding IT-dependent strategic initiatives.

Specifically, in this chapter we introduced the following frameworks:

- Industry analysis, focusing on the characteristics of the industry your firm competes in, seeks to help you identify opportunities to deploy information systems to improve the profitability of the industry.

- Value chain analysis focuses on the firm's own unique transformation process. It seeks to spur your thinking about how information systems and technology can be used to introduce new activities and/or change the way the firm's activities are currently performed.

- The customer service life cycle (CSLC) suggests that there is ample opportunity to create value by using information systems and technology to enhance the relationship with customers and enable superior customer service. The CSLC identifies four major phases and thirteen stages in which the relationship between the firm and its customer can be mapped. Each one offers opportunities for value creation.

- The virtual value chain recognizes the importance that the wealth of information available to today's organizations in the search for value creation. It identifies five sequential activities that a firm can use to transform raw data input into information outputs that have more value than the inputs. Using this approach, a firm can develop one of three classes of strategic initiatives: visibility, mirroring capability, and new digital value.

- Customer data can also offer the potential to create value with different strategies best fitting different organizations depending on two dimensions: the theoretical repurchase frequency of the firm's product or service, and its degree of customizability. Depending on where the firm finds its offer falling on these two dimensions, it will find a personalization, rewards, or attraction strategy to fit best. The viability of the chosen strategy depends also on the degree of difficulty the firm encounters in collecting and using the needed customer data.

Once the firm identifies a potentially value adding strategy, it must ensure that it can appropriate the value created over time. In other words, the firm that has created competitive advantage by way of an IT-dependent strategic initiative must ensure that the advantage is sustainable; this is the topic of next chapter.

STUDY QUESTIONS

1. Describe the focus and principal objectives of industry analysis applied to information systems. Select one of the five competitive forces, and offer an example of a firm that you believe has been able to influence it by way of an IT-dependent strategic initiative.

2. Describe the focus and principal objectives of value chain analysis applied to information systems. Why is it important to contextualize the value chain? Provide an example of a firm you think has been able to create competitive advantage using information systems. Identify the primary activities most impacted by information systems in this firm.

3. Describe the customer service life cycle (CSLC) and its primary objectives. Provide an example of a firm that, in your opinion, has created competitive advantage using information systems to enable superior customer service. What stages of the CSLC are mostly impacted by the firm's IT-dependent strategic initiative?

4. Describe the basic tenets of the virtual value chain. How does it differ from the physical value chain? Can you identify an example for each of the three applications of the virtual value chain?

5. Think about your last job, or the job you'd like to have once you graduate. Where would you place this firm's product or service on the dimensions of theoretical repurchase frequency and degree of customizability? How difficult is it for the firm to collect and use customer data? Is the firm engaging in a customer data strategy? If not, is it missing the boat?

FURTHER READINGS

1. Ives, B., and Learmonth, G. P. (1984). "The Information System as a Competitive Weapon." *Communications of the ACM,* Vol. 27, No. 12, pp. 1193–1201.

2. Piccoli, G., Spalding, B. R., and Ives, B. (2001). "The Customer Service Life Cycle: A Framework for Internet Use in Support of Customer Service," *Cornell Hotel and Restaurant Administration Quarterly* (42:3), pp. 38–45.

3. Piccoli, G. (2005). "The Business Value of Customer Data: Prioritizing Decisions." *Cutter Benchmark Review* (5:10), pp. 5–16.

4. Porter, M. E. (1980). *Competitive Strategy: Techniques for Analyzing Industries and Competitors.* New York, NY: Free Press.

5. Porter, M. E. (1985). *Competitive Advantage: Creating and Sustaining Superior Performance.* New York, NY: Free Press.

6. Rayport, J., and Sviokla, J. (1995). "Exploiting the Virtual Value Chain." *Harvard Business Review,* 73 (November–December), pp. 75–85.

GLOSSARY

- **Acquisition strategy:** A customer data strategy most appropriate for firms competing in industries characterized by a low theoretical repurchase frequency and a high degree of customizability.

- **Customer service life cycle:** A framework designed to draw managers attention to the potential for value creation offered by the relationship between the firm and its customers.

- **Degree of customizability:** The extent to which the product or service offered by a firm can be tailored to the specific needs and requirements of individual customers or a segment of the customer base.

- **Degree of unobtrusive data capture:** The extent to which, in the normal course of business, customer data can be collected and stored in a readily usable format by a firm.

- **Industry analysis:** A framework that identifies the five forces shaping the profitability potential of an industry.

- **IT-dependent strategic initiatives:** Identifiable competitive moves and projects that enable the creation of added value and that rely heavily on the use of information technology to be successfully implemented (i.e., they cannot feasibly be enacted without investments in IT).

- **Linkages:** The points of contact between the separate value chains of the firms in a value network.
- **Mirroring capabilities:** An application of the virtual value chain that enables the firm to perform some economic activities previously completed in the physical value chain to the information-defined world.
- **New digital value:** An application of the virtual value chain that enables the firm to increase customers' willingness to pay for new information-enabled products or services.
- **Personalization strategy:** A customer data strategy most appropriate for firms competing in industries characterized by both a high theoretical repurchase frequency and a high degree of customizability.
- **Reward strategy:** A customer data strategy most appropriate for firms competing in industries characterized by

a high theoretical repurchase frequency and a low degree of customizability.

- **Theoretical repurchase frequency:** The regularity with which the average customer acquires goods and services offered by the firms in the industry or segment of interest.
- **Value chain:** A framework that maps a firm's transformation process as a set of sequential value adding activities.
- **Value matrix:** A framework combining the physical value chain and virtual value chain models.
- **Virtual value chain:** A framework that uses the basic value chain structure to draw attention to data as a valuable input resource in the transformation process.
- **Visibility:** An application of the virtual value chain that enables the firm to "see through" organizational processes it was previously treating as a black box.

CASE STUDY: CANYON RANCH[10]

No matter what feeling better or feeling healthier means to you, Canyon Ranch is a place that helps you connect to a happier lifestyle. Everyone experiences a different Canyon Ranch; we'll meet you where you are.
    — Harley Mayersohn, Vice President of Marketing

The real challenge is: how do we get valuable information from a system that does not let it go easily and then use it for decision making?
    — Ben Campsey, Assistant Director of Finance

As the year 2004 began, Canyon Ranch remained the undisputed leader in the luxury segment of the spa industry. Its unparalleled breadth and depth of offerings, its integrated portfolio of treatments spanning traditional spa and fitness as well as health and healing services, and its incomparable attention to guest needs made Canyon Ranch the gold standard in the industry.

The spa industry in the U.S. was set to continue to grow. Competitors were also starting to attack Canyon Ranch more directly.

The challenge for Canyon Ranch was two-fold—to attempt to grow the business while maintaining the fundamental

characteristics of Canyon Ranch, and ensure that Canyon Ranch maintained its competitive advantage in the face of increasing competition.

Canyon Ranch Health Resorts was the brainchild of Enid and Mel Zuckerman, who, in 1979, sought to create a place where people would be inspired and motivated to translate their healthiest thoughts into action. As the company entered the twenty-first century, Canyon Ranch had grown into the leading health resort and spa with two destination resorts and three SpaClubs (see Exhibit 1). While the company grew larger, it remained true to its founders' original vision.

Canyon Ranch is more than just a fabulous vacation. It's an experience that can influence the quality of your life, from the moment you arrive to long after you return home. Canyon Ranch is a place to relax, enjoy yourself, and explore your potential for a happier, healthier, more fulfilling life.[11]

DESTINATION RESORTS

The two destination resorts were the backbone of the company. While they differed in their physical layout, both

---

[10] This case was originally published as: Piccoli, G., and Applegate, L. M. (2004), "Canyon Ranch," Boston, MA: Harvard Business School, Case #9-805-027.

[11] Canyon Ranch Web site, http://www.canyonranch.com/misc/whatis.asp (viewed on 6/9/04).

continued

CASE STUDY (*continued*)

Exhibit 1: Canyon Ranch Business Units

Destination/Health Resorts: Canyon Ranch Tucson, AZ (opened: 1979)

Facilities

- *62,000-square-foot spa complex:* Health and fitness assessment center; exercise physiology; fitness; men's program office; hiking and biking; six gyms, including an indoor cycling room; strength training and cardio-fitness equipment; yoga and meditation dome; wallyball, racquetball, squash, and basketball courts; locker rooms with steam and inhalation rooms, sauna, cold dip, sunbathing decks, and whirlpools; skin care rooms; beauty salon; art gallery
- *Life enhancement center:* Designed for small group interaction, home of Life Enhancement Program week-long experience
- *Aquatic center:* 11,000-square-foot facility with underwater treadmills, bikes, and cross-country ski simulators
- *Golf performance center:* Pitch, chip, and putting greens; computerized fitness evaluation and three-camera perspective; priority access to Arizona National Golf Club

Services—Spa

- *Massage and bodywork:* Ayurvedic herbal massage, herbal wrap, shiatsu, hydromassage
- *Skin care and beauty services:* Aloe-algae mask, European facial, seaweed paraffin body treatment

Services—Health & Healing

- *Nutrition classes and workshops:* Antioxidant evaluation, digestive wellness, hands-on cooking classes
- *Medical services:* Acupuncture, cardiac treadmill stress test, cholesterol and heart health consultation
- *Behavioral health services:* Biofeedback, hypnotherapy, adventure learning
- *Exercise physiology:* Basic fitness assessment, training for advanced and specialized needs
- *Movement therapy:* Aquatic therapy, Pilates

Services—Fitness

- *Fitness classes and activities:* Aerobics, biking, personal training, private aqua lessons
- *Outdoor sports:* Hiking, biking, aerobic walks
- Golf instruction for all levels
- Water exercise for sports conditioning, fitness, stress, and pain management

Destination/Health Resorts: Canyon Ranch in the Berkshires. Lenox, MA (opened: 1989)

Facilities

- *100,000-square-foot spa complex:* Health and fitness assessment center; six gyms; 75-foot indoor pool; exercise and weight training rooms; indoor tennis, racquetball, squash, basketball, and wallyball; locker rooms with steam and inhalation rooms, sauna, cold dip, and whirlpools; indoor running track; therapeutic massage and bodywork rooms; beauty salon and skin care services
- *Inn:* 126 guest rooms and suites

Services—Spa

- *Massage and bodywork:* Austrian moor mud therapy, Ayurvedic herbal rejuvenation, reflexology
- *Skin care and beauty services:* Glycolic skin treatments, hair care, makeup consultation and application

Services—Health & Healing

- *Nutrition classes and workshops:* Eating for weight loss, hands-on cooking classes, healing food
- *Medical services:* Acupuncture, cardiac treadmill stress test, cholesterol and heart health consultation
- *Behavioral health services:* Biofeedback, changing eating habits, emotional healing, smoking cessation
- *Exercise physiology:* Comprehensive musculoskeletal evaluation, posture analysis
- *Movement therapy:* Aquatic therapy, Pilates, etc.

Services—Fitness

- Over 40 fitness classes and activities each day (e.g., aerobics, basketball, cross training)
- Outdoor sports (e.g., biking, canoeing, cross-country skiing, hiking)
- One free round of golf at Cranwell Country Club

SpaClub: The Venetian. Las Vegas, NV (opened: 2000)

Facilities

- *65,000-square-foot spa complex:* Health and wellness center; massage, skin care, and body treatment rooms; therapeutic pools; three-story rock climbing wall
- *12,000-square-foot Living Essentials spa boutique:* Health-oriented store featuring in-store wellness education and demonstrations and environmentally sound merchandise

SpaClub: The Gaylord Palms. Kissimmee, FL (opened: 2002)

Facilities

- *20,000-square-foot spa complex:* 25 massage, body, and skin care treatment rooms; fitness facility with cardiovascular and weight-training equipment; locker rooms with steam and sauna; salon with beauty services for men and women
- *Living Essentials spa boutique:* Health-oriented store featuring in-store wellness education and demonstrations, and environmentally sound merchandise

SpaClub: The Queen Mary II—Cunard (opened: 2004)

Facilities

- *20,000-square-foot spa complex:* Located on two decks, 24 massage, body, and skincare treatment rooms; coed relaxation lounge; thermal suite and Rasul room; thalassotherapy pool with airbed recliner lounges; neck fountains; deluge waterfall; air tub and body massage jet benches; whirlpool; thermal suite with herbal and Finnish saunas; reflexology basins; aromatic steam room

Source: Company Documents.

resorts offered a similar portfolio of services and had the same organizational structure. Each was divided into three revenue-generating departments: Health and Healing, Hotel, and Spa, with a director overseeing each one.

As the company grew in size, so did its stunning array of services. The most recent guide to services for Canyon Ranch in the Berkshires, for example, detailed more than 230 different services in both the Spa and Health and Healing departments (see Exhibit 2). Guests also had access to numerous lectures and fitness classes, as well as multiple opportunities for outdoor activities at no extra charge (see Exhibit 3). Central to the mission of Canyon Ranch was the Health and Healing operation, a function staffed with medical doctors, nutritionists, behaviorists, and exercise physiologists. Canyon Ranch executives believed that, if properly integrated, the Health and Healing department could offer important synergies with other departments. Michael Tompkins, assistant general manager at the Lenox,

continued

Massachusetts resort, was in charge of all revenue generating departments. In early 2004, he explained:

> If Health and Healing recommends that you have shiatsu, that recommendation elevates the level of that service because a health professional recommended you do it. It raises the caliber of the spa services.

Of the three departments, Health and Healing showed the fastest growth but accounted for the lowest contribution to profitability. The leading department on the profitability front was the Hotel, followed by the Spa. Simon Marxer, Spa director, explained:

> When Health and Healing was started, it was accepted that we were going to lose money every year on it. This is no longer the case, but the flow-through remains much lower. A behaviorist makes around $60 out of the $105 you pay for the service, while a fitness instructor will make around $40 and a massage therapist around $30. As a result of the higher commissions paid to the Health and Healing professionals, the profit for Canyon Ranch is lower.

Exhibit 2 Services

Over 500 services, plus an average of 10 to 20 lectures a day and about 50 fitness classes, not including outdoor activities.

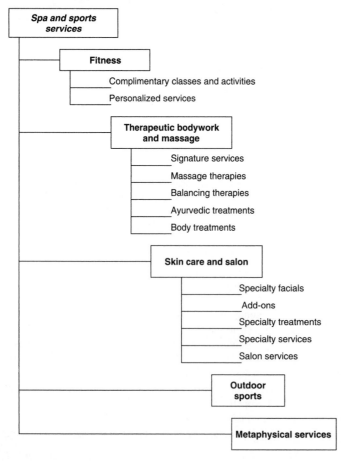

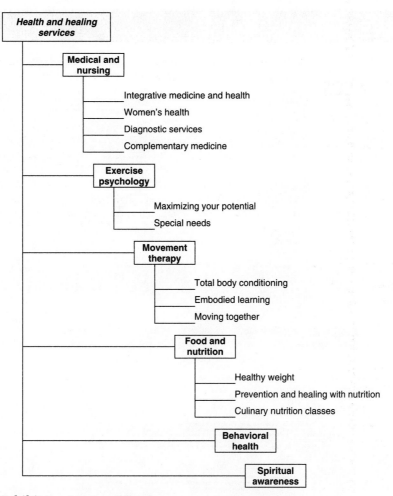

Exhibit 2   (*continued*) Services. (*Source:* Company documents.)

SPACLUBS

The SpaClubs complemented the Canyon Ranch destination resorts and focused on spa, fitness, and salon services but lacked a strong Health and Healing component. In 2004, the two SpaClubs were housed in third-party properties—the Venetian resort in Las Vegas, Nevada and the Gaylord Palms Resort & Convention Center in Kissimmee, Florida. The SpaClubs were designed to serve the needs of the guests of these properties—largely convention goers. A third SpaClub had recently been opened on the cruise ship Queen Mary 2. Mayersohn explained the role of the SpaClubs:

SpaClubs are "a touch of Canyon Ranch." They were designed to introduce customers to the brand. The synergy between the SpaClubs and resorts is still a little tenuous, but we expect the SpaClub on the Queen Mary 2 to be more of a feeder because the demographics are similar.

As a luxury destination, Canyon Ranch was extremely attentive to service with a 2.5:1 staff to guest ratio. For example, Canyon Ranch in the Berkshire Mountains of western Massachusetts had approximately 700 employees on property for an estimated "full house" count of 212 guests. But executives were quick to point out that a

continued

CASE STUDY (*continued*)

new services

special health packages
- Ayurvedic Health
- Brain Wellness: Preventive Medicine for the Mind
- Pregnancy Health

medical
- Breast Cancer Prevention
- Natural Medicine for the Home
- Pregnancy & Childbirth Counseling

movement therapy
- Align & Lengthen
- Energize Your Relationships
- Movement Principles for Yoga
- Real Bodies Moving

food & nutrition
- All About Carbohydrates, Insulin Resistance & Blood Sugar
- Beauty of Nutrition
- CustomVite™
- Digestive Wellness
- Eating for Energy
- Fastest Meals Imaginable
- Maximize Metabolism for Weight Loss
- Menopause Matters
- Neuronutrition, Stress & Brain Health

spiritual awareness
- Embodying Yoga
- Total Yoga

fitness
- Express Workout
- Forever Fit
- Weight Loss Workout

therapeutic bodywork & massage
- Bindi Shirodhara
- Canyon Hydra-Stone
- Integrative Bodywork
- Lymphatic Massage

skin care & salon services
- Ayurvedic Facial
- Ayurvedic Pedicure
- Buff Nails
- Gentleman's Scalp Renewal
- Hey Mom!
- Infusia Treatment
- Sisley Anti-Aging Facial

package allowances

Your package may include allowances for services in two categories, Health & Healing and Spa & Sports (refer to your confirmation information for allowance details). Your Program Coordinator can help you choose the services that you'll enjoy and benefit from most.

Health & Healing Services
- Medical & Nursing
- Behavioral Health
- Acupuncture & Energy Medicine
- Exercise Physiology
- Spiritual Awareness
- Movement Therapy
- Food & Nutrition

Spa & Sports Services
- Fitness & Sports
- Outdoor Sports
- Therapeutic Bodywork & Massage
- Skin Care & Salon
- Metaphysical

Complimentary
Many experiences at Canyon Ranch are available without charge. Lunch & Learn, hikes, bike rides, cross-country skiing are all complimentary. Check the postings in the Spa and *This Week at Canyon Ranch* for information.

SPECIAL HEALTH PACKAGES

Sign up: Ext. 5325 or 5439

OPTIMAL LIVING™ *4 nights or longer* — Fee: $985

Work with an integrated team of Canyon Ranch health professionals who will create a personalized plan to help broaden your awareness in health, fitness, nutrition, movement, stress management and creative expression.

Your package begins with an Optimal Health Consultation with a physician or psychotherapist and may include a combination of sessions with a physician, psychotherapist, movement therapist, Chinese medicine practitioner, exercise physiologist, nutritionist or dermo chef. You'll work closely with our team to develop a plan to take home.

These services are in addition to those in a spa package:
- Pre-arrival interview
- 50-minute Optimal Health Consultation
- $630 allowance for Health & Healing Services
- Final wrap-up and phone follow-up

Note: *For people over 50 who have not had recent health evaluations, we recommend the Ultraprevention package.*

ARTHRITIS/PAIN MANAGEMENT *4 nights or longer* — Fee: $1,250

If you have chronic pain from arthritis or any other condition, this package can help you live a fuller life. Our integrated approach uses nutritional and natural therapeutics, mind-body techniques, immune system modulation and musculoskeletal assessment.

We combine physical, behavioral, nutritional and spiritual approaches that lead to relief or better coping mechanisms. We can also provide follow-up communication with your primary care physician.

These services are in addition to those in a spa package:
- Pre-arrival interview
- 50-minute consultation with a physician
- Special Needs Assessment with a physical therapist
- Movement Therapy consultation
- Acupuncture or Chinese Herbal consultation
- Behavioral Health consultation
- Healing Foods nutrition consultation
- 30-minute follow-up with a physician
- Healing Touch
- Final wrap-up and phone follow-up

ULTRAMETABOLISM: NEW APPROACHES TO WEIGHT LOSS *3 nights or longer* — Fee: $1,800

Let an experienced team of Canyon Ranch specialists guide you through new approaches to diagnosis and treatment of obesity or weight problems. The latest clinical advances are available to help you balance the hormones, behavior, and brain chemistry that govern your eating pattern and weight loss or gain. Go beyond the frenzy of high-carb/low-carb, high-fat/low-fat and other confusing diets to unlock the gateway to healthy weight, increased energy and healthy aging.

These services are in addition to those in a spa package:
- Pre-arrival interview
- 50-minute Optimal Health Consultation
- Metabolic Exercise Assessment and Exercise Assessment follow-up
- DEXA Body Composition Test
- $500 allowance toward laboratory tests that may include:
  - Blood Glucose and Insulin levels before and after glucose challenge
  - Thyroid function
  - Cholesterol & Mean Health Profile

(Other specialized testing may be recommended for an additional fee.)
- Maximize Metabolism for Weight Loss
- Two Food Habit Management Consultations
- Final wrap-up
- 30-minute phone follow-up with physician
- 30-minute phone follow-up with nutritionist

SPA & SPORTS SERVICES • therapeutic bodywork & massage

Sign up: Ext. 5439

signature services

Canyon Ranch has created special treatments for you to enjoy at any of our properties.

MANGO SUGAR GLO — Fee: $120

The organic healing effects of the desert's aloe plant and the fragrant quality of the mango fruit combine in this truly luxurious Canyon Ranch original treatment. Derived from natural products – raw sugars, jojoba oil and aloe vera among others – this body scrub enhances your skin with rejuvenating and moisturizing effects. It begins with a light exfoliation to clear and balance skin. The vitamin-enhanced, hydrating qualities of the mango bodywash gently cleanse and condition. Ultimately, a vitamin-enriched mango moisturizer is applied to soften and smooth even the most sensitive skin. 50 minutes.

CANYON STONE MASSAGE — Fee: $165

Smooth, rounded basalt stones are heated in water then lubricated with essential oil and applied to the body as an extension of the therapist's hands. The heat within the stones penetrates your muscle tissue inducing deep relaxation without overheating. Only available from 10 a.m. to 5 p.m. 75 minutes.

EUPHORIA™ — Fee: $230

In the candlelit environment of our Spa Suite, music plays softly as you are draped in bath sheets, and your face is enveloped in towels dipped in sage oil. An aromatherapy scalp massage is followed by a warm botanical body mask. After the mask is gently buffed, you're immersed in a soaking tub for a revitalizing bath. Your experience concludes with a light, soothing massage using warm herb-infused oil. 100 minutes.

LULUR RITUAL — Fee: $230

This luxurious beauty ritual from Central Java begins with an effective combination of energetic massage techniques using jasmine frangipani oil followed by exfoliation with turmeric and a yogurt wash. Then enjoy a relaxing soak in a bath with floating rose petals. An application of jasmine frangipani aloe body lotion completes the ritual. Lulur leaves the skin with a radiant glow. 100 minutes.

massage therapies

Our therapists use a variety of subtle, stimulating and effective techniques to achieve overall relaxation and muscle rejuvenation.

CANYON RANCH MASSAGE — Fee: 50 minutes – $95; 100 minutes – $190

This classic full-body massage is a Canyon Ranch staple. Therapists adapt their eclectic massage techniques to your needs to increase circulation, relieve tense muscles and promote relaxation. Choose a 50- or 100-minute session.

SHIATSU — Fee: 50 minutes – $95; 100 minutes – $190

Shiatsu uses pressure and passive stretches throughout the body to shift the chi into better balance. This balances and improves the energetic system of the body, leaving you feeling centered and connected in mind, body and spirit. Please wear loose, comfortable clothing. Choose a 50- or 100-minute session.

SPORTS MASSAGE — Fee: $95

This personalized massage focuses on areas of need. The therapist applies specific techniques to reduce muscle tension, increase range of motion and provide a warm-up or cool-down for a particular activity. (Not a full-body massage.) 50 minutes.

Exhibit 3 New Services and Sample Packages and Services. (*Source:* Company documents.)

visitor to Canyon Ranch would receive a special kind of outstanding service. Tompkins explained:

> The service is not five-star-stuffy; there are no bell-men in white gloves here. Our staff are real people acting in a genuine manner to help you achieve your goals.

During recruitment, Canyon Ranch focused on finding people that would provide excellence in the position and would complement the set of skills currently available in the property. The fit of a new recruit's personality with the firm's culture was also an important factor. Applicants in Health and Healing were given a topic and were asked to give a presentation to the area directors and other members of the recruiting team. Applicants in the Spa department were asked to perform two or three services in their area of expertise.

Outstanding professional qualifications, though, had to be complemented by an outgoing personality, friendliness, and a genuine excitement for the job. Selecting people with the right personality was considered one of the critical factors for new hires at Canyon Ranch. Marxer aptly captured this culture: "We just don't say no. We'll find a way to meet guests' requests."

THE CANYON RANCH CUSTOMER

Canyon Ranch executives had developed substantial knowledge about customers over the years. This was particularly true of the approximately 17,000 customers (some returning multiple times) visiting each destination resort every year. Mayersohn explained:

> Our prototypical guest is a 47-year-old woman, with grown kids, with a high household income, active, generally fit, and who does not compromise on wanting the best.

While women represented about 75% of Canyon Ranch's customer base, men represented a growing segment. This growth was imputed to the aging of the baby boomer generation and the increasing attention that men paid to their health and well-being. This trend appeared to be confirmed by the growing interest customers showed in the Health and Healing department, with 6% of guests purchasing a package focusing on this area and generating about 16% of ancillary service revenue. Senior management was intent on fostering the trend. Tompkins explained:

> We have been in business for 25 years, and we have not been known for our wellness component. We

have been known for being the best spa in the world. The majority of our clientele comes here looking for the spa vacation. We are attempting to create an awareness of our Health and Healing component without disrupting the spa vacationers. Ideally, after customers try it, a whole new world opens up for them.

The primary feeder markets for both of the health resorts were the New York metro and the Eastern corridor areas. As a consequence, Tucson relied almost exclusively on fly-in customers, while Lenox served almost exclusively a drive-in market. Cross-property traffic was estimated to be just below 10%. Most customers bought packages. These included the hotel stay and meals, as well as some services or vouchers that could be used toward the purchase of services in specific areas (see Exhibit 4). Guests were required to stay for either three or four nights and spent $2000 to $2500 per stay, taking, on average, a little over two services a day (either included in their package or à la carte). Lectures, fitness classes, and outdoor activities were all complementary except when requesting a one-on-one session with the instructor. Some guests also purchased ancillary products such as books or CDs. Particularly popular were beauty supplies, generally purchased after service at the salon. The success of these sales, estimated to exceed half a million dollars at the Lenox, Massachusetts resort alone, had convinced Canyon Ranch executives to launch a proprietary line of skin care products.

At any given time, about 55% of the in-house guests had visited Canyon Ranch before. The firm calculated that 18% of the customers returned more than once to Canyon Ranch health resorts, with guests returning multiple times over their lifetime and some guests returning multiple times a year. Tompkins reasoned:

> People return over and over several times a year when they get what Canyon Ranch is all about and we become part of their lifestyle. We have a true integrative care model. When was the last time that you spent an hour with your physician? When you go see a doctor and you say, "I feel OK, I just want to feel better," they look at you like you are crazy, whereas here this is what Canyon Ranch is all about.

Particularly loyal customers had the option of becoming centennial members. Membership offered significant discounts and perks. After paying a flat fee proportional to the number of free nights the guest wanted to purchase, members were entitled to stay at Canyon Ranch for 50% of

continued

CASE STUDY (*continued*)

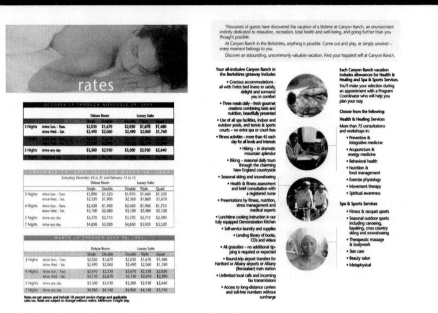

Exhibit 4   Canyon Ranch: Rates and Packages. (*Source:* Company documents.)

the room rate and receive a 10% discount on services purchased à la carte for the seven-year duration of the membership. The 798 current centennial members were also allowed to visit for only two nights when current occupancy levels allowed. Returning customers received tokens of appreciation (branded merchandise such as T-shirts and bags), but Canyon Ranch did not have a formal recognition or reward program.

Canyon Ranch did not advertise heavily, instead focusing on direct communication and affiliations with similar suitable partners. Mayersohn commented:

> We are a word-of-mouth referral business with a long sales lead time, not an impulse buy. Our core strategy is creating word-of-mouth. We do customer events and give parties with partners—like Williams Sonoma, for example. We invite customers and they bring a guest who has never been to Canyon Ranch. Partners will become the most important part of our growth in the next two years. We get one or two calls a week from people who want to do something with us, but we have to be carefully selective.

While Canyon Ranch did receive about 20% of its business from travel agents (including group business), the

firm had recently expanded the direct communication to the electronic space using e-mail and its Web site for direct marketing. Over two million unique visitors viewed the Canyon Ranch Web site in 2003. Executives were entertaining proposals to improve the Web site from its current static design to an interactive one. Mayersohn discussed the philosophy behind it: "Because your Canyon Ranch experience is customized to your needs, we want your Web site experience to be customized to your interests and needs as well."

THE SPA INDUSTRY

Since the time of Ancient Greece and Rome, humankind has enjoyed a variety of thermal and aquatic therapies for healing and relaxation purposes. The term *spa* originated from a town in Belgium renowned for its baths and mineral springs and has come to identify a place to receive a wide range of services. Yet the term has lost some of its meaning due to its broad use to include a wide range of services, traditional or modern, and sizes. In fact, in the U.S., the spa industry was dominated by many small operations and a few large companies. According to the International Spa Association (ISPA), in June 2002 there were 9632 spas in

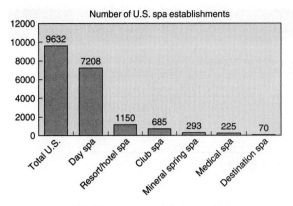

Exhibit 5   Composition of the Spa Industry.
(*Source:* The International SPA Association's 2002 Spa Industry Study, Price Waterhouse Coopers, p. 3.)

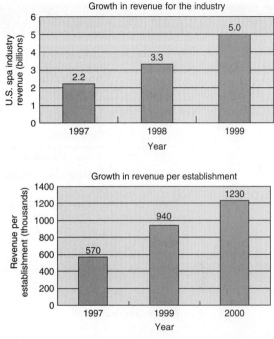

Exhibit 6   Industry Growth. (*Source:* Price Waterhouse Coopers/2001, The International SPA Association's 2000 SPA Industry Study.)

the U.S.—up from 1374 in 1990.[12] The census included such diverse outfits as day spas (outfits without a lodging element), spas housed in resorts and hotels, destination spas (outfits where the spa is the principal draw for customer), etc.—operated by approximately 7400 different organizations (see Exhibit 5).[13]

This growth in offerings was fueled by the growth in spa visits—from an estimated 57 million in 1997 to 155.8 million in 2001.[14] All this growth, attributed in large part to the aging baby boomer population seeking longevity, had propelled into a $10.7 billion industry by 2001,[15] up significantly from two years earlier (see Exhibit 6). This trend was confirmed by many customers no longer simply seeking a spa experience to be pampered, but as a way to a healthier life.[16] But while the spa industry was growing, the spa experience was still far from being "mainstream." According to the "The American Spa-Goer Survey," 11% of the U.S. population (over 16 years old) visited a day spa, 7% visited a resort/hotel spa, and 1% visited a destination spa in the 2002 to 2003 time frame (see Exhibit 6).

Despite industry growth, operations remained generally low-tech and relatively little attention was paid to the potential offered by information technology. Because of its very nature as a service business, characterized by personal attention and co-production,[17] the spa industry had traditionally been a high-touch, people-intensive business. Computerization was often seen as a threat, rather than an opportunity, due to its perceived potential to de-personalize and de-humanize the experience. Moreover, since many spa goers were seeking an escape from their increasingly stressful office lives, the industry was very careful to avoid any technology that might damage the carefully choreographed atmosphere of the setting.

---

[12] Price Waterhouse Coopers/2001, The International SPA Association's 2000 SPA Industry Study, p. 26.

[13] The International SPA Association's 2002 Spa Industry Study, Price Waterhouse Coopers, p. 3.

[14] Price Waterhouse Coopers/2001, The International SPA Association's 2000 SPA Industry Study, p. 29.

[15] Message Today, What Really Drives the Spa Industry? online at http://www.massagetoday.com/archives/2003/01/21.html (viewed on 1/14/04).

[16] The ISPA 2002 Spa Industry Study—Executive Summary (http://spas.about.com/library/weekly/aa090602f.htm (viewed on 1/14/04).

[17] The term *co-production* characterizes industries where the customer has to be actively present in the creation of the product or service.

continued

CASE STUDY (*continued*)

Table 2 Percentage of Spa Visitors

Visited Once or More in the Last 12 Months	1999*	2003*
Day spa	7%	11%
Resort/hotel spa	5%	7%
Destination spa	1%	1%

Source: The American Spa-Goer Survey, 2003

*People ages 16 or above

Table 3 Frequency of Visiting a Spa during the Last 12 Months (1999)

	Day Spa Visitor		Other Type of Spa Visitor	
	One or More*	Mean**	One or More*	Mean**
Day Spa	100%[†]	5.0[†]	44%	2.1
Resort/Hotel Spa	31%	1.8	84%[†]	2.5
Destination Spa	16%	2.1	41%[†]	1.9
Cruise Spa	8%	2.1	15%[†]	1.7

Source: Price Waterhouse Coopers/2001, The International SPA Association's 2000 SPA Industry Study

*Does not equal 100% due to multiple response.

**Among those who took one or more trips.

[†]Denotes a statistically significant difference from the comparison group at 95% confidence.

THE COMPETITION

Canyon Ranch was widely recognized as the gold standard in the industry. It commanded rates 25% to 30% higher than other destination spas—with the possible exception of Golden Door. Moreover, its astonishing array of services and its Health and Healing department set it apart from most competitors. Mayersohn discussed the competition:

> We do compete with the destination resorts that have spas. Two things differentiate us: the Health and Healing component that is unmatched in any similar setting, and the totality of all that is available under one roof. If a massage is all you want, there are many places to go. If you want to be open to the possibility of a life-enhancing experience, Canyon Ranch provides more options than anywhere else.

Customers who simply sought standard spa services such as massages, fitness, and salon services often included location as an important driver of the purchase decision and had a number of options to choose from (see Exhibit 7). Many of these guests also traveled to different destinations seeking variety of setting between purchases. Yet Canyon Ranch, because of its history and reputation, was able to attract a substantial number of spa goers, as Marxer explained:

> Over 50% of our customers visit Health and Healing because it is part of their package. But there is a big chunk of our guests that are here to get nothing but spa services and be pampered.

While senior management believed that no other spa resorts could currently compete head-on with Canyon Ranch, there were signs of increasing competition. Tompkins explained:

> Most of our competitors have either a very high spa component or a very high health and healing component. Because of our longevity, we have a huge menu of services that most spas don't have, as well as fitness classes and lectures. Our differentiator the whole time has been Health and Healing. It has become part of the spa, integrated under one roof.

Destination	Hotel and Resort (US)	Hotel and Resort (World)
Miraval, Catalina, Arizona	Hualalai Sports Club & Spa at Four Seasons Resort Hualalai, Hawaii	Four Seasons Resort Bali at Jimbaran Bay
Golden Door, Escondido, California	The Greenbrier, White Sulphur Springs, West Virginia	The Oriental, Bangkok
Canyon Ranch, Tucson, Arizona	Mauna Lani Spa at Mauna Lani Resort, Hawaii	Spa at Regent Chiang Mai Resort, Thailand
Canyon Ranch, Lenox, Massachusetts	Anara Spa at Hyatt Regency Kauai Resort	Ritz-Carlton, Bali Resort & Spa
Oaks at Ojai, California	Willow Stream Spa at Fairmont Banff Springs, Alberta	Four Seasons Hotel George V, Paris
Mii Amo, Sedona, Arizona	Spa Bellagio, Las Vegas	Banyan Tree Spa Phuket, Thailand
Rancho La Puerta, Tecate, Mexico	Golden Door Spa at the Boulders, Carefree, Arizona	Brenner's Park-Hotel & Spa, Baden-Baden, Germany
Ten Thousand Waves, Santa Fe, New Mexico	Plaza Spa, New York City	Le Sirenuse, Positano, Italy
Body Holiday at LeSport, St. Lucia	Four Seasons Resort Maui at Wailea	The Ritz, Paris
Palms at Palm Springs, California	Spa Grande at Grand Wailea Resort Hotel, Maui	Las Ventanas al Paraíso, Los Cabos, Mexico

Exhibit 7   Top Spas According to Travel + Leisure Magazine. (*Source: Travel + Leisure Magazine*, online at <http://www.travelandleisure.com/worldbest/pressrelease-spas.cfm>, (accessed 1/14/04.)

But there were signs that some competitors were beginning to encroach on Canyon Ranch's unique value proposition. Industry observers were seeing some convergence between medicine and spa. This trend was manifested in day spas aligning themselves with medical professionals, not only plastic surgeons and dermatologists, but also in many other branches of medicine, such as nutritionists, homeopathic doctors, physical therapists, and general practitioners. At the same time, some medical professionals were beginning to include spa treatments in their practice and some hospitals were including alternative treatments in their portfolio. While precisely estimating the extent of this trend remained difficult, management was watching it closely, as Mayersohn indicated:

These are potential threats to our uniqueness. Many of the large luxury destination resorts with sizeable spas now are building a medical or wellness component. On the other side, hospitals are adding spas and wellness centers with nutritionists.

Substantially more difficult was the analysis of competition from substitute luxury purchases. A destination spa was a big-ticket item that often competed with other vacation opportunities. But, as Mayersohn explained, the potential pool of substitutes was virtually unlimited:

We debate constantly what substitutes to our product are. We compete with trips to Europe, cruises . . . really, we compete with anything that may cost five grand of discretionary income . . . we could compete with a plasma-screen TV, for example.

INFORMATION TECHNOLOGY AT CANYON RANCH

The corporate IT function at Canyon Ranch numbered 20 professionals headed by Mike Randle, corporate IT Director, who reported to the COO and CFO. The function was responsible for internal software development and maintenance, as well as evaluating software packages and performing help-desk and support tasks. Randle recounted this evolution:

In 1996, the IT director position was created. At the time, Canyon Ranch had one programmer, one or two tech support people, and one manager who had worked her way up from the accounting department. The focus was on maintaining the only computer system—the Property Management System.

The growth came following the evolution of the role that IT played at Canyon Ranch. While the IT function had

continued

historically been regarded as a support function with the main goal of supporting the many operational systems—property management system, reservations, spa and wellness service scheduling, accounting, purchasing, payroll—IT was being viewed as increasingly strategic. This change was a result of the need for business intelligence, decision-support functionalities, and expected growth, as well as some turnover in senior management. The business expectation of what IT could deliver was growing rapidly. The pressure came from the top and from operational personnel who saw the potential value of information to enable better decision making. But, as Marxer explained, some difficulties remained:

> It can be a big transition to make decisions based on numbers rather than anecdotal information. In beauty services, for example, we found out that the utilization of therapists after 4:00 P.M. was high but utilization of facilities was low. This indicates that the few people on staff are booked all the time. But traditionally, beauticians believe that nobody wants a pedicure after four—it's late, their nails are wet before going to dinner. Using the utilization report, I was able to convince them.

Canyon Ranch relied on a decentralized IT infrastructure with both the destination resorts and the SpaClubs working relatively independently. The heart of the infrastructure at the destination resorts was the property management system—Computerized Lodging Systems (CLS)—a UNIX-based legacy application written in BASIC that the company had been using since 1986 through multiple versions. Canyon Ranch owned the source code to CLS, which made it easy to customize, and had worked in partnership with Computerized Lodging Systems Inc. to develop its complex and robust scheduling component for Spa and Health and Healing services. Other activities were not tracked by CLS. Like most operational computer systems, CLS focused on efficiently processing transactions rather than collecting decision-support data. This data was used to generate utilization reports for Spa and Health and Healing services. For popular services and activities, paper-based waiting lists were maintained. Campsey explained:

> To sign up for activities included in the rate such as fitness classes, outdoor sports, and lectures, the guests use a paper-based system. For reporting purposes, the instructors input the number of people who took the service in a database I have recently created.

CLS also represented the primary source of guest data. Traditionally, the company had been able to collect stay information (e.g., type of room, number of guests in the party, room rate and charges, address). Randle explained:

> We have guest history data dating back 10 years, even though beyond 1999 it gets questionable. We know when they were here and we know more or less what they spent, but we don't necessarily know what they spent it on.

The depth of this information had increased significantly with the 1999 upgrade of CLS to version 16. The firm could now track what paid services a customer scheduled, when, with whom they took the service, and similar transactional data. Like many luxury operations, the company had also been compiling significant amounts of data about guest stays (e.g., when guests asked for specific accommodations or visited on anniversaries or other important dates). This information was recorded in free-form text and could not be easily parsed by automated software.

To complement the functionality of CLS, Canyon Ranch in the Berkshires had recently implemented Guestware, a software application designed to collect preferences and support incident tracking, rapid response, and guest surveying. While Guestware had the potential to improve relationships with customers, it was currently a stand-alone application used primarily to record guest preferences. Campsey expanded on the current use of Guestware:

> We mainly use Guestware for preferences and incident tracking, but it does not integrate well with CLS yet. The manager on duty should be able to go in and look at what happened during the day and take action immediately. But this does not happen.

The firm did not have point-of-sale (POS) software either in the restaurant or the salon, where customers could purchase beauty products. A guest would schedule an appointment with the salon and the appropriate charge was posted to CLS. If a guest purchased beauty products, the value of the purchase would be added to the salon services, but it couldn't be tracked independently. As the profile of the IT function continued to rise, Randle explained his role: "One of the most important things I focus on is to enable management to use technology to answer operational questions without us being the bottleneck."

DELIVERING THE CANYON RANCH EXPERIENCE: CANYON RANCH IN THE BERKSHIRES

Typically a guest booked a Canyon Ranch vacation by calling the property they were interested in visiting. Three weeks prior to their scheduled arrival, the guest called a 1-800 number and spoke to pre-booking personnel (part of the reservation department). This call was designed to obtain some background information about the prospective guest's goals for their stay (e.g., relieve stress and relax, quit smoking, relieve back pain, lose weight) and some relevant background information (e.g., current exercise level, preferences for treatments such as time of day, preferred pressure level, therapist's gender). If possible, specific services were also booked at this time. Prospective guests were sent a health questionnaire that they were asked to return prior to their arrival.

Upon arrival, guests checked in at the security gate and were announced and greeted by name, once they drove up to the inn. After checking in and getting settled in their room, new guests received a brief orientation and a tour of the facilities. Then guests met with a program coordinator who could look up services pre-booked by the reservations department and counsel guests. This "hand-off" between reservations and program coordination was sometimes problematic, as Marxer, formerly a program coordinator, explained:

Ideally, program coordinators will know what you want upon arrival, you don't have to repeat what your goals are, what your history is. If you suffered from bulimia as a youth, you don't want to have to repeat yourself. The program coordinator should say: "I know that eating has been an issue for you before and here is how I think we should proceed."

Canyon Ranch in the Berkshires employed fifteen full-time coordinators, seven part-time, and a few on-call that could fill in during high-demand periods. As Marxer explained, the program coordinators served both as counselors, trying to connect with guests to understand their needs and make appropriate recommendations, and as concierge, helping the guest navigate the staggering array of services and options available:

Program coordinators need a unique blend of skills; they need to make the guest's entry into the environment as easy as possible. Sometimes they need to probe and connect with the guest, but they also need to be very practical and efficient in booking services. Tenure in the job helps a lot. When you are new and trying to remember what the heck the code was for

that one service, you are not really tuned into what the guest is telling you. You can't really connect with the guest.

Staffing the position was challenging, with a lead time of six weeks of training before the program coordinators could begin to interact with guests, and an estimated six months on the job for them to become proficient in the position. Turnover in the position was high, with the department turning over an estimated 50% every year and 20% of trainees not completing the preliminary six weeks. Reflecting on the causes of this high turnover, Marxer reasoned:

Right now the program coordinator is not a highly paid position. Paying them more would challenge our entire compensation scheme. Moreover, how many people want to make program coordinator their career? It can be stressful; some guests don't want to hear that 4:00 is prime time for a massage and their preference is not available.

Program coordinators needed to be very flexible and be able to think on their feet, as every scheduling request could pose conflicts that needed to be quickly and efficiently resolved. When conflicts arose, the coordinator tried to satisfy the guest request working in tandem with therapists on their schedules and using waiting lists, or they provided alternative options for the customer to evaluate. With their schedules worked out, guests were free to enjoy the many services that Canyon Ranch had to offer and returned to the program coordinators when they had changes in their plans. Guests met with therapists, instructors, or other service providers at the scheduled times.

Guests were provided with a daily schedule of services they had signed up for—printed from CLS. The service providers had individual vouchers, also printed daily from CLS, for each guest who would visit that day. The vouchers indicated the name of the guest, the service they had booked, and whether they were new or a returning guest. At the scheduled time the guest would either go to the Health and Healing department or to the Spa and Fitness locker room, depending on the service. If they needed Health and Healing services, they completed a short questionnaire and then were greeted by the service provider who would introduce him- or herself, welcome (or welcome back) the guest, and discuss any issues, concerns, or preferences regarding the service. Upon completion of the service, there was brief wrap-up session during which the service provider would provide any suggestions and referrals for other services before walking the guest back to the reception area.

continued

The experience in the spa was similar, with the guest being walked to the therapist by a locker room attendant. Any medical alerts or other noteworthy issues (e.g., three months pregnant, recent surgery) that had been noted by medical staff or program coordinators appeared in the form of a code, directly on the voucher. Before beginning the treatment therapist also introduced him- or herself and discussed any issues or preferences with the guest. Upon completion of the session, they walked the guest back to the locker room.

THE FUTURE

In early 2004, Canyon Ranch remained the undisputed leader in the destination segment of the spa industry. Yet in the face of increasing competition from within the industry as well as from substitutes, Canyon Ranch executives were constantly seeking ways to leverage this preeminent position to extend the Canyon Ranch brand and to maintain future dominance in the destination spa segment. The challenge, as Mayersohn framed it, was to grow the company by extending the brand and by improving the performance of the existing business units: "We must integrate our growing array of products under one brand, making sure that we continue to raise the level of consistency among all our business units."

Each business unit was intent on improving the level of customer service and personalization of the Canyon Ranch experience. Canyon Ranch in the Berkshires was at the forefront of this trend and its management was strongly committed to providing an unparalleled standard of customer service. Yet there existed no readily available blueprint for how to improve on the "best-in-the-business" spa experience. Canyon Ranch management was keenly aware of the potential that customer data offered, as well as the risks of not using it appropriately and with care. A number of questions remained unanswered: Should Canyon Ranch in the Berkshires develop a clear Customer Relationship Management (CRM) strategy and make it a cornerstone of its positioning as a preeminent destination spa? If so, what should this initiative look like? What is the value of the substantial amounts of data that are generated during the customer experience? Are there any opportunities to use this data during prospecting? Or during the customer stay? Or even after the stay?

CHAPTER 9

Appropriating IT-Enabled Value Over Time

What You Will Learn in This Chapter

General and functional managers have historically had a love-hate relationship with information technology. They recognize its potential to help the firm compete, but they often lack the tools to make sound decisions about its use. The plethora of pundits who comment on the strategic potential, or lack thereof, of information systems and IT only add to the confusion. In this chapter we provide a set of concepts and an analytical framework that will help you in establishing whether a given IT-dependent strategic initiative can be defended against competitors' retaliation. In other words, we will explore under what circumstance a competitive advantage rooted in an IT-dependent strategic initiative is sustainable.

Specifically, in this chapter you will learn

1. To analyze the potential of IT-dependent strategic initiative to ensure value appropriation over time.

2. To recognize the flaws in the arguments of those who suggest that information technology has lost its potential to enable sustained competitive advantage.

3. To recognize the four barriers to erosion that protect IT-dependent competitive advantage and to estimate their size.

4. To identify the response lag drivers associated with each of the four barriers to erosion, and to provide examples of each.

5. To recognize how each of the four barriers can be strengthened over time in order to protract the useful life of an IT-dependent strategic initiative.

6. To use the concepts and frameworks described in this chapter in the context of future IT-dependent strategic initiatives when your firm takes a leadership position.

7. To use the concepts and frameworks described in this chapter in situations where your firm may be evaluating whether to retaliate against a competitor who pioneered an IT-dependent strategic initiatives.

8. To identify the possible courses of action a firm should take based on your analysis, and to be able to recommend when the firm should or should not pursue a given IT-dependent strategic initiative.

MINI-CASE: RADISSON EXPRESS YOURSELF: SHOULD YOU FOLLOW SUIT?

In early 2006, five years after graduating, your information systems consulting business is thriving. At 6:45 A.M., when you power up your computer to check e-mail and start the day, you see a late-night message from Gregg Yves, the vice president of marketing and customer service initiatives at Big Chain of International Hotels (BCIH). He is an old friend you met through your university alumni network when you were in school and with whom you kept in touch.

Why would he be e-mailing so late? As you read his message, it becomes clear: "Do you remember when we discussed the Radisson Express Yourself[1] initiative? At the time we were focused on rolling out check-in kiosks in our properties and did not pay much attention. However, I noticed that Hilton quickly replicated and offered the service to its Gold- and Diamond-level Hilton HHonors program members. Now Hyatt launched the program for its North American properties.[2]

I have been thinking about this all night. Should we follow suit as well? Do we need to move rapidly? I'd rather take a wait-and-see approach here, but I am afraid that if we miss the boat on this initiative, the repercussions could be significant.

You are an expert on this strategic information systems stuff; can you give me your insight and direct my thinking a bit?"

DISCUSSION QUESTIONS

1. Do you believe that the Radisson Express Yourself initiative is sustainable?
2. What are the pros and cons of the wait-and-see approach that Gregg prefers?
3. What is your recommendation? What should BCIH do next?

INTRODUCTION

As we discussed in Chapter 7, when it comes to using information systems and IT, the primary objective of the modern general and functional manager is to use them to create added value. However, creating added value is just one facet of the job; the firm must be able to appropriate the value created over time to truly benefit. In other words, any competitive advantage the firm has created with the implementation of its IT-dependent strategic initiative must be defended over time to ensure that the firm will be able to reap the benefits of its innovation. Failing to do so will quickly lead to a situation where competitors match the leader and customers, rather than the innovator, end up appropriating the value created.

Can a firm really protect an advantage based on the innovative use of information systems and IT? Can IT-dependent strategic initiatives deliver sustained competitive advantage? These seemingly simple questions engender much debate and continue to stir up controversy—they have for over two decades now! On the one side are the skeptics who claim that, as the very success of IT continues (i.e., technology becomes cheaper, easier to use, and more pervasive than ever before), its strategic value declines.

Most information systems researchers and professionals disagree. Such disagreement is based on the findings of over thirty-five years of information systems research, which has demonstrated that not all information technologies are created equal or behave the same—particularly when used strategically.

---

[1] See the mini-case in Chapter 8 for a description of the Radisson Express Yourself initiative.

[2] Gilden, J. (2006), "Check Out the Web Check-Ins," *Los Angeles Times* (June 25, 2006).

NOT ALL IT IS CREATED EQUAL

The two examples described below show how two different IT-dependent strategic initiatives, based on two different technologies at their core, can produce opposite results when it comes to creating and appropriating economic value.

High-Speed Internet Access in Hotel Rooms

During the dot-com days of the late 1990s, as the number of Internet users was increasing at a staggering rate, a host of organizations—ranging from airport operators, to coffee shops, to malls—began offering high-speed internet access (HSIA) and wireless connectivity to their customers (Figure 9.1). Lodging operators also followed this trend, offering in-room HSIA capabilities in their hotels. Soon HSIA became one of the hottest technologies to hit the lodging industry in a while. Companies offered HSIA as a paid amenity, with $9.95 for unlimited daily use being the most popular pricing option.

While take rates (i.e., guests' actual usage) were much lower than expected, HSIA quickly became a "must-offer" amenity, based on the assumption that business travelers, who were used to high-speed connections at home and in the office, would snub hotels that could not have them surfing in the fast lane.

The inevitable result was an increasing number of properties that offered HSIA, and quickly the amenity became free of charge. For example, in February 2001 the Sheraton Vancouver Wall Centre announced that it was offering HSIA free of charge to all guests. In the press release introducing the initiative, the HSIA vendor declared, "Offering this service as an amenity with no charge to the guest will certainly differentiate the Sheraton Vancouver Wall Centre from its competitors." Any hoped-for differentiation did not last long, however, as more operators had to join the "HSIA as a free amenity" trend. Soon free HSIA moved from a property-level amenity to a brand-level free amenity. Omni Hotels began offering HSIA systemwide to all guests starting in February 2003, and Best Western and Holiday Inn quickly followed suit, as did many other major chains.

Following the trend of countless amenities before it, HSIA was rapidly becoming just another cost of doing business in the lodging industry and a competitive necessity. HSIA is valuable indeed; how hard is it to use a dial-up connection when you are used to high-speed at home and in the office?! However, because it could not be protected from rapid imitation, all of the value it created is now largely appropriated by hotel guests rather than the hotel companies that introduced it.

Figure 9.1 A High-Speed Internet Access Point For Hotel Rooms. (*Source:* Copyright to TeleAdapt displayed. This Product is a DeskBridge (R).)

Business Intelligence at Harrah's Entertainment

Harrah's Entertainment has been widely celebrated for its innovative use of information systems and IT in support of its efforts to better understand its customers—a type of initiative known as business intelligence (see Chapter 12). To do so, Harrah's had to invest heavily in IT—an investment estimated to exceed $100 million in 2000. While the expenditure may seem significant, the firm made a conscious decision to invest the money in technology rather than follow the industry trend of creating elaborate resorts that would "wow" visitors with their size and design (e.g., MGM Mirage's, The Bellagio, The Venetian) (Figure 9.2). Harrah's used a fraction of the money necessary for these developments, often exceeding the $1 billion mark, to create a sound technological and organizational brandwide infrastructure.

Technology is only the beginning of this story, though. Harrah's did not simply buy a bunch of computer systems, flip on the switch, and watch dollars roll in. Instead, the firm embarked on a large-scale reorganization, centralizing and focusing operations around the brand and away from individual property interests. As part of the reorganization, Harrah's hired a new breed of analysts, known as decision scientists. These individuals had the mindset and the skills to gather and analyze data about gamblers' characteristics and activities. By carrying out scientific experiments, Harrah's was able to become both more efficient (i.e., spend less) and effective (i.e., spend better) in its use of funds to attract and retain gamblers while also increasing share-of-wallet (i.e., the percentage of the gambling budget a gambler would spend with Harrah's rather than its competitors) and customer satisfaction.

The returns on Harrah's use of technology have been considerable, even in the face of a slowing economy. At the same time, the centralized IT infrastructure and the processes it has developed enable Harrah's to expand its distribution with relative ease and control. Clearly, Harrah's Entertainment has been able to reap significant long-term results from its IT-dependent strategic initiative and continues to appropriate a large portion of the value created.

The Need for A Priori Analysis

If nothing else, the above examples raise the questions of whether managers should approach distinct IT-dependent strategic initiatives differently. Put another way, is there a way, a priori, to reduce uncertainty about whether an IT-dependent strategic initiative can

Figure 9.2 The skyline of mega-properties in Las Vegas.

(*Source:* Courtesy of Udo Wolter, www.dicke-aersche.de/www.big-asses.de)

lead to a sustainable advantage? In the remainder of this chapter we introduce a framework designed to support this analysis.

APPROPRIATING VALUE OVER TIME: SUSTAINABILITY FRAMEWORK

The major criticism levied by the skeptics against the potential for sustained competitive advantage associated with IT innovation is that technology is easily replicated by competitors, who can quickly offer the same functionalities. Put in the framework of value creation, the accusation is that IT helps companies create value that they cannot appropriate over time because competitors can easily imitate any IT innovation.

By now it should be clear to the attentive reader of this book that this argument simply misses the point. Because information systems are not IT, as we established in Chapter 2, creating and appropriating value hinges on successfully deploying a defendable IT-dependent strategic initiative. It follows that the focus on the analysis of sustainability should be the IT-dependent strategic initiative, in all its facets, not just the IT core. In other words, even if the IT components used by the firm are (at least in theory) replicable by competitors, it does not follow that the firm's IT-dependent strategic initiative built on that (replicable) technology will be easily copied as well.

Sustainable Competitive Advantage

The ability of a firm to protect its competitive advantage, known as sustainability of the advantage, is often thought of as a binary condition—it is either possible or impossible for competitors to erode the leader's advantage by matching the added value it creates. However, this can be a misleading approach. After all, short of very few resources, such as patents or exclusive access to raw materials, almost anything is replicable—in theory! Thus, it isn't whether the advantage is *theoretically* replicable that matters in practice, but the difficulty that competitors face in matching the leader's offer.

Consider the example of Amazon.com, a firm that is famous for its relentless pursuit of customer service and customer satisfaction. In an effort to improve customer service and satisfaction, by 2000 Amazon had deployed nine highly automated distribution centers strategically located throughout the United States (Figure 9.3). While it is true that competitors (for

Figure 9.3   An automated warehouse

instance, Buy.com), could theoretically replicate Amazon's distribution, it would be very difficult—time consuming and expensive—for them to do so.

Rather than thinking about sustainability as a binary condition, you should think of it in terms of how much time and how much money would it take competitors to erode the advantage that the leading firm has been able to create with its IT-dependent strategic initiative. The higher the "time and money" obstacles—termed here barriers to erosion—the more resilient the firm's advantage.

Response Lag

Competitive retaliation occurs in stages. Once a firm's rivals find themselves at a disadvantage, they search for the sources of the firm's competitive advantage. If they are successful in identifying those sources, the competitors must decide whether they are able and willing to respond and, if they are, what approach they should take. Response lag, the time it takes competitors to respond aggressively enough to erode a firm's competitive advantage, is a measure of the delay in competitive response.

The longer the time and the higher the cost of replication, the more resilient is the firm's advantage. Thus, response-lag drivers are defined here as the characteristics of the technology, the firm, its competitors, or the value system in which the firm is embedded that combine to make replication of the IT-dependent strategic initiative difficult and costly. Response-lag drivers combine their effect to levy barriers to erosion.

Four Barriers to Erosion

Response-lag drivers can be grouped into one of the following four barriers to erosion of IT-dependent competitive advantage: (1) IT-resources barrier, (2) complementary-resources barrier, (3) IT-project barrier, and (4) preemption barrier. The magnitude of each barrier to erosion is determined by the number and strength of its response-lag drivers (Figure 9.4).

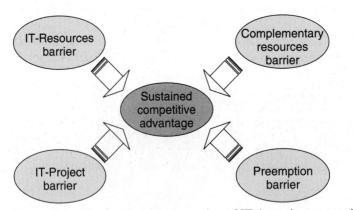

Figure 9.4 The four barriers to erosion of IT-dependent competitive advantage

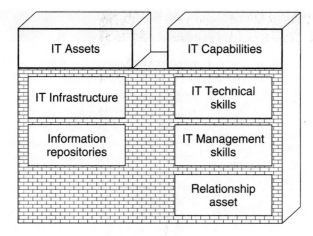

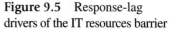

Figure 9.5 Response-lag drivers of the IT resources barrier

We briefly describe each barrier to erosion below and detail each of the response-lag drivers associated with them in the sidebars.

Barrier 1: IT Resources   IT-dependent strategic initiatives rely on access to the assets and capabilities necessary to produce and use the technology at the core. Two classes of response-lag drivers contribute to the height of the IT-resources barrier; these are IT resources and IT capabilities (Figure 9.5). As an initiative becomes more reliant on preexisting IT resources and capabilities, it becomes increasingly difficult to copy (Sidebar 1 lists and explains in detail all the response-lag drivers associated with this barrier).

Consider, for example, a firm that controls some highly specific and difficult to imitate IT resources, such as Wal-Mart Stores, Inc. In earlier chapters we described the notion of continuous replenishment, an IT-dependent strategic initiative pioneered by Wal-Mart in conjunction with Procter & Gamble. Continuous replenishment relies on real-time or near-real-time scanner data transfer between a retailer (e.g., Wal-Mart) and a supplier (e.g., P&G). Wal-Mart, having access to its satellite-based network infrastructure among its stores, found this initiative easier and less costly to implement than any of its competitors. In other words, it should not surprise us that continuous replenishment was pioneered by Wal-Mart, as it already had the network infrastructure to do so. Competitors who wanted to replicate this initiative had to first deploy the same (or a comparable) infrastructure.

Using the terminology of the sustainability framework, we can assert that the difficulty Wal-Mart competitors found in quickly and successfully imitating Wal-Mart's continuous replenishment strategy was in part due to the need to first acquire a prerequisite IT asset, the networking infrastructure enabling real-time scanner data transfer from stores. Wal-Mart's ownership of this unique asset translated in a response-lag driver (IT infrastructure) that contributed to increase significantly the magnitude of the IT resources barrier to erosion.

SIDEBAR 1: IT RESOURCES BARRIER

IT Assets

IT assets are technology resources available to the organization, including hardware components and platforms (e.g., a private network connecting globally distributed locations), software applications and environments (e.g., a proprietary software using custom-developed analytical models), and data repositories. These resources contribute to building response lag directly, by simplifying and speeding up the development and introduction of the initiative's IT core, or indirectly, by making it difficult for competitors who have no ready access to the needed IT resources to replicate the leader's initiative.

IT Infrastructure

An IT infrastructure is a set of IT components that are interconnected and managed by IT specialists with the objective of providing a set of standard services to the organization. Thus, the IT infrastructure provides the foundation for the delivery of business applications. With IT infrastructure-development times generally estimated to exceed five years, the response lag and ensuing barrier to imitation is likely to be substantial.

Information Repositories

Information is now widely recognized as a fundamental organizational resource, and firms are investing significantly to improve their ability to collect, store, manage, and distribute it. Information repositories are often large data stores containing extensive information about customers, suppliers, products, or operations, organized in a structured form that is accessible and useable for decision-making purposes. A firm's information repositories can contribute to the development of substantial response lag by supporting strategic initiatives. Competitors attempting to replicate the leader's strategic initiative must not only duplicate the IT at its core, but they must also accumulate a comparable information resource—a feat that often takes substantial time.

IT Capabilities

IT capabilities are derived from the skills and abilities of the firm's workforce. These capabilities directly influence the response lag associated with the introduction of IT at the core of IT-dependent strategic initiatives because they facilitate the technology's design and development. These capabilities

also play a fundamental role in enabling effective and timely implementation, maintenance, and use of the technology.

IT Technical Skills and Business Understanding

IT technical skills relate to the ability to design and develop effective computer applications. They include proficiency in system analysis and design, software design, and programming. Another element is the depth of business understanding of IT specialists. Business understanding enables the IT specialists charged with developing the technology supporting IT-dependent strategic initiatives to envision a creative and feasible technical solution to business problems. A high level of business understanding also contributes to the creation of response lag by mitigating the risks associated with the introduction of the strategic initiative and the relative investments in technology.

IT-Management Skills

IT-management skills refer to the firm's ability to provide leadership for the IS function, manage IT projects, integrate different technical skills, evaluate technology options, select appropriate technology sources, and manage change ensuing from the introduction of IT. IT-management skills, because of their idiosyncratic and socially complex nature and the learning curve associated with their development, are a source of sustainable competitive advantage. Managerial IT skills can contribute to creating substantial response lag when techniques and routines developed over time can substantially reduce development costs and development lead times. Competitors who attempt to replicate the initiative but lack the same high level of managerial IT skills as the innovator face substantial obstacles to imitation.

Relationship Asset

The relationship asset is accumulated over time and finds its roots in a mutual respect and trusting rapport between the IS function and business managers. When a firm has developed a substantial relationship asset, IS specialists and business managers are able to work together effectively by coordinating and communicating extensively. Having developed the relationship, they share a vision for the role of IT within the business. Business partners share the risk and accept the responsibility for IT projects, and IS specialists are able to anticipate a business's IT needs and devise solutions that support these needs.

Barrier 2: Complementary Resources   While IT is by definition a fundamental component of any IT-dependent strategic initiative, successful implementation of such an initiative requires that complementary organizational resources be mobilized as well (Figure 9.6). Thus, to implement an IT-dependent strategic initiative, the firm must develop or acquire the necessary complementary resources (e.g., physical assets such as warehouses and distribution centers, intangible assets such as a brand).

As an initiative becomes more reliant on distinctive complementary resources, the complementary-resource barrier to imitation strengthens, and replication of the strategy becomes slower, costlier, and more difficult. In this situation, competitors will have to acquire or develop not only the IT at the core of the strategy, but also the complementary resources that underpin the initiative (Sidebar 2 lists and explains in detail all the response-lag drivers associated with this barrier).

Consider again the example of Harrah's Entertainment and its business intelligence initiative. While the firm spent a significant amount of money to acquire IT resources, it also engaged in a radical reorganization when launching the initiative in the late 1990s. This reorganization challenged decades of casino management practice, where each casino within a chain operated in a highly independent fashion. Through its reorganization Harrah's asked the general managers of each property to report to divisional presidents, who in turn reported up to Harrah's Entertainment's chief operating officer. The firm also created transfer mechanisms and incentives to support cross-property traffic and a general sense that customers "belonged" to Harrah's corporate office, not to each individual casino that signed them up to the program. This change in organizational structure enabled the success of Harrah's brandwide initiative.

Fast forward now to the year 2001, when Harrah's was receiving substantial praise and attention for its use of guest data and putting pressure on competitors to imitate. How well positioned were its competitors to replicate Harrah's highly centralized customer data strategy? Not very well, since the typical competitor still treated each property as unique and independent, with a unique brand and little incentive to share customers and customer data with the other casinos in the chain.

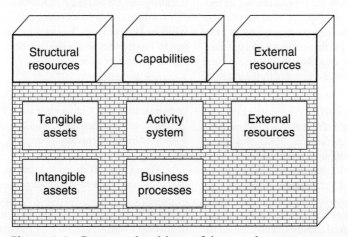

Figure 9.6   Response-lag drivers of the complementary resources barrier

Using the terminology of the sustainability framework, we can assert that Harrah's competitors are likely to find it costly and time consuming to successfully imitate Harrah's business intelligence initiative. This is because, at least in part, their organizational structure is not conducive to the strategy and a change would be very risky, costly, and time consuming. In other words, Harrah's has access to a unique complementary resource, such as its idiosyncratic

SIDEBAR 2: COMPLEMENTARY RESOURCES BARRIER

Structural Resources
Structural resources comprise non-IT-related tangible and intangible internal assets used by the firm in the enactment of its IT-dependent strategic initiative.

Tangible Assets
In theory, any tangible resource available to the firm can underpin an IT-dependent strategic initiative. Among these are competitive scope, physical assets, scale of operations and market share, organizational structure, governance, and slack resources.

Intangible Assets
As in the case of tangible resources, nearly any of a firm's intangible resources can support an IT-dependent initiative. Examples of commonly cited intangible resources that can be so applied include corporate culture, top management commitment, and the ability to manage risk. As with tangible IT resources, complementary intangible resources create response lag by making a strategic initiative difficult, costly, and time consuming to imitate.

Capabilities
A firm's capabilities define how the firm carries out its productive activities. These resources specify what activities are performed and what steps or business processes make up those activities. The activities that the firm performs and the manner in which it performs them contribute to response lag and help sustain the competitive advantage created by the initiative.

Activity System
A performance-maximizing activity system relies on a set of economic activities that are both interlocking and mutually reinforcing, expressly showing internal consistency (internal fit) and appropriately configured given the firm's external environment (external fit). Although IT is one of the fundamental components of the strategy, it still must fit within the entire activity system. When a firm has implemented a given configuration of activities and has developed the IT core supporting the linked activities, replication of the technology alone is insufficient for successful imitation.

Indeed, narrowly replicating just the IT core leads to further decline of the imitator's position by wasting time, money, and management attention without eroding the leader's competitive advantage. A classic example of a firm that has an idiosyncratic activity system is Southwest Airlines. Because Southwest does not cater flights, does not offer seat assignments, has a standardized fleet of aircrafts, uses less crowded airports, and focuses on point-to-point travel by price-sensitive customers, it is relatively resistant to competitive imitation. Merely imitating one aspect of Southwest's activity system will not suffice, but attempting to duplicate the entire package generates considerable response lag.

Business Processes
We defined a business process as the series of steps that a firm performs in order to complete an economic activity. The notion of business process is related to, but distinct from, that of the economic activities discussed above. Economic activities describe the set of undertakings that the firm performs, while business processes describe the way in which the firm performs them. The contribution that business processes make to response lag and to the height of barriers to imitation depends on their distinctiveness and strategic value. When a firm is able to introduce an IT-dependent strategic initiative built around a business process with characteristics of uniqueness and differentiation, the firm creates a significant barrier to erosion.

External Resources
External resources are assets (such as brand, reputation, and interorganizational relationship assets) that do not reside internally with the firm but accumulate with other firms and with consumers. Generally intangible, external resources are usually developed over time.

When a firm's IT-dependent strategic initiative can make use of or contribute to the development of these external resources, response lag increases considerably and barriers to imitation are augmented. Thus, the firm forces competitors to develop a comparable level of external resources before producing an effective response.

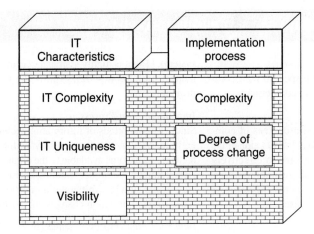

Figure 9.7   Response-lag drivers of the IT project barrier

organizational structure, which creates substantial response lag and contributes to heighten the complementary resource barrier.

Barrier 3: IT Project   IT-dependent strategic initiatives rely on an essential enabling IT core. Thus, they cannot be implemented until the necessary technology has been successfully introduced. The response-lag drivers of the IT project barrier are driven by the characteristics of the technology and the implementation process (Figure 9.7).

Information technologies are not homogeneous, undifferentiated entities. To the contrary, they differ substantially with respect to their intrinsic characteristics, their ability to complement other organizational resources, the context in which they are introduced and used, and the degree of organizational change that needs to occur during the implementation process (Sidebar 3 lists and explains in detail all the response-lag drivers associated with this barrier).

Consider, for example, a Web site. No matter how complex they are, Web sites are typically relatively quickly designed and deployed, particularly compared with large infrastructure projects (e.g., data warehouses) that are complex, lengthy, and prone to failure. Returning to the Harrah's Entertainment example, it should not surprise you that the IT project barrier associated with its $100 million investment in technology is substantial in and of itself.

Barrier 4: Preemption   You may now be wondering why we term the four forces ensuring sustainability as "barriers to erosion" rather than "barriers to imitation." We do so because in some cases, even if a competitor is able to replicate an IT-dependent strategic initiative, the response may bear no fruit for the laggard. A discussion of the preemption barrier will clarify this point (Figure 9.8).

In some cases the IT-dependent strategic initiative pioneered by the first mover creates a preferential relationship with customers or other members of the value system and introduces substantial switching costs. Under these circumstances it is not enough for competitors merely to imitate the leader's strategy; they need to either compensate the customer for the cost of switching or provide enough additional value to justify the customer's decision to incur the switching costs. That is, imitators must be "that much better," where "that much" is an amount

SIDEBAR 3: IT PROJECT BARRIERS

IT Characteristics
Information technologies differ with respect to their complexity, distinctiveness, and visibility to competitors.

IT Complexity
Different IT applications have different degrees of complexity. The complexity of the technology is a function of the bundle of skills and knowledge necessary to effectively design, develop, implement, and use it. Technology complexity raises the IT project barrier by increasing development lead times for a competitive response.

IT Uniqueness
On the low end of the IT uniqueness continuum are self-contained, off-the-shelf IT products that need little integration or customization (e.g., an electronic mail system). At the high end are custom-developed applications or infrastructure subsystems that are unavailable in the open market. When the IT underlying the innovator's strategy is not distinctive, competitors can engage consultants or service firms to aid them in reducing knowledge barriers, thereby reducing the imitation response lag. Unique IT makes this process much more difficult.

Visibility
Visibility is the extent to which competitors can observe the enabling technology. The visibility dimension can be conceptualized as a continuum spanning from custom developed internal systems, which are virtually invisible to competitors, to immediately visible interorganizational or customer-facing systems that require extensive education and selling to external users or customers (e.g., an online purchasing system). IT that is highly visible and is readily available for inspection by competitors limits the strength of the IT project barrier.

Implementation Process
Since different kinds of information technology are inherently dissimilar, the processes by which they are implemented and become available to the organization also differ. Depending on the implementation characteristics of the IT core of the strategic initiative in question, the strength of the barriers to imitation changes considerably.

Implementation-Process Complexity
Implementation-process complexity is a function of the size and scope of the project, the number of functional units involved, the complexity of user requirements, and possible political issues, among other things. IT infrastructure projects represent a powerful example of complex systems that have a substantial lead time. While the components may be commodity-like (e.g., personal computers, server, telecommunication equipment), it is difficult to integrate them in an effective system.

Degree of Process Change
Business processes often need to change to fit a new system—particularly in the case of large, highly integrated enterprise systems. The challenges escalate when several organizations or operations use the technology involved in the strategic initiative. The more departments are involved and the more organizational boundaries are crossed, the harder and the riskier the change becomes. Yet as complexity increases, so do the difficulties encountered by competitors in imitating the strategy.

---

greater than the current value of all co-specialized investments[3] that the customer has made (Sidebar 4 lists and explains in detail all the response-lag drivers associated with this barrier).

eBay, Inc., the dominant online auction site, provides a perfect example. Aware of its success, two formidable competitors, namely Amazon.com and Yahoo!, launched their own online auction sites. Despite having an e-commerce pedigree, brand recognition, and technical capabilities just as good as eBay's, both firms achieved lackluster results when imitating eBay's IT-dependent strategic initiative. Interestingly, a brief look at both competitors' Web sites would show that they were remarkably similar to eBay's own. Clearly an imitation strategy didn't pay, but why?

---

[3] The term *co-specialized investment* simply refers to investments made in conjunction with a specific IT-dependent strategic initiative. Because these investments are specific to the initiative, they will lose part or all of their value if those who made the investment switched to a competitor (see Sidebar 4).

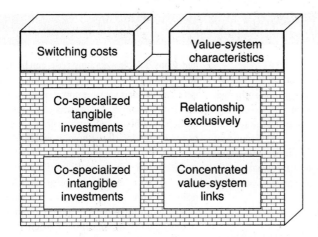

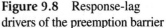

Figure 9.8 Response-lag drivers of the preemption barrier

The reason for eBay's dominance is to be found in its ability to harness a dynamic that occurs in its industry—strong network effects. As you recall from Chapter 4, when strong network effects are present, the dominant player will be the one that first reaches critical mass (in this case, eBay). At that point both buyers and seller face daunting switching costs, and only "wholesale defection" of a large portion of the customer base will enable competitors to catch up to the leader—an extremely unlikely event. Being second in the online auction market is not a good place to be![4]

With the language of the sustainability framework, we can assert that eBay, by virtue of being the first company to reach critical mass of buyers and seller in a market with strong network effects, was able to erect an insurmountable preemption barrier to erosion.

The Dynamics of Sustainability

As high as the barriers to erosion may be, when launching IT-dependent strategic initiatives, a firm has an advantage but can't "fall asleep at the wheel." Rather, general and functional managers proposing IT-dependent strategic initiatives should have a plan for continuously remaining ahead of the competition. This means looking for opportunities to reinvigorate and reinforce the barriers to erosion described above. Consider the example of Dell Inc., a firm that has been able to maintain its leadership position in personal computer manufacturing for more than a decade. At the heart of Dell's strategy is its high-velocity built-to-order production model for direct sales. The firm is continually improving the performance of its production system as well as introducing further initiatives that leverage its core advantage.

For example, in the mid-1990s Dell took its direct sales model to the Internet and began to sell to consumers. More recently the firm has extended its high-velocity production model to other products, such as high-end servers and consumer electronics.

There are two main dynamics for rejuvenation and strengthening of barriers to erosion over time: capability development and asset-stock accumulation. There is a mutually reinforcing dynamic between barriers to erosion and a firm's IT-dependent strategic initiative. Available

---

[4] Interestingly, the eBay example shows that using proprietary IT is not a necessary condition for superior long-term performance.

SIDEBAR 4: PREEMPTION BARRIER

Switching Costs

Switching costs represent the total costs borne by the parties of an exchange when one of them leaves the exchange. They include not only economic costs but also psychological and physical costs. "Switching costs are the norm, not the exception, in the information economy."[5] IT-dependent strategic initiatives, which rely heavily on the collection, storage, manipulation, and distribution of information, are particularly suited to the creation and exploitation of switching costs.

Co-Specialized Tangible Investments

When an IT-dependent strategic initiative is deployed, it may require that the firm's customers acquire the physical assets necessary to participate in the initiative. The total capital outlay necessary to obtain these assets is termed co-specialized tangible investments. These range from computer hardware and telecommunication equipment to software applications and interfaces between the existing customer's systems and the firm's IT. For example, hotel franchisees buy costly interfaces for the franchising brands' reservation system. These interfaces become valueless if the property is re-branded. The extent to which the IT-dependent strategic initiative requires co-specialized tangible investments determines the potential for strong barriers to imitation associated with the initiative.

Co-Specialized Intangible Investments

As is true of tangible investments, the deployment of an IT-dependent strategic initiative often necessitates a firm's customers or channel partners to invest time and money to take part in the initiative. An investment of this kind is known as a co-specialized intangible investment. For instance, to benefit from customer relationship management initiatives, customers often need to take the time to complete a profile. Co-specialized intangible investments might include "setup" costs as well as ongoing costs (e.g., retraining new travel associates using a reservation system). Data and information repositories represent perhaps the most important class of co-specialized intangible investments in the information

age. Considerable switching costs can be built on information accumulated over time. An interesting example is offered by information that is valuable only as long as the customer is using the firm's products or services (e.g., revenue-management models and historical records that are brand specific and become valueless if the hotel is re-branded).[6]

The same situation occurs even when switching costs are not readily apparent. Some forward-looking banks are attempting to take advantage of their long-standing relationships with customers to reach a position of "trusted consolidator" of top clients' complex financial positions. This strategy entails the collection of extensive information about customers' banking profiles and services used; insurance holdings; investment portfolio; mortgage, credit, and loan positions; and scheduled bill payments. The bank in this instance need not provide all of the services in question, but it strives to offer a consolidated view that customers find valuable and costly to transfer to competitors. Note that even when switching costs appear to be low, their presence can be critical for strategy development.

Value System's Structure

A firm does not engage in economic activity in isolation, but as a link in a larger value chain or system that includes upstream and downstream members. The structure of this value system can provide opportunities for preemptive strategies and for the exploitation of the response-lag drivers discussed here. The structure of the value system does not directly affect the strength of the preemption barrier to imitation, but instead magnifies or diminishes the preemptive effects of switching costs.

Relationship Exclusivity

An exclusive relationship exists when participants in the value system will elect to do business with only one firm that provides a particular set of products or services. The firm's counterpart (i.e., customer or supplier) places a premium on dealing with either the firm or one of its competitors, but not both. Relationship exclusivity is the norm with IT-dependent initiatives that provide integration services

---

[5] Shapiro, C., and Varian, H. (1998), *Information Rules: A Strategic Guide to the Network Economy* (Boston: Harvard Business School Press), p. 111. Also see this book for an excellent treatment of switching costs in the information age.

[6] The software here is neither proprietary nor brand specific, and the data are not acquired over a network or hosted by the brand. Yet the historic data and the models the hotel has developed assume that the hotel has a given brand (e.g., Four Seasons). If the hotel is re-branded, while the software, the data, and the models are retained, their value is much lower because the data and models are specific to the original brand and assume the hotel sports the related flag (e.g., has access to Four Season's brand equity, reservation systems, loyal customer base).

and that benefit from the accumulation of historical information. When first introduced, the American Airlines SABRE terminal for travel agents created strong incentives for relationship exclusivity, as travel agents did not want to waste valuable office space for competitors' proprietary terminals (e.g., United's Apollo), which were considered essentially duplicates of the SABRE terminal.

When a business relationship benefits from exclusivity, the customer faces penalties for hedging behavior and for sourcing the needed product or service from multiple firms, and when competitors introduce competing offers, customers are already invested in their relationship with the incumbent.

Concentrated Value-System Link
At each of the various stages or links of the value system, the degree of concentration in the link is inversely proportional to the number of suitable business entities populating that link—where suitability depends on whether the firm would find the products or services offered by the vendors populating the link acceptable. A highly concentrated link

is one where there are relatively few organizations or consumers available for the firm to use or serve. In the case of airline reservation systems, for instance, the total number of travel agents serving the market targeted by the airline sponsoring the system represents the concentrated link.

A market of given size will support only a finite number of competitors, and achieving a substantial penetration in the concentrated value-system link—by definition, a small market—is necessary to successfully preempt imitation. As the degree of concentration increases, the time necessary to secure a relationship with a substantial proportion of the link decreases—all else being equal. Consequently, the leader has a better chance of capturing a substantial proportion of relationships and being able to use switching costs to "lock out" competitors and maximize its barriers to imitation. Conversely, when a link in the value system comprises a large number of business entities, a firm is unlikely to effectively reach a critical mass of entities and raise substantial barriers to imitation in the same amount of time.

---

response-lag drivers offer the firm a "head start" on the competition. The enactment of the strategy enables the firm to engage in the capability development and asset-stock accumulation processes described below, in turn leading to further development of the response-lag drivers and the preservation of barriers to erosion (see Table 9.1 for a list of response-lag drivers affected by each dynamic).

Capability Development *Capability development* refers to the process by which an organization is able to improve its performance over time by developing its ability to use available resources for maximum effectiveness. When it comes to IT-dependent strategic initiatives, capability development consists of the ability to engage in "learning by using,"

Figure 9.9 Automated computer assembly

Table 9.1 Barriers to Erosion Response-Lag Drivers

Barriers to Erosion	Response-Lag Drivers
IT Resources Barrier	<u>IT Assets</u> • IT infrastructure* • Information repositories* <u>IT Capabilities</u> • Technical skills[†] • IT management skills[†] • Relationship asset*
Complementary Resources Barrier	<u>Complementary Resources</u>*[†]
IT Project Barrier	<u>Technology Characteristics</u> • Visibility • Uniqueness • Complexity <u>Implementation Process</u> • Complexity • Process change
Preemption Barrier	<u>Switching Costs</u> • Tangible co-specialized investments* • Intangible co-specialized investments* • Collective switching costs* <u>Value-System Structural Characteristics</u> • Relationship exclusivity • Concentrated links

*Response-lag drivers subject to asset-stock accumulation processes.

[†]Response-lag drivers subject to capability development processes.

defined as the process by which a firm becomes more effective over time in using and managing an information system and the technology at the core.

Note that capability development processes can only be set in motion once the IT-dependent strategic initiative is introduced. In the case of Dell Inc., repeated practice with its high-velocity, built-to-order production model enabled Dell to consistently increase inventory turns—thereby strengthening its direct sales initiative over time—and subsequently to leverage its advantage to reach the previously unserved consumers and small accounts through the Internet.

Asset-Stock Accumulation Critics of the sustainability potential of information systems and IT contend that information technologies today are easily imitable and readily acquirable in the open market. However, many of the assets underpinning an IT-dependent strategic initiative cannot be readily acquired, particularly when they are internally developed. For example, specialized databases and ad-hoc forecasting models need to be custom developed; the same goes for an IT infrastructure (e.g., Wal-Mart). The same holds for many complementary resources.

Figure 9.10   Casino floor

Asset-stock accumulation represents the process by which a firm accrues or builds up a resource over time. Assets of this kind must be built up and developed over time as a result of a consistent process of accumulation. For example, at the core of Harrah's initiative discussed throughout this chapter, there is a comprehensive centralized repository of personal and behavioral data about each gambler and a set of predictive computer models that forecast a gambler's projected worth. Harrah's ability to collect data and develop the predictive models depends on having the information systems for data collection, storage, analysis, and distribution. These only became available when Harrah's launched its IT-dependent strategic initiative. Moreover, no matter how committed a competitor may be, the process of data accumulation requires time to complete. Consider a destination customer who visits a Las Vegas property once per quarter to play blackjack (Figure 9.10), collecting six data points about her (i.e., information on six visits) requires one and one-half years.

For these reasons, sustainability often does not stem from visionary one-time initiatives, but from evolutionary initiatives predicated on a commitment to capability building and asset-stock accumulation. On this basis, the firm can develop the strategic initiative, offering a moving target to its competitors by reinforcing its barriers to imitation over time.

APPLYING THE FRAMEWORK

When looking to be innovative with information systems and IT, you can easily get wrapped up in wishful thinking about the potential of new ideas and new technologies. Importantly, the sustainability framework is as useful to decide when not to pursue an IT-dependent strategic initiative as it is to suggest when to do it.

You can use the framework when evaluating IT-dependent strategic initiatives either as the innovator looking to protect an existing advantage or as the laggard looking for ways to respond. This is done by asking a series of increasingly specific questions.[7]

---

[7] We frame the analysis here by referring to a proposed initiative. Thus, we take the perspective of the innovator evaluating a new initiative. The same script can be used, with minor adjustments, by followers.

Prerequisite Questions

Since the focus of the analysis here is on sustainability (i.e., appropriation of value over time), you must assume that the IT-dependent strategic initiative under investigation does indeed create value and is consistent with the firm's priorities. The set of prerequisite questions discussed next can be used as a check.

Is the Proposed Initiative Aligned with the Firm's Strategy? This crucial question often goes unasked until late in the analysis. (Sometimes it never gets asked!) This question is important because it is necessary for the proponents of the initiative to be able to formulate how the initiative advances the firm's positioning and strategy. If the firm has developed a strategic information systems plan (see Chapter 6), this question is relatively easy to answer by ensuring that the proposed initiative follows the information systems guidelines.

Is the Proposed Initiative Focused on Reducing the Firm's Cost or Increasing Customers' Willingness to Pay? Rare, but particularly coveted, initiatives have the potential to accomplish both—decreasing the firm's cost while increasing customers' willingness to pay. As we discussed in Chapter 7, the value of this question is in requiring managers to clearly define the value proposition of the planned initiative.

What Is the IS Design Underpinning the Proposed Initiative? This question is designed to formalize even more the analysis begun with the second question. At this stage in the analysis, one needs to achieve clarity with respect to the information processing functionalities of the information system supporting the proposed initiative. Each of the four components—IT, people, processes, and organization structures—also needs to be discussed to evaluate what changes to the current information systems and what new resources may be needed. This question is also crucial because it is the first step in evaluating the chances of implementation success of the needed information system (see Chapter 2).

Sustainability Questions

While it is impossible to estimate perfectly the magnitude of any particular barrier to erosion, the purpose of this analysis is refine the design of the IT-dependent strategic initiative, identify areas of potential weakness, and identify areas where changes to the initiative—often small ones at this stage—can substantially strengthen it.

Perhaps the most important aspect of this analysis is to identify initiatives that are not sustainable. Because it is important to understand when to avoid investing in expensive projects, the following questions can raise red flags before substantial resources are committed to the initiative.

What Competitors Are Appropriately Positioned to Replicate the Initiative? Based on a clear understanding of the characteristics of the proposed IT-dependent strategic initiative, the objective of this competitor analysis is to evaluate the strength of the IT-resource and complementary-resource barriers to erosion. Competitor analysis allows the innovator to identify sources of asymmetry that can be exploited and amplified through the deployment of the proposed initiative. The objective is to design the initiative so that it takes advantage of the existing sources of asymmetry and provides a basis to reinforce them over time through capability development and asset-stock accumulation.

A powerful opportunity here is to take advantage of competitors' rigidities, which are resources that hamper competitors' ability to replicate an innovation. A classic example is provided by firms with strong distribution ties (e.g., Compaq computers, Levi's), which could not easily replicate direct sellers' use of the Internet (e.g., Dell, Lands' End) because of channel conflict. While Compaq, for example, may have had the ability to sell directly from its Web site, as Dell does, it wasted precious time early on because it could not risk upsetting its dealers, who were responsible for the bulk of its distribution. As a consequence, it experienced a substantial delay in responding to Dell's move online.

The result of this analysis is a clearer understanding of which competitors are in a position to respond quickly to the IT-dependent strategic initiative and which will instead need first to acquire necessary resources or capabilities. This analysis may also provide guidance as to how hard it would be for competitors to acquire these prerequisite resources. It is clear that when fundamental resources are heterogeneously distributed, substantial response lag can be crated. Developing initiatives that amplify and leverage this heterogeneity is a critical step in your analysis.

How Long before Competitors Can Offer the Same Value Proposition?   This question is primarily concerned with the response lag associated with the creation, rollout, and infusion of the information systems at the heart of the IT-dependent strategic initiative. This analysis yields an assessment of the strength of the IT project barrier.

After a visioning stage, where the main characteristics of the initiative are envisioned by managers, the information system at the core needs to be developed and implemented. This process follows a sequential set of stages from inception to full functionality (see Chapter 11). It generally includes the following sequential stages: system definition, system build, and system implementation. Upon completion of the process, the cycle often restarts with maintenance and enhancements to the system.[8]

Competitors looking to have the same information processing functionality in place, and thus be able to offer the same value proposition, need to enter a similar development and implementation cycle. The only difference is that a follower will start the process with an awakening phase rather than a vision phase.

The awakening stage occurs when the competitor realizes that the innovator has an advantage. The timing of the awakening depends on the characteristics of the initiative and can occur when the competitor begins to witness losses (e.g., market share, revenue), when the innovation is first introduced (typically for customer-facing systems), or even before the innovator has launched the initiative. Knowledge of behavior patterns exhibited by competitors may help in gauging the timing of the awakening and of the subsequent stages.

For example, Burger King has traditionally shown a propensity to quickly enter geographical markets pioneered by McDonald's. While not technology related, this type of knowledge of the competition is what allows the innovator to more precisely estimate lead time. In some rare cases, some competitors will find imitation so daunting that they will elect not to follow. The SABRE reservation system, pioneered by American Airlines, and the Apollo reservation system, built by United Airlines, emerged as the dominant airline

---

[8] The attentive reader will note that the rationale offered by those who suggest that IT is not strategic because it is easily imitable is that the *technology* can easily be replicated. In other words, this rationale addresses only the build and implementation phases of the IT development cycle. The attentive readers of this book know that there is much more to IT-dependent strategic initiatives than simply technology development!

reservation systems because other airlines elected early on not to follow the lead of these two carriers. The decision not to engage in the design and development of their reservation systems was based on the expense and risk associated with such projects.

Will Replication Do Competitors Any Good?   Armed with an understanding of which competitors will be in a position to respond to the innovator's IT-dependent strategic initiative and a general idea of how long it may take them to have the same functionality in place, the innovating firm must estimate the magnitude of the preemption barrier to erosion. The fact is that being second sometimes means being left behind (remember the eBay example?). Exploiting the characteristics of the innovation and the industry in which they compete, innovators can sometimes preempt any meaningful response by competitors.

Even when outright preemption is not possible, the attentive innovator often has the ability to create substantial obstacles for any prospective imitator by levying switching costs. Preemption is strongest when the firm can identify a link in the value system where few customers or partners (e.g., suppliers) exist, and the partners that do exist place a premium on having an exclusive relationship with only one firm. In this scenario, they may eventually sever their relationship with the firm and do business with a competitor, but they won't trade with both at the same time.

Consider, for example, a five-unit restaurant operation that wants chainwide forecasts and historical analyses of trends, such as those offered by business intelligence-data consolidators like Avero Inc. In this case, for the software to be useful, all five units must use it (Figure 9.11). From Avero's standpoint, customers (in this case, the restaurant chain) place a premium on an exclusive relationship. The restaurant chain will either use Avero for all five restaurants or switch them all to a competitor's software program. In either case, it will not work with two software vendors at the same time, as that would defeat the original purpose of data consolidation.

When such conditions are present or can be created, switching costs have the most power in raising the preemption barrier. When switching costs are high, competitors must indemnify any newly won customers for the cost of switching. As we stated previously,

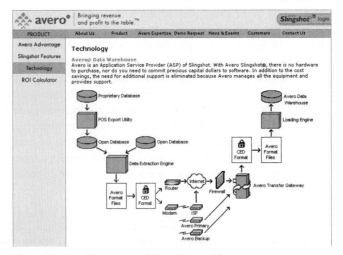

Figure 9.11   The Avero Slingshot architecture

competitors must be that much better than the leader, where "that much" is determined by the magnitude of the switching costs.

The set of three questions offered above should provide the innovator, or any follower who is using this analysis as a diagnostic tool to study the leader's IT-dependent strategic initiative, with an idea of how defendable the initiative is and the available options to improve its barriers to erosion. No initiative is static, though, and barriers to erosion decay over time as competition runs its course. As a consequence, you should ask one more question to complete the analysis.

What Evolutionary Paths Does the Innovation Create?   Sheltered by its lead time, the innovator can and should seek ways to reinforce its barriers to erosion. Based on their understanding of the capability development and asset-stock-accumulation processes described previously, the leading firm's managers can chart an evolutionary path for the initiative. While the evolutionary paths thus identified must be revised as the situation changes, the analysis to this point can highlight important response-lag drivers that can be strengthened over time. Performing this analysis will also ensure that the evolution of the initiative is intentional rather than haphazard and minimizes the likelihood that opportunities will be missed.

Consider, for example, the case of modern hotels. Because of the nature of the lodging service, where guests often volunteer preference and personal information, many hotels have assembled vast databases of guest needs and likes. Yet until recently the value of guest data for analyses (e.g., customer lifetime-value analysis) was not recognized by managers (cynics may suggest that it still largely isn't). A careful analysis of guest-reward initiatives may have shown that the substantial information repositories that accumulated as a byproduct of the initiative are subject to asset-stock accumulation.

MAKING DECISIONS

On the basis of the analysis discussed above, you are in a position to decide whether to go forward with a proposed initiative or shelve it for future reevaluation. The following are three possible broad outcomes from the analysis:

Develop the IT-Dependent Strategic Initiative Independently

Independent development is warranted if the analysis suggests that strong barriers to erosion exist and the firm foresees the ability to appropriate the value created by the initiative over the long term (i.e., sustainable advantage can be attained). Independent development is also warranted if the leader can reap an acceptable return on its innovation, even though the analysis shows that competitors will eventually be able to overcome the barriers to erosion.

Note once again that focus should be on the IT-dependent strategic initiative as whole. The determination of whether the technology at the core of the initiative should be developed in a proprietary manner will depend on the role that the response lags associated with it play in the sustainability of the advantage (i.e., the IT project barrier).

Develop the IT-Dependent Strategic Initiative as Part of a Consortium

When the initiative is unlikely to yield sustainable competitive advantage for the innovator, but, even after replication by competitors, it will improve the overall profitability of the industry, the firm should attempt to create a joint venture with competitors or engage them in a consortium. In this scenario, the leader should strive to minimize costs and risks associated with the initiative and seek to share them with competitors since all will benefit in the long term.

Shelve the IT-Dependent Strategic Initiative

When the analysis suggests that the initiative will not offer strong barriers to erosion, and retaliation by competitors will degrade the average profitability of the industry (e.g., any value created is driven to customers by competition), the firm should shelve the proposed initiative. If the firm does go ahead with the initiative, the likely outcome is competitors' imitation and the creation of value that will be competed away and appropriated by customers. For these types of initiatives, the firm should refrain from being the innovator and instead plan to follow only when strictly necessary. Because of the fast-declining costs of IT and IT implementations, being a follower with nonsustainable innovations enables the firm at least to replicate the leader's initiative at a much lower cost.

SUMMARY

In this chapter we demonstrated that quibbling about the strategic potential offered by information technology is not a productive use of management time and efforts. A large number of cases, including eBay Inc., Dell Inc., Harrah's Entertainment, and Wal-Mart, provide evidence that IT-dependent strategic initiatives, with technology at their core, can be a source of sustained advantage for the modern firm.

More importantly, though, this chapter armed you with the tools to make recommendations about whether a specific firm should pursue a specific IT-dependent strategic initiative or it is better served by forgoing the financial investment and implementation effort. Specifically, we learned that

- When analyzing the potential to defend a competitive advantage created by an IT-dependent strategic initiative, you must estimate the magnitude of the following four barriers to erosion: IT Resources Barrier, Complementary Resources Barrier, IT Project Barrier, and Preemption Barrier. The extent to which an IT-dependent strategic initiative can be protected from competitors' retaliation is a function of the presence and significance of the response lag drivers that underpin it.

- An IT-dependent strategic initiative is defendable when the magnitude, in terms of time and money, of one or more of the barriers to erosion is such to discourage imitation or to render it impossible or impractical.

- Information technology (IT) can be critical to the sustainability of competitive advantage. But, aside from rare occasions, it is not the IT itself that ensures sustainability, but the characteristics of the IT-dependent strategic initiative the technology enables.

- The useful life of an IT-dependent strategic initiative (i.e., the span of time while the firm is able to protect the added value it created) can be extended by rejuvenating the barriers to erosion. Two processes, capability development and asset-stock accumulation, enable the firm to maintain its leadership position.

- The outcome of the analysis is one of three recommendations: (1) Pursue the IT-dependent strategic initiative independently, when the firm can protect it or reap an acceptable return on investment before competitors can successfully retaliate; (2) pursue the IT-dependent strategic initiative as part of a consortium, when the firm cannot protect it, but all the firms in the industry will be better off once replication has occurred; and (3) do not pursue the IT-dependent strategic initiative, when the firm cannot protect it and industry profitability degrades once replication has occurred.

STUDY QUESTIONS

1. The CEO of your company, where you serve as the CIO, recently read the article title "IT Doesn't Matter" (see Further Readings list). He calls you into his office to "pick your brain," and asks, "Why do we invest money in IT when every one of our competitors can buy the same technology?"

2. Why is the difference between information systems and information technology so important to the analysis of sustainability?

3. Describe each of the four barriers to erosion.

4. For each barrier to erosion, provide an example of an IT-dependent strategic initiative that, in your opinion, leverages the barrier. Can you identify which response-lag drivers underpin the barriers to erosion in your examples?

5. Review your answers to the questions at the end of the opening mini-case. Have they changed? Why or why not?

FURTHER READINGS

1. Carr, Nicholas G. (2003). "IT Doesn't Matter." *Harvard Business Review,* May, Vol. 81, pp. 5–12.
2. Piccoli, G., and Ives, B. (2005). "IT-Dependent Strategic Initiatives and Sustained Competitive Advantage: A Review and Synthesis of the Literature." *MIS Quarterly* (29:4), pp. 747–776.
3. Porter, M.E. (2001). "Strategy and the Internet." *Harvard Business Review,* March, Vol. 79, pp. 63–78.
4. Tapscott, D. (2001). "Rethinking Strategy in a Networked World." *Strategy and Competition,* Third Quarter.

GLOSSARY

- **Asset-stock accumulation:** The process by which a firm accrues or builds up a resource over time.

- **Barriers to erosion:** The difficulty, expressed in time and money, that competitors must overcome to match the value proposition offered by the leading firm.

- **Capability development:** The process by which an organization is able to improve its performance over time by developing its ability to use available resources for maximum effectiveness.

- **Competitive advantage:** The condition where a firm engages in a unique transformation process and has been able to distinguish its offerings from those of competitors. When a firm has achieved a position of competitive advantage, it is able to make above-average profits.

- **IT-dependent strategic initiatives:** Identifiable competitive moves and projects that enable the creation of added value and that rely heavily on the use of information technology to be successfully implemented

(i.e., they cannot feasibly be enacted without investments in IT).

- **Resource:** Assets (i.e., things the firm has) and capabilities (i.e., things the firm can do) that the firm can deploy and leverage as part of its IT-dependent strategic initiatives.

- **Response lag:** The time it takes competitors to respond aggressively enough to erode a firm's competitive advantage. The delay in competitive response.

- **Response-lag drivers:** The characteristics of the technology, the firm, its competitors, or the value system in which the firm is embedded that combine to make replication of the IT-dependent strategic initiative difficult and costly. Response-lag drivers combine their effect to levy barriers to erosion.

- **Sustained competitive advantage:** The condition where a firm is able to protect a competitive advantage from competitors' retaliation.

CASE STUDY: CUSTOM MADE APPAREL AND INDIVIDUALIZED SERVICE AT LANDS' END[9]

ABSTRACT

The case describes a hugely successful example of IT-driven strategy, the Lands' End custom tailored apparel initiative. In less than a year, 40% of Lands' End customers buying chinos and jeans from the firm's Web site were buying tailored products. Over 20% of these customers had never made a purchase over the Web before. The case explores mass customization and Web-based customer service initiatives while providing a rich opportunity to discuss the sustainability of competitive advantage derived from IT-driven strategic initiatives. The case also describes the cross-organizational and cross-border supply chain that Lands' End and its business partner, Archetype Solutions, Inc., have constructed as well as Archetype's extension of that chain to other retailers.

INTRODUCTION

A tall man, Larry Cantera had always found buying clothes a frustrating proposition. Only the largest U.S. cities had high-quality big and tall men's apparel stores; the selection was usually small and the prices high. Cantera had been intrigued when Lands' End's custom tailored chinos program was announced in late October of 2001.

Using the Web-based service, customers could custom tailor trousers based on length, waist size, and a number of other fit variables. Customers could also select among a variety of color and style options (e.g., cuffs, pleats). Only men's and women's chinos were included in the initial offering. In April of 2002, customized jeans were added to the Land's End Web site,[10] and, in November of 2002, customized men's twill trousers and men's shirts were introduced. Cantera had ordered five pairs of trousers and a dress shirt with French cuffs.

Others had apparently found value in the program. By the end of September 2002, 40% of all jeans and chinos sold on the Lands' End Web site were custom made, far more than the 10% management had initially hoped for. While 20% of Lands' Ends' Web shoppers were new customers, an even higher percentage of customers choosing custom apparel were making their very first Web purchase [Bass,

2002]. These results had been achieved with no advertising other than on the firm's Web site and in its catalog [Tedeschi, 2002]. They also, at least temporarily, defied the predictions of one expert in mass customization who believed that suits were a better candidate than jeans for customization because, while suit buyers expect delays associated with alterations, jean buyers want instant gratification [Pine, 2000].

MASS CUSTOMIZATION

In the late 1990s mass customization had become increasingly popular.[11] A potentially industry-transforming extension of mass production, mass customization was defined as a *"process that uses the same production resources to manufacture a variety of similar, yet individually unique products"* [TC[2], 2002].

Among better-known examples were: made-to-order assembly of personal computers, first popularized by Dell Computer and later by Apple, Gateway, and others; customization of makeup and beauty care products, pioneered by Reflect.com [Swartz, 2002]; and customized automobiles, pioneered by Ford Motor Company (although the need to rely on dealer network inventories for order fulfillment had limited the initial success of that and similar initiatives). Peapod, WebVan, MyWebGrocer, FreshDirect, and others had also invested heavily in customized order picking and home delivery of groceries with mixed results [Ives & Piccoli, 2002; Kirkpatrick, 2002, Palmer et al., 2000].

A Kurt Salmon and Associates study in 1997 found that 36% of consumers were willing to pay 12 to 15% more for custom apparel and footwear [TC[2], 2002]. Shoe and jeans manufacturers were among the first to extend customization to apparel, much of it targeting teens. A privately held Internet company, Customatix, offered sneakers in thousands of combinations of colors, logos, graphics, and materials. In 1999, Nike introduced its version of customized sneakers; by 2002 they accounted for 20% of pairs purchased from the firm's Web site [Swartz, 2002]. Levi Strauss was another early entrant in apparel customization; in 1995 Levi had introduced its "Original Spin" program, which allowed customers to visit a Levi's store to be measured

---

[9] This case was originally published as Ives, B., and Piccoli, G. (2003), "Custom Made Apparel and Individualized Service at Lands' End," *Communications of the AIS* (Vol. 11, Article 3), pp. 79–93.

[10] http://www.landsend.com

[11] See Gillenson et al. [1999] for a tutorial on mass customization.

for jeans. These were then custom-tailored and subsequently home delivered [Tedeschi, 2001]. Levi's attempt to sell merchandise, tailored or otherwise, online from its own Web site had been curtailed in November of 1999 when the firm announced its intentions to instead sell through the Web sites of two of its major customers, J. C. Penney's and Macy's [*Wall Street Journal,* 1999].

In November of 2001, Brooks Brothers introduced a "Digital-Tailoring" system for customized suits, jackets, trousers, and shirts. In 12 seconds the system could scan the customer's body and record 200,000 data points. These were then translated into exact measurements for 45 specific tailoring measurements (e.g., collar, neck). The customer could then choose from hundreds of fabrics and a variety of styles. Products were shipped in about three weeks. The entry price for trousers was $200, with suits starting at $700—$100 more than Brooks Brothers own off-the-shelf suits and $400 less than the firm's traditionally tailored ones [Colman, 2002]. In January of 2003, the service was still only available in the firm's Madison Avenue store.

Apparel customization, according to Kurt Salmon Associates [TC^2, 2002], came in three varieties: personalization, fit, and design. A golf shirt customized with an owner's initials was an example of personalization. Customization by fit could involve asking the customer to provide measurements or, as with Brooks Brothers, to visit a measurement facility. The third type of customization, design, electronically drew the customer into the design process (for instance, at Nike) by specifying the colors of the various components of a pair of shoes.

While customized products could fetch higher prices and, presumably, higher margins, customization still had its detractors. Some felt that the many choices could be confusing for customers. Others feared for the integrity of the resulting customer-driven designs. Still others questioned whether there was enough customer demand for customization. An analyst at Jupiter Research observed that: *"For the most part, consumers are perfectly content with mass manufacturing"* [TC^2, 2002].

ABOUT LANDS' END

Lands' End, founded in Chicago in 1963 by its chairman Gary Comer, initially sold sailing equipment. It soon branched off into clothes and home furnishings and relocated to Dodgeville, Wisconsin. The company, according to one observer:

cruised through the 1980s, ringing up annual sales and profit gains of over 40% by selling traditional threads such as khaki pants and rugby shirts. Stressing

quality and value rather than fashion fads, it won loyal customers by setting a new standard for service: Calls to its phone centers were answered within 1.5 rings, merchandise was almost always available and orders were usually shipped within a day. [Merrick, 2001]

In its capsule description of the firm, Hoovers.com described Lands' End as marketing

its products through its folksy flagship catalog and specialty catalogs (such as Lands' End Kids and Business Outfitters). It also runs about 30 outlet and retail stores in the US, UK, and Japan. Its traditional, casual apparel for men, women, and children is generally immune to the changing tides of fashion. Lands' End also sells accessories, home goods, luggage, and corporate gifts to its primarily middle-aged customers. Lands' End is expanding its Web presence worldwide, but catalogs continue to be its primary means of marketing. [Hoovers, 2002]

Land's End had been one of the first major apparel firms to recognize the desirable economics of the internet. In his letter to the shareholders in the 1999 annual report CEO, David F. Dyer, had noted that:

more than 40 percent of our operating costs is spent in creating, printing and mailing catalogs. E-commerce selling costs are significantly less than catalog. Processing e-commerce orders is significantly less than taking a phone order . . . and unlike the bricks and mortar merchants, our investments in the distribution infrastructure are perfectly leveraged through e-commerce. Every e-commerce sale has the potential to be a more profitable sale than through the catalog. [Dyer, 1999]

While the following year's results had reaffirmed Dyer's assumption that Web sales were more profitable than catalog sales, his next letter to the Lands' End shareholders reflected a new understanding of the Internet market:

Based on results from fall 1999, circulation tests to Internet buyers confirmed the synergistic relationship of our catalog to the Web. We know that withholding catalogs from Internet buyers does not generate online sales. We believe that a smaller catalog (fewer pages) with sufficient mailing frequency may produce the best results over time. Still, we will continue to refine our tests to determine the optimum frequency and pages for keeping our Internet customers apprised of Lands' End's exciting new products. The Internet was the fastest growing source of new

continued

CASE STUDY (*continued*)

	Jan 02	Jan 01	Jan 00	Jan 99
Revenue	1,569.1	1,462.3	1,319.8	1371.4
Cost of Goods Sold	853.3	817.2	706.6	727.2
Gross Profit	715.8	645.1	613.2	616.7
Gross Profit Margin	45.6%	44.1%	46.5%	45%
SG&A Expense	575.7	560.0	515.4	544.4
Depreciation & Amortization	26.9	23.4	20.7	18.7
Operating Income	113.2	61.7	77.1	59.7
Operating Margin	7.2%	4.2%	5.8%	3.6%
Total Net Income	66.9	34.7	48.0	31.2
Net Profit Margin	4.3%	2.4%	3.6%	2.3%
Diluted EPS ($)	2.23	1.14	1.56	1.01

Exhibit 1 Lands' End Income Statements (1999–2002, in millions of U.S. dollars)

customer names to our file last year. It is less costly to bring these customers to the Lands' End file through e-commerce than through printed media. [Dyer, 2000]

From fiscal 1999 to fiscal 2002, Internet merchandise sales at landsend.com had progressed from $61M to $138M to $218M to $299M. An income statement and balance sheet are reproduced in Exhibits 1 and 2, respectively.

THE ORDERING PROCESS

Lands' End customers had the opportunity to customize certain elements of color, fabric, and design. The men's Chino trouser section on the Web site, for instance, offered trousers in four colors, with or without pleats, with or without cuffs,

loose or tight fitting, and with a short, regular, or medium height waist (rise). In addition, customers provided specifications for the length of their inseam, the width of their waist, and self-descriptions of the size of their thighs (slim, average, full), the shape of their seats (four options), and their leg to body proportions (five options). Weight, arm length, as well as collar and shoe size were also collected.

Shirt customization included plain or patterned cloth, three different types of fabric, various colors, two types of pleating, five collar styles, four cuff options, and with or without a chest pocket. The Web site included pictures of shirts or trousers that illustrated the various options. For custom shirt size, drawings of men's arms depicted various levels of musculature from which to select. Small browser windows also could be opened to provide larger images of

	Jan 02	Jan 01	Jan 00	Jan 99
Cash	122.1	75.4	76.4	6.6
Net Receivables	13.3	19.8	17.8	21.1
Inventories	227.2	188.2	162.2	219.7
Total Current Assets	402.6	321.7	289.4	294.3
Total Assets	599.1	507.6	456.2	456.0
Short-Term Debt	16.2	16.9	11.7	38.9
Total Current Liabilities	185.6	178.9	150.9	205.2
Long-Term Debt	0.0	0.0	0.0	0.0
Total Liabilities	198.4	193.5	159.9	213.7
Total Equity	400.7	314.2	296.2	242.5
Shares Outstanding (mil.)	30.0	29.3	30.1	30.5

Exhibit 2 Lands' End Balance Sheet (1999–2002, in millions of U.S. dollars)

color swatches, including some representation of fabric detail and patterns. Together the various options provided billions of variations for the customized products.

Bill Bass, Lands' End's senior vice president for e-commerce, had joined Lands' End in 1999 after three years at Forrester Research Inc., where he had most recently served as group director of research for consumer e-commerce and new media [Merrick, 2001].

Bass was attracted to the position at least partially because he saw at Lands' End the three elements that he felt were conducive to a successful electronic commerce offering: proprietary products, a strong distribution infrastructure, and an established brand. Their subsequent success on the Internet, he felt, had been driven by the firm not having set up its Internet division as a separate business unit and because of the exclusivity of the merchandise [Merrick, 2001]. The former avoided internal competition and the latter reduced competitive threats from other vendors.

Bass believed that in a few years no major apparel company could afford not to offer custom tailored apparel. He viewed the Lands' End custom tailoring program as

one of the most significant technology advances in the apparel industry . . . [that] allows the masses to get the perfect fit without hiring a tailor . . . no [apparel company] can afford not to use it. [Swartz, 2002]

According to Bass, Lands' End's approach to tailoring was quite different than the approach used by other automated tailoring systems such as that at Brooks Brothers:

Any type of custom clothes before, you've had to go into a store and get yourself measured and get [your] body scanned, which involved taking your clothes off, both of which for consumers is fairly inconvenient. Now compare that to what we've done online. You can now sit down in front of your computer and within two minutes answer questions that you already know. You don't have to break out a tape measure. [Rivera, 2001]

Customized products at Lands' End ranged in price from $49 to $69 plus shipping. Lands' End's margin was reportedly the same on custom and off-the-rack sales, but because the custom products were priced higher, they yielded more total profit [Tedeschi, 2002].

After an order was placed, customers were sent a confirmation message (see Exhibit 3). Another was sent when the order shipped. Among other things, this message included the Lands' End guarantee:

All Lands' End items are backed by our Guaranteed. Period.® promise: If you are not entirely satisfied with an item, return it to us at any time for an exchange or refund of its purchase price.

Lowering return rates was one claimed benefit for custom tailoring. While estimates of returns for traditional mail order goods varied widely,[12] and Lands' End did not share this number, they had reported that returns for their custom products were similar to that experienced for their ready-made sizes [Tedeschi, 2002]. This discrepancy in expectations might be explained by the fact that customers rating purchases as fair or worse were requested to return them for a refund and given a discount on a reorder. The details dissatisfied customers provided about product fit were then used to fine tune the algorithms used to create the patterns driving the design of custom made apparel, as well as to fine tune each customer's own electronic data models.

Another benefit of the customizing program was in customer loyalty. According to Bass:

Customer loyalty to our custom tailored clothing has surprised me. The level of feeling that customers have is amazing. This is particularly true for women. Fitting 100 some million women in the U.S. in 8 or 10 basic sizes as well as they would like is really impossible. Once they get a pair of jeans to fit some will order every color in every fabric. [Bass, 2002]

As new custom apparel categories were rolled out sales increased, as Bass explained: "Once a customer returns to the site to look at the new category, they are often inclined to also re-order from a category they had shopped before. [Bass, 2002].

CRAFTING CUSTOMIZED CLOTHES

Customized orders placed on the Lands' End Web site were entered into a form provided by Lands' End's partner, Archetype Solutions, Inc. (ASI). Using that form, the order, with a tracking barcode attached, was then transmitted to ASI's offices in California.

---

[12] Tedeschi [2001] reports that 30% of all apparel bought online is returned; an analyst with Kurt Salmon and Associates reports that the figure for Chinos bought online is closer to 20% [Tedeschi, 2001]; Bass of Lands' End reports that their returns are lower than the industry and that custom tailored returns are in line with those of standard products bought off the firm's Web site [Bass, 2002].

continued

CASE STUDY (*continued*)

Date: Thu, 07 Nov 2002 23:40:54 -0600 (CST)

From: Lands' End <orderinquiry@landsend.com>
Subject: Your Lands' End Order #999999
To: lcantera@aisnet.org

Thank you for shopping at Lands' End.

Your order #999999 is being processed.
Please refer to this number if you have any questions.

$ 69.00	Your merchandise total
$ 7.95	Shipping costs
$ 0.00	Taxes

$ 76.95	Total for this order

Payment:
$ 76.95   on Visa **** **** **** 9999

The following items will be shipped to:
LARRY   CANTERA
1 MAIL STREET UNIT 1
HOUSTON, TX 77000-0000
United States

Men's Regular Custom Classic Stripe Broadcloth Shirt
Blue, Size: Custom-made for Me
$69.00

NOTE: Your Lands' End Custom products will ship separately from other items sent to this address. They will be delivered in 3-4 weeks regardless of the shipping method you choose for the balance of your order.

If you have questions about your order, please call us at 1-800-963-4816 (USA), or 608-935-6170 (Intl). You can also reply to this e-mail.

Thank you for shopping at landsend.com.

Are you getting our free e-mail newsletter?
You can receive a periodic "heads up" e-mail with the latest word about new products, online overstocks specials, plus all the news from Dodgeville and environs. Visit our sign-up page and subscribe Today.

http://www.landsend.com/newsletter.cgi

Exhibit 3   Order Confirmation

For each clothing line ASI pattern makers were required to develop base patterns including allowances for the various styling alternatives. They then decided how the patterns would change based on the possible range of customer inputs. Software coders then automated all of these decisions.

A pattern for a particular customer's garment was a two-dimensional "drawing" of all the pieces to be cut and assembled into a garment. A pattern was designed using key measurements (e.g., for pants it would be waist, seat, front and back rise, thigh circumference, leg opening) and shape considerations (how curvy or straight, how much tapering, how much ease, etc.). Electronic patterns were precise representations of the garment to be prepared for a particular customer. Customer-specific patterns were retained by ASI and not shared across its retail partners.[13]

In November of 2001, *Bobbin Magazine,*[14] an apparel-industry trade publication, awarded ASI one of that year's ten *Bobbin* All-Star Awards, for the best innovations in the business. The following is the award certificate's description of what happens once an order is received by ASI.

"Using Gerber's[15] PDF 2000[16] and made-to-measure programs and Nester[17] software, patterns are swiftly drafted. The trio of software programs allows Archetype to match the specific measurements and styling demands of the consumer [and] make and manipulate the patterns. Then the pattern files are sent electronically to select contract manufacturing locations, where Archetype has already installed its systems, including Gerber's automatic, conveyorized, single-ply DCS 3500 cutters.[18] [McElwain, 2001].

It took less than 30 seconds to create a pattern for a particular customer. Individual patterns were then transmitted to a manufacturer, batched by the material selected. At the plant a roll of fabric was placed on the input end of the laser-driven cutter and then each pattern was automatically cut in single-ply, based on the pattern created by ASI [McElwain, 2001]. The specific stages in the selling, manufacturing and distribution process are shown in Exhibit 4.

According to Lands' End's Bass, the manufacturing process was challenging:

When people are used to doing it with mass production, it is very difficult. Moving from standard manufacturing to modular requires significant training and testing before production can be started; it takes several months. But, using technology and our experience we have been able to bring the cost of custom apparel to a level comparable with mass production. For example, setting up a fabric to be cut takes 15 minutes. Unless you can batch a certain number of orders for that fabric, it is not feasible to offer the fabric for selection by customers. [Bass, 2002]

According to Bass, the global reach of the tailored-apparel supply chain was long and expanding. The firm's chinos and jeans were currently produced in Mexico, and the firm was looking to add further capacity in Asia. Dress shirts and higher-end trousers were to be made in Costa Rica and the Dominican Republic [D'Innocenzio, 2002].

ABOUT ARCHETYPE SOLUTIONS

Robert Holloway founded Archetype Solutions Inc. in early 2000. Originally named DNAwear, the firm started in a small facility in Richmond, California. It soon changed its name and relocated to Emeryville, California, located in the San Francisco Bay Area. That same year, the firm raised

---

[13] Personal communication with Jeff Luhnow, ASI president, January 8, 2003. Luhnow notes that "they [retailers] have the customer information and sizing inputs, but the patterns and specifics are our property."

[14] http://www.bobbin.com

[15] http://www.gerbertechnology.com

[16] An expert system enhanced software package for developing patterns based on the entire garment rather than pieces of it (http://www.gerbertechnology.com/gtwww/01library/Literature/Apparel/PDS2000exE.pdf).

[17] Nester Software produces software for arranging elements of a pattern or patterns to minimize material waste (http://www.nestersoftware.com).

[18] The Gerber Technology DC3500 is an automated machine tool for cutting single (single-ply) or small layers of material (http://www.gerbertechnology.com/gtwww/01library/Literature/Apparel/dcs3500e.pdf).

continued

CASE STUDY (*continued*)

1. Archetype supplies retailer with sizing questions and answer choices.
2. Consumer answers questions on Web site, in store, or over phone.
3. Retailer sends Archetype the order file once a day.
4. Orders automatically processed by Archetype software in California.
5. Software produces electronic pattern and order file for each order.
6. Sent via e-mail to production facilities in Latin America or Asia.
7. Manufacturers are set up with one central server and five or six networked desktops located at different stages in production process.
8. Garments assigned unique ID.
9. Fabric is cut using supplied digital pattern and automated cutter
10. Barcode ID label printed out as fabric is being cut.
11. Label is attached to the product.
12. Production order also printed out as fabric is cut.
13. Production order has a bill of materials listing necessary pieces for each garment (zippers, buttons, labels, pockets, etc.).
14. Garments are made, inspected, and packed for shipping.
15. Garments scanned and status updated at each stage of process.
16. Garments shipped from factory to a third-party shipping center in the U.S.
17. Garments received by shipping center and individual items scanned.
18. Shipping labels are printed.
19. Items are express shipped to consumers.
20. Status report for all orders sent nightly to retailers.

Exhibit 4   Production and distribution process for custom-tailored clothes[19]

$1.5M in venture capital. In November of 2001, ASI attracted second-round financing of $6.25M from Carlyle Venture Partners. In early 2001, ASI approached Lands' End for a possible partnership and, later on that same year, signed a deal with Lands' End to provide custom tailored jeans and chinos [McElwain, 2001]. The arrangement gave Lands' End a six-month exclusive license to ASI's proprietary customizing solution for each new apparel category roll-out. Lands' End also made a significant, but noncontrolling, investment in ASI. In 2002, with Holloway still at its head, ASI employed over 40 people and held several patents pertaining to the customization process and the algorithms used to create custom made apparel.

Prior to founding ASI, Holloway had been President of Levi Strauss North America, a firm he had served for 17 years. His plan was to follow his vision about the future of apparel:

> What if you could go online to a store, or phone up a catalog, and in two or three minutes design your own pair of pants, design your shirt, whatever, and

have it made for you as an individual so it's exactly to your specifications, and it fits you absolutely? And what if you could do it at a price that was fairly similar to what you pay for off-the-shelf [goods]? That's what we set about doing for two years—solving this fundamental issue for the apparel industry. . . . Ultimately, what I'm excited about—and what we talk about—is redefining apparel. [McElwain, 2001]

ASI's president and cofounder was Jeff Luhnow, previously a management consultant at McKinsey & Company and, before that, an engineer at Gore Fabrics. Luhnow felt that finding manufacturers with the mindset to embrace customization was essential; so too was ensuring those manufacturers were also willing to invest:

> It does require some investment on their part up front—they are sharing part of the risk, hoping and assuming this idea will take off and that it will be something that they will be a part of for a long time. All our manufacturers need to be able to be adept and

---

[19] Personal communication with Jeff Luhnow, ASI president, November 18, 2002.

flexible, and able to learn new technologies fairly rapidly. They need to have automated cutting machines [because] part of what we send them is instructions for these cutting machines, along with all the files that help track the order through the manufacturing process. [McElwain, 2001]

Contracts between retailers and independent manufacturers were negotiated in the usual manner but manufacturers were then required to license manufacturing and tracking software from ASI. As Luhnow explained, the licenses did not yet generate revenues for ASI.

We recognize that [manufacturers] would more than likely pass that cost through to the retailer, and we like being in a position where we don't get anything from the manufacturer—it allows us to be more neutral and objective.[20]

According to Luhnow, ASI sought to provide its retail partners with flexibility in production partners:

Brands and retailers don't like to be locked into one apparel supplier for a category; we give them the flexibility to choose whichever manufacturer they want—then as long as that manufacturer can set it up and work with us, it will happen. The hard part is the set up of new products, styles and brands. That takes many months. Also, the brands and retailers have to trust us; we are making products with their name. That takes a while to build.[21]

Retailers paid ASI a license fee, as Luhnow explained:

There is an annual fixed component based on number of categories (men's chinos, women's jeans, etc.) and then a per unit fee. The annual fee only partly covers our costs . . . so we only succeed if they sell a lot of units. That way, incentives are aligned.[22]

Starting in the summer of 2002, ASI had begun to work with Bob's Stores,[23] a regional apparel company, to develop a service similar to Lands' End's. By October of 2002, Bob's was selling customized chinos from their Web site. Bob's chinos were priced at $39.95 plus shipping and included several elements not available from Lands' End, including the number and cut of the pockets. Initially the firm would rely on the same

manufacturing plants that produced the Lands' End jeans, but offer different choices in color and fabric [Tedeschi, 2002].

Setting up a new retailer was not an easy process, as an ASI executive had explained to a reporter:

There's a ton of work that has to be done for each customer before we can launch. A lot goes into getting to know each customer's brand, and how best to customize with them. [Tedeschi, 2002]

OTHER TECHNOLOGY-DRIVEN INNOVATIONS AT LANDS' END

Lands' End had long been a progressive user of technology for enhancing customer service. The firm's Web site, accessed over one hundred thousand times on a typical day, included several innovations intended to enhance service to Land's End's 2 million customers.

Bass had strong views about the use of innovative technologies:

I never, ever want anybody on our site to go, "Wow, what cool technology," I want the technology to be like the oxygen in the air—you don't even notice it because it works so well. [Merrick, 2001]

Nevertheless, the firm did try each year to roll out, usually in September or October, an innovation on the Web site that attracted attention. Bill Bass explained:

Nothing changes on a retailer's Web site once you get into November. So we launch in September or October—no one had time to copy our innovations.

For the 2001 holiday season, that innovation had been customized chinos. In 2002 it was custom-tailored men's shirts.

In 2000, the Smithsonian had recognized Lands' End for "outstanding achievements in leading the information technology revolution to enhance and enable the relationship between company and customer [Lands' End, 2000a]. These innovations included "ImageTwin"™, a body scanning system that created a precise virtual model of the consumer's body[24]; "My Virtual Model™", a visualization of the customer on which selected merchandise could be displayed; "My Personal Shopper," employing a

---

[20] Personal communication with Jeff Luhnow, ASI president, January 8, 2003.

[21] Personal communication with Jeff Luhnow, ASI president, November 18, 2002.

[22] Personal communication with Jeff Luhnow, ASI president, January 8, 2003.

[23] www.bobsstores.com

[24] Though popular with many customers the service was discontinued after a year of use because it was felt by Lands' End executives not to have improved service [Merrick, 2001].

continued

CASE STUDY (*continued*)

sophisticated modeling tool to make personalized recommendations based on responses to a few questions; and "Shop with a Friend," which permitted friends to shop together, but from different locations, on the Lands' End Web site.

Internet instant messaging service was another Lands' End innovation in technology-driven customer service:

> Lands' End uses real-time communication to help online shoppers find what they're looking for. Surfers visit the company's Web site and click on the Ask Us button if they have a question about chinos, T-shirts or jeans. After typing in their names, they are greeted by a cheery representative, whom they are introduced to on a first-name basis. Questions are answered promptly and courteously, with a healthy dose of exclamation points. [Dukcevich, 2002]

LANDS' END ACQUISITION BY SEARS

On May 13, 2002, Sears Roebuck announced [Sears, 2002] its intention to acquire Land's End for $62 per Lands' End share, or approximately $1.9 billion—an $11 premium over the stock's closing price the previous trading day [Lewis, 2002].

The terms of the agreement left day-to-day management of Lands' End in the hands of its current executive team though the members of Lands' Ends Board and founder Comer no longer were involved with the firm. The acquisition gave Sears an exclusive right to sell the Lands' End lines in their retail stores. By November of 2002, 180 stores would be carrying the line [*Milwaukee Journal Sentinel,* 2002] and by the fall of 2003, the Lands' End lines were to be available in all of Sears' full-line stores [Merrick, 2001]. Dave Dyler, Lands' End's CEO, took over responsibility for Sears' direct selling operations, including Sears' remaining specialty catalog sales operations as well as the Sears.Com Web site [Lewis, 2002]. Sales from these catalogs had amounted to about $500 million in 2001 [Merrick, 2001].

CONCLUSION

Cantera, a professor at a local business school, stood before a too-short full-length mirror and admired his new blue and white striped custom-tailored French cuffed shirt and black twill pants. While expensive at $69.00 each (plus $7.95 in shipping costs), they fit better and were far less expensive than he would have paid at the high-end big and tall men's store where he normally shopped in Houston.

Sitting down at his desk, Cantera's mind returned from fashion to his upcoming lecture on electronic retailing. He could predict some of the questions the Lands' End experience would raise for his students: How popular would custom-tailored clothing become and what would be the implications on apparel retail and catalog sales? And how, if at all, would Sears strategically leverage this element of its new acquisition?

He also wondered who in the retail channel would be the winners and who the losers if customization caught on. On the one hand, there were the giant retail chains, including Sears, who, with their acquisition of Lands' End, could now test the waters of customization. At the other extreme was Amazon's newly opened apparel store, where the customer could select from over 400 brands. Among these were Lands' End's lines, but also Levi's, Tommy Hilfiger, and Van Heusen. Just the previous day, Cantera had received a broadcast e-mail from Jeff Bezos, Amazon's CEO and founder, boasting the results of the firm's one-week pilot of the apparel store. In that short time, over 40,000 items of apparel had been sold.

Another question was the role, if any, Archetype Solutions and their likely future competitors would play.

"As usual," Cantera thought with bemusement, "this example raises far more questions than it answers."

REFERENCES

Archetype Solutions, Inc., Press Release: Archetype Closes $6.25 Million Round of Financing Led by Carlyle Venture Partners," November 6, 2001.

Bass, B. (December 11, 2002). Personal communication.

Colman, D. (2002). "For the Man with a 15.95-Inch Neck," *New York Times,* November 14, 2002.

Dukcevich, D. (2002). "Instant Messaging: Lands End's Instant Business," *Forbes,* July, 22, 2002.

Dyer, D. (1999). Letter to the Shareholders, *Lands' End Annual Report, 1999.*

Dyer, D. (2000). Letter to the Shareholders, *Lands' End Annual Report, 2000.*

Hoovers.Com (2002). "Lands' End, Inc.: Capsule," http://www.hoovers.com/co/capsule/3/0,2163,10883,00.html (current November 15, 2002).

D'Innocenzio, A. (September 9, 2002). "Lands' End adds more size options online," *San Jose Mercury News,* http://www.bayarea.com/mld/mercurynews/business/4035072.htm.

Gillenson, M. L., Sherrell, D. L., and Chen, L. (September 1999). "Information Technology as the Enabler of One-to-One Marketing." *Communications of the Association for Information Systems,* (2)18.

Ives, B., and Piccoli, G. (2002). "Rice Epicurean Online Shopping: Destiny or Decadence." *Communications of the Association for Information Systems* (Vol. 9), pp. 314–329.

Kirkpatrick, D. (2002). "Tech @ Work: The Online Grocer Version 2.0." *Fortune,* Monday, November 25, 2002.

Lands' End. (2002a). "Lands' End Introduces Latest Online Shopping Innovations: Setting New E-Commerce Standards for Customer Service." Press Release, Lands' End, October 18, 2002a.

Lands' End (2002b). "Press Release: Lands' End Agrees to Be Acquired By Sears for $62 per Share, or $1.9 Billion In Cash." May 23, 2002.

Lewis, M. (2002). "Sears Goes Back to the Future." *Forbes,* May 21, 2002.

McElwain, J. "Archetype Raises the Bar," *Bobbin Magazine,* December 1, 2001, http://www.archetypesolutions.com/contentpresentation.cfm?doc=archetype1201.htm&pagetype=news (Accessed Nov. 15th 2002).

Merrick, A. (December 10, 2001). "The People Behind the Sites: Lands' End: Keep It Fresh." *The Wall Street Journal,* p. R6.

Milwaukee Journal Sentinel (October 28, 2002). "Sears Hopes Shoppers Bite as It Begins Lands' End Brand Rollout."

Palmer, J. et al. (2000). "Online Grocery Shopping Around the World: Examples of Key Business Models, *Communications of the Association for Information Systems,* (4)3, December.

Pine, B. J. (2000). *Markets of One: Creating Customer-Unique Value Through Mass Customization.* Boston, MA: Harvard University Business Publishing.

Rivera, E. (November 29, 2001). "Perfect' Pants Online." *Tech Live Systems,* http://www.techtv.com/news/print/0,23102,3362661,00.html.

Sears (May 13, 2002). "Sears Agrees to Acquire Lands' End for $62 per Share, or $1.9 Billion in Cash." Sears, Roebuck and Company Press Release.

Swartz, J. (October 29, 2002). "Thanks to Net, Consumers Customizing More," *USA Today.*

TC² (2002). "Studies Reveal the Consumer, Manufacturer and Retailer All Win With Mass Customization." http://www.tc2.com/About/AboutMass.htm (current November 13, 2002).

Tedeschi, B. (November 5, 2001). "Selling Made-to-Order Clothing Online." *New York Times.*

Tedeschi, B. (September 30, 2002). "E-Commerce Report; A Lands' End Experiment in Selling Custom-Made Pants Is a Success, Leaving Its Rivals to Play Catch-Up." *New York Times.*

Wall Street Journal (November 1, 1999). "Levi's Plans to Stop Selling Merchandise on Own Web Sites." *Wall Street Journal.*

I V

Getting IT Done

The last part of this book is dedicated to the many issues that surround the management of information systems and technology in modern organizations—from budgeting and operational planning, to design and development, to ongoing operations. Keeping with the focus of the text, this section is not overly technical. Rather, it focuses on what general and functional managers need to know to be actively involved in the management of their firm's or function's information systems resources.

Your involvement with the decisions discussed in this section is essential. While you can typically avoid worrying about hardware decision making, the same cannot be said of software applications and the issues that surround them. Software applications enable and constrain how work is done and have a direct impact on successful operations. Thus, as the organizational expert and the person responsible for the success of your business function, you must have a say in the funding and prioritization of projects, you must be intimately involved in the design or selection of new systems, and you must be cognizant of the organizational risks associated with security and privacy failures.

In order to be an asset on the team making the aforementioned decisions, you must understand the processes that surround them, be up to date on the information systems trends that concern these decisions, and be well versed in the vocabulary and issues. Part IV of this book is devoted to these topics. Specifically,

- *Chapter 10: Funding Information Systems.* This chapter focuses on the decisions and techniques pertaining to the funding of information systems. It also discusses outsourcing decisions and the outsourcing decision-making process.

- *Chapter 11: Creating Information Systems.* This chapter describes the process by which IT-enabled information systems come to be. It discusses the three main avenues for new systems creation: systems design and development, systems selection and acquisition, and end-user development.

- *Chapter 12: Information System Trends.* This chapter introduces the enduring and emerging information systems trends that concern general and functional managers. It then describes and discusses the characteristics and implications of each one.

- *Chapter 13: Security, Privacy and Ethics.* This chapter makes the case for why general and functional managers need to be intimately involved in information security, privacy, and ethics decisions. It then provides the background to partake in the organizational debate of these issues.

10

Funding Information Systems

What You Will Learn in This Chapter

We begin Part IV by discussing how modern organizations support and fund their information systems efforts.

In this chapter you will learn

1. To describe the relationship between strategic information systems planning and the yearly budgeting and prioritization process.

2. To articulate the role that general and functional managers play in the yearly budgeting and prioritization process.

3. To define and use the appropriate vocabulary, including concepts such as total cost of ownership (TCO), business case, and steering committee.

4. To evaluate the three main funding methods used by modern organizations: chargeback, allocation, and overhead. You will also learn their respective advantages and disadvantages.

5. To understand the yearly budgeting and prioritization project. Be able to evaluate individual and portfolio risks of information systems projects.

6. To define the terms *outsourcing* and *offshoring* and identify the primary drivers of this enduring trend. You will also be able to articulate the principal risks of outsourcing and offer some general guidelines with respect to the outsourcing decision.

MINI-CASE: BUDGETING AT PERFORMANCE BOARDS, INC.

As the chief information officer (CIO), you chair the IT steering committee at Performance Boards, Inc. Performance Boards has recently been acquired by Big Sporting Manufacturer, Inc. and is currently operating independently as a wholly owned subsidiary. During the yearly IT budgeting process, or the "ultimate fighting championship," as you called it, you were the unwilling center of attention—the arbiter of all disputes. It was that time of the year again, as shown by the calls you were receiving from other managers you hardly heard from all year.

Every July the budgeting process started with a call for projects. Every functional area responded with a rank-ordered list of initiatives that needed funding, and their supporting business cases. Once the steering committee reviewed the preliminary proposals, each executive sponsor presented the case for his or her proposed projects. Armed with this information, the steering committee deliberated and chose the projects to be presented to the executive team for inclusion in the overall budget. Typically whatever the steering committee proposed, the executive team approved. The executive team's main concern was overall IT spending. Bjorn Dunkerbeck, the founder and CEO of Performance Boards, was adamant that the firm would be in line with the manufacturing industry benchmark of 3.3 percent of revenue as a yearly IT budget.

This year, the third of declining revenues for the firm, the ultimate fighting championship was shaping up as an all-time great—not a good thing for you! You had set aside 64 percent of the budget for the information systems function to control, in accord with industry allocation benchmarks. Your group needed the money for security, disaster recovery, general maintenance, infrastructure management, and administrative expenses. Yet, because of the tightening budgets, for the first time in your tenure as CIO you had been questioned and required to justify the allocation to the IS function.

At this point the human resource project and the inventory management projects seemed most likely to get greenlighted. The vice president of human resources had been asking for an upgrade to the benefits package management application for three years now. His business case showed both productivity improvements and higher retention of employees. The chief operating officer presented the business case for the manufacturing group. He had shown a substantial ROI associated with the proposed supply chain and just-in-time inventory management initiatives.

The VP of accounting and the new director of sales, Robby Naish, were exerting lots of pressure to obtain funding for their projects: the upgrade to the accounting management system and a sales force automation (SFA) application, respectively. Naish had just finished reiterating his case to you on the phone. Being new to the firm, he was becoming quite frustrated with Performance Boards' approach to budgeting: "How am I supposed to compete with a project that increases productivity and one that improves efficiencies through automation? They can easily compute an ROI, but my project is not suited to that type of analysis. I can surely come up with some fictitious ROI number. I can pull them out of the thin air if this is how you guys do business!"

As you review the current informal ranking of projects, you can't help but think that you need to find a way not to alienate the functional managers and project sponsors. The last thing you need is for the IS function to be perceived as a roadblock to the success of the other functional areas, and ultimately of Performance Boards, Inc.

DISCUSSION QUESTIONS

1. What should you do next? What are some of the options at your disposal to ensure that you do not alienate your colleagues?
2. Are there any structural problems with the budgeting process at Performance Boards, Inc.? What improvements would you suggest for next year—if any?

◼ INTRODUCTION

In Chapter 6 we discussed the information systems strategic planning process. Strategic information systems planning involves identifying the long-term direction of information systems use and management within the organization. It provides a framework for decision making and project selection. Within this framework the firm develops yearly operational plans and budgets in order to prioritize information systems spending.

As a general or functional manager, you need to understand how the budgeting and prioritization processes work so that you can make the most of it. All too often we see organizations funding information systems using simple metrics, like percentage of revenue or fixed increments over the previous year's budget. While these metrics have a place in the budgeting process, the yearly budget is an opportunity to formally evaluate competing projects and make the (sometimes tough) comprehensive prioritization decisions necessary to align information systems with the firm's strategy. The firm that fails to do so misses the opportunity to offer guidance and a clear mandate to the IS function. The consequence is that a lack of direction and cohesive effort will degrade service (in many cases leading to outright failure) and demoralize the firm's IS professionals.

Note that this prioritization role should not be delegated to the information systems group, but should be made in concert between business managers (i.e., those who need the information systems) and IS professionals (i.e., those who make and manage the information systems). An IT group that does not deliver consistently is often the product of an executive team that fails to provide clear priorities.

◼ FOUNDATION CONCEPTS

To engage in the discussion about information systems funding and to be more effective when you seek funding for projects that will benefit your department or functional area, you need to master the following essential concepts.

Total Cost of Ownership (TCO)

Given the characteristic of information systems and IT, one of the important concepts in the funding process is total cost of ownership (TCO). TCO is a financial estimate designed to explicitly recognize the full life cycle costs of IT assets. The costs of information systems and technology typically far exceed the costs of acquisition (e.g., selection, licensing, implementation) and include expenses that occur after the system is up and running but are necessary to maintain it in operation over its life span. These include ongoing training of users and support personnel, maintenance, upgrades, security, and business continuity investments. Even the end-of-life costs associated with retiring the asset should be included in TCO calculations.

TCO is an imprecise measure that depends on substantial estimation and assumptions about feasible configurations and future events. Nonetheless, it is essential to estimate TCO as comprehensively as possible when making funding and budgeting decisions. Today there is commercial software that can be used to aid in TCO computations (Figure 10.1).

Business Case

The business case is a formal document, prepared and presented by the general or functional manager sponsoring the project. It provides the rationale for pursuing the opportunity. Its primary objective is to explain and provide evidence to convince the executive team, typically during the budgeting process, that the initiative will pay off and its funding is warranted. Note that a firm will not only require a business case to be developed for new systems, but often the business case will be used to evaluate ongoing spending decisions and to evaluate existing systems.

CIOview | TCOnow! SNAPSHOT

Windows vs. Linux
Cost Savings: $1,048,751 | Users: 1000
Strategy: File and Print Consolidation

TOTAL COST OF OWNERSHIP OVER 3 YEARS

Windows Server 2003 Savings	Red Hat Linux	Windows Server 2003	Key Savings
Total: $1,048,751	Total: $1,606,671	Total: $557,920	In your Windows and Linux analysis, you stand to realize the greatest cost savings in the Personnel category. This savings of $465,424 is a result of managing fewer Windows/Intel servers that each handle more of your overall processing load. Additionally, you stand to save $170,687 in Support costs. This is primarily due to lower Windows Server 2003 operating system support needs giving you lower costs of $3,767 in year 1, and $5,213 in the final year of your analysis.

Servers ($23,912)
Software ($131,020)
Storage ($168,540)
Network ($14,070)
Services (–$16,336)
Facilities ($18,671)
Training ($108,196)
Personnel ($465,424)
Downtime (–$35,434)
Support ($170,687)

Acquisition: $.43 m
Ongoing: $.62 m

Red Hat Linux — TCA Acquisition $.71 m / ACO Ongoing $.89 m
Windows Server 2003 — TCA Acquisition $.28 m / ACO Ongoing $.27 m

RESULTS SUMMARY

Category	Red Hat Linux	Windows Server 2003	Assumptions
Consolidation Strategy	Single workload consolidation	Single workload consolidation	Failover cluster, scale up over time
Existing Servers	0	0	Purchase new hardware
New Production Servers or IFLs	22	2	Linux: 22 images Windows Server 2003: 2 images
New Non-Production Servers or Virtual Machines	1	0	Linux: 1 image Windows Server 2003: 0 images
Storage Cost $ /MB	$0.54	$0.21	500GB RAIDS in a Fibre Channel SAN
IT Staff (FTEs)	1.80	0.4	Linux: 12.8 images/FTE Windows Server 2003: 5 images/FTE
System Availability	99.992%	99.994%	9x5 hours of operations $1,568 per minute of downtime

Figure 10.1   TCO Computation for an Operating System Migration Project

Typical business cases require fact-based investment analyses grounded in financial indicators such as internal rate of return (IRR), return on investment (ROI), or net present value (NPV). They require an analysis of the timeline of the project and its future cash flow stream, and supporting evidence for project benefits and costs estimates. In order to provide these analyses, project proponents must make assumptions and arbitrary judgments (Figure 10.2).

Limitations of the Business Case   The traditional business case technique is increasingly receiving criticism. The skeptics suggest that business cases strictly based on fact will often require so many assumptions and speculations that they will become based on fiction. This problem is less likely with automation initiatives, but it is particularly evident for projects that rely on business or technical innovation. Financial projections are also difficult to make for projects that have mostly "soft" benefits.

The limitations of a traditional business case approach are clearly exemplified by the president of a large hotel chain explaining how his firm justified a recent customer relationship management project: "You can't justify such a project with traditional methods. There is too much uncertainty beforehand. You know this is the right project because it fits with your strategic positioning and brand. This is how we are going to differentiate our product in the marketplace."

In order to overcome the limitations of a traditional business case, some observers point to the value of heuristics. A heuristics is a simple rule that is good enough to make decisions, recognizing that adjustments along the way will be necessary. This approach offers another advantage: It systematizes the reevaluation of both the costs and benefits of projects during their development.

Another valuable approach consists of relaxing the focus on fact-based business cases and allowing proponents of a project to ground their request on faith (i.e., project rationale based on beliefs about market trends, customer expectations, competition, strategy, etc.) and fear (i.e., need to engage in projects to keep from falling behind the competition or to avert a likely negative outcome). Typically a well-crafted business case will include all of the above: fact, faith, and fear-based arguments.

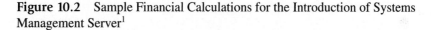

Figure 10.2 Sample Financial Calculations for the Introduction of Systems Management Server[1]

Steering Committee

Larger organizations often formalize management involvement in information systems decision making by forming a steering committee. The steering committee brings together representatives from the various functional areas, the CEO (or other general management staff), and key IS professionals (e.g., CIO) who convene regularly to provide guidance to the IS function and share the responsibility for aligning its efforts with business strategy. The steering committee is typically the venue where business cases are presented for approval or as a filter before the budgeting process.

FUNDING INFORMATION SYSTEMS

As with any other organizational asset, the firm must account for and fund information systems assets and expenses. Information systems are typically designed, built, implemented, and managed to achieve some business goal (e.g., improve factory floor efficiencies, increase

[1] A systems management server is a software program designed to aid IT specialists in managing software updates, patches, and configuration of applications in a business environment.

sales effectiveness and customer repurchase). The exception is provided by shared services (e.g., security, planning and administration, business continuity initiatives) and infrastructure investments. There are three main methods used by modern organizations to fund information systems: chargeback, allocation, and overhead. Each one offers advantages and disadvantages.

Chargeback

The chargeback approach calls for direct billing of information systems resources and services to the organizational function or department that uses them. It is grounded in the pay-per-use principle. For example, a department may be charged for networking expenses based on the volume of traffic it initiates, and for personal productivity software based on the number of concurrent software applications licenses it runs.

The main advantage of chargeback mechanisms is their perceived fairness and the accountability they create for both users and the IS function. Another advantage of such systems is the degree of control they afford to general and functional managers, who can proactively control their function's information systems expenses. However, maintaining such detailed costing mechanisms can generate substantial direct and indirect expenses, including the cost of the tracking mechanisms and those for auditing and dispute resolution of charges.

Chargeback systems typically treat the IS function as a cost center. That is, the units are billed on the basis of actual costs. In some occasions, particularly when the IS function has some unique skills, it may become a profit center and compete for service provision with external vendors. In rare cases it may also sell its services to other firms, not only to internal users, and return the profits to the organization.

Allocation

The allocation approach calls for direct billing of information systems resources and services to the organizational function or department that uses them. However, rather than a pay-per-use metric, it computes allocations based on more stable indicators such as size, revenues, and number of users. For example, a hotel chain may charge properties on the basis of the number of rooms. A chain of retail outlets may charge each unit a fixed percentage of revenue or square footage.

The allocation method seeks to strike a balance between the pay-per-use fairness and the high cost of the chargeback method. Since rates are typically set once a year, the expenses each unit can expect are also more predictable. Some functional managers prefer the predictability of fixed allocations, while others prefer the higher degree of control offered by the chargeback mechanism.

Overhead

The overhead approach treats information systems as a shared expense to be drawn from the organization's overall budget rather than to be paid for by each unit. This is the simplest approach to funding information systems since decisions are made once a year during the budget approval process. It also provides the most control to the IS function over spending decisions. As a consequence, the IS function is more likely to experiment and evaluate new technologies.

The main drawback of the overhead approach is lack of accountability for both the functional areas and the IS department. On the one hand, since users are not billed directly, they are less likely to proactively manage their usage and filter their requests for service and new projects. Moreover, they remain largely unaware of their impact on the overall IS budget, which often leads to misconceptions about the cost of IT resources and the reasonable expectations for service. On the other hand, since the IS function has little accountability to the individual functional areas, it is more likely to be less responsive and offer poorer service.

THE BUDGETING AND PROJECT PRIORITIZATION PROCESS

The yearly budgeting process is a tool organizations use to plan and control. As a planning tool, the budget provides an assessment of what the firm believes future financial flows will be. As a control mechanism, the budget helps encourage and enforce specific behaviors. More subtly, the budget can be used to allocate decision rights and power. In recent years, operational IT budget have hovered around 2 percent of revenue for a large cross section of firms surveyed by Computer Economics (Figure 10.3).[2]

For example, in an organization where the information systems function controls the bulk of the IT budget, decisions regarding the use of the resource will be highly centralized. In this case the information systems group will be able to identify and create efficiencies, but users will enjoy limited flexibility. Conversely, if much of the IT budget is controlled by individuals units, they will be able to fund tailored initiatives, but integration and firmwide efficiencies are left without a strong sponsor.

Typically control over the IT budget is split, with a portion allocated to the information systems function for infrastructural expenses and projects that enable the business to operate in a reliable and secure manner (e.g., disaster recovery planning, business continuity initiatives, information systems security management). The remainder is controlled by the individual units, for funding operations of existing systems and for funding new projects (Side bar 1).

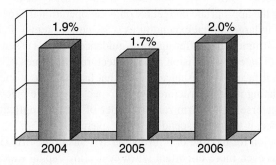

Figure 10.3 Operational IT Budget Trends. (*Source:* Computer Economics)

---

[2] http://www.infoedge.com/cei/iss/infocenter_main.asp

SIDEBAR 1: SAMPLE OPERATIONAL IT BUDGET

This sample operational IT budget is loosely based on that of a major hotel chain.

Expenses	*Amount (U.S. dollars)*	*Percentage*
Payroll	3,140,000	31.4
Travel & entertainment	270,000	2.7
Depreciation[1]	450,000	4.5
Amortization[2]	1,080,000	10.8
Training	30,000	0.3
Equipment/hardware/software purchases[3]	90,000	0.9
Maintenance	680,000	6.8
Telecommunications expense	520,000	5.2
Disaster recovery	10,000	0.1
Misc. other operating expense	180,000	1.8
Corporate IT allocation[4]	3,530,000	35.3

[1] Capitalized equipment is subject to depreciation.

[2] Capitalized software is subject to amortization.

[3] Equipment below the capitalization threshold.

[4] IT allocation from the parent company. For firms without a parent company, this line would spread over the other items in roughly the same percentages.

Making the Budget

The budgeting process requires trade-offs between diverging interests and the prioritization of projects under resource constraint. This can make a very stressful process within which executives must argue and rally support for their initiatives, all the while attempting to ensure that information systems resources are deployed to meet the strategic demands of the business.

The budgeting process varies by organization, but there are typically two decisions to be made: determining the appropriate budget for ongoing operational expenses (e.g., maintenance) and evaluating large capital expenditures (e.g., new systems). Published industry benchmarks can be instrumental in offering some guidance, but it is essential to stress that your firm's budget is dictated by its vision and architectural guidelines (Chapter 6) and the unique contingencies it faces. For instance, a firm that has been very successful in rationalizing and consolidating its infrastructure can be expected to have below-average ongoing IT expenses. Conversely, if a firm ran a number of legacy applications in need of substantial maintenance, it would be spending above average.

A sound appreciation for the role of information systems in the firm (i.e., the information systems vision) is even more important when evaluating capital expenditure and new information systems projects. This is critical not so much for the evaluation of individual initiatives, but for the evaluation of the aggregate degree of information systems risk the firm is willing to accept.

Individual Project Risk

The budgeting process, with its yearly review of the firm's information systems priorities, expenses, and risk, affords the opportunity to evaluate information systems resources as a whole. This is an important assessment, particularly when measuring the overall risk of the systems under development and the cost/benefits they are expected to deliver. Information systems projects are renowned for their high degrees of risk and incidence of failure. However, the risks associated with any one particular initiative can vary widely based on the following:

- *Project size.* Project size, expressed as the estimated monetary investment, is a proxy for project complexity and the potential consequences of failure. Note that you should focus less on the absolute size of the project (e.g., $12 million) than its size relative to the typical kind of project the information systems group in your firm undertakes. In other words, a $12 million initiative carries different risk for a firm that typically handles $20 million projects than one that is mostly familiar with $150,000 efforts.

- *Experience with technology.* The degree of experience a firm has with the technologies (e.g., hardware, development environment) at the heart of the project is a primary determinate of risk. Working with new and unproven technologies carries more risk than using mature ones. However, the relative novelty of the technology for the firm is also an important source of risk.

- *Organizational change.* The degree of organizational change that the project requires is another important determinant of risk. As we discussed in Chapter 2, third-order change is much more difficult (and risky) to implement than second- and first-order change.

With respect to the cost/benefits that a system is expected to deliver, different initiatives vary significantly with respect to the size of the investment they call for and the expected useful life over which they will deliver the benefits. A large enterprise system will require a significant up-front investment but will deliver its benefits over decades. Conversely, a redesign of the company Web site will typically require a fraction of the investment but will also obsolesce much more quickly.

A portfolio approach can be used to optimize the blend of projects under development and ensure a balance of the overall risk as well as proactively manage the cost/benefits of the applications under development.

Portfolio Management

After evaluating the risk of each proposed project, management should take a portfolio approach to information systems risk management. That is, during the budgeting process, when the firm evaluates the collection of initiatives for the coming year, it should determine the appropriate level of aggregate risks it should accept. Note that this evaluation is a managerial decision, not an IT decision. While information systems professionals must help in evaluating project risk, it is the responsibility of the steering committee or the board of directors to decide what overall degree of risk the firm should accept given its overall strategic information systems plan.

A portfolio approach to managing information systems risk ensures that the funded initiatives fit the risk profile the firm has deemed appropriate. For instance, firms in the strategic quadrant (Chapter 6) typically need to take on much higher aggregate risk than those in the support quadrant. This is due to the fact that in the first case information systems assets and initiatives are instrumental to the success and growth of the firm. The same cannot be said for those organizations that choose a very defensive approach to information systems use and management (e.g., support quadrant). In such a case, a high degree of aggregate portfolio risk is a signal that the firm is not managing information systems in accord with its strategic information systems plan. It may be that the organization needs to reevaluate and update its information systems vision, perhaps moving into the turnaround quadrant. However, it may be that the firm is failing to take advantage of the budgeting and prioritization process to enforce the existing (and appropriate) plan.

OUTSOURCING

Information systems outsourcing is often used as a means of funding information systems operations by engaging outside providers. Outsourcing is the process of acquiring products or services that used to be produced inside the organization from an outside provider. More specifically, information systems outsourcing is the process of contracting with an outside firm to obtain information systems services. Such services can range from automation of specific processes (e.g., payroll), to management of specific assets (e.g., data center), to development of new applications, to outright management of the IS function as a whole (i.e., full outsourcing). Outsourcing of information systems services is now estimated to be a $284.9 billion industry, as measured by worldwide spending.[3]

Drivers of outsourcing

Outsourcing information systems and IT to a specialist the outsourcing firm is typically driven by one or more of the following objectives:

Reduce Cost   Perhaps the primary driver for the outsourcing decision is the intention to capitalize on the provider's ability to create economies of scale in the production of IT services. Large providers of information systems services can consolidate their infrastructure (e.g., data centers) and enjoy superior bargaining power when dealing with technology vendors (e.g., hardware and software firms).

Access to Superior Talent   Many organizations find it difficult to attract top IT talent. The reason is simple: Top IT graduates want to be challenged and want to remain on the cutting edge of technological development. But many organizations cannot (and should not!) make this objective a priority. Conversely, IT service providers are in the business of continually seeking to improve their information systems operations, evaluate new technologies, and attract the best talent.

Because of these structural differences, outsourcing contracts offer the opportunity for organizations to access top IT talent and receive an infusion of technology and information systems management expertise.

Improve Control   In many organizations that resort to outsourcing, particularly full outsourcing, the driving force for the decision was an attempt to reclaim control over the IT

---

[3] Cathers, D. (2006), "Industry Surveys. Computers: Commercial Services," *Standard & Poor*'s *Industry Surveys,* May 4.

function when it was perceived to be inefficient and unable to provide the appropriate level of service to the organization. By engaging in a contractual arrangement with an outside provider, the theory goes, the firm can surface costs, making them explicit, and hold the provider to its service level agreements.

Improve Strategic Focus   For many organizations information systems operations are considered (rightly or wrongly) a nuisance rather than a core strength of the firm. For these organizations outsourcing has considerable appeal because it enables the firm to focus on what it considers its strengths and eliminate what is often a little understood function that generates significant frustration for senior management.

Financial Appeal   Outsourcing arrangements where the service provider acquires the infrastructure and IT professionals of the outsourcing organization liquidate some of the tangible and intangible assets tied up in the IT infrastructure. As such, these deals can strengthen the balance sheet and have considerable financial appeal.

The Risks of Outsourcing

While the drivers of outsourcing described above provide a strong case for the decision, the outsourcing literature and history have provided many examples of outsourcing deals gone bad. The following are the major potential drawbacks that must be carefully evaluated before taking the plunge:

The Outsourcing Paradox   Organizations that resort to information systems outsourcing often do so out of frustration with their current IT operations. Yet if you have little faith in your ability to manage information systems internally, how can you expect to be able to make sound outsourcing decisions (i.e., draft advantageous contracts) and monitor the performance of the service provider? How can you determine the appropriate amount to pay for the services and the service levels you should expect? How do you know that you are getting what you paid for?

The Dark Side of Partnerships   The word *partnership,* when used in a business context in particular, can be very misleading. While the outsourcing firm and the service provider are "partners," as they work together to ensure the success of the operation, each has a responsibility to shareholders to maximize its performance. This sometimes leads to friction and court battles. Imagine, for example, a service provider that is under pressure to cut costs and increase profitably. This result can be achieved by reducing customer service, particularly in areas where service levels are difficult to measure, hard to monitor, have no penalties attached, or have not been clearly specified in the contract.

Changing Requirements   One of the primary dangers in an outsourcing relationship is given by the length of the contracts in relation to the speed of technological and business needs evolution. For example, a ten-year contract will see significant change in organizational requirements before it is up for renewal. Yet outsourcing contracts are often very lengthy and specific in order to limit the possibility of self-interested behavior (e.g., service degradation).

Hidden Coordination Costs   One of the biggest surprises awaiting organizations that outsource information systems is the extent of coordination efforts needed to work with the provider. Coordination efforts include communicating requirements, monitoring and measuring the provider's activities and services, handling dispute resolution, and the like. These coordination efforts come at a cost of course, a cost that must be estimated beforehand and used in the decision-making phase.

The Deceptive Role of Information Systems   While many organizations outsource on the contention that they are not in the "IT business" or that "IT is not a core competency" for the firm, a lot of organizations underestimate the critical role that information systems play as enablers of business success.

Offshoring

Outsourcing has received substantial recent attention in the United States because of the prominence of the debate over loss of jobs to foreign countries allegedly brought about by one of its variants: offshoring. Offshoring, short for offshore outsourcing, is the process of engaging a foreign provider to supply the products or services the firm no longer intend to produce internally.

Offshoring has received much impetus after the commercialization of the Internet, which significantly lessened the impact of geographical and time differences on the transaction of information-based services (e.g., software design and development). Offshoring growth has been fueled by many of the same drivers of outsourcing, particularly cost and quality, with much of the business moving to India and China—countries that enjoy a significantly lower cost of living than the United States and offer a seemingly endless pool of highly qualified IT talent.

Making Optimal Outsourcing Decisions

As with any other complex and far-reaching managerial decision, there are no silver bullet solutions when it comes to outsourcing. The outsourcing decision requires a clear understanding of the characteristics of the organizing and of the relationship with the service provider—a debate that general and functional managers must be involved in.

The strategic grid (see Chapter 6) can provide helpful guidance by mapping the current and future role that information systems are expected to play in the firm. Typically, firms that find themselves in the support and factory quadrant may find it easier to outsource given the standardized and well-understood role played by information systems resources. More difficult is the decision for firms in the turnaround and strategic quadrants. Here, due to the critical role that information system assets must play in enabling the firm's strategy, outsourcing may be both challenging and risky. In this case, particularly for firms with limited access to new technologies or superior IT talent, outsourcing may be the only viable solution. However, these firms will typically provide critical information systems services in house.

In most cases a firm should not resort to full outsourcing, locking itself into one provider, but should rely on selective outsourcing arrangements. Selective outsourcing arrangements are those where the firm relies on multiple providers offering different services. In such arrangements the firm often retains an internal information system group and enables it to compete for the contract against outside service firms.

Perhaps the clearest advice that can be offered to firms considering outsourcing is to maintain a core group of information systems specialists and a strong CIO function: first, have the in-house expertise to match the organization's business needs to the appropriate information systems services—whether these services are provided in-house or not—is fundamental. Second, it is critical to have a group of internal employees, with their allegiance to your firm, who understand what the service firms are providing and how best to manage the relationship.

SUMMARY

This chapter begins our discussion of the techniques and methodologies modern organizations use to introduce and manage information systems within the framework provided by the strategic information systems plan. As a general or functional manager, you must understand this process in order to fund initiatives of interest to your area and to partake in the overall budgeting and prioritization process in partnership with other executives and information systems professionals.

Specifically, in this chapter we learned that

- Total cost of ownership (TCO) is a financial estimate designed to explicitly recognize the life cycle cost of IT assets. The costs of information systems and technology typically far exceeds the cost of acquisition (e.g., selection, licensing, implementation) and include expenses that occur after the system is up and running but are necessary to maintain it in operation over its life span.

- Project sponsors use TCO in the formulation of the business case. The business case is the formal documentation used to garner support and win funding for the initiative. The project sponsor presents the business case to the executive committee or, in larger organizations, to the steering committee. The steering committee, comprised of representatives from the various functional areas and IS professionals, provides guidance for the use of information systems assets and shares the responsibility for aligning IS efforts with business strategy.

- Modern organizations use one of three approaches to the funding of information systems operations and projects: chargeback, allocation, and overhead. The chargeback method, requiring direct billing based on actual usage, gives the most control to users but has the highest administrative costs. The allocation method, requiring direct billing based on measures such as size or revenue, seeks to strike a balance between fair billing and administrative overhead. Finally, the overhead method, drawing funding directly from the overall organization's budget, is the simplest to administer but reduces accountability of both the IS function and units using the services.

- The yearly budgeting process is the tool organizations use to assess future information systems requirements and prioritize funding. The budgeting process enables the firm to encourage and enforce specific behaviors and to allocate information systems decision rights and control. It can be a fairly stressful and emotionally charged process in which managers compete for funding of their projects.

- During the budgeting process the firm has an opportunity to evaluate the risk of proposed projects, both individually and as a portfolio. The firm must take this opportunity to evaluate whether the degree of risk associated with its current portfolio of projects matches the risk profile the firm deemed appropriate during strategic information systems planning.

- Information systems outsourcing is the process of contracting with an outside firm to obtain information systems services. Modern organizations outsource their complete IS function (i.e., full outsourcing) or some of their IS assets and services (i.e., selective outsourcing) seeking one or more of the following benefits: reduce costs, gain access to superior information systems talent, improve control over IS resources, free resources to focus on core competencies, and liquidate IT assets. When evaluating outsourcing of information systems services, you need to consider the following risks: A firm with admittedly poor IS management will have difficulties evaluating providers and negotiating good contracts; outsourcing partners seek to maximize their own performance, which often creates friction; IS requirements evolve rapidly; and information systems operations are often more strategic than executives realize.

STUDY QUESTIONS

1. Describe the relationship between strategic information systems planning and the yearly budgeting and prioritization processes. What is the objective of each?

2. Why should general and functional managers be involved in decisions about the funding of information systems assets and services?

3. What is a business case? What is its purpose? Who should be developing and presenting the business case for a new information system?

4. Define the following terms: *total cost of ownership* (TCO) and *steering committee.*

5. Describe each of the three main information systems funding methods and discuss the advantages and disadvantages of each.

6. What are the key drivers of new information systems project risk? Why should a firm evaluate the aggregate risk of its portfolio of projects? What should the organization do if the current level of portfolio risk is not aligned with the degree of risk deemed appropriate according to the strategic information systems plan?

7. Define and differentiate the following terms: *Outsourcing, information systems outsourcing, offshoring, full outsourcing,* and *selective outsourcing.* What are the principal drivers and risks associated with information systems outsourcing?

FURTHER READINGS

1. Huff, S. L., Maher, P. M., and Munro, M. C. (2006). "Information Technology and the Board of Directors: Is There an IT Attention Deficit?" *MIS Quarterly Executive* (5:2), 1–14.

2. Lacity, M., Willcocks, L., and Feeny, D. (1996). "The Value of Selective IT Sourcing." *Sloan Management Review,* Spring, vol. 37, no. 3, pp. 13–25.

3. Lacity, M., Willcocks, L., and Feeny, D. (1995). "Information Technology Outsourcing: Maximizing Flexibility and Control." *Harvard Business Review* (May–June), vol. 65, pp. 84–93.

4. McFarlan, F. W. (1981). "Portfolio Approach to Information Systems." *Harvard Business Review* (September–October), vol. 51, pp. 142–150.

5. McFarlan, F. W., and Nolan, R. L. (1995). "How to Manage an IT Outsourcing Alliance." *Sloan Management Review* 36, no. 2 (winter), pp. 9–24.

6. Nolan, R., and McFarlan, F. W. (2005). "Information Technology and the Board of Directors." *Harvard Business Review,* vol. 83, no. 10 (October), pp. 96–106.

7. Ross, J. W., and Weill, P. (2002). "Six IT Decisions Your IT People Shouldn't Make." *Harvard Business Review,* November vol. 80, pp. 84–92.

8. Rottman, J., and Lacity, M. (2004). "Twenty Practices for Offshore Sourcing." *MIS Quarterly Executive,* vol. 3, no. 3, pp. 117–130.

GLOSSARY

- **Allocation:** A method of funding information systems where the cost of services is billed to the organizational function that uses them based on some stable metric (e.g., size, revenues, number of users).

- **Business case:** A formal document, prepared and presented by the general or functional manager sponsoring the project. It provides the rationale for pursuing the opportunity.

- **Chargeback:** A method of funding information systems where the cost of services is billed to the organizational function that uses them based on actual usage.

- **Chief information officer (CIO):** The individual in charge of the information systems function.

- **Information systems outsourcing:** The process of contracting with an outside firm to obtain information systems services.

- **Offshoring:** Offshoring, short for offshore outsourcing, is the process of engaging a foreign provider to supply the products or services the firm no longer intends to produce internally.

- **Overhead:** A method of funding information systems where the cost of services is not billed to the organizational function that uses them. Rather information systems assets and services are funded directly from the organization's overall budget.

■ **Steering committee:** The steering committee, comprised of representatives from the various functional areas and IS professionals, provides guidance for the use of information systems assets and shares the responsibility for aligning IS efforts with business strategy.

■ **Total cost of ownership (TCO):** A financial estimate designed to explicitly recognize the life cycle cost of IT assets.

C H A P T E R

11

Creating Information Systems

What You Will Learn in This Chapter

This chapter covers a very important subject: the process by which organizational information systems come to be. While as a general or functional manager you may not concern yourself with hardware decisions, you must partake in the software design, acquisition, and implementation processes. Your involvement is essential because technology professionals rarely can evaluate the cost/benefit trade-off and impact of new information systems on the organization and its business success drivers.

Specifically, in this chapter you will learn

1. To appreciate how complex it is to design and implement information systems and the stable, robust, secure technology at their core.

2. To articulate the advantages and disadvantages of custom software design and development versus acquisition of an off-the-shelf product.

3. To describe and be able to use the main methodologies for custom software design and development. Specifically, you will be able to identify the major phases of the system development life cycle (SDLC) and discuss its advantages and disadvantages. You will also become familiar with the prototyping approach and will be able to identify its principal advantages and disadvantages.

4. To describe the systems selection methodology and be able to use it to choose a prepackaged software program for a specific organization.

5. To describe the reasons for the increasing prominence of end-user development in modern organizations and to articulate the benefits and risks of this approach to software development.

MINI-CASE: PROJECT MANAGEMENT BLUES

"What am I going to do now?" you found yourself asking out loud while staring at the ceiling in your office. "Should I de-escalate this project or press on?" It felt like you were in one of those management case studies—except that it was real and it was you!

You replayed the events leading up to this dilemma. It all started when you were appointed the lead of the HRBPS team—the project team in charge of creating the new human resources benefits package management system. You had made a very successful business case presentation and received public praise from the executive team. "Finally someone who does not speak techno-mumbo-jumbo but can present an IT project in business terms!" had exclaimed Margaret Weston, the CEO. It had been your ability to interface with both the developers and the business stakeholders that had landed you the project manager position. You were the first project manager in your firm to come from a functional area (human resources) instead of the information systems function.

The project had proceeded very well with great support from the user community—your former colleagues, of course. This was due in large part to your knowledge of HR and your stakeholder-friendly approach. You had made a conscious choice to seek user feedback and honor as many requests for enhancements as possible. "You have to freeze the requirements" had objected Erik Dinos, the lead system analyst, "otherwise it is going to be anarchy." But you had dismissed his complaints as "development team grumblings." Those guys were never happy with a little uncertainty anyway. Having been on "the other side," as a stakeholder in a number of system development projects, you knew full well that unhappy users were the fastest route to system failure.

Now you were beginning to second-guess your decision. The original schedule called for releasing the beta version of the application for user testing later this week. Instead you had only 40 percent of the approved functionality coded. Moreover, your team was looking at a list of twenty-two enhancements, two of which would require a change in the database structure that the users had identified as valuable. Projected completion, without the proposed enhancements, entailed seven more months (a 45 percent increase on the original).

It was now apparent that the original project had also been underfunded in the original budget. The current estimate for finishing the project with the approved set of requirements called for a 62 percent budget increase (over the original). It was unclear how much more it would cost to exceed the requirements since the twenty-two proposed enhancements had yet to be evaluated by the system architect.

You were due to present a progress report to Ms. Weston tomorrow afternoon, but you were still unsure about what course to take. The only certainty at this point was that you had to make your pitch for a project extension and ask for further funding at the meeting. Your plan was to report on the current state of affairs, paint a picture of the final product, and seek support. But what was the final product going to be?

DISCUSSION QUESTIONS

1. What should your agenda for tomorrow's meeting be? Should you press on with your strategy, or is a change of course in order?
2. What would you do differently, if anything, given the chance to start this project all over again?

◼ INTRODUCTION

Once a firm has developed a strategic plan for the use of information systems resources (Chapter 6) and has gone through the budgeting and prioritization processes (Chapter 10) to identify what specific information systems it needs, it is ready to act. Whether the information systems rely on custom-developed technology or off-the-shelf software, it is critical that you as a general or functional manager understand how information systems come to be. Armed with this knowledge, you can proactively participate in the process.

While general and functional managers need not be concerned with hardware decisions, they must take part in the software design, acquisition, and implementation processes.

Aside from the significant portion of your budget devoted to information systems management and development, general and functional mangers' involvement in information systems funding and design is essential because never before has a firm's success depended so much on the use of the right applications. Deciding what the characteristics of the "right" application are is a business decision. It is a decision based more on cost/benefit analysis and the understanding of the business processes the software will enable (or constrain!) than on technical considerations.

How Hard Can IT Be?

Consider the following three recent examples, each playing out in the last few years, and answer the question (write your answers on a separate sheet) before reading on to find out what really happened:

- The U.S. subsidiary of one of the major food producers in the world inked a deal to implement SAP (the leading enterprise system application), in an effort to centralize and rationalize operations across its nine divisions. The project required streamlining process, standardizing software applications, and implementing the same organizational structure across the units. How much time and how much money would you budget for this project?

- A large hospitality company with over 2000 units developed a customer information system to enable its customer relationship management (CRM) strategy. The custom-developed functionalities of the software application at the heart of the information system included a property-management system, the loyalty and CRM applications, and the reporting modules. How much time and how much money would you budget for this project?

- A major telecommunication carrier scheduled an upgrade of its customer service systems from version 6 to version 7 of a leading off-the-shelf application. The newer, more powerful version, exchanging information with fifteen other systems (e.g., billing), would simplify customer service representatives' access to customer data and would increase the amount of customer information available for sales and service transactions. How much time and how much money would you budget for this project?

There are few technologies and products that have evolved as far and as fast as information technology has. However, the astounding successes of IT can be misleading, tricking you into severely underestimating what it takes to build and implement a stable, robust, secure system that must work under a wide array of organizational conditions.

Should you check your answers one last time before reading on? OK, here's what happened:

- The implementation of SAP by the major food service company took over six years and over $200 million. It was mired by setbacks and dead ends, with high-profile casualties, including the project leader, who was reassigned midway through the implementation.

- The large hospitality firm invested over $50 million in the design and development of the application and in integrating it with the other applications in the firm's infrastructure. The project took about two years. The resulting system, the firm's largest investment in recent history, was considered a success.

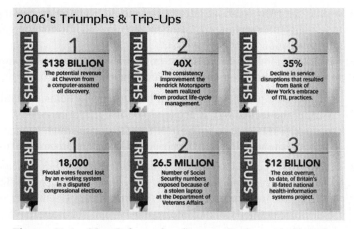

Figure 11.1 New Information Systems Projects are Complex and Risky Undertakings

- The upgrade at the telecommunication company was a complete failure. The new system was unstable, crashing for days at a time, and the old system was no longer usable. The customer service difficulties translated in an estimated $100 million in lost revenue during the three months it took to complete the upgrade. A rival acquired the firm, which was mired in difficulties, for half its original valuation.

The critical insight from this simple exercise is that organizational information systems usher in a wealth of complexities that go far beyond those associated with the personal computing environment most familiar to the typical end user (i.e., purchasing and installing Microsoft Office) (Figure 11.1). Unfortunately, managers are surrounded by the misleading rhetoric of statements like "IT is easy, the hard part is people." Or "today firms can easily develop or purchase technology to obtain the capabilities to rapidly match their competitors." Or "IT is a commodity."

These views are gross oversimplifications of reality. When they are held by those who have never been involved in large-scale information systems development efforts, they dangerously hide the truth: Organizational information systems development efforts are very complex and risky endeavors. They are complex and risky precisely because they involve both technical and social challenges—and the intersection of the two.

The interplay of many different actors (often with divergent agendas), the sheer size of many organizational systems, and the myriad of expected and unforeseen organizational conditions the system must support and the constantly evolving nature of the modern firm make these projects some of the most challenging that modern organizations face. These projects require technical expertise. They also call for a big dose of managerial skill and informed involvement by general and functional managers.

FULFILLING INFORMATION PROCESSING NEEDS

In Chapter 2, we stated that the primary reason why modern organizations introduce information systems is to fulfill their information processing needs. Information systems leverage IT at their core to optimize the manner in which the firm captures, processes, stores, and distributes information.

How does the firm go about introducing the information processing functionalities needed to fulfill its information processing needs? How do information systems come to be in modern organizations?

At the most general level of analysis, this process has two main components: technology development and information system development.

- *Technology development.* Modern information systems are built on an IT core. Whether the technology is acquired and integrated into the existing firm's infrastructure or it is custom built by (or for) the organization, generating the IT core is a prerequisite to delivering the needed information processing functionalities.

- *Information system development.* Creating the needed IT core is not sufficient to fulfill the information processing needs of the firm (see Chapter 2). The firm must successfully integrate the technology with the other components (i.e., people, processes, structure) to develop working information system. This is the implementation process.

The technology development and implementation processes are intertwined, not sequential. Because of systemic effects (Chapter 2), the components of an information system must interact with one another without friction. Thus, the design of a new software program (i.e., technology development) must take into account how the technology will be employed (i.e., processes), by whom (i.e., people), and with what purpose (i.e., structure).That is, technology development must take into account future implementation as it is being designed.

Three Approaches

There are three general approaches to the acquisition of information processing functionalities and the introduction of IT-based information systems. Note that each of these approaches encompasses both the technology development and implementation processes. However, the critical differences among them pertain to how the technology components, and more specifically the software that defines the capabilities of the system, are designed and developed.

1. *Custom design and development.* With this approach the organization implements a software application that is expressly made, whether internally or through outsourcing, for the unique needs of the firm.
2. *System selection and acquisition.* With this approach the organization implements an off-the-shelf software application that is mass produced by a vendor.
3. *End-user development.* With this approach the organization uses a software application created by its end users, rather than the firm's information systems professionals.

We describe the advantages and risks associated with each approach. We also introduce the most prevalent methodologies used to articulate the information systems design and development process in each case. Our objective here is not for you to become an expert in systems design and development. Rather, it is to help you nurture an understanding of the process so that you can successfully take part in it.

Make versus Buy

In some cases custom developing the software at the heart of a new information system is not an option for your firm, it is a necessity. This is the case when the system must enable a new initiative and no market for such products already exists. For example, when Amazon first introduced its personal recommendation system (Figure 11.2), electronic commerce was largely uncharted territory and the firm was indeed shaping the online retailing industry. Waiting for an off-the-shelf product to be developed was not an option.

Typically, though, the firm will have to weigh the choice between custom development and purchase of the needed technology. Each approach offers some advantages and disadvantages.

Advantages of Custom Development   While pre-packaged software is available in the marketplace, in many cases the firm will still engage in custom design and development to capitalize on the advantages of this process. Such advantages include the following:

Unique Tailoring   The defining characteristic of custom-developed software applications is that they are molded to fit the unique features of the firm that commissions them. A quote by Bill Bass, former senior vice president for eCommerce at Lands' End, provides an apt metaphor: "Fitting 100 some million women in the U.S. in 8 or 10 basic sizes as well as they would like is really impossible."[1] When we purchase clothes in standard sizes, they often fit well in one area and less well in another. Typically we accept this substandard fit. Yet those who find it hard to find fitting clothes (and can afford it) can purchase tailor-made garments—perhaps using the Lands' End Custom Web site.

The human body is unique, no two people are alike, and the same holds true for modern organizations. Thus, off-the-shelf software will "fit" well in some areas of the firm but may create problems in others and require some adjustment from the organization.[2] Conversely, custom-made software, like a tailor-made suit, can be designed to fit perfectly with the organization's characteristics and needs.

Figure 11.2   Amazon.com's Personal Recommendations

---

[1] Ives, B., and Piccoli, G. (2003), "Custom Made Apparel and Individualized Service at Lands' End," *Communications of the AIS* (vol.11, article 3) pp. 79–93.

[2] As we will see, this adjustment of the organization typically takes place during implementation when, taken the software as given, a working information system is developed.

Figure 11.3   Axigen Mail Server Software

Note that while every organization is unique, not all its processes are. For example, while Lands' End and Eddie Bauer are two different organizations, they both provide e-mail for their employees and do so in very similar fashion. Standard mail server software will likely serve the needs of both firms quite well (Figure 11.3). Conversely, if the business processes that the software is designed to enable are unique and value adding (i.e., a source of competitive advantage), commercial off-the-shelf software may undermine their uniqueness and be detrimental to the firm.

Flexibility and Control   Custom-developed software applications offer the highest degree of flexibility and control to the organization. Because the project team builds the system from scratch, the software can be molded into any form the stakeholders (e.g., management, end users) would like it to take and the firm owes no licensing fees to software vendors. Moreover, since the firm retains control over the code, the system can be evolved, at any time, in any direction the firm would like.

This level of control is not achievable with software purchased from vendors, since software houses need to develop applications that serve the needs of a large number of buyers. Moreover, the software house has to prioritize the features that will be coded into the upgrades. Typically they are the ones that have the broadest appeal, rather than niche request from individual clients.

Advantages of Purchasing   As the software industry has evolved and grown dramatically over the last twenty years, the off-the-shelf offer has become comprehensive. Purchasing software from a vendor yields a number of advantages to the organization.

Faster Roll-Out   An organization that purchases new software is typically interested in the information processing functionalities it enables, not in the IT itself. Thus, how quickly the firm can be "up and running" with the new information system is an important concern. Purchased software dramatically reduces the time it takes to obtain the software and begin the implementation process. Rather than engaging in the lengthy custom development process, the firm researches and evaluates existing packages before selecting one. Upon purchasing the selected application, the implementation phase is ready to start.

Knowledge Infusion   Another advantage offered by off-the-shelf applications is access to the expertise coded in the software. Because software programs can enable and constrain the manner in which users complete a task or execute a business process (see Chapter 2), an organization that purchases prepackaged software also acquires a "way of doing business."

Consider the example of a call center operator who takes orders from catalog shoppers. The design of the application will determine the order in which the interaction takes place (e.g., greeting, items to be shipped, verification of address, payment) and what data

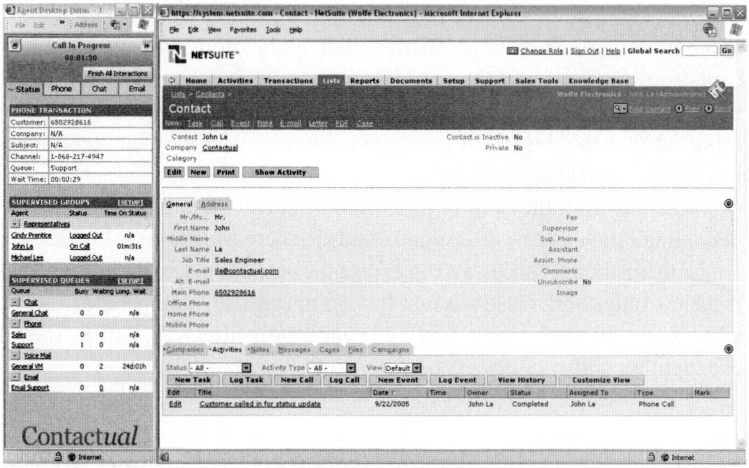

Figure 11.4   Call Center Software Application

are necessary to complete the transaction (e.g., no order can be completed without a valid phone number) (Figure 11.4).

This notion of knowledge infusion is now an important design and marketing tool for software vendors who proactively seek out best practices in order to code them into their applications. Returning to the call center example, an often mentioned best practice in call center operations is to enable personalized interactions with each customer. Thus, a call center software vendor may code a feature in its application that automatically brings up the customer's order history so that the representative may engage in conversation with the customer—after adequate training!

Economically Attractive   While it is always difficult to generalize when it comes to system design and development costs, purchasing off-the-shelf applications typically allows the firm to capitalize on the economies of scale achieved by the vendor. As with the example of mass-produced and tailor-made clothing, when a vendor can mass produce a software application, there are significant economies of scale that lower the unit cost. This is particularly true with software, a classic information good (see Chapter 4), with significant costs of producing the first copy and negligible reproduction costs.

High Quality   Significant debate surrounds the issue of software quality, with the skeptics pointing to the many examples of pre-packaged applications that have significant bugs. Yet large software houses with mature products will point to their significant testing budgets and large installed base of users for evidence that their applications have been put through the paces and thus all major problems have surfaced.

Buy and Make

The make versus buy decision is typically treated as a dichotomous one (i.e., the firm must chose one or the other approach).[3] Yet modern firms are increasingly adopting blended approaches first acquiring systems and then modifying them extensively.

---

[3] To simplify the discussion, we discuss each approach separately as well.

A recent Cutter Consortium survey found that, when asked about the degree of customization required by large off-the-shelf applications the firm purchased, less than 12 percent of respondents said they modified the software slightly or not at all. A quarter of them reported modifying the application "a great deal." Furthermore, half of the respondents reported that the degree of package customization they engaged in exceeded their pre-implementation expectations.[4]

Keeping with the current integration trends (Chapter 3), off-the-shelf applications are becoming larger and more complex and are increasingly crossing departmental boundaries. Under these circumstances we can expect the need for extensive customization of pre-packaged products only to increase—a fact lost on unsophisticated general and functional managers who expect the application to work immediately after installation, the way simple personal productivity software does (i.e., Microsoft Word).

BUILD YOUR OWN: SYSTEMS DESIGN AND DEVELOPMENT

Until the rise to prominence of the software industry, the acquisition of pre-packaged software was the exception, rather than the norm, for most organizations. Its long tradition notwithstanding, designing and developing organizational software applications and information systems has always been a complex, failure-prone undertaking. Viewed by many as more akin to alchemy than to a reliable science, systems design and development continues to frighten non-IT managers, who perceive it as a minefield of technical, behavioral, and managerial challenges (see Figure 11.5).

Figure 11.5   The Systems Development Process as Perceived by Many Managers

[4] Ulrich, W. (2006), "Application Package Survey: The Promise versus Reality," *Cutter Benchmark Review,* (6:9), pp 13–20.

In order to manage the risk and complexity associated with custom development, information systems specialists, academics, and consultants have contributed to the creation of a number of systems design and development methodologies.

Systems Development Life Cycle

The two dominant systems development methodologies today are the system development life cycle (SDLC) and prototyping. The SDLC approach is predicated on the notion that detailed justification and planning is the vehicle to reduce risk and uncertainty in systems design and development efforts. Thus, spending considerable time up front, the project team improves the chances of solving the right business problem with the right information system design. For this reason the SDLC is a highly structured methodology where the outputs of one stage become the inputs of the next, and where the project team strives to keep changes after the project has started to a minimum.[5]

The SDLC methodology is articulated in three phases—definition, build, and implementation—each one further divided into three steps (Table 11.1).

Definition   The definition phase of the SDLC is concerned with clearly identifying the features of the proposed information system. The critical actors in this phase are the prospective end users and the general or functional managers who represent the main stakeholders.

From the information systems staff, systems and business analysts get involved. Systems analysts are highly skilled information systems professionals who are well versed in both technology issues and communication. Their role is to help users identify and articulate the system requirements and serve as liaison with the technical staff (i.e., developers). Business analysts are individuals with expertise in business process redesign as well as technology.

Table 11.1   Principal Phases of the SDLC

Definition
Investigation
Feasibility analysis
System analysis
Build
System design
Programming
Testing
Implementation
Installation
Operations
Maintenance

---

[5] The SDLC is often called the waterfall model because, as water flowing down a waterfall never flows upward, there should be no going back once a stage has been completed.

They help ensure that the business processes and software programs at the heart of an information system are jointly optimized and work smoothly together.

Investigation During investigation, proponents of the new system must identify what business issues the system will pertain to. Managers who envision new ways of operating are the driving force at this stage as they formulate the main goals, scope, and value proposition of the new system. This stage is typically very informal. The next stage brings a greater discipline to the analysis.

Feasibility Analysis In order to ensure that scarce organizational resources are put to best use, the project team must heavily scrutinize the proposed project prior to giving the formal go-ahead. Specifically, the team must evaluate the technical, operational, and economic feasibility of the project.[6]

Technical feasibility is the evaluation of whether the proposed system is viable from a technology standpoint. The team must ask whether the state of the art in hardware, software, and telecommunication is such that the proposed system will work as intended (e.g., it will have enough storage capacity and an acceptable response time). The history of new systems development abounds with examples of technology implementations that predated their time, thus undermining system success.

Operational feasibility, sometimes called behavioral feasibility, is the evaluation of whether the information system as a whole, not just the technology component, is viable. This analysis requires an evaluation of the other three components to make sure that employees have the skills to utilize the new technology and that they will accept (or can be given incentives to accept) the new work system. During this phase the project team must envision how business processes will be redesigned and must foresee possible drivers of user resistance and rejection.

Economic feasibility is the evaluation of the financial viability of the proposed system. A number of techniques have been developed over time to justify the proposed investment, including ROI, payback, and net present value computations. Ultimately, evaluating financial feasibility consists of performing a cost/benefit analysis in order to ensure that the money to be spent on the system design and development project meets the firm's financial hurdles for investment. The business case provides the basis for this analysis (see Chapter 10).

The outcome of the feasibility analysis is a document culminating in a go or no-go recommendation. At this point the firm has invested a small amount of resources, relative to the full project cost; thus if the project is to be called off, this is an appropriate time to do so.

System Analysis Once a decision has been made that the system is worth pursuing, the project team needs to identify and articulate the system requirements. Systems analysts and the stakeholders (i.e., end users, management) take center stage at this point. If the system is not simply automating existing tasks but is instead designed to enable redesigned business processes, business analysts will join the team.

In large systems implementations, it is impossible to involve all users at this stage; rather a subset of the user population joins the team, sometimes full time. Note that it is critical to choose users who are representative of the broader population. That is, the

---

[6] Note that the feasibility analysis for a new system is informed by its business case (Chapter 10), but there are differences. The business case mainly focuses on justifying the pursuit of the project (i.e., cost/benefit analysis), while the feasibility analysis looks comprehensively at all the factors that can hamper system success—technical, operational, and economic.

Reservation functions	❖ Clear all fields by clicking a Reset button ❖ Retrieve guest profile[2] info for the selected main guest ❖ Modify guest profile info for selected main guest ❖ Retrieve previous reservations for modification ❖ Select a main guest by typing his/her name in full ❖ Select a main guest by typing the first few letters, then selecting from a suggested list of 5 names ❖ Add multiple rooms or a single room for multiple days to a reservation ❖ View the calculated tax for a reservation ❖ View the calculated total cost (before and after tax) ❖ Modify rates for individual room-nights on-the-fly ❖ Record pre-paid amount and method of payment ❖ Add notes specific to a reservation

Figure 11.6   User Requirements for a Hotel Property Management System (New Reservation Function)

team should include not only the users who are highest performing or most well versed with technology (so called super-users), but also underperforming and, most importantly, dissenting users (those individuals who may indeed resist rather than support the new system).

Another important aspect of user involvement is that it should not be "window dressing" or "impression management." Systems analysts must genuinely seek out and value stakeholders' input in the process. The system analyst is the specialist in this phase, not the user. It is therefore the system analyst's job to ensure a productive and comprehensive surfacing of requirements.

As the outcome of this stage, the project team produces the systems requirements document (Figure 11.6). This document details what inputs the system will accept, what outputs it will produce, what users will have access to what information, and so on. The document typically includes mock-up screens and scenarios (Figure 11.7) and is sent to the stakeholders for review and approval.

In a strict application of the SDLC methodology, once the stakeholders approve the document, the systems requirements are "frozen" and the cost of future changes, if any are requested, becomes the responsibility of the stakeholders. This step is necessary to minimize the impact of scope creep—the phenomenon by which stakeholders add or change requirements during the build phase of the SDLC, thus significantly increasing cost and considerably delaying development.

Build   The build phase of the SDLC is the most technical and the one that most people picture when they imagine how software is designed and developed. This phase is the primary domain of developers: systems architects and programmers. The objective is to take the system requirements document and produce a robust, secure, and efficient application.

System Design   The build phase begins with the system design stage. Taking the results of the definition phase (i.e., what the applications should do), systems architects create the structure of the system (i.e., how the application will perform its tasks). At this stage the team identifies what hardware will be used, what languages will be adopted, what data structures are needed, and so on. The output of this stage is a precise set of documents that programmers use to write code.

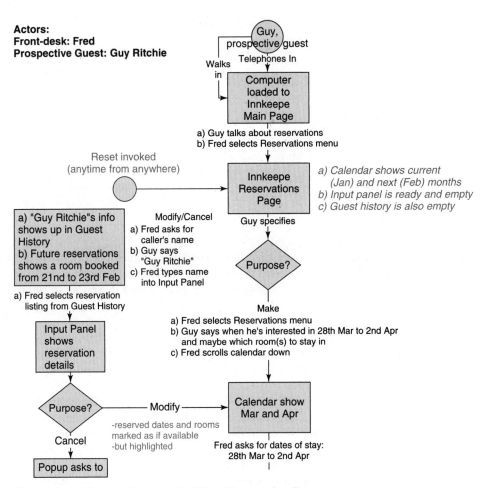

Figure 11.7 Sample Scenario for Hotel Reservation Process

Programming Programming is the process of translating the abstract software design into a set of commands or instructions that can be executed by the hardware. If the application requires the creation of new databases, their structure is also developed at this stage (Figure 11.8).

An important element of the programming stage, but one that developers often detest, is the documentation. Thorough and clear documentation is essential in organizational software programs because they are large, complex, and expected to last for a number of years. Without adequate documentation such systems become impossible to support and maintain, let alone upgrade and evolve over time.

Testing While testing of the program is a process that programmers are constantly engaged in as they develop the system, formalized assessment of components and subsequently of the complete applications is an essential stage in the SDLC. While most non–IT personnel rarely think about testing, this stage can take as much time and resources as the programming stage.

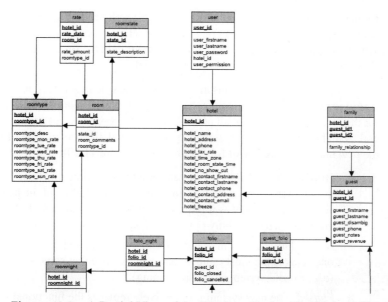

Figure 11.8   A Partial View of the Database Design Underlying a Hotel Property Management System

The testing phase is articulated in alpha testing, carried out by developers themselves, and beta testing, carried out by releasing the beta version to a limited set of actual users who use it and report any problems they identify (Figure 11.9).

Note that the objective of the testing stage is not to identify and correct all the possible bugs plaguing the system, as this is uneconomical and rarely needed. Rather, the testing phase is designed to stress the system, to make sure that it can perform under production circumstances, and to correct the most important errors. The objective is to release the application when it is good enough, not when it is flawless.

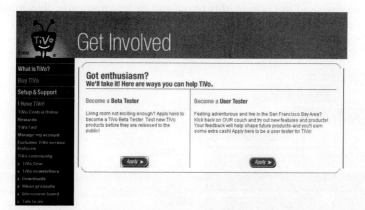

Figure 11.9   Many Organizations Enlist Users to Participate in their Beta Testing Programs

Implementation   Once the software has been developed and tested, the project team needs to ensure that it is properly integrated with the other components of the information system. This is the implementation phase, an extremely delicate time when project management skills and executives' involvement are essential.

Installation   During the installation stage, the system is loaded on the production hardware and the databases are populated. Installation typically takes place during slow periods for the organization and, if at all possible, while the system is not needed (e.g., over a weekend, at night). If an existing system is being replaced, the firm migrates from the old one to the new one following one of four approaches (Figure 11.10):

- *Parallel.* The old and new systems are run for a time together. This approach is the most conservative as it offers insurance against failure of the new application. It is also the most costly as it requires significant redundancy of efforts. In some cases this approach is the only option (e.g., systems that must operate 24 × 7 × 365).

- *Direct.* The old system is suddenly discontinued and the firm cuts over to the new one. This is the most radical approach, but one that sometimes cannot be avoided (e.g., the old system stops functioning).

- *Phased.* The new system progressively replaces the functionalities of the old one. This approach is best suited to modular or componentized applications that can be rolled out in stages.

- *Pilot.* Well suited for multiunit operations (e.g., hotels, chain retailers), this approach allows the firm to run the new system in one business unit or one of the firm's departments before rolling it out completely.

Beyond the technical aspects of the installation phase, there are two critical processes that take place at this time: end-user training and change management. End-user training typically occurs in formal settings, such as classrooms or make-shift computer labs.

Change management is the process of smoothing the transition from the way the various stakeholders interacted with the previous system and carried out their work to the new work practices. User resistance and inertia are the biggest dangers at this point. To the extent that stakeholders had been actively involved in the early stages of the SDLC and the design of the system, this phase will be less traumatic, thus minimizing risks of rejection.

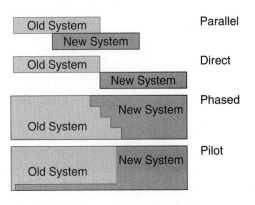

Figure 11.10   Migration Approaches

Operations   At this stage the system is up and running and the firm begins to use it. The project team is disbanded and the new system becomes a permanent asset of the firm to be maintained and managed.

Maintenance   Once the system is in place, up and running, both errors that had escaped the testing phase and enhancements that had escaped the requirements definition phase begin to emerge. Maintenance is the process of compiling this information, prioritizing requests, and implementing both fixes and improvements.

Note that, as comprehensive and well designed as a new system may be, the organization is in continuous evolution. As a consequence, over time, it is normal for a gap to emerge between current system's functionalities and the firm needs (remember this the next time you are tempted to ask, "What were they thinking when they designed this system?!?").

The functionality gap is closed on an ongoing basis by way of upgrades and additions until such ongoing maintenance becomes economically unfeasible and management makes the case for the development of a new system. For this reason some authors have begun to suggest that the traditional sequential SDLC approach needs to be reevaluated.[7]

Advantages of the SDLC Approach   The SDLC is a highly structured methodology that provides a systematic approach to reducing the uncertainty and risk associated with systems design and development projects. It clearly identifies roles and expectations for the members of the project team and it offers a blueprint for how these individuals should interact. By demanding a thorough justification and requirements definition, it is particularly well suited for large-scale projects where changes that occur during the project can be very costly.

The SDLC also offers a vehicle for communication and negotiation between the project team and the many project stakeholders. It does so by requiring evaluation and approval of deliverables for every phase thus stimulating discussion, facilitating the identification of priorities and surfacing hidden trade-offs.

Limitations   While the SDLC methodology has evolved from the traditional waterfall approach into a more iterative process (e.g., spiral model) in which designers and developers are allowed some reevaluation of previous stages, the SDLC remains a highly structured approach. Thus, its critics point out that it creates substantial overhead in time and cost and does not enable the project team to properly address the inevitable changes that occur during the life of such complex projects.

Prototyping

Recognizing the limitations inherent in the SDLC methodology, the prototyping approach is rooted in the notion that it is impossible to clearly estimate and plan in detail such complex endeavors as information systems design and development projects. Instead the team is better served by staying nimble and iterating quickly through multiple designs to zero in on the optimal one.

The growing acceptance of prototyping methodologies was enabled by tools that speed up the development process, such as nonprocedural programming languages. These tools

---

[7] Wagner, E., and Piccoli, G. (2007), "A Call to Engagement: Moving beyond User Involvement in Order to Achieve Successful Information Systems Design," *Communications of the ACM*.

allow developers to rapidly create working (or partially working) models of the proposed system and garner stakeholders' feedback about the system's design, functionalities, user interface, and so on.

Prototyping Life Cycle One of the applications of the prototyping methodology is within the confines of the SDLC, as a way to elicit user requirements and seek input in the design of the user interface. The value of this approach stems from the fact that it is simpler for users to react to a prototype than it is for them to envision and articulate requirements in the abstract. Moreover, by involving users in the development of the front end of the application, the design team can foster their support and increase the chances of acceptance of the final system.

However, prototyping can be used as an alternative to the SDLC to develop a complete system according to the following steps:

Requirements Definitions At this stage the development team seeks basic requirements. The degree of precision needed at this stage is much less than that needed in the SDLC because requirements are not frozen at this point. Rather, the understanding is that future feedback and modification will heavily shape the system.

Initial Prototype Armed with the basic requirements, the team develops a first iteration of the system. The system could be only a shell (i.e, nonfunctional user interface), a partially functional application, or a "first-of-a-series" fully functional prototype.

Evaluation At this time the stakeholders review the prototype and provide feedback on the current design as well as requests for enhancements and new functionality.

Revision Based on the feedback generated during the evaluation stage, the development team designs and codes the requested changes. This phase leads to a new prototype to be submitted to the stakeholders for evaluation. Note that at any time during these iterations the team and the stakeholders may conclude that no further investment in the system is warranted. In this case the project is halted.

Completion Once the stakeholders and the development team are satisfied with the functionalities of the system, the iterative evaluation/revision process stops and the development team finalizes the system. At this stage the developers code important features that users typically do not request (e.g., security, administration). Documentation and testing follow prior to the formal release of the system.

Advantages of the Prototyping Approach Given the characteristics of the prototyping approach, systems developed this way tend to be more quickly delivered and closer to the users' expectations since the stakeholders are more involved throughout the development effort. Thus prototyping is best suited to the development of smaller-scale projects and those that radically change the manner in which work is done. The prototyping approach also enables the firm to experiment with new technologies and new system functionalities because it requires a smaller investment of resources than the SDLC before the product can be evaluated—thus limiting the risk and sunk costs.

Limitations The premium that the prototyping approach puts on speed and functionality development may cause the team to release a system that is lacking from a security, robustness, and reliability standpoint. Systems built using the prototyping approach are typically less thoroughly tested and documented than those using a more structured methodology.

Moreover, the rapid pace of iteration and release of new prototypes can mislead stakeholders who underestimate the complexity of software development. The consequence is rampant scope creep. These limitations make the prototyping approach ill suited for large-scale and complex systems development efforts.

Outsourced Development

Custom-designed software programs are increasingly developed by software houses that "fill in" for the firm's information systems professionals. These arrangements, typically called software development outsourcing, vary greatly, with some firms only outsourcing the programming and testing stages while others resort to an external provider to see them through the entire system development life cycle.

The outsourcing of software development projects has increased dramatically in popularity following the widespread adoption of the Internet. Software programs, as a classic information good (Chapter 4), can be designed and developed anywhere in the world. As a consequence, an increasing proportion of U.S. firms' custom software development is now done overseas.

Consider virtual teams of developers as an example. Software projects are increasingly completed by development teams that work together but are not physically located in the same office. While cost considerations may come to mind as the principal reason to establish virtual teams, a recent Cutter Consortium survey shows that over 85 percent of the respondents see the ability to pool the most qualified talent on the project as the principal driver for their adoption.[8]

With the widespread adoption and internationalization of custom software development, a set of tools to evaluate the quality of providers has emerged. The most popular, the Capability Maturity Model (CMM), ranks software development organizations according to their ability to produce quality software on a scale of 1 to 5 by evaluating a set of standard processes thought to determine software quality.

The principal value proposition of custom software development outsourcing is in its superior cost/quality ratio. U.S. firms can outsource development to countries such as India, Ireland, or China, with a large pool of highly skilled software engineers and programmers and lower cost of living (i.e., lower wages). For example, while 70 percent of software development organizations are estimated to be at CMM level 1, 75 percent of the firms achieving the selective level 5 classification are based in India.[9] Outsourcing developments to these regions of the world enables the firm to receive superior-quality products at a fraction of the cost of internal development.

BUYING OFF-THE-SHELF APPLICATIONS

The SDLC provides the basis for the system selection and purchasing process that organizations use to design and develop information systems based on off-the-shelf software programs (Table 11.2). The systems selection process often starts when managers learn about the capabilities of a new application being advertised, being described in the press, or being

---

[8] Piccoli, G. (2006), "Virtual Teams: No Longer an 'Emerging' Organizational Form," *Cutter Benchmark Review* (6:7), pp. 95–96.

[9] http://en.wikipedia.org/wiki/Capability_Maturity_Model

Table 11.2 Phases in the Systems Selection Processes

Definition
Investigation
Feasibility analysis
System analysis
Formulate evaluation criteria

Compile Short list of vendors
Compile and distribute RFP
Evaluate alternatives
Negotiate contract

Build
System design (Customizations)
Programming (Customizations)
Testing

Implementation
Installation
Operations
Maintenance

promoted by consulting firms. Following the systems selection process is important because it enables a systematic investigation of these applications as well as competing products—thus ensuring that all issues are considered and the firm chooses the best solution for its current needs.

Definition

Both the investigation and feasibility analysis stages are qualitatively similar to those in the SDLC. At this time the proponents of the system articulate a vision for the proposed information system and evaluate its technical, operational, and economic viability. It is in the remaining stages of the definition phase that the major idiosyncrasies of the systems selection process occur.

System Analysis   During the system analysis stage, the selection committee focuses on eliciting the specific functionalities required of the proposed system. As with the SDLC, this phase entails the interplay of system analysts and stakeholders. However, the degree of precision and detail sought by the selection committee is less than that needed for custom development. The objective here is to have enough of an understanding of the systems requirements to formulate evaluation criteria.

Formulate Evaluation Criteria   Systems selection is the structured attempt to evaluate all commercially available software solutions that can enable the proposed information system.

In order to do so, it is necessary to develop a set of evaluation criteria that can be uniformly applied to all packages under investigation. The criteria must also be amenable to communication to software vendors by way of the request for proposal (RFP) process.

A common approach is to use the system requirements document to identify the features appropriate applications should have, and group them into three categories:

- *Essential features.* Those capabilities that the system must have. Systems that miss any one of these features are automatically discarded.

- *Value adding features.* Those capabilities that, while not essential, offer significant advantages for which the firm would be willing to pay a premium.

- *Nonessential features.* Those capabilities that are "nice to have" but produce small tangible advantages for which the firm is not willing to pay a premium.

Compile Short List of Vendors   Armed with the evaluation criteria, the selection committee seeks information about existing solutions. Web sites, trade press, vendor brochures, and trade expos are all viable sources of information. The information gathered is used to identify a preliminary short list of vendors.

This stage is important for two reasons. First, creating targeted RFPs that yield high-quality responses and evaluating those responses is time consuming. Second, products that fail to meet necessary requirements can be identified fairly quickly, and vendors will appreciate not being asked to respond to RFPs that they have no chance of fulfilling.

Compile and Distribute the RFP   The RFP is the formal communication document used to elicit substantial, detailed information from the short-listed vendors. Most organizations have a template for such documents. The RFP should explain what the selection committee has identified as the critical system requirements, the environment in which the system will be used, and any required performance metrics and expectations.

Upon its distribution to the short-listed vendors, those interested will respond to the RFP. The selection team should ask vendors to adhere to a template, making cross-comparison of the applications simple, and should ask for pricing information. Pricing information should also be provided according to the firm's template, ensuring that the pricing mechanisms for the applications, any customization, and ongoing maintenance and upgrades are clear and comparable across vendors. Finally, the selection committee should specify a deadline by which vendors must respond in order to be considered.

Evaluate Alternatives   Once all interested vendors have responded to the RFP, the competing solutions are evaluated using the criteria developed earlier. The selection committee compiles the list of top vendors and seeks any further information needed to make a final decision. This includes on-site demonstrations, evaluation of reference sites, and the like. The outcome of this stage in the selection process is a rank-ordered list of the acceptable candidates.

Negotiate Contract   Negotiations can be relatively quick and simple or be a very involved process requiring input from professionals and legal counsel. The objective of the selection committee is to draft and sign a contract that provides the firm with the needed solution and insulates it from future risks. Common elements of negotiation are the components and magnitude of costs (e.g., installation, training, customization, maintenance, upgrade), the eventual liabilities and service-level agreements, control over the intellectual property, and the extent to which modifications are allowed.

Build

The build phase in the system selection process mirrors that of the SDLC but is much narrower in scope. When the software program is to be installed without configuration or customization, as is the case with simple applications, the firm can move directly to formal testing and implementation. However, as we mentioned above, it is becoming increasingly common for organizations that purchase off-the-shelf applications to configure and customize them extensively.[10]

To the extent that customization is necessary, the firm will engage in system design and programming of the necessary enhancements. This is where a tightly written contract becomes important as the customization process can add significant time and cost to the project. The contract should specify who is responsible for customizing the application— the vendor, the firm, or a third party (i.e., independent consulting firm, integrator)—and the conditions of the customization effort (e.g., schedule).

Whether customized or not, the firm should test the system. In the case of off-the-shelf applications, the testing stage is mostly concerned with system performance rather than with the identification and correction of bugs.

Implementation

The implementation phase is also quite similar to the one described earlier regarding the SDLC. Note, however, that the degree of process change and training required to get buy-in from users is typically greater when implementing off-the-shelf applications. This is because a pre-packaged program is not designed with the idiosyncrasies of your organization in mind. Rather the software house builds the program to appeal to the broadest market possible.

Asking for stakeholders' input during the selection and evaluation of competing solutions is one way to enroll them in the process and reduce rejection risks. However, you should still plan to invest considerable resources during the implementation phase to set up the application, train employees, engage in change management—particularly when the application is larger in scope and forces a change in traditional work practices.

END-USER DEVELOPMENT

As we discussed in Chapter 1, the ease of use of information technologies has steadily increased while their cost has declined dramatically. These two forces have conspired to bring the power of software development to the masses in the form of end-user development. *End-user development* is an umbrella term capturing the many ways in which knowledge workers, not IT professionals, create software.

---

[10] Configuration is the process of tailoring a software program using built-in parameters. Customization is the process of changing the functionality of the software program beyond available options. Customization requires that the new functionalities be coded using a programming language.

End-user-developed systems range from spreadsheet models (e.g., an ROI calculator written in MS Excel), to personal or departmental databases, to full-fledged software programs built with user-friendly computer languages (e.g., Visual Basic for Applications) or development tools such as fourth-generation languages. These "shadow systems" are now prevalent in modern organizations.[11]

The Benefits of End-User Development

The chief benefits of end-user development stem from user empowerment and the fact that some of the burden on typically overworked information systems departments is lifted. The benefits include the following:

- *Increased speed of development.* The user community typically must direct requests for new systems and improvements to existing ones to the IS function. In turn, the IS function must prioritize the deployment of its scarce resources. As a consequence, those projects that end users can complete independently will be completed faster by virtue of not entering the cue.

- *End-user satisfaction.* One of the main problems with new systems is users' dissatisfaction or outright rejection. When users create their own applications, they are more likely to be satisfied with the result; they have either created the functionalities they wanted or have themselves decided what features to forgo.

- *Reduced pressure on the IS function.* End-user development can limit the number of requests the IS function receives, enabling them to be more focused on the projects that, because of their scope and complexity, require their attention.

The Risks of End-User Development

Unfortunately, end-user development presents a number of difficult-to-manage risks that limit its value to the organization.

- *Unreliable quality standards.* There is a reason why software development is a lengthy process. Quality software requires a number of activities that may not be readily apparent but are necessary—such as testing, documentation, security, and the like. Because of the limited skill set and knowledge of most end users, the quality of their work varies dramatically.

- *High incidence of errors.* Audits of spreadsheets used in organizations show that a sizable percentage, between 20 and 40 percent (sometimes 90 percent), of them contains errors.[12] The focus on outcomes (i.e., what the program does) and rapid development typically conspire to increase the likelihood of errors in end-user-developed applications.

---

[11] Ulrich, W. (2006), "Application Package Survey: The Promise versus Reality,"*Cutter Benchmark Review* (6:9), pp. 13–20.

[12] Panko, R. (2005), "What We Know About Spreadsheet Errors," http://panko.cba.hawaii.edu/SSR/Mypapers/whatknow.htm (Accessed 9/9/2006).

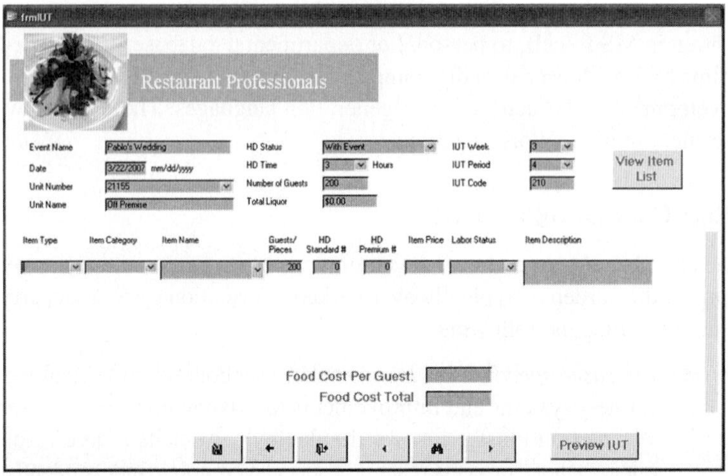

Figure 11.11 An End-User-Developed Database Application

- *Continuity risks.* Because end-user development often does not comply with traditional system development methodologies, it may be difficult for anyone but the individual who wrote the program to understand it, enhance it, and support it. Lack of documentation compounds this problem. A common scenario involves people like you, who develop great applications during internships only to see them fade into company oblivion once you leave the firm (Figure 11.11).

- *Increased pressure on the IS function.* While end-user development can relieve some of the development demands on the IS function, it often creates more requests for assistance during the development process and, over time, for help managing the applications after release.

SUMMARY

This chapter continued our discussion of the techniques and methodologies modern organizations use to introduce and manage information systems within the framework provided by the strategic information systems plan.

Specifically, in this chapter we focused on the three approaches used to introduce new organizational information systems: custom design and development, system selection and acquisition, and end-user development. We learned that

- The astounding progress that has characterized information technologies over the last forty years often misleads general and functional managers. Being mostly familiar with personal computing, they underestimate how much time and how much money it takes to build a stable, robust, and secure system that must work under a wide array of organizational conditions. In order to avoid these misconceptions, managers must become familiar with the process by which IT-based information systems come to be in modern organization.

- Introducing an organizational information system is a two-step process requiring technology development and the implementation process. These two processes, while often described separately, are complementary and intertwined.

- Modern firms introduce new information systems using one of the following approaches: custom design and development, system selection and acquisition, or end-user development. The critical difference among them is the manner in which the software applications at the core of the information system are developed. In the first approach, IT professionals within the organization or contracted develop uniquely tailored software for the firm's needs. In the second approach, the selection committee chooses an off-the-shelf application. In the third approach, it is the firm's end users, rather than IT professionals, who create the software.

■ The main methodology for custom system development is the system development life cycle (SDLC). The SDLC, predicated on the notion that detailed up-front planning is the vehicle to reduce risk and uncertainty in systems design and development efforts, is best suited for the development of large, complex software applications. The SDLC is articulated over three main phases—definition, build, and implementation—and nine stages. The primary limitation of the SDLC is the creation of substantial overhead and rigidity that limit the project team's ability to address the inevitable changes.

■ The prototyping methodology has emerged as a viable alterative to the SDLC. Prototyping is rooted in the notion that it impossible to clearly estimate and plan in detail such complex endeavors as information systems design and development projects. Instead the team is better served by staying nimble and iterating quickly through multiple designs to zero in on the optimal one. Prototyping's advantages include user satisfaction (particularly for small-scale applications or those that dramatically change work practices), rapid development, and experimentation. The drawbacks include the risk of lower-quality systems than those developed using a more structured methodology, and scope creep.

■ With the advent of the Internet and the growth of the software industry in countries with access to a large pool of talent and low cost of living, it is increasingly viable to outsource development of custom applications.

■ The software industry has grown to a point where almost any application a firm needs is available off the shelf. When building information systems around prepackaged software applications, the firm must engage in a formal systems selection and acquisition process. Doing so ensures that the selection team evaluates all possible solutions and acquires the one that is best suited to the firm's needs. The selection and acquisition process mirrors the SDLC, with some important variations during the definition and build phases.

■ The advent of powerful and easy-to-use computer languages and software development tools has enabled an unprecedented degree of software development by end users (i.e., non–IT professionals). The benefits of end-user development include increased speed, end-user satisfaction, and a reduced pressure on the IS function to develop new applications. The risks of end-user development include unreliable quality standards, high incidence of errors in the applications, continuity risks, and increased pressure on the IS function to support development and management of end-user applications.

STUDY QUESTIONS

1. Describe the reasons why general and user managers often fail to understand the complexities of organizational information systems development. Can you provide an example from your own experience?

2. What is the difference between technology development and information systems development? What is the relationship between these two processes?

3. How do the three information systems development approaches in use today in modern organizations differ? Can you provide an example of each?

4. Provide arguments in support of both the make and buy approaches. What are the principal advantages of each decision? Increasingly firms approach information systems development as a "buy and make" process. What do we mean by "buy and make"? Why is this approach gaining increasing popularity today?

5. Describe the systems development life cycle (SDLC) methodology in the context of a "real" example. In other words, think about (or imagine) a situation where you proposed the need for a new information system. For this system development effort, describe what happened (or should happen) during the definition, build, and implementation phases.

6. Repeat Question 5, this time using the prototyping methodology.

7. Repeat Question 5, this time using the systems selection and acquisition methodology.

8. Articulate the advantages and disadvantages of end-user development.

▪ FURTHER READINGS

1. Pink, D. H. (2004). "The New Face of the Silicon Age: How India Became the Capital of the Computing Revolution." *Wired Magazine* (12:02).
2. Wagner, E., and Piccoli, G. (2008). "A Call to Engagement: Moving beyond User Involvement in Order to Achieve Successful Information Systems Design." *Communications of the ACM.*

▪ GLOSSARY

- **Build:** The build phase of the SDLC is concerned with taking the system requirements document and producing a robust, secure, and efficient software application.

- **Business analyst:** Business analysts are individuals with expertise in business process redesign as well as technology. They help ensure that the business processes and software programs at the heart of an information system are jointly optimized and work smoothly together.

- **Custom software:** A software program that is created in single copy to address the specific needs and design requirements of an organization.

- **Custom software development:** The process by which an organization, or a contracted software house, creates a tailored software application to address the organization's specific information processing needs.

- **Definition:** The definition phase of the SDLC is concerned with clearly identifying the features of the proposed information system.

- **End-user development:** The process by which an organization's non–IT specialists create software applications.

- **Implementation:** The implementation phase of the SDLC is concerned with taking the technology component and integrating it with the other elements (people, process, structure) to achieve a working information system.

- **Off-the-shelf application:** A software program that is mass produced and commercialized by a software vendor.

- **Programmer:** A highly skilled IT professional who translates a software design into a set of instructions that can be executed by a digital computer.

- **Prototyping:** A systems development approach predicated on the notion that it impossible to clearly estimate and plan in detail such complex endeavors as information systems design and development projects.

- **Software application:** A software program or, more commonly, a collection of software programs, designed to perform tasks of interest to an end user (e.g., write a memo, create and send invoices).

- **Software development outsourcing:** An arrangement where an external provider (i.e., a software house) custom develops an application for an organization.

- **System analyst:** A highly skilled IS professional whose role is to help users identify and articulate the system requirements.

- **System architect:** A highly skilled IT professional who takes the system requirements document (i.e., what the applications should do) and designs the structure of the system (i.e., how the application will perform its tasks).

- **System development life cycle (SDLC):** A software development approach predicated on the notion that detailed justification and planning is the vehicle to reduce risk and uncertainty in systems design and development efforts.

- **System selection and acquisition:** The process by which an organization identifies and purchases an off-the-shelf software application to address its information processing needs.

CASE STUDY: DARTCOR MANAGEMENT SERVICES[13]

There is so much information technology out there, how do you decide what's appropriate for your company and how to measure the return it provides? Giving up short-term profits to take the resources and the time to implement new technology—when you are not sure of the payoff—is a hard decision to make.

— Michael Giamarino, VP of Operations

In the summer of 2002 Dartcor Management Services, an onsite foodservice provider, was poised for growth in the New York City and surrounding New Jersey areas. Executives believed that Information Technology (IT) could be a key enabler in its quest for expansion and a tool that would allow Dartcor to compete with its much larger competitors. Leading the charge on the technology front was a young Cornell graduate, Joey Essenfeld.

As Joey quickly learned, the IT challenge in a small company was identifying, selecting, and implementing new technology with limited resources and an eye to future expansion. In his search for appropriate technology, Joey had identified a software application that allowed catering orders to be placed online. After substantial data gathering and research, Joey was getting ready to present his findings and his recommendation to the executive team. With limited resources at his disposal, Joey knew that he had few opportunities for funding and should provide a balanced and convincing case.

DARTCOR'S BACKGROUND

In 1985 a Cornell Hotel School graduate, Warren Leeds, and his partner, Christopher Schiavone, started Dartcor as a retail gourmet deli store. The café had seats for about 25–30 people. "Our deli was similar to a Dean & Deluca operation. It had a real New York feel in the suburbs of New Jersey," Leeds recalled. As the young entrepreneurs learned the business, it soon became clear that an important component of the operation was off-premise catering. Describing the early days, Leeds said: "The retail side grew slow and steady, while the catering side really took off very quickly due to our close proximity to many *Fortune* 500 companies." As the catering business continued to grow, Dartcor decided to sell the retail business, largely because the firm felt the margins were much better on the catering side. Dartcor catering

soon began moving from pool parties and christenings to more and more sophisticated events such as weddings, high-society functions, and corporate events. After multiple requests from corporate clients to open up foodservice outlets—referred to as cafés at Dartcor—on their premises, Dartcor finally decided to begin accepting these requests. Leeds recalled:

> When I was at Cornell I really never focused on the onsite foodservice segment of the restaurant industry because it was not the most appealing to me. But we figured there was interest and it would be a nice complement to our core catering business, so we entered it.

In the early 1990s Schiavone shifted his focus from the day-to-day aspect of the operations to allow himself the opportunity to open a golf course management company. Shortly afterward, Leeds secured Dartcor's first account with a large multi-tenant class A office building. Entering the business and industry (B&I) segment of the on-site foodservice business provided a move ripe with lessons for the young entrepreneur. Leeds explained:

> The first place was fabulous, but we made a few mistakes. We paid for the entire build-out of the facility and did not negotiate exclusivity in the office park. The revenue could never support our substantial investment. Although we lost money, it was such a beautifully designed café with great food and service that many other real estate developers came to us and requested our services.

Without an active selling approach, but due to positive word of mouth, the contract foodservice venture continued to expand. Seeing the opportunities in the B&I segment, Leeds hired Michael Giamarino (see Exhibit 1 for Dartcor's organization chart). Charged with ensuring the reputation for service that Dartcor wanted to develop, Giamarino, a former Disney employee, spearheaded a centralized training program called DATES (Dartcor Approach To Excellent Service). The program, patterned after the Disney model, instilled a service culture at Dartcor. Since then, Leeds said, operating cafés with a service orientation became Dartcor's signature and its key competitive differentiator. Leeds explained:

---

[13] This case was originally published as: Piccoli, G., and Reynolds, D. (2002), "Dartcor Management Services," *Communications of the AIS* (vol. 9, article 17), pp. 298–314.

continued

CASE STUDY (*continued*)

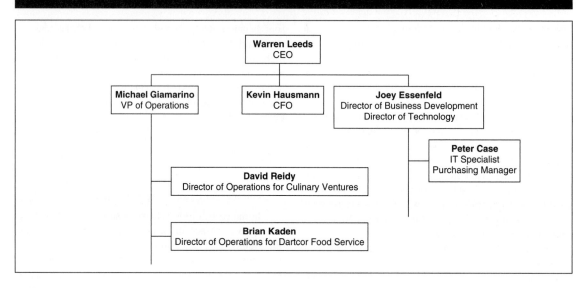

Exhibit 1 Organization Chart

I figured, if we were going to be great at this, what we must be sure to do is provide what I call "legendary service." We are so focused on service that we have a director of legendary service whose role is to make sure that all cafés achieve the Dartcor standards.

Given the intensity of both the foodservice and catering business, when an opportunity came to sell the catering side of the business in the late nineties, Leeds regrettably agreed. Following the sale, Dartcor focused wholeheartedly on the contract foodservice side of the business in an effort to expand the current portfolio of 15 locations. In 2000 Dartcor bought Culinary Ventures, an established foodservice management company with over 40 accounts. Culinary Ventures provided the opportunity for segmentation of the market as it was much more focused on industrial and factory accounts—the blue-collar side of B&I foodservice—and academic accounts. Speaking about the differences between the two brands, Giamarino said:

> Culinary Ventures accounts typically are more focused on industrial and manufacturing facilities. Employees at such facilities tend to prefer less complex "comfort foods," so we would be unlikely, for example, to have a sushi day or serve mahi mahi at these accounts. In terms of menu development and selection there is significant difference, but we have similar specs in terms of food quality and service.

Dartcor's management felt that they had been able to integrate Culinary Ventures into the Dartcor philosophy by dropping accounts that did not share its values of quality and service. Dartcor's management also reasoned that the company differentiated itself in the B&I marketplace by having taken a restaurant approach to the operations of the cafés rather than a cafeteria approach. This was evidenced by the firm's philosophy of hiring chefs with a restaurant background, rather than a noncommercial foodservice background, and by preparing high-quality foods à la minute rather than hours before consumption. Warren Leeds suggested:

> I thought there was tremendous opportunity for a great regional niche player in this market. Our goal was to take the Dartcor brand and target high-end multi-tenant class A office buildings and single tenant clients who really wanted high levels of service.

At the heart of Dartcor's operation was a restaurant approach that started with recruiting entrepreneurial employees who were challenged to understand the idiosyncrasies of their building's tenants, develop relationships with the client, and, as Leeds put it, "run the café as if it were their own restaurant." Dartcor believed that delegation of authority to the unit level improved the responsiveness and flexibility of the organization and enabled it to compete much more effectively with larger players. "Ultimately, we have to become part of the organizations we serve; we want to mesh with their culture and be perceived like just another organizational department rather than as an external entity," Giamarino concluded.

THE CONTRACT MANAGEMENT BUSINESS

The global on-site foodservice industry, spanning operations in B&I, healthcare, schools, colleges, correctional facilities, and sports and recreation venues, accounted for about $230 billion of the $800 billion global foodservice industry. The opportunity in the United States alone was enticing, with on-site foodservice sales approaching the $80 billion mark. These sales were divided almost equally between two types of operations: self-operated foodservice outlets—run by the same organizations they served—and contract-foodservice providers, also known as managed-services companies, that served those organizations outsourcing foodservice operations.

Since the 1980s, the number of contracted operations had increased steadily. Managed-services providers touted a systematized approach to a business in which most host organizations had little experience and competence. This was particularly true in B&I accounts. Large corporations generally realized the benefit of outsourcing foodservice to experts who could manage the enterprise more cost-effectively (based partially on the economies of scale associated with purchasing) and with higher quality (owing to the management expertise and systematized approach to the business' operations).

This propensity of outsourcing in B&I, however, created a competitive environment in which contract-foodservice operators managed more than 85 percent of all food outlets. In addition, businesses that had historically subsidized the foodservice, viewing it as an employee amenity and a method for enhancing productivity by keeping employees in the building, began passing the cost back to employees. Thus, organizations sought contract-foodservice companies that could offer high quality but at the lowest possible cost.

This trend created an important shift in the managed-services arena. Traditionally, organizations had outsourced their foodservice and paid the contractor a fixed fee for service. The total cost to the host organization was the same or less, but the quality generally improved. The contractor, in turn, provided foodservice to the organization's employees using a subsidized cost structure. So long as food and service quality was maintained, there was little risk to the contractor; if costs increased, they were passed along to the client. Even in extreme situations, such as when different businesses were combined or sections of plants were closed, contractors were able to pass along any added expenses without sacrificing their management fee. But as businesses focused more and more on their bottom line and short-term

financial returns, they began looking at ways to reduce nonessential operating expenses, such as those associated with providing foodservice to employees. Thus, many clients began asking contract-foodservice providers to assume more risk. This resulted in a greater number of accounts operated under a profit-and-loss (P&L) arrangement, wherein the contractor operates in a manner similar to a commercial restaurant. The contractor assumes more risk (if business declines, so do profits), but has the potential for greater gains if it manages the operation effectively.

This dynamic marketplace was dominated by three global companies: Aramark, based in the United States, Sodexho Alliance, with its corporate office in France, and Compass Group, PLC, operating out of the United Kingdom. In addition, regional players abounded, each focusing on close-to-the-customer relationships, offering customizable programs, and maintaining ever-flatter and leaner organizations. While many regional foodservice providers existed, the trend toward growth through acquisitions, which was shared by the big three, created an aggressive business climate. The overarching goal of many regional players was to build a critical mass of contracts such that the firm would be appealing as an acquisition by a larger managed-services company.

In order to survive, both global and larger regional foodservice providers had become adept at managing with either P&L or fee-based arrangements. The most savvy operators learned how to integrate quality guarantees to their contracts, further protecting clients. In every contractual arrangement, however, the focus continued to be the same: providing the highest quality of food and service, on a cost-effective basis, such that customers will choose to eat at the on-site outlet rather than leave the building and dine at commercial restaurants nearby.

From the contractor's side, the best contract was known as an "evergreen" agreement: a contract with no end date. Not surprisingly, most clients preferred fixed-term contracts in order to provide more leverage in reducing costs with each renewal period. Regardless of the type or duration of the contract, nearly all featured an "out" clause for both parties. Thus, if the contractor encountered a situation where profitability was impossible, or where a client was unable to meet its financial obligations, the managed-services provider could formally cancel a contract, typically with 30, 60, or 90 days notice. Giamarino noted: "The out clause is important. For example, if there are massive layoffs you don't want to be contractually obligated to serve food to 200 rather than 800 employees. That's how regional foodservice companies go out of business." Clients, too, could terminate the relationship, which generally occurred due to perceived low quality of food or service, or personal disagreement between the client and the on-site managers.

continued

The contract foodservice management industry was one with small margins, with after-tax income sometimes as low as 2 or 3 percent of sales. Even when an average of 50 percent of the building's population dined on-site (widely recognized as the industry average), the contractor still had to contend with labor issues and operating expenses. Moreover, clients sometimes made unreasonable demands, often rooted in their lack of understanding of foodservice operations, making financial profitability even more difficult. The final challenge was represented by tight cash flow. While most contracts dictated net 30 terms, many clients did not pay on time. Reticent to cancel a contract for late payment, contractors sometimes threatened to affix interest charges (as stipulated in most contracts) on outstanding receivables, only to be rebuffed by clients who knew the contractor would rather have the net amount, albeit late, than risk losing the entire contract. This situation led to managed-services providers—particularly smaller companies—to have problems with their payables. As a result, relationships with vendors often became strained when the contractor did not have adequate cash to cover a given month's invoices.

DARTCOR'S OPERATIONS

Since the acquisition of Culinary Ventures, Dartcor had segmented its core B&I business internally along two lines. Accounts that aligned with the business side of B&I were generally referred to as "Dartcor" units. Accounts in factories and similar host organizations were referred to as "CV" units. Further delineating these businesses, the company generally preferred the P&L model for Dartcor accounts and fee-based arrangements for CV accounts. Accounts in both segments featured a foodservice director, a chef, or chef manager for small accounts, and 6 to 20 employees. The largest accounts included a production supervisor as well as a sous chef. The pay varied by geography, but base salary for line employees generally exceeded minimum wage and was competitive with that paid to individuals in similar positions in nearby commercial restaurants. Foodservice directors and the chefs in high-end Dartcor accounts, such as the Avon account in New York City, commanded a salary ranging between $50,000 and $60,000. Smaller accounts were those that had a managed volume—sales in a P&L account and sales plus the subsidy in subsidized accounts—of less than $250,000. Large accounts were those with managed volume in excess of three-quarters of a million dollars. As Giamarino noted:

The greater the managed volume, the greater the challenges in managing the operation. But we pay our managers not just for the amount of money they manage, but also for the skills they bring to the table, not the least of which are an entrepreneurial approach and the ability to motivate the crew. Inevitably, these abilities translate to higher unit-level profit and, ultimately, stronger client retention.

In terms of strengthening P&L unit sales, Giamarino added:

Our focus is on building relationships so we can achieve our target capture rate of 55 to 60 percent. We want our managers on the floor, talking with customers, understanding what they want. The key is to be interacting with them, listening to their needs and immediately addressing their suggestions on improvements.

This focus on customer relations was also evident in the company's belief in a service-oriented approach to café operations as reflected in its continuous hours from 7:00 A.M. to 3:00 P.M. Breakfast was typically responsible for 25 percent of the total daily covers and staff arrived as early as 6:00 A.M. to begin preparations. Peak times for breakfast operations ranged from 7:30 A.M. to 9:00 A.M. while peak time for lunch ranged from 12:15 P.M. to 1:15 P.M.—when 60 percent of the lunch business was realized. Purchases were generally cash based, with some of them being charged to "house accounts." Credit cards for individual purchases were not accepted. Giamarino explained: "We don't accept credit cards because they slow down the checkout process. We have a target of 5 minutes from the customer entering the café to checkout." Cash transactions were handled using an electronic cash register, while house account charges were handwritten on a piece of paper. The cashier obtained the customer's name, company affiliation (in multi-tenant buildings), noted whether it was breakfast or lunch, obtained the account number to be charged, and noted the transaction amount. At the end of each day the paper was stored in an appropriate folder—the "weekly folder"— and charged sales were recorded in a spreadsheet along with other operational measures (e.g., total sales, number of breakfast and lunch covers, and outside purchases—known as the payout).

While the goal was to use the same accounting systems in units regardless of the Dartcor or CV designation, the businesses in each segment were different. For example, in Dartcor units, of which there were 22, the goal was to drive revenue in order to maximize the bottom line in a manner similar to restaurant operations. In the 20 CV accounts, the fee was dictated by the contract and was not subject to revenue variability. As Giamarino put it: "In a P&L account you look for a nickel on a dollar. In a subsidized account you want all costs in line in order to be able to charge your management fee knowing that you are delivering maximum value to the client." As in any food-service venture, food and labor costs represented the largest component of costs. Specific to Dartcor accounts, this combination represented some 85 percent of sales, with labor costs commonly exceeding food costs. These economics spurred a growing interest in technology that would automate any labor-intensive job.

Dartcor not only offered breakfast and lunch service in its cafés, but was also available to cater any events the tenants would host. These were generally high-end events, such as board meetings or corporate-sponsored functions that required a separate, more sophisticated menu of à la carte items. In its most important accounts Dartcor had access to the facilities and talent necessary to provide on-site catering. For the remaining accounts, catering was centralized for each geographic location and supplied by a commissary with the ability to produce the appropriate gourmet menu. Catering operations realized substantially higher margins than regular café operations. Joey Essenfeld, Director of Business Development and Technology, commented:

In high-end accounts, profit is mostly generated on the catering side. In these accounts we will cater anywhere from 150 to 250 catering events per week. An account can generate 20 to 30 percent profit on catering sales by utilizing the production staff from the café to complete the food preparation.

In aggregate Dartcor estimated that a total of 2,000 to 4,000 events would be catered each week by its units. The average catering ticket was $12/per person with a typical order serving 15 to 30 people. Analysis of the catering business indicated that catered events could be separated into routine events—recurrent events with little or no variation with respect to number of people attending, item selection, time of delivery, etc.—and complex events—irregular or very high-end events requiring accommodation of special needs and other special arrangements.

A catering transaction began when authorized administrative assistants called the manager and, menu in hand, provided their name, the date of the event, how many people would be attending, and listed the required items and any special request. Alternatively they used a fax or e-mail order form. The size and complexity of the order determined the necessary lead-time for preparation. True to its service orientation, Dartcor strived to honor any request,

even prioritizing catering orders in an effort to meet the customers' demands. The order was written down by the chef or manager on a catering slip and, at the appropriate time, prepared. Joey explained:

Catering at a typical high-end account is comprised of 95 percent routine events and 5 percent complex ones. A typical call for routine events lasts between three and five minutes. Complex orders require significant customization and discussion over unusual menu-item requests, service preferences, or merchandising. The calls for these orders typically last between five and ten minutes.

When the order was delivered, a copy of the original catering slip accompanied it. The administrative assistant would check the delivery for accuracy, provide the account number to be billed or the credit card number to be charged, and sign off on the catering slip while keeping a copy for his or her records. The manager kept the catering slips in the weekly folder and, at the end of the week, sent them to headquarters for billing.

The process of handling the weekly folders was very time consuming. At week's end, after each unit's weekly folder was received, a full-time employee at headquarters separated the documents (e.g., accounts receivable, accounts payable, sales) and typed the data in the appropriate accounts of Dartcor's accounting software, MAS 90. Once the data were input, a bill for every customer was generated and mailed to the appropriate customer address. If payment was not received within 30 days, the collection process was initiated and payment was solicited through e-mail, fax, or phone. Kevin Hausmann, Dartcor's Chief Financial Officer, estimated the labor intensity of this process:

Including the process necessary to record the entries that have to be made to record the sale, we have two people a day working every day on data entry. Including salary and benefits the two full time equivalents cost, in aggregate, about $80,000 a year. Of this time, catering accounts for 50 percent and charged sales make up the other 50 percent.

With some charges as small as three dollars, Hausmann estimated that the company lost money on some of them due to the laboriousness of the process:

We consider it part of the customer-service experience to be able to charge these small amounts, but at times it is a bit frustrating to see that such small figures generate so much work. You have to have someone input the charge, generate the bill, send it out, and then after sixty days the $3.75 still has not been

continued

paid and you have to have someone call and follow up. It is something that has always been an issue.

Joey also stressed the significant delay that accounts receivable generated: "The best we can do on a catering account receivable is seven days, when a customer provides a credit card number to charge the purchase to." Company officials did not believe that customers would delay payments as a matter of policy. Rather, it was the small nature of many of the invoices, and their significant human handling, that led to them being ignored, lost, or delayed. Hausman commented:

For what we are charging I don't believe our clients play the float. These amounts add up to thousands of dollars for us, but for each client they are quite small and most companies we deal with are fairly large. If anything, because our invoices are relatively small, they fall below the radar screen. The client gets a stack of invoices that need to be sent to the appropriate departments, approved, and returned to the accounting department. At every step there may be delays or something may go wrong and we end up having to follow up.

DARTCOR'S IT INFRASTRUCTURE

Joey joined Dartcor immediately after graduating from Cornell, in the summer of 2001. At the time, the firm's IT infrastructure was comprised of one file server running Microsoft Windows 2000 and providing a gateway to the Internet via a fractional T1 line. Workstations were provided to the officers and support personnel at headquarters but only the officers had access to e-mail. Each machine ran the Microsoft Office suite including Word and Excel. The payroll function was outsourced, and Dartcor ran only one specialized package—MAS 90—to support the accounting function. Dartcor's long-time senior accounting manager had set up the IT infrastructure and had been responsible for managing and overseeing IT operations until he left the company following the acquisition of Culinary Ventures.

Since his arrival, Joey had revised the agreement with Dartcor's Internet service provider (ISP) and had been able to secure enough e-mail accounts to ensure that all headquarter personnel, all managers and chefs in the field, and anyone else who requested it, could receive a personal e-mail account. Like many early Web sites, the original Dartcor site looked amateurish. Upon joining the company,

Joey made a successful case for engaging a design firm and secured $20,000 to completely redesign the Web presence of the Dartcor brands. Joey recalled his justification for the investment:

When we are handing out our business card trying to sell a multimillion dollar account and they go to our Web site and it fails to meet their expectations, they are going to say: "OK, these guys aren't professional." The Web site is going to be out there, people will look at it, and their impression must be positive.

Senior management believed that the Web site (http://www.dartcor.com), now comparable in quality to Dartcor's large competitors, had been a positive investment that enabled the firm to project a high-quality, service-oriented image. While successful, this effort provided some important lessons about the risks and challenges associated with technology projects. The designer originally commissioned to redesign the site did not produce work of appropriate quality and the relationship had to be severed with a settlement payment. But the designer registered the domain name dartcorfoodservice.com and held it hostage demanding to be paid further. Joey recalled:

I spent a significant amount of time calling him every day and talking to him, engaging our lawyer to put pressure on him, alerting our ISP, and so on. We finally put enough pressure on him and he released the domain.

While Joey had made an impact at headquarters, his strongest contribution to IT operations had been at the unit level. Each unit was equipped with one Windows-based personal computer running the Microsoft Office suite of productivity tools. These personal computers had Internet access at varying speeds—mainly depending on the speed supported by the tenant's own network. No other computing equipment was at locations, with sale transactions supported by one to three standalone cash registers.

Managers were provided Excel spreadsheets for reporting. Daily records were kept for sales, purchasing, and catering. Separate sheets were provided for weekly inventory and bi-weekly time cards reports. Joey explained:

At the end of each week, the managers produced sales and inventory reports. They printed the reports and faxed them to headquarters. At headquarters a clerk would receive the fax, key in the number, and throw away the fax, but they would only input certain numbers such as sales, catering, receivables, payables. In essence they were just picking certain numbers off a fax.

Joey wanted to streamline the process. Using free software that created a pdf file of the report and automatically attached it to an e-mail directed to headquarters, he enabled the creation and transmission of the reports to be collapsed into one step. At headquarters the e-mail software automatically filtered the messages in appropriate folders for easy access by the administrative assistants. Speaking about the challenges associated with the new process, Joey said:

> We originally filtered the reports by e-mail subject, but we had to rely on the managers and chefs to provide the correct subject line. They are computer novices and are also very busy. We had a two-day training session in a client's training lab. That worked for a couple of months but unfortunately, when you stop calling them and visiting them often, "operating report" becomes ops report, OR, or some other acronym. We now filter on brand and unit, which is more reliable because it minimizes human input.

A second initiative, still in beta testing, was the updating of the inventory reports. The current version of the report enabled the unit manager to input current inventory levels, but provided no checks for accuracy. Every week, managers would clear the report, manually check inventory, and input the new values. Joey explained: "Being a small company, we are very vigilant with our inventory, that's why we check it weekly. But input errors in the report are the biggest challenge. These errors are time consuming because they need to be caught and you need to follow up on them." The new report was designed to provide a four-week rolling snapshot of the unit's inventory. When managers ran a macro, the values for the last four weeks would shift and the new values could be input. This format enabled managers to view four weeks of inventory quantities on one screen, as Joey explained:

> With the new report they can see trends and identify input errors. If you had ten cases of tuna last week and today you have one hundred, there was clearly an input error. But the managers are having trouble visualizing the four weeks and understanding how the values shift and where to put the new values. When we are sitting in our office Peter [Case] and I are very computer literate, and what we think may work at the units may in fact not work.

Dartcor had evaluated an automated solution to some of its data transmission and information management challenges. It had recently evaluated a proposal from a local computer consulting company for a software interface that would

capture accounts receivable information and automatically input it into MAS 90. As Joey explained: "The quote came back for about $30,000, an amount we could certainly not devote to a software interface." Dartcor had also recently contemplated very seriously whether to upgrade its unit level IT infrastructure by replacing cash registers with point of sale (POS) terminals—available for about $3,000 per terminal (hardware/software bundle). After substantial debate and analysis, the firm decided not to invest in the initiative. Joey recalled many of the proposed benefits of the initiative:

> With a POS system replacing the cash registers we could completely remove the reporting processes. We could automatically generate all the reports, inventory could easily be input in the POS and we could eliminate the current spreadsheet-based reporting process.

Hausman also believed that POS terminals could improve the accuracy of data used for decision making while, at the same time, alleviating some of the needs for labor-intensive data processing and re-entry. Explaining his vision for technology use, Hausman noted:

> Ideally you would have a cash register or other terminal that could handle all the information we need such as what was purchased, by whom, on what account. A sophisticated enough terminal could then interface directly with our accounting software and feed information directly to it—we would not need to re-input the data.

Dartcor's leadership felt that the benefits of the POS project could only be reaped if the new technology was consistently deployed in all units. Giamarino explained:

> Unless we were able to absorb the significant expense associated with a full rollout, little benefit would ensue from the POS project. Its real value is in its ability to dramatically reduce duplication of effort and the need for significant data re-entry. But this can't happen unless all units implement the POS.

These early IT projects had surfaced many of the key challenges associated with new IT initiatives at Dartcor. Among them were the resource constraints typical of a small private company, the current IT infrastructure that limited the firm's ability to introduce new technology, and the difference in operations, processes, and technology that characterized different units. Giamarino explained:

> When TGIFriday, as an example, sets up its restaurants, they are all the same. Their kitchens are the same, their menus are the same, their cycles are the same. When you need to implement technology across units, it is

continued

straightforward. But every one of our facilities is different, catering menus can be different, billing processes are often different; it is much harder to standardize and leverage technology across the units.

The limited computer literacy typical of unit level personnel, coupled with the need for the staff to focus on operations, was another significant challenge noted by Leeds:

A lot of our chefs are very talented chefs, but they are not necessarily computer savvy. More importantly, there is only so much information we can ask our chefs and managers to absorb in a given week. Therefore, we make it management's priority to stay clearly focused on our goals and objectives.

Giamarino added:

We have managers that work very hard from 6:00 A.M. to 3:00 P.M., [and] technology must be easy to use and understand. If you put a system in that is burdensome, they are not going to use it.

THE NEW IT INITIATIVE

Reflecting on the role of technology at Dartcor, Leeds said:

The challenge on a daily basis is to raise the bar on service, quality, and create a fun working environment. On one front, information technology can help us minimize

the time that our managers spend on process and maximize the time management spends with our guests.

Joey was excited about IT and understood its potential for streamlining business processes and for taking advantage of new opportunities. His background prepared him for his role at Dartcor, both as a technology champion and as the driving force behind new IT projects and proposals. Giamarino explained:

One of the reasons we were very excited about Joey joining us was that he brought an understanding of technology and new ideas about its use. Joey is out there, I tend to be more conservative, and Warren is sort of in the middle. As a team this works out very well; that's what we want.

Since his arrival at Dartcor, Joey evaluated various possible applications of information technology. One—the online catering project—stood out for its potential.

THE ONLINE CATERING PROJECT

The online catering project consisted of a Web-based ordering system that allowed Dartcor to load the gourmet catering menu with pictures and make it available to administrative assistants to log on to (see Exhibit 2 for screenshots of a similar software application). The application was relatively small

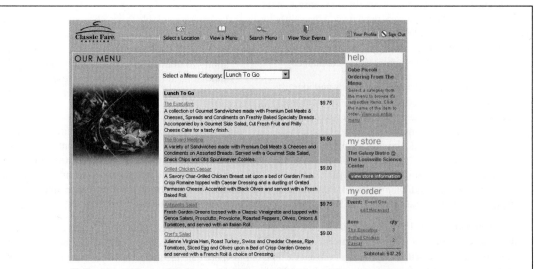

Online Menu. (*Source:* http://www.classicfare.com)

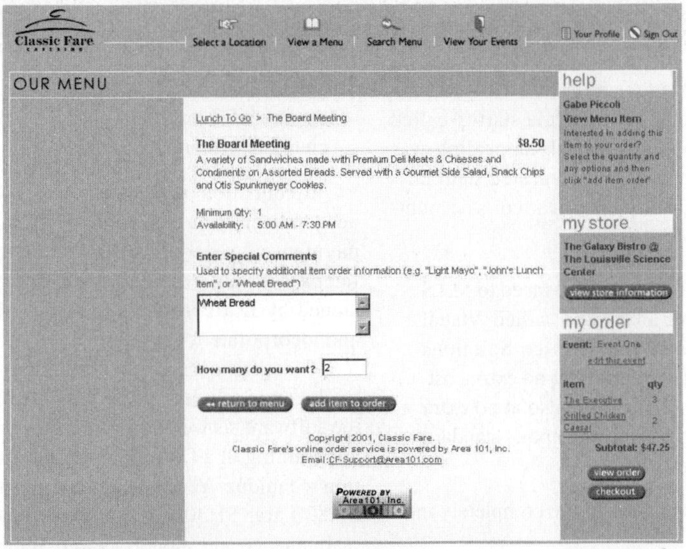

Event Ordering Screen (Source: http://www.classicfare.com)

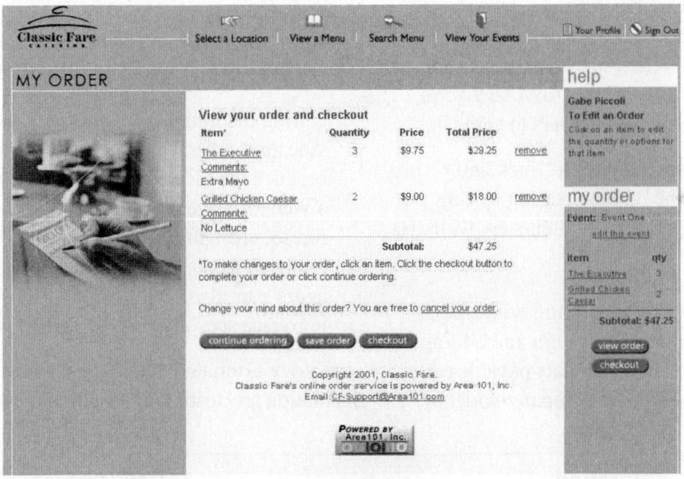

Order Summary (Source http://www.classicfare.com)

Exhibit 2   Online Catering Application

and could be easily hosted on a Web server provided by the client. Each assistant would receive a profile and had access to the history of previous catering orders. Joey noted:

> Chefs are very busy and it is difficult for them to come to the phone. The administrative assistant logs on to the catering ordering system. Now they don't have to wait for the chef. Menu items can be selected online and notes can be input for any customized request. If it is a repeating event they can pull up the previous order, modify it appropriately and submit it instantaneously. The software provides ordering convenience cueing ordering time, it can cross-sell by suggesting similar items, and it provides an audit trail so there is no doubt as to what was ordered.

continued

Joey was particularly interested in eCatering, a software application produced by a California startup called FoodService Solutions, Inc. Particularly appealing was the fact that the software could be integrated with customers' accounting software as well as Dartcor's accounting application. He explained:

> The eCatering application can be interfaced to MAS 90. We would purchase an add-on called Visual Integrator for $1,500 and FoodService Solutions would write an automated interface at no extra cost. Interfacing with client's software is also at no extra charge, assuming that their system supports standard data communication protocols.

Joey discussed the advantages of the completely integrated solution:

> If the client pays by credit card, the order is immediately charged, the software has a secure gateway to our merchant account, and we receive payment immediately. If the transaction is charged to a house account, the transaction is posted immediately to MAS 90. We don't have to wait for the weekly folders to come in.

Because of the software's ability to track and record orders, Joey believed that the online catering system provided significant advantages to the clients as well. He explained:

> They can reconcile all of their catering with a couple of clicks rather than going through and adding up all the catering slips. Their accounts payable can also produce all kinds of reports: company-wide, by

department, by administrative assistant, by type of event, and so on. They enjoy great operational efficiencies without having to support the software.

Acquisition of eCatering entailed the purchase of the needed licenses, a one-time configuration charge, and the payment of yearly hosting and maintenance fees. Two licenses would be required for the configuration envisioned by Dartcor, one enterprise suite license ($4,800) and a corporate location license ($3,600). Configuration fees for each license would be $6,000 and $2,400, respectively, and included the installation and configuration of the software, as well as the one-time creation of the menus and training of a Dartcor representative on the configuration technique. Yearly maintenance and hosting fees were $1,800 and $1,300, respectively, and included routine maintenance and support as well as the hosting of a secure connection to major credit card clearing houses to authenticate credit card transactions.

FoodService Solutions would be responsible for the creation of initial menus, but Dartcor had the ability to access them and modify them at will. Joey explained:

> During the initial configuration process we will provide text and graphics and FoodService Solutions will produce the menus. From then on, we have access to a Web interface that allows us to modify them. I don't foresee changing them often—maybe once a month—probably a couple hours of my work. Chefs and managers can also access the system via their PCs to introduce specials or highlight and push certain items.

Joey estimated that his involvement during the implementation and testing of the software would be up to eighty

Phase	Duration	Deliverables
Phase I	1 Week	Architecture design and documentation of the technology, data and data integration needs between existing applications and eCatering.
Phase II	3 Weeks	Implementation and configuration of the application, including features, graphics, and data.
Phase III	2 Weeks	Rollout, testing, and approval.
Phase IV		Application live in production environment.

Exhibit 3   Catering Software Proposed Implementation

Activity	Beneficiary	Time Savings (hrs)*		Time per Year	Savings per Year**
Event planning	B&I Client	6	per day	1,560	$ 39,000
Billing	Dartcor	8	per month	96	$ 2,400
Billing reconciliation	B&I Client	2	per week	104	$ 2,600
Monthly reporting	Dartcor	8	per month	96	$ 2,400
Monthly reporting	B&I Client	8	per month	96	$ 2,400
Approval and Payment	B&I Client	8	per month	96	$ 2,400
Food waste reduction	Dartcor				$ 5,000
			Total Operations Savings	**2,048**	**$ 56,200**
Incremental orders	Dartcor				**$ 10,000**
				Total Indirect Savings	**$ 10,000**
				Total Savings	**$ 66,200**

*Assumes 5 days/week and 52 weeks/year.

**Assumes labor cost of $25/hour.

Exhibit 4   Analysis of Benefits. (*Source:* FoodService Solutions, Inc.)

Year	1	2	3	4	5	Total
B&I Client savings	$ 46,400	$ 46,400	$ 46,400	$ 46,400	$ 46,400	$ 232,000
Dartcor	$ 19,800	$ 19,800	$ 19,800	$ 19,800	$ 19,800	$ 99,000
Total savings	$ 66,200	$ 66,200	$ 66,200	$ 66,200	$ 66,200	$ 331,000
Total corporate cost	$ 20,100	$ 3,300	$ 3,300	$ 3,300	$ 3,300	$ 33,300
Total savings	$ 46,100	$ 62,900	$ 62,900	$ 62,900	$ 62,900	$ 297,700
Annual ROI	329%	2006%	2006%	2006%	2006%	994%
NPV of total savings	$211,740					
Discount rate	12%					

Exhibit 5   ROI Calculator. (*Source:* FoodService Solutions, Inc.)

hours of work. After successful implementation and integration with Dartcor's IT infrastructure, he expected to be able to pass the responsibility to the account manager, whose ongoing involvement was estimated at one hour per week for troubleshooting and other maintenance tasks associated with the eCatering software.

FoodService Solutions, Inc. had an established track record in this market and a number of installations with large food service managers. Based on this experience, the firm felt comfortable providing an implementation plan (Exhibit 3), as well as cost estimates (Exhibit 4) and projected ROI calculations (Exhibit 5).

THE DECISION

Joey had done significant research and it was time to produce a recommendation for the executive team. Whether he recommended to purchase and install the eCatering solution or not, Joey had to provide a compelling case based on careful analysis. This care was necessary because at Dartcor many

continued

projects competed for limited company resources—pursuing only the ones with the highest potential was fundamental. Sitting at his computer, Joey pondered some of his own words:

> Working on the business development side as well, I can see that cash must be spent on many fronts:

upgrading the units, merchandising, IT, and so on. We must make investments in the most critical areas, those that differentiate us and allow us to compete. We can't go in and say that our back office system is better, because nobody is going to care, or believe us because of our size.

12

Information System Trends

What You Will Learn in This Chapter

In this chapter we introduce some emerging and some enduring trends in information systems and technology management. Understanding these trends and technologies, the associated vocabulary, and the benefits and risks they engender for modern organizations is critical for you as a general or functional manager. You will hear much of this vocabulary from consultants, at conferences, and in the media, and you must learn to navigate it successfully. More importantly, as a manager you will be (or should be!) called on to participate in the debate about whether your own firm should embark in the type of initiatives described in this chapter. Understanding these trends is therefore a prerequisite to being an asset in the discussion.

Specifically, in this chapter you will

1. Learn what has been the genesis of the *enterprise systems* (ES) trend and why so many companies are employing or introducing them. You will also be able to articulate the principal benefits and risks associated with these systems.

2. Define the term *supply chain management* and explain the role that supply chain management applications play in modern organizations.

3. Define the term *best of breed* and describe the benefits and drawbacks of this approach to systems integration. You will also be able to draw comparisons between the best-of-breed and enterprise systems approaches.

4. Describe what is meant by *knowledge management,* categorize the different types of knowledge commonly found in organizations, and explain why organizations feel the need to employ knowledge management applications.

5. Define the terms *business intelligence* (*BI*) and *BI infrastructure*. Be able to identify and describe the role of the technologies that comprise a modern BI infrastructure.

6. Define the term *customer relationship management* (*CRM*) and articulate both its benefits and limitations. Explain how the CRM and BI trends relate to one another.

7. Define the term *open source software* and be able to identify the primary commercial models that have been crafted around the open source movement. You will also be able to articulate the principal advantages and risks associated with the implementation of open source solutions in modern organizations.

8. Define the software as a service (SaaS) trend, identify its genesis, and discuss its principal characteristics.

MINI-CASE: INTEGRATION AT BIGPHARMA, INC.

As you walk out the board room, still shaking your head in disbelief, you mumble to yourself, "Boy, that was fun! They were really going at it today!" As you get to your desk, it hits you—you have to make sense of what just happened in there.

As the executive assistant to the CEO at BigPharma, Inc., the second largest pharmaceutical firm in the United States, you have had the luxury of attending all of the executive team meetings, and sometimes participating in the decision making with your analyses, without any of the responsibility that comes with making those decisions. However, far from what you had imagined the glamour of board room discussions to be, most meetings of the executive team were pretty boring. Not today!

Surprisingly, you had predicted this one to be a real snoozer. A pretty safe bet given the topic: the need to gain efficiencies by better integrating across functional areas. The meeting took a turn toward the exciting right out of the gates when Laura Jean Polly, your boss, announced that at PharmaMed (the premier industry trade event of the year) she had drinks with the senior VP of business development of BigCoSoft, the second largest vendor of enterprise systems.

She said that BigCoSoft was interested in breaking into the pharmaceutical market and was seeking to sign up a high-profile customer. They looked at this contract as a mutually beneficial partnership that would lead to lots of press and advantages for both firms. The client would be a "showcase customer," featured on the Web site and in case studies. BigCoSoft was willing to waive licensing fees for the first three years. "But the biggest advantage," the senior VP had said, "is that with you on board we will attract more customers. With critical mass we can put huge development resources into this product."

At this point you were thinking, "Yep, snoozer! I was right." Two seconds later the first salvo was fired. Jane Pinket, the senior VP of finance, said, "Everyone knows

that BigCoSoft's strength is manufacturing. Their financial package stinks. They will surely want to reuse that code and I am going to have to take the hit. We can cut the same deal with LargeCoSoft. They already have an enterprise system for pharmaceutical firms, and their financial module is top notch."

"Another option could be to write a bolt-on," chimed in Erik Dino, the chief operations officer (COO), "that should take care of the missing finance functionalities." "But the Human Resource module of BigCoSoft also leaves much to be desired," interjected Joe Cole, the senior VP of human resources. "Plus, we just spent $12 million on the overhauling of the benefits management system; am I going to get hit with more information systems service charges for an upgrade I don't need?"

This is about the time confusion set in, and the story is fuzzy as you got lost in the ping-pong volleys of comments, questions, and responses. With a heated topic on the agenda, it was painfully clear that the people in the room were more used to being listened to than to listening.

You were snapped back to attention when Ms. Polly closed the meeting by calling your name. She added, "Well, it looks like I had underestimated how much my staff cared about systems! I will need a report with an investigation of the top three most viable options; the need to integrate is not going away, so we have to do something. I told BigCoSoft I would get back to them in three weeks."

DISCUSSION QUESTIONS

1. Even as the lowly executive assistant to the CEO, it was apparent to you that there was some groupthink going on here. Was buying an enterprise system the only option?

2. You vaguely recall this idea of best-of-breed applications from your information systems class, two years ago. Could that approach work here?

Enterprise System: Focus on integrating the key internal business process of the firm. E.G. SAP, Oracle, People soft
โดยรวมเข้าด้วยกัน software module & common central data base และ เชื่อมโยงการไหลของ information ในทั่วๆแบบมาร์ทด้วยการ
business process ต่างๆ

ENTERPRISE SYSTEMS   359

INTRODUCTION

In this chapter we discuss the most relevant and influential trends in information systems and technology management. We focus on those emerging and enduring trends that are capturing media attention and that consulting companies are promoting today. These are the trends that you will need to confront as you join the workforce in the immediate future.

We organize this chapter around the technologies at the core of each trend. This is a conscious approach that mirrors how decisions are made in modern organizations. Typically, an organization will become aware of an emerging information systems trend through publications, consulting companies, or conferences and events. The trend is defined by the functionalities of the technology at the core or the features and characteristics of a new class of software applications—from which the trend typically takes its name. It is critical for you to realize that, no matter how sophisticated a technology may be, in order for it to have a positive impact on the organization, you must be able to design an information system around it (see Chapter 2). Thus, for each of the trends discussed in this chapter, we analyze the technology capabilities as a departure point to understand the organizational impacts that they engender.

ENTERPRISE SYSTEMS

Organizations have historically designed and custom developed software applications to support their unique work activities and business processes. This approach was necessary as computers became a staple of operations in large organizations in the 1970s and 1980s, but a stable software industry had yet to emerge. These custom-developed applications were typically designed and implemented at departmental or functional level, giving rise to what we have termed the functional perspective (see Chapter 3).

staple = principal & essential

Once organizational computing became prevalent, as software entrepreneurs identified more and more areas where operations of organizations could be automated using standardized software programs, the software industry grew dramatically. Today the worldwide software industry has surpassed the $200 billion mark and continues to grow at a tremendous pace (see Figure 12.1).

In the late 1980s and early 1990s, the proliferation of stand-alone applications began to highlight the limitations of the functional approach, giving rise to the process perspective, business process reengineering methodologies, and the integration imperative (see Chapter 3). The missing piece in the quest for integrated operations was a class of standardized software applications that would enable and support integrated business processes. Such applications are now known as enterprise systems (ESs).

The Genesis of Enterprise Systems

While enterprise systems have been the dominant trend in organizational computing over the last decade and a half, and continue to garner significant attention, their roots reach as far back as the 1960s, when computing resources began to be applied to manufacturing

Million

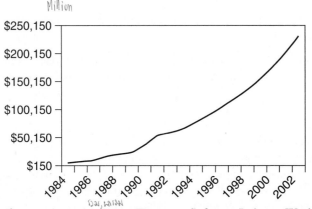

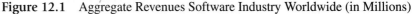

$250,150

$200,150

$150,150

$100,150

$50,150

$150

1984 1986 1988 1990 1992 1994 1996 1998 2000 2002

Figure 12.1 Aggregate Revenues Software Industry Worldwide (in Millions)

problems. At the time, manufacturing organizations applied information technology toward the optimization of inventory control, quickly realizing that in order for inventory to be efficiently managed, it would have to be linked to production schedules. Thus, the MRP (material requirement planning) approach was born and manufacturing firms wrote software designed to automatically translate master production schedules into requirements for subassemblies, components, and raw materials.

Under pressure to be increasingly efficient, in the 1980s manufacturing organizations introduced MRP-II (manufacturing resource planning), a concept that extended MRP to encompass the entire factory production process. At that time, software houses like German-based SAP began to seek integration of activities that have a bearing on manufacturing processes but span other functional areas, such as human resources, engineering, and project management. So what should we call a software application that extends the MRP concept to support integrated management beyond the manufacturing function and encompass other functions across the enterprise? Enterprise resource planning (ERP), of course, quite a confusing label that only makes sense based on its genesis.

With the relentless pursuit of efficiency by manufacturing firms under pressure from Japanese firms, the steadily declining cost of information technology assets, and the emergence of the client/server model, which allowed organizations to enable access to complex

Figure 12.2 A Factory Shop Floor

software applications such as ERPs through user-friendly personal computer terminals, the stage was set for ERP (or enterprise systems, as they were later renamed) to become widely accepted. A big contribution to the commercial success of enterprise systems came from the fear that twenty- and thirty-year-old legacy applications[1] would suddenly stop running on January 1, 2000 (known as the Y2K bug).

While much early development in this area was focused on functionalities (i.e., what the software applications could do), the parallel development of the business process reengineering (BPR) methodology (see Chapter 3), which called for a process focus and the use of IT to integrate activities across the organizational functions, led to an increasing focus on changing the way activities in the enterprise were performed. At this time, with the increasing focus on business processes and their redesign, ES vendors began focusing on incorporating "best practices" in their applications with the objective of offering a ready-made set of menus of business processes native to the application. Today the label "best practice software" is a pervasive and highly inflationed one.

As enterprise systems have continued to mature, the list of top vendors reads like a who's who of software companies, and consolidation has already begun to occur, with the top 5 vendors (Table 12.1) estimated to control over 70 percent of the market.[2] Competition is now fierce; with the market for larger *Fortune* 1000 organizations close to saturation, the main vendors have developed enterprise systems aimed at small and medium enterprises (SME).

As a consequence of the commercial success of enterprise systems, as you enter the workforce you will either be managing in an organization that already has an ES or a smaller firm that is evaluating such purchase. In either case you need to understand the characteristics of these applications—with the advantages and risks they engender—and their impact on the surrounding information system and the organization at large.

Enterprise Systems: Definition

It is clear from the genesis of modern enterprise systems that their defining feature is that of native integration and an effort to support all components of the firm's IT infrastructure. We define an enterprise system as a modular, integrated software application that spans (all)

Table 12.1   Top ERP Vendors (2004)

Vendor	2004 Revenue (millions of U.S. dollars)	2005 Market Share (%)
SAP	$9372	40
PeopleSoft[3]	$2880	12
Oracle	$2465	10
Sage Group	$1243	5
Microsoft Business Solutions	$ 775	3

[1] *Legacy* is a term that does not have a precise definition in information systems. It is typically used to refer to older functional applications based on traditional programming languages (e.g., COBOL) that run on mainframes.

[2] Reilly, K. (2005), "AMR Research Releases ERP Market Report Showing Overall Market Growth of 14% in 2004," June 14, http://www.amrresearch.com/Content/View.asp?pmillid=18358 (Accessed 8/8/2006).

[3] In 2005, Oracle complete the purchase of PeopleSoft, further consolidating the industry.

organizational functions and relies on one database at the core (Figure 12.3). An organization can theoretically build its own ES in house. For example, in 2003 Hilton Hotels unveiled OnQ, a custom-made enterprise system estimated to cost over $50 million. Describing it, Tim Harvey, CIO of Hilton, stated, "OnQ is comprised of six major business functions; the idea was to take all the business functions required in a hotel and make them all work together as one system so it's highly integrated."[4]

Some custom development notwithstanding, the great majority of firms will purchase an ES from one of the dominant vendors in an effort to capitalize on the economies of scale associated with off-the-shelf software applications (see Chapter 11).

The principal characteristics of enterprise systems are modularity, application and data integration, and configurability.

Modularity   Enterprise systems are modular in nature, thus enabling the organization that purchases one to decide which functionalities to enable and which ones not to. The modularity of enterprise systems is a necessity dictated by their size and scope. For as much as ES vendors strive to code comprehensive menus of configuration options and "best practices" into their applications, no single vendor can be the best at each module. For example, PeopleSoft (now owned by Oracle) has historically been known for the strength of its human resource module, while SAP R/3 is known for the strength of its manufacturing module (see Table 12.2 for a sample ES modules and functionalities).

Modularity enables customers of enterprise systems to exercise some flexibility with respect to the components of the application they intend to purchase and those that they don't need (and should not pay for). In the extreme, modularity also enables a firm to pick and choose individual modules from competing ES vendors, even though this approach defeats the very driver of ES implementations.

Application and Data Integration   Native integration is the defining characteristic of enterprise systems. More specifically, ESs enable application integration. With application integration, an event that occurs in one of the modules of the application automatically triggers an event in one or more separate modules.

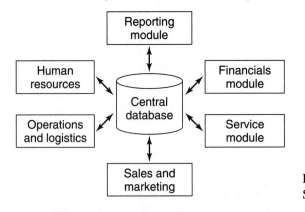

Figure 12.3   Enterprise System's Modules

[4] Shein, E. (2003), "Hilton Hotels CIO Talks 'OnQ'," *CIO Magazine,* July 15. http://www.cloupdate.com/insight/article.thp/2235231 (Accessed 6/6/07).

Table 12.2   Sample ES Modules and Functionalities

Financials

Accounts receivable and payable
Asset accounting
Cash management and forecasting
Financial consolidation
General ledger
Product-cost accounting
Profit-center accounting

Human Resources

Payroll
Personnel planning
Travel expenses

Operations and Logistics

Inventory management
Material requirements planning
Materials management
Plant maintenance
Production planning
Routing management
Shipping

Sales and Marketing

Order management
Pricing
Sales management
Sales planning

Consider the following example:

> A Paris-based sales representative for a U.S. computer manufacturer prepares a quote for a customer using an ES. The salesperson enters some basic information about the customer's requirements into his laptop computer, and the ES automatically produces a formal contract, in French, specifying the product's configuration, price, and delivery date. When the customer accepts the quote, the sales rep hits a key; the system, after verifying the customer's credit limit, records the order. The system schedules the shipment; identifies the best routing and then, working backward from the delivery date, reserves the necessary materials from inventory; orders needed parts from suppliers; and schedules assembly in the company's factory in Taiwan.

> The sales and production forecasts are immediately updated, and a material-requirements-planning list and bill of materials are created. The sales rep's payroll account is credited with the correct commission, in [euros], and his travel account is credited with the expense of the sales call. The actual product cost and profitability are calculated, in U.S. dollars, and the divisional and corporate balance sheets, the accounts-payable and accounts-receivable ledgers,

the cost-center accounts, and the corporate cash levels are all automatically updated. The system performs nearly every information transaction resulting from the sale.[5]

The above example, a sort of sales-pitch for the perfect world of ES, neatly highlights the notion of application integration. A number of modules—inventory, production, logistics, human resources, and financials—are engaged by one simple event: The sales-rep hits the enter key to confirm the order.

Data integration focuses on the information that is stored by the ES, instead of the processes it supports. ESs rely on one logical database at the core. That is, while there may be multiple physical data stores and locations where information resides, they will be treated as one, thus ensuring data integration. This feature is a critical selling point of ESs because one logical database ensures a high degree of data integrity (i.e., data are accurate), limitation of data redundancy (i.e., data are not repeated unnecessarily) and the enforcement of one data schema (i.e., all modules define the same piece of data, say customer, in the same way).

Configurable   Enterprise systems are parameterized. That is, because they are intended to serve the needs of a wide range of different organizations in an industry, ESs come with configuration tables that enable the adopting firm to choose among a predefined set of options during the implementation of the application. For instance, your firm may prefer to account for inventory on a last-in first-out (LIFO) basis, while another firm that purchased the same ES needs to use the first-in first-out (FIFO) method. During the implementation, you and your competitor will simply configure the application differently by choosing different options.

Enterprise systems also allow the firm to extend the capabilities of the standard application by creating "bolt-on modules." Bolt-on modules, typically written using a programming language that is native to the ES (e.g., ABAP in SAP), are used to further tailor the ES to the specific needs of the organization. While this tailoring of a standardized application may seem counterintuitive, a recent Cutter Consortium survey shows that it is a fairly common occurrence, with 48 percent of the respondents reporting the development of add-ons to supplement the functionality of the package.[6]

The Advantages of Enterprise Systems

At this point there is considerable literature and evidence describing the advantages of adopting enterprise systems, including efficiency improvements through direct and indirect cost savings, responsiveness, knowledge infusion, and adaptability.

Efficiency   Perhaps the biggest selling point of enterprise systems to an executive audience is their promise to rein in complex, generally hard-to-manage and support legacy IT infrastructures. Because of their support of business and data integration, ESs have the potential to dramatically reduce direct costs, such as those associated with the need for entering the same data in multiple applications. ESs also promise improved efficiency through the reduction of indirect costs achieved by streamlining business processes and operations.

---

[5] Davenport, T. H. (1998), "Putting the Enterprise into Enterprise System," *Harvard Business Review* (July/Aug.), pp. 121–131.

[6] Ulrich, W. (2006), "Application Package Survey: The Promise versus Reality,"*Cutter Benchmark Review* (6:9), pp. 13–20.

Responsiveness As the scenario presented earlier shows, one of the advantages of application integration, as delivered by enterprise systems, is a dramatic improvement in the firm's ability to respond to customers and market demands. With up-to-date information available in the field, the sales representative in the example was able to quote a delivery date and price on the fly. Moreover, application integration confirmed the order seamlessly and immediately engaged all processes necessary to fulfill the contract.

Knowledge Infusion As with most off-the-shelf applications, enterprise systems enable the infusion of knowledge into the adopting firm. That is, the application is thought to embed the state of the art in industry practice so that it can be used as a vehicle for updating business processes and operations within the firm. The appeal of knowledge infusion has traditionally been one of the primary selling points of enterprise systems because ES vendors have made it a cornerstone of their strategy to embed "best practices" in their software releases by vetting and selecting the parameters of the application.

ES vendors have been largely successful in these efforts, with 70 percent of respondents to a recent survey claiming that adopting the ES would help them to adopt best practices,[7] and the major vendors commercializing industry-specific ES that make industry best practices a key value proposition. In fact, many enterprise systems implementations have been justified on the basis of senior executives' frustration with the current state of operations. In these organizations the ES installation became a means to drastically reorganize the firm's operations using business process reengineering techniques and the software to enforce the new business processes.

Adaptability A final advantage offered by enterprise systems is their high degree of adaptability to the unique organizational context. While certainly not comparable to the adaptability of tailor-made applications, enterprise systems offer a degree of customizability rarely provided by off-the-shelf applications. The adaptability of ES is achieved through the use of configuration tables and bolt-on functionality.

Because of the size, scope, and complexity of ES, implementation and configuration processes are very complicated. For example, SAP R/3 has over 3000 configuration tables. Beyond configuration and the development of bolt-on functionalities, an ES implementation requires migration and consolidation of data repositories. For this reason every major vendor has a network of partners, called integrators, who have developed specific expertise in implementing the applications. Large integrators, such as Accenture or Earnst & Young, take ownership of the installation, implementation, and adaptation processes, and their fees (rather than software licenses) make up the bulk of the cost of an ES implementation.

The Limitations of Enterprise Systems

A massive undertaking of the kind that enterprise systems implementations bring about is bound to have significant drawbacks, and there is now a comprehensive literature on the limitations of enterprise systems. The critical issues to consider are the trade-off between

---

[7] Wagner, E. L., and Newell, S. (2006), "User Experiences with the Implementation and Use of Application Package Software," *Cutter Benchmark Review* (6:9), pp. 5–13.

standardization and flexibility, the limitations of best practice software, the potential for strategic clash, and the high costs and risks of the implementation process.

Standardization and Flexibility   Despite the potential for adaptability and the support for the development of bolt-on modules, when implementing enterprise systems organizations are highly encouraged to implement as close to a standard version of the software as possible. This "vanilla" implementation ensures that the organization capitalizes on the development economies of scale of the vendor and that implementation time and effort are kept to a minimum. Moreover, if the firm limits itself to configurations and adaptations that are native to the ES, it will find it easiest to transition when upgrading its current software during marketplace migrations.[8]

This approach is diametrically opposite to the custom development approach, where the technology is shaped to fit the unique needs of the organization. With "vanilla" enterprise systems implementations, it is the firm and its business processes that need to accommodate the characteristics of the packaged enterprise system—often requiring significant business process reengineering and change management.

The trade-off between standardization and flexibility is further amplified by the fact that there is significant premium associated with the consolidation of the firm's IT infrastructure around one enterprise system. The high degree of application and data integration promised by enterprise systems can only be delivered if the firm is willing to standardize on one vendor and install a sufficient number of modules. Yet as the reach of the application within the organization extends (i.e., more modules are implemented), so do the limitations to the flexibility of individual units. The high degree of integration of ESs requires that the separate units learn to coordinate their efforts and negotiate their preferences.

Finally, enterprise systems are often referred to as software concrete. Concrete is very adaptable and moldable while being poured yet very inflexible and difficult to modify after it has set. In other words, while it is true that enterprise systems offer degrees of adaptability that are not typical of off-the-shelf applications, it is important to note that much of the adaptability comes from configuration tables that can only be used during the implementation process.

Is the Best Practice Embedded in the ES Really Best?   One of the critical selling points of enterprise systems is the fact that they are thought to embed industry best practices. The notion of best practice software is predicated on the idea that it is possible to identify the technique or techniques that are optimal in delivering a given outcome, and that these techniques or methods can be codified in a software program. When the application is implemented in an organization, it will "force" the firm to adapt, thus putting into practice the optimal technique.

While the notion of best practice software is intuitively appealing, it is critical that you recognize some of its limitations. First, it is unclear how best practices are identified. In the case of enterprise systems, the best practice may simply be what the software design team deemed as the optimal set of processed to complete the activity. Second, as we discussed in Chapter 2, it is not enough to implement a software program to enact a new practice. Third, and most important, the unique approach your organization has developed to

---

[8] The term *marketplace migration* refers to the cyclical upgrades associated with new versions of the software.

carry out a given activity, your own best practice if you will, may not be supported by the ES. This limitation of the best practice approach can have dramatic impacts when it leads to a strategic clash.

Strategic Clash   When a firm adopts an enterprise system, it will have to choose amongst the set of business processes supported by the software—the best practices. Often they will be readily available within the existing set of configuration tables provided by the application (e.g., FIFO inventory management). In other cases, the established business processes of the firm may not be supported. This is not a problem when the traditional organizational processes are considered substandard. Indeed, as mentioned above, the case for ES implementation often stems from the need to update the firm's operations. But what if one of your unique practices, one that you think gives you a competitive edge, is not supported by the ES?

Consider the case of a spare parts manufacturer. The firm made customer service a cornerstone of its strategic positioning and was willing to "shuffle the cue" of orders when one of its best customers required a rushed order. The firm did not advertise this "best practice" and such practice was not coded into the ES the firm was considering implementing. Yet management thought that such a differentiating process was a source of competitive advantage. What would you do in this case?

As the example above illustrates, as a general or functional manager you must be extremely careful with enterprise systems installations. You need to be able to identify those highly unique business processes that differentiate your organization from the competition. Such processes will likely not be codified in the ES inventory of best practices. Thus, you will have to weigh one of the following options:

- Forgo the ES implementation.
- Implement the ES but build bolt-on modules to maintain support for your unique processes.
- Implement the ES without the modules that impact the unique processes and maintain the associated legacy systems.
- Implement the ES in standard fashion (i.e., vanilla installation) and sacrifice your unique processes to seek improved efficiency and preserve integration.

The appropriate course of action will depend on the number of unique business processes you identify and their impact on the firm's performance. The important consideration here is to evaluate the decision beforehand rather than during implementation or, even worse, afterward.

High Costs and Risks   Gartner, the technology advisory and consulting firm, has recently developed a tool it calls the hype cycle (Figure 12.4). The hype cycle describes the five phases of evolution of business technology:

- *Technology trigger.* The phase when a new technology becomes available.
- *Peak of inflated expectations.* The phase when overenthusism and unrealistic expectations fuel rapid adoption.[9]

---

[9] The irony of the fact that it is often organizations like Gartner that push technologies toward the peak of inflated expectations will not be lost on our most attentive readers.

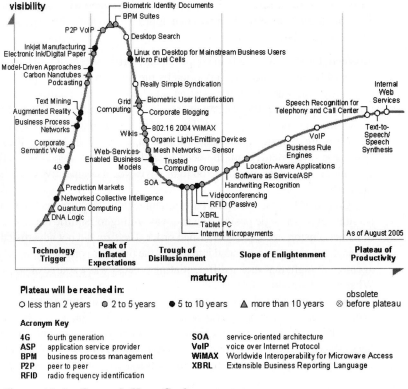

Figure 12.4 Gartner's Hype Cycle

- *Trough of disillusionment.* The phase when failures become public and the sentiment that the technology was incorrectly surrounded by too much optimism takes hold.

- *Slope of enlightenment.* The phase when the true benefits of the technology become apparent to the organizations that persist in applying them.

- *Plateau of productivity.* The phase when the benefits and risks of the technology become widely understood and accepted.

Enterprise systems have achieved a degree of maturity such that they are rapidly approaching the plateau of productivity. Yet over the years ESs made plenty of casualties. This is because enterprise systems, like most large-scale systems implementations, are costly, in terms of time and money and risky endeavors.

Consider the following well-documented case: "FoxMeyer Drugs was a $5 billion company and the nation's fourth largest distributor of pharmaceuticals before the fiasco. With the goal of using technology to increase efficiency, the Delta III project began in 1993. FoxMeyer conducted market research and product evaluation and purchased SAP R/3 in December of that year. FoxMeyer also purchased warehouse-automation from a vendor called Pinnacle, and chose Andersen Consulting to integrate and implement the two systems. [. . .] FoxMeyer was driven to bankruptcy in 1996, and the trustee of FoxMeyer announced in 1998 that he is suing SAP, the ERP vendor, as well as Andersen Consulting, its SAP integrator, for $500 million each."[10]

An enterprise system engenders a number of technical (e.g., migrating and integrating existing databases) and behavioral (e.g., significant degree of business process change) challenges that must be actively managed by the adopting firm with the help of a skilled integrator.

SUPPLY CHAIN MANAGEMENT

In its most general terms, a supply chain is the set of coordinated entities that contribute to move a product or service from its production to its consumption. From the standpoint of a given firm, the upstream supply chain is concerned with gathering and providing the organization with the resources it needs to perform its transformation process (e.g., raw materials, energy, and equipment). The downstream supply chain is concerned with moving the outputs of the firm's production process to its intended consumers.

For instance, the supply chain of a grocery store is the complex network of firms that produce the groceries consumers purchase at the individual stores (see Figure 12.5). Supply chain management (SCM) is the set of logistic and financial processes associated with the planning, executing, and monitoring of supply chain operations.

A Brief History of Supply Chain Management

The use of information technology to enable supply chain management has a long tradition, following a pattern of increasing integration of separate processes similar to that of

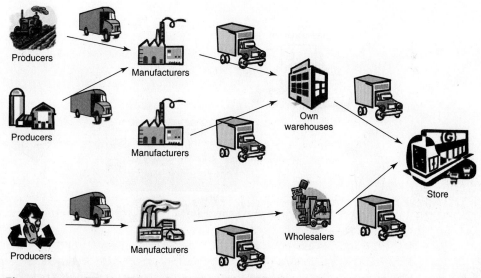

Figure 12.5   Supply Chain of a Grocery Store Chain

---

[10] Scott, J. (1999), "The FoxMeyer Drugs' Bankruptcy: Was It a Failure of ERP?" *Proceedings of The Association for Information Systems Fifth Americas Conference on Information Systems,* Computer Society Press, Milwaukee, WI, August 1999.

enterprise systems. Software support for supply chain management emerged to capture the strong linkages between the warehousing and transportation functions of the organization (see Figure 12.6). Integrated warehousing and transportation allowed the firm to create efficiencies due to the joint optimization of warehouse locations, layouts, transportation routes, and related processes. Something as simple as ensuring that delivery trucks leave the warehouse full, rather than half-empty, can have dramatic impacts on the firm's profitability because of the high fixed costs of this activity.

The next step in the evolution of integrated supply chain management was marked by the recognition that further efficiencies could be created by integrating the logistics processes (i.e., transportation and warehousing) with manufacturing schedules and processes (see Figure 12.7). At this stage, the financial and information flows associated with the management of the supply chain (i.e., procurement and order management processes) were also integrated.

This increasing degree of integration was enabled by the continued improvements in the power of IT and supply chain management software functionalities. The firm that is able to manage these activities in concert can minimize slack resources (e.g., costly slow-downs or stoppage in manufacturing due to lack of the needed raw materials), improve logistics, and make better purchasing decisions.

Modern Supply Chain Management

The last step in the evolution of supply chains consisted in the realization that tight linkages could be established with upstream (i.e., suppliers) and downstream firms (i.e., customers). Modern supply chain management systems are therefore interorganizational systems (Chapter 2) increasingly supported by the use of the Internet (see Figure 12.8). Typically a firm will establish an extranet in order to coordinate activities with its supply chain management

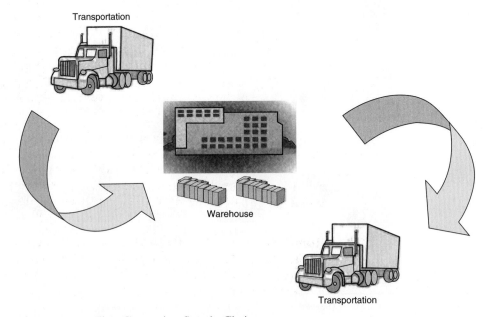

Figure 12.6   First-Generation Supply Chain

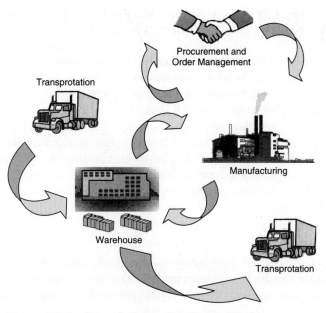

Figure 12.7   Second-Generation Supply Chain

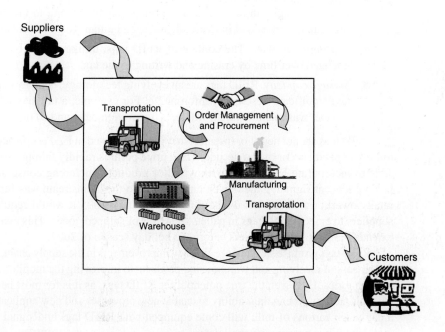

Figure 12.8   Third-Generation Supply Chain

partners. An extranet is a private network that uses the public Internet infrastructure and Internet technologies but spans the boundaries of the organization and enables secure transactions between a firm and its suppliers, vendors, customers, or any other partner.

The last stage in the evolution of supply chain management has been its integration with enterprise systems. As ERP applications have traditionally been focused on internal operations, merging with boundary-spanning supply chain management systems has been a natural evolution. Moreover, as the ES market is maturing and the majority of large organizations have deployed them, linking firms in the supply chain has become simpler.

The increasing attention to IT-enabled supply chain management has also given rise to focused intermediaries whose value proposition is providing the tools to enable integrated supply chain management in specific industry "verticals" (i.e., industry segments). Such B2B intermediaries facilitate coordination of the material, financial, and information flows in the supply chain.

Supply Chain Management Trends

The emergence of cost-effective radiofrequency identification (RFID) chips has opened a new frontier for supply chain management. RFID relies on a set of tag readers that detect and decode information contained in RFID tags using radio frequencies. RFID has a number of advantages:

- *No line of sight requirements.* Because RFID tags use radiofrequencies, they do not require that a tag be directly in contact or have an unimpeded path to the transponders, as is the case with bar code scanner, for example.

- *Embedding.* Because RFID tags need no line of sight to communicate with tag readers, RFID tags can be embedded in the products they are to identify. Moreover, tags can be embedded in livestock and even humans (e.g., patients in a hospital).

- *Writing capability.* The content of RFID tags, unlike that of bar codes, can be changed over time by erasing and writing to the tag.

- *Storage capacity.* RFID tags are an evolving technology, but they can already contain significant descriptive information. For example, a tag may tell us when the product was manufactured, where, its expiration date, and so on.

RFID tags are not new. For instance, they have been used in EZ Pass devices for highway toll booth payment for over a decade. Their price point is rapidly falling to where it is feasible to incorporate RFID tags in a myriad of products, including consumer goods. The landmark event signaling the movement of RFID to the mainstream was June 2003, when retail powerhouse Wal-Mart dictated that by January 2005 it would require its top 100 suppliers to embed RFID tags in pallets and cases of shipped goods. This mandate was later extended to over 1000 suppliers before the holiday season of 2007.

RFID tags promise substantial efficiency improvements in the supply chain, from speeding the process of receiving and warehousing products to improving the monitoring and control of inventories. However, the true potential for RFID tags, as it is for most new information technologies, may be in their ability to enable new processes and new applications. Imagine a day when cartons of milk will come equipped with RFID tags and signal to your fridge that this milk is nearing the spoil date.

BEST-OF-BREED INTEGRATION

Organizations have implemented enterprise systems and integrated supply chain management applications in response to the recent emergence of the integration imperative (see Chapter 3)—ES with predominantly an internal focus and SCM with an interorganizational one. Both of these solutions rely on the use of a single-vendor, highly integrated, modular software program that limits the firm's flexibility. While a firm can install a limited set of ES modules and use multiple vendors, this approach limits the advantages offered by the package. Thus, the firm typically will install modules that are not considered the best for the firm's needs in order to preserve integration.

Recognizing these limitations, a competing approach, known as best-of-breed, is becoming increasingly popular. The best-of-breed approach is designed to enable the firm to retain a high degree of flexibility with respect to the applications it decides to adopt while still being able to achieve tight integration among them. As the term suggests, best-of-breed allows the firm to choose the module or application that best suits its information processing need. As such, the best-of-breed approach enables a firm to achieve integration using applications from different vendors.

Enterprise Application Integration (EAI)

The best-of-breed approach is enabled by a new integration paradigm that focuses not on applications to be integrated, but on the linkages among them. Integration of separate systems has been traditionally achieved with point-to-point connections called interfaces. This approach engenders significant limitations as the number of interfaces grows dramatically with the number of applications that need to be connected. That is, the number of bilateral interfaces needed to connect n systems is $n(n-1)/2$ (i.e., 3 systems, 3 interfaces; 5 systems, 10 interfaces, 10 systems, 45 interfaces, and so on). Such an approach can quickly result in a messy infrastructure that is difficult and costly to maintain (see Figure 12.9). Note that anytime a change is made to one system, all interfaces that connect to it will need to be modified.

In order to achieve the promise of best of breed without the limitations of bilateral interfaces, the enterprise application integration (EAI) approach has recently emerged. EAI consists of "re-architecting" existing programs so that an intermediate layer, termed *middleware,* is developed between the applications and databases (see Figure 12.10). The existing applications are designed to make calls to the middleware layer rather than to one another, as with bilateral interfaces. Integrating applications and databases in this fashion provides the firm with the highest degree of flexibility when selecting applications and the ability to swap them independently when upgrades are needed.

The EAI approach also streamlines the maintenance process because changes to an application will not affect all the interfaces connected to it. Rather, as long as each application is able to make requests to, and receive requests from, the middleware layer, no other application needs to be modified.

While the EAI approach has intuitive appeal, it is a trend that is still in its infancy and is in substantial flux. As a consequence, EAI implementations require substantial technical expertise and engender a significant degree of risk. By some estimates, 70 percent of EAI projects

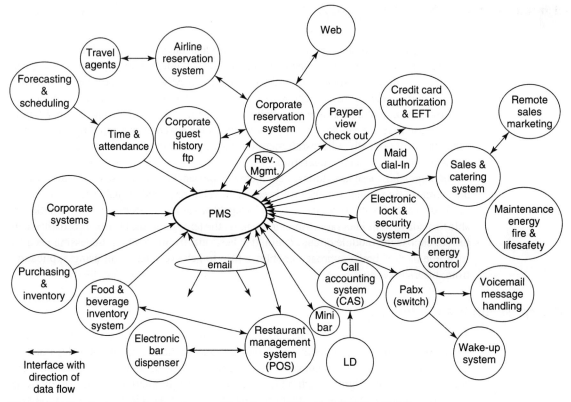

Figure 12.9 Systems Infrastructure and Interfaces of Typical Midsize Hotel

still fail.[11] While these figures are typically overinflated by considering overbudget and late projects as outright failures, it is clear that EAI is a technology that has not matured yet. However, with major vendors offering their flavor of EAI technology, EAI remains a promising trend for organizations seeking to achieve integration without sacrificing flexibility.

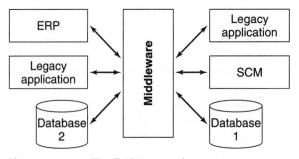

Figure 12.10 The EAI Approach

---

[11] Trotta, G. (2003), "Dancing Around EAI 'Bear Traps'," *eBizQ*, December 15. http://www.ebizq.met/topics/int_sbf/features/3463.html (Accessed 6/6/07).

Ultimate Flexibility: Service-Oriented Architecture

Business organizations are under constant pressure to become increasingly flexible and agile in order to respond to rapidly evolving customer needs and accelerating competition. IT professionals and the software industry have seized the opportunity to enable such increasing levels of agility and flexibility. The dominant solution goes under the broad label of service-oriented architecture (SOA).

SOA is a software design perspective focused on reusability of software components, interoperability, and ongoing optimization of business processes. SOA works by using standards to make independent services available on a network. These services, sometimes referred to as Web services, are made available as components to be accessed and used by application without knowledge of their underlying design or structure. In other words, SOA enables the rapid creation of application by the combination of pre-built services.

The SOA approach is different from EAI, even though it conceptually builds on the same ideas. EAI calls for integration of separate best-of-breed applications through middleware. With SOA the applications themselves, as well as the manner in which they communicate, are built using separate but interoperable components that can be modified and combined depending on the characteristics of the business process they are designed to support.

KNOWLEDGE MANAGEMENT

Recognizing the importance of knowledge as an organizational asset, Thomas Watson, the legendary CEO of IBM, stated, "All the value of this company is in its people. If you burned down all our plants, and we just kept our people and our information files, we should soon be as strong as ever."

Knowledge: Definition

In Chapter 4 we defined the term *data* as codified raw facts, and *information* as data in context. Knowledge can be thought of as a blend of actionable information built over time based on accumulated experiences and understanding of a phenomenon. We can categorize knowledge with respect to its object as follows:

- *Knowing what.* This type of knowledge is based on the ability to collect, categorize, and assimilate information. An example is the ability of a financial intermediary to articulate and explain what type of investment is best suited to the goals expressed by a given client.

- *Knowing how.* This type of knowledge is predicated on the ability to recognize or create the sequence of steps that are needed to complete a task or carry out an activity. An example is the ability of the financial intermediary to create the portfolio of investments described above by completing the appropriate forms and purchasing the appropriate securities.

- *Knowing why.* This type of knowledge is based on an understanding of cause-effect relationships and the laws that govern a given phenomenon. An example is the ability of the same financial intermediary to recognize why some investments are best suited for her various clients as they progress through life and conditions change.

This understanding will allow her to identify relevant changes and suggest the appropriate adjustments to each of them.

Knowledge has also been categorized with respect to its type in explicit and tacit knowledge.

- *Explicit knowledge.* Explicit knowledge can be articulated, codified, and transferred with relative ease. An example is provided by the training manual that the financial intermediary described above used to learn how to purchase securities for her clients. The manual enables the intermediary to know how to perform the transaction. She can then pass this knowledge on to her associates if necessary.

- *Tacit knowledge.* Tacit knowledge is the type of knowledge that individuals possess but find difficult to articulate, codify, and transfer. A classic example is offered by athletes who, when asked about the reasons for a specific decision during the game, often refer to instinct—an instinct developed through years of practice and handling of similar game situations, but, as such, hard to express in words and convey to others.

The above distinction is important because a firm that engages in knowledge management will find it easier to handle explicit rather than tacit knowledge. Whether explicit or tacit, knowledge is increasingly considered a critical asset for modern organizations and, as such, it needs to be protected and proactively managed. Knowledge enables a firm to interpret environmental signals, process these inputs, and identify and implement appropriate responses.

Knowledge Management: Definition

Given the increasing importance assigned to knowledge assets, the last decade has seen increasing attention to their active management. It is perhaps no coincidence that knowledge management became a full-fledged business trend in the mid-1990s, seemingly in response to the realization that the downsizing and "delayering" that followed the rise to prominence of business process reengineering engendered significant loss of organizational knowledge. As a consequence, business leaders—aided by consulting firms—concluded that institutional systems needed to be developed to preserve and communicate organizational knowledge in the face of change and over time.

The term *knowledge management* refers to the set of activities and processes used to create, codify, gather, and disseminate knowledge in the organization. The challenge is best articulated by the chief knowledge officer of a large, multinational consulting organization: "We have 80,000 people scattered around the world that need information to do their jobs effectively. The information they need is too difficult to find and, even if they do find it, is often inaccurate."[12] Thus, knowledge management is the set of activities and processes that an organization like this enacts to manage the wealth of knowledge it possesses and ensure that it is properly safeguarded and put to use to help the firm achieve its objectives.

Information technology has featured prominently in knowledge management initiatives since the inception of this trend, giving rise to the notion of knowledge management

---

[12] Leidner, D. E. (2006), "The Ongoing Challenges of Knowledge Management Initiatives," *Cutter Benchmark Review* (6:3), pp. 5–12.

systems. However, as is the case with most of the trends discussed in this chapter, no single software application can enable a firm to successfully implement a knowledge management initiative. Rather, a number of technologies are used in concert to enable the various aspect of a knowledge management initiative: creating, capturing and storing, and disseminating knowledge.

Creating Knowledge   Knowledge creation is the first phase in any knowledge management initiative. In this phase the organization's employees generate new information, devise novel solutions to handle existing problems, or identify new explanations for recurrent events. Such new knowledge is potentially very valuable to others in the organization who may be facing similar problems.

Consider, for example, the genesis of the now ubiquitous "to go" service at your local casual dining chain (e.g., Chili's Bar and Grill). A restaurant manager at Outback Steakhouse noticed a group of his customers opting not to wait for a table in the long line of people ahead of them. Rather, they would order their food from the bar and then set up a makeshift dining table in the bed of their pick-up truck. Identifying an opportunity for increased sales to customers willing to trade off eating on premise for speed, he set up a separate pick-up area and began to promote the take-out service. When corporate saw what he was doing, it formalized the program and encouraged all restaurant managers to establish separate take-out operations. This case exemplifies the potential far-reaching impact of locally developed knowledge.

Capturing and Storing Knowledge   The main objective of a knowledge management initiative is to consciously compile and use knowledge. The process of capturing and storing knowledge enables the organization to codify new knowledge and maintain an organizational memory. While this process may sound trivial at first glance, you need only to imagine the multiple forms that organizational knowledge can take (e.g., paper documents, computer files, hallway conversations, interactions with customers) to realize the complexity of the challenge. More insidiously, it is critical that the firm be able to create a culture that values knowledge and knowledge sharing in order to ensure that the firm's employees are willing to engage in knowledge management activities—activities that often do not have immediate and measurable impacts on firm performance.

Knowledge repositories and content management systems (CMSs) feature prominently among the technologies used to capture and store knowledge. A knowledge repository is a central location and search point for relevant knowledge. However, as the popularity of such repositories increases, so too does the volume of knowledge. As the volume of knowledge increases, so too does the difficulty of finding high-quality, relevant knowledge to address a specific problem. A CMS offers a partial solution to this problem. A CMS is a software program designed to organize and facilitate access to digital content such as text, pictures, and video.

Disseminating Knowledge   Knowledge dissemination is the last phase in a knowledge management initiative. It is at this stage that the investments made in knowledge creation and storage pay off. When knowledge is available in a format that is quickly searchable and readily usable for those employees confronted with a new problem, dramatic improvements in effectiveness and efficiency can be achieved.

BUSINESS INTELLIGENCE

Organizations have been managing data and information since the beginning of organized social life. In ancient Rome, for instance, the provinces would have to keep detailed records to account for taxes to be paid to the Emperor in Rome. With the emergence of computerized information systems, databases took center stage. In technical parlance, a database is a self-describing collection of related records. Modern organizations manage their databases using a database management systems (DBMS)—the software program (or collection of programs) that enables and controls access to the database. A DBMS equips a database administrator with the tools to manage the data (e.g., protect it through authentication, schedule backups) and enables application/data independence. That is, when using a DBMS, applications need not store the data themselves, but rather issue requests to the DBMS. The database can therefore be shared among multiple applications, and upgrades to the one of the applications or the database itself can be made independently.

You are perhaps most familiar with personal DBMSs, such as Microsoft Access, that allow individuals or small groups to create and manage relatively small databases (Figure 12.11). Such a system can be confusing because typically it embeds both the DBMS and the database applications (see Figure 12.12).

Now consider a large organization, say Sabre Holdings Corporation, the parent company of Travelocity, Sabre Travel Network, and Sabre Airline Solutions. Sabre manages what at one point in time was the second-largest computer system in the United States. Sabre was anchored by a database that supported a huge number of users, ranging from travel agents and individuals seeking to make airline and hotel reservations, to airline check-in agents issuing boarding passes and seat assignments, to airline employees routing planes and managing their maintenance schedules. The Sabre database was once estimated to perform 8000 transactions per second! For such large operations, and for much smaller ones like grocery stores, eCommerce Web sites, and the like, you will need a multiuser industrial-strength DBMS (e.g., Oracle Database 10*g*; Sybase ASE 15). Making requests to the DBMS are a set of separate database applications (see Figure 12.13).

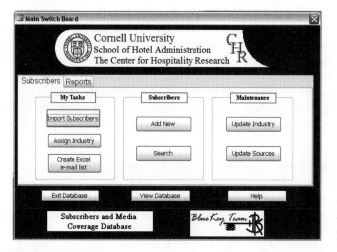

Figure 12.11 MS Access Database Application[13]

---

[13] Courtesy of Rohan Ashar and Daniel Gomez.

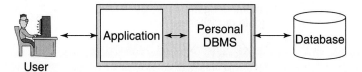

Figure 12.12   Individual Application and DBMS (e.g., MS Access)

While databases have been a staple of organizations' operations since their inception, data has only recently emerged as a critical organizational resource (Chapter 8). Recalling our discussion of the IS cycle (Figure 12.14) in Chapter 3, you will note that each of the examples described up to this point focuses on the first stage: handling the present. In other words, to this point we have only described transactional database applications.

As we described in Chapter 1, the declining cost of computing and storage, along with the increasing interconnectivity of computing devices, has given modern organizations access to more data and information then ever before. The business opportunities associated with this wealth of available information have spurred the emergence of a new trend: business intelligence (BI).

Business Intelligence: Definition

Business intelligence (BI) is one of the most recent buzzwords in a long tradition of business computing confusing lingo. Yet as with many of the acronyms and jargon in business computing, it is intuitively simple when stripped to its core. Intelligence, in the connotation used, for example, in the term *Central Intelligence Agency,* represents the ability to gather and make sense of information in a given area of interest—in the case of the CIA, it is the enemy and his or her behavior. Business intelligence is therefore the ability to gather and

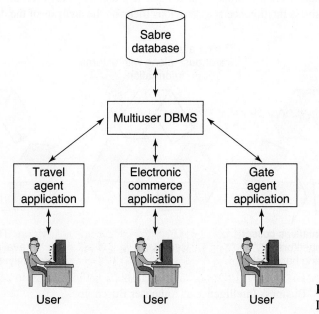

Figure 12.13   Multiuser Database Structure

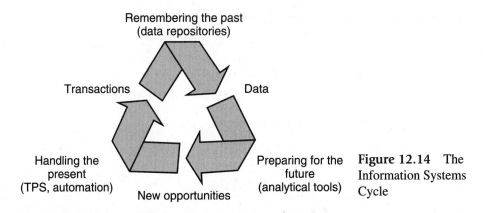

Figure 12.14 The Information Systems Cycle

make sense of information about your business. It encompasses the set of techniques, processes, and technologies designed to enable managers to gain superior insight and understanding of their business and thus make better decisions.

Consider the example of Anheuser Busch, Inc., the parent company of beer brands such as Budweiser and Michelob. Anheuser Busch's distributors carry hand-held devices, rather than the traditional clipboard, when they visit the stores they supply. They use the device to take orders, but also to gather much intelligence about the firm's and competitors' products. The data are immediately uploaded to Anheuser Busch's data warehouse, where they are married with demographic, marketing, and other external data to become available for analyses using an application called BudNet. Mapped to the IS cycle, this application shows how data progress through it, from collection as orders are taken (handling the present), to long-term storage in the data warehouse (remembering the past), to its employment for analytical purposes (preparing for the future) (see Figure 12.15).

As the example above shows, business intelligence encompasses transaction processing, since these transaction processing systems generate the data. However, the defining characteristic of business intelligence is a conscious focus on the analysis of the data generated.

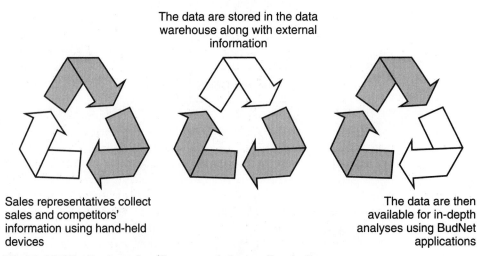

Figure 12.15 Business Intelligence at Anheuser Busch, Inc.

Components of the Business Intelligence Infrastructure

From our definition of business intelligence, it is clear that BI is not a technology or set of technologies. In fact, as was the case in the Anheuser Busch example, in order to engage in business intelligence, the firm must develop an information system paying particular attention to each of the four components (see Chapter 2). Yet given the sheer volume of data and information that a firm needs to manage as part of its BI initiatives, IT is a necessary component. As a consequence, business intelligence applications now represent a thriving segment of the software industry.

We use the term *business intelligence infrastructure* to refer to the set of applications and technologies designed to create, manage, and analyze large repositories of data in an effort to extract value from them. Beyond the transaction processing systems that generate the needed data, the main components of a BI infrastructure are data warehouse, data marts, query and reporting tools, online analytical processing (OLAP), and data mining.

Data Warehouse A data warehouse, or, more precisely, an enterprise data warehouse, is a data repository that collects and consolidates data from multiple source systems, both internal to the organization and external, with the purpose of enabling analysis. This succinct definition captures the essential characteristics of enterprise data warehouses:

- *Large in size.* Data warehouses easily spans into the terabytes scale—the rough equivalent of all the content of an academic library.

- *Large in scope.* By definition, a data warehouse draws information from a wide variety of source systems.

- *Enabling data integration.* A data warehouse compiles and collects data from multiple source systems, ensuring that data are accurate and current.

- *Designed for analytics.* The defining characteristic of a data warehouse, that what makes it different from a large transactional database, is its focus on data analysis.

A data warehouse is typically the cornerstone of a BI infrastructure, but the repository is only valuable insomuch as the data it contains is accurate—a condition that IT professionals like to call GIGO—garbage in, garbage out. Thus, the primary driver of complexity and cost of building a data warehouse is associated with the need to gather and clean the data to be compiled—the extracting, transforming, loading (ETL) process as it is known. What may appear to be a trivial process at first glance is in fact a length and complex undertaking designed to ensure that redundancy, data integrity violations, and inconsistencies are kept to a minimum.

As mentioned above, a data warehouse is optimized for analysis. While traditional transactional databases enable analysis and reporting, their structure is optimized for fast data retrieval at the atomic level. For example, if you asked a gate agent to change your seat assignment as you get ready to board an American Airlines flight, she will have to retrieve your individual record, make the change, and store it before issuing the new boarding pass. Such a transaction is focused on the present, accesses one record, and addresses a specific item in the record (see Table 12.3).

Now consider the example of Anheuser Busch. The firm was not interested in any one of its target customers (i.e., how much beer you buy). Rather, it focused on large groups of individuals who shared some characteristics, in an effort to identify patterns and draw conclusions

Table 12.3 Transactional Versus Analytical Databases

Transactional Database	*Analytic Database*
Atomic level	Aggregate level
Current data	Historical data
Individual record access	Multiple records access

about their collective behavior (i.e., how much, when, and how people like you in your neighborhood purchase a given brand of beer). Such transactions seek to access multiple (i.e., thousands of) historical records and aggregate them on several dimensions of interest (see Table 12.3).

While such aggregation is possible with transactional databases, and indeed it is performed every day in organizations to extract reports, as the size of the database grows, aggregating data in transactional databases can put a lot of strain on the system. There are situations where, beyond a certain size, the database will require more than twenty-four hours to create a report—clearly negating the possibility of daily reports.

Using techniques such as multidimensional representations and pre-aggregation, an analytical database is optimized for enabling complex querying and the analyses of large amounts of data with a response time of a few seconds. For example, using OLAP tools (described below) and an analytical database, a bank analyst would be able to identify which accounts are currently overdue, organizing the results by branch, type of loan, customer type, and so on. What's more, the analyst can expect the results within a few seconds of issuing the query.

Data Mart   A data mart is a scaled-down version of a data warehouse that focuses on the needs of a specific audience. Like a data warehouse, a data mart is a repository built explicitly to enable analyses. Unlike a data warehouse, though, a data mart is designed for the specific needs of a narrowly defined community of knowledge workers (e.g., marketing group, accounting). The advantages of a data mart over a data warehouse are that the data mart is smaller in scope, thus easier to build, and uses audience-specific data classifications and language. In very large organizations that have already created an enterprise data warehouse, data marts may be introduced to simplify and focus analyses by a department or function.

In many cases a firm will develop data marts in order to take an incremental approach to its BI strategy. In this case the firm will introduce one or more data marts before creating a data warehouse. The early data marts focus on areas that offer the highest potential return to the investment in data analysis. This incremental strategy can help generate buy-in from senior executives and momentum behind business intelligence initiatives. The drawback of this strategy is that a proliferation of data marts creates the potential for replicating the problem that centralized data storage was designed to eliminate—data redundancy and lack of data consolidation.

Online Analytical Processing   The term *online analytical processing* (OLAP) refers to a class of software programs that enable a knowledge worker to easily and selectively extract and view data from analytical databases. The defining characteristic of OLAP tools is that they are user driven. In other words, an analyst must issue a query that specifies what data items the user is interested in. Note that OLAP users need not be IT specialists; in fact, if you elect to become an analyst for a financial institution or a marketing organization, you stand a very good chance to use OLAP tools yourself.

For instance, as an analyst for Spalding, the sports equipment maker, you may be interested in viewing all the beach ball products sold in Florida in the month of July and compare revenue figures from these items with those for the same products in September in the same location and/or in California during the same period. The revolutionary aspect of OLAP is that you would no longer need to request such data from the IT department and wait for them to design ad-hoc queries for you. Rather, you can perform the analysis on your own and receive an immediate response employing a user-friendly application (Figure 12.16).

Data Mining   Data mining is the process of automatically discovering nonobvious relationships in large databases. The recent popularity of data mining is due to the availability of powerful computer systems that can quickly search through large volumes of data contained in data warehouses. A recent example of the power of data mining is offered by Wal-Mart, a company that built its data warehouse in the early 1990s. Using years of compiled data, Wal-Mart analysts recently sought to identify what the best-selling items were in areas under threat of an approaching hurricane. Much to everyone's surprise, the most important item needed to prepare for a hurricane was not water, wood, or nails. It wasn't even beer, a perennial favorite in audiences confronted with this question. Wal-Mart found that strawberry pop-tarts sold most! While it is relatively easy to make sense of this finding once we are told about it (i.e., pop-tarts have a long shelf-life, they need not be cooked, kids like them, etc.), it is a nonobvious and largely unexpected finding beforehand.

Like OLAP tools, data mining is used to analyze historical information. Unlike OLAP, though, data mining is more akin to a brute force approach enabling the software to identify significant patterns by analyzing all possible combinations rather than relying on an analyst to structure a specific query. Of course, analysts are still heavily involved in data mining as they must interpret the results. Yet, as in the Wal-Mart example, data mining is

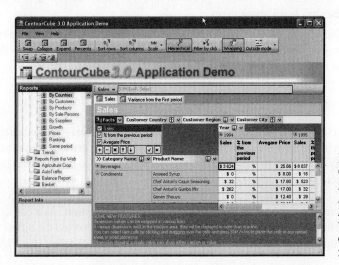

Figure 12.16 Sample OLAP Screen. (*Source: Business Benefits Through CRM: Hitting the Right Target in the Right Way* (2002). Goodhue, D., Wixom, B., and Watson, H. MIS Quarterly Executive, Vol. 1 Issue 2, pp.79–94.)

used to seek unexpected (i.e., nonobvious) relationships among data items. The following is a list of possible patterns a data mining application may identify:

- *Associations.* Associations occur when one event can be correlated to another event (e.g., beer purchasers are highly associated with chips purchases in the week leading up to the Superbowl).

- *Sequences.* Sequences occur when one event leads to another subsequent event (e.g., a rug purchase followed by a purchase of curtains).

- *Classification.* Classification occurs when categories are generated from the data (e.g., customer profiles based on historical spending).

- *Forecasting.* Forecasting occurs when patterns in the data can be extrapolated to predict future events.

CUSTOMER RELATIONSHIP MANAGEMENT

Customer relationship management (CRM) has been a dominant business trend over the last decade and, like enterprise systems, is still receiving substantial attention. CRM finds its roots in the proliferation of customer data and the efforts of modern business organizations to differentiate themselves through customer service (see Chapter 8).

As with many of the business technology trends that preceded it, CRM has been co-opted by vendors, consulting firms, and various other pundits and the term has increasingly lost a precise meaning. We define customer relationship management as a strategic orientation that calls for iterative processes designed to turn customer data into customer relationships through active use of, and learning from, the information collected. Thus, the defining characteristics of CRM are the following:

- CRM is a strategic initiative, not a technology. Information technology is an essential enabler of all but the smallest CRM initiatives.

- CRM relies on customer personal and transactional data and is designed to help the firm learn about them.

- The ultimate objective of a CRM initiative is to help the firm use customer data to make inferences about customer behaviors, needs, and value to the firm so as to increase its profitability.

Aspects of CRM

A CRM strategy needs to encompass front-office functionalities—termed *operational CRM*—which determine how the firm interacts with customers to create and maintain the relationship. Today customers in most industries expect to be able to interact with the firms through a multiplicity of touchpoints, such as the firm's Web site, stores, call center, and so on. Moreover, modern firms are increasingly expected to be able to provide consistency across these proliferating touchpoints and channels of communication. As a consequence, integration of the transactional databases that have historically supported the different channels into one operational data store is a priority in many organizations today (see Figure 12.17).

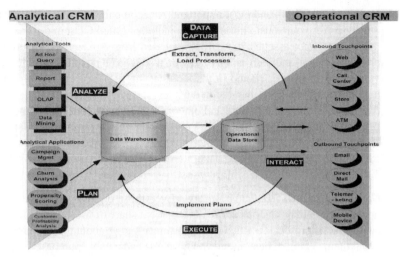

Figure 12.17 Example of CRM Infrastructure

A CRM strategy requires that the organization be able to actively manage and strengthen the relationship with profitable customers, while achieving efficiencies (and sometimes firing!) less profitable ones. This level of precision and granularity of interactions with customer require substantial data analysis—analytical CRM.

It should be clear at this point why it is nonsensical to be talking about a CRM system as a technology product that, once installed, allegedly enables the firm to establish and maintain relationships with customers. CRM is a highly customizable strategic initiative that will differ dramatically between companies. Thus, as with business intelligence, we need to talk about a CRM infrastructure as the collection of applications that support and enable the specific aspect of the firm's CRM strategy.

The Limitations of CRM

CRM is an intuitively appealing concept, but it may engender the very seed of its demise. If this is the case, companies that make it a cornerstone of their strategy may in turn be setting themselves up for failure.

CRM Is Firm Centric One of the main limitations of current CRM approaches is that a firm's CRM strategy only relies on transactional and behavioral customer data pertaining to the interactions of the customer with the firm. Consider what is probably the most celebrated example of CRM strategy: Amazon.com's collaborative filtering initiative. When a returning customer logs on to the Amazon Web site, he is personally greeted and receives suggestions based on prior purchases. However, as good as the Amazon CRM initiative is, there are some problems.

First, not all the products that customers purchase are for themselves; they also purchase gifts. Second, not all the products customers buy are for the same purpose; we may purchase items for work or leisure. Amazon has attempted to account for these potential problems by asking customers to qualify their purchases (i.e., shifting the burden of precise data collection to customers). Third, and most important, Amazon only knows customers' transactions with Amazon. Yet your music library surely includes gifted CDs, and it may include old vinyl records and tape cassettes, items you purchased from Amazon's competitors—online and in physical stores—and increasingly individual songs you download from Internet retailers.

This limitation is rooted in the fact that the firm has access only to transactions and behavioral data that is generated in the interaction between its customers and itself. Indeed, the firm can buy demographic and other personal data about customers from firms such as Acxiom and ChoicePoint, but it can't obtain customers' transactional data from competitors. Under these circumstances, the picture that the firm creates about each customer is irremediably partial, and drawing accurate inference or producing good advice based on it is difficult at best and impossible at worst.

CRM Has Limited Predictive Ability   Even those organizations that have exclusive relationships with their customers (i.e., 100 percent share of wallet) still face a challenge. Some events are unforeseeable and only the customer knows about their occurrence or future plans about them. Think of customers who have just had a baby, purchased a house, or those who just got divorced or were involved in a big accident. As good as the firm's inference systems may be, they rely on historical data and patterns and, unless the customer volunteers information about life-changing events, it will typically fall short on accuracy.

While there are many areas, industries, and organizations that have benefited and will continue to benefit greatly from their CRM strategy, the example above highlights an endemic problem. To the extent that the objective of a CRM strategy is personalization, inference, consultation, and advice, the battle may be an uphill one and the end result not as comprehensive as hoped.

Customer Managed Interactions

The concept of customer managed interactions (CMIs) may solve some of the limitations of CRM described above. CMI is predicated on a shift in the collection and control of the data. In the CMI approach, customer data are stored and managed by the customer—or on his or her behalf by an infomediary (see Chapter 5)—rather than by the firms who originally handled the transaction. Thus, customers maintain control over the decision to interact, the timing of the interaction, the channel to be used, and the data generated.

This approach solves the fundamental limitation of CRM initiatives because the customer's personal data warehouse holds a complete record of all relevant transactions, simplifies the data integrity and redundancy challenge, and, since the transaction is initiated by the customer, it reflects any unforeseeable or life-changing events that may be relevant.

When a customer is ready to transact with your organization, he or she will share the relevant data and his or her requirements with you and, perhaps, some of your competitors. Each of the interested organizations can elect to respond with an offer that the customer evaluates prior to making a selection. This scenario may appear overly futuristic, and it certainly is at this point for most goods. However, the process described above is no different from one that we are all very familiar with: the request for proposals (RFP) process.

Today the RFP process is relegated to big-ticket items because the economics of the process are such that it is not feasible for most consumer goods. Yet as the price-per-performance of computing equipment continues to fall and IT becomes more and more pervasive, both in business and homes, we can envision a time when the RFP process becomes feasible for the majority of consumer goods: airline tickets, music CDs, books, home appliances, and the like.

Note that the CMI approach is not necessarily about the lowest prices. Conversely, for most industries and most organizations, CMI success will likely stem from the quality of the recommendation and the fit of the solution to the customer need. As the firm has access to much better customer data, it is reasonable for customers to expect much better-fitting solutions.

CMI Technology The technology is now in place to support the move of CMI to the mainstream. The Internet has created the infrastructure for data transfer, the falling cost of storage justifies the development of comprehensive personal data repositories, and standards like XML provide the infrastructure for formatting messages among loosely coupled agents.

Consider, for instance, Quicken, the personal financial management software. While Quicken is typically focused on the financial side of the transaction, if you use credit cards as the exclusive form of payment and diligently download your statements to Quicken, you can develop a pretty comprehensive personal data repository. The leap to a situation where every transaction comes with an associated XML message describing it isn't big. For simple goods, such as airlines, this is already possible as the reservation fully defines the relevant characteristics of the product.

OPEN SOURCE

The use of open source software, another long-existing trend that gained significant momentum with the emergence of the Internet, is one of the most important IT trends currently confronting modern organizations. The open source movement has coalesced around the Open Source Initiative (OSI), an organization dedicated to promoting open source software, focusing on its benefits and qualities for the business community. According to the OSI Web site, "Open source software is an idea whose time has finally come. For twenty years it has been building momentum in the technical cultures that built the Internet and the World Wide Web. Now it's breaking out into the commercial world, and that's changing all the rules. Are you ready?"[14]

Open Source: Definition

Open source software is often confused with free software—as in free of charge. In fact, licenses for open source software may or may not be offered at no cost (free of charge software is called freeware). Rather, the term *open source* is used to differentiate the software from closed source, or proprietary, programs that prevent users from accessing and modifying the source code.

Software programs are created by software engineers, who design the algorithm, and programmers, who code it using a specific programming language. The code generated by the programmers, which can be understood by anyone who is well versed in the programming language used, is called the source code (see Figure 12.18).

---

[14] http://www.opensource.org/

```
dBDate = CDate(BirthDate)
dRelDate = CDate(RelativeTo)
iAns = Year (dRelDate) - Year (dBDate)

If Month(dBDate) <> Month (dRelDate) Then
    bSubtractOne = Month (dBDate) > Month (dRelDate)
Else
    bSubtractOne = Day (dBDate) > Day (dRelDate)
End If
```

Figure 12.18 Sample Visual Basic Source Code

In order for the program to work, the source code has to be transformed (i.e., interpreted or compiled) into a format that a computer can execute, called the object code. Typically, when you purchase a software license from a software company (e.g., Microsoft Office, Oracle Database 10*g*), you are given the object code and the right to run it on your computers, but you are not provided with the source code. In fact, any effort to reverse engineer the object code to gain access to the source code is considered a violation of the intellectual property of the software house and will land you a well-founded lawsuit.

Unlike proprietary software, open source programs are distributed with the express intent of enabling users to gain access to the source code and modify it. An open source license typically exhibits the following characteristics:

- *Free redistribution.* The software can be freely given away or sold.
- *Available source code.* The source code is published and freely obtainable.
- *Derived works.* Licensees can modify the software and redistribute it under the same license terms as the original.
- *No discrimination.* The license is available to any entity, including for-profit organizations and commercial users.
- *Technology neutrality.* The license, and all of its provisions, must be free of restrictions tied to the use of any technologies or type of interface.

Open Source Is Now Open for Business

Analysis of the open source licensing characteristics shows that the open source movement encourages, rather than opposes, commercial applications and commercial redistribution. This friendliness toward business applications has been the catalyst for widespread acceptance and growth of open source software as a viable alternative to proprietary programs.

A number of organizations have emerged in an attempt to capitalize on the open source movement. The following three models are currently being implemented:[15]

Sponsored Open Source A number of not-for-profit foundations provide support and coordination to open source efforts. For example, the Apache Software Foundation coordinates enhancements to the Apache Web Server, and the Mozilla Foundation supports the development of the FireFox Web browser and many other products (Figure 12.19).

---

[15] For a more in-depth analysis and treatment of them, see Watson, R., and Boudreau, M. C. (2005), "The Business of Open Source: A Strategic Perspective,"*Cutter Benchmark Review* (5:11) p. 5–12.

Figure 12.19   Mozilla Foundation

Some corporations also sponsor their own open source projects, typically "opening" their own software products by releasing the source code. The first example in this area was offered by Netscape Corp., which released the source code of its Web browser in 1998. More recently Sun Microsystems released the source code of its OpenOffice suite and NetBeans products and in November 2006 even released the source code of its Java programming language.

Open Source Service   The open source service model emerged in the late 1990s with the increasing attention being garnered by the Linux operating systems. While licenses to Linux had to be free, a number of firms, led by pioneer Red Hat, Inc., began charging for installation, support, training, and all the other ancillary services typically associated with software sales. Today a number of upstarts and established firms compete in this market, including big names such as HP, Unisys, and Novell. They support a whole stable of open source applications such as Linux (operating system), Apache (Web server), and MySQL (database management system).

Professional Open Source   The latest evolution in the open source model is professional open source. This label refers to organizations that, while being part of the open source movement and subscribing to the open source licensing terms, maintain fairly tight control over the software programs they sell. For example, a professional open source organization will have its own core set of programmers and developers who provide direction for the project. At the same time, though, the group will leverage the greater community of open source programmers, testers, and adopters. These organizations rely on their knowledge and understanding of the core source code to provide better services when a client adopts their software.

Advantages and Disadvantages of Open Source Software

As a general or functional manager, you will without a doubt be part of a system selection committee. Increasingly, such committees have the option of adopting open source software rather than purchasing proprietary programs. A recent Cutter Consortium survey found that 75 percent of organizations surveyed use at least one open source software program.[16] While decisions of this kind are very context specific, we identify next the main benefits and drawbacks of open source.

Advantages   The principal advantages of open source touted by the proponents are a function of the ability of open source projects to leverage a large community of developers, programmers, testers, and customers. These advantages include the following:

- *Robustness.* Proponents of open source software claim that mature projects (e.g., Linux) are more robust, more reliable, and generally higher quality than comparable proprietary applications (e.g., Microsoft Windows).

- *Creativity.* Open source software harnesses the creativity of thousands of developers around the world. As such, it is more likely to generate breakthrough new solutions (e.g., FireFox tabbed browsing) than traditional products created by a small community within one software house.

- *Limited lock-in.* Open source software is not without switching costs, but supporters claim that such costs are much lower than those associated with proprietary software. For example, customers of open source software can make their own modification to the source code rather than having to rely on the software vendor to do so.

- *Simplified licensing.* Because of the structure of an open source license, customers need not worry about complex legal constraints (e.g., number of concurrent users). They simply install as many copies of the program as they need.

- *Free license.* While not regarded as one of the chief benefits of open source by the open source movement, total cost of ownership is still an important factor to those firms that adopt open source applications. Because open source generally can be licensed for free, costs are lower than those associated with proprietary applications.

Disadvantages   Software is by no means simple (or cheap) to install and operate, and open source software is no exception. Thus, the skeptics respond by raising the following concerns:

- *Unpredictable costs.* Skeptics like to say that free software is like a free puppy— yes, you get it for nothing, but then you will encounter many (often unplanned) costs along the way. Thus, you need to carefully evaluate an open source installation based on total cost of ownership (see Chapter 10).

- *Support varies widely.* Depending on the product and where your firm acquired it, support can range from high quality to nonexistent.

- *Security.* Skeptics claim that publishing source code gives an advantage to those who want to break its security. Proponents of open source respond that a large community of developers will identify and close more weaknesses than a small team of company developers.

- *Compatibility.* Standardization of products using one or a few vendors simplifies compatibility and integration. There is no guarantee that open source solutions will be compatible with one another and/or with proprietary software.

---

[16] Piccoli, G. (2005), "Open Source: A Reality That Still Requires Careful Management," *Cutter Benchmark Review* (5:11), p. 19.

■ *The legal landscape.* Open source software requires that no portion of the code is protected by copyright. Recent court challenges have raised the specter that there is no way to ensure that copyrighted code will not make it into open source solutions, thus opening customers to liability. In response, some of the firms that support open source software (e.g., JBoss, HP, Red Hat) have adopted indemnification clauses in their licensing agreements.

In summary, the decision of whether to go with open source and with what products will depend on the characteristics of the organization and the maturity of the software program. Some products, such as the Linux operating system, are already so robust that in early 2005 the MIT Media Lab felt comfortable advising the Brazilian government to shun Microsoft products for open source software, contending that "free software is far better on the dimensions of cost, power, and quality."[17] Other products require a much stronger commitment in terms of support and investments. It is essential that organizations adopting such products have the expertise and resources to implement and maintain them.

SOFTWARE AS A SERVICE

Software as a service (SaaS) is not a new concept, but one that has gained significant currency with the renewed attention to outsourcing, the emergence of the open source movement, and the consolidation of the Internet as viable platform for business operations. Software as a service is a software delivery approach in which a provider hosts the application in its data centers and the customer accesses the needed applications' functionalities over a computer network. Thus, instead of licensing the application and requiring that the customer installs it, maintains it, and generally supports it, in the SaaS model it is the provider who shoulders these tasks. In other words, management of the application is outsourced to the provider, and the client simply takes advantages of the service. Perhaps the simplest example of SaaS is a class of applications you most likely use: Web-based e-mail systems such as Gmail (Figure 12.20).

The SaaS model focuses on the services (i.e., functionalities) being provided, not on the physical products (the applications) being sold. The metaphor for SaaS is the utilities we all use—such as electricity or water (Figure 12.21). We don't worry so much about the generation of power and the management of the delivery system (i.e., the wires and transformers), we simply plug in our appliances and expect to access the service (i.e., electrical power) that comes through the wire.

Historical Context

Business Process Outsourcing   The idea of accessing software as a service provided by an outside firm is not new. The concept of business process outsourcing (BPO) has been around, on and off, since the mainframe era and the 1960s. In a BPO agreement, a client, say the local independent convenience store, engages a provider to provide and manage a given business process—say accounting and payroll.

---

[17] "MIT Urges Brazil to Adopt Open-Source." Reuters, 17 March 2005 (Accessed 6/6/07 http://msnbc.msn.com/id/7220913).

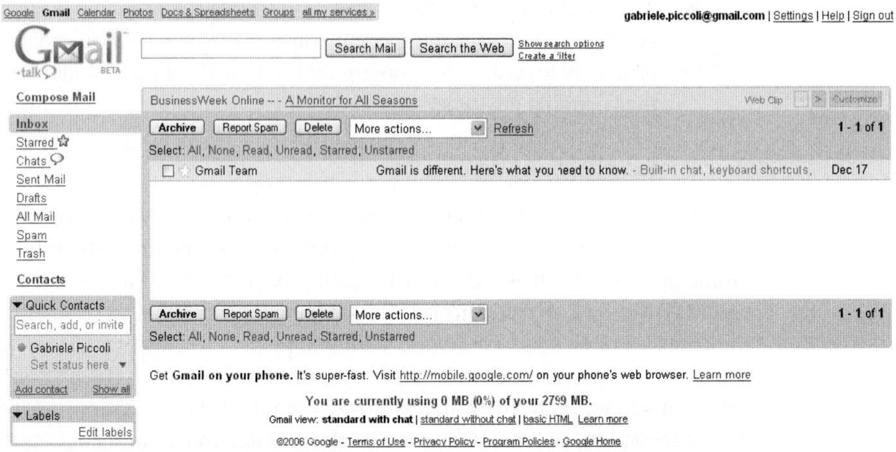

Google **Gmail** Calendar Photos Docs & Spreadsheets Groups all my services »   gabriele.piccoli@gmail.com | Settings | Help | Sign out

[Gmail interface screenshot]

Figure 12.20   Gmail, a Web-Based E-Mail System by Google

In the traditional BPO approach, management at the convenience store would pass the provider the time cards detailing hours worked by each employee as well as invoices from suppliers and cash register records. The BPO provider would feed this information into its accounting and payroll applications and compute accrued vacation, benefits, and tax withdrawals and cut the checks for the employees. The provider would also be able to produce financial statements for the business and accounting reports. In this case, not only the payroll and accounting software applications are outsourced, but the entire business process that they enable.

Figure 12.21   A Transformer on the Power Grid. (*Source:* Courtesy of Kuhlman Electric Corporation.)

As the BPO model evolved over time, a number of other business processes became viable candidates for outsourcing. Today they include accounting, human resources and payroll, call center operations, and the like.

Application Service Providers   With the emergence of the commercial Internet during the dot-com days in the mid-1990s, application service provision emerged on the wings of the slogan "the network is the computer." This slogan captured the idea that, with the availability of widespread, increasingly reliable, and cheap computer networks (i.e., the Internet), it would not matter much where computer processing would happen—at the user's workstation, on the firm's premises, or somewhere else in cyberspace.

Application service provision (ASP) is a software delivery model where a provider hosts and manages a standard application, say Microsoft Office, and enables clients to access it and use it over a computer network. This application is often purchased and licensed by the customer but managed and supported by the provider on its infrastructure. Strictly speaking, ASP is a special case of software as a service, where the provider offers hosting services on behalf of the customer.

SaaS Today

Today the software as a service model has evolved to encompass the ASP model as well as to include providers who develop applications with the explicit objective of hosting them and providing them as a service to clients—sometimes referred to as software on demand. Moreover, the SaaS movement has received further impetus from the increasing popularity of open source software, with providers who now deliver open source applications as a service—thus shouldering the effort and costs associated with managing the open source application.

Today there is a wealth of SaaS providers offering software programs ranging from basic personal productivity tools to highly specialized and customized applications. The advantages and disadvantages of the SaaS model parallel those that are inherent to any type of outsourcing agreement with the added risks and rewards associated with the delivery of the application through a network.

On the positive side, SaaS applications reduce setup time and can be up and running relatively quickly. Their pricing can be more flexible, with charges based on actual usage rather than fixed licensing fees. As with any other outsourcing arrangement, SaaS reduces the local staff needed to maintain and support the application.

The above advantages come at a cost, of course. The chief limitation of SaaS arrangements is the added reliability risk associated with the availability of the Internet. If the firm's Internet connection experiences an outage, the applications become unusable, even though they are actually up and running. Another limitation of SaaS is that it is more difficult to integrate remote applications with the existing IT infrastructure of the firm and with its other applications. Thus, while there are providers who offer ERPs on a SaaS basis, stand-alone applications may be most suitable to this model.

Finally, as with any other outsourcing arrangement, the performance of the firm is directly impacted by the performance of the service provider. For example, many Salesforce.com (Figure 12.22) customers blamed the firm for lost sales when Salesforce.com experienced an outage lasting almost a day on December 20, 2005—during the holiday season's final days.

Figure 12.22 Salesforce.com, One of the Leading Providers of SaaS Solutions

SUMMARY

In this chapter we introduced some emerging and some enduring trends in information systems and technology management. Understanding these trends and technologies, the associated vocabulary, and the benefits and risks they engender for modern organizations is critical for you as a general or functional manager as you will be called upon to participate in the debate about whether your own firm should embark in the type of initiatives described in this chapter.

Specifically, in this chapter we learned that

- Enterprise systems (ESs), also known as ERP, are modular, integrated software applications that span (all) organizational functions and rely on one database at the core. The defining characteristics of ESs are their large scope (seeking to support all aspects of an organization's IT infrastructure in an integrated fashion), their modularity (enabling adopting firms to select what components they need), and their configurability (allowing adopting organizations to choose among a predefined set of options during the implementation of the application).

- While enterprise systems offer much promise in terms of efficiency improvements, increased responsiveness, knowledge infusion, and adaptability, they have some significant limitations, including: the trade-off between standardization and flexibility, the limitations of best practice software, the potential for strategic clash, and the high costs and risks of the implementation process.

- Enterprise systems have traditionally focused on internal organization processes. Conversely, supply chain management applications have been introduced to enable interorganizational business processes across the supply chain. Supply chain management applications have become increasingly integrated in an effort to create efficiencies through tight relationships between suppliers and customers.

- Best-of-breed integration approaches have emerged in response to the limitations of enterprise systems. Specifically, enterprise systems limit the adopting firm's ability to maintain a flexible IT infrastructure by restricting available options. In contrast, best-of-breed, enabled by the enterprise application integration (EAI) approach, allows an organization to purchase applications from multiple vendors and integrate them with its existing legacy systems using middleware.

- Knowledge management is the set of activities and processes that an organization enacts to manage the wealth of knowledge it possesses and ensure that such knowledge is properly safeguarded and put to use to help the firm achieve its objectives. A knowledge management initiative evolves over three phases: knowledge creation, capture and storage, and distribution. While knowledge management has intuitive appeal, knowledge management initiatives are deceptively complex and prone to failure. This is due to the sheer quantity and variety of organizational knowledge, and to the fact that most organizations lack a culture of knowledge sharing and management.

- Business intelligence has been one of the dominant trends in organizational computing over the last decade. It encompasses the set of techniques, processes, and technologies designed to enable managers to gain superior insight and understanding of their business and thus make better decisions. A firm that intends to engage in business intelligence needs to create a business intelligence infrastructure that typically is centered on a data warehouse. Feeding the data warehouse are internal transaction processing systems and external sources. Once the data have been structured for analysis in the data warehouse, or a data mart, they can be examined using analytical tools such as OLAP and data mining.

- Customer relationship management (CRM) represents another enduring business trend of the last decade. We have defined CRM as a strategic orientation that calls for iterative processes designed to turn customer data into customer relationships through active use of, and learning from, the information collected. While the term *CRM* has lost much of its original meaning as of late, it is critical that you realize that CRM initiatives are unique to the characteristics and objectives of the implementing organization. Thus, the set of technologies and applications the firm will use (i.e., the CRM infrastructure) to enable both the operational and analytical aspects of its CRM strategy will vary dramatically.

- In our discussion we also identified some of the principal limitations of CRM initiatives: firm centricity and limited predictive ability. In response to these limitations, the customer managed interactions (CMI) trend is emerging. In the CMI approach, customer data are stored and managed by the customer—or on his or her behalf by an infomediary—rather than by the firms who handled the transaction.

- Open source software programs, those programs that enable the adopting firm to receive and modify the source code, are increasingly becoming a viable option for organizations. When weighing the decision to adopt open source instead of a proprietary software program, you need to evaluate the following advantages and disadvantages of open source projects. The pros include robustness, creativity, limited lock-in, simplified licensing, and free licenses. The cons include unpredictable costs, varying degrees of quality support, security concerns, compatibility concerns, and a potentially complex legal landscape.

- Software as a service (SaaS) is a software delivery approach in which a provider hosts the application in its data centers and the customer accesses the needed applications' functionalities over a computer network. Instead of licensing the application and requiring that the customer installs it, maintains it, and generally supports it, in the SaaS model it is the provider who shoulders these tasks—customers simply gain access to the needed applications in much the same way they gain access to utilities (e.g., water, electricity).

STUDY QUESTIONS

1. What is an enterprise system (ES)? Can you describe its genesis? Identify the principal advantages and risks that a firm considering the installation of an ES should consider.

2. What is a supply chain? Why is it important to actively manage the supply chain? If you were the CEO of a hospital, would you consider using RFID technology? If not, why? If yes, for what applications?

3. Define the term *best-of-breed integration*. Why has best-of-breed integration recently emerged as a business trend? Explain how enterprise application integration (EAI) works. What are its primary advantages over competing integration approaches?

4. Define the following terms: *knowledge, explicit and tacit knowledge, knowledge management.* What are the principal phases of a knowledge management initiative? Describe the essential benefits of knowledge management for modern organizations. Why are so many organizations struggling with their knowledge management initiatives?

5. Define the following terms: *business intelligence, business intelligence infrastructure, data warehouse, data mart,*

OLAP, data mining. What is the relationship among the various elements of BI infrastructure?

6. Define the term *customer relationship management* (CRM). What are the essential objectives of a CRM initiative? Explain why using the term *CRM system* is misleading. Differentiate the concept of operational and analytical CRM. What are the principal limitations of modern CRM initiatives? How does the CMI trend respond to these limitations?

7. What is open source software? What are the main advantages and disadvantages of open source software? When would you consider an open source software implementation in your organization? When would you not?

FURTHER READINGS

1. Davenport, T. H. (1998). "Putting the Enterprise into Enterprise System." *Harvard Business Review* (July/Aug.), pp. 121–131.
2. Davenport, T. H. (2006). "Competing on Analytics." *Harvard Business Review,* January, pp. 98–107.
3. Watson, R. T., Piccoli, G., Brohman, M. K., and Parasuraman, A. (2004). "I Am My Own Database." *Harvard Business Review* (81/11), pp. 18–19.
4. Watson, R. T., Piccoli, G., Brohman, M. K., and Parasuraman, A. (2005). "Customer-Managed Interactions: A New Paradigm for Firm-Customer Relationships." *MIS Quarterly Executive* (4:3), pp. 319–327.

GLOSSARY

■ **Business intelligence:** The ability to gather and make sense of information about your business. It encompasses the set of techniques, processes, and technologies designed to enable managers to gain superior insight and understanding of their business and thus make better decisions.

■ **Business intelligence infrastructure:** The set of applications and technologies designed to create, manage, and analyze large repositories of data in an effort to extract value from them.

■ **Customer managed interactions (CMI):** A paradigm where the customer retains control over the decision to interact, the timing of the interaction, the channel to be used in the interaction, and the data generated.

■ **Customer relationship management (CRM):** A strategic orientation that calls for iterative processes designed to turn customer data into customer relationships through active use of, and learning from, the information collected.

■ **Database:** A self-describing collection of related records.

■ **Database management system:** The software program (or collection of programs) that enables and controls access to the database.

■ **Data mart:** A scaled-down version of a data warehouse that focuses on the needs of a specific audience.

■ **Data mining:** The process of automatically discovering nonobvious relationships in large databases.

■ **Data warehouse:** A software program that collects and consolidates data from multiple source systems, both internal to the organization and external, with the purpose of enabling analysis.

■ **Enterprise system (ES):** Enterprise systems, also known as ERP, are modular, integrated software applications that span (all) organizational functions and rely on one database at the core.

■ **Explicit knowledge:** The type of knowledge that can be articulated, codified, and transferred with relative ease.

■ **Extranet:** A private network that uses the public Internet infrastructure and Internet technologies but spans the boundaries of the organization and enables secure transactions between a firm and its suppliers, vendors, customers, or any other partner.

■ **Knowledge management:** The set of activities and processes that an organization enacts to manage the wealth of knowledge it possesses and ensure that such knowledge is properly safeguarded and put to use to help the firm achieve its objectives.

- **Integrators:** A consulting firm that partners with an enterprise systems vendor and becomes a specialist in the implementation of the ES vendor's products.

- **Online analytical processing (OLAP):** A class of software programs that enable a knowledge worker to easily and selectively extract and view data from an analytical database.

- **Open source:** A type of software licensing agreement that enables the licensee to obtain and modify the source code of the software program.

- **Software as a Service (SaaS):** A software delivery approach in which a provider hosts the application in its data centers and the customer accesses the

needed applications' functionalities over a computer network.

- **Supply chain:** An organization's supply chain is the set of upstream firms that produce and sell the resources the organization needs to perform its transformation process (e.g., raw materials, energy, and equipment).

- **Supply chain management (SCM):** The set of logistic and financial processes associated with the planning, execution, and monitoring of supply chain operations.

- **Tacit knowledge:** The type of knowledge that individuals possess but find difficult to articulate, codify, and transfer.

CASE STUDY: CARNIVAL CRUISE LINES[18]

We have been attentive to our relationships with customers since we started the company. We listen to customers, we cater to their needs, we respond to them.
                    — Bob Dickinson, President and CEO
CRM has been a four-letter word around here. But it's not CRM itself. It's this concept of big bang. Look at the low success rate of many companies who tried this big-bang CRM approach.
    — Brenda Yester, Vice President Revenue Management

With the 2004 winter holiday season in full swing, the management team at Carnival Cruise Lines had much to celebrate. More than 3 million passengers would sail with Carnival this year, an all-time high (Exhibit 1 presents passenger numbers for Carnival and the industry). Before year's end, Carnival was set to launch the 110,000-ton, 2,974-passenger *Carnival Valor,* the 20th ship in the fleet (Exhibit 2). When the *Carnival Liberty* joined the fleet in early 2005, Carnival's cruise capacity would lead the industry (Exhibit 3 on page 414–415 presents cruise capacity by brand). The fortunes of Carnival Corporation and PLC, the parent company of Carnival Cruise Lines, reflected the strength of its most visible brand. Carnival Corporation was having the best year in its history, due in part to a rebound in ticket prices following recent industry-wide discounting. The company authorized a $1 billion stock buy-back in the fourth quarter of 2004 and a 20% quarterly dividend increase to 15 cents per share. They would easily beat Wall Street earnings forecasts, despite

a still-sluggish North American economy, higher fuel prices, the war in Iraq, and a devastating hurricane season that had disrupted operations in the company's main Caribbean cruising waters (see Exhibit 4, pages 415–418 for Carnival Corporation and PLC financials).

Indeed, there was much fun taking place at the Miami-based headquarters of the "Fun Ships." Nevertheless, a seasoned team of senior managers (Exhibit 5, pages 419–422), many of whom had been with the company since its formative years in the 1970s, were already looking ahead to opportunities and challenges. Among these was a branding initiative designed to narrow the gap between Carnival's ongoing quality improvements and consumer perceptions of the Carnival cruise experience. Carnival strategists were also contemplating the next-generation of Carnival cruise ships that would be needed to keep up with the seemingly insatiable demand for cruise vacations. Less glamorous decisions, though equally important, involved how to handle friction in evolving cruise distribution channels, where a growing direct-marketing effort had rankled some travel agents.

Simmering under the surface of these and other initiatives were questions about how Carnival could best manage customer relationships now and into the future. The company had long practiced a successful market-expansion strategy, with growth fueled by selling the mass-market cruise category to first-time cruisers. Less emphasis had

---

[18] This case was originally published as: Applegate, L. M., Kwortnik, R., and Piccoli, G. (2004). "Carnival Cruise Lines." Harvard Business School Publishing, Case #9-806-015.

continued

CASE STUDY (*continued*)

	Carnival		CLIA Lines*	
Year	Passengers Carried	Annual Growth (%)	Passengers Carried	Annual Growth (%)
1994	1,035,037	15.33	4,448,000	−0.71
1995	1,185,588	14.55	4,378,000	−1.57
1996	1,343,356	13.31	4,656,000	6.35
1997	1,517,330	12.95	5,051,000	8.48
1998	1,535,359	1.19	5,428,000	7.46
1999	1,837,764	19.70	5,894,000	8.59
2000	2,044,563	11.25	6,882,000	16.76
2001	2,290,801	12.04	6,906,000	0.35
2002	2,482,231	8.36	7,640,000	10.63
2003	2,854,476	15.00	8,300,000	8.64
2004	3,037,948	6.43	8,980,000	8.19

Note: CLIA lines are the cruise lines that belong to Cruise Lines International Association, the main trade association representing the cruise industry in North America. Cruise Lines that are members of CLIA comprise approximately 95% of the cruise capacity marketed from North America.

Exhibit 1 Annual Passengers Carried by Carnival Cruise Lines Compared to the North American Cruise Industry. (*Source:* Carnival Cruise Lines and CLIA.)

Ship	Class of Ship	Year Launched	Gross Tonnage	Staterooms	Double Occupancy
1 *Holiday*	Holiday	1985	46,052	743	1,452
2 *Celebration*	Holiday	1987	47,262	743	1,486
3 *Fantasy*	Fantasy	1990	70,367	1,026	2,056
4 *Ecstasy*	Fantasy	1991	70,367	1,026	2,052
5 *Sensation*	Fantasy	1993	70,367	1,026	2,052
6 *Fascination*	Fantasy	1994	70,367	1,026	2,052
7 *Imagination*	Fantasy	1995	70,367	1,026	2,052
8 *Inspiration*	Fantasy	1996	70,367	1,026	2,052
9 *Carnival Destiny*	Destiny	1996	101,353	1,321	2,642
10 *Elation*	Fantasy	1998	70,367	1,021	2,052
11 *Paradise*	Fantasy	1998	70,367	1,026	2,052
12 *Carnival Triumph*	Triumph	1999	101,509	1,379	2,758
13 *Carnival Victory*	Triumph	2000	101,509	1,379	2,758
14 *Carnival Spirit*	Spirit	2001	88,500	1,062	2,124
15 *Carnival Pride*	Spirit	2002	88,500	1,062	2,124
16 *Carnival Legend*	Spirit	2002	88,500	1,062	2,124
17 *Carnival Conquest*	Conquest	2002	110,000	1,487	2,974
18 *Carnival Glory*	Conquest	2003	110,000	1,487	2,974
19 *Carnival Miracle*	Spirit	2004	88,500	1,062	2,124
20 *Carnival Valor*	Conquest	2004	110,000	1,487	2,974

Exhibit 2 The Carnival Cruise Lines Fleet. (*Source:* Carnival Cruise Lines.)

been placed on repeat business. Though the segment of potential first-timers remained large, competition for the mid-market vacation dollar was fierce. Carnival had amassed a large past-cruiser database, though the company had done little with it to date.

THE CRUISE INDUSTRY

Cruise vacationing was the fastest-growing category of the North American leisure travel industry. In 1970, cruise lines carried about 500,000 passengers; in 2004, the industry was projected to embark more than 10 million guests. Cruising remained, though, a relatively small industry. Bob Dickinson explained:

> Overall, there were 300-plus million person trips per year taken in the U.S. and Canada that involved at least three nights' stay away from home in a hotel or a cruise ship. We carried 3 million guests. Orlando and Las Vegas did 70 million visitors last year—almost a quarter of the vacation market. We are in the vacation business, not the cruise business; they are our biggest competitors.

Dickinson noted further that only 16% of the North American market had ever cruised, leaving a large untapped base of potential customers. Though he admitted that some people will never cruise, his message had been clear and unwavering for years: cruise lines must develop the first-timer segment in order to convert land vacationers to cruisers.

INDUSTRY EVOLUTION

Shipping companies have transported passengers for centuries, but it was only since the mid-1960s that the core product shifted to pleasure cruising. Marking this transition were dramatic changes in the cruise ships (or the "hardware," in industry parlance). Famous vessels such as the *Queen Mary,* the *Normandie,* and the *Empress of Britain* were richly appointed, but even these icons paled in comparison to modern hardware. New mega-ships typically ranged in size from 70,000 to 140,000 GRT,[19] with Cunard Line's 150,000-ton *Queen Mary 2* owning the title of the largest ship ever built. Ships of this scale carried anywhere from 1,800 to 3,800 passengers, as well as 700 to 1,200 crew members.

These floating resorts also featured a remarkable array of activities designed to suit guests' increasingly diverse interests. In addition to the varied dining options, casinos, bars, cabaret acts, pools, shuffleboard, and bingo—long a staple of pleasure cruising—now passengers experienced themed eateries, spas, state-of-the-art fitness facilities, rock-climbing walls, inline skating, video game rooms, basketball and tennis courts, high-tech discos, Las Vegas- and Broadway-style productions, wine tasting, art auctions, Internet cafes, cigar bars, sports bars, in-cabin movies, guest-chef cooking demonstrations, and educational enrichment programs of all types. Beyond these onboard options, guests enjoyed many other activities when the ships reached ports of call.

Cruising grew rapidly, with more than 70 brands serving the North American market since the 1960s.[20] A period of heavy consolidation left Carnival Corporation, Royal Caribbean International, Ltd., and Star Cruises dominating the seascape with 10 major brands that controlled nearly 95% of the market. Carnival Corp. became the largest cruise company in the world (see Exhibit 3). This consolidation was completed when post-9/11 pricing pressures hastened the demise of several budget cruise lines, and Carnival Cruise Lines emerged as the low-price leader.

Cruise lines targeting the North American market operated in four segments: contemporary (mass market), premium, destination (specialty), and luxury.[21] The recent relabeling of the mass-market segment as "contemporary" reflected the departure of the budget lines and their older vessels from the market. Although brands in the premium category tended to offer more sophisticated, traditional, higher quality, and higher priced products, the new ships being introduced by these brands were larger than in the past and featured many of the same amenities as ships sailing in the contemporary category. Christine Arnholt, Vice President of Marketing Services, explained:

> There's a wealth of great product out there today. The premium and contemporary segments are really merging—the premium brands are implementing some of the proven mass-market strategies, and we're reaching higher by improving the quality of our product, our service, and the cruise experience overall.

At $1,651 per person (including onboard spending), the average 7-day cruise was hardly inexpensive;[22] however, the

---

[19] GRT stands for gross registered tonnage and represents the volume of space within the hull of a ship, or a ship's total internal capacity (1 vessel ton = 100 cubic feet).

[20] North America accounts for three-quarters of cruise passenger capacity (74%), while Europe accounts for 23%, with Asia/South Pacific making up the balance.

[21] The luxury and destination segments accounted for only about 5% of the market and included such brands as the Yachts of Seabourn (luxury) and the masted-sailing vessels of Windstar (destination/specialty).

[22] Source: Cruise Lines International Association 2004 Cruise Market Profile, Presented by TNS/NFO Plog Research. *continued*

per diem price was less than the daily rate at many destination hotels and all-inclusive resorts. Plus, cruise fares included the cost of lodging, transportation to multiple destinations, dining, entertainment, and other amenities. Shorter cruises, popularized by Carnival, not only allowed first-timers to sample the product with less risk, but often offered a better value. Indeed, during the shoulder season in the fall of 2004, Carnival's 3-day Miami to Bahamas cruises were advertised for just $299 per person.[23] As Bob Dickinson put it: "Unlike the hotel business, a cruise line drives price to fill the ship. Our pricing model is different."

Vicki Freed, Carnival's Senior Vice President of Marketing and Sales, commented:

> Cruising is not the low end of the vacation market. Even though Carnival is a mass-market, value cruise line, at $100 a day per person, we're not at the low, low end. We're not a $39-a-night Motel 6. We're not dining at McDonald's. In the vacation segment, we're already in the middle.

As demand for cruising boomed, so did supply. Since 1990, more than 130 new cruise ships were launched worldwide and 20 new ships were under contract or planned to be launched before 2008, which would increase the industry's capacity another 20%.[24] Carnival's direct rival, Royal Caribbean, had announced plans for an even larger version of its massive, innovative Voyager class ships, with their signature rock-climbing walls and other active-adventure amenities.

Despite the success of the cruise industry, the events of September 11, 2001 did not leave cruise lines unharmed. Public fears of flying led to a sharp decline in occupancies that had typically reached 100%. This event only exacerbated softness in the market caused by the increase in supply, the weak economy, and other factors. Cruise lines were forced to cut fares to fill newly built ships. But these hardships also showed the flexibility inherent in cruise operations and the strength of brands like Carnival that had tight control on costs. For example, some cruise lines redeployed their ships to North American ports (e.g., New Orleans,

Galveston, TX, and Charleston, SC) within driving distance of feeder markets to capture customers still afraid to fly, but ready to vacation again. This "homeporting" reduced the price barrier to cruising even further, and occupancy levels quickly returned to normal, though five years later prices had yet to return to the high-water mark set in 1999.

CARNIVAL CRUISE LINES

The Carnival Corporation portfolio of 12 cruise lines and 75 ships covered each of the four North American market segments, as well as Europe (Exhibit 6). With the exception of the Vacation Interchange Privileges program (VIP)— where past guests on any sister brand were treated as past guests on Carnival and vice versa—the brands under Carnival Corp.'s "World's Leading Cruise Lines" umbrella remained independent, especially with respect to sales and marketing. Senior management believed that this internal competition was good for the parent company, as it forced each brand to maintain an edge in the marketplace and to clearly define a unique value proposition. On the back end, where synergies driven by economies of scale could pay dividends (e.g., purchasing), cooperation and coordination among the brands were more welcomed.

On any given week, Carnival carried more than 60,000 passengers; by comparison, the luxury sister brand, Seabourn, carried 21,000 passengers per year. Bob Dickinson, who also serves on the board of directors of Carnival Corporation, recalled how the cash flow generated by the Carnival brand had allowed the purchase of its sister brands. He commented:

> We are the 800-pound gorilla in the industry. We carry more guests than anybody else, we make more money than anybody else, we have the highest return on invested capital, and we are the only supplier in the travel business that calls on all travel agents.

Carnival was also the largest feeder to all other cruise lines in North America—including the competition. Furthermore, the Carnival experience was often the standard

---

[23] Cruises are usually priced per person, double occupancy, exclusive of taxes and fees. This means a "lead-in price" of $599 is for a lower-category cabin (e.g., an inside stateroom) with the expectation that two guests would use the room ($599 3 2). Government taxes and fees might be an extra $15 to $70 per person depending on which ports the ship sails from and visits.

[24] Cruise ship passenger capacity is defined by the number of "lower berths," which is typically two per cabin. Because many cabins can accommodate more than two passengers with sleeping arrangements in fold-out sofa beds or pull-down bunk beds, it is not unusual for ships to sail at more than 100% occupancy.

Cruise Brand	Inception (Acquisition)	Ships	Double Occupancy	Geographic Market(s) Served
Carnival Cruise Lines*	1972	20	44,934	North America
Princess Cruises*	(2003)	14	28,050	North America
Holland America Line*	(1989)	12	16,937	North America
Costa Cruises*	(1997)	10	18,287	Europe
P&O Cruises U.K.	(2003)	4	7,506	United Kingdom
AIDA	(2003)	4	5,316	Germany
Cunard Line*	(1998)	2	4,411	North America, UK
Ocean Village	(2003)	1	1,620	United Kingdom
P&O Cruises Australia	(2003)	1	3,374	Australia
Swan Hellenic	(2003)	1	684	United Kingdom
Yachts of Seabourn*	(1992)	3	624	North America
Windstar Cruises*	(1989)	3	604	North America
Total		**75**	**132,347**	

*A set of Carnival Corporation brands that serve the North American market have been collectively branded as the "World's Leading Cruise Lines" (Carnival Cruise Line, Princess Cruises, Holland America Line, Cunard Line, Costa Cruises, The Yachts of Seabourn, and Windstar Cruises)

Exhibit 6   Carnival Corporation and PLC Cruise Brands. (*Source:* Carnival Cruise Lines.)

against which repeat cruisers judged their later cruise experiences. Vicki Freed offered this insight:

> There are many experienced cruisers out there who may have cruised on Carnival 10 years ago or who have never tried Carnival and who would say, "ABC—Anything But Carnival." We've grown up as a company and the product has evolved. We want recognition for that in terms of the guests and prospects understanding that evolution.

Carnival had a humble launch in 1972 as the vision of Ted Arison, father of the current chairman of the board and CEO of Carnival Corp, Micky Arison. Christine Arnholt, a member of Carnival's management team since 1991, painted a colorful picture of the line's history:

> The story of the "Fun Ships" started because we began with one converted transatlantic liner that ran aground on a sand bar on its inaugural voyage for Carnival, so we opened the bar, and gave everybody drinks. Everybody had fun, and that's our legacy. And here we have this fleet of beautiful new ships, but some of the old misperceptions do

not change, although we're making steady progress.

Throughout its history, one driver of Carnival's success was a clear vision about the industry it operated in and an unwavering commitment to the brand essence. Bob Dickinson remarked:

> We own the psychographic of fun. Based on research, fun is the thing most people look for in a vacation. Even our sister companies are very traditional. That's fine—floating country clubs at sea, a little elitist, true to a heritage of a posh, very affluent, upscale deal. We're unabashedly Orlando and Vegas.

As the definition of what made a ship a "Fun Ship" depended on customer expectations and needs, Carnival considered product design one of its critical success factors. For example, the *Carnival Holiday,* built in 1985 and still with the company today, was the first ship created with entertainment architecture in mind. The *Holiday* was themed throughout and was anything but a typical ship when it was built. Carnival's ship design was known for being bright, with neon lighting and vibrant colors. Senior management believed in

continued

having the right product that was consistently executed in terms of both hardware and software (with software being the service personnel and delivery). Equally important was being able to look into the future and position products to fit the changing interests of Carnival's varied customer base. Maintaining a clear message that captured the firm's positioning was also deemed crucial to the firm's success.

Carnival "Fun Ships" were designed to include a wide range of activities and options for guests. (Exhibit 7 provides an example of a typical daily cruise itinerary as published in *Carnival Capers.*) Beyond enabling guests to tailor their Fun Ship experience, Carnival also offered product variety through cruise duration (Carnival's core business was 3-, 4-, 5-, and 7-day cruises), destinations and the ports of call along the way (Carnival sailed from 19 homeport cities and sailed to ports of call in The Bahamas, Canada, the Caribbean, Mexico, New England, Panama Canal, Alaska, and Hawaii), and themed sailings (Carnival hosted cruises for fans of NASCAR, the Florida Marlins, and even the rock bands Journey and Styx).[25] But all this variety notwithstanding, Carnival was a frugal and efficient company. Terry Thornton, Vice President of Marketing Planning, explained:

> We are very disciplined when buying new hardware and invest the smallest amount per bed. Most of our competitors buy ships for 25%–30% more per bed than what we do. That difference is going into bells and whistles that we don't think produce a return.

THE CARNIVAL CUSTOMER

According to research by Cruise Lines International Association (CLIA), the industry's main trade association, the average cruiser was 50 years old and affluent, with a household income of $99,000 per year. Cruisers were typically married and sailed with their spouses (78%). More than half (54%) had taken their first cruise within the past five years and, on average, took 2.6 cruises in this time period. Carnival's customer profile was similar, but with some notable differences. The average age of the Carnival cruiser was somewhat lower at 46, though the age distribution was widespread, with 24% of guests 55 or older, 40% between 35 and 55, and 36% 35 or younger. The Carnival product was popular with families, singles, honeymooners, and multigenerational families—indeed, a

wide spectrum of ages. The average annual household income of the Carnival cruiser was about $65,000. Carnival also carried fewer married passengers (55%). The company pursued this broad market via a variety of promotional channels, including national TV and cable advertising, promotions in more than 200 newspapers, direct marketing to the past-guest database, as well as the industry's largest field sales force that called on travel agents.

Bob Dickinson believed that profiling the prototypical Carnival customer using demographic characteristics was less important than understanding the customer's mindset:

> We try to position ourselves in the mainstream vacation market. We're the Fun Ships. We're for Everyman with a capital E.

Brendan Corrigan, the Senior Vice President of Cruise Operations, further explained:

> We don't go fishing for the big tuna; we cast the wide net of fun and attract all kinds of fish. Our guests make the Carnival experience. They say, "I'm going to enjoy myself. I'm on vacation." In my opinion, competitors of ours have guests who have a different mindset regarding cruising. They cruise because, traditionally, the "rich and famous" cruise. These guests are the pseudo rich. They have the same money as the majority of our guests, and from afar, you might say they're the same as our guests, but if you really look, they're not the same. They aspire to something different—to sail on the "royal ship." On our ships we have people who really want to enjoy themselves.

Although targeting the "fun" psychographic had been a constant for Carnival, the type of customer attracted to the brand had changed over the years, in part because the product had changed. During the early years, Carnival, like the cruise industry overall, attracted an older customer. Soon, though, Carnival developed a reputation as a no-frills party cruise line and began to attract a much younger demographic. Vicki Freed, who had been involved with Carnival's sales and marketing since 1978, offered some perspective:

> Some of our travel agent partners who have been in the business for a long time still have this perception of Carnival. They say, "I put all of my people under

---

[25] Some customized cruises are organized and marketed by a travel packager, not by Carnival.

Exhibit 7 Typical Activities Available on a Carnival Cruise

Source: Carnival Capers for the *Carnival Valor,* January 18, 2005.

30 on Carnival, or I'll put all of the honeymooners on Carnival." They don't realize that an empty-nester is a very good guest to send on Carnival or that the average age on our longer cruises is 47, which means that people in their 60s and 70s are cruising with us.

For most cruise lines it is estimated that one out of three guests is a first-timer. Carnival's Terry Thornton estimated that half of the line's guests were first timers. Of the 50% of guests who were repeaters, two-thirds were repeaters to the brand and one-third were cruisers who had not previously sailed Carnival. Thus, on any given cruise, roughly one-third of guests had sailed Carnival before. Although the company courted new cruisers, there was a desire to increase within-brand repeat rates and to strengthen loyalty to the brand. However, executives were puzzled as to why loyalty was low, given a 98% guest satisfaction rating. Thornton commented:

The loyalty issue is a big question. Our repeat-cruiser numbers are not much different than our sister brands on common itineraries, but we shake our heads

because guests had a great time, and we offer so many options—we'd expect more.

Carnival's analysis of repeat cruisers found that the majority had cruised with the brand twice, repurchasing every 12 to 25 months on average; however, repeat rates dropped fast after that—less than 20% of guests who cruised with the brand during the past seven years returned more than once. Repeaters spent an average of about 15% more on their cruise vacations. Because most costs associated with cruising were fixed, increased guest spending typically flowed right to the bottom line.

The generally held belief in the industry was that experienced cruisers understood the value offered by the product—the ability to unpack once in an all-inclusive resort that magically appeared in a different destination at the dawn of every day. While first-timers were unsure about what to expect and wanted to test the waters, repeaters were willing to spend extra for a balcony cabin, premium dining, wine at dinner, shore excursions, spa treatments, and the like. Thus, driving repeat purchases appealed to many Carnival executives. Vicki Freed explained:

continued

We want guests to stay loyal to the brand. We already have the marketing acquisition costs in the Carnival experienced cruiser. Our call centers spend more time with first-timers than with repeaters. The repeat guests are more educated about the product, so they understand the value proposition better.

Not everyone was sold on the idea that significant resources should be directed to attracting repeat guests. Bob Dickinson, for one, argued that past guests "just come to us automatically."

DISTRIBUTING THE CARNIVAL PRODUCT

Customers bought Carnival cruises through two main channels—travel agents, accounting for about 85% of the company's bookings, and direct. The travel agency portion was everything from large internet agents like Travelocity and Expedia to independent "mom and pop" agencies and at-home agents. Cruise lines viewed agents as a vital external sales force, but also an expensive one. Agents earned a commission of 10% or more on the ticket price of a cruise, which made the agent's commission one of the largest individual line items on a cruise's P&L statement. Nevertheless, Carnival's marketing team was sensitive to relationships with travel-agents and recognized the value that professional agents added through their marketing of the brand, education of consumers, and hand-holding of clients during the purchase process. Vicki Freed explained:

> We're very sensitive to channel disharmony. We're not in competition with travel agents. We need them. Some consumers are happy booking through their travel agent, and we're happy to let them. And some consumers want to book direct with the supplier. I think that just shows you the evolution of the consumer.

Carnival's direct-marketing channel comprised inbound and outbound avenues. Inbound included 1-800-Carnival and Carnival.com. These direct channels involved interactions initiated by the customer and thus provided qualified leads. However, few customers booked online at Carnival.com, in part because of the complexity of the product and the purchase process, but also because most cruise customers still preferred to speak to a "live" person when buying a cruise.

The outbound channel was a separate division, started just over four years prior, that had grown rapidly to more than 200 professional telemarketers called Personal Vacation Planners (PVPs). Leads for the PVPs came from a number of sources, including the Carnival.com Web site and other consumer inquiries. The outbound-direct marketing by PVPs had proven to be an effective sales channel for Carnival, especially for moving unsold inventory as sailing dates drew near. However, Carnival was reluctant to be too aggressive with using PVPs to market directly to past guests out of fear that this would upset travel agents. A PVP only contacted a past guest if the customer had subsequently visited the Carnival.com site to make an inquiry about a cruise or was already in the PVP's "book of business" as a customer or sales lead. On the other hand, Carnival's marketing department sometimes communicated directly with past guests (e.g., with e-mail promotions), but the call to action always included the travel agent. Brenda Yester underscored Carnival's commitment to agents:

> There's been a lot of discussion in the industry about who owns the guest. No one owns the guest, frankly. Still, we've been very careful about marketing to agents' guests. When we run a past-guest promotion, we say, "Contact your travel agent, call Carnival, or visit Carnival.com." Our media always says, "See your travel agent." We always include them.

DELIVERING THE CARNIVAL EXPERIENCE

The Carnival experience began for travelers long before the ship set sail. Guests typically booked their cruises 3 to 5 months before the sailing date, though a growing segment of shoppers waited for last-minute deals. Prospects increasingly got cruise information via the Web, but generally went to travel agents for assistance with the reservation. Once a customer purchased a cruise, the travel agent collected their name, age, and dining-time preference and relayed this information to the cruise line reservations department, either by calling 1-800 Carnival or using Carnival's "Bookccl.com" travel-trade portal. Travel agents often had access to significant customer information, including travel and activities preferences, demographic data, contact information, and e-mail addresses. However, the hand-off to the cruise line wasn't always smooth. Carnival's reservations office sometimes knew only customers' first and last names, dining preferences, and maybe a made-up birth date.

Carnival obtained more information about first-time guests who booked directly with the company. A new online registration process for cruise boarding passes (the "Fun Pass") facilitated capture of demographic data (e.g., guest name, address, phone number, e-mail address, and birth date). Carnival estimated that 80% to 90% of passengers completed their Fun Pass registration online, though usually not until the week before their scheduled departure. The remaining guests provided their Fun Pass data in a written form during embarkation.

Carnival was experimenting with several e-commerce applications, including pre-cruise online sign-up for shore excursions and spa appointments. Though Carnival outsourced the operation of these revenue centers, each was quite profitable for the cruise line. Scheduling for excursions and spas traditionally took place on the ship, which could lead to sign-up lines or frequent promotional announcements onboard by the cruise director as he or she tried to stir up demand. Having customers sign up for excursions online before they boarded the ship provided significant advantages. Shannon Balliet-Antorcha, Manager of Revenue Enhancement, explained:

> Now that Carnival enables people to manage their vacation prior to sailing, we can apply revenue management to a process that was previously purely an onboard thing. If we see that an excursion is selling out, we could raise the price and allow it to sell out, or we could go to the vendor and ask to increase our inventory. We also will get people out of line and hopefully in the photo gallery, casinos, (and) the bars spending more money and having more fun.

The relationship between Carnival and its guests most visibly started at embarkation—when thousands of travelers converged at the cruise port. Embarkation was often a chaotic process that combined elements of an airline-like check in and security clearance. For the process to run smoothly, Carnival needed guests to arrive a few hours before the scheduled sailing time (though not too early, as this would interfere with the debarkation of prior guests), and with their cruise documents properly completed. Most guests arrived via shuttle or taxi and were dropped off at the cruise terminal. Assuming that they had properly filled out their luggage tags, a small army of porters directed the guests to the embarkation area and moved upward of 8,000 pieces of luggage to be loaded onto the ship. Guests then passed through a security area with X-ray machines[26] and entered a queue

to await processing of their boarding passes, have their picture taken, and receive their "Sail & Sign" card. The picture was electronically tied to the card, which also had a magnetic strip. The Sail & Sign card had come a long way from its origins. Dwayne Warner, Vice President of Strategic Automation and a 20-year veteran of the industry, recalled:

> The Sail & Sign card started as a cash-control tool onboard the ship. As the technology improved we started doing more with it, and it rapidly became a one stop shop for all onboard transactions.

The modern Sail & Sign card was all encompassing, serving as a pass to board/deboard the ship and to sign up for excursions, as well as acting like a credit card to pay for anything purchased onboard and against which gratuities were automatically charged.[27] Once guests had their Sail & Sign card in hand, their vacation officially started. It was not uncommon for the embarkation process to take one to two hours. However, members of Carnival's Skipper's Club (VIPs and buyers of the high-end staterooms and suites) enjoyed an expedited embarkation. These guests were escorted to a private area where they were checked in by attentive staff in a well-appointed, air-conditioned room and then through security and directly onto the ship, making for a speedy process.

From Carnival's standpoint, embarkation was the continuation of the debarkation process, and capped off a strenuous day where the crew had to turn the ship around in only a few hours. Debarking guests were offloaded to the dock with their luggage and had to clear customs. Foreign-national guests and crew also needed to clear immigration. As guests left their rooms, stewards (who generally were responsible for 26 cabins each) had to clean and refresh the rooms so that these would look brand new to the guests arriving later the same day. The public areas on the ship presented an even bigger challenge, since these were the last areas occupied by debarking guests and the first ones seen by embarking ones.

Beyond these guest-facing processes, turning around a floating resort housing 3,000 guests and 1,100 international crew members (from 40-plus different countries) was extraordinary. Crew leaving service had to be processed out, and replacements had to be processed in; luggage had to be offloaded and loaded; tons of food, fuel, and water had to be loaded and directed to proper storage facilities. With storage

---

[26] Stringent security screening was not used, nor was it necessary, prior to the 9/11 terrorist attacks.

[27] Carnival charged each guest $10 per day to pay gratuities to the crew. Guests were free to increase or decrease gratuities, but had to see the ship's Purser's office to make such adjustments to their folio.

continued

and staging space on the ship at a premium, sequencing of these activities was crucial. Unannounced inspections from the health and safety department provided occasional disruption to an otherwise amazing example of well-orchestrated chaos.

Given the increasing scale of ships and the tight cruise turnaround time, Carnival relied on cruise staff to quickly learn guests' names and preferences. Cruise travelers were increasingly sophisticated and had high expectations. At the same time that cruise lines tried to deliver a higher-quality, higher-variety experience, there was the need to control costs to ensure that customers perceived good value received for their vacation dollar. Still, there were limits to cost-cutting tactics Carnival could employ before the guests' vacation experiences began to deteriorate. Thus, management sought ways to better direct guest spending onboard toward higher-margin purchases, as well as to provide more opportunities for guests to spend money on the ship. Brenda Yester quipped:

> The biggest driver of profitability is our ability to influence yields, both pre-board, which is what we sell the tickets for, and onboard, which is when we take you on the ship, hang you upside down, and shake every dollar out of your pocket, so to speak. . . . We certainly have no shortage of fun ways for our guests to spend their money on the ship.

A Carnival cruise offered many opportunities for guests to augment their cruise experience—and for Carnival to net ancillary revenues. Bar waiters circled the deck areas, ready to sell all manner of drinks, from soft drinks to buckets of beer (four to a bucket for $14) or frozen cocktails in special souvenir cups ($6.75). The ship's shops sold everything from souvenir trinkets to fine jewelry. Duty-free shops sold discounted alcohol that was made available at the end of the cruise, and sommeliers sold a huge selection of wines at dinner—from an $18 Walnut Crest Merlot to a $425 Chateau Lafite Rothschild. The spa sold a range of treatments, from a $25 manicure to a $297 "ionithermie algae detox" treatment. There were also art auctions, wine tastings with the sampled vintages for sale, airbrush art (temporary tattooing), Internet cafés, video arcades, and golf simulators. A new option offered by Carnival was "alternative bistro dining," where for $20–$25 per person, guests would enjoy different dining experiences than those found in the main dining rooms. The biggest onboard revenue centers for cruise lines—and Carnival in particular—were the casinos, shore excursions, and bars. Other high-margin, though lower-volume profit centers were ship-to-shore telephones, laundry, and the ship's photo gallery. Carnival's photographers took hundreds of high-quality pictures of guests during the cruise, from candid shots to posed portraits. The photos were sold for $4 for a 5 × 7 and $20 for an 8 × 10. Many of these prints were discarded at the end of the cruise if unsold.

It was possible for a Carnival guest to enjoy a cruise complete with food, most nonalcoholic beverages, entertainment, lodging, and outstanding service, and to spend little more for this than the cruise fare, taxes, and gratuities. However, it was also easy to spend more to enhance the cruise experience and customize it to one's needs, preferences, and desires. According to Carnival estimates, the average cruiser spent an additional $30–$50 per day on board, not including gratuities. Carnival was always looking for new ways to offer guests variety and choice—and to derive increased revenue in the process.

Carnival executives believed that, at the end of a cruise, if there was a positive gap between customer expectations and product delivery at good value, this created a passionate consumer base. Bob Dickinson reinforced this view:

> We try to create the minimum level of guest expectation—just high enough for them to buy our product. We then deliver a product that goes far beyond that level of expectation. Our vision statement is to "Provide quality cruise vacations that exceed the expectations of our guests"—that's a recipe for success.

CARNIVAL'S INFORMATION SYSTEMS

The information systems (IS) group at Carnival counted about 275 full-time employees shoreside, plus about 45 shipboard IS managers in charge of the enabling technology onboard. With a large number of applications in the portfolio that were custom-developed, Carnival devoted a substantial amount of resources to maintenance and operations (Exhibit 8 presents Carnival's IS infrastructure). The typical on-board infrastructure revolved around two key guest management applications: the property management system (PMS) and the point of sale (POS). These two applications shared the underlying Oracle database. The POS, a custom-made application called Fun Sales System (FSS), enabled staff to ring up sales in the many outlets the guests could use to make purchases (e.g., bars, shops, photo

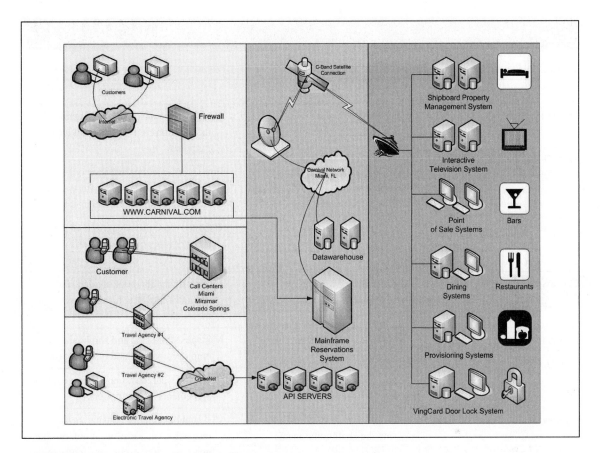

Exhibit 8 Carnival Cruise Lines IS Infrastructure. (*Source:* Company data.)

gallery). FSS offered a graphical user interface allowing employees to choose the items to be charged, accepted Sail & Sign cards as form of payment, and post the charge to the guest folio (Exhibit 9). The outlets that ran as a concession, like the Internet Café, spa, and casino, did not use FSS and posted charges directly to the Oracle database that generated the guest folios. Thanks to the use of Sail & Sign cards (backed by credit cards or cash deposits), a cruise ship was a cashless society. A guest could engage in the myriad activities that onboard life offered and not have to worry about payment until the day prior to debarkation when a folio was delivered to the cabin for verification and approval.

Once the ship arrived to port on the last day of the cruise, a data cable was connected to the shoreside network, and the voyage data was downloaded from the onboard systems. Guest data was downloaded by operations accounting personnel from the PMS and rolled-up into financial statements in order to "close the voyage."

Table 4 Shipboard Hardware (Approximate Number Per Ship)

Description	*Number*
Clients (PC + POS terminals)	120–150
Servers	16

continued

Table 5 Principal Shoreside Software Systems

Shoreside Computer System	Description	Use
Oracle Financials	A/P, A/R, GL, and Purchasing modules	Collects and consolidates financial information for reporting and legal purposes.
Reservations	Custom made mainframe application	Powers reservations and the booking engine for the Carnival.com Web site, call center and travel agents.
Revenue Accounting	Custom made application	Used to "close the voyage." It enables account reconciliation, reporting by revenue center, payment of partners.
Cornerstone	Oracle Data Warehouse	Loads pricing and booking data and produces forecasts for use by revenue management.
Lawson	Payroll and Benefits package application	Manages shore side and shipboard employee payroll and benefits programs.
i2	Supply Chain package	Aggregates purchases and manage master agreements with suppliers.
Carnival.com	Combination of in-house and off-the-shelf components	CCL's public site for consumers to research CCL vacations, book on-line, purchase shore excursions, register for Fun-Pass, etc. Site also provides travel-agent portal, bookccl.com, for online agency bookings.

Closing the voyage entailed the balancing and reconciliation of accounts and the aggregation of financial data in order to produce voyage reports by revenue center (e.g., bars, shops, casino), as well the processing of payments to external vendors and operators (e.g., for tours and excursions). Thus, once debarkation began, the focus shifted from the guest—and ensuring that each guest was accurately billed for the transactions they had completed—to the revenue centers—and ensuring that accurate financial statements could be produced and financial analyses could be performed. While Carnival did not have a guest data warehouse, and could not easily retrieve guest transactional and behavioral data for analysis, the IS group had the foresight to start saving individual voyage data before it was

rolled up to the financials and much of the granularity was lost. Thus, the company had accumulated two years worth of voyage data that could be analyzed when loaded into a guest data warehouse at a future date. Hidden in this data was a picture of household-level onboard spending obtained by way of the Sail & Sign cards.

Aware of the potential benefits of selective IT deployment, Carnival maintained a group of experienced business analysts and architects who worked with users on developing the business case for new applications. These business cases were then taken to the IS steering committee, which included Bob Dickinson, for evaluation and approval based on expected benefits and ROI. One of the biggest challenges faced by Carnival, beyond the traditional low IT spending

Table 6 Principal Shipboard Software Systems

Shipboard Computer System	Description	Use
Shipboard Property Management System (SPMS)	Custom developed Carnival application	The core shipboard system housing guest information (e.g., room, credit card) and where transactional guest related transactional data must flow to produce the folio.
Fun Ship Sales (FSS)	Point of Sale (POS) system. Custom developed Carnival application.	The primary point of sale system used onboard Carnival ships. Supports transaction processing at most guest touch points (e.g., bars, shops, photo gallery)
Silverware	Off-the-shelf application	Used by the maître d' to create seating arrangements based on the manifest (guest list) and seating preferences communicated by reservations.
Iverson	Casino Financial System (CFS). Owned and operated by Carnival Corp.'s casino unit.	Used by Carnival Corp.'s casino unit to manage the casinos on the ships.
Ocean Player Club	Player tracking system. Owned and operated by Carnival Corp.'s casino unit.	Used to track accrual and redemption of "ocean points"—player reward points that can be accrued and redeemed in casinos on any ship within the Carnival Corp. family.
Concession Systems	Terminal access to SPMS, operated by concessionaires.	Used to post charges to the individual guest's folios.
Consumer Response System (CRS)	Off-the-shelf application	Used to track incidents and interactions with guests throughout the cruise.
Interactive Television	Off-the-shelf application with custom interfaces	Enables guests to order in-room movies, as well as perform simple transactions through the TV set (e.g., order tours and shore excursions, room service, check statements online).
Crew Personnel System (CPS)	Custom developed Carnival application	Crew management and scheduling system.

continued

Table 6 *continued*

Shipboard Computer System	Description	Use
Crew Pay Gratuity (CPG)	Custom developed Carnival application	Used to allocate gratuities left by customers to the appropriate personnel according to guest wishes or, if unspecified, according to predetermined formulas.
Fun Time	Time card system. Custom developed Carnival application	Allows crew to sign in and out at the beginning and end of a shift.
InfoSHIPsql	Inventory and purchasing. Off-the-shelf application.	Enables requisitioning and purchasing for technical items
VingCard Door Lock	Off-the shelf application	Used to manage cabin door locks

Source: Authors' research.

in the hospitality and travel industry, was driven by the wide variation in the sophistication of channel partners. Dwayne Warner explained:

> We assume nothing. We have to be able to interface with large distributors using XML, but the fax is state of the art for many of the other travel agencies. We need a tiered approach.

Despite being the biggest cruise line, Carnival's management did not feel that it had to set the competitive IT agenda for the industry or strive to be the IT innovator; still, the company was careful not to fall behind. The value of this approach was evident when the big travel distributors turned to the cruise industry as a growth avenue and started selling the cruise product online. Carnival was able to develop interfaces in order to stay competitive. Carnival's conservative stance toward IT was also thought to have paid dividends when the customer relationship management (CRM) fad swept the industry at the dawn of the 21st century. Myles Cyr, Chief Information Officer, explained:

> The large consulting firms were laying out multi-million dollar, multi-year projects that required substantial integration of systems across all touch points with the objective of intimately knowing customers to increase their loyalty. But it all starts with the data. If you don't have accurate data, then the so-called

state-of-the-art CRM application that sits on top of the data will be useless.

An appreciation for the business value of data and information wasn't new to Carnival. The firm had a sophisticated revenue management group, started in 1999, that included analysts and decision scientists who leveraged daily inventory, pricing, and booking data available in Carnival's revenue management data warehouse to optimally price each cruise. The group had custom-developed forecasting and pricing models, and was now turning its attention to onboard spending as part of a new "revenue analytics" project. Beyond pricing decisions, Carnival used data to understand the performance of travel agents. The company knew productivity by agent, what products each travel agency booked, and when they booked them. This information allowed Carnival's sales force to manage the firm's relationship with the channel very efficiently by creating incentives and rewards systems that increased booking flow. Because of the reliance on the travel-agent channel, Carnival had not actively cultivated direct relationships with customers until recently. Cyr explained:

> For a long time cruise lines did not even own their customer lists, which were in the hands of the fulfillment houses that mailed out the brochures and welcome home letters. Moreover, the boarding passes were keyed in by a third party company that was paid per boarding pass— there were no checks and balances on data accuracy.

Statement for: MR Freddy Funship					Cabin#: S1	
					Authno: 5251	
Chgdate	Description of item	Check#	Folio	Sale Amt	Tip	Total
12/06/2004	SERVICE GRATUITY	957472	9574	40.00	0.00	40.00
12/06/2004	SERVICE GRATUITY	957477	9575	40.00	0.00	40.00
12/06/2004	SERVICE GRATUITY	957484	9576	40.00	0.00	40.00
12/06/2004	SERVICE GRATUITY	957487	9577	40.00	0.00	40.00
12/06/2004	SE / DR WATER	957487	9575	25.00	3.75	28.75
12/06/2004	PUT ON RITZ 108	528741	9577	4.25	0.64	4.89
12/06/2004	INTERNET CAFE	307568	9575	25.00	0.00	25.00
12/08/2004	FORMALITIES SHOP	530815	9575	85.00	5.00	90.00
12/08/2004	PHOTO GALLERY	533691	9577	19.99	0.00	19.99
12/08/2004	SE / DR WATER	953878	9575	6.25	0.94	7.19
12/08/2004	LIDO DECK	534047	9575	8.90	1.33	10.23
12/08/2004	FORMALITIES SHOP	536399	9577	10.34	0.00	10.34
12/08/2004	VIDEO ARCADE	450968	9577	5.00	0.00	5.00
12/08/2004	VIDEO ARCADE	451288	9577	5.00	0.00	5.00
12/08/2004	VIDEO ARCADE	452333	9577	5.00	0.00	5.00
12/09/2004	SHORE EXCURSIONS	445474	9575	156.00	0.00	156.00
12/09/2004	SHORE EXCURSIONS	445477	9575	458.00	0.00	458.00
12/09/2004	ART AUCTION	462129	9577	18,637.02	0.00	18,637.02
12/10/2004	GIFT SHOP	889494	9577	14.95	0.00	14.95
12/10/2004	DIAMONDS LOUNGE	901213	9577	2.5	0.38	2.88
12/11/2004	GIFT SHOP	962165	9577	42.00	0.00	42.00
12/11/2004	SERVICE GRATUITY	962892	9575	100.00	0.00	100.00

TOTAL CHARGES:	19,782.24
Less Cash Deposits:	0.00
Plus Cash Refunds:	0.00
NET BALANCE: $	19,782.24

Exhibit 9 Sample Guest Folio[28] and Detailed View of Charges. (*Source:* Carnival Cruise Lines.)

---

[28] The folio presents highly aggregated data. Those same transactions could yield substantially more information when the individual systems were queried.

continued

CASE STUDY (*continued*)

Row #	VOYAGE	FOLIO	BOOK#	SEQ#	SALE_DATE	RECEIPT#	TRANS_LINE#	LOC_NAME	ITEM_NAME	AMOUNT	GRATUITY	TOTAL
1	FS20041206004	9574	6B17C0	4	12/6/2004 1:29:43 PM	957472	1	SERVICE GRATUITY	UNDEFINED ITEM	0	0	0
2	FS20041206004	9574	6B17C0	4	12/6/2004 1:29:43 PM	957472	2	SERVICE GRATUITY	CABIN STEWARD	14	0	14
3	FS20041206004	9574	6B17C0	4	12/6/2004 1:29:43 PM	957472	3	SERVICE GRATUITY	DIN ROOM SERV TEAM	22	0	22
4	FS20041206004	9574	6B17C0	4	12/6/2004 1:29:43 PM	957472	4	SERVICE GRATUITY	DIN ROOM MGMT	2	0	2
5	FS20041206004	9574	6B17C0	4	12/6/2004 1:29:43 PM	957472	5	SERVICE GRATUITY	ALTERNATE DIN STAFF	2	0	2
6	FS20041206004	9575	6B17C0	1	12/6/2004 1:30:17 PM	957477	1	SERVICE GRATUITY	UNDEFINED ITEM	0	0	0
7	FS20041206004	9575	6B17C0	1	12/6/2004 1:30:17 PM	957477	2	SERVICE GRATUITY	CABIN STEWARD	14	0	14
8	FS20041206004	9575	6B17C0	1	12/6/2004 1:30:17 PM	957477	3	SERVICE GRATUITY	DIN ROOM SERV TEAM	22	0	22
9	FS20041206004	9575	6B17C0	1	12/6/2004 1:30:17 PM	957477	4	SERVICE GRATUITY	DIN ROOM MGMT	2	0	2
10	FS20041206004	9575	6B17C0	1	12/6/2004 1:30:17 PM	957477	5	SERVICE GRATUITY	ALTERNATE DIN STAFF	2	0	2
11	FS20041206004	9576	6B17C0	3	12/6/2004 1:31:10 PM	957484	1	SERVICE GRATUITY	UNDEFINED ITEM	0	0	0
12	FS20041206004	9576	6B17C0	3	12/6/2004 1:31:10 PM	957484	2	SERVICE GRATUITY	CABIN STEWARD	14	0	14
13	FS20041206004	9576	6B17C0	3	12/6/2004 1:31:10 PM	957484	3	SERVICE GRATUITY	DIN ROOM SERV TEAM	22	0	22
14	FS20041206004	9576	6B17C0	3	12/6/2004 1:31:10 PM	957484	4	SERVICE GRATUITY	DIN ROOM MGMT	2	0	2
15	FS20041206004	9576	6B17C0	3	12/6/2004 1:31:10 PM	957484	5	SERVICE GRATUITY	ALTERNATE DIN STAFF	2	0	2
16	FS20041206004	9577	6B17C0	2	12/6/2004 1:31:22 PM	957487	1	SERVICE GRATUITY	UNDEFINED ITEM	0	0	0
17	FS20041206004	9577	6B17C0	2	12/6/2004 1:31:22 PM	957487	2	SERVICE GRATUITY	CABIN STEWARD	14	0	14
18	FS20041206004	9577	6B17C0	2	12/6/2004 1:31:22 PM	957487	3	SERVICE GRATUITY	DIN ROOM SERV TEAM	22	0	22
19	FS20041206004	9577	6B17C0	2	12/6/2004 1:31:22 PM	957487	4	SERVICE GRATUITY	DIN ROOM MGMT	2	0	2
20	FS20041206004	9577	6B17C0	2	12/6/2004 1:31:22 PM	957487	5	SERVICE GRATUITY	ALTERNATE DIN STAFF	2	0	2
21	FS20041206004	9575	6B17C0	1	12/6/2004 11:13:58 PM	307568	1	INTERNET CAFE 315	WIRELESS BLK MINS#3	25	0	25
22	FS20041206004	9575	6B17C0	2	12/7/2004 5:00:57 PM	960372	1	ROOM SERVICE	MILK	0	0	0
23	FS20041206004	9575	6B17C0	1	12/7/2004 5:49:59 PM	452693	1	ROOM SERVICE 340	DECAF COFFEE	0	0	0
24	FS20041206004	9575	6B17C0	1	12/7/2004 5:49:59 PM	452693	2	ROOM SERVICE 340	SWEET & LOW	0	0	0
25	FS20041206004	9575	6B17C0	1	12/7/2004 5:49:59 PM	452693	3	ROOM SERVICE 340	SUGAR	0	0	0
26	FS20041206004	9575	6B17C0	1	12/8/2004 6:07:57 AM	454061	1	ROOM SERVICE 340	HOT TEA	0	0	0
27	FS20041206004	9575	6B17C0	1	12/8/2004 6:07:57 AM	454061	2	ROOM SERVICE 340	COFFEE	0	0	0
28	FS20041206004	9575	6B17C0	1	12/8/2004 6:07:57 AM	454061	3	ROOM SERVICE 340	CREAM	0	0	0
29	FS20041206004	9575	6B17C0	1	12/8/2004 6:07:57 AM	454061	4	ROOM SERVICE 340	SUGAR	0	0	0
30	FS20041206004	9575	6B17C0	1	12/8/2004 6:07:57 AM	454061	5	ROOM SERVICE 340	SWEET & LOW	0	0	0
31	FS20041206004	9575	6B17C0	1	12/8/2004 6:07:57 AM	454061	6	ROOM SERVICE 340	MILK-SKIMMED	0	0	0
32	FS20041206004	9575	6B17C0	1	12/8/2004 8:15:19 PM	454452	1	ROOM SERVICE 340	DECAF COFFEE	0	0	0
33	FS20041206004	9575	6B17C0	1	12/8/2004 8:15:19 PM	454452	2	ROOM SERVICE 340	CREAM	0	0	0
34	FS20041206004	9575	6B17C0	1	12/8/2004 8:15:19 PM	454452	3	ROOM SERVICE 340	SUGAR	0	0	0
35	FS20041206004	9575	6B17C0	1	12/8/2004 8:15:19 PM	454452	4	ROOM SERVICE 340	HOT TEA	0	0	0
36	FS20041206004	9575	6B17C0	1	12/8/2004 8:15:19 PM	454452	5	ROOM SERVICE 340	APPLE	0	0	0
37	FS20041206004	9577	6B17C0	2	12/8/2004 10:15:19 PM	450968	1	VIDEO ARCADE 710	VIDEO ARCADE	5	0	5
38	FS20041206004	9577	6B17C0	2	12/8/2004 10:25:19 PM	451288	1	VIDEO ARCADE 710	VIDEO ARCADE	5	0	5
39	FS20041206004	9577	6B17C0	2	12/8/2004 10:49:19 PM	452333	1	VIDEO ARCADE 710	VIDEO ARCADE	5	0	5
40	FS20041206004	9575	6B17C0	1	12/9/2004 5:56:42 PM	445474	1	SHORE TOURS 500	REEF & WRECK SNORKEL	156	0	156
41	FS20041206004	9575	6B17C0	1	12/9/2004 5:58:27 PM	445477	1	SHORE TOURS 500	MAYAN RUINS A	158	0	158
42	FS20041206004	9575	6B17C0	1	12/9/2004 6:01:53 PM	445480	1	SHORE TOURS 500	JUNGLE RIVER TUBING	300	0	300
43	FS20041206004	9577	6B17C0	2	12/9/2004 11:30:07 PM	462129	1	ART AUCTION 380	ART SALES	18041.6	0	18041.6
44	FS20041206004	9577	6B17C0	2	12/9/2004 11:30:07 PM	462129	2	ART AUCTION 380	SHIPPING & HANDLING	545.42	0	545.42
45	FS20041206004	9577	6B17C0	2	12/9/2004 11:30:07 PM	462129	3	ART AUCTION 380	APPRAISALS	50	0	50
46	FS20041206004	9577	1B29D2	1	12/11/2004 9:27:55 AM	962165	1	GIFT SHOP 600	SHIP MODEL ORN	8	0	8
47	FS20041206004	9577	1B29D2	1	12/11/2004 9:27:55 AM	962165	2	GIFT SHOP 600	POLY 3D MAGNET	5	0	5
48	FS20041206004	9577	1B29D2	1	12/11/2004 9:27:55 AM	962165	3	GIFT SHOP 600	CCL DOLPHIN LO	14.5	0	14.5
49	FS20041206004	9577	1B29D2	1	12/11/2004 9:27:55 AM	962165	4	GIFT SHOP 600	CCL VERTICAL K	14.5	0	14.5
50	FS20041206004	9575	6B17C0	1	12/11/2004 1:16:26 PM	962892	1	SERVICE GRATUITY	CABIN STEWARD	20	0	20
51	FS20041206004	9575	6B17C0	1	12/11/2004 1:16:26 PM	962892	2	SERVICE GRATUITY	DIN ROOM SERV TEAM	40	0	40
52	FS20041206004	9575	6B17C0	1	12/11/2004 1:16:26 PM	962892	3	SERVICE GRATUITY	DIN ROOM MGMT	10	0	10
53	FS20041206004	9575	6B17C0	1	12/11/2004 1:16:26 PM	962892	4	SERVICE GRATUITY	ALTERNATE DIN STAFF	30	0	30

Exhibit 9 (*continued*)

When one of the fulfillment houses filed for bankruptcy in 2001, Carnival purchased its own customer lists and vowed to never lose control of its customer database again. With the size of the database at 20m individual records—representing about 10m households—cleansing the data required more than a year of work. Several executives at Carnival felt data could be a strategic resource in the future. Yet, the company currently only devoted a fraction of a full-time equivalent (FTE) employee to customer data analysis, though several data analytic projects were currently in the works. Myles Cyr explained:

When data is not available a company conditions itself to work around the uncertainty and without the data. As soon as the data becomes available light bulbs start to go off and all of a sudden you have this pent-up demand for this information.

Brenda Yester offered more insight:

If you go back to how this business started and where we are today, the concept of data warehousing is still new. But people are learning more about what we can do with data and sharing data, and it's part of the evolution in terms of where we're going. Our biggest challenge is prioritizing. Approval for the revenue analytics project took me three passes with the IS Steering Committee. They kept saying, "What are you going to do with this data, Brenda?" The truth is, I don't know yet, but I do know that there's a wealth of information there and we need to take this leap of faith.

THE POTENTIAL VALUE OF CUSTOMER DATA

Carnival's management team had differing views about the use of customer data for creating, evaluating, and managing relationships with guests, let alone what the nature of these relationships should be. Bob Dickinson offered this caveat:

If we did a cruise itinerary designed for Polynesian frog worshippers, and there weren't enough Polynesian frog worshippers to fill that ship, and if in the process of marketing to try and get Polynesian frog worshippers, people said, wait a minute, Carnival's the line for Polynesian frog worshippers, I don't want to be on board with Polynesian frog worshippers, then you wind up with some disconnects. You don't mind having a few Polynesian frog worshippers on every ship, but you don't want to have a ship exclusively for one group—this sends mixed messages.

Carnival was just beginning to experiment with loyalty programs. Its first foray was offered as part of the Carnival Vacation Club. This program, sold on selected ships, enabled guests to purchase cruise points redeemable for cruises or timeshare products over the following five years. Terry Thornton explained:

The value of this program for us is that it locks in future purchases. Once you bought into the Carnival Vacation Club you are not going to cruise with a competitor. Moreover, because the ticket was purchased with points—it's funny money—we see these customers spending much more onboard the ship during their cruises.

A second initiative being pilot tested was a recognition card. Cruisers who sailed with Carnival at least once before would receive a gold Sail & Sign card, instead of the standard red, white, and blue one. The gold card provided a cue to the crew to offer differentiated service, not in its quality, but in its kind. For example, a bartender who saw a gold card would welcome the guest back to the Carnival family and ask what ships or itineraries the guest had sailed before. Thought was being given to a platinum card for high repeat guests. However, the underlying question about loyalty was whether the return from

rewarding it would be worth the investment. Brenda Yester explained:

If you're a repeat customer with other cruise lines, maybe they'll give you all kinds of goodies or a discount every day of the week. At Carnival, we have past guests that we talk to often about the product, past-guest rates, and special "reunion cruises." But we couldn't justify spending a lot of money on a past-guest program because we couldn't see the upside for Carnival or for our guests.

Marketing intelligence collected by Carnival suggested that other cruise lines saw little return on loyalty spending. Diana Rodriguez-Velazquez, Director of Internet and Database Marketing, offered this example:

When I worked at a competitor, we designed a textbook CRM program. But when we went to the ship, they said, "You must be crazy! You want me to put a mint on this passenger's pillow, but because the guest four cabins down has cruised five times, I need to put a mint AND a pen?" Operationally it can be excessive with no tangible ROI.

Carnival had no concerted program for attracting repeat guests. The company mailed out a magazine a few times a year and used direct marketing when there was a need. For example, if demand for Alaska cruises was soft, Carnival PVPs might e-mail or call past guests living in western North America. However, such efforts were not targeted based on past guests' preferences, seasonal travel patterns, or onboard purchase behavior, and Carnival did not segment customers based on profitability. The objective of repeat-guest marketing was to fill ships today. Vicki Freed offered additional justification for Carnival's broad-based approach to market targeting and customer-relationship management.

We're still in a growth stage of our business. Although some customers spend very little while on board, we treat and value those customers in the same way that we value a guest who has a higher onboard spend. After all, they bought the cruise; they bought it at a price that we set, good—bad, high—low. Plus, there's positive word-of-mouth promotion even in less profitable customers.

However, there was growing recognition at Carnival of the value of business intelligence about customers. Freed recounted a recent incident:

I just dealt with somebody who had sailed with us three times, and the third time was not a good experience. I

continued

was able to access his information: He was in a suite. He brought 24 people with him. He had a very high onboard spend in many areas on the ship. I wanted to win this guy back! He had some valid complaints, so I decided to give him a discount on a future cruise to win him back.

When a complaint occurred onboard, any effort by shipboard crew to resolve the issue and to compensate the guest was logged in to the consumer response system (CRS). It was only recently, though, that the shoreside guest relations department was able to access the CRS, thus enabling Carnival to track service recovery efforts, as well as those guests with a propensity to "dial for dollars" by complaining about problems onboard and then when they got home.

THE FUTURE

Sailing into the future, the horizon looked bright for Carnival Cruise Lines. Advance booking trends were strong and

ahead of prior-year levels. The company was set to take delivery of the *Carnival Liberty*—the 21st ship in the fleet, and the first Carnival ship to sail a European itinerary. The company kicked off 2005 with a slate of television commercials featuring the classic Bobby Darin song, "Somewhere Beyond the Sea," and intended to continue the repositioning of the brand as a more sophisticated, but still fun, vacation experience.

Yet, Carnival's management team wrestled with how to leverage the brand's market leadership into an even stronger competitive position with higher margins. Carnival ships almost always sailed full, and guests were very satisfied. Executives wondered, how could "The Most Popular Cruise Line in the World" attract even more loyal customers? Did repeat-purchase rates simply reflect the nature of cruise customers in general—or specifically the nature of Carnival's customers? Perhaps overarching this issue was the question of how Carnival could leverage its substantial access to customer data to better understand, serve, and profit from cruise guests.

Carnival Corporation	Ships	Double Occupancy	Market Share (%)	Market Positioning
Carnival Cruise Lines	20	44,934	23.2	Contemporary
Princess	14	28,050	14.5	Premium
Holland America Line	12	16,937	8.8	Premium
Costa Cruises (U.S. market)	2	4,224	2.2	Contemporary
Cunard Line (U.S.)	2	4,411	2.3	Luxury
Windstar Cruises	3	604	0.3	Destination
Yachts of Seabourn	3	624	0.3	Luxury
Total:	56	99,784	51.6	
Royal Caribbean International				
Royal Caribbean International	19	45,570	23.5	Contemporary
Celebrity Cruises	10	16,116	8.3	Premium
Total:	29	61,686	31.9	
Star Cruises				
Norwegian Cruise Line	10	17,890	9.2	Contemporary
Orient Lines	1	845	0.4	Destination
Total:	11	18,735	9.7	

Exhibit 3   North American Cruise Capacity and Market Positioning by Brand as of Year-End 2004.

(*Source:* Cruise Lines International Association "Five Year Cruise Industry Capacity Outlook" report, March 2005.)

Other CLIA-Affiliated brands				
Crystal Cruises	3	2,960	1.5	Luxury
Disney Cruise Line	2	1,754	0.9	Contemporary
Carnival Corporation	Ships	Double Occupancy	Market Share (%)	Market Positioning
MSC Cruises	2	3,180	1.6	Contemporary
Oceania Cruises	2	1,368	0.7	Premium
Radisson Seven Seas Cruises	6	2,764	1.4	Luxury
Silversea Cruises	4	1,356	0.7	Luxury
Total	19	13,382	6.9	
Grand Total	115	193,587		

Exhibit 3 *continued*

Carnival Consolidated Balance Sheets (2003–2004)

(in millions, except par/stated values)	November 30, 2004	November 30, 2003
Assets		
Current Assets		
Cash & Equivalents	$ 643	$ 610
Short-term investments	17	461
Accounts Receivable, net	409	403
Inventories	240	171
Prepaid expenses and other	266	212
Fair Value of derivative contracts	153	275
Total current assets	**1,728**	**2,132**
Property and Equipment, Net	20,823	17,522
Goodwill	3,321	3,031
Trademarks	1,306	1,324
Other Assets	458	482
	$27,636	**$24,491**
Liabilities and Shareholders' Equity		
Current Liabilities		
Short-term borrowings	$ 381	$ 94
Current Portion of long-term debt	681	392
Convertible debt subject to current put options	600	
Accounts Payable	631	634
Accrued liabilities and other	721	568
Customer deposits	1,873	1,358
Fair value of hedged firm commitments	147	264
Total current liabilities	**5,034**	**3,310**
Long-Term Debt	**6,291**	**6,918**
Other Long-Term Liabilities and Deferred Income	**551**	**470**

Exhibit 4 Financials Statements. (*Source:* Carnival Corporation & PLC 2004 Annual Report.)

continued

Shareholders' Equity

Common stock of Carnival Corporation; $.01 par value; 1,960 shares authorized; 634 shares at 2004 and 630 shares at 2003 issued and outstanding	6	6
Ordinary shares of Carnival plc; $1.66 stated value; 226 shares authorized; 212 shares at 2004 and 210 shares at 2003 issued	353	349
Additional paid-in capital	7,311	7,163
Retained earnings	8,623	7,191
Unearned stock compensation	−16	−18
Accumulated other comprehensive income	541	160
Treasury stock; 42 shares of Carnival plc at cost	−1,058	−1,058
Total shareholder' equity	**15,760**	**13,793**
	$27,636	**$24,491**

Income Statement Summary

	FY End 11/04	FY End 11/03	FY End 11/02	FY End 11/01	FY End 11/00
Revenue	$9,727	$6,718	$4,383	$4,549	$3,779
Cost of Sales	$4,244	$2,880	$1,764	$1,888	$2,058
Gross Profit	$5,483	$3,838	$2,619	$2,661	$1,720
Operating Expenses					
Selling, General & Administrative	$2,498	$1,870	$1,195	$1,397	$450
Operating Profit Before Depreciation & Amortization	$2,985	$1,968	$1,424	$1,264	$1,271
Depreciation & Amortization	$812	$585	$382	$372	$288
Operating Income after D & A	$2,173	$1,383	$1,042	$892	$983
Other Income (net)	($5)	$8	($4)	$109	$8
Interest Expense	($267)	($168)	($79)	($87)	($25)
Pre-Tax Income (EBT)	$1,901	$1,223	$959	$914	$967
Net Income from Continuing Operations	$1,854	$1,194	$1,016	$926	$965
Net Income from Total Operations	$1,854	$1,194	$1,016	$926	$965
Normalized Income	$1,854	$1,194	$1,036	$1,066	$965
Total Net Income	$1,854	$1,194	$1,016	$926	$965
Net Income available for Common Shareholders	$1,854	$1,194	$1,016	$926	$965
Earnings per Share (in Dollars)					
Basic EPS from Continuing Operations	$2.31	$1.66	$1.73	$1.58	$1.61
Basic EPS from Total Operations	$2.31	$1.66	$1.73	$1.58	$1.61
Basic EPS from Total Net Income	$2.31	$1.66	$1.73	$1.58	$1.61
Basic Normalized Net Income/Share	$2.31	$1.66	$1.76	$1.82	$1.61
Diluted EPS from Continuing Operations	$2.18	$1.65	$1.73	$1.58	$1.60
Diluted EPS from Total Operations	$2.24	$1.66	$1.73	$1.58	$1.60
Diluted EPS from Total Net Income	$2.24	$1.66	$1.73	$1.58	$1.60

Exhibit 4   *continued*

Note: FY = fiscal year.

Source: http://www.carnivalcorp.com/Sections/FinancialStats/FinancialStats.aspx

| Diluted Normalized Net Income/Share | $2.24 | $1.66 | $1.76 | $1.82 | $1.60 |
| Dividends Paid/Share | $0.53 | $0.44 | $0.42 | $0.42 | $0.42 |

Consolidated Statements of Cash Flow

| | Years Ended November 30, | | |
(*in millions*)	**2004**	2003	2002
Operating Activities			
Net Income	**$ 1,854**	$ 1,194	$ 1,016
Adjustments to reconcile net income to net cash provided by operating activities			
Depreciation and amortization	**812**	585	382
Impairment charge			20
Accretion of original issue discount	**21**	20	19
Other	**16**	8	14
Changes in operating assets and liabilities, excluding business acquired; Decrease (increase) in			
Receivables	**11**	−91	−5
Inventories	**−73**	−17	2
Prepaid expenses and other	**−54**	82	−81
(Decrease) increase in			
Accounts payable	**−28**	43	−12
Accrued and other liabilities	**178**	−16	−28
Customer deposits	**479**	125	142
Net cash provided by operating activities	**3,216**	1,933	1,469
Investing Activities			
Additions to property and equipment	**−3,586**	−2,516	−1,986
Sales of short-term investments	**1,216**	3,745	4,598
Purchases of short-terms investments	**−772**	−3,803	−4,637
Cash acquired from (expended for) the acquisition of P&O Princess, net		140	−30
Proceeds from retirement of property and equipment	**77**	51	4
Other, net	**−24**	−50	−10
Net cash used in investing activities	**−3,089**	−2,433	−2,061
Financing Activities			
Proceeds from issuance of long-term debt	**843**	2,123	232
Principal repayments of long-term debt	**−932**	−1,137	−190
Dividends paid	**−400**	−292	−246
Proceeds from short-term borrowings, net	**272**	94	
Proceeds from exercise of stock options	**142**	53	7
Other	**−4**	−15	−1
Net cash (used in) provided by financing activities	**−79**	826	−198
Effect of exchange rate changes on cash and equivalents	**−15**	−23	−5

Exhibit 4   *continued*

continued

	33	303	−795
Net increase (decrease) in cash and equivalents	**33**	303	−795
Cash and equivalents at beginning of year	**610**	307	1,102
Cash and equivalents at end of year	**643**	610	307

Consolidated Statement of Operations

		Years Ended November 30,	
(in millions, except per share data)	**2004**	2003	2002
Revenues			
Cruise			
Passenger tickets	**$7,357**	5,039	3,346
Onboard and other	**2,070**	1,420	898
Other	**300**	259	139
	9,727	6,718	4,383
Costs and Expenses			
Operating			
Cruise			
Passenger tickets	**1,572**	1,021	658
Onboard and other	**359**	229	116
Payroll and related	**1,003**	744	458
Food	**550**	393	256
Other ship operating	**1,763**	1,237	734
Other	**210**	190	108
Total	**5,457**	3,814	2,330
Selling and administrative	**1,285**	936	609
Depreciation and amortization	**812**	585	382
Impairment charge			20
	7,554	5,335	3,341
Operating Income	**2,173**	1,383	1,042
Nonoperating (Expense) Income			
Interest Income	**17**	27	32
Interest expense, net of capitalized interest	**−284**	−195	−111
Other income (expense), net	**−5**	8	−4
	−272	−160	−83
Income Before Income Taxes	**1,901**	1,223	959
Income Tax (Expense) Benefit, Net	**−47**	−29	57
Net Income	**1,854**	1,194	1,106
Earnings Per Share			
Basic	**$2.31**	$1.66	$1.73
Diluted	**$2.24**	$1.63	$1.69
Dividends Per Share	**$0.53**	$0.44	$0.42

Exhibit 4   *continued*

Exhibit 5 Partial Organizational Chart. (*Source:* Carnival Cruise Lines.)

continued

CASE STUDY (*continued*)

Bob Dickinson, President and Chief Executive Officer

Bob Dickinson joined Carnival Cruise Lines in 1972 and has handled all sales and marketing activities for more than 30 years. In May 1993, Dickinson was promoted to president and in 2003 to CEO. In that position he oversees all operations of Carnival Cruise Lines. He also serves on the board of directors of parent company Carnival Corporation. Prior to joining Carnival he held positions on the finance staff of Ford Motor Company and in the corporate planning office of RCA. Among his honors and awards, Dickinson was named "Travel Executive of the Year" and "Travel Person of the Year" by *Travel Trade* Readers (the only travel industry executive to win both honors the same year), and one of the 100 Best Marketers in the Nation by *Advertising Age Magazine.* He is a former vice-chair of the United States National Tourism Organization and a former chairman of Cruise Lines International Association (CLIA) and of Travel Industry Association (ITA). Dickinson coauthored *Selling the Sea: An Inside Look at the Cruise Industry* (1997) and *The Complete 21st Century Travel & Hospitality Marketing Handbook* (2004) with Andy Vladimir. He holds a BSBA in management from John Carroll University and an MBA from Duquesne University. He was awarded an Honorary Doctor of Business Administration Degree from Johnson & Wales University in 1995.

Vicki Freed, Senior Vice President of Sales and Marketing

Vicki Freed joined Carnival Cruise Lines in 1978 and was appointed to her current position, senior vice president of sales and marketing, in 1993. In this capacity, she has overall responsibility for all sales and marketing objectives for Carnival. Freed has earned numerous awards and accolades for her outstanding achievements in sales and marketing, including Travel Trade magazine's "2004 Executive of the Year"—the first woman to receive the honor. Freed was also the first female chairman of Cruise Line International Association (CLIA), the marketing and travel-agent training arm of the North American cruise industry. Florida Governor Jeb Bush appointed Freed to serve on the Florida Commission on Tourism, a private/public partnership that is responsible for promoting Florida tourism. Freed earned a bachelor's degree in business with an emphasis in marketing from the University of Colorado and holds a Certified Travel Counselor (CTC) designation.

Brendan Corrigan, Senior Vice President of Cruise Operations

Brendan Corrigan joined Carnival Cruise Lines 1978. He worked aboard several ships as a sanitation officer until 1982, when he became shoreside ship supervisor of the *Festivale.* He has since served as operations manager and director of operations. In 1992, Corrigan was promoted to vice president of operations. In May 2000 he was promoted to his current position as senior vice president of cruise operations. Prior to Carnival, he was a marine and fumigation surveyor for the British company, Rentokil Limited. Corrigan received his Bachelor of Science degree from Glasgow University.

Myles Cyr, Chief Information Officer and Vice President of Information Technology

Myles Cyr joined Carnival Corporation in 1998 as vice president of technology planning and was promoted to chief information officer of Carnival Cruise Lines in 1999. Prior to Carnival, he served as a manager with KPMG Consulting from 1994 to 1998, where he specialized in technology benchmarking, assessment, and operation improvement initiatives for both national and international corporations. From 1990 to 1994, Cyr worked as an account manager with the IBM Global Network in Tampa, where he assisted customers with planning, managing, and implementing EDI projects. Cyr received his bachelor's degree in computer engineering from the University of Florida.

Terry Thornton, Vice President of Marketing Planning

Terry Thornton's background in the cruise industry spans more than 20 years, beginning with financial and marketing positions at Norwegian Cruise Line from 1977 to 1982. He then moved on to five years at Sea Goddess, where, as co-founder and chief operating officer, Thornton played an

Exhibit 5 (*continued*) Biographies of Personnel Quoted in the Case

continued

integral role in launching that operation. He then served as vice president of finance for Windstar Cruises for two years until joining Carnival Cruise Lines in 1989 as manager of special projects. Thornton was promoted to vice president of marketing planning in 1992 and is responsible for Carnival's marketing and revenue planning functions.

Christine Arnholt, Vice President of Marketing Services

Chris Arnholt joined Carnival Cruise Lines in 1991 as the company's first advertising manager. In 1994, she was named director of partnership marketing and was promoted to director of marketing services a year later. In 2000, Arnholt was named vice president of marketing services. In this capacity, she is responsible for all aspects of Carnival's marketing communications, including advertising and promotions, as well as partnership marketing (travel agency co-op program and compensation/commissions). She also oversees Carnival's in-house desktop publishing/creative department and develops marketing strategies for the company's Web site. Prior to Carnival, Arnholt spent five years at McFarland & Drier, a Miami-based advertising firm which included Carnival among its clients. She serves on the marketing committee for Cruise Line International Association (CLIA) and was recently named one of *Travel Agent Magazine*'s "Rising Stars." Arnholt holds a bachelor's degree in communications from Florida State University.

Brenda Yester, Vice President Revenue Management

Brenda Yester joined Carnival Cruise Lines in 1999 and was promoted to VP revenue management two years later. Prior to joining Carnival, Yester spent three years at Royal Caribbean Cruise Lines (RCCL), most recently as the director of revenue management. Presently, she oversees all of Carnival's revenue management functions, including pricing, inventory management as well as both ongoing development of Carnival's revenue management system and improvement of revenue performance. She is a certified public accountant and has been recognized as one of *Travel Agent Magazine*'s "Rising Stars." Yester graduated from the University of Miami with a bachelor's in business administration and received her master's in business administration from Nova University.

Dwayne Warner, Vice President of Strategic Automation

Dwayne Warner joined Carnival Cruise Lines in May 1986 as part of the Applications Development group within the Information Systems Department. During his career he has held various management positions within the Information Systems department. In January 2001, he was promoted to the newly created position of Vice President of Strategic Automation. He leads a team of business analysts and application architects responsible for ensuring alignment of project efforts to Carnival's business and information technology strategies. In addition, Warner participates on the Carnival Information Systems Steering Committee, which is responsible for reviewing, approving and prioritizing Carnival's IT initiatives.

Diana Rodriguez-Velasquez, Director of Internet/Database Marketing

Rodriquez-Velasquez joined Carnival Cruise Lines in 2000 as manager of direct response and was named to her current position in 2001. She is responsible for managing the content of Carnival's web sites for consumers and travel agents as well as overseeing the company's past-guest loyalty and marketing programs, including a multimillion-name database. Prior to joining Carnival, she held a number of positions within the integrated marketing/technology arena. One of these positions was as the direct marketing account executive at Royal Caribbean Cruise Lines (RCCL), where she helped develop and manage the cruise line's loyalty and direct mail programs. She was also a direct response account executive for Hann & DePalmer, a fulfillment house that included Carnival among its clients. She is a graduate of Loyola University–New Orleans.

Shannon Balliet Antorcha, Manager of Revenue Enhancement

Shannon Balliet Antorcha has been in the field of yield management in the cruise industry for nine years. She began her career with Royal Caribbean International, joined Carnival Cruise Lines in

Exhibit 5 *continued*

continued

2000, and soon thereafter assumed the newly created position of manager of revenue enhancement. In this role, Shannon oversees projects related to operations analysis, policy and process improvement, e-commerce, and data warehousing, all with the goal of enhancing revenue performance. Shannon has a bachelor's degree in accounting from Florida International University and an MBA from Nova Southeastern University.

Exhibit 5 *continued*

13

Security, Privacy, and Ethics

What You Will Learn in This Chapter

This chapter discusses some important topics of managerial interest that are often delegated to IT specialists: security and IT risk management, privacy, and information systems ethics. The first objective of this chapter is to convince you that, as future general and functional managers, you will have to be involved in these decisions. The second objective is to help you gain an understanding of the circumstances in which choices and trade-offs are made so that you can actively participate in decision making. Specifically, in this chapter you will

1. Learn to make the case that information systems security, privacy, and ethics are issues of interest to general and functional managers, and why it is a grave mistake to delegate them exclusively to IT professionals.

2. Understand the basic IT risk management processes, including risk assessment, risk analysis, and risk mitigation.

3. Understand the principal security threats, both internal and external, and the principal safeguards that have been developed to mitigate these risks.

4. Be able to identify the nature of privacy concerns that modern organizations face and be able to articulate how general and functional managers can safeguard the privacy of their customers and employees.

5. Define ethics, apply the concept of ethical behavior to information systems decisions, and be able to articulate how general and functional managers can help ensure that their organization behaves ethically.

MINI-CASE: REINVENTRAVEL.COM COMES UNDER FIRE

As you watch the sun setting over the San Francisco skyline from your hotel room window, you can't avoid feeling that you really dropped the ball this time. You can still hear Clive Sturling, your CIO, as he tells you, "Don't worry about security, this is techie stuff, I'll take care of it. Just grow the business, that's what you are good at." You had not asked about security again after that conversation, perfectly happy to leave the "techie stuff" to him, and that was before you launched the company over two years ago!

Well, it was him on the phone a minute ago, ruining what had been a perfectly good day. In a daze you replay the conversation in your mind: "We have been attacked," Clive had said. "It was a distributed denial of service attacks, not much we could do with our current security infrastructure. The site was unavailable for about 70 minutes it was not defaced or otherwise ruined, just down. I don't think many people noticed. The attack ended about an hour ago, I did not want to call you before checking if they had compromised any files. It doesn't look like it."

Not much we could do? Isn't he the one who said not to worry about security? The site was down for "only 70 minutes." Does he know that in that amount of time ReinvenTravel.com typically processed 19,000 transactions? Granted, evenings were a bit slower, but there must have been at least 4500 customers who noted the outage. Your emotions kept mixing at a dizzying pace. You were angry at Clive; you trusted him and he let you down. However, you felt sympathetic to his position as well. You had been the one who told him to "run IT on a shoestring," to help you speed the path to profitability as much as possible.

Oddly enough, as you begin to recover from the shock of the news, your college days flash in your mind, bringing a smile to your face. You had started in this field only three and a half years before when you learned about the opportunity to revolutionize how people seek and purchase travel products. That day in your Information Systems class seemed like decades ago; now you were the CEO of a growing company with 52 employees, over 70,000 active customers and members, and revenues approaching $8 million. Clive had built the search engine in just eight months, alone! He was a wizard with that kind of stuff. Half the time you had no idea what he was doing . . . but that user interface, you certainly appreciated and understood that part of his work; everyone did! So far superior to anything that had been seen before . . . it

was that fabulous demo that got you your first round of venture capital financing.

Financing . . . that word snapped you back to reality! You had to get ready for dinner. The meeting with your VC was in less than an hour, and you had yet to take a shower. With first round of financing beginning to run out and minimal profits, a second round was a must. You had hoped to spend the evening discussing your plan for growing the customer base and beginning to monetize your membership, seeking their guidance and help with regard to the three potential partners you were evaluating. "Well, that ain't going to happen," you mumbled.

What should you do? Should you tell your VC about the denial-of-service attack? It may not be your choice; these guys liked to do their homework, and the odds were good that they were poking around the site when the outage happened. No time to call your legal counsel; you had to go it alone on this one.

Clive had been very unclear about whether an intrusion had occurred along with the denial-of-service attack. At this point you had little faith with regard to his staff's ability to find out; it seems that security and monitoring had not been ranking very high on their priority list! ReinvenTravel.com stored quite a bit of personal information about customers, including identifying information and credit card data. Should you communicate to the customers that an attack had occurred? Should you issue a press release? There was no evidence that security had been compromised and even less that personal data had been stolen. A denial-of-service attack only made a Web site unavailable for some time . . . did it not? "No way, Clive and his staff would know if data had been stolen," you told yourself.

This was increasingly looking like a situation you were ill prepared to address. But, as your father always said, "You wanted the bicycle? Now you have to pedal." As you began to feel the adrenaline pumping again, you exclaimed, "Here we go!" and jumped up from your chair. You had 55 minutes to develop your plan before dinner.

DISCUSSION QUESTIONS

1. Do you agree with the assessment that you had dropped the ball? Or are you being unduly harsh on yourself?
2. Who do you think should be making security calls at ReinvenTravel.com? Shouldn't this be the CIO's job?

3. What should you do tonight? Should you approach the topic at dinner or wait and see if anyone else raises the issue?

4. What should you do in the next few days? Should you issue a press release? Should you contact your customers directly? Should you focus on overhauling your security safeguards to prevent future similar problems and forget today's incident?

INTRODUCTION

This chapter focuses on three topics: information systems security and IT risk management, privacy, and information systems ethics. These topics, while distinct, are connected by a common thread. Information systems security, privacy, and ethical concerns were born along with the introduction of computer systems and information technology in organizations. However, the recent widespread adoption of the Internet and the proliferation of information for business use have dramatically amplified these threats. The computer security industry, for example, is estimated to be already in the billion-dollar range, and a recent ComputerWorld survey found that almost half of the organizations studied spend more than 5 percent of their IT budget on security.[1] This level of spending notwithstanding, the 2006 *InfoWorld* Security Report found that over 50 percent of individuals in charge of their organization's security are at best "somewhat confident" in their enterprise's security systems.[2] Yet a recent Cutter Consortium survey found that ensuring privacy was a key prerequisite to gaining customer trust and building loyalty (Figure 13.1).[3]

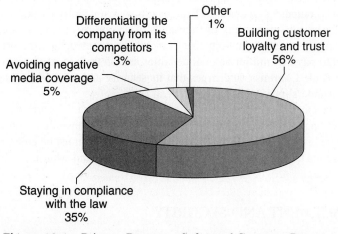

Figure 13.1   Primary Reason to Safeguard Customer Data. (*Source:* This figure was orginially published by Cutter Consortium, www.cutter.com © 2005 Cutter Consortium. All rights reserued. Reproduced with permission.)

---

[1] Brandel, M. (2006), "Avoid Security Spending Fatigue," *ComputerWorld* (April 17). Accessed 6/7/07:
http://www.computerworld.com/securitytopics/security/story/0,10801,110504,00.html

[2] Goodin, D. (2006), "Crisis in Confidence," *InfoWorld* (October 30). Accessed 6/7/07:
http://www.infoworld.com/article/06/10/30/44fesecsurvey_1.html

[3] Piccoli, G. (2006), "Doing Privacy Right: Using Data and Preserving Trust," *Cutter Benchmark Review* (6:1), pp. 3–5.

A failure in security, privacy, or ethics can have dramatic repercussions on the organization both because of its potentially damaging direct effects (e.g., computer outages, disruptions to operations) and its increasingly negative indirect effects (e.g., legal recourse, image damage). Consider the following three recent examples:

HostGator, a Web-hosting service firm that provides the tools for individuals and organizations to create and maintain a Web site, found itself under siege on a Friday afternoon. Customers began to (angrily) report that visitors to their legitimate Web presence would be automatically redirected to malicious sites that delivered viruses to the hapless visitor. It took HostGator over twelve hours to clean up the mess.

RealNetworks, the maker of streaming audio and video products, faced significant backlash in the late 1990s when it was perceived as violating its customers' privacy. The company's new streaming audio/video player Real Jukebox was shipped with a feature that allowed it to capture information about what CDs the user was listening to, and send such data to RealNetworks servers over the Internet. RealNetworks contended that it was simply trying to provide its customers with a more personalized experience, and the feature could be disabled relatively easily. However, it faced significant backlash motivated by the perception that RealNetworks had attempted to collect the data surreptitiously, without the customer's express authorization. In other words, the company gave its customers reason to doubt its trustworthiness.

ChoicePoint is a data collection company that accumulates public record information on all U.S. residents to resell it to organizations that use the data for research and marketing purposes, and to the government. In February 2005 ChoicePoint sold personal information on about 163,000 individuals in its databases to identity thieves posing as legitimate small businesses. While not a classic example of information systems security breach (the company's computer systems and IT safeguards were not violated), the incident was certainly a security breach—the safety of thousands of private records was indeed compromised! Aside from the negative publicity that ChoicePoint attracted, the firm lost a lawsuit and was required to pay $10 million in civil penalties and $5 million in consumer redress to settle Federal Trade Commission charges that its security and record-handling procedures violated consumers' privacy rights and federal laws.

As we mentioned in Chapter 6, security, privacy, and ethics are areas where, as general and functional managers, you cannot abdicate your responsibility. Yet in order to actively participate in decision making on these three fronts, you must be able to understand under what circumstances choices and trade-offs are made and what the principal threats and responses are.

IT RISK MANAGEMENT AND SECURITY

Information systems security refers to the set of defenses an organization puts in place to mitigate threats to its technology infrastructure and data resources. IT risk management is the process by which the firm attempts to identify and measure information systems security risks, and to devise the optimal mitigation strategy.

Security is an area that has increased in importance along with the widespread adoption of information technologies and even more so with the development and growth of networks. More recently security and IT risk management have come to the forefront of managerial attention because of the increasing threat of cyber-terrorism. For instance, a recent survey by Pew Internet & American Life and Elon University shows that two-thirds of the experts they polled believe the United States will suffer "at least one devastating attack to its national information network or power grid" in the immediate future.[4] As computer systems are increasingly underpinning the infrastructure of developed economies, they become legitimate targets of terrorism threats.

Why Is Security *Not* an IT Problem?

The pervasiveness and possible cost of the security threat should suffice to convince general and functional managers that security is a matter of strategic interest, not something that "the IT people should worry about." Speaking to the prevalence of such threats, a recent *InfoWorld* survey found that the 430 firms polled staved off a collective average of 331 network attacks in the previous 12 months.[5]

However, security should be on managers' radar screen also because of its peculiar characteristics that run the risk of leaving it underfunded, unless general and functional managers get directly involved in the threat assessment and mitigation process.

The game of chess offers a great metaphor for the information security management and IT risk management processes. In the game of chess the objective of the players, some more skilled than others, is to circumvent the defenses of the opponents in order to checkmate him. Security is a constantly evolving game of chess, one where current defenses, and their limitations, are the basis for future attacks. A difficult game indeed. But what do you get if you win the security chess game? Nothing. In fact, the best security is the one that leads to nothing happening. As in the opening mini-case, all the "excitement" occurs when your security has been breached.

More specifically, security is a negative deliverable. In other words, all the money spent on managing IT risk and securing the firm's IT infrastructure and the data repositories produces no revenue and creates no efficiencies. It has no ROI. Instead it limits the possibility that a future negative fallout will happen. As a consequence, it is difficult to secure funding for security efforts, a tendency nicely captured by Gene Spafford, a professor of computer science and security expert: "People in general are not interested in paying extra for increased safety. At the beginning seat belts cost $200 and nobody bought them."

Moreover, it is difficult to take credit for doing a great job when all you have to show for your efforts is that nothing bad happened. This is particularly true when "lucky" firms around you also have not suffered an attack (or have yet to notice that one has taken place!) and skeptics in your organization can point to them as "proof" that you are overinvesting in security.

Consider the hurricanes that hit the coast of Louisiana and Mississippi in the summer of 2005 (Figure 13.2). One of the reasons for the devastation of the city of New Orleans was the underfunding of the levy system protecting the city. However, seeking funding for such a protective system is about asking for money for projects designed to avert a possible negative outcome that may occur sometime, at an imprecise time in the future. This is a difficult task and one that officials who are in power for relatively short periods of time have little incentive to fight for— particularly when many other (more appealing) projects compete for the same funding.

---

[4] Piccoli, G. (2005), "Security and Risk Management: The Never Ending Game of Chess," *Cutter Benchmark Review* (5:12), pp. 3–5.

[5] Goodin, D. (2006), "Crisis in Confidence," *InfoWorld* (October 30). http://www.infoworld.com/article/06/10/30/ 44fesecsurvey_1.html

Figure 13.2 A Satellite Image of Hurricane Katrina

Because security is the type of investment that is difficult to gain funding for, particularly when competing for limited resources with projects that promise big results—efficiency improvements, revenue enhancements, and the like—it is all the more critical that it is not left to the IT group to make the case. General and functional managers must get involved in the security discussion, understand the threats, and assess the degree of risk that the firm should be allowed to take.

Forward-looking IT managers have begun to better "sell" security benefits. As Robert Charette, director of the Enterprise Risk Management and Governance practice of the Cutter Consortium, noted in a recent interview, "[Senior executives] don't care about the different levels of encryption—they care about the harm it will keep the company from suffering and how much it's exposed in the different scenarios."[6] Yet whether you are blessed with the help of "forward-looking" IT professionals or not, it is your responsibility as a general or functional manager to weigh in on the difficult trade-off decision between purchasing more security and accepting higher risks. If you are to do so, you must understand the basic threats and fundamental trade-offs engendered by computer security. This does not mean that you must develop an extraordinary amount of technical knowledge, as you will not be called on to implement the security measures. Instead you must understand the managerial process of IT risk management and information systems security decision making.

Risk Assessment

The risk assessment process consists of auditing the current resources, technological as well as human, in an effort to map the current state of the art of information systems security in the organization. An understanding of the current resources will provide an idea of the current set of vulnerabilities the firm is facing.

---

[6] Brandel, M. (2006), "Avoid Security Spending Fatigue," *ComputerWorld* (April 17). http://www.computerworld.com/securitytopics/security/story/0,10801,110504,00.html

For instance, Dell is a firm with a very prominent Web site. Dell's Web site is not only the face of the company, but it is also one of its main sources of livelihood. If customers cannot access it, Dell loses revenue by the minute. Thus, for Dell the risks associated with a denial-of-service attack that brings the Web site down is a very tangible one. The same could not be said for the Boat Yard Grill, a restaurant in Ithaca, New York, and its Web site (boatyardgrill.com).

The risk audit is useful because it provides the basis for a risk analysis. Risk analysis is the process by which the firm attempts to quantify the risks identified in the audit. We use the word *attempt* to indicate that precisely quantifying the monetary consequences of some of these risks is impossible. What do you think is the value of the loss of customer confidence in the Visa and Mastercard brands after the February, 18, 2003 announcement that an intrusion in their system allowed hackers to gain access to the accounts of 5.6 million customers? What is the value of the loss of confidence your customers may feel if they log on to your Web site one morning only to see it defaced with questionable pictures and comments? (Figure 13.3)

The impact of some security risks is harder to measure than others. However, the exercise is useful insomuch as rational decision making suggests that the amount you invest in security safeguards should be proportional to the extent of the threat and its potential negative effects. This is a critical point. Because security risks are really business risks—nobody would argue that loss of customer confidence is "an IT issue"—general and functional managers must be deeply involved in information systems security prioritization decisions.

Risk Mitigation

Risk mitigation is the process of matching the appropriate response to the security threats your firm identified. As Bruce Schneier, the noted computer security and cryptography expert, aptly put it, "There are two types of encryption: one that will prevent your sister from reading your diary and one that will prevent your government."

Figure 13.3   One of Microsoft France's Sites was Defaced in 2006

Risk mitigation allows your organization to devise the optimal strategy given the set of security risks it faces. Such optimal strategy is the one that yields the best trade-off between the degree of security the firm attains and the total investment in countermeasures necessary to achieve it (Figure 13.4). The total cost for security is a combination of anticipation costs, those expenditures designed to anticipate and mitigate the threats (e.g., purchasing and installing antivirus software), and failure costs, the negative financial fallout ensuing from a breach of security (e.g., loss of revenue during a Web site outage).

When faced with a security threat, the firm has three mitigation strategies available. Note than none of the three strategies described below is superior or inferior to the other in the absolute. The typical organization uses, consciously or unconsciously, a blend of all three.

1. *Risk acceptance.* This strategy consists of not investing in countermeasures and not reducing the security risk. The more an organization gravitates toward this strategy, the higher the potential failure cost it faces while minimizing anticipation costs.
2. *Risk reduction.* This strategy consists of actively investing in the safeguards designed to mitigate security threats. The more an organization gravitates toward this strategy, the higher the anticipation cost it faces while actively reducing failure costs.
3. *Risk transference.* This strategy consists of passing a portion (or all) of the risks associated with security to a third party (for example, by outsourcing security or buying insurance).

As the firm seeks to identify the optimal IT risk management and information systems security strategy, it will endeavor to identify the optimal blend of the three mitigation strategies. The optimal portfolio of security and risk management measures is based on the specific security threats the organization faces, as well as management's willingness to accept these risks. The major threats confronting the modern organization and safeguards available to respond to these threats are discussed below.

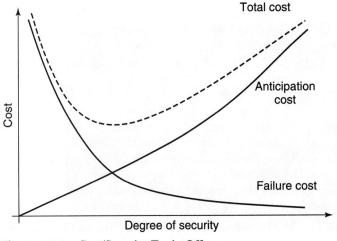

Figure 13.4   Cost/Security Trade-Offs

The Internal Threat

Internal security threats are those posed by individuals who have direct, on-premise access to the firm's technology infrastructure, or those who have legitimate reasons to be using the firm's assets. Internal security threats are important because the firm that is able to secure its assets against improper internal use not only has mitigated an important risk, but it is well on its way to mitigating the outside threat (i.e., the external threat can be seen a subset of the internal one). When addressing internal security threats, we can separate them in two broad categories: intentional malicious behavior and careless behavior.

Intentional Malicious Behavior   This type of threat is typically associated with disgruntled or ill-willed employees. This is a particularly troublesome threat because it is almost impossible to prepare for. Imagine, for example, that a member of the sales and direct marketing team is selling customer e-mail addresses to spammers. Unless this person makes a careless mistake or discusses his behavior with others, his actions may go undetected for a long time.

Careless Behavior   This type of threat is typically associated with ignorance of, or disinterest in, security policies. Consider a recent case. In May 2006 the U.S. Department of Veterans Affairs made public that a laptop containing personal information on as many as 26.5 million veterans had been stolen from the home of an employee. The data, including names, social security numbers, and dates of birth, were not supposed to be transferred onto an unsecured laptop or taken off of the Department's premises.

In this category fall a number of other behaviors that are more or less dangerous. For example, failing to modify default passwords, breaking the organization's policy on Internet and Web usage, not following guidelines about saving data on personal or portable devices, or failing to destroy sensitive data according to planned schedules.

The External Threat

Before the advent of the Internet and widespread connectivity, the importance of internal security threats far outweighed the danger posed by hackers and other outsiders. Mitigating the outside threat prior to pervasive networking simply amounted to physically securing the firm's IT assets. This is not the case anymore.

Today there is an incredible array of ways in which your firm's infrastructure can be attacked and compromised. Viruses, trojan horses, worms, time bombs, spyware, keystroke tracking tools, spoofing, snooping, sniffers—these are some of the most popular examples of malicious code and techniques that modern organizations find themselves fighting off. Couple this seemingly unabated tide of new releases and new forms of harmful software with human threats like crackers, thieves, social engineers, and industrial espionage contractors and you realize why security is continually ranked as one of the top worries for the modern CIO.

Those individuals who attack an organizations' IT infrastructure are typically called hackers. While some consider this a misnomer, contending that the term *hacker* simply means someone who possesses superior computer skills, the term has come to be associated in the media and general terminology with more or less maliciously intentioned individuals who attempt to subvert computer security defenses.

Below we address some of the external security threats confronting modern organizations.

Intrusion Threat   The intrusion threat is perhaps the most commonly envisioned when thinking about computer security. It consists of any situation where an unauthorized attacker gains access to organizational IT resources. Consider the following example. In the late 1980s a group of teenage hackers was found guilty of gaining unauthorized access to surveillance satellites and of using them for unauthorized purposes. As the story goes, the kids were discovered because the satellites were found marginally out of position at the beginning of every working day and the matter was further investigated. When the intruders' behavior was logged and monitored, it was discovered that upon taking control of the satellites, they were redirecting them on a nudist beach and taking pictures.

While the story screams urban legend, it is a great example of a (harmless) intrusion by individuals who did not attempt to inflict losses on the organization. Yet it is an intrusion nonetheless, as individuals without the authority gained access to one of the organization's resources and used it for unintended purposes. More common, and less fun, examples include individuals who access private information by stealing or guessing legitimate passwords. This can be done by "sniffing" a network connection with specialized software and intercepting passwords that are not encrypted.

Social Engineering　An even simpler method is what is now called "social engineering," which is a fancy name to describe a very simple practice: lying to and deceiving legitimate users. Social engineering is roughly defined as the practice of obtaining restricted or private information by somehow convincing legitimate users or people who have the information to share it. This is typically done over the telephone or other communication medium, and its success depends on the skills of the "social engineer," coupled with the gullibility and lack of training of the victim. Once the information has been obtained, say a password, the social engineer perpetrates the intrusion.

Phishing　The process of social engineering can be "automated" using a technique called phishing. Phishing consists of sending official-sounding spam (i.e., unwanted mail) from known institutions (e.g., Wells Fargo Bank). The message indicates that the institution needs the recipient to confirm or provide some data and contains a link to a Web page, a copy of the original, with fields for providing the "missing" information.

The act of phishing is the act of collecting the personal information, and a number of creative methods have been devised to direct traffic to the phony Web site (e.g., using links or fake promotions) and fool people into complying by crafting official-sounding messages from reputable institutions (Figure 13.5). Once on the target page, the user is asked to input some sensitive information—such as user name and password (Figure 13.6)— with the sole objective of stealing it for later use. While this appears simplistic, phishing has turned out to be a very effective way to obtain personal data—a 2004 study by the Gartner Group estimated that almost two million people, in the United States alone, had had their bank account compromised in the past 12 months due to phishing scams.[7]

Note that the low degree of sophistication of the phishing e-mail in Figure 13.5—which hit my inbox with great timing as I was writing this chapter—led to warnings from both the e-mail client (Figure 13.7) and the Web browser opening the page (Figure 13.8). As in any high-stakes game of chess, the security game is replete with moves and countermoves, but a more sophisticated attack would likely have gone undetected.

---

[7] Christie, L. (2004), *Going Phishing: Cyber-Crime is on The Upswing,* CNN/Money (Accessed 6/7/07: http://money.cnn.com/2004/08/03/pf/security_pi

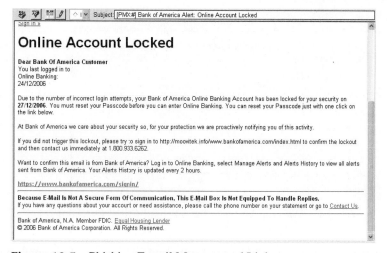

Figure 13.5   Phishing E-mail Message and Link

Backdoors and Security Weaknesses   Another way to gain unauthorized access is to exploit weaknesses in the software infrastructure of the organization under attack. Commercial software typically comes with "backdoors." A backdoor is code built into software program to allow access to the application by circumventing password protection. Backdoors are built into software in the event that high-level accounts, such as administrative accounts, are for some reason inaccessible (e.g., the password has been lost, a disgruntled employee is blackmailing the firm and will not unlock the software). While backdoors must be changed during the installation process, sometimes this step is forgotten and the default backdoor is allowed to exist while the program is operational. Hackers can

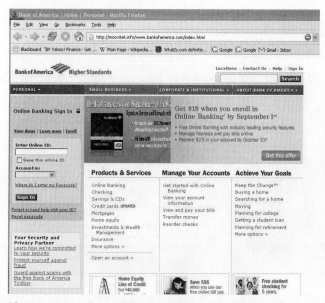

Figure 13.6   Capture Page Posing as a Legitimate Business

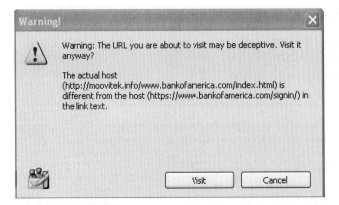

Figure 13.7   Warning Message from E-mail Client Detecting a Forged Web Address

then easily gain access to the application and take control of the application, giving themselves high-level access rights.

Beyond default backdoors, software programs have weaknesses (i.e., bugs). Typically these bugs are annoying because they prevent the application from functioning normally. For example, a program will shut off unexpectedly, or freeze. At times though, they can be extremely dangerous as they create security holes that an ill-intentioned intruder can exploit.

The intrusion threat is particularly troublesome because it has significant and long-lasting potential impacts. First, it may go undetected for a long period of time, enabling the intruder to perpetrate her crime(s) over time. Second, the intruder may be able to gain access to private information and even steal records. Third, when intrusion is discovered, it will require a thorough investigation in order to identify where the intruder came from, whether

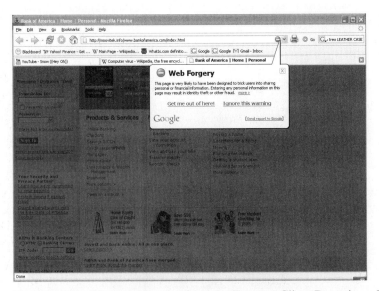

Figure 13.8   Warning Message from the Browser Client Detecting a Forged Web Address

she created backdoors that can be exploited in the future, and so on. Fourth, if information about the intrusion becomes public, something that is required by law in many states in cases where individuals' private information has been compromised, the firm will likely suffer significant damage to its reputation.

Going back to the opening example, it is now clear that even when intrusion by pranksters occurs (e.g., kids taking pictures of nude beaches, funny fellows who deface your Web site, or talented computer users who enjoy the challenge of breaking in and all they want is bragging rights with their friends), the expense in time, money, and trust recovery effort your organization must engage can be quite high.

The Threat of Malicious Code   Another security threat that modern firms face daily is presented by malicious code—also known as malware. The term *malicious code* refers to software programs that are designed to cause damage to individuals and/or organizations' IT assets. Below we identify the main categories of malicious code and discuss their characteristics.

Viruses   Computer viruses are an increasingly pervasive security threat. By some accounts there are more than 350 new viruses being produced and unleashed every week. These viruses are more and more often produced by putting together "component parts," malicious scripts that can be assembled into complete viruses by relatively unskilled individuals—aptly called script kiddies.

A computer virus is a type of malicious code that spreads by attaching itself to other, legitimate, executable software programs. Once the legitimate software program runs, the virus runs with it, replicating itself and spreading to other programs on the same machine. By dong so the computer virus, much like a biological virus, is able to prosper. If the infected files are shared and executed by others, their machine will be infected as well.

Following the infection phase, the payload delivery phase occurs. The payload is the typically harmful set of actions that the virus is designed to perform. They may range from simply annoying the user (see Figure 13.9)—a famous early virus dropped letters from the screen and nothing more—to wreaking havoc and bringing significant damage to the user—a popular one is the wiping out of all data on the hard disk. Some viruses deliver their payload immediately after infection, while others, known as time bombs, deliver it at a specific point in time or when a certain action is performed by the user. For instance, the Michelangelo virus discovered in 1991 was designed to deliver its payload on March 6, the birthday of the Italian master.

With the advent of the Internet and the widespread use of electronic mail, virus authors have found a new way to spread their "work." An e-mail virus is malicious code that

Figure 13.9   Alert Issued by the DROL Virus

travels attached to e-mail messages and has the ability to self-replicate, typically by automatically e-mailing itself to multiple recipients (see Figure 13.10).

Trojan Horses   A Trojan horse is a computer program that claims to, and sometimes does, deliver some useful functionality. However, like the legendary war machine the Greeks used against the people of Troy, the Trojan horse hides a dark side and, like a virus, delivers its malicious payload. Unlike a virus, a Trojan horse does not self-replicate, but it is passed on by those who share it with others.

Worms   A worm is a piece of malicious code that exploits security holes in network software to replicate itself. Strictly speaking, a worm does not deliver a payload, like a virus. A worm simply replicates itself and continues to scan the network for machines to infect. The problem is that, as the worm infects more and more machines on the network, the traffic it generates quickly brings the network down—with substantial damage. The original Internet worm, originating at Cornell University, was estimated to cost infected sites from $200 to $53,000 for repairs.

Spyware   Spyware applications have sprung up with the advent and widespread adoption of the Web. The term *spyware* suggests that the software runs without the awareness of the user and collects information. Broadly speaking, spyware is software that, unbeknownst to the owner of the computer, monitors behavior, collects information, and either transfers this information to a third party via the Internet or performs unwanted operations.

Typical examples of spyware include adware, software that collects information in an effort to use it for advertisement purposes by opening pop-ups or changing a users homepage; keyboard tracking, software that logs keyboard strokes in an effort to steal passwords and other sensitive information; and stealware, software that redirects payments legitimately belonging to an affiliate and sends them to the stealware operator.

While spyware differs from viruses, in that it cannot self-replicate, it can create significant problems for an organization. Beyond the malicious and often fraudulent effects of spyware, these programs divert resources and often slow down the user's legitimate work.

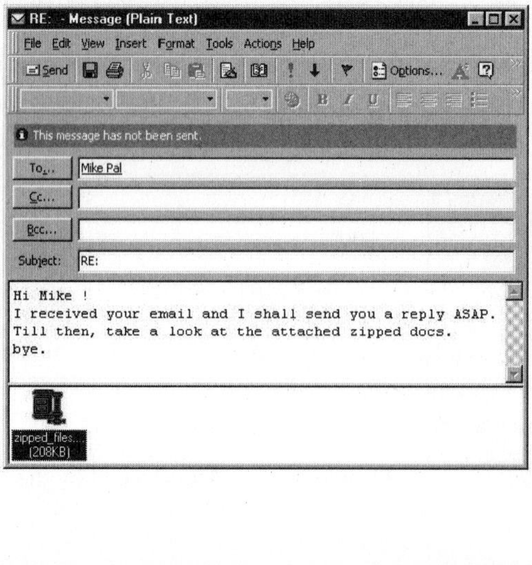

Figure 13.10   E-mail Virus Automatically Sending Itself

Denial-of-Service Attack   Denial-of-service attacks are particularly powerful today given the predominance of online operations and the number of firms that use Web sites and other online services for their operations. A denial-of-service attack is a digital assault carried out over a computer network with the objective of overwhelming an online service so as to force it offline.

Consider a Web site as the service of interest. A Web site is managed by a Web server that receives requests from clients all over the Internet and sends them the pages they request. When a Web server receives more requests that it can handle, it will attempt to serve them but begin to slow down, like a waiter who has been assigned too many restaurant tables and is scrambling to serve them all. If the number of requests is high enough, the service will likely shut down, thus becoming unavailable to legitimate traffic as well.

Denial-of-service attacks can be extremely dangerous because a skilled intruder will employ a denial-of-service attack to divert attention and occupy resources of the attacked organization. While the firm is busy averting the denial-of-service attack, the intruder can exploit available security breaches or create backdoors to be exploited later.

Responding to Security Threats

The management of computer security is a continuous effort. The principal objective is to identify the different threats and develop safeguards that match up with them and limit their incidence of success.

Internal Security Threats   Prevention of internal threats is no simple feat since security products and technologies can only partially help. Prevention of internal threats requires the development and enforcement of security policies and auditing standards designed to ensure that such policies are understood and respected by those in the organization.

Security Policies   The most easily preventable security risks are those caused by ignorance of sound security practice. A security policy spells out what the organization believes are the behaviors that individual employees and groups within the firm should follow in order to minimize security risks. They include what computing services will be made available and what computing services will not be made available within the firm. They specify what password standards the firm should follow (e.g., length, characters to be used, renewal schedules) and what rights different types of users will have. They specify the level of care that employees need to use with their passwords (e.g., do not share password with anyone, do not send passwords over clear channels such as not encrypted mail messages), what computing resources and what data should be accessible within the organization, what data can be downloaded to personal devices and what needs to remain within the company. The policy should address legitimate uses of portable devices, what data can be downloaded to them, and how such devices should be secured by those who own them. A security policy may even address what care employees should exercise when they leave the premises (e.g., not reviewing sensitive data on laptops while on airplanes).

Beyond having comprehensive security policies in place, the organization must audit them to ensure compliance. For example, accounts of terminated employees need to be swiftly deleted or made unavailable to prevent access from former employees who at best will see material they should not, and at worst will be able to damage company resources (e.g., delete data).

External Security Threats

Intrusion   A number of techniques and technologies to prevent intrusion have been developed over the years. The cornerstone of securing against intrusion is the use of passwords. Passwords ensure that resources are only made available to those who have the appropriate authentication levels. Thus, a password can be used to block unauthorized external users as well as discriminate to whom resources should be available among the legitimate users.

Organizations typically enforce standards to ensure that passwords are reasonably difficult to guess. For example, many security policies require that passwords have minimum length; they use letters, numbers, and special characters; they don't use dictionary words, and so on. However, there is an inherent trade-off between the complexity of a password and human ability. In other words, if passwords are too difficult to remember, people will write them down, creating a new security risk! For this reason the computer security industry is hard at work devising more robust identification schemes, such as biometrics—the use of physical traits (e.g., fingerprints, iris scans) as a means to uniquely identify users (Figure 13.11).

A firewall is a software tool designed to screen and manage traffic in and out of a computer network. Thus a firewall is used to secure the perimeter of the organization's computing resources employing a number of technologies and techniques. Firewalls can also be used to enforce security policies (for example, blocking traffic from Web sites deemed risky and blocking the download of some file types; see Figure 13.12).

Firewalls are a very important security tool, but you need to remember that perimeter protection is only as strong as its weakest link—much like the perimeter protection of a castle. For example, no matter how powerful your firewall is, if there are unsecured modems that an attacker can dial into, the network is not secure. Once the attacker gains access to the organization's resources through the unsecured modem, the strongest perimeter security is made useless—the intruder is working on the inside now.

Consider as well that any resource that is brought outside the perimeter is not secured by the firewall—hence the inherent danger associated with the proliferation of mobile devices. For instance, if an employee copies sensitive data to her laptop and takes the machine

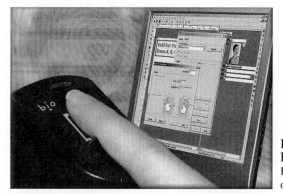

Figure 13.11   A Fingerprint Reader. (*Source:* Courtesy of The Euro Kiosks Network (EKN), "The Global Voice of Kiosking.")

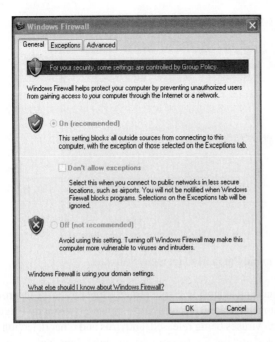

Figure 13.12   Microsoft Windows Built-in Firewall

on the road, the firm's firewall is useless in protecting such data. With data increasingly prevalent and portable devices achieving widespread adoption, perimeter security is increasingly insufficient.

Another technique that has been developed to safeguard against the intrusion threat is encryption. Through the encryption process, content is scrambled in such a way that it is rendered unreadable to all recipients, except those who hold a key to decrypt it. Encryption ensures that if the wrong individuals gain access to the data, they will be unable to make out its meaning. Encryption techniques are used to secure transmissions as well as to secure stored data. Consider once again the example of the lost laptop discussed above. If the data it contained had been encrypted, the loss to the firm would simply amount to the cost of the asset—less than a thousand dollars in most cases.

Security policy and audits will help a firm ensure that no backdoors are left open after installation of a new software program. With respect to security holes and weaknesses in software that are due to bugs, the IT staff in the organization must monitor bug reports and install patches—pieces of add-on code published by the software house that wrote the program designed to eliminate weaknesses that surface after the release of the software program. The problem is that many organizations lack the staff to constantly monitor this information and may fall behind in patch installations, thus opening the firm to unnecessary risks. To obviate to this problem, many of the large software houses (e.g., Microsoft) have now developed patch management software that automatically alerts users to the availability of newly released patches—and, if configured to do so, downloads and installs them automatically (Figure 13.13).

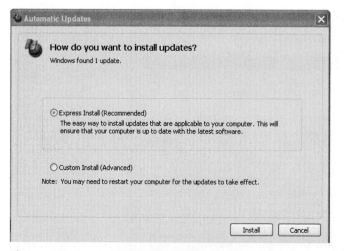

Figure 13.13   Automatic Patch Management Software

Malware   Safeguarding against malware requires that the firm's IT professionals install the appropriate detection software (e.g., antivirus, spyware sweepers) (Figure 13.14). With the large number of new viruses being released, antivirus and other detection software is only as good as its most recent update. For this reason, organizations that manage their own networks increasingly attempt to centralize these applications and push updates to individual users so as to ensure that safeguards against malware are up to date.

Training and policies can also be very helpful in mitigating the malware threat. Simple behaviors, such as not opening e-mail attachments from accounts you don't recognize (e.g., intriguing@sexylips.com), or limiting downloads from the Internet to trusted Web sites go a long way in preventing infection

Denial-of-Service Attack   Preventing a denial-of-service attack is very difficult. This is because in a well-orchestrated denial-of-service attack, the requests for the service are not

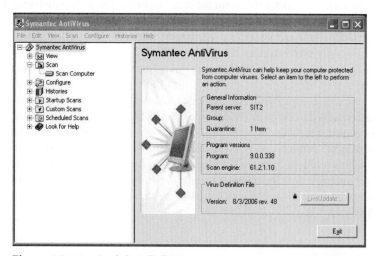

Figure 13.14   Antivirus Software

issued from the same few locations, making it easy to recognize and block. Instead, in what's called a distributed denial-of-service attack, the attacker will hijack or spoof multiple machines and initiate the attack from these multiple locations.

Managing Security: Overall Guidelines

As a general or functional manager, you are not likely to be involved in the technical details of the procedures and safeguards chosen to mitigate the specific security threats identified in the risk assessment. However, you should expect to be involved in setting the agenda for how the overall set of risks is to be addressed. In this role it is paramount that you recognize one important characteristic of security investments: Security is a negative deliverable, one that produces no upside, but helps in limiting damage ensuing from an uncertain negative event. For these types of investments it is difficult to obtain appropriate funding.

Moreover, when it comes to security, it is impossible to ensure success. In other words, it is impossible to claim that the organization is "secure." Rather it is possible to find out that the organization was not secure after a breach has occurred. Amid all these difficulties general and functional managers play a critical role.

Have a Plan and Specify Responsibilities   You would be surprised to find out how many organizations do not devise formal plans to be enacted during an attack or fail to assign formal responsibility for security design and enforcement (Figure 13.5). This is particularly true for the design of new applications as requirements requested by the business sometimes weaken the security of the applications. In this case the overall responsibility for security choices and trade-offs should reside with a business owner or other appropriate senior person, not with IT. When outside contractors are engaged in the development, security requirements should be spelled out in the contract.

A crisis management plan should specify who needs to be contacted in an emergency and what their roles should be. The plan must address questions such as what the first reaction measures should be (e.g., should the systems under attack be shut down or left operational). When and how should authorities, such as the FBI, be contacted? What will the firm disclose about the attack, if anything, and who should be in charge of press releases or of customer communication? What recovery plans need to be enacted under the various scenarios? In short, the plan should script all those decisions that are difficult to make when the firm is under attack.

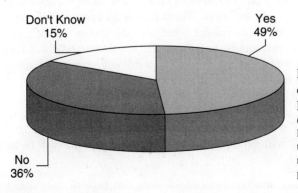

Figure 13.15   A Large Number of Organizations Lack an Overall Risk Management Strategy[8].
(*Source:* This figure was originally published by Cutter Consortium, www.cutter.com ©2005 Cutter Consortiun. All rights reserved. Reproduced with permission.)

---

[8] Piccoli, G. (2006), "Doing Privacy Right: Using Data and Preserving Trust," *Cutter Benchmark Review* (6:1), pp. 3–5.

Revisit Often Security is a constantly evolving area for a number of reasons: first and foremost, the breathtaking pace of technical evolution. Every new technology and software program your firm adopts ushers in a unique set of security and risk management challenges that should be proactively addressed—whether that means taking specific steps to manage it or consciously accepting the risk.

A recent security survey found that a large number of organizations update their overall risk strategy at least annually and roughly half of them have decided in the past to forgo the acquisition of a computer system due to security concerns.[9] Thus, you must ensure that security audits and reassessment of security plans are done periodically.

Develop a Mitigation Plan A well-architected security infrastructure and plan can go a long way toward tempering the many security threats modern firms face. But no matter how good your security, there is always the chance that your firm will be successfully attacked and that your defenses will be breached. What you do in this case can be critical, particularly when you become vulnerable to an intrusion.

The first reaction to an attack is often to shut everything down. This is a mistake since diagnosing where the attack is coming from, its severity, and its reach is much easier if the system is maintained operational and the attacker is maintained unaware of the fact that you spotted the security breach.

The first order of business at this point should be to determine how the attack took place in order to eliminate its chance of occurring again. The next step requires an assessment of the damage, particularly as it pertains to the loss of sensitive data. A series of laws have been recently passed in the United States requiring the firm to immediately notify those whose data may have been compromised. Whether this is a necessity or not in your jurisdiction, it is a wise move to immediately communicate the problem to those affected. As much as you would like to keep the matter private, to avoid the negative publicity, people understand that security breaches may occur, but they will be much less forgiving if they discover an attempt to cover up the problem.

PRIVACY

Privacy concerns emerge in the relationship between individuals and organizations because, when dealing with business firms or nonprofit and governmental organizations, customers (and employees) often provide personal information under the assumption that the organization will take "good care" of it. We, as customers and/or employees, provide personal information in order to receive the benefits of the transaction (e.g., employment, value proposition). Yet a prerequisite to the transaction is that we hold some degree of trust in the organization that we are dealing with. We trust that our information is reasonably secure and the organization has taken steps to prevent unauthorized use of it by those who have no legitimate reason to access it.

In other words, we must have trust in the firm's information systems security. Even more importantly, we must trust that the organization will be a steward of our personal information and that it will refrain from employing it in ways that will be harmful to us or our

---

[9]Baskerville, R. L. (2005), "Best Practices in IT Risk Management: Buying Safeguards, Designing Security Architecture, or Managing Information Risk?" *Cutter Benchmark Review* (5:12), pp. 5–13.

interests. For instance, even if we have great faith in the firm's security, we still must believe that the firm is ethical enough not to collect our data and immediately turn around and sell it to spammers in order to make a "quick buck."

Consider the following, more subtle incident: "In 2003, the public learned that JetBlue Airways had turned over records on more than a million of its passengers to a government contractor. The contractor sought the information to test a security application designed to identify suspected terrorists. However, the sharing violated JetBlue's privacy policy, which promised that the company would not provide personal information to third parties. The CEO issued a public apology and indicated that he had no knowledge of the data transfer at the time it was made. Nonetheless, JetBlue had to confront a lawsuit from privacy groups and passengers."[10]

What was the problem? After all, JetBlue was only trying to aid in efforts to prevent terrorist attacks and ultimately improve the safety of its own passengers! The problem is that JetBlue had not developed an appropriate process for dealing with privacy concerns in the face of the proliferation of customer data it stewards and the mounting number of potential (perhaps legitimate) uses of the data.

Privacy Defined

If there could be some doubt regarding whether computer security is an "IT issue" or a "business issue," there is no such doubt regarding privacy. Given the ethical concerns and the potential for liability associated with privacy, general and functional managers should be front and center in identifying and responding to the privacy concerns of the organization. This is not surprising when, by some estimates, nearly 80 percent of organizations collect information and half of them indicate that this information is sensitive in nature.[11] But what is privacy exactly?

Privacy can be defined as the ability of individuals to control the terms and conditions under which their personal information is collected, managed, and utilized. Private information is that information that can be traced back to the individual—for instance, a person's name, picture, address, social security number, or medical history.

It is evident from the above definition that privacy is not security, even though there is much confusion between the two terms. Privacy subsumes security. That is, a firm that is unable to secure customer or employee data will not be able to ensure privacy. More specifically, privacy is about informed consent and permission to collect and use identifying information, while security is about safekeeping of the collected data.

Privacy Risks

Privacy risks are a byproduct of the success that firms have been enjoying with their use of information technology. In a world where competition is global and it is not possible to have a personal relationship with the thousands or millions of customers your firm is trying to reach, IT-enabled information systems have created the ability to "know" individuals we do not interact with directly.

In many cases these developments have been welcomed by those involved (e.g., customers[12]). Many of us enjoy the personal recommendations that Amazon (Figure 13.16) is

---

[10] Culnan, M. J. (2006), "Privacy in Search of Governance," *Cutter Benchmark Review* (6:1) p. 5.

[11] Piccoli, G. (2006), "Doing Privacy Right: Using Data and Preserving Trust," *Cutter Benchmark Review* (6:1), pp. 3–5.

[12] While the arguments here can be extended to other entities, such as employees or suppliers, we use the example of customers throughout for simplicity.

Figure 13.16   Amazon.com's Personal Recommendations

able to provide us or the fact that we don't have to repeat our preferences every time we book a reservation with the same hotel chain (Figure 13.17). But these very advances in technology that allow us to better compete and better suit our customer needs create the potential for highly damaging privacy violations.

Function Creep   As we discussed in Chapter 4, information is not consumed by use and can thus be employed multiple times in different applications and for different purposes. For example, information about the number of soda cans sold by a vending machine can be used to compute revenues at one time and forecast future sales at another.

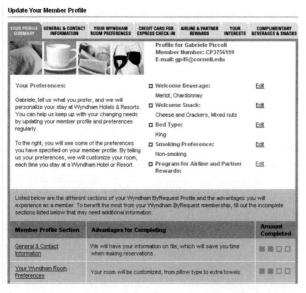

Figure 13.17   Personal Profile at Wyndham ByRequest

Function creep occurs when data collected for a stated or implied purpose are then reused for other, unrelated, objectives. In the case of the soda vending machine, this is not a problem, but when individuals' personal information is concerned, privacy issues take center stage.

Consider the recent example of Eckerd Corporation, the drugstore chain. Eckerd settled a lawsuit with the Florida attorney general's office contending that the firm had engaged in deceptive trade practices and breached customers' privacy by sending unsolicited promotions based on the prescriptions customers had filled in the past. The firm now obtains express permission from customers before sending them marketing material on behalf of pharmaceutical companies. It also endowed a $1 million chair in ethics at Florida A&M School of Pharmacy as part of the settlement.

While the above incident could be ascribed to the heightened sensitivity of medical information, the quick backpedaling reaction and image damage the firm suffered are not much different than what was experienced by RealNetworks in the case described in the introduction to this chapter. At the heart of both cases is a perceived breach of trust due to the fact that information the customer had provided with one intent was being used for other aims. The intention of the firm may be a good one—to provide valuable personalized information, for instance. However, the customers' perceived loss of control over their personal data opens the door to concerns of abuse and negative reactions.

Proliferating Data Sources Perhaps even more difficult to manage than the potential for function creep is the dizzying proliferation of data sources and technologies that generate customer data. Consider modern cellular phones. Such devices enable a fairly precise estimation of their physical location. This capability can be life saving in the case of 911 calls. Yet the potential for privacy invasion is just as significant. Can you imagine walking down a street and being pestered with "eSolicitations" from "nearby businesses"?

Beyond technology advances and the adoption of devices that surreptitiously generate the data, modern consumers themselves seem to revel in providing more and more information on a voluntary basis. Whether this is plain old self-expression, the need to feel part of a community, or the fact that we are becoming increasingly used to voicing our preferences to get tailored offers is irrelevant. The amount of personal information individuals are posting to sites like MySpace.com or Flickr is unprecedented. Navigating this landscape in a legal and ethical manner without missing opportunities for business success is becoming increasingly difficult.

Improving Data Management Technologies Not only is personal data easier to generate than ever before and proliferating, but it is increasingly simple, and cost effective, to merge data repositories. Consider one of the most celebrated examples of successful organizational use of customer data: Harrah's Entertainment, Inc. Harrah's collects individual demographic data that its customers provide when signing up to its loyalty program, and individual behavioral data when its customers stay at property, gamble, and redeem offers. Harrah's also collects nongambling data from external data providers such as Acxiom. It then merges all this information in its data warehouse to develop a complete profile of each customer.

The development of data management technologies enables initiatives of this kind and has created an unprecedented level of opportunity for data-driven strategies. It also creates much pressure for and risk of function creep if not managed carefully.

The Legal Landscape In an environment as difficult to navigate as privacy, it would be quite helpful to have comprehensive legal guidance. Unfortunately, though, with some exceptions, information technology evolution outpaces legal development. To further compound the problem, the Internet has all but destroyed traditional geographical boundaries, making legislation difficult to enforce and easier to circumvent.

It used to be that a community, a state, or an entire nation would be able to easily regulate behavior within its jurisdiction. For example, if a state did not want to allow its residents to gamble, it would simply not issue gaming licenses. Today this level of legislative control is no longer possible, when everyone with a computer can travel to any Web site in the world with the click of a button.

Safeguarding Privacy

Fair information practices have been proposed as a basis for privacy governance. Fair information practices are based on the five principles of notice, choice, access, security, and enforcement.

- *Notice* refers to the right of individuals to be informed when their personal data is being collected and to be informed about how it is or will be used.

- *Choice* calls for the ability of individuals to be informed of, and object to, function creep whether within one firm or across firms who share information.

- *Access* refers to the right of individuals to be able to access their information and correct any errors that may have occurred in their records.

- *Security* calls for organizations that house individuals' private information to ensure its safekeeping and to protect it from unauthorized access.

- *Enforcement* calls for organizations that collect and use private information to develop enforceable procedures to ensure that the above principles are upheld.

Noted privacy expert Mary Culnan offers the following straightforward guidelines for organizations that seek to comply with the above fair information practices: Say what you do, do what you say, and be able to prove it.[13]

Say What You Do   This first guideline requires that the firm develop a codified set of policies and procedures for safeguarding privacy. It also requires that the firm communicates these policies to affected individuals (e.g., customers, employees). Being able to follow this guideline is predicated on the firm's ability to audit and identify the personal information it collects and stores. It also necessitates a clear understanding of how the information is used today, how it may be used in the future, and whether it is transferred or otherwise shared with partners.

Do What You Say   The second guideline requires that those who represent the firm know, understand, and can enact the policies the firm has developed. Ensuring this level of compliance requires both training, so that the employees are aware of the policies and know how to best enact them, and follow-up, so that procedures are audited and behavior is monitored.

Be Able to Prove It   The third guideline requires that the firm document its policies and the processes it has developed to ensure privacy. This guideline acts as a sort of insurance against possible privacy violations. It enables the firm to demonstrate that it takes privacy concerns seriously and has been diligent in minimizing the possibility of privacy violations.

---

[13] Culnan, M. J. (2006), "Privacy in Search of Governance," *Cutter Benchmark Review* (6:1), pp. 5–13.

ETHICS

Many of the judgment calls about privacy that were discussed in the previous section are really ethical choices. But what is ethics? What does it mean to be ethical? How do you as a general or functional manager ensure that the people you manage act in an ethical manner when it comes to information systems use?

Ethics: Definition

Webster's Dictionary defines *ethics* as "the discipline dealing with what is good and bad and with moral duty and obligation." Ethics is the branch of philosophy that concerns itself with morality by studying right and wrong and attempting to draw a distinction between good and evil.

Recent examples of unethical behavior in business abound. The corporate scandals that have led to the demise of one-time stock market darlings like Enron Corp. and Global Crossing have clearly shown that we cannot assume that today's managers are equipped to make appropriate ethical choices. These corporate scandals have led to legislation—such as the Sarbanes-Oxley Act in 2002, which increases the scope of management and director's responsibilities, as well as the reporting requirements that public firms have to comply with. However, unethical behavior in business circles has roots that go beyond a legislative vacuum.

While many react with outrage to unethical behavior, arguing that "everyone knows what's right and what's wrong," this stance oversimplifies reality. Because of the intense technical training that most business and management schools focus on, the fact that managers will make ethical decisions is often mistakenly taken for granted. Most managers are ill equipped to make ethical decisions because they typically lack formal training in the area and because their attention is typically on the objective they are trying to reach. Aptly capturing this dilemma was a former CIO at Metro-Goldwyn-Mayer Studios: "When your job is building the best-performing database you can, you don't always think about the ethical implications of how that data will be used."[14]

Moreover, aside from those spilling over into illegal behavior, ethical choices are rarely straightforward. In fact, ethical dilemmas are typically rooted in the choice between multiple suboptimal courses of action that force well-intentioned individuals to make difficult trade-offs.

Fortunately, many business and management schools are formally introducing ethics in the curriculum. This education is necessary to enable future business leaders to confront ethical dilemmas and develop a sophisticated understanding of ethics before joining the workforce.

Information Systems Ethics

Information systems and new technologies, with their penchant for enabling new ways of doing business, constantly introduce the potential for ethical dilemmas. Moreover, because of the rapid pace of the evolution of IT and the slow pace at which legislation is passed,

---

[14] Wilder, C., and Soat, J. (2001), "The Ethics of Data," *InformationWeek,* May 14. Accessed 6/7/07: http://www.informationweek .com/837/dataethics/htm

formal explicit rules lag behind the possibilities offered by new technologies. Ethical guidelines fill (or should fill) the void, providing direction in the absence of explicit laws. Consider the following scenarios:

- As you are driving home, you hear a song from your youth. You had totally forgotten about that one head-banging band . . . memories of friends and happy times fill your mind. As you walk into your house, you think about downloading an mp3 version of the song from one of the many file-sharing networks available today on the Internet.

  While you know that downloading the song is "technically" illegal, you are confident that you will not have the time and interest to find and purchase the CD. You just want to listen to the song again and daydream a bit more . . . and what was the name of that other hit the band had . . .?

- As the IT director for your organization, you have some leeway with the priorities you assign to various projects. You recently reallocated resources and delayed the CRM implementation to speed up the ERP roll-out that is already running considerably behind schedule. You have reason to believe that Jack, one of your project managers, forwarded your e-mail about the shift of resources to the VP of marketing.

  As the IT director, you are well aware that all the company e-mails are backed up on the mail server and you know the backdoor that enables access to every account. As you walk over to the mail server late one evening, you tell yourself that it is critical that a General be able to fully trust his troops . . . you must find out whether you can trust Jack.

- It was your college-days dream, running your own company! ReinvenTravel.com had been *it* for the last four and half years. An industry magazine called it "the intermediary that reshaped how people buy travel." Your dream had turned into a nightmare. After filing for Chapter 11 bankruptcy protection and trying to restructure, it was now clear that ReinvenTravel.com would not make it.

  The decision was tough. You had been offered $7.2 million by your largest competitor—MightyTravel—for the preferences and historical transaction data of your customers. While you never liked the folks over at MightyTravel, they assured you that they would use the data to offer a more targeted and personal travel experience to your former customers. Your privacy policy never explicitly addressed what you would do with customer data, and the $7.2 million will allow you to honor salary and pension commitments to your employees. As you sign the contract, you reassure yourself, thinking that your customers will appreciate receiving more targeted offers from MightyTravel . . . everyone prefers targeted offers . . . right?

What is common to all three scenarios is the fact that each of the ethical dilemmas they capture would not have been possible just a few years ago. New technologies brought them about as a byproduct of their enabling new ways to collect, process, store, and distribute information. More importantly, all three scenarios paint an accurate picture of typical ethical dilemmas: The appropriate course of action is far from clear and no choice is without a negative impact on other individuals.

Ensuring Ethical Uses of Information Systems

There are no silver bullets to ensure ethical behavior in the context of organizational information systems. Developing a culture of ethical decision making is critical. Such a culture should create the preconditions and reward behavior that strives for harm minimization, respect, and consistency.

Ethical dilemmas typically pit the interest of one person or group (e.g., shareholders) against that of another (e.g., customers). Applying the principle of harm minimization, one needs to weigh the relative impact that the decision will have on all individuals affected and strive to moderate damage to any one individual or group. The principle of respect requires that information systems decisions be made in an effort to treat each of the affected parties with the outmost consideration. Finally, the principle of consistency provides a test for evaluating decisions. It requires a person confronted with an ethical dilemma to consider whether he would approve if everyone else made the same choice he is considering.

A practical, and pragmatic, approach to foster a culture of ethical decision making is to establish an information systems ethics code of conduct. A code of conduct, typically used by professional associations, offers two advantages. On the one hand, it communicates to all parties the organization's principles of ethical information systems use. Thus, it can be used as an educational mechanism to point employees in the right direction. On the other hand, it identifies the firm's formal stance, thus enabling detection of, and distancing from, unethical choices made by any member of the organization.

SUMMARY

In this chapter we focused on three topics of interest to general and functional managers: information systems security and IT risk management, privacy, and information systems ethics. A failure in security, privacy or ethics can have dramatic repercussions on the organization both because of its potentially damaging direct effects (e.g., computer outages, disruptions to operations) and its increasingly negative indirect effects (e.g., legal recourse, image damage).

In this chapter we sought to convince you that, as future general and functional managers, you will have to be involved in these decisions. We also helped you gain an understanding of the circumstances in which choices and trade-offs are made so that you can actively participate in decision making.

- Information systems must be secured against both internal and external threats. The internal threat is due to either ill-willed or careless members of the organization and it is mitigated by way of security policies and training. The external threat comes from skilled individuals, referred to as hackers. The external threat takes the form of malware, intrusion attempts, and denial-of-service attacks. Each of the threats is matched by the appropriate safeguard.

- Information systems security and risk management are not "IT issues." Because of the impact of the security breaches on the current and future viability of the organization, it is critical that general and functional managers take an active role in security decision making. This is done by participating in risk assessment, the process designed to evaluate the potential impact of threats confronting the firm, and risk mitigation, the process of identifying the appropriate response to these security threats. This involvement is necessary in order to make the appropriate trade-off decision among risk acceptance, risk reduction, and risk transference.

- Privacy concerns, like security threats, need general and functional managers' full attention. This is because privacy, like security, is a negative deliverable. That is, investments in privacy help the organization avoid a possible negative occurrence (e.g., lawsuit, loss of customer trust, negative impact on the firm's image) rather than generate benefits such as improved efficiency or increased revenues.

■ In order for the firm to safeguard the privacy of its employees and customers, it must subscribe to fair information practices. Fair information practices are based on the five principles of notice, choice, access, security, and enforcement. Moreover, the firm should produce a codified set of security policies, monitor and enforce compliance with them, and document both the policies and the processes it has developed to ensure privacy.

■ The recent flurry of corporate scandals has ignited interest in business ethics. When it comes to information systems, ethics becomes a crucial guiding light for management behavior as legislation often lags technology improvements. Thus, developing a culture of ethical decision making is essential for modern organizations.

STUDY QUESTIONS

1. Imagine that you have just been hired by a retail financial institution. How would you explain to your CEO that she needs to get involved in information security decisions?

2. What are the three costs associated with information systems security? What is the relationship among them?

3. Define what is meant by internal and external threats. How do the two differ? How are they related?

4. Define and provide an example of each of the different types of intrusion threats. Describe the appropriate countermeasure for each of your examples.

5. Define and provide an example of each of the different types of malicious code threats. Describe the appropriate countermeasure.

6. What is a denial-of-service attack? Why are these attacks particularly dangerous?

7. Imagine that you have just been hired by a retail financial institution. How would you explain to your CEO that she needs to get involved in privacy decisions?

8. How is privacy defined? What are the principal privacy risks? Can you provide examples of each one?

9. What is ethics? What are the principal challenges associated with information systems ethics?

FURTHER READINGS

1. Austin, R. D., and Darby, C. A. (2003). "The Myth of Secure Computing." *Harvard Business Review,* June, pp. 120–126

2. Dutta, A., and McChronan, K. (2002). "Management's Role in Information Security in a Cyber-Economy." *California Management Review* (45:1)., pp. 67–87

3. Purcell, R., and Fusaro, R. (2000). "Chief Privacy Officer."*Harvard Business Review,* November/December, pp. 20–22.

4. Wilder, C., and Soat, J. (2001). "The Ethics of Data." *InformationWeek,* May 14. Accessed 6/7/07: http://www .informationweek.com/837/dataethics.htm

GLOSSARY

■ **Backdoor:** Code built into software programs to allow access to an application by circumventing password protection.

■ **Biometrics:** In the context of computer security, the term *biometrics* is used to refer to the use of physical traits as a means to uniquely identify users.

■ **Denial-of-service attack:** A digital assault carried out over a computer network with the objective to overwhelm an online service so as to force it offline.

■ **Encryption:** A technique designed to scramble data so as to ensure that if the wrong individuals gain access to the data, they will be unable to make out its meaning.

■ **Firewall:** A hardware or software tool designed to screen and manage traffic in and out of an organization's computer network.

■ **Hacker:** The term *hacker* simply means someone who possesses superior computer skills. It has come to be associated in the media and general terminology with more or less maliciously intentioned individuals who attempt to subvert computer security defenses.

- **Information systems security:** The set of defenses an organization puts in place to mitigate threats to its technology infrastructure and data resources.

- **Intrusion:** The intrusion threat consists of any situation where an unauthorized attacker gains access to organizational IT resources.

- **IT risk management:** The process by which the firm attempts to identify and measure information systems security risks, and to devise the optimal mitigation strategy.

- **Malware:** The general term *malicious code,* or *malware,* refers to software programs that are designed to cause damage to individuals and/or organizations' IT assets.

- **Phishing:** The process of collecting sensitive information by tricking, in more or less automated ways, those who have it to provide it thinking that they are giving it to a legitimate concern.

- **Privacy:** In the context of information systems, privacy is the ability of individuals to control the terms and conditions under which their personal information is collected, managed, and utilized.

- **Risk analysis:** The process by which the firm attempts to quantify the risks identified in the risk assessment.

- **Risk assessment:** The risk assessment process consist of auditing the current resources, technological as well as human, in an effort to map the current state of the art of information systems security in the organization.

- **Risk mitigation:** The process of matching the appropriate response to the security threats your firm identified.

- **Social engineering:** The practice of obtaining restricted or private information by somehow convincing legitimate users or people who have it to share it.

- **Spyware:** Software that, unbeknownst to the owner of the computer, monitors behavior, collects information, and either transfers this information to a third party via the Internet or performs unwanted operations.

- **Trojan horse:** A computer program that claims to, and sometimes does, deliver some useful functionality. But the Trojan horse hides a dark side and, like a virus, delivers its malicious payload.

- **Virus:** A type of malicious code that spreads by attaching itself to other, legitimate, executable software programs.

- **Worm:** A piece of malicious code that exploits security holes in network software to replicate itself.

CASE STUDY: GIANT FOOD AND ELENSYS: LOOKING OUT FOR CUSTOMERS OR GROSS PRIVACY INVASIONS?[15]

INTRODUCTION

Russell B. Fair, Vice President of Pharmacy Operations for Giant Food Inc., was walking his dog early on a Sunday morning in February. As was his custom, he had brought the newspaper with him to read. When he unfolded the front section of the *Washington Post,* the headline leaped out at him: "Prescription Sales, Privacy Fears; CVS, Giant Share Customer Records with Drug Marketing Firm." The story began:

> Using technology in a new way to market drugs, CVS Corp. and Giant Food Inc. are sending confidential prescription information to a Massachusetts company that tracks customers who don't refill prescriptions, a practice that some experts say raises new questions about medical privacy. The company, a computer

database marketing specialist, uses the data to send personalized letters–written on pharmacy letterhead and sometimes paid for by drug manufacturers–that either remind customers to keep taking their medicine or pitch new products that will treat the customer's ailment. [O'Harrow, 1998]

The article quoted a noted physician,

> It's a gross invasion. . . . Do you want the great computer in the sky to have a list of every drug you take . . . all without your permission?

"This is trouble," Fair thought to himself as he folded up the newspaper and headed for home. Within a few hours, he began receiving phone calls from the supervisors in the stores who reported they were receiving many complaints from irate customers. Fair knew immediately that Giant had

---

[15] This case was originally published as: Culnan, M. J. (2006), "Giant Food and ElenSys: Looking Out for Customers or Gross Privacy Invasions?" *Communications of the AIS* (16), pp. 317–328.

continued

a problem with the fledgling alliance Giant's pharmacy established with Elensys Care Services, Inc. to run a patient education and prescription drug compliance program. When Fair reached Giant's CEO at home and explained the situation, the CEO asked him, "What do you want to do?"

THE COMPANIES

Giant Food, Inc.

In February 1936, N. M. Cohen and Samuel Lehrman opened the first Giant food store on Georgia Avenue in Washington, D.C. The store was based on a novel concept for the times: a large self-service store that could offer lower prices to consumers by substituting high volume for high markups. As of 2005, Giant operated 203 supermarkets, including 174 full-service pharmacies in Virginia, Maryland, the District of Columbia, Delaware, and New Jersey. The Delaware and New Jersey stores operated under the name Super G. Giant also operated two large distribution centers, a bakery, a dairy processing plant, an ice cube processing plant, as well as a soda bottling plant, all in suburban Maryland. The company's extensive private label line included as many as 9,000 products carrying the Super G label.[16] Giant was the market leader in the Washington metropolitan area.

Giant's reputation is as a family business with a strong history of service to the community and innovation. In the late 1980s, Giant was the first supermarket chain to install front-end scanning in all of its stores, a feat which as of December 1991 had been duplicated by only a few others.[17] In 1970 it was one of the first food retailers to hire a consumer advocate, former Presidential advisor Esther Peterson. Giant's current Vice President of Consumer Affairs, Odonna Mathews, was a familiar figure from Giant's newspaper and television ads, in-store promotions, and educational materials. Giant contributed more than $6 million annually in cash, goods, and services to support charitable and community organizations in the markets it served.[18]

In 1964, N. M. Cohen, one of the founders, turned the reins of the business over to his son Izzy, who served on the Board of Directors since its founding. Izzy Cohen served as chairman, president, and CEO until 1992, when he tapped Pete L. Manos to serve in the role of company president. Izzy Cohen died on November 22, 1995. Cohen's commitment to the customer—"There is nothing too good for a Giant customer"—permeated Giant's corporate culture. Cohen's guiding principles endure today: quality, value, and especially service in a warm and friendly atmosphere.[19]

In October 1998, Royal Ahold NV, a large conglomerate, Dutch grocery completed a $2.7 billion cash purchase of Giant. Giant's stock was delisted on the American Stock Exchange on October 30. Pete L. Manos, Izzy Cohen's successor as Giant's Chairman and CEO, announced his retirement after four decades with the firm. In 2003, Royal Ahold announced it would merge Giant and its corporate sibling, Stop & Shop Supermarket Co., consolidating the corporate offices at Stop & Shop's headquarters in Massachusetts.

Elensys Care Services, Inc.

Elensys, located in Burlington, Massachusetts, was founded in late 1993 by Dan Rubin and Mike Evanisko. Evanisko was an executive with a management consulting firm. Rubin was also a management consultant with extensive experience in the pharmaceutical industry. Based on his experience, he saw an opportunity to address the health care problem of prescription noncompliance, primarily with chronic conditions such as hypertension (high blood pressure), asthma, diabetes, and high cholesterol. Rubin knew that more than half of all patients on these types of medications stopped taking their prescriptions prematurely.

The Elensys programs focused on the development and management of patient compliance programs that educated patients about their medications and reminded patients to refill their prescriptions. The services Elensys offered to its customers, retail pharmacies, included compliance program strategy and planning, communications design, program

---

[16]Giant Food [1998], Corporate Profile, May 1998.

[17] Giant Food [2005b], The History of Giant.

[18] Giant Food [2005a], Press release, April 19, 2005.

[19] Giant Food [1995], "Izzy," We News Special Edition, Giant Food publication, November 1995.

implementation, and performance analysis to ensure maximum program impact. All of Elensys' programs were designed to provide clear therapeutic or economic benefits for patients, as their core values illustrate (Table 1).[20]

Better compliance potentially benefited everyone. For patients, it meant better health. For pharmacies and pharmaceutical companies, it meant increased revenues. Pharmaceutical manufacturers often earned very high gross margins on branded products. These companies made significant sales and marketing investments, typically focused on inducing doctors to write prescriptions for their products. For these firms, noncompliance resulted in billions of dollars in lost revenues. Retail pharmacies would increase their revenues through better compliance due to increased prescription refills plus whatever additional purchases their customers made in the stores with each store visit. As a result of managed care, gross margins in the retail pharmacy industry had declined from 35% to 17–20%. The health care system in general and the managed care system in particular would also benefit through reduced costs that resulted from better health of the public. The question was, Who should pay the costs of running compliance programs?

In developing his business model, Rubin spoke with a representative from a major managed health care organization but quickly learned that managed care was not likely to be a viable vehicle for implementing his idea. While increased prescription compliance would likely lead to lower overall costs for these plans, the head of pharmacy at most managed care plans was primarily concerned with controlling prescription costs (i.e., utilization); the programs Rubin envisioned running would lead to increased utilization of prescription medications and therefore drive pharmacy costs up for the managed care plans. Further, people switched health care plans approximately every 18 months, meaning the next plan would reap the benefits of the former plan's investment in the compliance program.

Rubin subsequently identified retail pharmacies as the potential partner with both a financial interest and a "professional obligation" to provide such services. This business model was attractive because pharmacies maintained an electronic record of every pharmacy transaction.

These data were needed to allow for timely communications with patients and to measure the effectiveness of these communications in improving compliance. The pharmacy data could help identify specific points or activities in a patient's therapy, such as missing a refill or obtaining their last refill without a new prescription. Further, many pharmacies did not possess the in-house information systems resources to develop the database and tracking capabilities needed to manage compliance programs. In the Gallup surveys of public perceptions of the most trusted professions conducted early in 2002 and 2003, the public rated pharmacists in the top ten.[21] Elensys' business model would build on this relationship between the consumer and the pharmacist by providing communication and prescription education materials about the consumer's specific medications to the consumer from their local pharmacy.

The Elensys compliance programs were funded in one of two ways. Many were funded by the pharmaceutical manufacturers who approached a pharmacy to run a compliance program for all of the pharmacy's patients for whom a specific drug was prescribed. Pharmacies could also pay Elensys themselves to run a program on their behalf.

The business was launched in July 1995 with two regional pharmacy chains as customers. Employees included two former Vice Presidents of Pharmacy at major pharmacy chains, and clinical pharmacists with both research and practical experience. By 1998, the firm grew to approximately twenty employees. At that time, Elensys received prescription data from approximately 15,000 pharmacies [O'Harrow 1998]. New customers were acquired primarily by making sales calls and by exhibiting at trade shows.

All communications to patients were sent on behalf of and at the direction of Elensys' customers, the pharmacies. Thus, nothing was ever sent to a patient that hadn't been previously reviewed and approved by the participating pharmacy chain. For example, once the pharmacy decided to run a compliance program for a particular medication, Elensys would enable the mailing of personalized letters to a pharmacy's patients on the pharmacy's letterhead, educating patients as well as reminding them to refill their

Table 1 Elensys Core Values

- Focus on patient health.
- Patient confidentiality must be absolute.
- Physicians are the focal point of all patient treatment decisions.
- Pharmacists play a critical role in counseling and educating patients about their medications.

---

[20] Elensys Care Services, Inc. [1998].

[21] Veverka [2000]. In this survey, pharmacists ranked second, after nurses.

continued

CASE STUDY (*continued*)

prescriptions. The format of the letter could be customized based on the patient's demographics using research on effective communication strategies for that demographic subgroup.

PHARMACEUTICAL INDUSTRY TRENDS

In the 1990s, the move to managed care brought significant changes to the healthcare system and placed enormous pressures on the profits of the pharmaceutical industry. In the U.S., which constituted one-third of the world's pharmaceutical market, 80% of the population was covered by managed care in 1993. In 1995, managed care organizations controlled 75% of the drug purchases in the U.S. The majority of these organizations employed formularies, a list of approved medicines, as one method of cost control; the insurance company would only pay for drugs listed on the formulary. By the mid-1990s, the same price pressures had also reached Europe, with governments imposing price reductions on many drugs.[22]

Further, by 1996, approximately 86% of health maintenance organizations (HMOs) routinely substituted generic products for patented drugs whenever possible, further reducing the profitability of the drug manufacturers. This trend away from the need to prescribe more expensive branded drugs was accelerated by the 1984 Waxman-Hatch Act, which reduced barriers to entry in the pharmaceutical industry by accelerating the FDA approval process for bringing generic drugs to market. As a result of formularies, generics, and other cost pressures, pharmaceuticals appeared to be headed for commodity status. In an effort to combat these trends and to address a public health problem, prescription medicine noncompliance, the pharmaceutical companies initiated patient education programs.[23]

PATIENT EDUCATION PROGRAMS

During the 1990s, recognition of the importance of patient education concerning their conditions, their prescribed treatments, and their treatment options grew. This recognition was reflected in two regulatory programs:

1. In 1990, Congress required pharmacists to offer to discuss any information they deemed significant with any patients receiving benefits under Medicaid. Subsequently, some states adopted laws requiring counseling for all patients.

2. In 1996, Congress required pharmacists to disseminate "useful written information" to all consumers about their prescription drugs. Pharmacists responded to this requirement with a variety of tailored printed materials that they provided to consumers in a face-to-face encounter when people received their prescriptions. Because of the costs associated with developing and disseminating this information in a format that satisfies the requirements of the law, the materials were often funded by pharmaceutical manufacturers.[24]

Pharmacies also engaged in three other kinds of direct-to-patient (DTP) messaging.

1. Compliance messaging encouraged proper use of prescribed medications. In particular, the pharmacy or the pharmacist might remind a patient to finish a course of treatment such as taking all prescribed antibiotics, or to refill a prescription. In developed countries, on average only 50% of prescriptions are taken as prescribed, and nearly half of all patients stop taking their medication within the six months of being prescribed.[25] Further, noncompliance, or the failure of an individual to take medication as prescribed, was estimated to account for over $100 billion in costs to the U.S. healthcare system.

    Compliance programs were particularly important for chronic conditions such as diabetes, high cholesterol, or hypertension (high blood pressure). For example, a study conducted by the University of Southern California School of Pharmacy found that non-compliant patients with high blood pressure cost the California Medicaid system $591.46 more per patient than those who maintained their therapy during a twelve-month period.[26]

2. The second DTP program involved messages about treatment alternatives or adjunctive therapies. For example, the pharmacy might notify a consumer about a lower-cost generic drug that was equivalent to a more expensive brand

---

[22] Harvard Business School [1998].

[23] Castagnoli [1995], pp. 46–53.

[24] National Consumers League [2004].

[25] World Health Organization [2003].

[26] McCombs et al. [1994].

name drug the patient was currently taking, or the pharmacy might notify the patient about alternative medications that were covered by the individual's health insurance plan. These types of messages were sometimes viewed as controversial if they were sponsored by a pharmaceutical manufacturer. These messages also raised concerns about interfering with the doctor-patient relationship.

3. The third type of DTP messaging involved educating consumers about their conditions; for example, educating people with diabetes about ways to manage their disease. Pharmacists traditionally viewed this type of messaging as central to their professional responsibilities. However, these messages could also be viewed as controversial when they were funded by third parties such as pharmaceutical manufacturers.

The pharmaceutical companies were losing approximately $35 billion annually to unfilled prescriptions. DTP messaging programs potentially provided a way for pharmaceutical companies to reduce these losses. For example, prior research found that reminders, either by mail or telephone, increased prescription refill compliance.[27] McKesson, a healthcare supply management company, operated a Patient Care Enhancing Program (PCEP) in collaboration with 500 pharmacies nationwide. Compliance for Coumadin, a blood thinner from Dupont Pharma, increased 25% after patients received a PCEP reminder to refill their prescriptions.[28]

However, a letter from a physician to the editor in the *Journal of the American Medical Association* raised ethical concerns about compliance programs financed by pharmaceutical companies that only included consumers who were prescribed a specific drug from that manufacturer, excluding the rest of the pharmacy's customers who suffered from the same condition. "It appears that the true motivation for this campaign lies in the drawers of their cash registers," the physician wrote.[29]

PRIVACY ISSUES

The use of DTP messaging also potentially raised privacy issues. In 1993, the *Harris-Equifax Health Information Survey* found that 60% of the public felt it was not acceptable for pharmacists to provide names and information of customers taking certain medications to pharmaceutical companies for direct marketing without first obtaining the individual's consent.[30] The Direct Marketing Association, a trade association that represented pharmaceutical companies through its healthcare marketing group, formulated voluntary privacy guidelines for marketing use of health and medical data. Because of the sensitivity of medical data, information derived from the patient–care provider relationship should never be used for marketing purposes. Other health and medical data voluntarily disclosed by the consumer should be treated as sensitive, and rented, sold, transferred, or exchanged only where appropriate safeguards were in place. To participate in the McKesson PCEP, for example, patients needed to register for the program and could "opt out" of the program at any time by calling a telephone number found in all mailings they received.

On April 14, 2001, the U.S. Department of Health and Human Services (HHS) issued a Privacy Rule which meant that for the first time, the privacy of medical information in the United States was protected by law. HHS issued final modifications to the Privacy Rule on August 14, 2002. The Privacy Rule was required by the Health Insurance Portability and Accountability Act of 1996 (HIPAA) and covered health insurance plans, healthcare clearinghouses, and healthcare providers who conducted healthcare transactions electronically. The majority of covered organizations were required to comply with the Privacy Rule by April 14, 2003. Small health plans were given until April 14, 2004 to comply. Appendix 1 provides an overview of the provisions of the final Privacy Rule. A separate rule on information security took effect on April 20, 2005 for most covered entities. Small health plans had until April 14, 2006 to comply with the security rule. The security rule required organizations to "reasonably safeguard" protected health information from intentional or unintentional use or disclosure that violated the standards and further specified implementation standards for administrative, physical, and technical standards.[31]

---

[27] Stockwell and Schulz [1992].

[28] McLaughlin [1998].

[29] Hirsch, Sherwood, and Denman [1998].

[30] Louis Harris & Associates [1993].

[31] See http://www.hhs.gov/ocr/hipaa/ for complete information about the HIPAA Privacy Rule. A summary of the Rule is available at http://www.hhs.gov/ocr/privacysummary.pdf. The marketing provisions of the Rule are available at http://www.hhs.gov/ocr/hipaa/guidelines/marketing.pdf. Information about the Security Rule is available at http://www.cms.hhs.gov/hipaa/hipaa2 [accessed April 23, 2005].

continued

CASE STUDY (*continued*)

Rubin knew from day one that privacy would be an issue for Elensys. The following steps were taken to protect the privacy of the pharmacies' customers.

1. The database for each pharmacy was split into two parts: One part contained name and address information, the second part contained prescription information but no personally identifiable information, so analysis could be done without knowing the patient's identity. To generate mailings, the two files could be linked through a unique I.D. assigned to each patient's records. The database had extraordinary security; even the CEO did not have access to the information.

2. Postcards were never used for mailings. Instead, all mailings were sent by first-class mail using window envelopes so there was no chance of the wrong letter getting into an envelope. The pharmacy signed off on all communications.

3. Elensys considered itself a true partner and it would caution pharmacies not to accept any inappropriate programs to avoid potential trouble.

4. Patients could "opt out" of any compliance program at any time through a number of easy methods including a postage paid business reply envelope (BRE) and a toll free phone number included on all mailings.[32]

5. Elensys did not run marketing programs, it only ran compliance programs. It did not send coupons to patients, nor did it run any "switch" programs where letters would be sent to patients taking one drug suggesting they ask their doctor to switch them to another drug or engage in other forms of direct marketing. These switch programs were a legal form of DTP communication and while other firms in this industry were running these types of programs, all of Elensys' programs provided information only about the specific drug prescribed by the patient's physician.

6. Elensys never provided or sold patient prescription information to pharmaceutical companies. Such an action would violate the contract between Elensys and the pharmacy.

GIANT AND ELENSYS

Giant began investigating the feasibility of providing a prescription compliance program in early 1997. In addition to the public health issues noncompliance raised, unfilled prescriptions resulted in lost revenue streams for Giant. The companies viewed compliance programs as benefiting consumers through better health in addition to increased sales for retailers and manufacturers.

Like other large chains, Giant was previously approached by pharmaceutical companies hoping to gain access to Giant's customers to do DTP marketing. Giant declined these offers because it was not comfortable with what the pharmaceutical companies wanted to do and felt these offers were not appropriate. Giant also was concerned about mailing reminders to their customers. However, the trade publications suggested that everyone was running compliance programs, and no legal or other problems were reported with consumers. State Attorney Generals and consumer advocates had not raised any concerns about these programs. Russell Fair talked to other chains and found they were running similar programs. Further, Giant's own customers would bring in letters they received from competitors such as CVS. In short, nothing suggested that these programs raised a red flag.

Giant first investigated the feasibility of running a compliance program in-house. However, the information systems requirements were too large. For example, to develop the tracking database needed to monitor compliance would tie up too many resources versus partnering with an organization that already developed this technology. Giant decided to outsource the compliance program.

Fair learned about Elensys from reading articles about what other companies were doing in trade journals such as *Drugstore News and Chainstore Age,* and from attending trade shows where Elensys exhibited. He liked that fact that Elensys was the only independent company running compliance programs. The others all were associated with a pharmaceutical manufacturer. Fair didn't trust the firewalls these companies established between the compliance programs and the other parts of the business.

Fair decided to partner with Elensys. In his discussions with legal and risk management professionals, all agreed the program raised privacy concerns. They were also concerned about other business risks. However, since so many other pharmacies were already participating in similar programs, they decided the downside risks were manageable. Giant's legal department negotiated the contract with Elensys. With many of its other customers, Elensys negotiated directly with the pharmaceutical companies for program funding. However, Giant chose to tightly control the environment by negotiating its own agreements directly with the pharmaceutical companies. Giant alone would determine what communications were sent to its customers. They would avoid offers for "controversial" drugs such as Prozac. Giant did not want to risk customers inferring that "Giant knows 'X' about me."

---

[32] The national "opt-out" rate for programs administered by Elensys was less than 3%.

Once Giant negotiated with a pharmaceutical company to do a compliance program for a particular drug, the relevant consumers would be identified using Elensys' proprietary database software. Each consumer would be sent a letter introducing the program and inviting them to participate. An 800 number was provided for the consumer to opt out of the program. If no response was received, additional educational letters would go out on Giant letterhead. Separate letters were sent for each drug; no mass mailing was to go out to all Giant customers.

Elensys also provided periodic measurement reporting so Giant could assess the performance of the compliance program. Analysis was performed using nonidentifiable data through proprietary techniques which used the Elensys database software, and could quantify the impact of the compliance programs statistically on increasing patient retention on their prescribed medications.

In December 1997, Giant began sending its pharmacy transaction data to Elensys to test the database design and so that Elensys could begin to identify trends. Each week, Giant would send the transactions for that week. Giant did not provide Elensys with its entire customer database (Appendix 2 lists the fields that were provided for each customer transaction). To track compliance, a baseline of 6–8 weeks of transaction data was needed. At Elensys, Giant's data were stored in a separate database that only contained data from Giant, running on hardware that was only used for processing Giant's data. Fair felt it was essential that no one else could gain access to Giant's customer data. However, as of mid-February when the article appeared in the *Washington Post* about the program, Elensys had yet to send out a single communication on behalf of Giant.

DEALING WITH THE IMPENDING CRISIS

Fair arrived at work early Monday morning. He met with Odonna Mathews, Giant's Vice President-Consumer Affairs, who was not involved in the original Elensys decision. The two of them quickly agreed on a course of action.

REFERENCES

Castagnoli, William G. (1995) "Is Disease Management Good Therapy for an Ailing Industry?" *Medical Marketing & Media,* January 1, pp. 46–53

Elensys Care Services (1998) "Patient Compliance & Education Services: Description of Services?" Woburn, MA: Elensys

Giant Food (1995) "Izzy," We News Special Edition, November

Giant Food, 1998. Corporate Profile, Giant Food, Inc. May

Giant Food (2005a) Press release, April 19

Giant Food (2005b) The History of Giant. http://www.giantfood .com/corporate/ company_aboutgiant2.htm (accessed July 25, 2005).

Harvard Business School (1998) *The Pharma Giants: Ready for the 21st Century?* Case 9-698- 070, Boston, MA: HBS Press, May 6.

Hirsch, Ronald L., L. M. Sherwood, and J. Denman (1998), "Merck-Sponsored Simvastatin (Zocor) Compliance Program for Patients Using Wal-Mart Pharmacy: Of Benefit to Whom?" *JAMA,* (279)23, pp. 1875–1876, June 17.

Louis Harris and Associates (1993) *Harris-Equifax Health Information Privacy Survey,* Atlanta: Equifax.

McCombs, Jeffrey S. et al. (1998) "The Costs of Interrupting Antihypertensive Therapy in a Medicaid Population," *Medical Care* (32) pp. 214–226.

McLaughlin, Mark (1998) "Pharmacy Database Program Helps Consumers Keep Their Refills Current," *DM News,* November 9, p. 10.

National Consumers League (2004) *Health Care Communications Provided by Pharmacies: Best Practices Principles for Safeguarding Patient Privacy.* http://www.nclnet.org/pressroom/ pharmacy_privacy_practices_report.htm (accessed April 23, 2005).

O'Harrow, Robert Jr. (1998) "Prescription Sales, Privacy Fears: CVS, Giant Share Customer Records with Drug Marketing Firm," *Washington Post,* February 15, p. A1.

Stockwell, M. L., and R. M. Schulz (1992) "Patient Compliance: An Overview," *Journal of Clinical Pharmacy and Therapeutics* (17), pp. 283–295.

Veverka, A. (2000) "Gallup Poll Shows Fewer Americans Trust Accountants," Knight Ridder Tribune Business News, December 20, p. 1.

World Health Organization (2003) *Adherence to Long Term Therapies: Evidence for Action,* Geneva: WHO, http:// www.who.int/chronic_conditions/ adherencereport/en/ (accessed April 23, 2005).

APPENDIX 1: OVERVIEW OF THE FINAL HIPAA HEALTH PRIVACY RULE[33]

The regulation establishes national standards to control the flow of sensitive patient information and penalties for the misuse or disclosure of the information. The regulation covers medical records and other individually identifiable health information related to treatment, payment and healthcare operations held or disclosed by a covered entity (health care providers and health plans which transmit health information for standard transactions electronically). The regulation includes the following protections.

---

[33] See: http://www.hhs.gov/ocr/hipaa/ for complete information about the HIPAA Privacy Rule. A summary of the Rule is available at http://www.hhs.gov/ocr/privacysummary.pdf. The marketing provisions of the Rule are available at http://www.hhs.gov/ocr/hipaa/guidelines/marketing.pdf. Information about the Security Rule is available at accessed 4/23/05: http://www.cms.hhs.gov/hipaa/hipaa2/.

continued

CASE STUDY (*continued*)

Consumer Control Over Health Information

Patients must be provided with notice of the patient's privacy rights and the privacy practices of the covered entity. Consent for routine healthcare delivery purposes is not required. However, treatment providers are required to make a good faith effort to obtain the patient's written acknowledgment of the notice. Consent is required for other uses of personal information.

Boundaries on Medical Record Use and Release

With limited exceptions, an individual's health information can be used or disclosed for health purposes only. Entities covered by this regulation may disclose health information to a business associate, and may allow a business associate to create or receive health information on its behalf if the entity obtains satisfactory assurance that the business associate will appropriately safeguard the information. A business associate is a third party that may provide services on behalf of the entity on a contractual basis (e.g., outsourcing).

Establish Accountability for Medical Records Use and Release

Entities covered by the regulation must adopt written privacy policies, train employees, designate a privacy officer, and establish grievance processes for patients. The detailed policies and procedures for meeting the standards specified in the regulation are left to the discretion of each covered entity.

Health plans, providers, and clearinghouses that violate these standards are subject to civil penalties. Federal criminal penalties apply if covered entities knowingly and improperly disclose information or obtain information under false pretenses.

Rules Related to Marketing

Health organizations covered by this rule (covered entities) must obtain the patient's written authorization to use or disclose protected health information for marketing. Marketing is defined as "communication about a product or service that encourages the recipient to purchase or use the product

or service." Excluded from this definition are communications related to treatment, payment, or operations:

■ That describe a health-related product or service that is provided by the covered entity;

■ That describe health-related products or services available to health plan enrollees that add value to (and are not part of) the plan's benefits; or

■ Are related to treatment of the individual including to direct or recommend alternate therapies, providers or settings of care.

Examples of communications that are not considered marketing include:

■ A health plan sends a mailing to its subscribers approaching Medicare age with materials describing its Medicare supplemental plan;

■ A pharmacy or other health care provider mails prescription refill reminders to patients, or uses a business associate to do so;

■ A hospital uses its patient list to send a mailing announcing the acquisition of new equipment

For any permitted communications, a covered entity is allowed to disclose protected health information to a business associate to assist with the communication. The business associate is prohibited from using the information for any other purposes.

Protected health information may also be used for fundraising under a limited set of circumstances. In this case, the fundraising materials must describe how the individual can opt out of future fundraising communications.

Covered entities may not sell lists of patients or enrollees to third parties for the marketing activities of the third party without the individual's authorization. For instances where authorization is required, the authorization must disclose if the marketing involves remuneration to the covered entity by a third party. Simply put, an entity covered by HIPAA may not sell health information protected by HIPAA to a business associate or any other third party for that party's own purposes. Further, covered entities may not sell lists of patients or enrollees to third parties without obtaining authorization from each person on the list.

APPENDIX 2: TRANSACTION DATA SUPPLIED TO ELENSYS

Customer Name

Customer Address

Date of Birth

Gender

Prescription Components:

- Drug
- Prescription #
- Quantity
- Date Supplied
- Number of Refills
- Doctor

Elensys' proprietary database was structured in two separate parts. One part contained the patient's name, address information, and an indicator of whether or not the patient had "opted in" or "opted out"[34] of the program. The second part contained prescription and analysis information. This separation made it possible to do data mining operations on the prescription information without ever linking this information to specific patients. Data mining operations involved sophisticated analysis based on the unique medical and pharmaceutical knowledge of Elensys employees, and went well beyond simple rules of the type "If patient X has prescription Y, send mailing."

Elensys did not own any of the patient data in their database. They were legally prohibited from selling or providing in any way any of the data they acquired from the pharmacies to pharmaceutical manufacturers or others.

ABBREVIATIONS

BRE: Business reply envelope

CRM: Customer relationship marketing

DTC: Pharmaceutical direct to consumer advertising

DTP: Pharmacy direct to patient messaging

HHS: U.S. Department of Health & Human Services

HIPAA: Health Insurance Portability and Accountability Act

HMO: Health Maintenance Organization

---

[34] With "opt-in" the patient will not receive any mailings unless they have consented. With "opt-out" the patient will be sent mailings unless they object.

INDEX